THE LIFE AND WORK OF SIGMUND FREUD

VOLUME II

1901–1919

YEARS OF MATURITY

Books by Ernest Jones

DAS PROBLEM DES HAMLET

HAMLET AND OEDIPUS

PAPERS ON PSYCHO-ANALYSIS
(*5 volumes*)

TREATMENT OF THE NEUROSES

DER ALPTRAUM

PSYCHO-ANALYSIS AND THE WAR NEUROSES
(*with Abraham, Ferenczi and Simmel*)

ESSAYS IN APPLIED PSYCHO-ANALYSIS
(*2 volumes*)

HOW THE MIND WORKS
(*with Cyril Burt*)

ZUR PSYCHOANALYSE DER CHRISTLICHEN RELIGION

ON THE NIGHTMARE

WHAT IS PSYCHO-ANALYSIS

THE LIFE AND WORK OF SIGMUND FREUD
(*Volume I*)

Translations

CONTRIBUTIONS TO PSYCHO-ANALYSIS
by Sandor Ferenczi, M.D.

The Life and Work of

SIGMUND

FREUD

By Ernest Jones, M.D.

VOLUME

2

Years of Maturity

1901-1919

New York

BASIC BOOKS, INC.

Publishers

Copyright, © 1955, by Ernest Jones
Manufactured in the United States of America
Library of Congress Catalog Card Number: 53–8700
ISBN: 465–04015–2 (3 vols.)
ISBN: 465–04016–0 (vol. 1)
ISBN: 465–04017–9 (vol. 2)
ISBN: 465–04018–7 (vol. 3)
DESIGNED BY MARSHALL LEE

To Anna Freud,

TRUE DAUGHTER OF AN IMMORTAL SIRE

Contents

Illustrations

Preface

The years here under discussion may fairly be called Freud's years of maturity. He had overcome any personal inhibitions and corrected early mistakes. He had perfected the instruments of research he had devised and was now free to exploit them by exploring in detail the new world of knowledge they had opened to him—in a word, the Unconscious. The perplexities of youth were past and were succeeded by a greater serenity and a more critical judgment.

Freud's emotional life was by now far more contained than it had been in earlier years. The turmoil of those years had largely subsided, though it was to give signs of re-emerging in an intellectual form during the last phase of his life; and events, including personal relationships, did not touch him so nearly as they had in earlier times. His inner life, containing no secrets, was taken up with the further development and application of the ideas he had already formulated, and his outer life proceeded harmoniously in the public eye, or at least in that of a considerable circle.

The technical problem I have found most troublesome in the present volume concerns the matter of Freud's extensive writings, for after all this Biography purports to deal with both his Life and his Work. Yet the writings of this period are so well known and so accessible, both in the original and in numerous expositions of them, that it would seem otiose to offer still another account of them. I have always held that Freud's work is best understood if studied chronologically, though this applies more particularly to his earlier writings. It might be thought that the account of those of this period should best be woven into the chronology of his life in the hope that the development of his ideas might in this way be more closely followed. But I should remark to this that the writings in question represent a steadily progressive unfolding of his ideas, with ramifying applications of them, rather than a great deal in the way of novel development. That was to come once more in the last period of his life. So after much reflection I think I shall be doing the best by my readers in again, as in the first volume, grouping the main themes under separate rubrics, the contents of which are then in turn related chronologically. It becomes possible to consider various topics as a whole and to observe the developments that took place in, for instance, the matters of technique, theory and so on, in a more ordered fashion than if each item were interposed in the midst of the general story of his life; the latter contains only a brief mention of the literary productions of each year in turn. I have, moreover, tried to lighten the reading of this familiar material by selecting only the high lights of each essay, by adding any knowledge I have about the circumstances and dates of its production, and by quoting any comments Freud himself may have made on the various items.

Naturally there can be no question of the condensed accounts given here being, especially for serious students, any substitute for the fuller ones available elsewhere. Nor is there any need here to reproduce the meticulous Bibliography of them which Mr. Strachey is preparing for the *Standard Edition* of Freud's works. A few of the topics Freud discussed in this period, notably those on religion, are reserved for more extensive consideration in the third volume of this biography.

A further remark about Freud's writings of this period may be in place. They seem on the whole to fall into three broad groups. There were first many occasional pieces, written by request or to fill up gaps in the Society's agenda or the pages of his periodicals; several of these, notably the "Thoughts on War," are of abiding interest. Then there were those in the direct line of his intellectual evolution: the change in theory that came with the conception of Narcissism, and above all the five papers on Metapsychology which rounded off an epoch. Lastly there were a few non-medical writings concerned with themes that moved him personally, such as his books on Leonardo and Totemism, which opened even wider perspectives than the more technical psychological papers.

The biographical material available for the present volume is much more extensive than was so for the previous one. Not only have we many accounts of eyewitnesses, such as Freud's family, friends and pupils, but I have also at my disposal some five thousand letters from his correspondence. Only one holocaust of them took place in this period, in the spring of 1908 when Freud was changing his domestic arrangements. Of the correspondence the most valuable is that between Freud and Abraham, Ferenczi, Jung, and myself; fortunately the letters on both sides have been preserved, thus making various allusions much more intelligible. The number of letters in this last-mentioned correspondence is respectively: 495 (of which 220 are from Freud); 1,234 (of which 547 are from Freud); 368 (of which 171 are from Freud); and 1,347 (of which 656 are from Freud). The widows of my friends Karl Abraham, Max Eitingon and Sandor Ferenczi placed after their deaths their correspondence at my disposal; Ferenczi's literary executor, Michael Balint, was good enough to arrange and make available the material in his possession, as did Hilda Abraham. Professor Jung has generously made available his extensive correspondence with Freud. *Pfarrer* Pfister has also kindly let me read his very interesting correspondence. The letters Freud wrote in English I have distinguished from those translated by adding an asterisk. I have not ventured to amend his English grammar; if one started making such improvements one would end by defacing the original style. I have even left Freud's "yours truly" in the letters where in German he would have written *"Ihr getreuer"* (yours loyally). Then Ernst Federn and Hermann Nunberg have allowed me to read the valuable collection in their possession of the Minutes of the Vienna Psycho-Analytical Society from 1906-1914. I have read Brill's letters to Freud, but in his will he stipulated that Freud's letters to him should not be read for fifty years. In addition to these sources there is an immense number of letters written to the most diverse people, since Freud was a tireless correspondent and faithfully answered all letters addressed to him. I am grateful to the many people who have sent me such letters and to those who have helped me in many other ways. Among them I must specially single out the names of Anna Freud, Marie Bonaparte, Kurt Eissler, Edward Hitschmann, James Strachey, Alfred von Winterstein, and of course my own dear wife. I would also express my gratitude to the Bollingen Foundation for a grant which materially facilitated the preparation of this volume.

Happy is he who can search out the causes of things,
For thereby he masters all fear, and is throned above fate.

Alfred Noyes after Virgil

1

PART

LIFE

1

CHAPTER

Emergence from Isolation

(1 9 0 1 – 1 9 0 6)

IN 1901 FREUD, AT THE AGE OF FORTY-FIVE, HAD ATTAINED COMPLETE
maturity, a consummation of development that few people really
achieve. Intellectually he had been precocious enough, but balance in
the emotional sphere had been compassed much more slowly. For at
least twenty years, certainly from the time of his falling in love when
he was twenty-six, there had been continual periods of restlessness, uncertainty, instability and even more definitely neurotic disturbances.
A profound self-confidence had been masked by strange feelings of
inferiority, even in the intellectual sphere, and he had tried to cope
with these by projecting his innate sense of capacity and superiority
on to a series of mentors on some of whom he then became curiously
dependent for reassurance. Thus he idealized six figures who played an
important part in his early life: Brücke, Meynert, Fleischl, Charcot,
Breuer and Fliess, all of whom were good friends to him. The first four
of these died in the early nineties before Freud had published anything
in psychopathology. One of them, the highly neurotic Meynert, had
turned against Freud in the end, being incensed at Freud's advocacy
of hypnotism. The last two, of whom Freud had thought extremely
highly for many years, forsook him to his great disappointment when
he persisted in his unpopular work on sexuality.

In 1897 he embarked, all alone, on what was undoubtedly the greatest feat of his life. His determination, courage and honesty made him
the first human being not merely to get glimpses of his own unconscious mind—earlier pioneers had often got as far as that—but actually
to penetrate into and explore its deepest depths. This imperishable

feat was to give him a unique position in history. But three or four years of herculean struggles with those powerful forces in the mind that so strenuously resist such an endeavor brought their reward. He obtained the insight and knowledge that made possible the life's work for which his name has become famous. It was dearly bought: some idea of the pain and sufferings Freud's great achievement cost him has already been given in the first volume of this biography.

Of more immediate importance to himself was the gain in mental harmony, in the integration of his personality, that was to enable him later to buffet his way through the many storms, stresses and tribulations that lay ahead—if not with equanimity, at least with unshaken fortitude. No self-analysis, it is true, however ruthlessly pursued, can completely resolve the deepest unconscious conflicts, but all that remained in later years of Freud's early troubles were a few personal idiosyncrasies, on which we may presently have occasion to comment, and some vexatious disturbances, probably "psychosomatic" in nature, in the functioning of his alimentary organs—little enough to show for the years of mental turmoil through which he had passed.

On the intellectual side there had been much to record from the past quarter of a century. Under the influence of Brücke and Meynert Freud had done notable work in the field of neuro-physiology. By means of ingenious and delicate methods he had finally established some of the most difficult points in the microscopic anatomy of the pons area of the brain. More important were the contributions he made to the theory of evolution by determining the way in which the spinal and some of the cerebral sensory (and sensorial) nerve ganglia emerge from the central nervous system to their adjacent sites outside it. Furthermore, he had pointed out the unitary nature of the neurone, a conclusion which is the foundation of all later neuro-physiology, although it was reserved for another neurologist, Waldeyer, to coin that name for it. Through a very comprehensive study Freud brought the medicinal value of cocaine to the notice of the medical profession, but it was a friend of his to whom he had given the idea who obtained the credit for its chief use—local anaesthesia. So Freud had just missed fame on two occasions, both times in his early twenties.

All this work had occupied some seven years. After it the need to earn a living and to maintain a married state had driven him into clinical practice in neurology. He did not like this occupation, but he became a competent clinical neurologist and in one department, that of children's paralyses, he was the leading authority in Europe. Very much against his inclination he had to go on writing monographs on this topic as late as 1897, which we may call the end of his neurological period. The acme he reached in it, however, was in 1891 when he published a very remarkable and original book, *On Aphasia*,[a] one which in many ways foreshadowed the psychological theories he was soon after to develop.

As happens to most neurologists, Freud's private practice consisted largely of neurotic patients. To be successful in it he therefore had to pay special attention to therapy. After trying the more conventional methods of the time he began at the end of 1887 to use hypnotism, of which he had had some experience in Obersteiner's private Clinic where he had worked for a time in 1885 and still more when studying under Charcot shortly afterwards. Some months of this monotonous treatment, however, began to bore Freud; what he wanted was to understand something about the meaning and source of neurotic symptoms. So he bethought himself, rather belatedly, of an experience Breuer had related to him some seven years before. It was the "cathartic" method of treatment which Breuer had learned from his famous patient Frl. Anna O. This led to collaboration with Breuer, and the two men published in 1895 an epoch-making book entitled *Studies in Hysteria*. Breuer, however, could not follow Freud in the conclusions he was drawing concerning the sexual causation of neurotic disturbances, and the old friends began to draw apart. To his own great surprise, and against his personal puritanical predilections, Freud was finding himself more and more compelled by the results of his investigations to attach importance to the sexual factors in aetiology, and the next ten years only confirmed and extended his conclusions. It was no sudden discovery, and—in spite of what his opponents have suggested—it was quite unconnected with any preconceptions. Only very gradually, and as it seems to us now—slowly, did Freud become convinced of the significance of sexual factors and of the extensive part they play in buried mental life. The importance of sexuality in early childhood, and its essentially incestuous nature, ideas which brought down such a storm on his head, he learned of in a curiously inverse way. He at first accepted his patients' stories of their parents' sexual overtures towards them when they were children, but came to realize that the stories were simply phantasies derived from his patients' own childhood.

In the nineties Freud wrote several papers on these topics and indicated the complicated mechanisms of distortion that forbidden impulses undergo when kept from consciousness by "repression." And in

[a] A translation of it by E. Stengel has recently appeared.[1]

the last year of the century there appeared his magnum opus, *The Interpretation of Dreams*, without any doubt Freud's greatest work and one which contains the germs of all his later work. Its importance lay not merely in the interesting fact of its finally solving the age-old riddle of dream life, but far more in Freud's being able, by means of this particular study, to expound the hitherto unknown nature of the unconscious mind with all its peculiarities. The rest of his life was to be devoted to extending this knowledge in detail and working out the numerous ways in which it can be used to throw light on all manner of previously obscure aspects of human life.

For some years—he said ten—Freud had suffered greatly from intellectual loneliness which the warm contact of his family and social life only partly alleviated. There was no one at all with whom he could discuss his novel findings except to some extent his sister-in-law, Minna Bernays, and in the correspondence and occasional meetings with his great friend, Wilhelm Fliess, the Berlin rhinologist. They were years of what he later called "splendid isolation"; it was apparently Fliess who, to console his friend for his acute loneliness, adopted this phrase of Goschen's, one which Lord Salisbury was using to describe Britain's foreign policy in those days.[2]

Freud later described the advantage of this period: [3] the total absence of competition or of "badly informed opponents," his having no need to read or collate extensive literature as in his neurological years, since none at all existed in the new field he was opening up. In his description he certainly idealized this time. "When I look back on those lonely years from the confusion and harassment of the present [b] it seems to me to have been a beautiful heroic era." The sufferings and hardships he had then passed through, as we have since learned from the correspondence with Fliess, were now apparently forgotten or else obliterated in rosy retrospect. Perhaps the chief result of his painful experiences in those ten years was that in them Freud developed or consolidated an attitude of mind that was to remain one of his most distinctive characteristics: an independence of other people's opinion. He had learned to stand alone in the world and, after the friendship with Fliess was broken, really alone.

When did the ten years come to an end? Like most happenings in Freud's life the emerging from isolation was a gradual process. More and more abstracts of his writings appeared in psychiatric periodicals, and this by the end of the first decade of the century was to turn into

[b] Spring of 1914.

a flood of lengthy reviews, sometimes hundreds of pages long. From the beginning there had been signs of interest in his methods, principally in Anglo-Saxon countries, but most of them do not seem to have come to his notice. A couple of sympathetic papers had been published in Germany, which we shall mention later, but they were very elementary and concerned only the early tentative methods which he had long abandoned.

It is not indeed clear which ten years Freud had in mind in his eulogy of them. In his *Autobiography* he wrote: "For more than ten years after my separation from Breuer I had no followers." [4] The separation from Breuer we know took place in 1894, the year before their joint *Studies in Hysteria* actually appeared, and that would bring us to 1904. Elsewhere, on the other hand, he related how a number of young doctors gathered about him to learn the practice of psychoanalysis "from 1902 on," and other evidence confirms this.

The beginning of what was later to become the famous Vienna Psycho-Analytical Society, the mother of so many subsequent ones, has not been altogether easy to elucidate. Among those who listened to Freud's University lectures on the psychology of the neuroses at the turn of the century there were two men, both doctors, whose interest persisted: Max Kahane and Rudolf Reitler. The latter became the first person to practice psychoanalysis after Freud. Kahane worked in a sanatorium for psychoneurotics, but confined himself to the use of electricity and other conventional methods of treatment; he left the Society in 1907. In 1901 he mentioned Freud's name to Wilhelm Stekel as that of a neurologist who had devised a radical method of treating neurotic affections. Stekel had himself written a paper in 1895 on coitus in childhood,[5] but he had not then heard of Freud. Freud later made a reference to this paper, though, incidentally, quoting the wrong year.[6] Stekel was at that time suffering from a troublesome neurotic complaint, the nature of which I need not mention, and appealed to Freud for help. The help was forthcoming and was very successful. Stekel himself said that the analysis lasted only eight sessions,[7] but this seems very unlikely and I had the impression from Freud that it was much more extensive. Stekel says that he read a long review, evidently that by Burckhardt in *Die Zeit*,[8] adversely criticizing Freud's recently published *Interpretation of Dreams*, and that he promptly wrote a defense of it to the *Neues Wiener Tagblatt*.[9] Actually this was two years later, presumably after his analysis. In 1913 Freud referred to Stekel's analysis having been carried out "about ten years ago";[10] I should surmise it was in 1901. The essay was written in Stekel's most flowery style. He began to practice psychoanalysis in 1903.[11] He was the only member of the Society who referred to Freud by his surname instead of "Herr Professor."

Alfred Adler asserted that he did the same service for Freud at this time by writing to the *Neue Freie Presse*,[12] but it has proved impossible, even after a thorough search, to confirm this statement or the accompanying one about there having been a review of Freud's book in that newspaper to which Adler was alleged to have replied. Nor is there any family memory of his ever having been Freud's family doctor.

In the autumn of 1902 Freud addressed a postcard to these four men, Adler, Kahane, Reitler and Stekel, suggesting that they meet for discussion of his work at his residence. Stekel said it was he who had first made that suggestion to Freud,[13] and this is borne out by Freud's remark that "the stimulus came from a colleague who had himself experienced the beneficial effect of analytic therapy." [14] So Stekel may be accorded the honor, together with Freud, of having founded the first psychoanalytic society. At all events, from then on they formed the habit of meeting every Wednesday evening for discussions in Freud's waiting-room, which was suitably furnished for the purpose with an oblong table. The meetings were given the modest title of the "Psychological Wednesday Society." Stekel used to report its discussions every week in the Sunday edition of the *Neues Wiener Tagblatt*.

In the next couple of years others joined the circle, but often only temporarily. The only names that would now be remembered were those of Max Graf; Hugo Heller, Freud's future publisher; and Alfred Meisl. Then better known ones appear: in 1903 Paul Federn; in 1905, Eduard Hitschmann, introduced by his old schoolfellow Federn; in 1906 Otto Rank, who presented himself to Freud with an introduction from Adler and the manuscript copy of his little book *Art and Artist*, and Isidor Sadger; in 1907 Guido Brecher, Maximilian Steiner and Fritz Wittels,[c] who had been introduced by his uncle, Sadger; in 1908 Sandor Ferenczi, Oskar Rie and Rudolf Urbantschitsch; in 1909 J. K. Friedjung and Viktor Tausk; in 1910 Ludwig Jekels, Hanns Sachs, Herbert Silberer, and Alfred von Winterstein.

I need hardly say that I know of no evidence for the remarkable statement that the famous writers Karl Kraus, Hugo von Hofmannsthal, Arthur Schnitzler and Jakob Wassermann "joined the psychoanalytic circle and made their different contributions to its theories." [15] The first named of these was actually one of Freud's bitterest opponents.

[c] Wittels resigned from the Society in 1910.

The early guests of the Society were: Max Eitingon, January 30, 1907; C. G. Jung and L. Binswanger, March 6, 1907; Karl Abraham, December 18, 1907; A. A. Brill and myself, May 6, 1908; A. Muthmann, February 10, 1909; M. Karpas of New York, April 4, 1909; L. Jekels, November 3, 1909; L. Karpinska, December 15, 1909. As an example of how occasions may become glorified in retrospect I may mention Eitingon's statement, when thirty years later he described his first visit to the Society, that there were twenty or thirty-five members present;[16] actually there were ten. Although at the beginning of 1908 there were twenty-two members, it was rare for more than eight or ten of them to attend meetings.

In the spring of 1908 the little Society began to collect a library. This had grown to impressive proportions by the time the Nazis arrived to destroy it in 1938. At the same time (April 15, 1908) it acquired a more formal designation: the old "Psychological Wednesday Society" now became the "Vienna Psycho-Analytical Society," by which name it is still known.

In the early days a social evening would be arranged just before Christmas. This was changed later to a more sumptuous repast in the summer, first in the Schutzengel on the Hohe Warte, just outside Vienna, and then on the Konstantinhügel in the Prater.

There was one feature of the Society that is perhaps unique. It was one that so well illustrates Freud's delicacy of feeling and considerateness that I will quote in full the circular letter in which he made the proposal; it was dated from Rome, September 22, 1907.

"I wish to inform you that I propose at the beginning of this new working year to dissolve the little Society which has been accustomed to meet every Wednesday at my home, and immediately afterwards to call it into life again. A short note sent before October 1st to our secretary, Otto Rank, will suffice to insure a renewal of your membership; if we hear nothing by that date we shall assume that you do not wish to renew it. I need hardly emphasize how very pleased I should be at your re-entry.

"Allow me to give the reason for this action which may well seem to you to be superfluous. We are only taking into account the natural changes in human relationships if we assume that to one or another member in our group membership no longer signifies what it did years earlier—whether because his interest in the subject is exhausted, or his leisure time and mode of life are no longer compatible with attendance, or that personal associations threaten to keep him away. Presumably he would still remain a member, fearing lest his resignation be regarded as an unfriendly action. For all these cases the dissolving and reorganizing of the Society has the purpose of re-establishing the personal freedom of each individual and of making it possible for him to stay apart from the Society without in any way disturbing his relations with the rest of us. We have further to bear in mind that in the course of years we have undertaken (financial) obligations, such as appointing a secretary, of which there was no question at the beginning.

"If you agree after this explanation with the expediency of reconstituting the Society in this way you will probably approve of its being repeated at regular intervals—say every three years."

This delicate fashion of accepting resignations was in fact repeated in 1910, but not afterwards. It was, however, made use of by other Societies in later years, e.g. the Swiss and British, when it was desired to restrict their membership to serious students of psychoanalysis.

In April 1910, the growth of the Society made Freud's waiting-room over-crowded, so they used then to meet in the *Doktoren Collegium* (College of Physicians) at 19 Rothenturmstrasse, in the same building as where Max Steiner then lived. At the end of 1911 the College moved to the Franz-Josefs Quai.

The Viennese soon began to publish contributions of their own to psychoanalysis, or at least expositions of it. In 1905 Adler gave examples of how an apparently random choice of numbers could be unconsciously determined.[17] In the same year he expounded the importance of sexual problems for education.[18] His first book, the one that made his name, appeared in 1907.[19]

Meisl expounded the importance of repression in one paper[20] and of the theory of dreams in another.[21] Sadger began a series of valuable contributions by an exposition of Freud's method.[22] Stekel opened his extensive literary career with two books. The first was a general account of hereditary and environmental factors in the aetiology of the neuroses, stress being laid on the importance of sexual factors.[23] The other was a solid contribution to our knowledge of anxiety states in which he laid more stress on psychological factors than Freud had. It appeared first as a short paper[24] and was a year later expanded into a considerable book with the same title.

The years we are concerned with were very productive ones, both internally and externally. Freud was constantly improving and refining his technique and thus acquiring an ever increasing mastery of the psychoanalytic method. Then besides writing five valuable papers, mostly expository in nature, he published one book in 1901 and no fewer than four more in the years 1905-1906, one of which ranks next only to *The Interpretation of Dreams* in importance. We shall later consider in appropriate sections the contents and provenance of these writings, but in order to keep in touch with Freud's progress some mention of them should be made here also.

First may be mentioned the little-known fact that Freud published an autobiographical notice of himself in 1901 in a compilation edited by Professor Julius Pagel under the title of *Biographisches Lexicon hervorragender Ärzte des neunzehnten Jahrhunderts* (Biographical Dictionary of Outstanding Physicians of the Nineteenth Century).[25] Freud had evidently composed it in the autumn of 1899, since it refers to *The Interpretation of Dreams* being in the press. He rather mournfully recorded the fact that he had in 1897 been proposed as Extraordinary Professor to the University; we know that it took five years for this to be accepted.

The first of the books, a brochure called *On Dreams*, has already been described in the first volume of the present work.[26] The next, entitled *The Psychopathology of Everyday Life*, 1904, is perhaps the best known of Freud's books among the general public. It had appeared in a periodical three years before.

In the same year he contributed anonymously a chapter entitled "Freud's Psycho-Analytic Method" to a book of Löwenfeld's. It was the fullest account of this practical topic he had yet written and so was of great value to those who were already tentatively beginning to apply his mode of treatment.

The year 1905 was one of the peaks of Freud's productivity, which, as he once half-jocularly remarked, occurred every seven years. In it appeared four papers and two books, one of the latter being of outstanding importance.

Three of the four papers were also expository, and two of them were contributory chapters to books. One, on "Mental Treatment," was written for a popular medical encyclopedia called *Die Gesundheit* (Health). Another, "On Psychotherapy," was an address he had delivered in the previous December 1904 to a medical audience in Vienna, the last time he ever did so. Then there was a chapter entitled "My Views on the Part Played by Sexuality in the Aetiology of the Neuroses," which formed part of another book of Löwenfeld's.

One of the two books published in 1905 was *Jokes and Their Connection with the Unconscious*, usually referred to, not quite correctly, as Freud's book on wit. The book with its rather surprising title deals with the psychological mechanisms and significance of wit and humor as illustrated in the field of jokes. It is the least read of Freud's books, perhaps because it is the most difficult to apprehend properly. But it contains some of his most delicate writing. Like the one to be mentioned next it was derived from the ideas expressed in the great *Interpretation of Dreams*, so we perceive a direct continuity of Freud's thought and studies in the early years of the century.

This book was written simultaneously with the one presently to be mentioned, the *Three Essays*. Freud kept the manuscript of each on two adjoining tables and wrote now on one and now on the other as the mood took him. It was the only occasion I know of when Freud combined the writing of two essays so close together, and it shows how nearly related the two themes were in his mind.

The other book, which was to cause a great sensation and to make Freud almost universally unpopular, was *Three Essays on the Theory of Sexuality*, one of the two most important books Freud ever wrote. There for the first time Freud put together, from what he had learned by analyses of patients and other sources, all he knew about the development of the sexual instinct from its earliest beginnings in childhood. The book certainly brought down on him more odium than any other of his writings. *The Interpretation of Dreams* had been hailed as fantastic and ridiculous, but the *Three Essays* were shockingly wicked. Freud was a man with an evil and obscene mind. Naturally the main opprobrium fell on his assertion that children are born with sexual urges, which undergo a complicated development before they attain the familiar adult form, and that their first sexual objects are their parents. This assault on the pristine innocence of childhood was unforgivable. In spite of the contemporary furor and abuse, however, which continued for perhaps twenty years, time worked its way with the book, and Freud's prediction that its conclusions would before long be taken for granted is approaching fulfillment. Today anyone who denied the existence of a sexual life in children would run the risk of being looked on as merely ignorant.

At about the same time Freud filled his cup of turpitude in the eyes of the medical profession by, after *four* years of hesitation, deciding to publish a case history which is generally referred to as the "Dora analysis." [27] This fascinating application of dream analysis to the elucidation of an obscure case of hysteria was again a by-product of *The Interpretation of Dreams*. But his colleagues could not forgive the publication of such intimate details of a patient without her permission, and still more the imputing to a young girl tendencies towards revolting sexual perversions.

After this burst of literary production in 1905 Freud contented himself in the following year with publishing only one fresh paper, a lecture he had given to an audience of young jurists on the ascertaining of truth. Apart from his books on dreams and on jokes this may be called his first excursus outside the purely medical field, but it was very far from being his last. In the same year he published the first of his five volumes entitled *Sammlung Kleiner Schriften zur Neurosenlehre* (Collected Short Papers on the Theory of Neuroses). They comprised the scattered writings of the past ten years on this topic, which were now gathered together in a convenient and accessible form.

Freud did very little journalistic work in this period. He had given up the regular reviewing and abstracting he had done for years for German neurological periodicals. The only record I can find is of four book reviews in the *Neue Freie Presse*, their dates being February 8, 1903; two on February 4, 1904; and the last one on August 31, 1905.

The only important event in Freud's personal life in the period under consideration was the final resolution of his intimate friendship with Fliess. The unpleasant scene between the two in 1900[28] and the Swoboda-Weininger affair in 1904 were followed by Fliess's public denunciation of Freud in 1906, to which, as his letters to the press show, Freud responded with considerable indignation. Soon, however, he not only recovered his calm, but achieved a far more objective view of his old friend than had hitherto been possible. He retained his admiration for his striking personality and gifts, and also his gratitude for the invaluable support Fliess had accorded him at a critical period of his life, but he freed himself from his former dependence on Fliess's opinions and judgment.

In 1906, on the occasion of his fiftieth birthday, the little group of adherents in Vienna presented him with a medallion, designed by a well-known sculptor, Karl Maria Schwerdtner, having on the obverse his side-portrait in bas-relief and on the reverse a Greek design of Oedipus answering the Sphinx. Around it is a line from Sophocles' *Oedipus Tyrannus*.[d]

ὃς τὰ κλείν' αἰνίγματ' ᾔδει καὶ κράτιστος ἦν ἀνήρ.

When he showed it to me a few years later I asked him to translate the passage, my Greek having rusted considerably, but he modestly

[d] "Who divined the famed riddle and was a man most mighty."

said I must ask someone else to do it. Thanks to Dr. Hitschmann's kindness I am happy to possess a duplicate of this medallion.

At the presentation of the medallion there was a curious incident. When Freud read the inscription he became pale and agitated and in a strangled voice demanded to know who had thought of it. He behaved as if he had encountered a *revenant,* and so he had. After Federn told him it was he who had chosen the inscription Freud disclosed that as a young student at the University of Vienna he used to stroll around the great arcaded court inspecting the busts of former famous professors of the institution. He then had the phantasy, not merely of seeing his own bust there in the future, which would not have been anything remarkable in an ambitious student, but of it actually being inscribed with the *identical* words he now saw on the medallion.

Not long ago I was able to fulfill his youthful wish by presenting to the University of Vienna, for erection in the court, the bust of Freud made by the sculptor Königsberger in 1921, and the line from Sophocles was added. It was unveiled at a ceremony on February 4, 1955. It is a very rare example of such a daydream of adolescence coming true in every detail, even if it took eighty years to do so.

Freud's private practice had by this time increased to full-time work. Few patients came, either then or later, from Vienna. The majority came from eastern Europe: Russia, Hungary, Poland, Roumania, and so on.

Freud continued his University lectures during these years. We happen to possess a list of those attending in the year 1906. They were seven in all: Carl Furtmüller, Franz Grüner, Gustav Grüner, Paul Klemperer (who kindly gave me this information), H. Oppenheim, Emmy Pisko (Sachs's future wife), Hanns Sachs and Richard Wagner. Four years later all these, except Emmy Pisko, became members of the Vienna Society, but in October of the same year (1910) four of them resigned with Adler, all except Sachs and Wagner.

The early years of the century were relatively peaceful and happy ones. They were an interval between the storms before and after. Freud was never again to know such a peaceful and enjoyable period. The even tenor of his life passed between professional work, including the literary work, and private relaxations. There was the weekly game of cards on Saturday, his favorite tarock; after giving his weekly University lecture from seven to nine he would hire a cab at the hospital and drive to his friend Königstein's house for the game. He could not see much of his children except at meal times and on Sundays, so they all greatly looked forward to the lengthy summer holidays together. The family would move out of Vienna in June when the hot weather began and he usually joined them in the middle of July for a month or longer.

Freud was very fond of mountain scenery and of climbing, though he would hardly be called a mountaineer in the strict sense of the word. Still, someone who could climb the crampons of the Dachstein must have had a good head for heights as well as the other necessary attributes. The family spent their summer holidays in Bavaria in the first years of the century: in 1901 at Thumsee near Bad Reichenhall and close to Salzburg; in 1902, 1903 and 1904 in the Villa Sonnenfels, near Berchtesgaden. In 1905 the holiday was at Alt-Aussee in the Salzkammergut. In 1906 they were at Lavarone (Hotel du Lac), "where the laburnum flowers in August," a hilly spot in the Trentino or what was then called the South Tyrol.

His son Martin tells me of an incident on the first of these holidays which is worth recording. On returning from a walk they found their way home, which meant crossing the Thumsee to get to their hotel, barricaded by a noisy crowd who were shouting anti-Semitic slogans at them. Swinging his walking-stick Freud unhesitatingly charged into them with an expression on his face that made them give way before him. It was by no means his first experience of the kind. I recall a particularly unpleasant one where he also cowed a hostile group that happened on a train journey from Hamburg to Vienna during his engagement time. Freud could on occasion create a formidable impression with a stern and somewhat scowling glance. The last time when it was displayed, and with success, was when he faced the Nazis in his home in 1938.

But he also loved to roam farther afield for his own edification. It not being feasible to cart the whole family along on distant tours he would nearly always choose some companion, for he greatly disliked traveling alone. His wife, busy with other duties, was seldom mobile enough to travel, nor was she equal to Freud's restless pace or his omnivorous passion for sightseeing. At times he thought it unfair that he should have such enjoyable experiences without her and wished she could race along with him. Thus in a letter from Sorrento[29] he consoled her with the promise to take her along with him to England next year, a trip, however, which did not come off. But almost every day on such tours he would send a postcard or telegram to her and every few days a long letter; these communications have all been faithfully preserved. There was always a special congratulatory telegram on the anniversary of their wedding day, September 14. It was very important to him to keep in constant touch with her, to hear the home news and to let her know the details of his movements and doings. From those communications it has been possible to reconstruct a narrative of the tours.

In the late summer of 1901 there took place an event which had the highest emotional significance for Freud, one which he called "the high-point of my life." [30] It was the visit to Rome, so long yearned for. It was something vastly important to him and consideration of it must therefore yield some secret of his inner life.

Of the lasting strength of the longing there is not the slightest doubt. It is a theme that kept recurring in the correspondence with Fliess,[31] particularly in the late nineties, and Freud wrote openly and at length about it in *The Interpretation of Dreams*, since it played an extensive part even in his dream life.[32] It was one that evidently began in his boyhood, and, as he himself put it, "It became the symbol for a number of warmly cherished wishes." [33] In a letter of October 23, 1898,[34] he mentioned how he was spending his spare time in studying the topography of Rome, and four months later he spoke of a secret wish that would mature if he could only get to Rome.[35] He added that to gratify it he was prepared to surrender his docentship. One can only surmise what that wish was. My own guess is that it was one more of his numerous wishes to get away from Vienna for good, since in a later letter to his wife on a subsequent visit to Rome he expressed the hope that they might be able to settle there permanently.[36]

Another measure of its strength is the great happiness and even exaltation he experienced on every visit to Rome. Its fascination never palled for a moment, and letter after letter speaks of it in the most glowing language.

Yet on the other hand there is plenty of evidence that the fulfillment of this great wish was opposed by some mysterious taboo which made him doubt if the wish could ever be realized. It was something too good to be true. At times he tried to rationalize his inhibition by saying that the climate in Rome in the summer made it impossible, but all the time he knew there was something deeper holding him back. So his years of extensive travels in northern and central Italy brought him little nearer to Rome than Trasimeno (in 1897). Thus far and no farther said the inner voice, just as it had spoken to Hannibal at that spot two thousand years ago. But he did at least surpass Hannibal in catching sight of the Tiber.

It was inevitable that people should wonder about this deep conflict in Freud's mind, and various explanations, analytic and otherwise, have been proferred. Since I disagree with all of them I feel
called upon to offer one of my own, and I promise I shall not indulge
in any speculative play on words such as that crucifers in a dream must
refer to the Cross of Christ, that respect for his teacher Brücke concealed awe of the Pope because Brücke is the German for pons and
pons refers to Pontificus, or that Freud's agile habit of darting up-
stairs three at a time was an expression of his secret adoration of the
Trinity![37] The suggestion which has been made that the thought of
Rome covered that of Jerusalem, as the "promised land," has little
to commend it. It is true that he once wrote to Fliess:[38] "Were I to
close my letter with 'next Easter in Rome' I should appear like a
pious Jew,[e] so let me rather wish for a meeting in summer in Berlin."
But Jerusalem meant little to the unorthodox Freud until after the
Zionist settlement there following the Balfour Declaration, and that
was twenty years ahead. He certainly had no longing to go there.

Then there is the most astonishing explanation of all: Freud is supposed to have had a secret longing, which he concealed from himself,
to join the Roman Catholic Church and thus further his worldly
prospects! As Velikovsky puts it: "In order to get ahead he would have
to conclude a Faust-like pact; he would have to sell his soul to the
Church."[39] It is linked with the notion that Freud resented being a
Jew and wished he were a Gentile, a notion supported by Oehlschlegel[40] and Puner.[41] Both these ideas I find frankly absurd; they are
incompatible with all we know of Freud. Worldly advancement meant
very little to him, and it would never have occurred to him to sacrifice
any principle for such a reason. Then those Viennese Jews who were
"converted" for worldly motives nearly always became Protestants,
not Catholics. As long as they were baptized the Catholic authorities
accepted them as Christians, and being a Protestant was a far milder
step to take than becoming a Catholic. Freud did once, it is true, for
five minutes toy with this idea, but for anti-religious reasons;[42] a
Protestant was allowed to have a civil wedding, and Freud detested
religious ceremonies of any kind, Jewish as much as Christian. The
picture of Freud accepting the ceremonies and beliefs of the Catholic
Church provokes only risibility in anyone who knew him. Nor is there

---

[e] Referring to the sentence at the end of the Passover Service from which
many Jews employ the sentence: "Next year in Jerusalem" to express
various genuine or even illusory hopes.

any justification for twisting his very natural resentment at the unjust treatment meted out to Jews into the notion that he resented *being* a Jew; his whole personality was identified with the fact that he *was* one, and wholeheartedly so.

Let us keep closer to the facts. To Freud, as to everyone else in the world, Rome meant two things; in fact there are two Romes (apart from the present political one). There is ancient Rome, in whose culture and history Freud was deeply steeped, the culture that gave birth to European civilization. This alone would appeal powerfully to Freud's interest, which ever turned to the matter of origins and beginnings. Then there is the Christian Rome that destroyed and supplanted the older one. This could only be an enemy to him, the source of all the persecutions Freud's people had endured throughout the ages. But an enemy always comes between one and a loved object and if possible has first to be overcome. Even after reaching his goal Freud related how the sight of that second Rome, with the evidences all around him of what in his forthright manner he called "the lie of salvation," impaired his enjoyment of the first.[43]

I do not propose to reinterpret any of Freud's dreams, a proceeding which I should stigmatize as at least hazardous, but one dream of his may be cited as being pertinent in this connection. This is the dream labeled "My son, the Myops." In discussing it Freud wrote: "Incidentally, the situation in the dream of my removing my children to safety from the City of Rome was distorted by being related back to an analogous event that occurred in my own childhood: I was envying some relatives, who, many years ago, had had an opportunity of removing their children to another country." [44] Freud was here plainly referring to his two half-brothers' move to England when he was three years old. He never ceased to envy them for being able to bring up their children in a country far freer from anti-Semitism than was his own. It is clear, therefore, that Rome contained two entities, one loved, the other feared and hated.

We have two other incontrovertible facts to take into account. One is that he quoted Rank's study of the symbolism of cities and Mother Earth[45] in which the following sentence occurs.[46] "The oracle given to the Tarquins is equally well known, which prophesied that the conquest of Rome would fall to that one of them who should first 'kiss' his mother." This passage, which Freud cites as one of the variants of the Oedipus legend, is evidently a reversal of the underlying idea that in order to sleep with one's mother one has first to conquer an enemy.

The second fact is Freud's ancient and passionate identification of himself with the Semitic Hannibal.[47] Hannibal's attempt to gain possession of Rome, the "Mother of Cities," was thwarted by some nameless inhibition when he was on the point of success. For years Freud could get little nearer to Rome than Trasimeno, the place where Hannibal finally halted.

Freud had no compunction in admitting his love for the first Rome and his dislike of the second, but there were formidable resistances against linking these emotions with the corresponding primordial figures whom they had come to symbolize. It was only after four years of determined and unsparing self-analysis that Freud at last conquered those resistances and triumphantly entered Rome. With his characteristic understatement he added a footnote in the second edition of *The Interpretation of Dreams* which ran: "I discovered long since that it only needs a little courage [!] to fulfill wishes which till then have been regarded as unattainable."[48]

One sign of the heightened self-confidence that Freud's entering Rome betokened was his willingness to take appropriate steps to circumvent the clerical anti-Semitic authorities who had for so many years denied his well-earned entry into the ranks of University professors. Announcing to his friend Fliess his success in this undertaking he admitted he had been a donkey not to achieve it three years before, and added: "Other people are clever enough to do so without having first to get to Rome."[49]

After these preliminaries let us take up the narrative itself. Leaving his family in Thumsee and, accompanied by his brother Alexander, he broke his journey in Trient, where he visited the Castello and the museum; it was a town he had always been fond of and he was loth to leave. They took the overnight train, however, and at noon on Monday, September 2, 1901,ᶠ Freud had reached his heart's desire and found himself in Rome. It was the first of seven visits to the Holy City. He immediately wrote home saying that within an hour he had had a bath and felt himself a proper Roman; it was incomprehensible that he had not got there years ago. And the Hotel Milano had electric light and charged only four lire a day.

The next morning he started at half-past seven by visiting St. Peter's and the Vatican Museum, where he found the Raphaels "a rare enjoyment." "And to think that for years I was afraid to come to Rome." He soon tossed a coin into the fountain of Trevi, vowing that he would

ᶠ Not in 1913, as Mrs. Puner says.[50] Nor is she correct in saying that 1913 was the first of many visits; there was only one subsequent one (in 1923).

soon return to Rome, which indeed he did the very next year. He also thrust his hand into the Bocca della Veritá in S. Maria in Cosmedin, a superfluous gesture for a man of such integrity.

On the following day he put in two and a half hours in the Museo Nazionale and then rode in a fiacre, at two lire an hour, from three to seven, getting a general impression. It was all more splendid than he could say. He had never felt so well in his life. And the next day he caught his first glimpse (first of how many later!) of Michelangelo's statue of Moses. After staring at it for a while he suddenly had a flash of intuition, at reflecting on Michelangelo's personality, that gave him an understanding of it, though it was probably not quite the same explanation he was to expound thirteen years later. It was a busy day, since he also inspected the Pantheon and again explored the Vatican Museum, where he specially noted the Laocoon and the Apollo Belvedere. He was still in an exalted mood. On the following day came the Palatine, which he told me became his favorite corner of Rome. Alexander wanted to dash to Naples for a day, but they found that the museum in Pompeii would be closed just then for a festival, so they spent a day in Tivoli. Freud was by now somewhat of a connoisseur of Italian wine and he had hard things to say about the local wine there; it tasted like potassium manganate!

On September 10 he was again in the Vatican Museum and came away from it exhilarated by the beauty of what he had seen. The next day was spent in the Alban hills and the children must be told that he rode for two hours on a donkey.

His old misgivings about the climate of Rome in the summer were not entirely unjustified. On his third morning there was a terrific thunderstorm—"of the kind that Michelangelo might have made"; the lightning was so brilliant that he could read the hieroglyphics on an obelisk some way off—or at least would have been able to were he not in the position of the peasant who thought he could read if only he wore spectacles. Two days before leaving there was a sirocco that gave him the feeling of being terribly tired, and he was also depressed to think the end of the wonderful holiday was so near.

After twelve unforgettable days in Rome Freud set out on September 14 and reached Vienna after two nights in the train.

At the end of August 1902, emboldened by his triumph over the heat in Rome the year before, he planned to visit Naples and its neighborhood, and, if possible, also Sicily. His friend Paul Hammerschlag had primed him with information about Naples. Setting off on August 26 from Königssee he sent a card to his sister-in-law, Minna

Bernays, from Rosenheim before crossing the frontier into Austria; Breuer and Fleischl were on the same train. An overnight journey brought him to Bozen where he was to meet his brother, Alexander, again the companion of his tour. There he related meeting his double (adding, "another one, not Horch" [g]), and in one of his superstitious moods asked: "Does this signify *Vedere Napoli e poi morire?*" [h] Death was seldom far from his thoughts. The next morning they dashed off via Trient to Venice, which again he found "indescribably beautiful"; they were there from noon to nine in the evening. Then overnight to Orvieto, but at half past two in the morning, when they had to change trains at Bologna into the express from Munich, there was time for another postcard. Orvieto was reached at eleven in the morning and the day spent there, since the train for Rome did not leave until nine at night. Only twenty-four hours were spared for Rome, and this time they stayed at the Hotel Rosetta. So they got to Naples at two in the afternoon of the thirty-first.

Naples, however, proved to be "inhumanly hot," so they contented themselves with a visit to the famous aquarium and two days later moved on to Sorrento. There the Hotel Cocumella charged them only ten lire a day all found. It was hot enough there also, so they gave up the idea of Sicily and decided to have a lazy time for a week and enjoy the bathing. The letter that follows gives his impressions of Sorrento.

"September 3, 1902

"My Dear Ones:

"*Kennst du das Land wo die Citronen blühen?* [1]

"If not, I will describe to you what I can see from the terrace in front of our room on the first floor of the Cocumella. On my left there is the shade from another wing of the building, which is a good thing, or otherwise I shouldn't be sitting here. To the right, beyond the end of the terrace, there is a maze of tree-tops above which three pines stand out most elegantly. In between I can see tall walnut trees, fig trees, (the nearest of which I can almost reach), chestnut trees, etc. The darkest green, which doesn't quite come to the top of the wall, belongs, as I well know, to orange and lemon trees laden with green fruit, and when I stand up and look down into the garden I can see

[g] Evidently someone who closely resembled Freud
[h] See Naples and die.
[1] From Goethe's *Mignon*. Thomas Carlyle has translated this as "Know'st thou the land where lemon-trees do bloom?" [51]

on the farthest trees the great orange-yellow balloons '*im dunkeln Laube glühend*'.[j] One of these trees has achieved a strange color effect by being clothed with a clematis with enormous blue bell flowers. Just imagine all that.

"The woods to the left reach to a quite presentable mountain, around which a road has been marked out like a white girdle. Up above there are the gleaming white walls of an old castle. I believe the hill must be the Monte San Angelo. I don't propose to linger at the sight of it, since beyond my third and highest pine I catch sight of another mountain above which a tiny cloudlet hovers. At its foot there is a cluster of little houses beyond which one can catch a glimpse of the sea. It is of course His Majesty Mount Vesuvius himself, with the Torre Annunziata near which lies Pompeii. Vesuvius is clearer than usual; it has been misty in the last few days. Finally, just in front I need only look over the roof of a Russian villa to see the blue sea, the surface of which is slightly troubled. It ends in a long white strand which can be reached by boat in an hour and a quarter. That is where Naples is, a dog's kennel or monkey's cage, where it was quite impossible to stay; but by night its lights look almost as beautiful as Vienna from the Bellevue. The finest pine of all divides the view into two equal parts. Far to the left is an uneven rock, the Island of Ischia, and were it not for the house in the way I should have to describe Capri, three quarters of an hour away.

"All that is very beautiful, but it is different from what we had pictured. It is impossible to move about to look at the different views or to change one's outlook. It is frightfully hot, though everyone says it has been so for only four or five days. From eleven to four one simply can't move, and even before and after that time one can only drive or bathe; woe to him who tries to walk. Our first two days here have been given up to bathing and *dolce far niente*.[k] All the same there has been something else. Last evening we were at the theatre, where we saw a light opera from a quarter to ten till a quarter to one. It was of course in the open, in a courtyard, and the wings were formed by plants of a kind that we hire for weddings or funerals. The best society of Sorrento was present, displaying the best manners. One can see that the people here like to live by night."

(The rest of the letter is taken up with instructions for postal communication.)

[j] From the same poem of Goethe's, (*Mignon*). The Carlyle translation is "And oranges like gold in leafy gloom."
[k] Sweet idleness.

But the eager Freud could not laze for long, especially when there were such wonderful things within reach. The very next day they sailed to Naples to explore the Pompeian relics in the museum there, and spent the following day in Pompeii itself, "a ravishing experience." They were back in Sorrento that evening, September 5, and the next day sailed to Capri. A night was spent there and of course the Blue Grotto properly visited. After a full day's rest in Sorrento they embarked on a two and a half days' excursion to Amalfi, Salerno and the celebrated temples of Paestum. The weather having broken, they returned to Naples on the twelfth, and on the next day climbed Vesuvius. They left on the evening of the fourteenth for Venice, where they were to meet Minna Bernays, and so back to Vienna.

In 1903 his traveling companion was his sister-in-law, Minna Bernays, but the holiday was only for a fortnight. The first week they spent in Munich and Nuremberg, where it was so hot that they longed for the mountains and left for Bozen. There, however, there were too many thunderstorms and Minna was in poor health, so they spent the remaining days at Meran, a favorite resort of the women of the family.

In 1904 he joined the family in Königssee on July 12, and a fortnight later his wife left there for a stay of a couple of weeks in Hamburg with her mother. His brother Alexander announced that he could only get a week's leave that year. They planned to spend it in Corfu, but fate had a more exciting experience in store for them. Freud parted from his family on August 28, arrived at Graz the same day and left there at midnight for Trieste. There he met his brother at the Hotel Buon Pastore and they took the funicular to Opcina to lunch there. Alexander now met a friend who advised them not to go to Corfu where it would be impossibly hot, and instead to take a trip to Athens by a steamer leaving the next morning.[1] Both the brothers saw only difficulties in the idea, about passports, etc., but when the time came, without saying a word to each other, they went to the shipping office and booked tickets. They had visited Miramar, the Emperor of Mexico's palace, and bathed at Barcola. This had been so enjoyable that they hesitated about going away, but at half-past ten the next morning, August 30, they sailed for Brindisi, a twenty-four-hour trip. Among the passengers was Professor Dörpfeld, the assistant of the famous archaeologist, Schliemann. Freud gazed with awe at the man who had helped to discover ancient Troy, but he was too shy

[1] Not the same afternoon, as Freud said in relating the story thirty-two years later.[52]

to approach him. The day after they had three hours at Corfu, which Freud likened to Ragusa; he had time to visit the two old Venetian fortresses there. The ship stopped at Patras the next morning, went on to the Piraeus, and at noon on September 3 they were in Athens. The first impression was an unforgettable and undescribable one of the temple of Theseus.

The following morning they spent two hours on the Acropolis, for which visit Freud had prepared himself by putting on his best shirt. In writing home he related that the experience there had surpassed anything he had ever seen or could imagine, and when we remember the wealth of classical lore with which his mind had been stored from boyhood onward and his sensitive feeling for beauty we can well understand what the impressions meant to him. More than twenty years later he said that the amber-colored columns of the Acropolis were the most beautiful things he had ever seen in his life.[53] When standing there he had a curious psychological experience, one which he analyzed many years later in a letter to Romain Rolland.[54] It was a peculiar disbelief in the reality of what was before his eyes, and he puzzled his brother by asking him if it was true that they really were on the Acropolis. In the delicate analysis he published later Freud traced this sense of disbelief to the incredulity with which he would have greeted in his impoverished student years the idea that he should ever be in a position to visit such a wonderful place, and this in turn was connected with the forbidden wish to excel his father in achievement. He compared the mechanism at work with that he had described as operative in the people who cannot tolerate success,[m][55] a mechanism of which we shall hear more later. If anyone knew the importance of a father for a child's development it was Freud.

On this occasion Freud had to learn how different ancient Greek was from modern Greek. He was so familiar with the former that as a youth he had written his diary in Greek, but now when directing the driver of his carriage to take him to the Hotel Athena he failed, despite all varieties of pronunciation, to make himself understood and was humiliatingly reduced to writing the word down.[56]

Freud spent the whole of the next day again on the Acropolis. They left Athens on the morning of September 6, took a train to Corinth and then went along the Corinth Canal to Patras where they joined the ship that sailed at ten that evening. Then home via Trieste.

At Easter 1905 Freud undertook a few days' walking tour with his brother Alexander, evidently to explore the possibility of a summer

[m] *"Die am Erfolge scheitern."*

residence. From Bozen they did a stiff climb on the west side of the Adige Valley past St. Barbian to Bad Dreikirchen, nearly four thousand feet high, but the desirable pension there was closed. On the following day they marched up the Grödner Thal (now the Val Gardena) past St. Ulrich as far as Wolkenstein. Then back to their starting point at Waidbruck on the main line and so home.

For the summer expedition he left Alt-Aussee on September 3, accompanied by his sister-in-law Minna, and spent the night at the Hotel Europa, Innsbruck. At noon the next day they went on to Bozen, and after a break of three hours there to Rovereto. On the 5th they explored Verona and pushed on to Milan. The following day they sailed up Lake Como and stayed at the Villa Serbelloni, Bellagio, where they arrived at eight in the evening. There was an enjoyable day resting there, but in the evening they got across to Lugano. Without a pause they doubled back to Bellagio the next day and reached Pallanza on Lake Maggiore. This meant four journeys, two by train and two by boat, but they had a view of two "magic islands," the Isola Madre and the Isola Bella. In a postcard written on the Isola dei Pescatori he mentioned that Minna, who had not been in the best of health, had stood the tiring journey pretty well. The next day, September 10, they moved across to Stresa. They spent the whole of two days there, or rather in the Hotel Alpino, 2600 feet high. Then they were off again: Bergamo was visited and once more Milan. They got to Genoa that evening, without, however, missing the Villa Pallavicini at Pegli on the way. There was a good deal to see in Genoa, so they put in eight days, staying at the Hotel Continental, before returning to Vienna where work started on the 26th.

In 1906 Freud did not leave the family. They spent the first few weeks of the holiday at Lavarone, a charming spot in the Lower Dolomites, some thirty-five miles east of Trient. Freud had marked it down on discovering it in 1900,[57] but it was six years before there was a chance of getting there.

His son Martin has written, in a very literary style, an account of a somewhat ill-starred expedition on which he accompanied his father during this stay, and with his permission I shall extract from it the following features of the trip. At four in the afternoon on August 14 they left Lavarone and tramped ankle deep in dust the nineteen miles to Caldonazzo where they took a train to Trient. There they spent the rest of the evening studying architectural sights, particularly the Cathedral, during which Freud explained to his eager fifteen-year-old son the stylistic features and historical associations of the various buildings. After the coolness of the mountains they found the air in Trient stifling, nor was the prospect of sleep improved by the night-long singing beneath their window; in fact the father got only an hour's sleep and the son none at all. Undeterred, however, they set out before breakfast on an ambitious tour. The plan was to walk to Monte Gazza, climb over it and descend to Molveno. The object was to find out whether Molveno would serve as a suitable resort for the next year's holiday. They proceeded through Cadine, where they break-fasted, past Terlago and around its lake to Covello, and then they began to climb the mountain. Now Monte Gazza is a particularly arid mountain with no trace of either shade or water. A good walker can cross it in six hours in favorable circumstances, but to attempt to do so in a burning August sun did not reveal much knowledge of local conditions. After a while Martin, who was slowly making his way ahead, noticed that his father was not following, and after a short search found him reclining on a stone by a low bush. He was "purple-red, almost violet" in the face and could only make a gesture begging for a drink. The son, well-trained not to make superfluous remarks, did not ask him if he felt ill, but handed him the flask of Chianti. His father was so far gone that he drank out of the flask without using the aluminum beaker he carried in his pocket, and he so far forgot the conventions as to open his collar and throw off his tie. This struck his son as something so unusual as to indicate a serious emergency. There was, however, no other sign of his customary calm being disturbed. After a rest the trouble, presumably a heat stroke, passed off, but they wisely decided to leave the mountain for another day, retraced their steps to Terlago where they obtained a carriage that took them back to Trient and then, by another route, through San Michele to Mezzo-Lombardo. There another carriage was found that climbed to Andalo and finally to Malveno, their goal. The drive alone had taken eight hours.

After they had cooled down from the heat of Trient they all left Lavarone for Riva on Lago di Garda, a wonderful drive that took a full day. There they stayed until work once more called.

Freud had now begun to emerge from his years of isolation. A time was to come when he looked back nostalgically on the freedom and quietude of those lonely days, but once embarked on his career of recognition there was no going back. The few who had gathered around him in Vienna were to prove the forerunners of a steadily in-creasing throng of followers who, before his life ended, were to be found in every country of the world.

2

CHAPTER

The Beginning of International Recognition

(1 9 0 6 – 1 9 0 9)

FOR SOME YEARS FREUD'S WRITINGS HAD BEEN EITHER IGNORED IN THE German periodicals or else noted with contemptuous comment. Some reviews in English-speaking countries had, however, been friendly and respectful, even if they did not for a time lead to any definite acceptance of his ideas.

The first writer in English to give an account of Breuer's and Freud's work was certainly F.W.H. Myers. Only three months after it was published in the *Neurologisches Centralblatt* (January 1893) he described their "Preliminary Communication" [1] at a general meeting of the Society for Psychical Research, and his account was published in its *Proceedings* for June of that year. So the first discoveries in what later became psychoanalysis were accessible to English readers within six months of their being announced. Four years later (March 1897) he delivered an address before the same Society on "Hysteria and Genius," in which he gave an account of the *Studies in Hysteria*. This was summarized at the time in the Society's *Journal* and published at much greater length in the author's *Human Personality* which appeared in 1903, two years after his death.

The year before Myers's review of the *Studies* Dr. Mitchell Clarke, a Bristol neurologist, had published a full one in *Brain*,[2] a periodical to which Freud himself had contributed a neurological study many years before.[3] Most neurologists passed it by, but two readers made a serious mental note of it. One was Havelock Ellis. Two years later he published a paper in an American periodical in which he gave an account of the *Studies* and accepted Freud's views about the sexual aetiology of hysteria.[4] It was then reprinted eight years later in the second volume of his *Studies in the Psychology of Sex*.[5] In 1904, in the first volume of his *Studies in the Psychology of Sex*, he had devoted several pages to what he called "Freud's fascinating and really important researches." He also alluded in this and the next volume (1906), though without giving any bibliographical references to them, to Freud's papers on neurasthenia and anxiety states. In later life he often dealt with Freud's work, towards which he then developed an increasingly negative attitude.

The other was Wilfred Trotter, the famous surgeon whose name is familiar to psychologists through his book, *Instincts of the Herd in Peace and War* (which was actually composed in 1904, though not published till 1916).[a] He called my attention to Clarke's review in 1903 when I was beginning to specialize in psychopathology, and in the same year I read the much fuller account of the *Studies* in Myers' *Human Personality* which had just appeared. Havelock Ellis' discussion of the new findings appeared in the year following, and then further study necessitated the acquiring of German. The first case to be analyzed outside German-speaking countries (1905-1906) was one of conversion hysteria. One upshot of the analysis was the patient's decision to divorce her husband, a well-known New York neurologist, on the grounds of cruelty. To finish the story I may add that when I lived later in America he formed the habit of following me from one congress or medical meeting to another in order to exercise his very considerable powers of vituperation, and on one occasion Dr. James J. Putnam, Professor of Neurology at Harvard, magnanimously traveled a thousand miles to support me; between us we got on quite well. It was Dr. Putnam who published, in the first number of *The Journal of Abnormal Psychology* (February 1906), the first paper in English specifically on psychoanalysis, and the first adequate account of it in that tongue; his summing-up, however, was at that time on the whole adverse. The year before Dr. Morton Prince, of Boston, had in a letter to Freud spoken of Freud's "well-known work" and asked him to write a paper for the first number of his new periodical. In New York two immigrant Swiss psychiatrists, Adolf Meyer and August Hoch, had been following Freud's writings, the latter even with sympathy; they could hardly have failed to have mentioned them to their students.

Little of all this, however, was within Freud's ken at the time. Be-

---

[a] He has been described as "an intellect of brilliance outshone in our century by none in medicine, science and philosophy."[6]

fore 1906 the only happenings he knew of outside Vienna were the brief and cutting references in German neurological and psychological periodicals and a few elementary attempts to test some of his early ideas. The first of these was by W. Warda of Blankenburg, who was the first non-Austrian to lend any support to Freud's ideas. As early as 1900 he published a full study of a case he called "hypnoid-hysteria" which he treated by Breuer's method of catharsis; he was therefore the first foreigner to substantiate the Breuer-Freud findings through personal investigation.[7] In the next three years he published three casuistic studies on the obsessional neurosis, but he never applied the psychoanalytic method itself. He did not make much impression on Freud; a letter (unpublished) to Fliess in April 28, 1900, speaks disparagingly of Warda's effort. "He deals only with my early *Sturm und Drang* [b] period, and even brings up the old hypnoid conception that had been forced on me" (by Breuer). In 1903 Wilhelm Strohmayer, of Jena, described an obsessional case in terms of Freud's early "defense" theory,[8] and five years later published a long study with many illustrative cases that confirmed Freud's views about the relation of sexuality to anxiety and obsessions.[9] Here again, however, there was no question of psychoanalysis proper. The same applies to two other writers a little later: Otto Juliusburger, who made two confirmatory contributions in 1907 and 1909 respectively,[10] and Muthmann. Muthmann was a guest at Freud's home on February 2, 1909. He wrote the first, and I think the only, book on Breuer's cathartic treatment,[11] but he never ventured any further. Freud dryly remarked of him that he did not live up to his name.[c]

1904

In 1904, however, we come to two workers who had advanced further. Otto Gross of Graz, a genius who later unfortunately developed schizophrenia, published a paper [12] in which he ingeniously contrasted the dissociation of ideas described by Freud with the dissociation in conscious activity displayed in dementia praecox, and followed it by a very original book in which Freud's libido theory, with the concepts of repression, symbolism, etc., was fully recognized.[13] He was my first instructor in the practice of psychoanalysis and I used to be present during his treatment of a case. Later I prevented him from dragging the great Kraepelin into the courts where he proposed to discredit him by exposing his ignorance of psychoanalysis! In 1908 he

[b] Storm and Stress.
[c] "Man of courage."

was treated in the Burghölzli Mental Hospital in Zurich, where Jung, after weaning him from morphinism, conceived the ambition of being the first to cure a case of schizophrenia. He worked hard and told me that once the session continued for twenty-four hours until both their heads were nodding like China mandarins. One day, however, Gross escaped over the asylum wall and the next day sent a note to Jung asking for money to pay his hotel bill. In the First World War he enlisted in a Hungarian regiment, but before it was over his life came to an end through murder and suicide.

The other worker in question was A. Stegmann, of Dresden. In 1904 he described several successes with cases of hysteria and obsessional neurosis which he had treated by the psychoanalytic method.[14] He was the first to write about unconscious factors in asthma.[15] He died in 1912.

1906

All this was a very faint dawn. But in 1906 the westward began to brighten. In the autumn of 1904 Freud had heard from Eugen Bleuler, the Professor of Psychiatry in Zurich, that he and all his staff had for a couple of years been busily occupying themselves with psychoanalysis and finding various applications for it. The main inspiration was coming from Bleuler's chief assistant, C. G. Jung. Jung had read *The Interpretation of Dreams* soon after publication and had even made three casual references to it in a book he wrote on occultism (*absit omen!*) in 1902.[16] From 1904 on he was applying Freud's ideas in various directions. He had devised some ingenious association tests which confirmed Freud's conclusions about the way in which emotional factors may interfere with recollection[17] and by means of which he was able to demonstrate experimentally the presence of repressed material in the form of what he called "affective complexes"—adapting Theodor Ziehen's word "complex" for this purpose. In 1906 he had published his *Diagnostische Assoziationsstudien* (Diagnostic Studies in Association), a collection of valuable studies by himself and his pupils, and in the following year a book that made history in psychiatry, *The Psychology of Dementia Praecox*, which extended many of Freud's ideas into the realm of the psychoses proper. Jung of course sent him copies of both books, but so eager was Freud to read the first one that he had bought it himself before Jung's copy could arrive.

In April 1906 a regular correspondence began between Freud and Jung which lasted for nearly seven years. For some years it was a most friendly and even intimate exchange of both personal thoughts as well as scientific reflections.

The news that his researches of the past thirteen years, so scorned and despised elsewhere, were finding enthusiastic acceptance in a famous psychiatric clinic abroad warmed Freud's heart. His elation at it, and the favorable impression he soon afterwards gained of Jung's personality, made it hard to retain a cool judgment. How could he foresee that the resistances which inevitably accompany the pursuit of psychoanalysis, with which he was familiar enough in his patients, could also hamper and deflect analysts themselves?

Doubtless encouraged by the growing interest in his work Freud published in this year the first of his five *Sammlung kleiner Schriften zur Neurosenlehre.* After his outburst of activity in the previous year there were, as one might expect, no important contributions in 1906. He gave two lectures by request, one on "Sexual Abstinence" before a sociological society, and one on "Psycho-Analysis and the Ascertaining of Truth in Legal Proceedings" before the Juristic Faculty of the University; the latter was published in an anthropological journal. Then, apparently for his own amusement, since he never published it, he wrote a little essay full of fresh ideas on "Psychopathic Characters on the Stage"; it first saw the light in an English translation three years after Freud's death.

1907

In 1907 Freud had three visitors from Zurich. There were not only Swiss working under Jung's leadership in Zurich. And it happened that the first emissary from there to visit Freud was one of the strangers. It was Max Eitingon, then a medical student completing his studies in Zurich where he had come in contact with the new psychology. Born in Russia he had been brought up in Galicia and Leipzig and after leaving Zurich he settled down in Berlin, retaining, however, the Austrian nationality his father had acquired. He was to become in later years one of Freud's closest friends. The occasion for his visit was to consult Freud over a severe case he was interested in. He wrote to Freud about the case, one which, however, turned out to be unsuitable for analytic treatment, and accompanied the patient to Vienna late in January 1907. He was the first swallow of what in later years became an enormous flock of visitors. Eitingon stayed there for nearly a fortnight and attended the Wednesday meetings of the little group on January 23 and 30. He passed three or four evenings with Freud and they were spent on personal analytic work during long walks in the city. Such was the first training analysis! I remember the swift pace and rapid spate of speech on such walks. Walking fast used to stimulate the flow of Freud's thoughts, but it was at times breathtaking for a companion who would have preferred to pause and digest them. In October 1909 Eitingon spent three weeks in Vienna. Twice a week he had an evening walk with Freud, continuing his training analysis. In November of that year he moved from Zurich to Berlin, intending to stay for a year, but he remained there until he left for Palestine in 1932. He was intensely loyal to Freud, who recognized this in a letter he wrote to him on January 1st, 1913: "You were the first to reach the lonely one and will be the last to leave."

On February 22nd, 1907, Freud told his little group that Dr. Johannes Bresler, the Editor of the *Psychiatrisch-Neurologische Wochenschrift*, had invited him to become Co-editor of a new periodical he was founding, the *Zeitschrift für Religionspsychologie*. Freud assented and contributed a paper to the first number, his first one on the subject of religion.[18]

Far more exciting, however, was Jung's first visit to Freud, which took place on February 27, 1907, at ten on a Sunday morning. In the following July at the International Congress of Neurology in Amsterdam, at which we were both reading papers, Jung gave me a lively account of his first interview. He had very much to tell Freud and to ask him, and with intense animation he poured forth in a spate for three whole hours. Then the patient, absorbed listener interrupted him with the suggestion that they conduct their discussion more systematically. To Jung's great astonishment Freud proceeded to group the contents of the harangue under several precise headings that enabled them to spend the further hours in a more profitable give and take.

Jung attended the weekly meeting of the Vienna group on March 2, and was accompanied there by a Swiss pupil of his, Dr. Ludwig Binswanger, later the Director of the Kreuzlingen Mental Hospital. Binswanger had already the year before published a paper in support of Freud's theories.[19]

For two or three years, as correspondence between them shows and my own memories confirm, Jung's admiration for Freud and enthusiasm for his work were unbounded. His encounter with Freud he regarded as the high point of his life, and a couple of months after first meeting him he told him that whoever had acquired a knowledge of psychoanalysis had eaten of the tree of Paradise and attained vision.

Freud on his part was not only grateful for the support that had come to him from afar, but was also very attracted by Jung's personality. He soon decided that Jung was to be his successor and at times called him his "son and heir." He expressed the opinion that Jung and Otto Gross were the only truly original minds among his followers.[20] Jung was to be the Joshua destined to explore the promised land of psychiatry which Freud, like Moses, was only permitted to view from afar.[21] Incidentally, this remark is of interest as indicating Freud's self-identification with Moses, one which in later years became very evident.

What, I think, most attracted him to Jung was Jung's vitality, liveliness and, above all, his unrestrained imagination. This was a quality that seldom failed to captivate Freud, just as in the cases of Fliess and Ferenczi. It echoed something of great significance in his own personality, something over which his highly developed capacity for self-criticism had to exercise the strictest control. But neither with Jung nor Ferenczi did he become emotionally involved in a personal sense as he had with Fliess; he merely warmed in their presence.

That when the International Association was founded in 1910 Freud should designate Jung to be its President, and, as he hoped, for an indefinite period, was only natural. To begin with, Jung with his commanding presence and soldierly bearing looked the part of a leader. With his psychiatric training and position, his excellent intellect and his evident devotion to the work, he seemed far better qualified for the post than anyone else. Yet he had two serious disqualifications for it. It was not a position that accorded with his own feelings, which were those of a rebel, a heretic, in short a "son," rather than those of a leader, and this consideration soon became manifest in his failure of interest in pursuing his duties. Then his mentality had the serious flaw of lacking lucidity. I remember once meeting someone who had been in school with him and being struck by the answer he gave to my question of what Jung had been like as a boy: "He had a confused mind." I was not the only person to make the same observation.

Jung's admiration for Freud's personality, with its penetrating acumen, was very far from extending to his group of followers. These he described to me as a medley of artists, decadents and mediocrities, and he deplored Freud's lot in being surrounded by them. They were no doubt somewhat different in their demeanor from the professional class to whom Jung was accustomed in Switzerland but, rightly or wrongly, I could not help suspecting that some "racial" prejudice had colored his judgment. At all events the antipathy between the Swiss and the Viennese was mutual and only increased with time, a circumstance that was to cause Freud much distress.

Freud and Jung were to come together on nine or ten further occasions, including four Congresses and the journey to America together, but the freshness of the first meeting could never be experienced again. The last time they saw each other was at the Munich Congress in September 1913.

Before this memorable year was over another and more permanent friend was to visit Freud, Karl Abraham. He had held a post under Bleuler and Jung in Zurich for three years, but not being Swiss he had no prospects of further promotion there and so decided in November 1907 to settle in Berlin and practice as a psychoanalyst. Like Jung he had been studying Freud's work since 1904. He had sent Freud in June a reprint of the first of the valuable series of papers he wrote on psychoanalysis,[22] which he had read before the *Deutscher Verein für Psychiatrie* (German Psychiatric Society) at Frankfurt on April 27, 1907, and it had made a very favorable impression on Freud. It started a regular correspondence and Freud invited him to visit him. This Abraham did on December 15, 1907, and in the next few days had several animated talks with him. He also attended a meeting of the little Freud group on the 18th. The two men soon cemented what was to be an unbroken friendship, and Abraham was one of the three people (the others being Ferenczi and myself) whose constant correspondence with Freud elicited the most valuable scientific comments of any.

The next foreign visitor was an equally valuable acquisition. Sandor Ferenczi, of Budapest, who was to become Freud's closest friend and collaborator, was a general practitioner who had experimented with hypnotism. He had read *The Interpretation of Dreams* on its appearance, but had dismissed it with a shrug of his shoulders. In 1907, however, Dr. F. Stein of Budapest, a psychopathologist who, through an introduction from Jung, was slightly acquainted with Freud personally, induced Ferenczi to give him another chance, and this time the effect was electric. He wrote to Freud and, accompanied by Stein who introduced him, called on him on Sunday, February 2, 1908, shortly before the Salzburg Congress. The impression he made was such that he was invited to spend a fortnight in August with the Freud family, with whom he soon became a special favorite, on their holiday in Berchtesgaden.

Freud was early attracted by Ferenczi's enthusiasm and lively speculative turn of mind, qualities which had previously fascinated him in his great friend Fliess. This time, however, his emotions were less involved in the friendship, though he always took a keen fatherly interest in Ferenczi's private life and difficulties. They spent many holidays together, and between 1908 and 1933 exchanged more than a thousand letters, all of which have been preserved. From the very first Ferenczi discussed scientific problems in these letters, and the two men in their talks and correspondence evolved several important conclusions in psychoanalysis between them.

Hanns Sachs of Vienna had already attended Freud's University lectures for several years, and early in 1910[d] he ventured to call on him personally to present him with a little book he had just published. It was a translation of some of Kipling's *Barrack-Room Ballads*—incidentally an excellent one.

By then the members of the little circle who for many years were to be close friends of Freud's had come to know him personally: Rank in 1906, Eitingon and Abraham in 1907, Ferenczi and myself in 1908 and Sachs in 1910.

The family had enjoyed their holiday in Lavarone so much in the previous year that they went back to it in 1907. Toward the end of August they moved, first to Wolkenstein (Selva in Gardena) in the Dolomites, and then to Annenheim on the Ossiacher Lake just north of Villach in Carinthia, where they spent a fortnight. On September 12 Freud left for Bozen, his sister-in-law joining the train at the junction of Franzensfeste. The rest of the family had in the meantime gone to Thalhof, Payerbach-Reichenau, to await his return. From Bozen Freud wrote saying he had not yet made any plans. He always preferred traveling as freely as possible. The next day he wrote saying they were leaving for Rome on the following morning and would arrive there in the evening, but he must have changed his mind, since two days later, on the 15th, a letter arrived from Florence. On the 16th, after showing Minna something of Florence and his beloved Fiesole, he announced that she was leaving that evening to continue her recuperation at Meran, spending the night at Verona. In the meantime Freud had left for Orvieto, and on the following day reached Rome. Freud wanted some time alone on this trip in order to get some writing done.

In the first letter from Rome Freud told his wife he couldn't understand why she should think he was so very venturesome, since he was extremely comfortable in the Hotel Milano and could work there.

* Not 1909, the date Sachs gave in his book.[28]

He spent the whole morning of the first day in the Forum and worked in the afternoon. The next day he visited the Garibaldi monument to get his favorite view of Rome. He had not yet been able to get to the Villa Borghese and had visited St. Peter's first, since the next day was a festival. Eitingon, who was passing through Rome, called on him that evening, but they missed each other; they had met in Florence a few days before. The following day was devoted to the Catacombs where Freud naturally was most interested in the Jewish ones. On the shelves were still candlesticks "which I believe are called Menorahs," a remark that illustrates his unfamiliarity with synagogues. The next letter is worth quoting as a rather typical one from his travels.

"Rome, 22.9:1907

"Dear Family,

"On the Piazza Colonna, behind which, as you know, I am staying, a couple of thousand people congregate every night. The evening air is truly delicious; wind is hardly known in Rome. Behind the column is a bandstand and there is music every night. At the other end of the square a screen is put up on the roof of one of the houses; there on the screen an Italian advertising company projects pictures. They are actually advertisements, but to bribe the public to give its attention they are interspersed with pictures of landscapes, negroes of the Congo, ascents of glaciers and so on. But that isn't enough to fill in the time. So they show short films for the sake of which the children (your father included) suffer quietly the advertisements and the monotonous photographs. They are mean with those titbits; I had to see the same piece over and over again. When I turn back to go a certain tension in the crowd recalls me; I look again and indeed a new performance has begun. And so I stay on. Until nine the magic works; then I begin to feel lonely in the crowd and go home to write to you after I have ordered a bottle of fresh water. The others who promenade in twos or *undici, dodici* stay on as long as the music and pictures continue.

"In a corner of the square one of those awful flashing pictures is still making its disturbing appearance. I think the medicine is called Fermentine. Two years ago when I was in Genoa with your aunt it was called TOT; it was an indigestion remedy and the look of it was really unbearable. But it doesn't seem to disturb the people. They often feel free to stare at the pictures and listen at the same time to the talk of their friends behind them. There are a lot of small children among them, of whom many women would say that they should have been in bed a long time ago. Strangers and natives mix in the most easy fashion. The customers of the restaurant behind the column and of the confectioner's on one side of the square enjoy themselves too; besides that there are deck-chairs to be had near the music, and a lot of people like sitting on the stone balustrade at the fountain. I am not sure at the moment whether I haven't forgotten another fountain in the square; it is such a large square. In the middle of it the Corso Umberto, of which it is in fact an enlargement, runs through. Coaches and electric tramways pass, but they don't do any harm, for a Roman never moves for any vehicle and the drivers don't seem to know they have the right to run people over. When the music stops everyone claps loudly, even those who haven't listened. From time to time a horrible shouting breaks out in the otherwise quiet and rather distinguished crowd. It comes from half a dozen or so newspaper boys who hurl themselves into the crowd with the evening edition of a paper, breathless like the herald of Marathon; the idea is that with their news they relieve an almost unbearable tension. When they have an accident to report, people wounded or killed, they feel they are masters of the situation. I know those papers and buy two of them every day for five centesimi each; they are cheap, but I must say they never contain anything that could interest a sensible person from abroad. Occasionally there is something like a riot, all the youngsters run in one direction. But there is no need to be afraid, nothing has happened and they return peacefully. The women in the crowd are very beautiful, so far as they are Roman. Roman women are, strange to say, even beautiful when they are ugly, but not many of them are that.

"I can hear the music plainly in my room; the pictures I cannot of course see. Just now the people are clapping again.

"With my best love
"Papa"

Immediately after this came a letter to his daughter Mathilde apologizing for his having overlooked a fountain in the Piazza, "which shows how hard it is to observe accurately." The next day was taken up with "overpowering impressions" from the museums, so much so that he now felt tired of sight-seeing and began to think of getting back home. But he was pleased to have recognized the Gradiva plaque in the Vatican. In the last letter, of September 24, he gave an amusing description of a presentation of *Carmen,* in which among other things his attitude to music is displayed. The first of the orchestra to arrive was a violinist, who started tuning his instrument "having evidently forgotten to do so at home." The conductor stood absolutely motionless for several minutes, but it was only "the calm before the storm, which presently broke loose." Rome was as heavenly as ever. If only he could live there. On the last day he climbed the Castel S. Angelo for a view of Rome, visited the Sistine chapel once more and revelled in the wonderful antiquities of the Vatican Museum. He left on the 26th, after having had only eight days in Rome, and started work on the 30th.

In 1907 he was asked by Dr. Fürst, the Editor of a periodical devoted to social medicine and hygiene, to express his views on what was then a new question, that of the sexual enlightenment of children. Freud was naturally in favor of it, having seen so many painful results of withholding such information from children, and he related some poignant examples of them. A more important publication, however, was Freud's first contribution to the study of religion, in which he compared and contrasted certain religious practices with the compulsive acts performed by obsessional patients. The main production of the year was his book on Jensen's novel *Gradiva*. The contents, as well as those of Freud's other writings will be considered later in the appropriate chapter. The book formed the first of a new series of publications, the first of several he was to edit, the *Schriften zur angewandten Seelenkunde* (Papers on Applied Psychology) (Deuticke). It was replaced by other series in 1920, when the twentieth volume of the *Schriften* was published. This in itself is significant of the change in Freud's prospects from ten years before when there seemed little in store for him but a lonely life in his scientific work.

1908

At the end of November 1907 I had spent a week in Zurich with Jung, where I met, among others working there, Brill and Peterson of New York. At the early stages of an acquaintance Jung could be very charming. As an example I might quote the following recollection. They were working at Burghölzli just then on Otto Veraguth's psychogalvanic phenomenon, and Brill started to explain it to me. Knowing that I was pretty well informed Jung interrupted him with the words: "We didn't invite Dr. Jones here to teach him, but to consult him." This short note from him at the time illustrates the same feature.

"Burghölzli, Zürich, 23.XI.1907

"Dear Dr. Jones,

"I should be very glad to see you as soon as possible. If you arrive Sunday evening, let me know it by telephone Monday morning at 9ʰ. I expect you for lunch at eleven. If you arrive Monday evening I will meet you in the Hotel Baur au Lac between 11 and 12. I hope we will have many interesting talks.

"With best greetings
"Yours very truly
"Dr. Jung"

He could also be very witty. I recollect asking him once whether he thought the vogue of Dadaism, just then beginning in Zurich, had a psychotic basis. He replied: "It is too idiotic for any decent insanity."

A little "Freud Group," as it was called, had just been started in Zurich at that time. With a few exceptions, such as Edouard Claparède of Geneva and Binswanger of Kreuzlingen, all the members came from Zurich. Jung was, of course, the leader of the group, which included among others his chief, Professor Bleuler, a relative of Jung's called Franz Riklin, and Alphonse Maeder. All of these were making useful contributions to psychoanalytical knowledge.

The little group used to meet at the Burghölzli Mental Hospital to discuss their work, and there were generally one or more guests present. I remember attending an early meeting in November 1907—I think it was the second of the meetings—when the famous neurologist C. von Monakow was present. I don't know what he made of it, but I fancied that after scaling the mountain he must have feared he had got to a witches' sabbath. He maintained, however, that he had been practicing psychoanalysis for twenty-five years, so that Freud had nothing new to teach him.

I suggested to Jung the desirability of arranging a general gathering of those interested in Freud's work, and he organized one that took place in Salzburg in the following April; it was intended to hold it in Innsbruck, but Salzburg was more convenient for the Viennese. I wanted to give it the name of "International Psycho-Analytical Congress," by which it and all subsequent ones have since been called, but he insisted on heading the invitations he sent out as *Zusammenkunft für Freud'sche Psychologie* (Meeting for Freudian Psychology), an unusual personal title for a scientific meeting. It represented an attitude which presently was to give his chief, Bleuler, a handle for criticism. Incidentally, when Abraham afterwards asked Freud under what title he was to refer to the Congress when he published the paper he had read there,[24] Freud answered that it was merely a private meeting and that Abraham was not to mention it.

Nevertheless it was an historic occasion, the first public recognition of Freud's work. Since no account of it is extant it would seem apposite to give one here. The Congress differed from all subsequent ones in having no Chairman,[e] no Secretary, no Treasurer, no Council, no kind of sub-committee whatever, and—best of all—no business meeting! It occupied only one day.

On Sunday, April 26, 1908, we assembled in the Hotel Bristol, Salzburg. Freud had arrived from Venice that morning. Among the other guests staying there were Dr. Aldren Turner, a well-known London neurologist, who must have wondered whatever was going on, and Professor Alfred E. Hoche of Freiburg, whom we shall encounter later as both a secret admirer and bitter enemy of Freud's.

The meeting was truly international, as will appear from the following facts. Nine papers were read: four from Austria, two from Switzerland, and one each from England, Germany and Hungary. There were forty-two present, half of whom were or became practicing analysts. At the time of writing the only survivors are, besides myself, Graf, Hitschmann, and Jung. The names of those attending, checked by enquiries, were:

From America[f]

    A. A. Brill, New York

From Austria

    Alfred Adler, Vienna
    D. J. Bach, Vienna
    Guido Brecher, Gastein-Meran
    Frau Professor Erismann, Vienna
    Paul Federn, Vienna
    Sigmund Freud, Vienna
    Josef K. Friedjung, Vienna
    Max Graf, Vienna
    Frieda Gross, Graz and Munich
    Otto Gross, Graz and Munich

---

[e] Freud had wanted Bleuler to preside but Jung was so sure he would refuse that he did not even ask him.

[f] Jung had got Peterson to invite Morton Prince of Boston to attend the Congress. Prince actually announced a paper on "Psychogalvanic reactions in a case of Multiple Personality," but he was unable to attend.

Eduard Hitschmann, Vienna
Hugo Heller, Vienna
Edwin Hollerung, Vienna
Ludwig Jekels, Bielitz
Max Kahane, Vienna
Paul Klemperer, Vienna
Professor Leopold Königstein, Vienna
Hans Königstein, Vienna
Otto Rank, Vienna
von Redlich, Vienna
Rudolf Reitler, Baden near Vienna
Isidor Sadger, Vienna
Maximilian Steiner, Vienna
Wilhelm Stekel, Vienna
Hugo Schwerdtner, Vienna
Fritz Wittels, Vienna

From England

Ernest Jones, London
Wilfred Trotter, London[g]

From Germany

Karl Abraham, Berlin
Arend, Munich
Professor A. Löwenfeld, Munich
A. Ludwig, Munich
A. Stegmann, Dresden

From Hungary

Sandor Ferenczi, Budapest
F. Stein, Budapest

From Switzerland

Hans Bertschinger, Schaffhausen
Prof. E. Bleuler, Zurich
Edouard Claparède, Geneva
Max Eitingon, Zurich
C. G. Jung, Zurich
Franz Riklin, Zurich

The papers, in the order they were given, were as follows:

Freud: "Case History"
Jones: "Rationalization in Everyday Life"

[g] This famous surgeon-psychologist did not meet Freud again for thirty years, when he was consulted by him in London.

Riklin: "Some Problems of Myth Interpretation"
Abraham: "The Psychosexual Differences between Hysteria and
                Dementia Praecox"
Şadger: "The Aetiology of Homosexuality"
Stekel: "On Anxiety Hysteria"
Jung: "On Dementia Praecox"
Adler: "Sadism in Life and in Neurosis"
Ferenczi: "Psychoanalysis and Pedagogy"

In addition Otto Rank read a passage he had discovered in Schiller's correspondence[25] in which he advised a friend to release his imagination from the restraint of critical reason by employing a flow of free association.

Most of the papers were subsequently published, but the only one that concerns us here is Freud's. Jung had begged him to relate a case history,[26] so he described the analysis of an obsessional case, one which afterwards we used to refer to as that of "The Man with the Rats." [27] He sat at the end of a long table along the sides of which we were gathered and spoke in his usual low but distinct conversational tone. He began at the Continental hour of eight in the morning and we listened with rapt attention. At eleven he broke off, suggesting we had had enough. But we were so absorbed that we insisted on his continuing, which he did until nearly one o'clock. Someone who can hold an audience engrossed for five hours must have something very worthwhile to say. What riveted us, however, was not only the novelty of what he had to tell us, but also his extraordinary gift for orderly presentation.

Among the ideas he put forward were the alternation of love and hate in respect of the same person, the early separation of the two attitudes usually resulting in repression of the hate. Then commonly follows a reaction to the hate in the form of unwonted tenderness, horror of bloodshed and so on. When the two attitudes are of equal strength there results a paralysis of thought expressed in the clinical symptom known as *folie de doute*. Obsessive tendencies, the great characteristic of this neurosis, signify a violent effort to overcome the paralysis by the utmost insistence. Another interesting feature he commented on is the regression that takes place in this neurosis from action to pure thought, this being aided by the attraction of early curiosity. It explains why most symptoms of the neurosis remain on an exclusively mental level.

Some more personal reminiscences and impressions on this first occasion of meeting Freud may perhaps be pertinent. His first remark when I was introduced (by Jung) was that from the shape of my head I could not be English and must be Welsh.[h] It astonished me, first because it is uncommon for anyone on the Continent to know of the existence of my native country, and then because I had suspected my dolichocephalic skull might as well be Teutonic as Celtic. During our long evening talk he pressed me to expound his dream theory in English; it seemed to mean more to him than other aspects of his work.

At the age of fifty-two Freud was only beginning to show slight signs of greyness. He had a strikingly well-shaped head, adorned with thick, dark, well-groomed hair, a handsome moustache, and a full pointed beard. He was about five feet eight inches tall, somewhat rotund—though probably his waist did not exceed his chest measurement—and he bore the marks of a sedentary profession. Since I am mentioning figures I may add that the circumference of his head was fifty-five and a half centimetres, the diameters measuring eighteen and fifteen and a half centimetres respectively. So with a cephalic index of eighty-six he was decidedly dolichocephalic. He had a lively and perhaps somewhat restless or even anxious manner, with quick darting eyes that gave a serious and penetrating effect. I dimly sensed some slightly feminine aspect in his manner and movements, which was perhaps why I developed something of a helping or even protective attitude towards him rather than the more characteristic filial one of many analysts. He spoke with an absolutely clear enunciation, a feature appreciated by a grateful foreigner, in a friendly tone of voice, more pleasing when low than on the rare occasions when he raised it. He was clever at elucidating my English mispronunciation of German words, but seemed sensitive to mistakes in gender;[i] I can recall, for instance, his impatience when I spoke of *"die Schnee."*

It was natural that Freud should make much of his new Swiss adherents, his first foreign ones and, incidentally, his first Gentile ones. After so many years of being cold-shouldered, ridiculed and abused it would have needed an exceptionally philosophical disposition not to have been elated when well-known University teachers from a famous Psychiatric Clinic abroad appeared on the scene in wholehearted support of his work. Fires, however, were always smoldering behind Freud's calm exterior, and his possibly excessive elation was not pleasing to the Viennese, who after all had been the first to rally round him when he stood alone in the world. Their jealousy inevitably cen-

---

[h] Only recently have I learned that Jung had already told him that!
[i] He referred in *The Interpretation of Dreams* to his own embarrassment at saying "he" instead of "it" in English.[26]

tered on Jung, about whom Freud was specially enthusiastic. Their attitude was accentuated by their Jewish suspicion of Gentiles in general with its rarely failing expectation of anti-Semitism. Freud himself shared this to some extent, but for the time being it was dormant in the pleasure of being at last recognized by the outer world. The Viennese predicted even at that early date that Jung would not long remain in the psychoanalytical camp. Whether they at that time had any justification for this is another matter, but the Germans have a good saying, "*der Hass sieht scharf.*" [j]

The papers were followed that evening by a convivial banquet, which was enlivened by an amusing speech from Brecher of Meran. He followed this custom for a few years until Hitschmann took over from him with equal success. In the middle of the dinner Freud spied someone in the hall whose back seemed familiar to him, so he went to inspect more closely. It was his half-brother Emmanuel, then seventy-four years old, who was springing a surprise on him. Freud spent the next day with him and then saw him off to Berlin before taking the night train to Vienna himself.[29]

At a small gathering after the papers, it was decided to issue a periodical, the first one to be devoted to psychoanalysis; the number of such periodicals went on increasing until the catastrophes of the Second World War, but there are still nine, apart from many "fellow-travelers." It was the *Jahrbuch für psychoanalytische und psychopathologische Forschungen*, which ceased at the outbreak of the First World War. It was directed by Bleuler and Freud and edited by Jung. Freud had the year before urged Jung to found a periodical, for which Jung then proposed the title *Archiv für Psychopathologie*.[30] I suggested it should be international, accepting papers in three languages, but negotiations with Morton Prince to amalgamate it with *The Journal of Abnormal Psychology* failed. The Viennese were offended at being ignored in the production of the new periodical, and especially at not even being consulted; it had been discussed with the Swiss, with only Abraham, Brill, Ferenczi and myself being present as well. The Viennese resentment grew and came to open expression two years later at Nuremberg.

To have a periodical to which he had free access for his publications meant a great deal to Freud. It made him feel more independent. He could now afford to laugh at his opponents. A few months later he wrote to Jung: "I quite agree with you. Many enemies, much honor.[k]

[j] Hate has a keen eye.
[k] *Viel' Feind, viel' Ehr!*

Now when we can work, publish what we like and get something out of our companionship it is very good, and I hope it will continue like that for long. If the time of 'Recognition' should arrive it would compare with the present as the weird glamour of the Inferno does with the blessed boredom of Paradise. (Naturally I mean this the other way round.)" [31]

After the Congress Brill and I went on to Vienna, where we experienced the delightful hospitality of the Freud family, and then to Budapest to visit Ferenczi. We had attended a meeting of the Vienna Society on May 6th, the anniversary of Freud's birthday. Brill sailed for New York, where a bride was awaiting him, while I spent six months working in Munich and Paris before taking up my new post in Canada.

It was at this time that Brill asked Freud for the translation rights of his writings, which Freud willingly, but rather unthinkingly, granted. It was to be the source of endless personal and even legal difficulties in the future. My own response was one of considerable relief, since I was engrossed in plans for works of my own on which I was already engaged and knew from experience what a time-robbing occupation translating could be. Freud himself was a highly gifted and swift translator, but he translated very freely, and I do not think he ever understood what an immense and difficult task it was going to be to render accurately and edit (!) his own writings. Brill's evidently imperfect knowledge of both English and German soon aroused my misgiving, so I offered to read through his manuscript and submit for his consideration any suggestions that occurred to me; my name was not to be mentioned. After all, English was my mother-tongue, whereas Brill had picked it up in the unfavorable surroundings of his early days in New York. But he rejected the offer, probably because he took it as a reflection on his linguistic capacities; he had some knowledge of half a dozen languages and in his early days had earned a living by giving lessons in them. There is no need for me to stigmatize Brill's translations; others have done so freely enough. When I remarked to Freud a couple of years later that it was a pity his work was not being presented to the English-speaking public in a more worthy form, he replied: "I'd rather have a good friend than a good translator," and went on to accuse me of being jealous of Brill. That I had no need to be, but it was never easy to change Freud's opinion on anything, and I did not speak of the matter again. It took years of protests coming in from abroad before he would acknowledge to himself the truth of my remark.

Brill's relative lack of polish in his early days could not conceal the all-important fact that he had a heart of gold. From the outset I perceived that we should get on well together in the common work we had in front of us in America, and I have never had a more loyal friend than he consistently proved to be.

At the beginning of 1909 Freud made another friendship of a very different kind; it lasted without a cloud to the end of his life. It was with *Pfarrer* Oskar Pfister of Zurich, with whom he carried on an extensive correspondence later. Pfister's first visit to Freud was on Sunday, April 25, 1909. Freud was very fond of him. He admired his high ethical standards, his unfailing altruism and his optimism concerning human nature. Probably it also amused him to think he could be on unrestrainedly friendly terms with a Protestant clergyman, to whom he could address letters as "Dear Man of God" and on whose tolerance toward "an unrepentant heretic"—as he described himself—he could always count. Pfister, on his side, felt unbounded admiration and gratitude towards the man who he insisted was a true Christian.[32] The only concession Freud could make to that gentle impeachment was to remark that his friend, Christian von Ehrenfels of Prague, who had just written a book on sexual ethics, had christened himself and Freud as "Sexual Protestants." [33]

There were a few other foreign visitors to Vienna in this period. At the beginning of July 1908, Dr. Macfie Campbell, a Scotchman who was just off to America to take up the position of director of the New York Psychiatric Institute, called on Freud.[34] He joined our group later in America, but had too cautious a temperament to go beyond taking a benevolent attitude towards psychoanalysis. Early in the following year Dr. Muthmann, one of the first Germans to follow Freud, paid him a visit in Vienna.[35] Then there was a less welcome visitor, Moll, the sexologist from Berlin, who came that April.[36] Freud thought very poorly of him and he said he gave Moll a bad time.

The after-echoes of the Salzburg Congress were mostly very pleasant, but there was one that was not. That was a clash between Abraham and Jung, which revealed their personal incompatibility and, especially on Abraham's side, considerable antagonism. He had spent happy years in Zurich but had of late been discontented with what he regarded as unscientific and mystical tendencies among those working there. The actual occasion for trouble was that Freud had, in personal talks with Abraham and Jung, expressed his opinion that dementia praecox differed from any neurosis merely in having a much earlier point of fixation, one which was at that time called simply "auto-erotism," to which regression took place in the disease process. It was a conclusion he had reached some nine years before.[37] The two men read papers on dementia praecox at the Congress, but whereas Abraham took full advantage of Freud's hints and even came to the conclusion that what was called "dementia" in this disease was due, not to any destruction of intellectual capacities, but to a massive blocking of the feeling process, Jung on the other hand merely repeated his opinion that the disease was an organic condition of the brain produced by a hypothetical "psycho-toxin."

It was one of those stupid little disputes over priority that have so often marred scientific progress, from Newton and Leibnitz onward. It arose from Abraham's omitting to mention or give any credit to Bleuler and Jung in his Congress paper for their psychological investigations into dementia praecox, which Jung took very much amiss at the time. The only interest about it is the light it throws on Freud's attitude towards such matters and the persons concerned. This is best seen by quoting the actual letters between Freud and Abraham.

"Lieber und geehrter Herr College,

"I am glad to hear that you regard Salzburg as a gratifying event. I myself cannot judge, since I stand in the midst of it all, but my inclination is also to consider this first gathering to be a promising test.

"In connection with it I would make a request to you on the fulfillment of which all sorts of things may depend. I recollect that your paper led to some conflict between you and Jung, or so at least I gathered from a few words you said to me afterwards. Now I consider some competition between you unavoidable and within certain limits quite harmless. In the matter at issue itself I unhesitatingly thought you were in the right and I attributed Jung's sensitiveness to his own vacillation. But I shouldn't like any bad feeling to come between you. We are still so few that disharmony, especially because of any personal complexes, should be out of the question among us. It is also important for us that Jung should find his way back to the views he has just forsaken, of which you have been such a consistent advocate. I believe there is some prospect of that, and Jung himself writes to me that Bleuler is showing himself amenable and almost inclined to abandon again the conception of the organic nature of dementia praecox. So you would do me a personal favor if you would communicate with Jung before publishing your paper and ask him to discuss his objections with you so that you can take them into account. A friendly gesture of that kind will assuredly put an end to the nascent disagreement between you. It would greatly please me and would show that all of us are able to gain from psychoanalysis practical advantages for the conduct of our own life. Don't make the little victory over yourself too difficult.

"Be tolerant and don't forget that really it is easier for you to follow my thoughts than for Jung, since to begin with you are completely independent, and then racial relationship brings you closer to my intellectual constitution, whereas he, being a Christian[1] and the son of a pastor, can only find his way to me against great inner resistances. His adherence is therefore all the more valuable. I was almost going to say it was only his emergence on the scene that has removed from psychoanalysis the danger of becoming a Jewish national affair.

"I hope you will give your attention to my request and I greet you warmly.

"Yours,
"Freud"

Getting no answer to this Freud became anxious and wrote again.

"May 9, 1908

"*Sehr geehrter Herr College,*

"Getting as yet no response to my request I am writing again to reinforce it. You know how willingly I put what I have at your disposal, as I do at that of others, but nothing would be more painful to me than that sensitiveness about priority among my friends and followers should be the result. If everyone plays his part it should be possible to prevent such things. I expect that you will wean yourself from them for the sake of the cause[m] as well as for myself.

"With cordial greetings,
"Yours
"Freud"

"May 11, 1908

"*Sehr verehrter Herr Professor,*

"I was just going to write to you when your second letter arrived. That I hadn't answered earlier was for a reason conducive to our mutual interests. When I read your first letter I did not entirely agree with it and so put it aside for a couple of days. Then I was able to

[1] The customary Jewish expression for "non-Jews."
[m] Freud always used the expression "*die Sache*" for psychoanalysis.

read it *sine ira et studio* and convince myself of the correctness of your arguments. I delayed no longer in writing to Zurich, but did not post the letter at once. I wanted to make sure after a few days' interval that there was nothing concealed in it that would turn the friendly overture into an attack. I know how hard I find it to avoid polemics entirely, and after reading the letter again found I was right in my suspicion. Yesterday I composed the letter afresh in its final form and I hope it will serve our cause. I wanted to write to you only after dealing with the letter to Jung and am sure you will excuse my silence. Now, when I can view the matter calmly, I have to thank you for your intervention and also for the confidence you reposed in me. You need not fear that the matter has left me with any sort of bad feeling.

"Actually I got into the conflict quite innocently. I had asked you last December whether there was any risk of my colliding with Jung, since you had communicated your ideas to both of us. You dissipated my misgiving. My Salzburg manuscript contained a sentence that would have gratified Bleuler and Jung, but following a sudden impulse I omitted it when delivering the paper. I deceived myself for the moment by a cover-motive—of saving time—while the real reason lay in my animosity against Bleuler and Jung. This came from the unduly propitiatory nature of their recent publications, from Bleuler's address in Berlin where he did not even mention you, and from various trivialities. That I did not mention Bleuler and Jung evidently signified 'Since you are turning away from the sexual theory I won't cite you when I am dealing with it.'

.   .   .

"Yours sincerely,
"Karl Abraham"

Abraham's friendly overture did not meet with the success it deserved: there was never any response to it. He then made some criticisms of Jung, but Freud told him his own opinion of Jung was more favorable. He added: "We Jews have an easier time, having no mystical element." [38] In his next letter[39] he wrote: "I will do all I can to put matters right when I go to Zurich in September. Do not misunderstand me: I have nothing to reproach you for. I surmise that the repressed anti-Semitism of the Swiss, from which I am to be spared, has been directed against you in increased force. But my opinion is that we Jews, if we want to cooperate with other people, have to develop a little masochism and be prepared to endure a certain amount of injustice. There is no other way of working together. You may be sure that if my name were Oberhuber my new ideas would despite all the other factors have met with far less resistance. . . . Why can't I pair you both together, with your keenness and Jung's enthusiasm?" Abraham then sent him the unfavorable news he had been receiving from Zurich to the effect that psychoanalysis was being put into the background as something they had got over.[40] But in September Freud spent several days in Zurich and talked with Jung for eight hours a day. He told Jung—unwisely, as one would think—of Abraham's doubts and rumors, at which Jung said he was very sorry to hear of them. He maintained that Jung had got over his oscillations and was fully committed to his (Freud's) work. He had parted from Bleuler, who was entirely negative, and had given up his post as Assistant. So Freud came away rejoicing.

In December, however, there was fresh trouble. Abraham was incensed at Jung's informing him that some important reviews he had written for the *Jahrbuch* would, because of lack of space, have to appear in the second number instead of the first. Abraham took this personally and was again suspicious of Jung's good intentions. Freud this time took Jung's side and admonished Abraham very severely. I have read all the letters he wrote in these years to his followers and consider this one to be the most censorious rebuke he administered to any of us. Since many people have declaimed about Freud's dictatorial attitude towards us it will be interesting to see if the following letter comes up to their expectations. I may add that the omitted parts of the letter were written in his usual friendly style.

"December 26, 1908

"Lieber Herr College,

"Now for the painful part. I am very sorry that you are again quarreling with Jung. In Zurich I pressed him hard and found him quite accessible. Only recently he wrote saying how glad he was to have achieved an easy relationship with you. This time I do not find you are in the right. Jung made a decision which plainly falls within his province as Editor, and in my opinion anyone who assumes responsibility and administrative powers should be allowed a certain elbow-room. His act had certainly nothing in it that was hostile to you. You are represented in the first number with your paper on the marriage of relatives, and the postponing of your review to the second number does not signify any disregard of you. I am afraid you show too much distrust of him. I should be very sorry were you to give him grounds now for justifying his earlier behavior towards you. I have

purposely refrained from exercising any influence over the arrangements of the *Jahrbuch* and think you could well do the same without
any derogation. . . . After all, our Aryan comrades are quite indispensable to us; otherwise psychoanalysis would fall a victim to anti-
Semitism.

> "With many cordial greetings
> "Yours friendlily
> "Freud"

Abraham, being a man of sense, took the criticism in the right
spirit. Jung returned Freud's visit in the following spring, and, with
his wife, stayed in Vienna from March 25 to March 30, 1909.[41]

Freud's wife was in Hamburg at the time of the Congress, visiting
her old mother, so there are several letters of the time to her. In them
Freud described the Congress as having been "a great success," mentioned Brill's and my visit to Vienna, and told her of his having seen
the *Tannhäuser* parody (by Nestroy) in the Karltheater on the afternoon of Sunday, May 10, which he had found very amusing.

At about the time of the Congress a change was being made in
Freud's domestic arrangements. At the end of 1907 his sister Frau
Rosa Graf vacated her flat which was opposite his on the same land-
ing, and Freud planned to simplify his life and also obtain more accommodation by taking it over. This meant giving up the little flat
of three rooms on the ground floor where he had worked and seen his
patients for some fifteen years. In the general clearance he took the
opportunity, for the second time in his life, to destroy a mass of
documents and letters, greatly to our loss.

After living in Vienna for nearly fifty years Freud decided to become officially a "citizen" of that city. This happened on March 4,
1908. It gave him the right to vote, which I should surmise was
the reason for his application; he only voted on the rare occasions
when a Liberal candidate put up for his constituency, and I should
not be surprised to learn that this was the first opportunity.

The family spent their summer holiday this year, 1908, at Diedfeld
Hof near Berchtesgaden in Bavaria. Freud joined them on July 15,
and so did Ferenczi. He had planned a trip to Holland followed by a
visit to his half-brother Emmanuel in Manchester, but he had to renounce the former. He left for England on September 1, traveling
both ways via the Hook and Harwich. However, he broke the journey[n]

[n] Freud later related how he managed to do this by means of a "symptomatic action" that defeated his conscious intention.[42]

so as to see the Rembrandts in The Hague, and they made an "incomparable impression" on him; Rembrandt and Michelangelo seemed to have been the painters who most deeply moved him. It was the first time he had been to England since the inspiring visit at the age of nineteen,[43] and it was to be his last before he settled there in 1938. He now spent a fortnight in England and there are half a dozen long letters written from there. He and Emmanuel went first to Blackpool and Southport and then spent four days at St. Anne's, a small resort on the Lancashire coast. It had been their intention to visit the Isle of Man, but the weather was unpropitious. They returned to Manchester on September 7 so that Freud could see his other half-brother Philipp, and he went on to London alone that evening.

Freud stayed at Ford's Hotel, Manchester Street. London was simply splendid, and he was full of praise for the people and everything he saw; even the architecture of Oxford Street met with his approval (!). He bought an English pipe and the cigars were wonderful. There was a long description of Hyde Park with the accuracy and fullness of a Baedeker; what struck him most about it was the "fairy-like beauty" of the children. The city was of course visited, but what meant most to him was the collection of antiquities, particularly the Egyptian ones, in the British Museum. He did not go to any theatre, because the evenings were given up to reading in preparation for the next day's visit to the museums.

He would have liked to spend months exploring London, but he was terribly lonely and he referred to the almost unbearable loneliness he had experienced in the week he had passed in Rome without a companion in the previous year. Also he yearned for the sun of the South. The last day in London he spent in the National Gallery, where it was the English school of Reynolds and Gainsborough that specially interested him; after all he was familiar enough with Italian pictures.

He left London on September 15 and Emmanuel joined him at Harwich. They traveled together to Berlin, where Emmanuel planned to stay for a few months, but after a day there Freud himself left for Zurich.

He stayed in Zurich for four days as Jung's guest in Burghölzli, and they had a happy and enjoyable time together. Jung took him on a motor tour to see Mount Filatus and the Rigi, and they had many walks together. He looked forward to being a guest in the new house Jung was building at Küsnacht. The two men came closer together on this visit than at any other time with perhaps the exception of their first meeting.

After the excitement of all this talking, following on the new impressions of England, Freud felt in need of a few days pure rest in the sun. So on the evening of September 21 he took the over-night train for Milan, where he changed for Besenzano. He arrived there at noon and met Minna, with whom he proposed to spend a few days on the Lago di Garda. Salo, on the west side of the lake, was the spot chosen. That was Tuesday evening and he left for home on the following Sunday morning. On the Friday there was a trip in a motor boat across the lake to San Vigilio, passing on the way the fascinating little islands whose possession he envied Prince Borghese. On the way home there was half a day at the well-known Bozen and he reached Vienna on Tuesday morning, September 29.

In 1908 Freud published five papers. The first of them, and the most original one, proved to be a bombshell and aroused more derision than anything he had hitherto written. It was a short paper, only a couple of pages, in which he pointed out that anal sensations in infancy, on the erotic nature of which he had long insisted, were capable of affecting character traits in a quite specific way. That any feature of one's character could proceed from such lowly origins seemed then to the outside world purely preposterous, although the truth of the conclusion is now widely recognized.

A paper on the relation between sexual morality and civilization foreshadowed more profound studies on the nature of civilization which came to fruition more than twenty years later.

One of the papers was an exposition on the curious hypotheses young children often form concerning the nature of sexual activity, including impregnation. Another was on the relation of hysterical phantasies to bisexuality. Then he boldly tackled an aesthetic problem in a discussion of the relation of poets to phantasy, in which he came to some striking conclusions.

About this time Freud wrote a Preface to Stekel's book on anxiety states, the only interest of which is that it was he who suggested to Stekel the term "anxiety-hysteria," thus distinguishing it from the well-known anxiety neurosis.

1909

In December 1908 an event occurred that was to introduce Freud's personality and work to a far wider and more distant circle. Stanley

Hall, the President of Clark University, Worcester, Massachusetts, invited him to give a course of lectures on the occasion of the University's celebration of the twentieth year of its foundation. Traveling expenses would be paid. But the date proposed was the first week in July and Freud considered he was "not rich enough" to lose three weeks' practice in Vienna. "America should bring in money, not cost money." [44] So, evidently with reluctance, he declined.

A couple of months later, however, Stanley Hall announced that the celebration had been postponed to the first week of September, which made it possible for Freud to accept; he was to receive three thousand marks ($714.60). He invited Ferenczi to accompany him, and his brother Alexander also expressed the wish to do so—though later this proved impossible. Freud said he felt very worked-up at the prospect.[45] Ferenczi was still more excited, started to learn English and ordered books on America for them to get a proper orientation on that mysterious country. Freud could not bring himself, however, to read them, but he learned from a book on Cyprus which he was studying that the best collection of Cyprian antiquities had found its way to New York where he hoped to see it. Commenting on his disinclination to read travel books he said: "The thought of America does not seem to matter to me, but I am looking forward very much to our journey together. It is a good illustration to the profound words in the *Magic Flute:* 'I can't compel you to love.' " [46] All he wanted to see there, he added, was Niagara Falls. I think there was here some suppression of the earlier elation lest it lead to some apprehensiveness about his task. He pretended it was not really important. He did not prepare anything for his lectures, saying he would do that on the ship.[47]

The traveling plans were also very complicated. They tried hard to secure passages on a ship from Trieste, calling at Palermo, so as to enjoy the Mediterranean, but the final decision was to sail from Bremen on the Norddeutscher Lloyd ship, the *George Washington,* on August 21. Ferenczi was concerned over whether he should bring a silk hat with him, but Freud told him that his plan was to buy one there and heave it into the sea on the way back.

In the middle of June Freud heard that Jung had also received an invitation, and he commented, "That magnifies the importance of the whole affair." [48] They at once arranged to travel together.

In the spring of that year a domestic event had taken place that gave Freud great pleasure. His eldest daughter, Mathilde, who was very close to her father, had got engaged in Meran, where she had been staying for six months, to a young Viennese, Robert Hollit-scher.[49] The wedding took place on February 7. Thanking Ferenczi for his congratulation on Mathilde's wedding Freud confessed he had wished the previous summer, when Ferenczi visited the family (for the first time) in Berchtesgaden, that he had been the lucky man;[50] his attitude towards him was always most fatherly.

The family spent their summer holidays in 1909 in Ammerwald, in a remote valley of the North Tyrol close to the Bavarian Alps. Freud left there on August 19, reaching Munich via Oberammergau in the afternoon. After he left, the family moved on to Riva on the Lago di Garda. He got to Bremen early the next morning, where he met Jung and Ferenczi. There he insured his life during the adventurous journey for twenty thousand marks ($4764.00) and Ferenczi did the same for ten thousand. He wrote four long letters to his wife the following day, three from Bremen, which he described at length, and one from Southampton, which they reached that evening. Freud had a poor night in the train from Munich to Bremen, which partly accounted for a curious incident the significance of which will be discussed later. He was host at the luncheon in Bremen and after some argument he and Ferenczi persuaded Jung to give up his principle of abstinence and to join them in drinking wine. Just after that, however, Freud fell down in a faint, the first of two such attacks in Jung's presence.[51] In the evening Jung played the host, and the next morning they went on board.

Freud started to keep a traveling diary of the trip, but gave it up after three days. Every day, however, he wrote long letters to his wife, to be posted when the opportunity came. He evidently enjoyed the voyage and they had discussions and pleasant laughter all day long. They had good weather but for fog. Freud asserted he was the best sailor of the three. During the voyage the three companions analyzed each other's dreams—the first example of group analysis—and Jung told me afterwards that Freud's dreams seemed to be mostly concerned with cares for the future of his family and of his work. Freud told me he had found his cabin steward reading *The Psychopathology of Everyday Life,* an incident that gave him the first idea that he might be famous.

Brill was, of course, on the quay when they arrived in New York on Sunday evening, September 27, but he was not allowed on board. So he sent a friend, Dr. Onuf, who had an official position, to greet the travelers. Interviews with the reporters gave little trouble, and the only account in next morning's paper baldly announced the arrival of a certain "Professor Freund (*sic*) of Vienna." They stayed at the Hotel Manhattan, paying two and a half dollars. On his first day ashore Freud called on his brother-in-law, Eli Bernays, and his old friend Lustgarten, but they were both still on holiday. So Brill showed them around. First came Central Park and then a drive through the Chinese quarter and the Ghetto; the afternoon was spent in Coney Island, "a magnified Prater." On the next morning they got to the place Freud most wanted to visit in New York, the Metropolitan Museum, where he was chiefly interested in the Grecian antiquities. Brill also showed them Columbia University. I joined the party on the following day and we all dined together in Hammerstein's Roof Garden, afterwards going on to a cinema to see one of the primitive films of those days with plenty of wild chasing. Ferenczi in his boyish way was very excited at it, but Freud was only quietly amused; it was the first film they had seen. There were more museums the next morn-ing, but in the afternoon Freud decided it was time to prepare his first lecture. By this time the rich American food had done its work on all three and they took it in turns to fast for a day.

On the evening of September 4 we all left for New Haven, an over-night journey in a curious combination of ship and hotel, and then by train to Boston and Worcester. Freud stayed with Stanley Hall, and we others at the Standish Hotel. Next morning the lectures began.

New England was by no means unprepared to listen to Freud's new doctrines. In the autumn of 1908, while staying with Morton Prince in Boston, I had held two or three colloquiums at which sixteen people were present: among others, Putnam, the Professor of Neu-rology at Harvard University; E. W. Taylor, later his successor; Werner Munsterberg, the Professor of Psychology there; Boris Sidis; and G. W. Waterman. The only one with whom I had any real suc-cess was Putnam. Then in May of the following year, not long before Freud's visit, there was an important Congress in New Haven at which Putnam and I read papers that provoked much discussion. So Freud's arrival was awaited with a good deal of eagerness.

Freud had no idea what to talk about, or at least so he said, and at first was inclined to accept Jung's suggestion that he devote his lectures to the subject of dreams,[52] but when he asked my opinion I advised him to choose a wider one and on reflection he agreed that Americans might regard the subject of dreams as not "practical" enough, if not actually frivolous. So he decided to give a more general account of psychoanalysis. Each lecture he composed in half an hour's

walk beforehand in Ferenczi's company—an illustration of how harmoniously flowing his thoughts must have been.

Freud delivered his five lectures in German, without any notes, in
a serious conversational tone that made a deep impression. A lady in
the audience was very eager to hear him talk on sexual subjects, and
begged me to ask him to. When I passed on her request he replied:
"*In Bezug auf die Sexualität lasse ich mich weder ab- noch zubringen.*"
That goes better in German, but it means he was not to be driven
to the subject any more than *away from* it.

The lectures have since been published in many different forms.[o]
Their initial reception was very mixed. The pronouncement, which I
sent Freud, from the Dean of the University of Toronto, was by no
means atypical: "An ordinary reader would gather that Freud advo-
cates free love, removal of all restraints, and a relapse into savagery." [53]

A particularly affecting moment was when Freud stood up to thank
the University for the Doctorate that was conferred on him at the
close of the ceremonies. To be treated with honor after so many years
of ostracism and contempt seemed like a dream, and he was visibly
moved when he uttered the first words of his little speech: "This is
the first official recognition of our endeavors." [p]

His pathetic encounter with William James, then fatally ill, Freud
has himself described. [54] William James, who knew German well,
followed the lectures with great interest. He was very friendly to us
and I shall never forget his parting words, said with his arm around
my shoulder: "The future of psychology belongs to your work"—
a remarkable saying when one reflects on his puritanical background.

Stanley Hall himself, the founder of experimental psychology in
America and the author of a massive work on adolescence, was en-
thusiastically complimentary to both Freud and Jung. After his return
from America Freud wrote to Pfister about him:[55] "It is one of the
pleasantest phantasies to imagine that somewhere far off, without
one's having a glimmering of it, there are decent people finding their
way into our thoughts and efforts, who after all suddenly make their
appearance. That is what happened to me with Stanley Hall. Who
could have known that over there in America, only an hour away
from Boston, there was a respectable old gentleman waiting im-
patiently for the next number of the *Jahrbuch*, reading and understanding it all, and who would then, as he expressed it himself, 'ring

o See Chapter 8, No. 4.
p "*Dies ist die erste offizielle Anerkennung unserer Benmühungen.*"

the bells for us?' " Soon afterwards I got Hall to accept the position of President of the new American Psychopathological Association I was just founding, but his interest in psychoanalysis did not last. A few years later he became a follower of Adler, the news of which hurt Freud very much.[56]

There was one little episode to do with Stanley Hall which is worth recording, since it seems to have been made the basis of an extraordinary rumor that Freud sometimes advocated parricide! The following is the translation of a letter written many years after in response to a question about the possible origin of this rumor. "Stanley Hall, who understood very little about neuroses, got me to investigate a man of his acquaintance whose agoraphobia was so severe as to make it impossible for him to earn a living. It turned out that he could not overcome a longing to be supported by his father, who, incidentally, was a stern patriarch. When Stanley Hall then asked me what he could do for the poor man I jestingly replied 'kill his father.' Hall was so alarmed that I had to assure him I had not made the same remark to the patient." [57] How many times have Freud's jokes and ironies been misunderstood by being taken seriously!

Freud made, however, a more enduring friend on this occasion. That was J. J. Putnam, the Professor of Neurology at Harvard. I had had long talks with him earlier when staying in Boston as Morton Prince's guest, and had got him to reconsider his initial objections to psychoanalysis. For a distinguished man in the sixties he was singularly open-minded, the only man I have ever known to admit in a public discussion that he had been mistaken over some point. A collection of his writings was the first volume in our International Psycho-Analytical Library series.

During the Worcester time Freud formed an exaggerated idea of my independence and feared, quite unwarrantably, that I might not become a close adherent. So he made the special gesture of coming to the station to see me off to Toronto at the end of the stay and expressing the warm hope that I would keep together with them. His last words were "You will find it worthwhile." [q] Naturally I was able to give him full assurances and he never doubted me again.

On September 13 the three friends, Brill and I having departed, visited Niagara Falls, which Freud found even grander and larger than he had expected. But in the Cave of the Winds he had his feelings hurt by the guide's pushing the other visitors back and calling out: "Let the old fellow go first." He was always sensitive to such

* *"Sie werden sehen, es wird sich lohnen."*

allusions to his age, and he quoted himself a good example of it in connection with a remark of Putnam's made about this time.[58] After all he was then only fifty-three. They took a trip in the Maid of the Mists below the Falls and also set foot in Canada, to Freud's great pleasure.

The three then proceeded to Putnam's camp in the Adirondack Mountains near Lake Placid, where they stayed for four days. Freud sent his wife a long description of the novel surroundings, a collection of huts in a wilderness. His enjoyment of the visit was somewhat marred by a definite, though mild, attack of appendicitis.[59] He did not mention it to anyone, not wishing to cause his host any embarrassment or to make Ferenczi anxious. Nevertheless it was otherwise a merry time, and Jung enlivened it by singing German songs. It was there that, greatly to Freud's satisfaction, they sighted a wild porcupine, on which incident hangs a tale. He had made the interesting observation that, when faced with an anxious task, such as the present one of describing his startling conclusions to a foreign audience, it was helpful to provide a lightning conductor for one's emotions by deflecting one's attention on to a subsidiary goal. So before leaving Europe he maintained that he was going to America in the hope of catching sight of a wild porcupine *and* to give some lectures. The phrase "to find one's porcupine" became a recognized saying in our circle. Having achieved his double purpose he was ready to return home.

They got to New York on the evening of September 19 and sailed on the *Kaiser Wilhelm der Grosse* on the 21st. This time they ran into the equinoctial gales, and although he was not seasick Freud went to bed at seven on a couple of evenings. Freud was never seasick in his life. Bremen was reached at noon on the 29th.

Despite his gratitude for his friendly reception there, with the recognition of his work and the honor bestowed on him, Freud did not go away with a very favorable impression of America. Such prejudices were very apt to last with him, and this one never entirely disappeared; it was years before close contact with Americans visiting Vienna even softened it. He was so obviously unfair on the subject that one is bound to seek some explanation of his attitude. There were several superficial ones, but, as we shall see later, they covered a more fundamental personal one which actually had nothing to do with America itself. Freud himself attributed his dislike of America to a lasting intestinal trouble brought on, so he very unconvincingly asserted, by American cooking, so different from what he was accustomed to. But this ignores the important fact that he had suffered from this complaint most of his life, many years before he went to America and many years after. His complaint, however, had this much in it, that during his time in America he constantly suffered from a recurrence of his old appendicular pain which in any case must have impaired his enjoyment of the great experience. Another physical trouble at the same time was prostatic discomfort. This was naturally both painful and embarrassing, and of course the fault of American arrangements. I recall his complaining to me of the scarcity and inaccessibility of suitable places to obtain relief: "They escort you along miles of corridors and ultimately you are taken to the very basement where a marble palace awaits you, only just in time." For some years Freud ascribed many of his physical discomforts to his American visit. He even went so far as to tell me that his handwriting had deteriorated since the visit to America.[60]

An amusing instance of this prejudice transpiring was when in one of his fanciful moods he predicted the extinction of the white race in a few thousand years and its probable replacement by the black one. Then he jocularly added: "America is already threatened by the black race. And it serves her right.[r] A country without even wild strawberries!" [61]

A more personal reason for his disgruntlement was his difficulty with the language, which repeated his disagreeable experiences in Paris years before.[62] He was always sensitive about making himself understood and understanding others. I recollect an occasion when one American asked another to repeat a remark he had not quite caught. Freud turned to Jung with the acid comment: "These people cannot even understand each other." He also found it hard to adapt himself to the free and easy manners of the New World, of which I have just quoted an example.[s] He was a good European with a sense of dignity and a respect for learning which at that time was less prominent in America. He said to me afterwards in his terse way: "America is a mistake; a gigantic mistake, it is true, but none the less a mistake."

Freud maintained from the start a close interest in the development of psychoanalysis in America, and from 1908 kept up a regular correspondence with Brill and myself, later on with Putnam also. He was often amused at the stories we had to tell him. For instance when I read a paper on his theory of dreams before the American Psychologi-

<hr>

[r] This sentence was in English.

[s] p. 58.

cal Association at the end of 1909 I mentioned the feature of egocentricity, whereupon a lady rose and indignantly protested that it might be present in Viennese dreams but she was sure that American ones were altruistic. This was capped by another psychologist who insisted that a patient's associations largely depended on the temperature of the room, and since Freud had omitted to state this important detail his conclusions were not worthy of scientific credence. Freud related these stories with gusto to the Vienna group.

Another one was of Munsterberg. He maintained that Freud overlooked the element of trauma (!) and related a case of hysterical vomiting which he had traced to the patient's having swallowed a hot potato. The audience laughed when I confessed that Freud had unaccountably omitted hot potatoes from the list of aetiological factors.

He was also amused at the following passage from one of my letters. "The current view here about hysteria is that it is a discreditable form of imitating diseases, partly so as to make medical diagnoses harder than they need be and partly from a reprehensible desire to gain sympathy by unfair means. Treatment consists in telling them that they have been found out."

Nor can I resist, in this repertoire of entertainment for Freud, quoting the following delectable passage from an editorial in the *Interstate Medical Journal* on my Hamlet essay. "He teaches that natural affection for the mother should be carefully watched lest unawares it steals a march on us. . . . Now this note of warning, we understand from Dr. Jones's essay, was never brought home to Hamlet by any of his medical friends; hence he nurtured what was in the beginning a natural affection into that phase of abnormal sexuality whose bitternesses are the one thing that invariably fasten the attention of the modern psychologists . . . who add to the burdens of modern civilization by weighting us with theories that destroy our faith in human nature."

A slight disagreement between us arose over the personality of Morton Prince, a man whom I had known through correspondence in London days years before and with whom I always stayed on my visits to Boston. He had been the first American pioneer in psychopathology, a fact which I felt deserved some recognition. Furthermore he freely opened his periodical, *The Journal of Abnormal Psychology*, to papers on psychoanalysis, almost the only one then available for that purpose. He was a thorough gentleman, a man of the world, and a very pleasant colleague, as I found in cooperation with him for some years in editing his *Journal*. But he had one serious failing. He was rather stupid, which to Freud was always the unpardonable sin. When he rejected an abstract of Brill's on the quite legitimate ground that its language was too unseemly for his lay audience, which included many clergymen and old ladies, Freud was very angry and wanted me to dissociate myself from him. He insisted that Prince was a man with whom one had to be prepared for "bad intentions veiled by friendly speaking" (February 22, 1909), and nothing I could say would shake his opinion. With all his knowledge of the complex intricacies of the mind Freud was rather apt, when it was a question of conscious judgment, to take a black or white view of a person's character, and it took a great deal to modify it.

Since I had not yet acquired the art of deciphering Gothic handwriting I asked him to use Latin characters. Here is his reply, together with a couple of examples of his early English, which greatly improved later.[t]

"Nov. 20, 1909

"My dear Dr. Jones,*

"Since you want me to avoid german characters I might as well try to write you in English; you are responsible for my mistakes.

"(1) Your critical remarks on Stekel's book are obviously true; you have hit the mark. He is weak in theory and thought but he has a good flair for the meaning of the hidden and unconscious. His book cannot satisfy me personally, but it will do immensely good among the outsiders, his level being so very much nearer to theirs. I am glad you like Abraham's work far better; he is a sharp thinker and has set his foot on fertile ground. The next number of the collection will continue to accost the subject of mythology which I guess is to be conquered by our views.

"(2) Do write the '*Wunscherfüllung in Kinderspielen*' [u] for the series. Do it in English. I will get it translated here or translate it myself if it suits my purpose, as it is sure to do.

"(3) It is interesting for me that you prefer the broader aspects of the theory, the normal, psychological and cultural relations to the pathological. Sometimes I feel the same way.

"(4) I am sorry you will be disappointed at my answers to the questions you put me. As for Anaesthesia I am inclined to think that it is a secondary effect of the psychical changes brought about by

[t] Throughout this volume, an asterisk has been used to enable the reader to identify that correspondence which Freud wrote in English.
[u] Wish-fulfillment in Children's Play.

withdrawal of interest ('*Besetzung*'), perhaps the erogene zone of the skin being particularly involved in the complexes. I know nothing better, because Anaesthesia never is a direct object of analysis: it is no 'symptom' but a 'stigma.'

"As for '*Angstträume*'[v] I do not think it wants a special character to explain their occurrence. I find them occasionally with all sorts of people. But I could state that dreams of painful contents (not exactly filled by anxiousness) are very frequent with *masochistic* men and women, as the chastisement is a clear '*Wunscherfüllung* for these characters. I have a hint on this point in the second edition of the *Traumdeutung*.

"I miss more news about your own position and doings and how you are satisfied by your new home.

"Yours very truly,
"Freud"

"Febr. 2nd, 1909

"Dear Dr. Jones,*

. . .

"As for your diplomacy I know you are excellently fitted for it and will do it masterly. But I am afraid it is easy to do too much in this way. Consider it is a piece of psycho-analysis you are performing on your countrymen. You are not to say too much at once or at too early a moment, but the resistance cannot be avoided; it must come sooner or later, and it is best to provoke it slowly and designedly.

"Yours sincerely
"Freud"

"May 18, 1909

"Dear Dr. Jones,*
"I heartily acknowledge the receipt of a big heap of printed matter containing your valuable contributions to organic neuropathology and foreshadowing another lot neither smaller nor less in value of your communications about neuroses and psychoanalysis we do expect you will produce in the next years.

"I can give you the information that we—Dr. Ferenczi and I— intend sailing from Bremen August 21 on board the *George Washington*. N.D.L. I cannot know if this term may coincide with your return to America. In any case you know we are fixed.

"I have not yet made up my mind about the subject of my lectures

[v] Anxiety dreams.

in Worcester. Sometimes it occurs to me as the best expedient to treat dreams and their interpretations. I am ready to take up your hints, if you are of other opinion.

> "I am with best love to you
> "Yours sincerely
> "Freud"

> "March 10, 1910

"Dear Dr. Jones,*

"I am very fond of your letters and papers. Indeed your Hamlet article is excellent. I did not recognize it, having read the manuscript in Worcester, as you remember; it is so much improved. . . . Perhaps it will be news to you, as it was to me, that Jung has left Europe for America yesterday on board the *Kronprinzessin Caecilie*. He has called to Chicago, has to leave the 22nd of this month and be present at the Congress^w the 30th. . . . Have you read the article of Bernard Hart on the Unconscious? The first clever word upon the matter.

> "I am yours sincerely,
> "Freud"

> "15.4.10

"Dear Dr. Jones,*

"You must not expect too much of Leonardo, who will come out next month, neither the secret of the Vierge aux Rochers nor the solution of the Mona Lisa puzzle. Keep your hopes on a lower level, so it is likely to please you more. Many thanks for the page from Pater. I knew it and had quoted some lines out of the fine passage.

"As for Hart's paper I found it the best on the damned topic of the Unconscious I had read in the last years and enormously superior to Morton Prince's trash. It is a merit to have driven him into this line of work. As for Pearson and Clifford, both of whom I only know by name, I have formed the intention to get better acquainted with them, but I have to postpone the execution of this wish until summer, my receptivity being now strained to the utmost by eleven cases of neuroses so that I must react by productive work in order to keep my equilibrium. . . .

"I am retiring to the background as behoves an elderly gentleman.

> "Yours sincerely
> "Freud"

* At Nuremberg.

"May 22nd 1910

"Dear Dr. Jones,*

". . . The Leonardo is to come out in the last days of this month. I am very busy and by no means well these weeks, suffering from influenza and the consequences of my American dyspepsia. So I do not much work of value. As regards your call to write on character formation, I must confess that I feel myself not competent to the task. Jung could do it better, as he is studying men from the superficial layers downwards, while I am progressing in the opposite direction. Besides, any kind of systematic work is inconsistent with my gifts and inclinations. I expect all my impulses from the impressions in the intercourse with the patients.

"I am, dear Dr. Jones, *mit herzlichen Grüssen*

"*Ihr*

"Freud."

The three friends traveled back to Bremen by the same route. Jung went home and the other two proceeded to Berlin where they both had relatives to visit, as well as Abraham. It was there that they had their first telepathic séance with a clairvoyant, over which Ferenczi was specially excited. It is a topic that will appear in a later chapter.

And so on October 2nd back to Vienna, the only part of the civilized world that never recognized him.

In November Freud told Jung he was joining what he called "Forel's *Verein*," by which he meant the International Congress of Medical Psychology of which Forel was the President.

Gustavo Modena of Ancona, whom I had interested in psychoanalysis when we worked together at Kraepelin's clinic in 1907, had published an excellent exposition in Italian of Freud's theories.[63]

In spite of the excitements of 1909 Freud managed to get a good deal of writing published. He put together a volume that counts as the second of the series of five *Sammlung kleiner Schriften,* and he also wrote two fresh short papers and two very long ones. The former were: one entitled "The Family Romance of Neurotics," which appeared as a section in Otto Rank's fascinating book *The Myth of the Birth of the Hero;* the other contained a number of general statements on the essential nature of hysterical attacks.

The longer papers were both classical contributions to his series of case histories. One was popularly known as the "Little Hans Case" and contained the first analysis of a child. The other was a close study of the mechanisms in the obsessional neurosis.

By this time Freud was in a position where he could look forward to a career of recognition and fame on which he had never counted in his lifetime. From now on he might meet with misunderstanding, criticism, opposition and even abuse, but he could no longer be ignored. He was at the height of his powers and eager to employ them to the full. All this, together with the harmonious home with its endless joy of the growing children, must have made the first decade of the century the happiest one of Freud's life. But they were to be his last happy years. They were immediately followed by four years of painful dissensions with the colleagues nearest to him; then by the misery, anxiety and privation of the war years, followed by the total collapse of the Austrian currency with the loss of all his savings and insurance; and, very little later, by the onset of his torturing illness which finally, after sixteen years of suffering, killed him.

3

CHAPTER

The International Psycho-Analytical Association
(1 9 1 0 - 1 9 1 4)

IN THESE YEARS WAS LAUNCHED WHAT WAS CALLED THE "PSYCHOANA-lytical Movement"—not a very happy phrase, but one employed by friends and foes alike. They were distressing years for Freud and it was during them that he looked back at what seemed then, through rosy spectacles, the halcyon years of "splendid isolation." The enjoyment of the increasing success and recognition was greatly impaired by the sinister signs of growing dissension among valued adherents, a topic that demands a chapter to itself. Freud was immensely troubled and also bewildered by the insoluble problems this gave rise to and the perplexity of coping with them. We shall, however, confine ourselves here to the brighter side of the story, the gradual diffusion of the new ideas that naturally meant so much to Freud.

1910

Freud's thoughts were at this time moving in the direction of a wider organization than a local society. He wrote to Jung saying he was playing with the idea of getting his supporters to join "some larger group working for a practical ideal." [1] An apothecary called Knapp, from Berne, had called on him and tried to enlist his support for an "International Fraternity for Ethics and Culture" which he had just founded and of which Forel was the President. Freud advised him to discuss the matter with Jung and asked Jung's opinion about the advisability of joining them. He wrote: "What attracted me was the practical, aggressive as much as protective, feature of the program: the obligation to fight directly against the authority of the State and the Church in cases where they are committing manifest injustice." [2] He added, however, that in no event would he be willing to join any anti-alcohol movement, such as the one Forel was so zealous about. Nothing came of this scheme, and it was soon displaced by the formation of a purely psychoanalytical association.

It was generally taken for granted among us that the Salzburg Congress would be the first of a series. At the moment of writing (1954) it ranks as the first of eighteen that have so far been held. In 1909 both Freud and Jung, the organizer of the first Congress, were so preoccupied with the Worcester lectures in America that the question of a Congress being held in that year did not seriously arise. But the eagerness to hold another Congress as soon as possible led to one being arranged for the following spring. Only one other Congress (Salzburg, 1924) has been held at that time of year. It was one that would have suited Freud best as not interfering with his long summer vacation, but it was an impossible time for Americans to travel and the desirability of their presence has made us defer to their convenience. That is also the reason why the 1910 International Congress has been so far the only one I have been unable to attend, being prevented by the course of University lectures I was just then giving at Toronto. The only American present at it was Trigant Burrow, who had been studying with Jung at Zurich. G. A. Young of Omaha, who had also been studying there, had already returned to America.

The arrangements were, as before, entrusted to Jung, and the Second International Psycho-Analytical Congress took place at Nuremberg on March 30 and 31, 1910. Freud arrived early the morning before the Congress began in order to spend some hours with Abraham.[3] Because of certain administrative proposals, which will be mentioned presently, the second Congress passed off in a far less friendly atmosphere than had the first. The scientific part itself was highly successful and showed how fruitful the new ideas were. Freud gave an interesting address on "The Future Prospects of Psycho-Analytic Therapy," with valuable suggestions concerning both its internal development and its external influence. His old critic and friend, Löwenfeld of Munich, read a paper. The Swiss contributions by Jung and Honegger were first class. I had written to Freud beforehand suggesting that a collective study of symbolism be instituted. He was pleased with the idea and promised to instigate Stekel to raise the matter at the Congress.[4] Stekel did so, and a committee consisting of Abraham, Maeder and Stekel was appointed for the purpose. Little came of this later, but I still consider that much could be learned from such a comparative study from all sources, dreams, jokes, myths and so on, so as to ascertain the precise points of resemblance on which symbols are constructed.

Freud had for some time been occupied with the idea of bringing together analysts in a closer bond,[5] and he had charged Ferenczi with the task of making the necessary proposals at the forthcoming Congress. After the scientific program Ferenczi addressed the meeting on the future organization of analysts and their work. There was at once a storm of protest. In his speech he had made some very derogatory remarks about the quality of Viennese analysts and suggested that the center of the future administration could only be Zurich, with Jung as President. Moreover, Ferenczi, with all his personal charm, had a decidedly dictatorial side to him, and some of his proposals went far beyond what is customary in scientific circles. Before the Congress he had already informed Freud that "the psychoanalytical outlook does not lead to democratic equalizing: there should be an *élite* rather on the lines of Plato's rule of philosophers." [6] In his reply Freud said he had already had the same idea.[7]

After making the sensible proposal that an international association be formed, with branch societies in various countries, Ferenczi went on to assert the necessity for all papers written or addresses delivered by any psychoanalyst to be first submitted for approval to the President of the Association, who was thus to have unheard-of censoring powers. It was this attitude of Ferenczi's that was later to cause such trouble between European and American analysts which it took me, in particular, years to compose. The discussion that arose after Ferenczi's paper was so acrimonious that it had to be postponed to the next day. There was, of course, no question of accepting his more extreme suggestions, but the Viennese, especially Adler and Stekel, also angrily opposed the nomination of Swiss analysts to the positions of President and Secretary, their own long and faithful services being ignored. Freud himself perceived the advantage of establishing a broader basis for the work than could be provided by Viennese Jewry, and that it was necessary to convince his Viennese colleagues of this. Hearing that several of them were holding a protest meeting in Stekel's hotel room he went up to join them and made an impassioned appeal for their adherence. He laid stress on the virulent hostility that surrounded them and the need for outside support to counter it. Then, dramatically throwing back his coat, he declared: "My enemies would be willing to see me starve; they would tear my very coat off my back."

Freud then sought for more practical measures for appeasing the two leaders of the revolt. He announced his retirement from the presidency of the Vienna Society in which he would be replaced by Adler. He also agreed that, partly so as to counterbalance Jung's editorship of the *Jahrbuch,* a new periodical be founded, the monthly *Zentralblatt für Psychoanalyse,* which would be edited jointly by Adler and Stekel. They then calmed down, agreed to his being Director of the new periodical and to Jung being made President of the Association. Jung appointed Riklin as his Secretary, and also Editor of the new official publication it was now decided to issue. This was the *Correspondenzblatt der Internationalen Psychoanalytischen Vereinigung* (Bulletin), which would convey to all members news of interest to them, society meetings, publications and so on. The first number was issued in July 1910. There were only five of them, since it was merged with the *Zentralblatt* at the Weimar Congress in September 1911. Specimens of them must now be very scarce.

None of these choices of officials, though they all seemed inevitable at the time, proved a happy one. Within five months Adler withdrew and Stekel was to follow him a couple of years later. Riklin neglected his duties, so that administrative affairs got into a complete muddle, and Jung, as is well known, was not destined to lead his psychoanalytical colleagues for long.

As soon as he returned home Freud sent Ferenczi the following "epilogue," as he called it, on the Congress.

"April 3, 1910

"Dear Friend:

"There is no doubt that it was a great success. And yet we two had the least luck. Evidently my address met with a poor response; I don't know why. It contained much that should have aroused interest. Perhaps I showed how tired I was. Your spirited plea had the misfortune to evoke so much contradiction that they forgot to thank you for the important suggestions you laid before them. Every society is ungrateful: that doesn't matter. But we were both somewhat to blame in not reckoning with the effect they would have on the Viennese. It would have been easy for you to have entirely omitted the critical remarks and to have assured them of their scientific freedom; then we should have deprived their protest of much of its strength. I believe that my long pent up aversion for the Viennese [a] combined with your brother complex to make us shortsighted.

"That, however, is not the essential thing. What is more important is that we have accomplished an important piece of work which will have a profound influence in shaping the future. I was happy to see that you and I were in full agreement, and I want to thank you warmly for your support which after all was successful.

"Events will now move. I have seen that now is the moment to carry out a decision I have long had in mind. I shall give up the leadership of the Vienna group and cease exercising any official influence. I will transfer the leadership to Adler, not because I like to do so or feel satisfied, but because after all he is the only personality there and because possibly in that position he will feel an obligation to defend our common ground. I have already told him of this and will inform the others next Wednesday. I don't believe they will even be very sorry. I had almost got into the painful role of the dissatisfied and unwanted old man. That I certainly don't want, so I prefer to go before I need, but voluntarily. The leaders will all be of the same age and rank; they can then develop freely and come to terms with one another.

"Scientifically I shall certainly cooperate until my last breath, but I shall be spared all the trouble of guiding and checking and can enjoy my *otium cum dignitate.*

. . .

"I spent an enjoyable day with Jung in Rothenburg. He is at the top of his form, and it is to be hoped he will prove himself. . . . The personal relationships among the Zurich people are much more satisfactory than they are in Vienna, where one often has to ask what has become of the ennobling influence of psychoanalysis on its followers.

"With the Nuremberg *Reichstag* closes the childhood of our movement; that is my impression. I hope now for a rich and fair time of youth.

"Au *revoir*

"your

"Freud"

[a] Only a few weeks previously he had unburdened himself to Abraham: "I no longer get any pleasure from the Viennese. I have a heavy cross to bear with the older generation. Stekel, Adler, Sadger. They will soon be feeling that I am an obstacle and will treat me as such, but I can't believe that they have anyone better to substitute for me."[8]

Only a few months later, when there had been further criticism of the new organization, Freud half regretted having brought it into being so soon. He thought that perhaps he had overstimated his supporters' understanding of psychoanalysis, but he had been impatient to see Jung placed at the head of the movement and wanted to lessen the weight of his own responsibility.[9]

Deuticke, who had hitherto always been Freud's publisher, refused to undertake the *Zentralblatt* on the ground that the association with Stekel might impair the scientific character of the periodical.[10] So recourse was had to Bergmann of Wiesbaden. It is possible that Stekel conducted these negotiations, which gave him later, as he thought, the right to claim that it was *his* periodical. The first number appeared in October 1910.

After the Nuremberg Congress the psychoanalytical groups already existing enrolled themselves as Branch Societies of the International Association, and before long new groups were also formed. The first to enroll was Berlin, on the last day of the Congress, March 31. Abraham of course was the President and there were nine other members: Eitingon, Magnus Hirschfeld, Juliusburger, Heinrich Koerber, J. Marcinowski, Simon, Stegmann, Strohmayer and Warda. The next to join was Vienna, in April. Adler had just been made President, and there were twenty-one other members. Zurich joined in June with nineteen members. Binswanger was the President and Ewald Jung the Secretary. Bleuler and a few others resigned from the Society because it was against their principles to belong to an international body—a forerunner of Switzerland's attitude towards the League of Nations and the United Nations Organization. Evidently that was only a rationalization on Bleuler's part.

Bleuler's fluctuating attitude distressed Freud considerably. He would write papers now supporting and now criticizing psychoanalysis. As Freud said, it was no wonder that he attached so much importance to the conception of ambivalence which he had introduced into psychiatry. Because of the increasingly prominent position Bleuler held among psychiatrists Freud was eager to retain his support. But Bleuler and Jung never got on well together and there came a time, only a year later, when their personal relations practically ceased. Jung attributed Bleuler's unfriendly attitude towards him, and consequently his refusal to join the society Jung had founded, to his annoyance at Jung's having allowed Freud to wean him to imbibing alcoholic drinks.[b] Total abstinence was a religion with Bleuler, as it

^b See Chapter 2, p. 55.

had been with his predecessor Forel. Freud found this interpretation of Jung's "clever and plausible." "Bleuler's objections are intelligible there, but when directed against our International Association they make nonsense. We can't in addition to the furtherance of psychoanalysis inscribe on our banner things like the providing of clothes for freezing schoolchildren. That would remind one too much of certain inn signs: Hotel England and the Red Cock."

With Bleuler, in spite of Freud's constant efforts through correspondence, matters dragged on. Toward the end of the year Freud wrote to Pfister: "I have taken great trouble over Bleuler. I cannot say that I want to hold him to us *at any cost,* since after all Jung is rather closer to me, but I will willingly sacrifice for Bleuler anything provided it would not harm our cause. Unfortunately I have little hope." [11]

He then induced Bleuler to meet him at Munich during the Christmas holidays. Bleuler had suggested meeting at Innsbruck, but Freud ruled it out because of the "horrid [c] memories" the town had for him from painful experiences there; [12] This can only refer to his discussions with Fliess at Innsbruck in the Easter of 1899. They had a long and very personal talk, with the result that excellent relations were established and Bleuler promised to join the International Association. Bleuler must have opened his heart to Freud, since in a letter to Ferenczi we read: "He is also only a poor devil like ourselves and in need of a little love, a fact which seems to be neglected in certain quarters that matter to him." [d] [13]

Unfortunately this state of affairs did not endure and a year later Bleuler again resigned,[14] this time for good. His interests then moved elsewhere, from psychological to clinical psychiatry.

Something should be said about the early progress of such groups, in which Freud took a week-to-week interest. After all, apart from his own writings, they represented the hope of the future for the dissemination of his ideas.

In Vienna itself, where the Society was now eight years old, the business meeting of October 12, 1910, elected Adler as President, Stekel as Vice-President, Steiner as Treasurer, Hitschmann as Librarian and Rank as Secretary. Freud was called the Scientific President and it was agreed that the three Presidents should in turn act as Chairman at the scientific meetings.[15] The doings of the Society and the

[c] *scheussliche.*
[d] F. g. Jung.

papers read have been recorded in the literature. Soon there were thirty-six members.

Berlin was naturally much slower in developing. It had been founded by Abraham on August 27, 1908, with four other members: Ivan Bloch, Hirschfeld, Juliusburger and Koerber. For the first couple of years Eitingon preferred to remain alone in Berlin and it was some time before he began to practice. Even four years later Abraham counted himself as the only active analyst in the Society.[16] Hirschfeld resigned in 1911,[17] as did two new members, Warda and Strohmayer, who objected to the subscription being increased to pay for the official organ of the International Association.[18] At that date there were still only four members besides Abraham. Freud was friendly with Hirschfeld, the Editor of the *Jahrbuch für sexuelle Zwischenstufen*, and there are records of his inviting him to lunch at his home on at least two occasions.[19]

The "Freud Society" in Zurich had existed since 1907, its first meeting having been held on September 27 of that year.[20] It had started its life with twenty doctors, soon to be joined by Reverends Keller and Pfister. In 1910 there were a few non-Swiss among the members: Assagioli from Florence, whom I had interested in psychoanalysis when we were fellow students under Kraepelin a few years before: Trigant Burrow from Baltimore; Leonhard Seif from Munich, also a friend of mine from Kraepelin days; and Stockmayer from Tübingen. It was now decided to hold public meetings from time to time, so that interest might be aroused in a wider audience. In November 1910, Bleuler, Binswanger and Riklin read papers before the Swiss Society of Alienists.[e] They were well received, and the President, Dr. Ris, welcomed the introduction of the new ideas.

Ferenczi read a paper on "Suggestion" before the Budapest Society of Physicians on February 12, 1911, but the response was entirely negative. For several years Hungary did not seem favorable soil for psychoanalysis, but later on it relieved Ferenczi from his loneliness by providing a number of excellent analysts.

Psychoanalysis was by now widely discussed at various medical meetings and Congresses in Europe, but the only paper in favor of it I can find in that year was one by myself on the psychoanalytical theory of suggestion read at the International Congress of Medical Psychology and Psychotherapy in Brussels in August.

In the United States, on the other hand, the new ideas were already being more widely received. The interest aroused by Freud's and Jung's

___

[e] Published in the *Correspondenzblatt für Schweizer Aerzte*.

lectures at Worcester in the previous year kept growing. Putnam had published a personal and very favorable account of their lectures.[21] In the course of his description he had made the unfortunate remark that Freud was "no longer a young man." This hurt Freud a good deal. He wrote to me: "You are young, and I already envy your restless activity. As for myself the phrase in Putnam's essay 'He is no longer a young man' wounded me more than all the rest pleased me." [22] When I consoled him with the thought that his mind was younger than any of ours he replied sadly that Putnam was more likely to be right about his age than I was. He took a slight revenge when he translated a paper of Putnam's for the *Zentralblatt* shortly afterwards by saying in a footnote that Putnam was "far beyond the years of youth." [23] He admitted this motive later in his writings in connection with an instance of "forgetting" a name in which the word "veteran" occurred.[24]

Brill, Putnam and I had also begun our career of lecturing and writing on psychoanalysis, and the first volume of Brill's translations had already appeared, in 1909. Besides his translation work Brill put up a gallant fight in various expository lectures and debates. Our spheres of activity overlapped very little; he concentrated mainly on New York, and with great success, while I ranged more widely, to Baltimore, Boston, Chicago, Detroit and Washington. No periodical refused our papers, and in particular the Editors of *The Journal of Abnormal Psychology* and *The American Journal of Psychology*, Morton Prince and Stanley Hall respectively, opened their pages freely to us and welcomed our contributions. The first number of the latter periodical for 1910 contained my Hamlet essay; the next number brought translations of Freud's and Jung's lectures at Worcester, a paper by Ferenczi on dreams, and a comprehensive account I wrote of Freud's theory of dreams with illustrative examples. The same volume contained a valuable paper by E. A. Acher on resemblances between children and primitive man.[25] It was not, it is true, written from a psychoanalytical point of view, but in the following year the same author published a lengthy and favorable review of psychoanalytical work.[26] The former periodical contained a paper by Bernard Hart of London on the theory of the unconscious.[27] So by now Americans had a pretty free access to the new ideas. Things were going well, and Freud remarked to Ferenczi on my "superb letters, full of victories and fights." [28]

The time not yet being ripe for a purely psychoanalytical society, I proposed to Putnam that a wider association be formed where psychoanalytical ideas could be discussed. I then approached Morton Prince, promising him that he should be the first President, and circulars were sent round to suitable people. Since psychiatrists were at that time even less interested in psychology than were neurologists we decided to hold our meeting immediately after the annual meeting of the American Neurological Association. So on May 2, 1910, at the Willard Hotel in Washington, the American Psychopathological Association came into being. There were forty present at the meeting. The following officers were elected: President, Morton Prince; Secretary, G. A. Waterman (his Private Assistant in Boston); Council, A. G. Allen of Philadelphia, August Hoch of New York, Adolf Meyer of Baltimore, J. J. Putnam of Boston, and myself. Five honorary members were elected: Claparède of Geneva, Forel of Zurich, Freud of Vienna, Janet of Paris, and Jung of Zurich. So Switzerland did well. I was not elected an honorary member until later. *The Journal of Abnormal Psychology* was made the official organ of the Association.

Signs of interest were appearing in Russia also. M. E. Ossipow and a few other colleagues were busy writing about and translating Freud's works, and we learned that the Moscow Academy had offered a prize for the best essay on psychoanalysis.[29] Ossipow sent in his application for it in March 1910, but I never heard whether he was successful. He visited Freud in June of that year and Freud reported that he was "a splendid fellow."[30] M. Wulff, who had studied with Juliusburger in Berlin, had been dismissed from his position at an institution there on account of his "Freudian views."[31] He then moved to Odessa, where he established contact by correspondence with Freud[32] and Ferenczi.[33]

Although the names of Ossipow and Wulff are those most worthy of remembrance in connection with the early days—and, as it was to prove, also the last days—of psychoanalysis in Russia, there were several other workers there also. A special periodical, *Psychotherapia,* was founded in Moscow in 1909 in which a number of psychoanalytical papers and reviews appeared. Pownizki, a military doctor in Odessa, was the first to publish an actual psychoanalysis, though of an elementary kind, in a lecture he gave in St. Petersburg in March 1908, and he subsequently contributed several other papers. Wirubow of Moscow made some useful contributions, and Berg and Assatiari also wrote; the latter two had visited Jung in Zurich.

The only news from France was a letter Freud received from R. Morichau-Beauchant towards the end of the year;[34] nothing further was heard from there for another couple of years, but in Italy the first paper on psychoanalysis was published by Baroncini as early as 1908.[35] About the same time Modena of Ancona, whose interest I had also aroused when working in Munich and with whom I have continued to correspond for many years, sent Freud the reprint of a paper,[36] which Freud praised highly,[37] and then set about translating the *Three Essays on the Theory of Sexuality*. Ferenczi mentioned an agreeable visit from him in 1910.[38] Assagioli of Florence read a paper on sublimation before the Italian Congress on Sexology in November 1910.

Things were stirring also as far off as Australia. In 1909 Freud reported having received a letter from Sydney telling him there was a little group eagerly studying his works. Dr. Roy Winn, of Sydney, has been good enough to conduct some laborious research and has supplied the following information about this remote episode. A Dr. Donald Fraser had established a little group and had lectured many times before various societies on psychoanalysis. Before acquiring a medical qualification in 1909 he had been a Minister of the Presbyterian Church, but had had to resign his position on account of his "Freudian views"—the first instance, but far from being the last, of this kind of victimization. The spark died out, as mine in Canada was to, shortly afterwards.

Two years later, however, Dr. Andrew Davidson, the Secretary of the Section of Psychological Medicine and Neurology, invited Freud, Jung and Havelock Ellis to read papers before the Australasian Medical Congress in 1911. They all sent papers which were read there; Freud's will be mentioned in the appropriate place.[f] He had suggested to Jung that they send a joint one, but Jung preferred them to be "independent."[39] Freud's paper was sent off on May 13, 1911.

The reader need not fear that I am embarking on the formidable task of describing the history of the International Psycho-Analytical Association or the accompanying "Movement," except in so far as it concerns Freud, but I thought the earliest beginnings, in which he was so interested, might well be recorded here. Enough has been said to show that by 1910, only a few years after Freud began to emerge from his era of isolation, his work was being widely discussed in many countries and that a number of doctors were already obtaining experience in the use of his methods. On the other hand, as we shall see presently, the interest in Freud's work was more than counterbalanced by the strenuous opposition it was at that time encountering.

In 1910 Freud published the lectures he had delivered at Worcester,

[f] Chapter 8, No. 5.

the *Five Lectures on Psycho-Analysis*, the paper he had given at the Nuremberg Congress, and a number of other slighter papers. In addition to this there were three more original publications. One was on "The Antithetical Sense of Primal Words," a discovery that gave him great pleasure in confirming an observation he had made years before about a mysterious feature of the unconscious. Another was the first of his three essays on the "Psychology of Love." But the outstanding literary event of 1910 was his book on Leonardo da Vinci. There he not only illuminated the inner nature of that great man, with the conflict between his two main motives in life, but showed how it had been influenced by the events of his earliest childhood. More than that, Freud contributed a general study of motivation which has a special interest for us. For, as I shall point out later, in doing so Freud was expressing conclusions which in all probability had been derived from his self-analysis and are therefore of great importance for the study of his personality. His letters of the time make it abundantly clear with what exceptional intensity he had thrown himself into this particular investigation.

In May Freud was rather flattered by the great Wilhelm Ostwald inviting him to contribute a paper on his work to the *Annalen der Naturphilosophie,* and he told Jung that if he were ambitious he would write one.[40] A few weeks later he accepted the invitation,[41] but he never wrote the paper. At about the same time the *Neue Freie Presse* made a similar request. This one he refused, feeling that he was already conspicuous enough in Vienna.

Freud was very tired after the strain of the Nuremberg Congress; the Easter "holiday" there had not been a recreation. At Whitsun he spent a few days in Karlsbad with his wife and his daughter Sophie. His plans for the summer had been to go first to Karlsbad in the hope of dispelling the after-effects of the American cooking the year before,[42] then to take his family to French Switzerland,[43] which would have been quite new to all of them, and finally to pay Jung a visit at Zurich.[44] These plans were all changed by the dangerous illness of his wife's mother in Hamburg, as it was thought desirable to be within reach of her.[45] She died of cancer on October 27 of that year. They therefore arranged to spend the summer in Holland.

Freud and his two younger sons went on ahead—the eldest was in the Dolomites—and they got to The Hague on July 17. They stayed at the Hotel Wittebrugh, Scheveningen. His plan was to spend six weeks in Holland and then sail from Rotterdam with Ferenczi on

August 29 for Naples. The three men had a most enjoyable time together in Holland, and Freud praised the delightful kindness with which his sons treated their old father. They bathed daily and Freud celebrated the second edition of his *Sammlung Kleiner Schriften* by spending a florin and a half on a horse ride for them. Of course Freud had to visit all the museums within reach, in Haarlem, The Hague and so on. His favorite town was Delft.

But nevertheless he greatly missed his women folk. His wife had gone from Vienna to Hamburg to be with her mother; for the first time in twenty-four years they were apart on her birthday (July 26). The unmarried daughters, with Tante Minna, were spending a holiday at Jekel's sanatorium at Bistra in Austrian Silesia. The women arranged to meet at Leyden on July 29, where Freud greeted them. They then went on to the Pension Noordsee on the coast at Noordwijk, where they spent a happy month. I spent a few days there with them in the second week of August and had many interesting talks with Freud. It was an exciting experience and I poured out a stream of questions which he answered most patiently. There were all sorts of technical problems to discuss about the cases I had been analyzing, and I had to give all the latest news from America. Then there was my report on our progress at the International Congress of Medical Psychology in Brussels, where I had just read a paper. On our long walks on the edge of the sea he would stride along swiftly, and I noticed he had to poke every bit of seaweed with his stick, his quick eyes darting here and there all the time. I asked him what he expected to find, but got the noncommittal answer "Something interesting. You never know." Freud was only three times at the seaside in his life (apart from the Mediterranean); the other occasions had been his short stay in Lancashire at the age of nineteen and one the year previously (1909). His sons had never seen the open sea before and were correspondingly excited about it. But the flatness of the landscape palled on Freud after a time, and he longed for his beloved mountains.

Among the letters Freud left behind after his death I was astonished to find my "bread and butter" letter to his wife thanking her for her hospitality. In the spring of 1908, when changing his domestic arrangements, he had destroyed all his previous correspondence, but after that he kept almost everything.

About this time Gustav Mahler, the famous composer, was greatly distressed about his relationship to his wife, and Dr. Nepallek, a Viennese psychoanalyst who was a relative of Mahler's wife advised him to consult Freud. He telegraphed from the Tyrol to Freud asking for an appointment. Freud was always very loth to interrupt his holidays for any professional work, but he could not refuse a man of Mahler's worth. His telegram, making an appointment, however, was followed by another one from Mahler countermanding it. Soon there came another request, with the same result. Mahler suffered from the *folie de doute* of his obsessional neurosis and repeated this performance three times. Finally Freud had to tell him that his last chance of seeing him was before the end of August, since he was planning to leave then for Sicily. So they met in an hotel in Leyden and then spent four hours strolling through the town and conducting a sort of psychoanalysis. Although Mahler had had no previous contact with psychoanalysis, Freud said he had never met anyone who seemed to understand it so swiftly. Mahler was greatly impressed by a remark of Freud's: "I take it that your mother was called Marie. I should surmise it from various hints in your conversation. How comes it that you married someone with another name, Alma, since your mother evidently played a dominating part in your life?" Mahler then told him that his wife's name was Alma Maria, but that he called her Marie! She was the daughter of the famous painter ᵍ Schindler, whose statue stands in the Stadtpark in Vienna; so presumably a name played a part in her life also. This analytic talk evidently produced an effect, since Mahler recovered his potency and the marriage was a happy one until his death, which unfortunately took place only a year later.

In the course of the talk Mahler suddenly said that now he understood why his music had always been prevented from achieving the highest rank through the noblest passages, those inspired by the most profound emotions, being spoiled by the intrusion of some commonplace melody. His father, apparently a brutal person, treated his wife very badly, and when Mahler was a young boy there was a specially painful scene between them. It became quite unbearable to the boy, who rushed away from the house. At that moment, however, a hurdy-gurdy in the street was grinding out the popular Viennese air "*Ach, Du lieber Augustin.*" In Mahler's opinion the conjunction of high tragedy and light amusement was from then on inextricably fixed in his mind, and the one mood inevitably brought the other with it.[46]

It was in this month of August that Freud first met van Emden in Leyden. He was to prove another of Freud's many life-long pupils and friends.

During this time Freud was conducting an agitated correspondence

ᵉ In German "*Mahler.*"

with Ferenczi over their complicated plans to travel to southern Italy. They were neither of them very expert in such matters, Ferenczi even less so. Freud had suggested that he invite Brill to accompany them on their trip to Naples and Sicily, and Ferenczi after expressing his misgiving at having to share Freud's society with someone else had to consent. It turned out, however, that Brill's timetable in Europe was such as made it impossible to conform to the Italian plan, so nothing came of the idea. By the middle of August they found that their project of sailing to Naples from Holland was not very practicable, and they decided to take the long train journey. Ferenczi got to Leyden on August 28 and spent a couple of days with the family in the Noordwijk Pension.

The plan arranged was to travel overnight from Leyden to Basel and on to Rome. But at the last minute his son Oliver, who was really expert, discovered a more convenient route via Paris and Milan. So they spent the night of September 1 in Paris, at the Hotel du Louvre. Paris was "much more magnificent than in my memory." [47] They lunched at the Café de Paris,[48] and Freud showed Ferenczi, who had never been there, what he could of the town in the short time. It was the third of Freud's visits to Paris. The high light was of course the Louvre, where Freud, whose mind was still full of Leonardo, made a minute examination of his pictures there.[49]

In the meantime the family moved to the Hotel Wittebrugh near The Hague, where, with the exception of Ernst and Anna who had to get back to Vienna, they remained for another fortnight before returning to Vienna.

After a day and a half in Paris the two companions traveled to Florence. They stayed there, at the Grand Hotel, from the evening of the third to the afternoon of the fifth. Then came forty-eight hours in Rome, where there was so much to show Ferenczi. The letters to his wife were as full as ever of the magic Freud always felt of that wonderful city. Naples was as rowdy as usual, but they drove out to Monte Posilipo to enjoy the panorama from Ischia to Capo Miseno. On the evening of their arrival there, September 8, they embarked on the S.S. *Syracuse* for an overnight voyage to Palermo. The Hotel de France there charged them fifteen lire ($2.90) each for full board, and for that they had three rooms and a bathroom. But there was a frightful lot to see. And he simply could not describe the beauty of the scene and the scent of the flowers. On the 12th there was an expedition to see "some ruins," and on the next morning a longer one began. They visited the Temple at Segesta and spent the night in Castelvetrano.

the forgetting of which name gave him trouble on a later occasion.[50] On the next day they saw the temple of Minerva at Selinunte, "which had been preserved by Hannibal," and got back to Palermo that night.

The following day, the 15th, brought a trip in another direction, to the temple of Girgenti. They got to Syracuse on the 17th, where the hotel cost only eleven lire. This spot Freud counted as the chief goal of the whole journey. After three wonderful days there, however, the sirocco was proving too unpleasant, so they decided to return rather prematurely. To save time they traveled back to Palermo, sailed to Naples and dashed through it so as not to be quarantined there on account of the cholera prevailing, spent only one night in Rome and reached Vienna on the morning of the twenty-sixth. There Freud took a few days rest before starting work. These few days he spent in translating a paper of Putnam's for the *Zentralblatt*. He did not sign the translation because it contained some complimentary references to himself.[51]

The time the two men passed together in Sicily was fateful for their subsequent relationship. Since the bond between them was the most important Freud was to forge in his later years it is necessary to mention briefly the beginning of their difficulties. What actually happened in Sicily was merely that Ferenczi was inhibited, sulky and unreliable in the day to day arrangements; Freud described his attitude as one of "bashful admiration and mute opposition." [52] But behind those manifestations lay severe trouble in the depths of his personality. As I well knew from many intimate talks with him, he was haunted by a quite inordinate and insatiable longing for his father's love. It was the dominating passion of his life and was indirectly the source of the unfortunate changes he introduced into his psycho-analytic technique twenty years later, which had the effect of estranging him from Freud (though not Freud from him). His demands for intimacy had no bounds. There was to be no privacy and no secrets between him and Freud. Naturally he could not express any of this openly, so he waited more or less hopefully for Freud to make the first move.

Freud, however, was in no such mood. He was only too glad when on holiday to dismiss from his mind all the irksome problems of neuroses and deep psychological conflicts, refreshing his mind with the enjoyments of the moment. Most of all was that so on such a journey as the present when there were so many interesting and beautiful new sights to explore. All he wanted was an agreeable companion with tastes similar to his own.

After they got home Ferenczi wrote one of his long explanatory letters of self-analysis in which he expressed his fear that after his recent behavior Freud might have no wish to have any more to do with him. But Freud was as friendly as ever, as the following answer shows.

                                                   "October 6, 1910

"Dear Friend:

"It is remarkable how much more clearly you can express yourself in writing than in speaking. Naturally I knew very much or most of what you write and now need to give you only a few explanations. Why I didn't give you a scolding and so opened the way to a mutual understanding? Quite true, it was weak of me. I am not the psycho-analytical superman that you construed in your imagination, nor have I overcome the counter-transference. I couldn't treat you in that way, any more than I could have my three sons because I am too fond of them and should feel sorry for them.

"You not only noticed, but also understood, that I *no longer* have any need to uncover my personality completely, and you correctly traced this back to the traumatic reason for it. Since Fliess's case, with the overcoming of which you recently saw me occupied, that need has been extinguished. A part of homosexual cathexis has been withdrawn and made use of to enlarge my own ego. I have succeeded where the paranoiac fails.

"Moreover, you should know that I was less well, and suffered more from my intestinal trouble, than I was willing to admit. I often said to myself that whoever is not master of his Konrad [h] should not set out on travels. That is where the frankness should have begun, but you did not seem to me stable enough to avoid becoming over-anxious about me.

"As for the unpleasantness you caused me, including a certain passive resistance, it will undergo the same change as memories of travels in general: one refines them, the small disturbances vanish and what was beautiful remains for one's intellectual pleasure.

"That you surmised I had great secrets, and were very curious about them, was plain to see and also easy to recognize as infantile. Just as I told you *everything* on scientific matters I concealed very little of a personal nature; the incident of the *Nationalgeschenk* [1] was, I think, indiscreet enough. My dreams at that time were concerned, as I

[h] The word Freud used for "bowel."
[1] A jocular allusion to his fondness for acquiring antiquities.

hinted to you, entirely with the Fliess affair, which in the nature of things would be hard to arouse your sympathy.

"So when you look at it more closely you will find that we haven't so much to settle between us as perhaps you thought at first.

"I would rather turn your attention to the present. . . .

"Herzlich
"Ihr Freud."

The generosity and tactfulness Freud constantly displayed towards Ferenczi, and his great fondness for him, preserved a valuable friendship for many years until, long after this episode, Ferenczi's own stability began to crumble.

1911

This was the year of the break with Adler, a painful episode which will be described in a later chapter. It was Freud's main preoccupation in that year, one that caused him great distress. His continued friendship with Jung and his closer contact with Putnam were prominent features of the year. The International Congress at Weimar in September was one of the most successful. Psychoanalysis continued to gain both friends and foes in various countries. Freud founded a new periodical, *Imago*. He took no long holiday away from his family. He wrote very little in 1911.

That is the brief summary of the year. The only domestic incident of note was that while skiing on the Schneeberg in the Salzkammergut Freud's eldest son Martin broke his thigh in a lonely spot.[53] Luckily he had a stout friend with him, who stayed five hours by his side at the cost of having two toes frozen. Then Jäger, the friend, managed to get help, but it took two and a half days to get the invalid to a hospital. Martin made an uninterrupted recovery, but his accident had given Freud considerable anxiety.[54]

Freud himself had about that time a curious experience which might well have ended fatally. For a month he had been suffering from a constantly increasing mental obfuscation with unusually severe headaches every evening. Ultimately a leak was discovered between the gas tubing and the rubber connection to his lamp, so for several hours every evening he was inhaling gas which his cigar smoke prevented him from detecting. Three days after the leak was seen to he was quite well.[55]

Early in the year Freud announced that his originality was unmistakably vanishing.[56] The remark is interesting, since it preceded by only a few months one of his most original contributions, that on the psychology of religion. By August, even in the holidays, he had to admit that he was "wholly totem and taboo." [57]

The outstanding event of the year was the Weimar Congress. Jung had first intended to hold it at Lugano,[58] but Abraham thought Weimar was both more central and more interesting.[59] It took place on September 21 and 22. It brought back the friendly atmosphere of the first Congress. No Viennese opposition obtruded itself. Freud had been staying beforehand with Jung in his new house at Küsnacht and Putnam had come to Zurich to meet them. Other Americans present at the Congress were T. H. Ames, A. A. Brill and Beatrice Hinkle. The total attendance was fifty-five, including some visitors. They included Bleuler; Magnus Hirschfeld, the Berlin authority on homosexuality; the Reverends Keller and Pfister from Switzerland; Lou Andreas-Salomé, then at Göttingen; and from Holland, van Emden of Leyden (later The Hague) and van Renterghem of Amsterdam, the latter an acquaintance of Freud's from the old hypnosis days. Above all there was Putnam.

The papers were of a high order. Among them were several classics of psychoanalytical literature, such as Abraham's study of manic-depressive insanity, Ferenczi's contribution to our understanding of homosexuality, and Sachs's paper on the interrelationship between psychoanalysis and the mental sciences. Then there were notable papers by Bleuler on "Autism" and by Jung on "Symbolism" in the psychoses and mythology. Rank's excellent paper on "The Motif of Nudity in Poetry and Legends" brought about an amusing episode. In a short report of the Congress in the local newspaper we read that "interesting papers were read on nudity and other current topics." It was the occasion that inclined us to discourage reporters at subsequent Congresses.

The high light of the Congress was certainly Putnam's appearance. The Europeans knew of his noble fight in America and of the high esteem in which Freud held him. His support had gone some way to compensate Freud for the way he was ignored in Vienna. His distinguished and modest personality made a deep impression on them. He himself reciprocated it. In the course of his many talks with Freud he congratulated him on the quality of his followers. Freud dryly replied: "They have learned to tolerate a piece of reality." Putnam opened the Congress with a paper on "The Importance of Philosophy for the Further Development of Psychoanalysis," one which led to some controversy afterwards in the *Zentralblatt*. His burning plea for the introduction of philosophy—but only his own Hegelian brand—into psychoanalysis did not meet with much success. Most of us did not see the necessity of adopting any particular system. Freud was of course very polite in the matter, but he remarked to me afterwards: "Putnam's philosophy reminds me of a decorative centerpiece; everyone admires it but no one touches it."

Freud opened the second day's meeting with a paper which he modestly called a postscript to his famous Schreber case.[60] It was of historical interest as being the first occasion when he dealt with the myth-making tendencies of mankind, made a reference to totemism, and uttered the dictum that the unconscious contains not only infantile material but also relics from primitive man.

Freud and Jung were still on the best of terms. I recollect someone venturing to say that Jung's jokes were rather coarse, at which Freud sharply answered, "It's a healthy coarseness."

While at Weimar, Sachs and I took the opportunity of calling on Nietzsche's sister and biographer, Frau Elisabeth Förster-Nietzsche. Sachs told her about the Congress and commented on the similarity between some of Freud's ideas and her famous brother's.

In his Business Report to the Congress Jung informed us that there were now 106 members of the International Association. A few remarks may be added on the happenings in the various groups.

The Vienna Society was in this year torn by jealousies and dissensions. Even after Adler's resignation in July there were left Stekel, Sadger and Tausk, all of whom gave Freud a deal of trouble. Federn and Hitschmann were growing in stature, and the latter published in this year an excellent exposition of Freud's work.[61] Nevertheless Freud was of the opinion that of them all only "little Rank" had any scientific future.[62] Hitschmann had been elected Vice-President and Sachs replaced him as Librarian.

In the spring Freud was shocked to hear that Honegger, in many respects the most promising of the Swiss analysts, had committed suicide on March 28.

Early in the year Leonhard Seif founded a little group in Munich with six members, but it did not have a long life. Later on Seif joined Jung, and Hans von Hattingberg continued the Freudian tradition in Munich.

On May 2 Drosnes of Odessa called on Freud and reported that, together with Ossipow and Wirubow of Moscow, he had founded a Russian Psycho-Analytical Society.[63] Drosnes himself afterwards settled in St. Petersburg, but there was little development there.

Signs of life were appearing this year in three new European countries. At the beginning of 1912 I got an enthusiastic letter from Professor Morichau-Beauchant of Poitiers, with a reprint of the first psychoanalytical paper to be written in France, at the end of 1911.[64] I then learned that he had been corresponding with Freud for some months.[65]

In Sweden, Poul Bjerre had begun his career there by reading a paper on "Freud's Psycho-Analytic Method" before the Association of Swedish Physicians on January 17.

At a meeting on March 19, 1910, of the Neurological-Psychiatric Section of the Warsaw Medical Society, Jaroszynski read a paper on obsessional neuroses and quoted several cases in which he had been able to confirm the aetiology and mechanisms of this disorder described by Freud. So Freud's work was getting known in Poland.

Holland was also moving. Freud had two visitors from there in May.[66] Van Emden had come to Vienna to study, and both he and August Stärcke were admitted to the Vienna Society. Freud was astonished to learn that the latter had been practicing analysis since 1905 and had written a good deal about it in Dutch periodicals.[67] Van Renterghem had joined the Berlin Society.

In America much was happening. Freud had been urging me to start an American Branch Society of the International Association, so I discussed the matter with Brill and Putnam. The latter agreed to be President if I would be Secretary.[68] My plan was that the new body should include all the analysts in America and that any local Societies that might be formed later for the purpose of holding more frequent meetings would become branches of the parent Association. It took, however, more than twenty years before this plan was finally adopted because, despite Freud's pressure to the contrary,[69] Brill was eager to have the prestige of the Society he intended to found in New York being itself a *direct* Branch Society of the International Association; perhaps he did not like the idea of "his" Society being in any way subordinate to "mine." So we quite amicably agreed to differ. He founded the New York Society on February 12, 1911, with twenty members, and it was at once incorporated under the State laws. He became President, B. Onuf Vice-President, and H. W. Frink Secretary. C. P. Oberndorf was the last survivor of the charter members who continued association with psychoanalysis.

I then sent out circular letters to the analysts outside New York, and the first meeting of the American Psychoanalytic Association took place at Baltimore on May 9, 1911. There were eight present: Trigant

Burrow, Baltimore; Ralph Hamill, Chicago; J. T. MacCurdy, Baltimore; Adolf Meyer, Baltimore; J. J. Putnam, Boston; G. L. Taneyhill, Baltimore; G. A. Young, Omaha; and myself, then at Toronto. Half of the members came from Baltimore. Such was the modest beginning of the present mighty organization! At our second meeting in the following year, however, there were already twenty-four members, with a number of applications pending. Both Societies were officially accepted by the Weimar Congress in September 1911.

In June Putnam was invited to give the Harvey Lecture and was asked that it should be devoted to psychoanalysis.[70] It was an indication of the progress we had made in the past couple of years.

From England there was, as before, little to report. At the beginning of the year Freud had been made an Honorary Member of the Society for Psychical Research,[j] and the year after he contributed a very concise paper to a special number on medical psychology.[72] When I announced to him my intention of returning to England from Canada he wrote: "You have, as it were, conquered America in no more than two years, and I am by no means assured which way things will go when you are far. But I am glad you are returning to England, as I expect you will do the same for your mother-country, which by the way has become better soil since you left it. I have had to refuse no less than three offers for translating the *Traumdeutung* [*The Interpretation of Dreams*] from Englishmen, expecting as you know that Brill will do it soon. I have got to answer letters from towns like Bradford, and one of the medical men at least, Osler,[k] did actually send me a patient, who is still under the care of Federn. So your task may prove less hard than you seem to judge it." [73] Moreover, *Brain*, the famous journal of neurology, devoted a special number to the subject of hysteria in which appeared a masterly essay by Bernard Hart on "Freud's Conception of Hysteria" with a list of 281 references to the psychoanalytical literature. Then M. D. Eder read a paper before the Neurological Section of the British Medical Association in July 28, 1911.[74] It was the first account published in England of a psychoanalysis, though by no means the first carried out. Eder had an audience of eight, but they left the room when he came to the sexual aetiology. An interesting follow-up study of this very case has recently been published, forty-two years after the original treatment.[75]

Other continents also were coming into view. In March Freud wrote to Ferenczi: "Last Sunday I had the visit of our distant be-

[j] He called this "the first sign of interest from dear old England." [71]
[k] Sir William Osler, then Professor of Medicine at Oxford.

ginner Sutherland from Sagar in India, a splendid fellow. He is translating the *Traumdeutung*. Behind him stands another, younger man, Berkeley-Hill, who is psychoanalyzing Hindus and confirming everything. He is also publishing his work. Then two days ago a new continent, Australia, announced itself. The secretary of the Neurological Section of the Australian Congress discloses himself as a subscriber to the *Jahrbuch* and asks for a short account of my theories which is to be printed in the *Reports of the Congress*[1] since they are still quite unknown in Australia. No sign of life yet from Africa!"[76] This had to wait for nearly forty years.

At the Weimar Congress it was decided to make the *Zentralblatt* the official organ of the International Association and to incorporate the former *Correspondenzblatt* in it. Then in the spring of that year Freud decided, in conjunction with Rank and Sachs, to start a new periodical that should be devoted to the non-medical applications of psychoanalysis.[77] It was an aspect of his work that specially attracted him and the reason why this proposal came into his mind just then was that he was already fully preoccupied with the study of religion that was to produce the essays on totemism in the following year. He told me that the new periodical was to be called *Eros-Psyche*,[78] a name I heard later had been suggested by Stekel. This was replaced later by one Sachs proposed, *Imago*, taken from Spitteler's profound novel with that title. Freud had great difficulty in finding a publisher for such a novel undertaking, and the first four he approached all refused: Bergmann, Deuticke, Barth, and Urban und Schwarzenberg.[79] Finally he persuaded his friend Heller to undertake it, and it proved a complete success. The first number appeared in January 1912.

In addition to the time-robbing Adler controversy, and largely perhaps because of it, Freud's mind was occupied this year with plans for writing papers expounding his technique. Thoughts about the psychology of religion were also beginning to ferment. So there was very little actual production in 1911. The chief contribution published was his exposition of the relationship between the two great principles of mental functioning: the pleasure principle and the reality principle.[80]

There were some very enjoyable holidays in 1911. At Easter he made an expedition in the neighborhood of Trient and Bozen searching for suitable accommodation for the summer. He left Vienna on the morning of Friday, April 14 and was back on the Tuesday morn-

[1] See p. 77.

ing.[81] Ferenczi met him in Bozen and helped in the search, which proved most successful.

On July 9 he left for Karlsbad to obtain relief for what he persisted in calling his "American colitis." [82] A letter of four large pages was despatched to his wife as soon as he arrived. The family had gone direct to Klobenstein. In Karlsbad Freud had the company of his daughter Sophie who was undergoing treatment as well. The van Emdens, of whom he was very fond, were also there. He was not in a good mood and could not do the writing he had expected to.[83] He wrote bitterly to his wife: "The emptiness of a life devoted to the care of a full bowel is becoming unbearable."

Traveling via Munich, Freud joined his wife at the Hotel Post, Klobenstein (or Collalbo) at the beginning of August. This is a little village in the Dolomites situated on a hilly plateau of porphyry called the Ritten or Renon, some seven miles north-east of Bozen. It has superb views over the whole mountain range south of the Brenner. Ferenczi joined the party on August 20 for a fortnight. The weather was unusually hot, so they gave up their original plan of descending to the lower level of Caldonazzo, in the Trentino, at the end of the month.

Ferenczi had to go back to work, so Freud traveled alone to Zurich where Jung met him in the early morning of September 16. Freud had wanted his wife to accompany him, but she evidently shirked the long journey and stayed on in the mountains. He stayed in Küsnacht for four days before leaving for the Weimar Congress. There were of course seminars, visitors and receptions, so it was by no means a pure holiday. Putnam, who stayed in Zurich, not Küsnacht, participated in all these activities. Freud stayed on in Weimar after the Congress to have talks with Abraham. He was not due back in Vienna before the thirtieth of the month.

1912

The separation from Adler had been completed in the previous year. It was a great relief to Freud, since the unpleasant scenes at the Society meetings had been most trying. After the break very little, if any, personal feeling about Adler remained, but for several years Freud was concerned to put Adler's conclusions to the test in various ways and finally to explicate the significance of the scientific differences between Adler and himself. There remained Stekel, and towards the end of the present year Freud was forced to separate from him also. 1912 was also the year when the personal relations between

Freud and Jung began to be less friendly than before, and there were two painful years ahead before that separation also came about. All these topics, however, are reserved for a special chapter.

In the days when the arrangements for the Congress were relatively simple it had been intended that they should be held annually. The reason why there was no Congress in 1912 was that Jung had under-taken to deliver a course of lectures in New York in the late summer, and a Congress without its President was considered unthinkable. It is also a measure of Jung's personal importance at that time.

Smith Ely Jelliffe had induced Fordham University, a Jesuit College, to invite Jung to give a course of eight lectures in September; it was an invitation I had myself refused on the ground of its being an unsuitable venue for a discussion on psychoanalysis. Jung's military service was early in August, so the third week of that month would have been the only possible time to hold a Congress. That, however, would mean interrupting everybody's summer holiday, so it was agreed to postpone the Congress for a year. Freud was not very pleased about this and distinctly dubious about the propriety of Jung's going to New York at that time. Actually it proved to be the turning point in the relationship between the two men. When I met Freud in June I asked him why he had not arranged to preside at the Congress him-self. He said he hadn't thought of the idea, and anyhow it should have been Jung's place to make such a suggestion.[84]

Freud counted 1912 as one of his most productive years; that was because of his great work *Totem and Taboo*. The new periodical, *Imago*, began its career in January, and before the end of the year he had founded yet another, the *Zeitschrift*. It was on the whole an anxious and unhappy year and also one when he suffered much from ill-health. Perhaps all these matters are obscurely inter-related.

Sending New Year's wishes to Abraham he added: "As for myself I have no great expectation. We have a gloomy time in front of us. It is only the next generation that will reap the reward of recognition. But we have had the incomparable joy of the first vision." [85]

Early in the year he heard from Jung that there had been a stormy agitation in the Zurich newspapers; psychoanalysis was being angrily attacked. *Pfarrer* Pfister was called to account by his superiors and it looked as if he might be expelled from the ministry; fortunately this did not happen. Riklin told Freud that the campaign had had a disastrous effect on their private practice, even on Jung's, and begged him to send them some patients.[86] Freud always believed that the vituperation was one of the reasons for the change of heart that occurred soon after among his Swiss adherents. It is always hard for Swiss to stand out against their fellow-countrymen.

At Easter there was a short but highly enjoyable holiday on the delightful island of Arbe in Dalmatia. Freud left Vienna on the evening of Friday, April 5, met Ferenczi in Fiume the next morning and after breakfast took the ship for Arbe, which they reached after a five hours' voyage.[87] They returned to Fiume on the Tuesday, from where it was only an overnight journey to Vienna.

Rank had gone on a student's tour to Greece, whence he returned "in a state of bliss." Freud does not mention the fact, but I happen to know he had made the journey possible for Rank by paying all his expenses.

In May Freud was greatly annoyed by the personal attack Allen Starr, the well-known neurologist, had launched on him, quoted in a New York newspaper.[88] Nor were things much pleasanter at home. Freud reported that he was being ostracized more than ever in Vienna, and Heller dare not display his new periodical, *Imago*, for fear of offending customers.[89] Nevertheless *Imago* had secured 194 subscribers after the first number, and the *Zentralblatt* had some 500.

That Whitsuntide Freud spent two days as Binswanger's guest at Kreuzlingen on Lake Constance.[90] He had notified Jung of the visit, but nothing was heard of him; what had happened we shall presently learn. This Kreuzlingen visit proved to be a fateful one in his relationship to Freud. On the Sunday Binswanger took Freud for a long automobile ride along the lake, and Freud wrote one of his detailed accounts of it, with of course literary and historical associations.[91] He mentioned among other things that they had been sumptuously entertained by the "Queen Widow" on her Brunegg estate. Naturally I wondered who that could have been, so I wrote to Professor Meng and asked him what royalties lived in that neighborhood at that time. He could only suggest the Empress Eugénie (at Arenberg), but I was sure Freud would not have confounded an Empress with a Queen. Then I found out from Dr. Binswanger that the title was a jocular one Freud had bestowed on his (Binswanger's) step-mother who was living on the family estate. I mention all this to show that even a faithful biographer can be misled into taking Freud's humorous remarks seriously—how often have other readers done so!

On the return journey he had two hours between trains at Munich, from ten to twelve P.M., and used the interval to get his old friend the *Hofrat* Professor Löwenfeld out of bed for a few minutes' greeting.

I was in Vienna for June that summer. It was the occasion when I had the idea of the "Committee" which played an important part in Freud's life for the next fifteen years.[m] Freud himself left for treatment in Karlsbad on July 14. He was accompanied by his wife and the van Emdens, who worked with him there as in the previous year; they stayed at the Goldener Schlüssel. On the following day there was a visitor from Hamburg to whom Freud's second daughter, Sophie, had just got engaged. An announcement of the happy event appeared in the *Neue Freie Presse* on the 28th. Freud remarked to Ferenczi that it afforded an unintentional over-determination of the theme he had just been working at—the three daughters of Lear.[92] For the remaining daughter, Anna, it was not lucky. Freud had arranged that as a reward for her hard work in the previous year she should spend some months in Italy "seeing something nice when she is young."[93] But the preparations for the marriage interfered with that plan, so there was no Italian trip. Freud, however, made it up to Anna later on by taking her himself. Sophie's mother spent a good deal of time in Hamburg helping her daughter to furnish her future domicile, so Tante Minna had to stay in Vienna to look after the household. Besides, there was much sewing and embroidery to be done for the trousseau.

Freud was given to interlarding his letters with semi-jocular remarks. On this occasion, for instance, after describing how terribly hungry he felt in the morning after taking his daily dose of the Karlsbad waters he added: "You notice the total abandonment of a sublimation."[94]

Freud and his wife left Karlsbad on August 14, traveled via Munich to Bozen where they met the rest of the family. They then settled in the Hotel Latimar, Karersee. Karersee (Lago di Carezza), in the Northern Dolomites, is situated some fifteen miles north-east of Bozen. It is some five thousand feet high and lies close to the jagged cliffs of the mighty Latemar, which is four thousand feet higher. Freud assuredly had a flair for beautiful spots.

There being no Congress, Freud wondered what expedition he and Ferenczi could make in September. Before leaving Karlsbad he had hit on the idea of spending a week in London, where I promised to act as guide, and inviting Abraham, Brill and Rank to accompany them. The first two, however, found it impossible to fit in with their other plans, but Freud wrote and asked me to engage rooms for the three—Ferenczi, Rank and himself—definitely on September 10. After the week in London Freud and Ferenczi were to spend another

<hr>

[m] See Chapter 6.

one in Scotland, a country that even Freud would have found it hard to exhaust in the time.

The family left Karersee on August 30 for Bozen, where Ferenczi met them in the Erzherzog Heinrich Hotel. They were then to travel to S. Cristoforo (Hotel Seehof) a village on the Lago di Caldonazzo about a dozen miles east of Trient.

I was staying at Seif's villa in Partenkirchen at the time and was surprised to get a letter there announcing a change in Freud's plans. His eldest daughter had been taken ill in Vienna, so Freud and Ferenczi had gone there from Bozen, leaving the rest of the party to go on to S. Cristoforo.[95] I still hoped the London plan was only delayed for a few days; a week later, however, I heard from him that his daughter was better, he was joining the family at S. Cristoforo, but: "So I could have kept my date at London had I been in better condition myself: I felt increasing fatigue and inactivity since Karlsbad, sleeping badly and spirits rather low and had looked for London as an analeptic. The excitement of this last week did mightily increase my weakness so that I feel I am in need of rest and unfit to produce myself in clever society. Even Ferenczi, kind as he is, who would not leave me for his own pleasure and recreation, is sometimes too much for me. He is reading in the next compartment and must not know it. I cannot remember a similar condition, which I am prone to ascribe to the strong action of the hot waters, and I expect something from time and sunshine." The lack of grip on his English shows how tired he was, and it was also hard to decipher. However, as he said, "No sudden attack of old age makes my hand shaky. I am writing you in the train from Vienna to Italy[n] and my hand plays the part of a seismometre's needle." [96]

In the meantime I had been busy in Zurich, where the Second International Congress of Medical Psychology had taken place, presided over by Bleuler. Psychoanalysis had secured a good footing, two out of the three members of the Council—Bernheim (the famous hypnotist), Seif and myself—being analysts. Then I got a letter from S. Cristoforo announcing a further sudden change of plan:

"September 14, 1912

"My dear Jones,*

"I have passed through some days of very bad health. Now I feel recovered and intend going to Rome tomorrow to catch a last dose of beauty and self-collection. I got a nice letter from Maeder about the

* He evidently already had this intention.

Congress and I am sure I have to thank *your* influence for it. Mrs. Jung who had been silent for a long time added some very kind words to sending her husband's famous paper in *Separatabdruck.*° So the prospects seem rather clearing—if all this be not the immediate effect of your personal intercourse with the Zurich people.

"I expect to meet Ferenczi on the line to Rome.

<blockquote>

"With my best love
"yours truly
"Freud"

</blockquote>

Two days later came a postcard showing that Rome had worked its old magic.

<blockquote>

"Rome.
"September 16, 1912

</blockquote>

"Dear Jones *

"I am glad to be here and I feel quite recovered."

<blockquote>

"Best love
"Yours truly
"Freud"

</blockquote>

I had suggested that his trouble was partly at least psychological, and that his anxiety about his daughter had stirred also his anxiety, because of Jung, about the fate of his mental child—psychoanalysis. Here is his reply:

<blockquote>

"Sept. 22, 1912

</blockquote>

"My dear Jones,*

"I am glad I have received all your letters as you have mine and hasten to answer the two last ones from your side before we can exchange writing for talking. I am very sensitive indeed to your kindness shown during my last troubles and glad to let you know that my daughter is slowly improving, while I feel strengthened and relieved by the air and the impressions of this divine town. In fact I have been more happy than healthy at Rome, but my forces are coming back and I feel

> *wieder Lust mich in die Welt zu wagen,*
> *der Erde Leid, der Erde Glück zu tragen.*ᴾ

° Reprint.
ᴾ "I feel the urge to face the world again,
   To bear life's happiness, to stand its pain."

"What you construed about the *Verdichtung*[q] of the two daughters sounds so ingenious that I dare not contradict it, the more so as it gave you the occasion for promises which touch my ear as music might another man. Of course there is a great difficulty, if not impossibility, in recognizing actual psychical processes in one's own person. To me the physical side must be more evident, the sudden intolerance of the heart muscle for tobacco and it seems even more for wine. My last improvement here is due to a great restriction of that delicious Roman wine I was indulging in. . . . We will shake hands in a few days.

"Yours truly
"Freud"

In the letters to his wife from the Hotel Eden in Rome he expressed the same happiness in being there. "It feels quite natural to be in Rome; I have no sense of being a foreigner here." [97] A few days later he was feeling so gay that he had taken to sporting a fresh gardenia in his buttonhole every morning. He even proposed to his wife that when they retired it should be to Rome, not, as they had hitherto planned, to the "cottage" suburb of Vienna, and he expressed the conviction that it would please his wife and her sister as much as himself—a most optimistic assumption.[98] He was visiting Moses daily and might write a few words about him.[99] Ferenczi had spent a day in Naples, and they were about to travel home together, at least as far as Udine.

His daughter Anna has preserved several picture postcards from this Rome visit, addressed to "my future traveling companion." So in 1912 Freud already had the plan of taking her with him to see Rome, one that did not get fulfilled until eleven years later.

How much Rome meant to Freud! A few months later when I was spending several weeks there he wrote: "I am glad you are getting so deep an impression of Rome and quite sure you did feel pretty unhappy in the first days as every honest man is bound to do. Your enjoyments will come out clearer every day. I know the restaurant on the Aventine pretty well, but there are more curious spots on the Coelius near by. My favourite spots are on the Palatine but it is better not to begin about this divine city. As for the beauty of the women it needs some days to detect it." [100]

There was plenty of work waiting for Freud on his return. His waiting list of patients was overflowing. The audience for his lectures had

[q] Condensation.

increased to fifty or sixty.[101] The trouble with Stekel came to a head in November and will presently be narrated in detail.[r] The final solution was arrived at in a meeting in Munich on November 24, which is also a story in itself.

Freud's despondency over Stekel and Jung at this time did not prevent his moods showing considerable variation. Thus in October he wrote: "I am in excellent spirits and envy you for all your sight-seeing, but especially for what is waiting for you in Rome." [102] Yet a couple of weeks later the other side is manifest in the elated response with which he greeted the first book on psychoanalysis in English, *Papers on Psycho-Analysis*.[s] It was the most natural thing in the world that I should dedicate it to him. He not only, however, felt impelled to telegraph thanks to me, but also to write as follows: "I have been so deeply emotioned by your last letter announcing the dedication of your book that I resolved not to wait for its material appearance to react by a letter of pride and friendship." [103] There were not many bright moments in his life about this time, and doubtless the loss of previous colleagues made him value contact with the remaining ones all the more. He had a consultation in Budapest at the beginning of December, and of course took the opportunity of seeing Ferenczi and of meeting the latter's future wife.[104] Abraham came to Vienna on a visit of three days at the end of December,[105] and I spent the following month of January in Vienna.

The Society for Psychical Research invited in this year first Freud and then Ferenczi to write a paper for them. Freud's will be described presently,[t] but the Society refused to publish Ferenczi's on account of its sexual content.[106]

Freud published a number of short papers in 1912, but there were two topics that dominated his thinking in that year: the exposition of his technique and the psychology of religion. I can perceive a connection between these apparently disparate topics. They had both to do with the increasing dissension of the Swiss school. Freud believed that much of this, as also with that of Adler and Stekel, came from an imperfect knowledge of the technique of psychoanalysis, and that it was therefore incumbent on him to expound this more fully than he ever had. Then the revival of his interest in religion was to a considerable extent connected with Jung's extensive excursion into mythology and mysticism. They brought back opposite conclusions from

[r] Chapter 5.
[s] One which the publishers post-dated on the title page.
[t] Chapter 13, No. 3.

their studies: Freud was more confirmed than ever in his views about the importance of incestuous impulses and the Oedipus complex, whereas Jung tended more and more to regard these as not having the literal meaning they appeared to, but as symbolizing more esoteric tendencies in the mind.

1913

The main event in Freud's life in this year was his final break with Jung, which took place at the Munich Congress in September. The two men never met again, although some formal relations continued until the following year. It was altogether a very anxious and distressing year, and Freud put it mildly when he wrote to me in October: "I scarcely can recall a time so full of petty mischiefs and annoyances as this. It is like a shower of bad weather, you have to wait who will hold out better, you or the evil genius of this time." [107] In the same month he had described himself to Pfister as a "cheerful pessimist." [108]

The record may now proceed more or less chronologically, as with the previous years. The first occurrence was Eder's going to Vienna from London for a three weeks' analysis.[109] Freud had no free hour, so he referred him to Tausk. In the middle of the month we heard there had been a panic in Boston. The police there, no doubt with some instigation, had threatened to prosecute Morton Prince for the "obscenities" he was publishing in his *Journal of Abnormal Psychology*.[110] So his generosity to psychoanalysts was ill rewarded, and there was some justification for his misgivings which Freud had wrongly attributed to his "puritanical prudishness." But Prince, who had not long before been Mayor of the city, knew how to weather such storms without having to appear in court.

In that month, on January 14, an exciting event took place in the Freud household. It was the marriage of his second daughter Sophie, to Max Halberstadt of Hamburg, a son-in-law who was as welcome to the parents as the first one had been.

In February Freud took the novel step of buying a typewriter, one which his daughter still uses. But it was not for himself, for there was no question of his employing an amanuensis and giving up his beloved pen. It was simply to help Rank to cope with his increasing editorial duties.

Ferenczi had wanted him to join him with another friend, Schaechter, on a three weeks' tour to Corfu and Greece at Easter, amplifying the trip Freud had made with his brother Alexander nine years before, but Freud said he could not afford to be away from work so long. His intention was to make a short visit to his half-brother Emmanuel in England, returning via Hamburg; Emmanuel was then eighty.[111] However, he chose instead to take his daughter Anna to Venice as a slight recompense for the Italian journey she had missed through her sister's engagement. She had been staying at Meran with a sister-in-law of Mathilde's since November and joined her father at Bozen on March 22. They had a look at Verona and then spent four days in Venice (staying at the Hotel Britannia), a town Freud knew and loved so well. From there they even had time to pay a visit to Trieste on the way home. He had left Vienna on the evening of March 21 and got back on the 27th.

The first half of the year was fully occupied in the writing of *Totem and Taboo*. I was present when he addressed the Vienna Society on the third section of the book on January 15, 1913, as I had been when he described the second section in the previous year (May 15, 1912). In May, when he was completing the book, he wrote to Abraham that he was writing it only for four or five men.[112] His doubts about his conclusions and his final conviction of their truth will be narrated in the appropriate place when describing the book itself.ᵘ

On June 29 there was the annual social evening at the Konstantin-hügel in the Prater, and I remember an ex-patient presenting Freud with an Egyptian figure which he kept in front of his plate as a totem. It was probably the last of these pleasant outings.

Freud left Vienna on July 13, but this time for Marienbad (Villa Taube) in place of Karlsbad. There were only his three womenfolk with him, since he no longer felt up to analytic work with the van Emdens as before. His daughter tells me it was the only time she ever remembers her father being depressed.

Freud kept on urging me to improve my German, but my progress with reading the Gothic handwriting was slow. He wrote: "I am sorry I must go on abusing your fine English as you have kept the Alexia Gotica while giving up the Aphasia mot. and sensor."ᵛ [113]

In the first week of August there was a duel between Janet and myself at the International Congress of Medicine, which put an end to his pretensions of having founded psychoanalysis and then seeing it spoiled by Freud. This was Freud's response to the news.

ᵘ Chapter 14, No. 19.
ᵛ I had learned to speak German and to understand spoken German but **not** yet to read it when written in Gothic characters.

"Marienbad
"August 10, 1913

"My dear Jones.*

"I cannot say how much gratified I have been by your report of the Congress and by your defeating Janet in the eyes of your countrymen. The interest of psychoanalysis and of your person in England is identical, and now I trust you will *'schmieden das Eisen solange es warm ist.'* ᵂ

" 'Fair play' is what we want and likely it may be got better in England than anywhere else.

"Brill will not come over. He writes, it is his family, wife and daughter, who want his presence this year. He has been appointed chief of the clinic of Psychiatry at the Columbia University, and so is settled and independent at last.

"I am leaving Marienbad for S. Martino di Castrozza, Hotel des Alpes. We had a bad time here, it was too cold and wet. I can scarcely write from rheumatism in my right arm. Perhaps we are to have more freezing in the mountains.

"Go on giving me your good news during these four weeks. You make me feel strong and hopeful.

"sincerely yours
"Freud"

Just then Havelock Ellis asked me to write a book of five to six hundred pages on the non-medical aspects of psychoanalysis for the Contemporary Science series, of which he was the Editor.

"August 22, 1913

"My dear Jones.*

I am glad you are entering with full sails into English scientific life. As you are kind enough to consult me about Havelock Ellis' offer I will not postpone to answer that you cannot decline it, but must do it first of all. Napoleon can wait, even the translation of Ferenczi's may; the translation of Pfister is no work for you. Your work is enough for one man, but your capacity for doing work is immense; it ought to be directed into urgent channels.

"Glad to see you in a few days.

"yours faithfully
"Freud"

▾ Strike while the iron is hot.

I signed the contract with Havelock Ellis, and came across it the other day, but cannot remember now how it was I never wrote the book. Nor did that on Napoleon ever reach the light. How few of one's plans ever come to fruition.

San Martino di Castrozza, which Freud reached on August 11, is nearly 5000 feet high; it is in the heart of the Dolomites, at the end of the Primiero valley. Ferenczi joined the family there on August 15 —Abraham was also there for a few days—and he traveled together with Freud to the Munich Congress, arriving at the Bayerischer Hof on the evening of September 5.

Ferenczi and I had many talks that summer with Freud about how best to cope with the situation Jung had created by renouncing the fundamental tenets of psychoanalysis. There were no longer any friendly feelings on either side between him and Freud, but the matter was far more important than any personal question. Freud was continually optimistic about the possibility of maintaining at least a formal cooperation, and both he and Jung wished to avoid anything that could be called a quarrel. So we approached the Congress, which was to meet on September 7, in that mood and in the expectation that there would be no open break.

Freud had been very unwilling to read a paper at the Congress, and it took all Abraham's persuasion to induce him to do so. It was on "The Predisposition to Obsessional Neurosis," [114] an important contribution in which he established the anal-sadistic phase as a regular pre-genital stage in the development of the libido.

My paper was the only one directly criticizing Jung's recent views, so I submitted it to Freud beforehand. In doing so I wrote: "I am not satisfied with the parts dealing with Jung directly. When I say I cannot understand why he goes on analyzing phantasies that are purely secondary in nature, and not causal, he could easily reply: because the libido and energy necessary for the performance of the *Aufgabe*[x] have got anchored there and have to be released through analysis. This is not easy to meet without overstepping the bounds of therapeutics and dealing with other parts of his theory." Here is his reply.

"August 29, 1913

"My dear Jones.*

"Your paper is excellent, unsparingly clear, clever and just. I feel some resistance against writing you in English after reading your German. You ought to learn Gothic letters too.

[x] Task.

"You are right in saying that there is some scarcity in your remarks about an important point against Jung. You might add that there is a special interest in abstaining from decisions in the *Zwangs*-cases,[7] where the patient is lying in wait to renew his play with the precepts given from without, which he had performed hitherto with those given from within. As regards the question of the importance of the unconscious fantasies I see no reason why we should submit to the arbitrary judgment of Jung instead of the necessary one of the patient himself. If the latter values those productions as his most precious secrets (the off-spring of his day-dreams), we have to accept this position and must ascribe to them a most important role in the treatment. Let aside the question if this importance is an etiological one: that is out of joint here, it is rather pragmatical.

"Your remarks on the esteem psycho-analysis is enjoying from afar in England made me laugh heartily; you are quite right.[8]

"In a few days I will have the pleasure of talking with you upon more topics. Don't forget: it is Bayerischer Hof.

"I received a good paper on psycho-analysis by one Becker of Milwaukee. The first papers of the newcomers seem always pretty good; now let us wait to see what the man may write two years later.

"Au *revoir*

"yours

"Freud"

There were 87 members and guests at the Congress. The scientific level of the papers was mediocre, although there were two interesting ones by Abraham and Ferenczi. One of the Swiss papers, containing many statistics, was so tedious that Freud remarked to me: "All sorts of criticisms have been brought against psychoanalysis, but this is the first time anyone could have called it boring." Jung conducted the meetings in such a fashion that it was felt some gesture of protest should be made. When his name came up for re-election as President, Abraham suggested that those who disapproved should abstain from voting, so he accepted the re-election with 52 votes against 22. He came up to me afterwards, observing that I was one of the dissidents, and with a sour look said: "I thought you were a Christian" (i.e. non-

[7] Cases of obsessional neuroses.
[8] I had written: "The references to ps-a in the magazines are usually highly complimentary, with that respect for the distant that is likely to change when matters are brought to closer quarters."

Jew). It sounded an irrelevant remark, but presumably it had some meaning.

Freud had been somewhat anxious about what Putnam's attitude was going to be concerning the dissension with Jung. I sent him a long letter I had just received from Putnam, and here is his comment on it. "Putnam's letter was very amusing. Yet I fear, if he keeps away from Jung on account of his mysticism and denial of incest, he will shrink back from us (on the other side) for our defending sexual liberty. His second-thought pencil-written question is very suggestive about that. I wonder what you will answer to it. I hope no denial that our sympathies side with individual freedom and that we find no improvement in the strictness of American chastity. But you could remind him that advice plays no prominent part in our line of treatment and that we are glad to let every man decide delicate questions to his own conscience and on his personal responsibility." [115] It is well known that Putnam remained a loyal and convinced adherent to the end of his life, so Freud's apprehension had been unnecessary.

In the meantime two other groups had been founded and accepted as Branch Societies of the International Association. The first was Budapest, which was formed on May 19, 1913, the officers being: Ferenczi, President; Hollós, Vice-President; Rado, Secretary; and Levy, Treasurer. I was present at the second meeting, when Ferenczi informed me in his usual witty manner that the remaining member, Ignotus, functioned as the audience.

The other Society was founded in London on October 30, 1913, with myself as President, Douglas Bryan as Vice-President and M. D. Eder as Secretary. There were nine members, of whom, however, only four ever practiced psychoanalysis (Bryan, Eder, Forsyth and myself). Bernard Hart joined a week later, but William McDougall and Havelock Ellis declined.

Immediately after the Congress Freud traveled to Rome, his sister-in-law, Minna Bernays, joining the train at Bologna.[116] He spent "seventeen delicious days" there,[117] from the tenth to the twenty-seventh, visiting his old haunts and discovering new ones, notably "the delicious Tombe Latine missed hitherto." As always he instantly recovered his spirits and health. Since Minna could stand only a little sightseeing, Freud was able to get through a good deal of work. Besides correcting the proofs of his long essay for *Scientia*, he wrote a Preface to the *Totem* book, wrote out and extended the paper he had given at Munich and, above all, a complete draft of his long paper on

"Narcissism." While in Rome he got a letter from Maeder assuring him of his continued veneration, but adding, in allusion to his changed views, "Like Luther, here I stand; I can do no other." Freud dryly commented: "A suitable remark for someone taking a risk, but hardly for someone drawing back from a risk."

In October Albert Moll invited Freud to join a Society, the *Gesellschaft für Sexualwissenschaft* (Society for Sexology), he had just founded in Berlin. Freud was very dubious about doing so, but on Abraham's advice consented.[118] When, however, the first number of its official organ, the *Zeitschrift für Sexualwissenschaft*, appeared shortly afterward, the allusions to psychoanalysis were not encouraging enough for Freud to be willing to have any more to do with the undertaking. Psychoanalysis was evidently to be kept in the background. "The Society is designed to achieve recognition for Fliess; that is quite right, since he is the only active thinker[aa] among them and the possessor of a piece of unrecognized truth. But to subordinate our psychoanalysis to a Fliessian sexual biology would be no less a misfortune than to subordinate it to an Elfitt metaphysics, etc. You know him with his incapacity in the psychological field and his logical consistency in the physical field. The left side equals woman, equals the unconscious, equals anxiety. We must in any event keep our independence and claim equal rights. In the end we can come together with all the parallel sciences." [119]

At Christmas Freud paid a visit to his daughter Sophie in Hamburg. He left Vienna on the evening of December 24 and got back on the morning of the 29th. On his way he broke his journey in Berlin for six or seven hours on Christmas Day and so had time to call on Abraham, Eitingon and his sister Marie. There were at that time many consultations, either personally or by correspondence, with members of the Committee about the Swiss situation, and Freud's mind was full of his polemical "History of the Psycho-Analytic Movement" which he was just then composing.

1914

The dissension with Jung came to an end in 1914 with his resignation from the editorship of the *Jahrbuch*, the presidency of the International Association, and finally from its membership. We all agreed that Abraham should function as temporary President and that he should arrange the next Congress. It was at first arranged to take place in Dresden on September 4, the date being later changed

[aa] *Ingenieur.*

to September 20,[120] but by then most of Europe was at war. Practically all the Swiss had joined Jung, and Abraham was even suspicious of the good Pfister's intentions. Freud could only say: "I have been warned against contradicting you in the judgment of the people." [bb] But in this case Abraham proved wrong, for Pfister remained a staunch supporter of Freud.

Early in the year Freud's daughter in Hamburg presented him with his first grandson, the first of six he was to have.[121] That grandson is now a psychoanalyst.

Freud had invited Ferenczi to repeat their pleasant sojourn of the previous year in Arbe and suggested bringing his daughter Anna along with him.[122] She had been running a temperature for some time and he was anxious about her. Brioni was then chosen as being more accessible (from Pola). At the last moment Anna was found to have whooping cough, so Freud took Rank with him instead. They left Vienna on the evening of April 9 and got back on April 13, a long journey for a taste of sea air.

In February Freud was surprised by a reprint from Holland of the Rector's official address on the occasion of the 339th anniversary of the founding of the University of Leyden. It was concerned with Freud's theory of dreams, which the author, G. Jelgersma, the Professor of Psychiatry, supported. "After 14 years the first recognition at a university of my work on dreams." [123] It was followed by a polite letter inviting Freud to lecture at the University that autumn. Freud was excited and wrote: "Just think. An official psychiatrist, Rector of a University, swallows psychoanalysis, skin and hair. What more surprises are we to expect!" [124]

In May things were not so good. His bowel trouble had been so disturbing that he had to undergo a special examination to exclude cancer of the rectum. It was carried out by Dr. Walter Zweig, a Docent for intestinal disorders. Freud remarked: "He congratulated me so warmly that I inferred he had fully expected to find a cancer. So this time I am let off." [125]

In the same month there was sad news from America. Stanley Hall had proclaimed his adherence to Adler. Freud wrote: "for personal reasons I felt this accident sharper than others." [126] It was after all Stanley Hall who had been so enthusiastic about Freud's work only five years before and had done so much to bring it to the notice of the world. Freud was evidently very disappointed, and in the same letter he added: "I badly want a few hours talk with you." Some six

[bb] Referring to Abraham's early prediction about Jung.

years later, however, Stanley Hall paid a handsome tribute to Freud's work and called him "the most original and creative mind in psychology of our generation. . . . His views have attracted and inspired a brilliant group of minds not only in psychiatry but in many other fields, who have altogether given the world of culture more new and pregnant *aperçus* than those which have come from any other source within the wide domain of humanism." [127]

On the other hand there was good news from France. Professor Régis of Bordeaux had, together with his Assistant, A. Hesnard, written a book containing a favorable description of psychoanalysis.[128] Hesnard had sent a letter two years before to Freud apologizing for the neglect of his work in France.[129]

In June Freud was in Budapest for a couple of days. He and Rank had gone there to attend the wedding of an ex-patient, Loe Kann.[130] It is perhaps worth mentioning, because of its being one of the two weddings he ever attended outside his immediate family.

Sachs stayed with me in London that May for a couple of weeks' holiday, and Ferenczi and Rank arranged to do the the same in August. But in August 1914 there were no holidays.

4

CHAPTER

Opposition

IN THE PRECEDING CHAPTER I HAVE DESCRIBED THE FAVORABLE ASPECTS of the psychoanalytical movement, of the gradual dissemination of Freud's work. I have next to give some account of the storm of opposition that he had to endure, particularly in the years before the First World War but to some extent for all the rest of his life.

There are two great difficulties in the way of describing at the present day the nature and extent of this opposition. The first is that the greater part could not find its way into print; it was simply unprintable. Not that Freud was spared hearing of it. Patients in a state of negative transference, not to speak of "kind friends," saw to it that he was kept well informed. And after all, being cut in the street, ostracized and ignored are unescapable manifestations.

Freud's name had by now become a by-word of sensation—or rather of notoriety—to German psychiatrists and neurologists, and his theories were having a profoundly disturbing effect on their peace of mind. Some day a student of the history of science may wade through the outpourings of abuse and misunderstanding that served as a vent for the explosive emotions that had been aroused. But even so he would get a very imperfect picture of the amount of anger and contempt with which those intellectual circles strove to cover the more panicky emotions that agitated them, since only a small part of the flood seeped through into scientific periodicals, and then only in a relatively civilized form. Most of the invective was to be encountered in unrecorded outbursts at scientific meetings, and still more in the private conversations outside these. Ferenczi well remarked that if the oppo nents denied Freud's theories they certainly dreamed of them.

The intense wave of hostility that greeted Freud's work in the years before the First World War now seems very remote, but those who experienced it cannot easily forget it. I passed through it not only in America and later on in England, but also in Germany. First as a research worker at Kraepelin's Psychiatric Clinic in Munich, and then on my annual visits from Canada to Germany, where I was a member of several learned societies, I had ample opportunities for sensing it. Furthermore, for some years I attended every International Congress in those allied subjects, where Freud's evil ideas were a staple topic of conversation and often of official discussions as well.

The second difficulty is that the nature of opprobrium has vastly shifted its ground in the past half century, and indeed largely as the result of Freud's own work. If nowadays it were being said of a prominent person that he was "obsessed with sex," that he had the habit of reading the filthiest and more repulsive aspects of sexuality into every little happening or act, most people would think it rather queer on his part, but would still judge him on other grounds, whether he was personally agreeable or whether he did valuable work. Even if it were hinted that he personally indulged in various sexual perversions, the rumor alone would hardly rule him out as an impossible creature, one not fit to speak to or to admit into decent company. I do not think he would be regarded as essentially evil-minded and *wicked*, an enemy of society.[a]

Yet that is what such a stigma would have meant forty or fifty years ago, and indeed for the half century before. The moral loathing thus aroused might perhaps find its counterpart nowadays in the attitude general in many countries towards the news that an apparently respectable citizen was really a "Communist" or a "Trotskyite." And if such a person were to go further and follow his principles to their logical end of assisting a foreign country against his own, we know many parts of the world where he would be judged literally unfit to live. So the conception of wickedness has undergone a considerable change in the past couple of generations.

Freud lived in a period of time when the *odium theologicum* had been replaced by the *odium sexicum* and not yet by the *odium politicum*. It will be for the future to assess which of the three should rank as the most disreputable phase in human history.

In those days Freud and his followers were regarded not only as

[a] It is fair to remember however, that a relic of this attitude is still reserved for the case of male homosexuality, particularly when it concerns the seduction of boys.

sexual perverts but as either obsessional or paranoic psychopaths as well, and the combination was felt to be a real danger to the community. Freud's theories were interpreted as direct incitements to surrendering all restraint, to reverting to a state of primitive license and savagery. No less than civilization itself was at stake. As happens in such circumstances, the panic aroused led in itself to the loss of that very restraint the opponents believed they were defending. All ideas of good manners, of tolerance and even a sense of decency— let alone any thought of objective discussion or investigation—simply went by the board.

At a Congress of German Neurologists and Psychiatrists that took place in Hamburg in 1910 Professor Wilhelm Weygandt, a *Geheimer Medizinalrat*, gave forcible expression to the state of alarm, when Freud's theories were being mentioned, by banging his fist on the table and shouting: "This is not a topic for discussion at a scientific meeting; it is a matter for the police." Similarly when Ferenczi read a paper before the Medical Society of Budapest he was informed that Freud's work was nothing but pornography and that the proper place for psychoanalysts was prison.[1] The only police action ever taken, however, that in Boston in 1913, was balked at the last moment.

Nor was the vituperation always confined to words only. At the Neurological Congress in Berlin in 1910 Professor Oppenheim, the famous neurologist and author of the leading textbook in that subject, proposed that a boycott be established of any institution where Freud's views were tolerated. This met with an immediate response from the audience and all the directors of sanatoria present stood up to declare their innocence. Whereupon Professor Raimann went further and declared that "the enemy should be sought out in his lair." All cases unsuccessfully treated by psychoanalysis should be collected and published.[2] Raimann was an Assistant at the Psychiatric Clinic in Vienna. He pursued Freud unrelentingly from 1904 to 1916 when Freud at last protested to his chief, Wagner-Jauregg, who put a stop to the invective.

The first material victim was, oddly enough, in far-off Australia where a Presbyterian clergyman, Donald Fraser, had to leave the ministry on account of his sympathy with Freud's work. In the same year, 1908, I was forced to resign a neurological appointment in London for making inquiries into the sexual life of patients. Two years later the Government of Ontario ordered the *Asylum Bulletin* to cease publication. It had been reprinting all papers written by the staff, and my own were declared "unfit for publication even in a medical periodical." In 1909 Wulff was dismissed from an institution in Berlin and in August emigrated to Russia, which was then a freer country than Germany in such matters. Pfister was more than once, in 1912 and again in 1917, in trouble with his superior authorities, but managed to survive the ecclesiastical examinations. His colleague, Schneider, was less fortunate and was dismissed from his directorship of a Seminary in 1916.[3] In the same year, Sperber, the distinguished Swedish philologist, was denied his docentship because of an essay he had written on the sexual origin of speech, and his career ruined.[4]

A curious feature in this campaign of contumely was that there was a certain specialization in the targets of the protagonists. Freud of course was the chief villain who started all the evil, but, perhaps for personal reasons, many of the opponents concentrated their attacks elsewhere. Friedländer, Hoche and Raimann aimed their shafts directly at Freud; Abraham had to contend with Oppenheim and Ziehen; Jung with Aschaffenburg and Isserlin; and Pfister with Förster and Jaspers; while Vogt and I had a corner to ourselves. In America Brill had to face the New York neurologists, Dercum, Allen Starr and Bernard Sachs; Putnam was harried by Joseph Collins and Boris Sidis; while I had a wide choice there which was soon to be extended when I returned to England in 1913.

In the first years of the century Freud and his writings were eithei quietly ignored or else they would be mentioned with a sentence or two of disdain as if not deserving any serious attention. At the Congress of Mid-German Psychiatrists and Neurologists held at Halle in 1900 there was a symposium of the pathogenesis of hysteria, but Freud's name was not even mentioned by any of the speakers. When the same Congress met in 1904 Stegmann gave an account of cases he had treated by Freud's method[b] and was severely castigated by Professor Binswanger[c] of Jena, the author of the standard textbook on hysteria.

But after 1905 when the *Three Essays on the Theory of Sexuality* and the Dora analysis appeared this attitude of silence soon changed, and the critics took a more active line. If his ideas would not die by themselves they had to be killed. Freud was evidently relieved at this change of tactics. He remarked to one of his favorite patients—no

[b] See Chapter 2, p. 30.
[c] Ludwig Binswanger, the psychoanalyst of Kreuzlingen, was a nephew of his.

other than the "Wolfman" [d]—that open opposition, and even abuse, was far preferable to being silently ignored. "It was a confession that they had to deal with a serious opponent with whom thy had *nolens volens* to thrash matters out." He could at times laugh at the moral indignation displayed, such as when he told the same patient that a meeting at which his views had been decried as immoral ended by the audience relating the most obscene jokes among themselves.

Even in the first review of the Dora analysis Spielmeyer declaimed against the use of a method that he described as "mental masturbation." [5] Bleuler protested that no one was competent to judge the method without testing it,[6] but Spielmeyer in an angry retort overwhelmed him with moral indignation.[7]

The first person to take independent action was Gustav Aschaffenburg. At a Congress in Baden-Baden in May 1906 he expressed himself vigorously and came to the conclusion that "Freud's method is wrong in most cases, objectionable in many and superfluous in all." [8] It was an immoral method and anyhow was based only on auto-suggestion. Hoche joined in. According to him psychoanalysis was an evil method proceeding from mystical tendencies and full of dangers to the medical profession; it was wrong-headed and one-sided. Jung replied to this outburst in the periodical that published Aschaffenburg's paper, but not very effectively.[9]

In the same year Ostwald Bumke[10] made great play of quoting the first devastating denunciation of Freud, which Rieger had published ten years previously on Freud's contribution to the theory of paranoia.[11] According to Rieger Freud's views were such as "no alienist could read without feeling a real sense of horror." The ground of this horror lay in the way Freud treated as of the greatest importance a paranoid rigmarole with sexual allusions to purely accidental incidents which, even if not invented, were entirely indifferent. All that sort of thing could lead to nothing other than "a simply gruesome old-wives' psychiatry." [12] This quotation was to be dug up again in yet another ten years' time by Professor von Luschan of Berlin. Some years later Bumke extended his denunciation into a book,[13] the second edition of which was to serve in Nazi times as a standard reference work on the subject.

In November of that year Jung and Hoche had a set-to at the Congress of South-West German Psychiatrists in Tübingen.

In the following year there was a more serious duel between Aschaf

[d] See Chapter 11, Case V.

fenburg and Jung at the First International Congress of Psychiatry and Neurology which took place in Amsterdam in September 1907.

Freud himself had been invited to take part in the symposium, but he had unhesitatingly refused. He wrote to Jung about it: "They were evidently looking forward to my having a duel with Janet, but I hate gladiator fights in front of the noble mob and find it hard to agree to an unconcerned crowd voting on my experiences." [14] Nevertheless he had some misgiving later at the thought of how he was enjoying a pleasant holiday when someone was fighting on his behalf. So just before the Congress he wrote an encouraging letter to Jung: "I don't know whether you will be lucky or unlucky, but I should like to be with you just now, enjoying the feeling that I am no longer alone. If you needed any encouragement I could tell you about my long years of honorable, but painful, loneliness that began for me as soon as I got the first glimpse into the new world; of the lack of interest and understanding on the part of my nearest friends; of the anxious moments when I myself believed I was in error and wondered how it was going to be possible to follow such unconventional paths and yet support my family; of my gradually strengthening conviction, which clung to *The Interpretation of Dreams* as to a rock in the breakers; and of the calm certainty I finally compassed which bade me wait until a voice from beyond my ken would respond. It was yours!" Freud also predicted that Jung would come across some sympathizer at the Congress, a prediction my presence there unexpectedly fulfilled.

Jung could certainly do with any encouragement before such an ordeal. Aschaffenburg repeated his previous dictum about the untrustworthiness of Freud's method because of every single word being interpreted in a sexual sense. This was not only painful for the patient but often directly harmful. Then, striking his breast with a gesture of self-righteousness, he asseverated how he forbade his patients ever to mention any sexual topic. In the course of his address Aschaffenburg made this revealing slip of the tongue: "As is well known, Breuer and *I* published a book some years ago." He did not appear to have noticed it himself, and perhaps Jung and I were the only people to have done so, or at least to perceive its significance; we could only smile across at each other. Jung said in his address that he had found Freud's conclusions correct in every case of hysteria he had examined, and he remarked that the subject of symbolism, although familiar to poets and the makers of myths, was new to psychiatrists. Unfortunately he made the mistake of not timing his paper and also of refusing to obey the chairman's repeated signals to finish. Ultimately he was compelled to, whereupon with a flushed angry face he strode out of the room. I remember the unfortunate impression his behavior made on the impatient and already prejudiced audience, so that there could be no doubt about the issue of the debate. Both papers were subsequently published.[15] Aschaffenburg was not able to be present on the following day when the discussion took place, but Konrad Alt and Karl Heilbronner seconded his attack in a fashion that made Jung feel it was useless to reply. Alt said that, apart from Freud's methods, it had always been known that sexual traumata influenced the genesis of hysteria. "Many hysterics had suffered severely from the prejudice of their relatives that hysteria can only arise on a sexual foundation. This widely spread prejudice we German neurologists have taken endless trouble to destroy. Now if the Freudian opinion concerning the genesis of hysteria should gain ground the poor hysterics will again be contemned as before. This retrograde step would do the greatest harm." [16] Amid great applause he promised that no patient of his should ever be allowed to reach any of Freud's followers, with their conscienceless descent into absolute filth.[e] The cheering was renewed when Ziehen rose to congratulate the speaker on the firm stand he had taken.

Jung was naturally extremely disgusted at the whole performance and very glad that Freud had not been present to be exposed to such contumely.

Even Jung's work on association experiments was thought to be moving in a dangerous direction. Ziehen of Berlin, who had a proprietory interest in the word "complex" which he had first introduced, protested against using this method for reaching the unconscious and asserted that "psychologists could not be warned too strongly against such deviations from association-psychology." To apply their results to dementia praecox was erroneous, artificial and even dangerous.[17]

When Jung's book on *The Psychology of Dementia Praecox* appeared in 1907, M. Isserlin of Munich delivered lengthy and violent polemics against it. He denied any causal connection in free association, and described the process as one of "guessing riddles." Nor did he think there could be such a thing as mental dissociation; "the unity of consciousness was a fundamental maxim." [18]

Daring attempts were made about this time to introduce psychoanalytical ideas into Berlin. On December 14, 1907, Juliusburger read a paper defending them before the *Psychiatrischer Verein* (Psychiatric Association) there and managed to survive the unanimous opposition

[e] *Schweinerei.*

he encountered.[f] A year after, on November 9, 1908, Abraham read a paper before the same Society on the erotic aspects of consanguinity.[19] It led to a furious outburst on the part of the famous neurologist Oppenheim who declared he could not express himself harshly or decidedly enough against such monstrous ideas. Ziehen was also shocked at "such frivolous statements," and announced that everything Freud wrote was simply nonsense. Braatz, alluding to Sadger's study of the influence of his mother in C. F. Meyer's life, cried out that German ideals were at stake and that something drastic should be done to protect them. Shortly afterwards Oppenheim published a paper in support of an attack Dubois of Berne had made on psychoanalysis.[20] Freud's false generalizations made his method dangerous, and the reports he and his followers published impressed one as a modern form of witchcraft-mania.[g] It was their urgent duty to wage war against this theory and its consequences, since they were spreading rapidly and the public would get hopelessly confused. Wulff ventured to send a reply to Oppenheim to this same periodical, but it was sent back to him by return of post; a few years later I was to have the same experience at the hands of the *British Medical Journal*. Shortly afterwards Wulff lost his position in Berlin. Oppenheim then arranged for a symposium to take place at the next Congress of German Neurologists on the theme of anxiety states, in which he played a prominent part.[21] Being affections of the bulb they were inaccessible to any form of psychotherapy. Incidentally it was known in his circle in Berlin that Oppenheim had recently suffered from a severe anxiety condition himself,[22] so this may have both stimulated his interest in the topic and also affected his scientific conclusions; furthermore, his wife was a bad case of hysteria.

In 1908 Moll, the Berlin sexologist, published a book entitled *The Sexual Life of Children*. It was so vehement in its denial of infantile sexuality that Freud said in a letter "There are several passages that would justify a libel action, but silence is the best answer." [23]

The indefatigable Abraham read another paper before the same Society on November 8, 1909, this time on "Dream States." It was met with superior smiles, and the President, Professor Ziehen, forbade any discussion but expressed his own emotions in an angry outburst.

Ziehen's qualifications for passing judgment on Freud's work may be estimated from the following episode. A patient came to the Berlin Psychiatric Clinic, of which Ziehen was the Director, complaining of

[f] Chapter 2.
[g] *Hexenwahn.*

an obsessional impulse to lift women's skirts in the streets. Ziehen said to his pupils: "This is an opportunity to test the supposed sexual nature of such obsessions. I will ask him if it applies to older women as well, in which case it evidently cannot be erotic." The patient's reply was: "Oh yes, to all women, even my mother and sister." On which Ziehen triumphantly ordered the entry in the protocol to describe the case as "definitely non-sexual." [24]

It would take us too far afield to follow the disputes about psychoanalysis all over the world, and we are concerned here only with those that more nearly touched Freud. Perhaps in time the history of the early development of psychoanalysis will be written in each country separately. But naturally Freud followed closely everything that went on, and he seemed to take a special interest in what happened in America—perhaps because it was the only place where he had ever in his life spoken to a public audience. So I may relate three incidents from that far-off continent which happened in 1910, the year we have now reached.

At the meeting of the American Psychological Association in December 1909 in Baltimore, Boris Sidis made a fiercely abusive attack on Freud's work and inveighed against the "mad epidemic of Freudism now invading America." Freud's psychology took one back to the dark Middle Ages and Freud himself was merely "another of those pious sexualists" of which there were many examples in America itself (Oneida Creek, Mormonism, etc.). Putnam was so angry that he could not trust himself to speak, but I managed to give a fairly quiet reply. However, a little later in the meeting Putnam and Stanley Hall answered him in an annihilating and final fashion.

At the annual meeting of the American Neurological Association in Washington in May, 1910, Joseph Collins, a New York neurologist, distinguished himself by making an after dinner speech at the usual banquet which was a scurrilous personal attack on Putnam in the worst possible taste. He protested against the Association having allowed Putnam to read the paper he had just done which was made up of "pornographic stories about pure virgins"; incidentally Collins himself was notorious for his proclivity to indecent jokes. "It was time the Association took a stand against transcendentalism and supernaturalism and definitely crushed out Christian Science, Freudism and all that bosh, rot and nonsense." [25] Naturally the speech offended the American sense of fair play, and the next morning when someone got up in the meeting and said how thankful the Association should be that a man of Dr. Putnam's high ethical standing had probed and tested this new work there was the heartiest applause.

A couple of years later another New York neurologist, Allen Starr, made an unprovoked personal attack on Freud before the New York Academy of Medicine.[h]

On March 29, 1910, there was a violent explosion of contumely at a meeting of the Medical Society of Hamburg.[26] Weygandt, the gentleman who talked of calling in the police, was particularly virulent. Freud's interpretations were on a level with the trashiest dream books. His methods were dangerous since they simply bred sexual ideas in his patients. His method of treatment was on a par with the massage of the genital organs. It was important to expose such things wherever possible. Embden, supported by Ernst Trömner and Max Nonne, warned all institutions against admitting such methods. Trömner made the original criticism that there could be no sexual factors in hysteria since most hysterics were frigid. Nonne was concerned about the moral danger to the physician who used such methods. Boettiger maintained that the only patients who felt well during the treatment were women given to psychical exhibitionism. Alfred Saenger showed how with the mention of anal erotism Freud's theories were assuming the most fantastic and grotesque shape. Fortunately, however, the North German population were very far from being as sensual as that of Vienna.

Freud's comment was: "There one hears just the argument I tried to avoid by making Zurich the center. Viennese sensuality is not to be found anywhere else! Between the lines you can read further that we Viennese are not only swine but also Jews. But that does not appear in print." [27]

Under the sensational title of "A Psychical Epidemic among Doctors," Hoche read a much-quoted paper at a Congress in Baden-Baden on May 28, 1910.[28] He announced that "psychoanalysis was an evil method born of mystical tendencies and full of dangers for the standing of the medical profession." Psychoanalysts were ripe for certification in a lunatic asylum. Freud found it simply amusing and told Ferenczi it was the greatest recognition he had yet achieved.[29] Writing to me on the same day he said: "It is a valuable symptom of the uneasiness our enemies feel in face of the growth of psychoanalysis." [30] To Jung he called it "a magnificent advertisement," [31] and a sign that we were fifteen years ahead of the rest.[32]

[h] See p. 122.

Another opponent who caused us more merriment was Friedländer of Frankfurt. He had already made several attacks on psychoanalysis.[33] The one published in America in which he listed a large number of unfavorable opinions did us a good deal of harm there, since it gave the impression that Continental authorities had made extensive investigations of the subject and universally condemned it. Although all his publications were extremely adverse to psychoanalysis it seemed to have some peculiar fascination for him. He would visit Jung, be sugary sweet to him and express the hope they would come to an understanding. What pained him most was that none of us would reply to his writings. Knowing this craving of his for acknowledgment we decided to ignore him entirely, and he found that very distressing. In a paper he gave at Budapest he complained bitterly about the way he was neglected.[34] "My review of the Freudian theory was announced several months ago, so why does not Freud, who did not mind traveling to America, give himself the trouble of coming to Budapest to refute me? Why does he dispose of his opponents in only a footnote?"

Friedländer was a curious man, a doubtful personality with a shady past, of which Freud was informed. When I was with Freud in Holland in the summer of 1910 he told me the following story. One Saturday, May 28, 1910, the telephone rang and a Professor Schottländer, a psychiatrist, asked for an interview. Freud said he might call that evening, but he was extremely puzzled since he knew the names of all the German psychiatrists and could not recollect this one. At nine o'clock Professor Friedländer appeared and assured Freud he had misheard his name on the telephone. Talk proceeded and soon came on to the topic of the Dora Analysis, which Friedländer referred to under the name of the Anna Analysis. Freud pricked up his ears, leaned forward and said: "If you please, Herr Professor, we are not on the telephone now. I suggest that we analyze this slip of the tongue." From there on he did not spare the visitor and he kept him on the rack until one in the morning. He admitted to us that he had given him a hard time—he had a good deal to work off and it was a rare opportunity—and his final summing up was that Friedländer was "a liar, a rascal and an ignoramus." [35]

Freud could not keep his opinion to himself, and Friedländer, hearing of a remark he had dropped in Switzerland a few years later, threatened to bring an action for slander against Freud.[36] Nothing, however, came of it.

In the same year Professor Robert Sommer of Giessen made a vigorous protest against the idea of the neuroses having a sexual aetiology, and he urgently warned against the danger of transferring such ideas to other fields, particularly that of education.[37]

Oscar Vogt was another bitter opponent. Between 1899 and 1903 he had published a series of papers maintaining the superiority of his "causal analysis" over Freud's psychoanalytic method. Intellectual self-observation was quite sufficient without invoking any affective agencies; Freud was simply a hide-bound bigot when he introduced the latter.[38] Vogt was President of the International Congress for Medical Psychology at Munich in September 1911 when Seif and I had a sharp set-to with him. He was a tyrannical person and got red in the face with anger when in the discussion on hypnosis I expounded Ferenczi's view of the regression to the child-patient situation. He interrupted me with the remark: "It is pure nonsense to suggest that my power of hypnotizing patients lies in *my* father complex—I mean, of course, in *their* father complex." Whereupon for the benefit of the audience I carefully explained the significance of the slip; I told Freud that if they encountered us often enough they would learn some psychoanalysis from practical experience.[39]

In the evening, however, in the more amicable atmosphere of a beer garden we got on to less strained terms. A number of obscene jokes were the order of the day by way of relaxation from the strenuous meetings, and Vogt told some good ones himself. I disturbed the harmony by remarking that the jokes would have had no point at all were it not for various symbolic meanings identical with those the existence of which he had vigorously denied the same afternoon. He was taken aback, but promptly gave the reply, which seemed to him quite convincing: "But this is outside science."

On January 12, 1910, Fritz Wittels read a paper before the Vienna Society analyzing the character of the well-known writer and poet, Karl Kraus. Freud found it clever and just, but urged special discretion in the study of a living person lest it deteriorate into inhumanity. Somehow or other Kraus got to hear of Wittels' paper, and he responded by making several fierce attacks on psychoanalysis in the lively periodical of which he was the editor, *Die Fackel.* Freud, however, did not take them seriously enough to be worth replying to.[40]

At the end of 1910 Freud could remark that "it rains abuse from Germany," [41] and a couple of years later he added: "It needs a good stomach." [42] This sort of thing, of which I have given some indication, went on for several years until the outbreak of the World War in 1914, but it would be tedious to go on multiplying examples. Not that the war itself entirely put a stop to it. In 1916 Professor Franz von Luschan of Berlin published a pronunciamento under the now familiar title "Old Wives' Psychiatry." [43] He praised Rieger for having been the first to perceive the danger and warn against it twenty years before, and he allotted severe blame to Bleuler for his astonishing behavior in helping to promulgate the epidemic. "Such absolute nonsense should be countered ruthlessly and with an iron broom. In the Great Times in which we live such old wives' psychiatry is doubly repulsive." Freud stoically remarked on this: "Now we know what we have to expect from the Great Times. No matter! An old Jew is tougher than a Royal Prussian Teuton." [44]

Much could be written about the opposition psychoanalysis encountered in England, but it belongs to my autobiography, if that is ever written, rather than to a biography of Freud. It is easy to predict that opposition to psychoanalysis will not vanish, or even much diminish in our lifetime or in that of our immediate descendants. As I write these lines I come across a book recently published in America which rivals in blindness and stupidity anything Germany itself ever produced, though its ill-nature does not degenerate into the same degree of malice.

So far nearly all the "criticism" we have noted could be reduced to two dicta, constantly reiterated in the most ex cathedra fashion: Freud's interpretations were arbitrary and artificial, and his conclusions, being repulsive, must be untrue. But there was a small group of writers who felt that a fuller understanding of his work was desirable, if only for the purpose of disproving it through arguments that purported to be objective. Incidentally, Freud once remarked to me how curious it was that his opponents should so calmly arrogate to themselves this quality; *he* was never allowed to be objective. The writers we are here concerned with published several lengthy expositions of Freud's work as it appeared in their eyes, and they will be briefly mentioned in order.

The first of them had the least claim to be considered objective. It was a review Friedländer published in 1907.[45] It was full of gross misunderstandings, some of them evidently tendentious. A typical example of the latter is the giving of Dora's age as fourteen instead of eighteen when inveighing against the wickedness of talking about sexual matters with adolescents.

A more serious attempt was made in 1909 by J. H. Schultz.[46] It is a review, with some serious value, of the early phases of psychoanalysis and the opposition it met. It contained 172 references. On the whole it refrained from passing any final judgment on the issues at stake, although the general tone was a negative one. He expanded it later into a chapter in a volume edited by C. Adam.[47] In the following year Isserlin published a full critical review[48] in which he had no doubt about a final judgment. The whole of Freud's procedure, both in its basis and its aims, was quite untenable. His conclusions concerning the unconscious could only be regarded as "a relapse into pre-scientific phases of understanding."

We then come to two more valuable contributions. In 1911 Arthur Kronfeld published a full summary of psychoanalysis considered as an organic whole.[49] He dealt very little with the historical aspects of the subject, but presented a cross section of it at the stage it had then reached. The critical aspects were of a philosophical and abstract nature, the conclusions being on the whole more than skeptical. When Freud read it he wrote: "Kronfeld has demonstrated philosophically and mathematically that all the things we plague ourselves over don't exist because they can't exist. So now we know."[1][50] This is what he told Stärcke: "I have also read Kronfeld's work. It displays the customary philosophical technique. You know with what assurance philosophers refute each other after fleeing far enough away from experience. That is just what Kronfeld does. He asserts that our experience counts for nothing, and then it is child's play for him to refute us."[51]

A year later Kuno Mittenzwey wrote an enormously lengthy review of the whole subject.[52] It ran, in continued parts, through every volume of Specht's short-lived *Zeitschrift*, which succumbed under its weight before Mittenzwey came to the end. So we possess only a torso of 445 pages of what is perhaps the best historical review of the early development of Freud's ideas.

So with the reviews just mentioned, the growing psychoanalytical literature, and the constant polemical discussions and diatribes conducted by his opponents at every meeting of psychiatrists and of many general medical meetings, no educated person in Germany could have failed to know of the existence of Freud's work in the period before the World War and have perhaps some rough idea of its nature.

Freud himself was well out of this hurly-burly and wasted little thought on it. The only reply he ever deigned to make to the flood of criticism was the same as Darwin's: he merely published more evi-

[1] *Da haben wir's.*

dence in support of his theories. He despised the stupidity of his opponents and deplored their bad manners, but I do not think he took the opposition greatly to heart. After all, he had had by then many years in which to harden himself, and his confidence in his own observations provided him with a good protective layer. But it did not improve his opinion of the world around him, particularly that part of it consisting of German scientists. Many years later, in his *Autobiography*, he was to write these words: "I fancy that when the history of the phase we have lived through comes to be written German science will not have cause to be proud of those who represented it. I am not thinking of the fact that they rejected psychoanalysis or of the decisive way in which they did so; both these things were easily intelligible, they were only to be expected, and at any rate they threw no discredit upon the character of the opponents of analysis. But for the degree of arrogance they displayed, for their conscienceless contempt of logic, and for the coarseness and bad taste of their attacks there could be no excuse. It may be said that it is childish of me to give free rein to such feelings as these now, after fifteen years have passed; nor would I do so unless I had something more to add. Years later, during the Great War, when a chorus of enemies were bringing against the German nation the charge of barbarism, a charge which sums up all that I have written above, it none the less hurt deeply to feel that my own experience would not allow me to contradict it." [53] Fortunately for him he had no opportunity to comment on Auschwitz and the other "camps" where some of his sisters perished.

Naturally the topic often came up among us in conversation, so I can speak at first hand of Freud's reactions to these various "criticisms." It was quite obvious to him that it was completely useless to reply to such diatribes and the thought of doing so never crossed his mind. That there should be general incredulity concerning his startling discoveries was fully intelligible to anyone who had for many years struggled with the intense opposition ("resistances") of his patients, and he had long realized that in this respect they did not differ from other people. Jung also had observed that normal people "had to fight with the same complexes as neurotics," a statement based on the optimistic assumption that normal people were sometimes to be found. Nor did it surprise Freud that the so-called arguments brought forward by his opponents were identical with his patients' defenses and could show the same lack of insight or even of logic. All this was therefore in the natural order of things and could neither shake Freud's convictions nor disturb him personally. After all, he had for years assumed that no one would believe him in his lifetime and that the same discoveries would be made by someone else, perhaps long after his death. It might even be called an agreeable surprise that the contrary happened and that he now had around him a growing group of convinced supporters.

He wrote to Pfister, who was commiserating with him on some opposition: "Please do not suppose that the derision and misunderstandings that appear in the literature are a matter of much concern to me. There are days when the uniformity of the reactions somewhat affect my mood, but never an hour when I despair of the insight we have gained ultimately making its way." [54] When Ferenczi, knowing he was not fond of compliments, apologized for making some eulogistic remarks he got the terse reply: "I am only insensitive to censure, not to recognition." [55] A few years later, on the occasion of receiving some critical suggestions Ferenczi and I had jointly sent him on the manuscript of his book on totemism, he wrote: "I have been interested to observe that I am no longer, as formerly, inaccessible to the judgments of others. At all events when you are the critics." [56]

All that I have just said about Freud's attitude to criticism is true enough, but it is by no means the whole truth. It would be misleading to portray Freud as a model of Olympian calm. In the face of criticism he was for the most part calm enough and would toss it off with some good joke or ironic comment. But with all his iron self-control he was more capable of strong emotions than most people, and there were certain aspects of the criticisms that could move him deeply enough. Thus he minded adverse and misunderstanding criticism from someone he liked or thought well of. Here is an example: "By way of exception I have been depressed[j] at what Forel recently wrote." [57] His depression at Stanley Hall's defection was another. Then, as the quotation given above from his *Autobiography* shows, he must have found it depressing that his psychiatric colleagues in Germany could descend to the depths they did. And he was evidently shocked to find a similar example of bad manners in America where he hoped for better behavior. On April 4, 1912, a well-known New York neurologist, Allen Starr, had denounced him as a typical "Viennese libertine" before the Neurological Section of the New York Academy of Medicine,[58] and the next day the New York *Times* reported him as saying he had worked in the same laboratory as Freud for a whole winter and therefore knew him well, ascribing his theories to the im-

[j] *verstimmt.*

moral life he led then. I have given the reasons why the two former statements could not be true, and there is not the slightest ground for supposing there is any truth in the third one either.[59]

To one accusation he appeared to be rather sensitive: namely, the idea that he had evolved all his conclusions out of his inner consciousness. It was the main motive that impelled him to answer Löwenfeld many years before in the only controversial reply he ever made to any criticism.[60] In a letter to Pfister he wrote: "If only we could get our opponents to understand that all our conclusions are derived from experiences—experiences, which, so far as I am concerned, other workers may try to interpret otherwise—and are not sucked out of our fingers[k] or put together at a writing table. That is really what they all think, and it throws a peculiar light, by way of projection, on their own manner of working." [61] One may suspect that this particular criticism affected Freud because of his deep fear or guilt about the imaginative, and even speculative, side of his nature which he had striven so hard to suppress or at least to control.

Another sensitive area was the ostracism he had to endure in his own city of Vienna. This he never really got accustomed to. One result of it was to make him specially grateful to recognition from abroad. Thus he wrote to me once: "Putnam's papers are excellent and his Preface to the 'Sexual Theory' very kind and appropriate . . . Yet I was astonished myself that the constant depreciations I am suffering here should have rendered me so sensitive to being acknowledged by some one both honest and clever. It is true, I thought I had more internal resistance." [62]

But what could really infuriate him on occasion was the hypocrisy in the lofty ethical pretensions of some of his opponents. Answering a letter in which Pfister had enclosed the proofs of a reply he had written to an attack Förster had made on him, Freud wrote: "I admire the way you can write, so gently, so humanely, so full of considerateness, so objectively, so much more written for the reader than against your enemy. *That* is obviously the right way to produce an educative effect, and it is also more becoming to a man in your position. I thank you specially for leaving my personality as much as possible in the background. But I could not write like that; I should rather not write at all, i.e. I don't write at all. I could only write to free *my* soul, to dispose of *my* affects, and since that would not turn out to be very edifying—it would give a deal of pleasure to the opponents, who would be happy

[k] A German idiom.

to see me angry—I don't reply to them. Just think! A fellow has been playing the part of an ethical and noble creature who turns against low things and so acquires the right to babble the greatest nonsense, to parade his ignorance and superficiality, to pour out his gall, to twist everything and to raise all kinds of suspicions. All that in the name of the highest morality. I couldn't keep calm in the face of it all. But since I cannot artificially moderate my wrath or convey it in a pleasantly infectious manner I keep silent. What I could never do would be to lower its temperature." [63] As soon as he calmed down, however, Freud knew perfectly well that the only effective reply was that of Darwin, and that is the one he consistently followed.

Freud could afford to do so, but the matter was different for those of us whose professional work brought us into inevitable personal contact with opponents. One could not always refuse invitations to read papers at meetings and Congresses; even as it was we were often enough regarded as exclusive hermits. Freud's advice on such occasions may be illustrated by a passage in a letter to Stärcke, one which also illustrates his absolute integrity of character.

"Your task at the Dutch Congress will not be an easy one. Allow me to express the opinion that it could be carried out in a better way than the one you propose. Your idea of convincing society, or persuading it through suggestion, has two things against it. In the first place it contemplates something impossible, and in the second place it departs from the prototype of psychoanalytic treatment. One has really to treat doctors as we do our patients, therefore not by suggestion but by evoking their resistances and the conflict. Moreover, one never achieves anything else. Whoever surmounts the first 'No' of the repressions and then the second and third will reach a true relationship to the relevant matters of psychoanalysis; the rest will stay bogged down in their resistances until they veer by the indirect pressure of the growth of public opinion. I think, therefore, one has to be content to state one's point of view and relate one's experiences in as clear and decided a way as possible and not trouble too much about the reaction of one's audience.

"To compile statistics, as you propose, is at present impossible. Surely you know that yourself. To begin with, we work with much smaller numbers than other doctors, who devote so much less time to individuals. Then the necessary uniformity is lacking which alone can form a basis of any statistics. Should we really count together apples, pears and nuts? What do we call a severe case? Moreover, I could not regard my own results in the past twenty years as comparable, since my technique has fundamentally changed in that time. And what should we do about the numerous cases which are only partially analyzed and those where treatment had to be discontinued for external reasons?

"The therapeutic point of view, however, is certainly not the only one for which psychoanalysis claims interest, nor is it the most important. So there is a great deal to be said on the subject even without putting therapy in the forefront." [64]

5

CHAPTER

Dissensions

THIS IS A PAINFUL AND DIFFICULT TOPIC TO EXPOUND; PAINFUL BECAUSE
of the distress the dissensions caused at the time and of the unpleasant
consequences that lasted for many years after; difficult because it is
hard to convey their inner meaning to the outside world and because
the personal motives of the dissidents cannot even yet be fully exposed. The outside world quite rightly attempts to judge the differences between Freud's theories and those of his followers who separated from him on the objective merits of the respective theories,
though it does not always succeed in this laudable endeavor. In the
nature of things, however, it is bound to overlook, or underestimate,
an essential element in the situation.

Investigation of the unconscious, which is a fair definition of psychoanalysis, can be carried out only by overcoming the "resistances"
which ample experience has shown are displayed against such a procedure. In fact, as Freud has remarked, psychoanalysis consists in an
examination of these resistances and of the "transferences" that accompany them, and of little else.[1] When the resistances have been
overcome the subject has insight into aspects of his personality to
which he had previously been blind.

Now it might be supposed that this is an act that is accomplished
once and for all, and this was Freud's first expectation. It was disappointing to find it is not so. The forces in the mind are not static
but dynamic. They can vary and shift in unexpected fashion. Thus it
may come about that the insight at first gained is not necessarily permanent and may once more be lost; it proved to have been only

partial insight. Only when the manifold resistances have been thor-oughly worked through is the insight of a lasting nature.

All this is equally true for the analyst as for the patient, since for him a clear and permanent insight is even more important. This consideration is sometimes overlooked by the public, who often assume that someone who is practicing analysis and has read the necessary books on the subject will not be prone to any fluctuations in his personal emotions and insight. Analysts were indeed themselves slow to appreciate this and perceive the need for a preliminary "training analysis" that should clear the obstacles present in every mind. I happened to be the first analyst to undergo a training analysis, although it was much less thorough than is nowadays demanded. Freud himself had been able to achieve the difficult feat of making a very extensive self-analysis, but none of the other pioneers had had much personal experience with their own unconscious or only in glimpses. Theoretically it should have been possible to anticipate the possibility of relapses among analysts such as we were familiar with in our patients, but nevertheless the first experiences of the kind were unexpected and startling. Nowadays we are less astonished.

When an analyst loses insight he had previously had, the recurring wave of resistance that has caused the loss is apt to display itself in the form of pseudo-scientific explanations of the data before him, and this is then dignified with the name of a "new theory." Since the source of this is on an unconscious level it follows that controversy on a purely conscious scientific level is foredoomed to failure.

The "divergencies" from psychoanalysis that have occurred in the past forty years have all been characterized by two features: repudiation of the essential findings made by means of psychoanalysis and exposition of a different theory of the mind. The latter must of course be judged on its merits by general psychologists and philosophers; the former is what specifically concerns psychoanalysts.

This being a biography rather than a discussion of scientific differences, it is necessary to comment on some personal considerations. The scientific divergencies in question have not always been confined to objective problems. There has been at times a propensity to link differences of opinion and interpretation with personal reactions to Freud himself. Then we are told that such and such a person left Freud and his circle not simply because of a difference of opinion but because of Freud's tyrannical personality and his dogmatic insistence on each of his followers accepting precisely the same views as himself. That such accusations are ridiculously untrue is demonstrable from his correspondence, his writings, and above all from the memories of those who worked with him. I may quote a passage from a letter written many years later to Binswanger: [2] "Quite unlike so many others you have not allowed the fact of your intellectual development moving away more and more from my influence to disturb our personal relationship, and you do not know how agreeable I find such decent behavior." [a]

Those of us who, like myself, remained close to Freud while openly disagreeing with many of his conclusions have been described as timid and docile people who have submitted to the authority of the great Father. It is, however, possible that they should be better described as men who had come to terms with their childhood complexes and so could work in harmony with both an older and a younger generation, whereas the dissidents may include those who still feel obliged to perpetuate the rebelliousness of childhood and to keep searching for figures to rebel against.

I would expressly say that these last remarks apply far more to colleagues who renounced psychoanalysis in later years than to the three whose dissension will be presently related. Some of these later writers have gone beyond drawing a picture of Freud as an irritable, disagreeable old man, and have invented remarks of his which are so out of character as to be utterly impossible for him ever to have made. I would issue a formal warning against believing everything that may appear in print about Freud, even if it purports to be a memory of Freud's conversation, since much of it is so untrue as to convey a quite mistaken impression of his personality.

Among these various divergencies two in particular have caught the attention of the general public; those instituted by Adler and by Jung respectively. Whether this was because of their being the first ones or because of some intrinsic quality it is hard to say. At all events these divergencies were promptly labeled "different schools of psychoanalysis" and their existence extensively exploited by all opponents, lay and professional, as reasons for not taking psychoanalysis seriously. How could they do so, they insisted, and how could any trust be reposed in psychoanalytic findings, if their supposed exponents differed so much among themselves as to find it necessary to establish different schools? For skeptics and for active opponents it was the repudiation of Freud's findings and theories that constituted the essential feature of the "new theories," and indeed in that judgment they were perhaps not far wrong.

[a] *wie sehr eine solche Feinheit einem Menschen wohl tut.*

It is to be hoped that these preliminary remarks will have prepared the reader for the fact that dissensions concerning psychoanalysis are even harder to resolve than those in other fields of science where it is not so easy to continue re-interpreting data in terms of some personal prejudice. On that basis we may now consider more coolly the stories I have to unfold.

Alfred Adler (1870–1937)

Freud greatly disliked occupying any prominent position, especially if it might bring with it any duties that implied the ruling of other people. As he remarked to Jung just after the Salzburg Congress: "I am certainly not fitted for the role of leader; [b] the 'splendid isolation' of such decisive years has been stamped on my character." [3] Anyone temperamentally less fitted to resemble the dictator he has at times been depicted as being I should find it hard to imagine. But, as the founder of his new methods and theories, and with his wealth of experience and knowledge behind him, his position in the little circle of Viennese followers could not fail to be an exceptionally dominating one. So much so that it was years before anyone felt equal to rebelling against such an obvious father figure. Any unresolved infantile complexes could find expression in rivalry and jealousy for his favor. This clamor to be the favorite child had also an important material motive, since the economic basis of the younger analysts depended in large part on the patients Freud could refer to them from his own surplus. Thus as time went on the atmosphere became more and more unpleasant. There was backbiting, acid remarks, quarrels over priority in small matters, and so on. The most troublesome members in this respect were Adler, Stekel, Sadger and Tausk.

The situation was greatly exacerbated after the first two Congresses, at which Freud's undisguised and perhaps unwisely extreme preference for the foreigner Jung was very evident. For a time this led the discordant Viennese to band together in a common complaint against Freud. It was probably the turning point when their former mutual jealousies began to develop into rebellion against him. The most prominent rebel was undoubtedly Adler, and it was he who provoked the first scission in the psychoanalytical movement.

Freud's endeavor to appease the disgruntled Viennese by putting Adler and Stekel, his oldest followers, in charge of the newly founded *Zentralblatt* in the autumn of 1910, and by handing over the presi-

---

[b] *Ich tauge gewiss nicht zum Chef.*

dency of the Society to Adler at the same time, was only partially and temporarily successful. He had little choice at that time of prominent colleagues, but the choice he made was certainly unfortunate. It was in that autumn also that the meetings of the Society, which had grown too large for Freud's private apartment, were transferred to the auditorium of the *Medizinisches Doktoren-Kollegium* which perhaps conduced to a chillier and more formal atmosphere. I observed myself that it was very different from what I had witnessed in the earlier years of the Society.

There is ample evidence to show that after the time of the Nuremberg Congress, in 1910, Freud was feeling the strain of the bickerings and recriminations of which he was the unwilling cause. He unburdened himself particularly to Ferenczi. Referring to the tension between Vienna and Zurich he wrote: "The tactlessness and unpleasant behavior of Adler and Stekel make it very difficult to get along together. I am chronically exasperated with both of them. Jung also, now that he is President, might put aside his sensitiveness about earlier incidents." [4] Complaining that it interfered with giving himself to his writing he went on: "I am having an atrocious time with Adler and Stekel. I have been hoping that it would come to a clean separation, but it drags on and despite my opinion that nothing is to be done with them I have to toil on. It was often much pleasanter when I was alone." [5] Ferenczi had suggested that Freud was living over again the unpleasant experience of Fliess's desertion of him ten years ago, and Freud confirmed this: "I had quite got over the Fliess affair. Adler is a little Fliess come to life again.[c] And his appendage Stekel is at least called Wilhelm." [d] After the long Adler debate in the following spring Freud complained: "I am continually annoyed by the two—Max and Moritz[e]—who are rapidly developing backwards and will soon end up by denying the existence of the unconscious." [6]

My own impression of Adler was that of a morose and cantankerous person, whose behavior oscillated between contentiousness and sulkiness. He was evidently very ambitious and constantly quarreling with the others over points of priority in his ideas. When I met him many years later, however, I observed that success had brought him a certain benignity of which there had been little sign in his earlier years. Freud apparently had thought rather highly of him in the earlier years; he was certainly the most forceful member of the little group.

[c] Redivivus.
[d] Fliess's first name.
[e] The two naughty boys in Wilhelm Busch's *Die bösen Buben*.

Freud thought well of his book on defective organs and also considered he had made some good observations in the study of character formation. But Adler's view of the neuroses was seen from the side of the ego only and could be described as essentially a misinterpreted picture of the secondary defenses against the repressed and unconscious impulses. Then his whole theory had a very narrow and one-sided basis, the aggression arising from "masculine protest." Sexual factors, particularly those of childhood, were reduced to a minimum: a boy's incestuous desire for intimacy with his mother was interpreted as the male wish to conquer a female masquerading as sexual desire. The concepts of repression, infantile sexuality, and even that of the unconscious itself were discarded, so that little was left of psychoanalysis.

Adler's theory was essentially one of the psychology of the ego. The way in which this may be manipulated and influenced by unconscious processes, i.e. the contribution made by psychoanalysis, was quite neglected and before long entirely ignored. Freud several times likened the ego, as described by Adler, to the clown who claims to have himself accomplished all the difficult feats of the circus.

Adler was never an intimate friend of Freud's, nor can the story of his having been Freud's own personal doctor [7] be confirmed by any member of the family; it sounds most improbable.

Adler's scientific differences with Freud were so fundamental that I can only wonder, as I did in the Fliess case, at Freud's patience in managing to work with him for so long. Adler had two good ideas in terms of which, however, he interpreted everything else: a tendency to compensate for feelings of inferiority (Janet's *sentiment d'incomplétitude*), the spur to do so being reinforced by an innate aggressivity. There was little search into the source of such feelings, which psychoanalytic investigation has had no great difficulty in ascertaining. At first Adler connected them with the feminine side of human beings, labeling the subsequent compensation his famous "masculine protest." So all conflict was between the masculine and feminine components, a pan-sexualistic view of the human mind that far outdid the stress Freud had laid on sexuality.* Soon, however, he rushed to the opposite extreme and interpreted everything in terms of Nietzsche's will to power. Even sexual intercourse itself was not impelled by sexual desire so much as by pure aggressiveness.

Freud took Adler's ideas very seriously and discussed their possi-

*Actually Freud had thought of this idea fifteen years before and had discarded it after carefully testing it with his cases. [8]

bilities at length. Even ten years later, when he had some particularly apposite clinical material with which to put them to the test, he published a very conscientious and thorough criticism of them.[9] Other members of the Society, however, were more vehement in their criticism, or even denunciation, of them, and Hitschmann suggested that they have a full-dress debate on the subject. The minutes of this, including the discussions, have been preserved and will shortly be published, but Colby has already made accessible the gist of them.[10] The first two evenings, on January 4 and February 1, 1911, were devoted to lengthy expositions by Adler. The first paper was entitled "Some Problems of Psychoanalysis," the second "The Masculine Protest as the Nuclear Problem of Neuroses." Two other evenings, February 8 and 22, were given up to discussions, which were forthright enough. Freud himself was unsparing in his criticism. Stekel gave it as his opinion that there was no contradiction between Freud's theories and Adler's, to which Freud replied that unfortunately for this view both Adler and Freud thought there was. Adler's insistence that the Oedipus complex was a fabrication was evidence enough of it.[11] Adler had said among other things that since, according to Freud, repression comes from civilization and also that civilization comes from repression then all this talk about repression was only playing with words. Freud had no difficulty in clarifying this caricature of his views, and he added: "I feel the Adlerian teachings are incorrect and therefore dangerous for the future development of psychoanalysis. They are scientific errors due to false methods; still they are honorable errors. Although one rejects the content of Adler's views one can recognize their consistency and significance."

After the last of those meetings, on February 22nd, there was a Committee meeting, at which Adler and Stekel resigned their positions as President and Vice-President respectively. The other officials thereupon resigned also, and a special meeting was held on March 1 with Hitschmann in the chair, to clear up the situation. Freud was asked to resume his previous presidency, to which he somewhat reluctantly agreed.[g] Hitschmann became Vice-President, and Sachs replaced him as Librarian. Rank and Steiner retained their former positions. A resolution was unanimously passed, thanking Adler and Stekel for their past services and expressing the hope that they would remain in the Society. Heller proposed an additional clause, which was also passed, affirming that Adler's views were not incompatible

---

[g] Stekel's memory was at fault when he said that he succeeded Adler in this position, though he may have taken the chair at the interim meeting.[12]

with psychoanalysis, although Freud pointed out that this was a criticism of Adler inasmuch as he had resigned on the ground of incompatibility.

Adler remained in the Society for a while longer; his last attendance at a meeting was on May 24. Then, however, Freud suggested to him that he resign his position as Co-editor of the *Zentralblatt* and wrote to the publisher, Bergmann, to the same effect.[13] Adler jibbed at this at first and got his lawyer to put forward conditions which Freud described as "displaying ridiculous pretensions of a quite unacceptable nature." [14] He and his friends also demanded that a discussion take place in an extraordinary meeting. He nevertheless resigned from the Society and from the *Zentralblatt*.[15] Freud wrote a couple of weeks later: "How the Adler affair passed off is too long-winded to relate in detail. I will tell you about it in Bozen. Enough that he is out of the Society and *Zentralblatt* and that I am on good terms with Stekel who has shown himself consistently loyal." [16]

In the biography of Adler the author states that Freud begged Adler to reconsider his decision and asked him to a private dinner so that they might seek a common field.[17] The truth about this is that Jekels had with great difficulty persuaded Freud, who was convinced of the uselessness of the suggestion, to hold a meeting *à trois* with Adler and himself, but it degenerated into such petty reproaches on Adler's side that it had no issue.[18]

Adler's response was to exploit the situation by forming a group under the rather tasteless name of "Society for Free Psychoanalysis," putting forward the claim that he was fighting for the freedom of science. Now that is certainly a worthy cause. It presumably means the freedom to pursue any investigation by any means, to form any conclusions one wishes on the results and to publish them to the world. Few scientific bodies anywhere, if any, have power to interfere with such freedom, least of all the tiny "Wednesday Society" in Vienna. The only issue was whether it was profitable to hold discussions in common when there was no agreement on the basic principles of the subject-matter; a flat-earther can hardly claim the *right* to be a member of the Royal Geographical Society and take up all its time in airing his opinions. Adler had drawn the correct inference by resigning. To accuse Freud of despotism and intolerance for what had happened has too obvious a motive behind it to be taken seriously.

The extraordinary meeting in question took place on October 11 at the beginning of the new session, and Freud announced the resignation of Adler, Bach, Máday and Baron Hye. The Committee proposed that members should decide to which of the two Societies they would adhere, the implication being that no member would belong to both. This represented a strong desire for a clean break. Sachs and other members supported the resolution, while Furtmüller made an impassioned speech against it. It was passed by eleven votes to five, whereupon the remaining adherents of Adler—Furtmüller, Franz Grüner, Gustav Grüner, Frau Dr. Hilferding, Paul Klemperer and Oppenheim—resigned from the Society.

It is not irrelevant to recall that most of Adler's followers were, like himself, ardent Socialists. Adler's wife, a Russian, was an intimate friend of the leading Russian revolutionaries; Trotsky and Joffe, for instance, constantly frequented her house.[19] Furtmüller himself had an active political career. This consideration makes it more intelligible that Adler should concentrate on the sociological aspects of consciousness rather than on the repressed unconscious.

A couple of years later Freud heard that Stanley Hall had invited Adler to lecture in America and added: "Presumably the object is to save the world from sexuality and base it on aggression." [20] Adler's endeavors in this direction continued throughout the rest of his life, but with only limited success. Nevertheless his name has been of service in the numerous attempts to discredit psychoanalysis.

Wilhelm Stekel (1868–1940)

The relief afforded by Stekel's professions of loyalty unfortunately did not last very long. The trouble he gave Freud was of quite a different nature from that provided by Adler. Stekel was extraordinarily unlike Adler. He had none of his heaviness, and far from being engrossed in theory alone, he had very little interest in it. He was above all practical and empirical, but the most important difference between him and Adler was that he had a ready access to the unconscious whereas Adler had so little that he soon came to disbelieve in its existence. Stekel was a naturally gifted psychologist with an unusual flair for detecting repressed material, and his contributions to our knowledge of symbolism, a field in which he had more intuitive genius than Freud, were in the earlier stages of psychoanalysis of very considerable value. Freud freely admitted this. He said he had often contradicted Stekel's interpretation of a given symbol only to find on further study that Stekel had been right the first time.[21] Unfortunately these talents went with an unusual incapacity for judgment. Stekel had no critical powers at all, and when he once cut himself loose from the amount of discipline that common work with colleagues imposed, his intuition degenerated into wild guess work. Some of it might be penetrating, much of it obviously not, and none of it to be depended on. In the spring of 1911 he published a large book on dreams.[22] It contained many good and bright ideas, but also many confused ones. Freud found it "mortifying for us in spite of the new contributions it makes." [23] Ferenczi stigmatized it as "shameful and dishonest." When he proposed that Putnam be asked to review it Freud told him he must do it himself: "We ask so much of Putnam that we cannot possibly expect him to deal with our own dirty linen." [24] Actually, Putnam had formed his own opinion of the book and described it as "frivolous and base." [25] The truth was that Stekel, who was a fluent if careless writer, was a born journalist in a pejorative sense, someone to whom the effect produced was much more important than the verities communicated, and indeed he earned part of his living by writing regular feuilletons for the local press.

Freud's difficulty in getting on with Stekel lay not in the scientific field, where Stekel spun speculations enough, if no serious theory of his own, but in that of personal behavior, a matter which, as he said, did not lend itself to description in print.[26] Wittels complained of this remark that "the reader might imagine that on one of the Wednesday evenings he had been caught pocketing the spoons," [27] but his misdemeanors were quite other than that. Stekel was, as Freud admitted,[28] a thoroughly good fellow at bottom, and, as I can bear out, he was a very agreeable companion. Unlike Adler, he was always cheerful, lighthearted and very amusing. Freud said of him once to Hitschmann: "He is only a trumpeter, but still I am fond of him." [h] [29]

Stekel had, however, a serious flaw in his character that rendered him unsuitable for work in an academic field: he had no scientific conscience at all. So no one placed much credence in the experiences he reported. It was his custom, for instance, to open the discussion on whatever the topic of the day might happen to be with the remark: "Only this morning I saw a case of this kind," so that Stekel's "Wednesday patient" became proverbial.

Two of Stekel's pronouncements at the Society meetings which caused much merriment are perhaps worth preserving. When asked how he could prove the truth of some startling assertion he proclaimed: "I am here to discover things; other people can prove them if they want to." On a similar occasion, when the topic concerned the body, he announced his intention of buying a few guinea pigs for someone to prove the truth of his assertion by experimenting on them.

[h] *"Er ist nur ein Trompeter und doch hab' ich ihn lieb."*

Naturally "Stekel's guinea pigs" became a favorite synonym for "evidence."

In a paper he wrote on the psychological significance people's surnames have for them, even in the choice of career and other interests, he cited a huge number of patients whose names had profoundly influenced their lives. When Freud asked him how he could bring himself to publish the names of so many of his patients he answered with a reassuring smile: "They are all made up," a fact which somewhat detracted from the evidential value of the material.[1] Freud refused to let it appear in the *Zentralblatt*, and Stekel had to publish it elsewhere.[31]

Perhaps what annoyed Freud as much as anything was a habit Stekel had of quoting at the Society meetings episodes and tendencies from his own life which Freud knew from his previous analysis of him to be entirely untrue and then gazing defiantly at Freud as if daring him to depart from professional discretion by contradicting him. I once asked Freud if he regarded an "ego-ideal" as a universal attribute, and he replied with a puzzled expression: "Do you think Stekel has an ego-ideal?"

Enough has been said to indicate that Stekel was an unsatisfactory editor of a serious periodical, and that to a man of Freud's literary good taste and scientific integrity working with such a collaborator could only be extremely irksome. But what brought about the break was something rather indirect. It happened that for some reason Stekel and Tausk hated each other, and at the last meeting of the session 1911-1912 (May 30, 1912) there was a very ugly scene between them.[32] Now Freud, although he once designated him as a "wild beast," had a very high opinion of Tausk's capacity, and just then wanted him to supervise the reviewing department of the *Zentralblatt* which had been sadly neglected. (Incidentally, the only reviews Freud himself wrote for it were of a popular book by Neutra[33] and a Spanish one from Chile.[34]) Stekel was at once up in arms and declared he would not allow a line from Tausk's pen to appear in *his Zentralblatt*.[35] Freud reminded him that it was the official organ of the International Association and that such personal claims were out of place. But Stekel was on his high horse and would not give way. His success in the field of symbolism made him feel he had surpassed Freud. He was fond of expressing this estimate of himself half-modestly by saying that a dwarf on the shoulder of a giant could see farther than the giant himself. When Freud heard this he grimly commented: "That may be true, but a louse on the head of an astronomer does not."

¹ Naturally Stekel gives a different account of this in his *Autobiography*.[36]

Freud wrote to Bergmann, the publisher, asking that the Editor be changed. Stekel, however, also wrote, and the puzzled publisher replied that matters should stay as they were till the end of the present volume, after which he intended to cease publishing the periodical altogether.[36] I asked Freud why he did not exercise his right as Director to appoint another Editor, for which he would have had every support. The excuse he gave me was that Stekel had too much influence with the publisher, but it may well be that he preferred withdrawing to having an open fight. He sent a circular asking us all to withdraw our names from the *Zentralblatt*, which nearly everyone did, and he got Jung to call a meeting of the available Presidents of the Branch Societies, as well as the officers of the International Association, to lay the whole matter before them. In the meantime, at the meeting of November 6 Stekel's resignation from the Vienna Society was announced.

We met in Munich on Sunday, November 24, 1912, and of course readily promised Freud our support. So the *Zentralblatt* was left in Stekel's hands, but there was so little demand for it that it ceased publication a year or so later. In its place there arose the *Internationale Zeitschrift für Psychoanalyse* under the editorship of Ferenczi, Rank and myself. This survived the First World War, but not the second.

Writing to Abraham Freud said: "I am so glad that now Stekel is going his own way. You cannot imagine how I have suffered from the labor of having to defend him against the whole world. He is an unbearable fellow." [37] Many years after Freud referred to him in a letter as a case of "moral insanity." [38]

C. G. Jung (1876–   )

Freud's response to the separation from Adler and Stekel was purely one of relief from difficulties and unpleasantnesses. The matter was quite otherwise with Jung. The break there was far more important, both personally and scientifically. What Adler had to offer was so superficial and indeed banal that it could seldom make any appeal to serious investigators. He simply ignored the methods and findings of psychoanalysis, so it was only a question of time before the pretense of a "rival school" became too threadbare to sustain. Jung, on the other hand, began with a far more extensive knowledge of psychoanalysis than Adler ever had, and what he offered the world was an alternative explanation of at least some of its findings. His intellectual ability and the width of his cultural background far transcended

Adler's equipment, so that in every way he had to be taken much more seriously.

From 1906 to 1910 Jung gave the appearance of being not only a wholehearted but also a most enthusiastic adherent of Freud's work and theories. In those years only a very keen eye could have perceived any signs of the future rift, and Freud himself had the strongest motives for turning a blind eye to them. The impression Jung made at the Salzburg Congress, in April 1908, was not altogether satisfactory. His paper on dementia praecox in which he ignored the suggestions Freud had made to him on the subject[j] and substituted the hypothetical idea of a "psychical toxin" that damaged the brain was disappointing. Jung had recently written to me that he had found the Freudian mechanisms to be common to both the normal and the abnormal, so the essence of "disease" could only lie in some small organic cerebral disorder, a view with which I could not agree.[39] But the suspicions the Viennese had of him at that time had probably more subjective than objective sources. Abraham, who had been working under Jung for a few years, had been already disconcerted at what he called the tendency to occultism, astrology and mysticism in Zurich, but his criticisms made no impact on Freud, who was building such high hopes on Jung. "I should not like to share your unfavorable prognosis about cooperative work with Burghölzli. The cessation of the Society's meetings there, it is true, struck me also; I don't know if it is final. I agree with you about Bleuler. He made an uncanny impression on me in Salzburg; the situation can't be agreeable for him. I agree with your description of his character. But it is a different matter with Jung. We have personal bonds on which I count, and he wrote to me about his Chief in the same words as you did. Besides, he can hardly go back now; he cannot undo his past even if he wanted to, and the *Jahrbuch* he edits is an unbreakable tie. I hope he has no intention whatever of separating from me and that you do not see aright from motives of a competition you have not yet overcome." [40]

That there was a certain antipathy between Vienna and Zurich on both sides was plain enough, but we all hoped that this would be smoothed over by our common interests. In those years Jung was very friendly to me personally and we had an extensive correspondence which I have preserved. He welcomed my distinctly premature idea of starting in London, in 1907, a Freud Society akin to that in Zurich and also my suggestion, for which I had already won over Henri Flournoy and Claparède of Geneva, of founding an international psychoanalytical periodical in three languages.[41] We had, the month

[j] See Chapter 2, p. 47.

before, discussed in Zurich the feasibility of holding an international congress.

On the Worcester visit in 1909 Jung startled me by saying he found it unnecessary to go into details of unsavory topics with his patients; it was disagreeable when one met them at dinner socially later on. It was enough to hint at such matters and the patients would understand without plain language being used. It seemed to me very different from the uncompromising way in which we had been dealing with very serious matters; but this is the first occasion of my mentioning the remark, deep as was the impression it made on me. It is of interest, as Ira Progoff points out in *Jung's Psychology and its Social Meaning*, which appeared in 1953, that Jung himself gave this American visit as the date of his first dissension from Freud's work, though Freud did not perceive it until a couple of years later. Some three years later, however, we heard from Oberholzer that this idea of not going into details had become a regular part of Jung's teaching.[42] I should like to contrast it with the following uncompromising passage Freud wrote a little later to Pfister when commenting on his analysis of the Graf von Zinzendorf. "Your analysis suffers from the hereditary weakness of virtue. It is the work of an over-decent man who feels himself obliged to be discreet. Now these psychoanalytical matters need a full exposition to make them comprehensible, just as an actual analysis can proceed only when one descends to the small details from the abstractions that cover them. Discretion is thus incompatible with a good presentation of psychoanalysis. One has to become a bad fellow, transcend the rules, sacrifice oneself, betray, and behave like the artist who buys paints with his wife's household money, or burns the furniture to warm the room for his model. Without some such criminality there is no real achievement." [43]

Jung had struck a different note only a few months earlier: "Evidently we shall be gradually cut off from the official scientists. One cannot hope for any contact. Still youth and the future belong to us, so we will march forward." [44] Nevertheless he was already concerned about the danger of laying stress on the sexual factors. "We should do well not to burst out with the theory of sexuality in the foreground. I have many thoughts about that, especially on the ethical aspects of the question. I believe that in publicly announcing certain things one would saw off the branch on which civilization rests; one undermines the impulse to sublimation. . . . The extreme attitude represented by Gross is decidedly wrong and dangerous to the whole movement. . . . Both with the students and with patients I get on further by not making the theme of sexuality prominent." [45]

In 1909 came the combined visit to America where the three friends got on excellently.[k] In 1910 Jung dashed off in March to a consultation to Chicago, but he was only seven days in America and was back in time to preside at the Nuremberg Congress on the 30th. He took a holiday afterwards, and he and his wife visited Freud in Vienna on April 19. As we have related, that Congress proved to be the starting point of Freud's worst troubles with the Viennese, but with Jung he was still on excellent terms. In August he wrote: "Yesterday I got an epistle from Jung which showed him to be at the top of his form and in full possession of those qualities that justified his election." [46] At the end of the year Freud had gone to Munich to have a talk with Bleuler. This seems to have been very successful. "I came to a complete understanding with him and achieved a good personal relationship. After all he is only a poor devil like ourselves and in need of a little love, a fact which perhaps has been neglected in certain quarters that matter to him. It is almost certain that he will join the Zurich Society and then the division there will be healed. The day after he left Jung came. He was magnificent and did me a power of good. I opened my heart to him, about the Adler affair, my own difficulties and my worry over what to do about the matter of telepathy . . . I am more than ever convinced that he is the man of the future. His own investigations have carried him far into the realm of mythology, which he wants to open up with the key of the libido theory. However agreeable all that may be I nevertheless bade him to return in good time to the neuroses. There is the motherland where we have first to fortify our dominion against everything and everybody." [47] The last remark was characteristic of Freud's attitude. Interested as he himself was in the history of mankind, and wishful at times to devote himself to such studies, he recognized that those other fields were what he called "colonies" of psychoanalysis, not the motherland. I was myself doing much work just then in the field of mythology, and he uttered the same warning to me as he had addressed to Jung.[48]

In 1911 things also went well at first. Jung was paying another visit to America, which made Freud express his regret that the "Crown Prince" should be so long out of his country.[49] Jung invited me to stay with him before going on to the Weimar Congress, which unfortunately I was not able to do.[50] In the autumn Freud was puzzled by a letter from Frau Jung to Ferenczi expressing the hope that Freud was not displeased with her husband.[51] There were no real grounds for this at that time, but possibly she was beginning to sense divergent

[k] See Chapter 2.

tendencies in her husband's views which could not be expected to please Freud.

The five happy years had now come to an end, and early in 1912 the clouds began to darken. In that year Freud was forced to see that his hopes of Jung's continued comradeship were doomed to be disappointed, and that Jung was moving in a direction that might well end in both a personal and a scientific separation. The following two years were taken up with cudgelling his brains about how to meet this new situation. He had just passed through two distressing years with Adler and Stekel and now he had nearly three still more distressing ones in front of him.

The background of this change cannot be altogether irrelevant. For the past two years the recriminations against Freud's sexual theories had been permeating Switzerland as well, where they could not fail to bring about both practical and moral difficulties for the Swiss analysts. Articles began to appear in the daily press denouncing the wickedness coming from Vienna and expressing the hope that they would not corrupt the pure-minded Swiss.[52] Now an outstanding peculiarity of the Swiss is the intimate bond subsisting among them; very few outsiders ever succeed in becoming Swiss. There are few parts of the civilized world where it is harder for an individual to stand apart from the prevailing moral standards of the community than in Switzerland. So the Swiss analysts soon had a very unhappy time, of which Pfister's letters to Freud bear ample witness. At all events we have to record the fact that within two years all the Swiss analysts, with two or three exceptions, had renounced their "errors" and had abandoned Freud's sexual theories.

Far more important, however, were various personal factors. Jung had certainly been more deeply involved emotionally in the relationship with Freud than Freud ever was with Jung despite his fondness for him and his admiration for his qualities. As often happens in such circumstances, it was the more labile member of the partnership who first felt the need to withdraw, and for the past year or two there had been signs of this happening. Jung had had an early fondness for archaeological studies and as far back as 1898 had also been interested in every branch of occultism. Towards the end of 1909 he announced his intention of plunging into profound studies of mythology which would take him a few years to complete. He admitted he would find it hard to work alongside the pioneer in that field. Freud was sympathetic to the plan, but advised Jung to concentrate on some single theme and not to wander diffusely over the whole field, advice which Jung unfortunately did not take. At first Jung was sure that the impulse towards incest and the fear of it would prove to be the key to all the problems of mythology, but before long he sent out vague warnings that perhaps something surprising would come out of his studies and there were hints that this was connected with the conception of libido.

Freud did not take these very seriously. What affected him more in the year 1910, and to a still greater extent in 1911, was his finding that Jung's intense absorption in his researches was gravely interfering with the presidential duties he had assigned to him. He had thought of Jung as a direct successor to himself and had pictured him, besides continuing the contributions to psychoanalysis he had already made, as acting as a central focus for all psychoanalytical activities. He was to be the liaison officer between the various societies, advising and helping wherever necessary, and supervising the various administrative work of Congresses, editorial work and so on. Freud would thus in this way be relieved from the active central position for which he had no taste. Unfortunately neither had Jung. Jung often said he was by nature a heretic, which was why he was drawn at first to Freud's very heretical work. But he worked best alone and had none of the special talent needed for cooperative or supervisory work with other colleagues. Nor had he much taste for business details, including regular correspondence. In short he was unsuited to the position Freud had planned for him as President of the Association and leader of the movement.

Nor were Freud's more personal wishes to be gratified much longer. Jung was at all times a somewhat erratic correspondent; his absorption in his researches made him increasingly remiss in this respect. It was a matter on which Freud was always very sensitive. He not only enjoyed getting letters and wrote profusely himself, but any delay in receiving a reply was apt to evoke various fears, of illness or accident and so on. The present situation must have reminded him—in fact he said as much to Jung a little later—of the same course of events with Fliess where the first sign of Fliess's cooling towards him was his delay in answering Freud's letters. So he had to face the painful conclusion that the period he had so much enjoyed of a warm, personal, regular and harmonious contact with a fellow-worker he greatly liked was drawing to a close. He very sensibly decided to resign himself to the inevitable, a few mild protests being of no avail: to lessen his expectations; and to withdraw a certain amount of his former personal feeling. And a psychologist such as Freud was could not have been re-assured by Jung's habit of from time to time, as early even as 1909, swearing he would never desert him as Fliess had or, later on, never as Adler had; it was only too reminiscent of Lady Macbeth.

Freud never spoke of such matters until the end of 1911 when he began dropping hints to Ferenczi about his dissatisfaction with Jung's conduct of affairs. Yet it was barely a year since he had told him confidently that he was more than ever convinced Jung was the man of the future.[53]

Jung's famous essay on "Symbols of the Libido," published later in book form, appeared in two parts;[54] it was in the second part that his divergence from Freud's theories became manifest. Freud read a draft of the first part in June 1910, and sent Jung several pages of criticisms and suggestions together with some commendatory remarks. But Frau Jung remarked that when Freud stayed with them that summer he seemed very reserved on the subject. He was evidently not enthusiastic about the essay. It appeared in July 1911.

In May 1911 Jung told Freud he regarded the term libido merely as a designation of *general* tension. They had some correspondence about this, but in November he announced he was "widening" the conception of libido. In the same month his wife wrote to Freud expressing her fear that Freud would not like what her husband was writing in the second part of the essay. This was the part where the idea of incest was no longer to be taken literally but as a "symbol" of higher ideas. Other divergencies, such as the belief in "prospective tendencies" and the need for "psycho-synthesis," dated from 1909. This second part of the essay I read in proof at Seif's house, and sent a full account of it to Freud in September 1912. This made him eager to read it himself, so he sent for a copy of the *Jahrbuch* in which it appeared, and wrote saying he could tell me the very page where Jung went wrong (p. 174); having discovered that he had lost further interest.[55] It is not my intention, however, to expound here the technical questions of the scientific differences between Freud and Jung. They are very generally known, and the reader may be referred to either the reviews of Jung's work by Abraham, Ferenczi and myself which appeared at the time in the *Zeitschrift* [56] or, better still, to a recent book by Edward Glover which considers also Jung's later works.[57]

The year 1912 was decisive in the personal separation between Freud and Jung. Three episodes in that year played a part in bringing about the final dissociation of their personal relationship. The first of these was Freud's visit at Whitsun to Binswanger at Kreuzlingen, near Constance. Freud had long promised this in return for Binswanger's visits to Vienna, but the occasion of the present visit was a dangerous operation on the latter for a condition that held the threat, fortunately never fulfilled, of an early death. Freud's feeling of friendliness was such that he did not shirk two long and tiring journeys to give Binswanger some pleasure. Because of his own daughter's illness he was not sure till the last that he would be able to go, but on Thursday, May 23, he wrote to both Binswanger and Jung saying he was leaving on the following day. Having only forty-eight hours for the visit he did not propose to undertake the further journey to Zurich, but he assumed Jung would take the opportunity to join the party at Kreuzlingen. He was there from midday on Saturday to midday on Monday. To his surprise and dissappointment there was no news of Jung.

In the following month and several times later Jung made sarcastic remarks in letters to Freud about "understanding his gesture of Kreuzlingen," a phrase that completely puzzled Freud and which he only managed to elucidate six months later.

A sign of the deteriorating relationship was Freud's change in his mode of addressing letters. June of this year was the last time he wrote "*Lieber Freund*"; after that he reverted to the more formal "*Lieber Herr Doktor.*"

The next event was Jung's course of lectures in New York in September, an invitation which he had accepted in March at the cost of postponing the Congress to the following year. Reports kept coming in from New York of his antagonistic attitude there to Freud's theories and even to Freud personally, who was being represented as an out-of-date person whose errors Jung was now able to expose. In May of that year Jung had already told Freud that in his opinion incest wishes were not to be taken literally, but as symbols of other tendencies; they were only a phantasy to bolster up morale. After that there was complete silence for five weeks.[58] Freud told Abraham that his old prediction about Jung, to which he had at the time refused to listen, was coming true, but that he himself had no wish to provoke a break.[59] On Jung's return from America he sent Freud a long account of his experiences and of how successful he had been in making psychoanalysis more acceptable by leaving out the sexual themes. To which Freud tersely replied that he could find nothing clever in that; all one had to do was to leave out more still and it would become still more acceptable.[60] In the previous June he had told Jung that their differences in matters of theory need not disturb their personal relations,[61] but these were evidently deteriorating from month to month. As late as September Freud expressed the opinion that there was no great danger of a separation, but that former personal feelings could not be restored.[62]

The third and decisive event was their meeting at Munich in November, their last except for the Congress in the following year in the same town. Jung had called a meeting of prominent colleagues to settle formally the plan of leaving the *Zentralblatt* to Stekel and founding a new *Zeitschrift* in place of it. There were present in addition to us three: Abraham, Ophuijsen (replacing Maeder), Riklin and Seif. I had been spending the month in Florence, where my address was easily available, but Jung sent the notification of the meeting to my father's home in Wales and also gave the date as November 25 instead of November 24. In the meantime, I heard the correct date from Vienna, and so arrived in time. The look of astonishment on Jung's face told me the mistake belonged to the class called "parapraxes," but when I told Freud of Jung's unconscious slip he replied: "A gentleman should not do such things even unconsciously." I mention the little incident because of its bearing on what followed. At the meeting at nine o'clock Jung proposed that Freud's plan of changing the journals be accepted without discussion, but Freud preferred to give first a full account of his difficulties with Stekel and the reasons for his action. Everyone amicably agreed with the steps he proposed, and the meeting finished before eleven.

Freud and Jung then took a walk together for the two hours before lunch. This was the opportunity to find out about the mysterious "gesture of Kreuzlingen." Jung explained that he had not been able to overcome his resentment at Freud's notifying him of his visit there in May two days late; he had received Freud's letter on the Monday, the day Freud was returning to Vienna. Freud agreed that this would have been a low action on his part, but was sure he had posted the two letters, to Binswanger and Jung, at the same time on the Thursday before. Then Jung suddenly remembered that he had been away for two days on that week-end. Freud naturally asked him why he had not looked at the postmark or asked his wife when the letter had arrived before leveling his reproaches; his resentment must evidently come from another source and he had snatched at a thin excuse to justify it. Jung became extremely contrite and admitted the difficult traits in his character. But Freud had also steam to let off and did not spare him a good fatherly lecture. Jung accepted all the criticisms and promised to reform.

Freud was in high spirits at the luncheon, doubtless elated at winning Jung round again. There was a little discussion about Abraham's recent paper on the Egyptian Amenhotep, with some difference of opinion, and then Freud started to criticize the Swiss for their recent publications in Zurich where his work and even his name were being ignored. This episode, including the fainting attack, I have already narrated and need not repeat an account of it here, but I have something to add to the interpretation I gave then.[63] Ferenczi, on hearing of the incident, reminded Freud of a similar one that had happened in Bremen when the three men were setting out for their voyage to America in 1909.[64] The occasion was, just as now, when Freud had won a little victory over Jung. Jung had been brought up in the fanatical anti-alcoholic tradition of Burghölzli (Forel, Bleuler, etc.), and Freud did his best to laugh him out of it. He succeeded in changing Jung's previous attitude towards alcohol—incidentally with serious after-effects on the relations between Jung and Bleuler—but then fell to the ground in a faint.[1] Ferenczi was so far-seeing as to wonder himself beforehand whether Freud would not repeat this in Munich, a prediction which was confirmed by the event. In his reply Freud, who in the meantime had analyzed his reaction of fainting, expressed the opinion that all his attacks could be traced to the effect on him of his young brother's death when he was a year and seven months old.[65] It would therefore seem that Freud was himself a mild case of the type he described as "those who are wrecked by success," in this case the success of defeating an opponent—the earliest example of which was his successful death-wish against his little brother Julius. One thinks in this connection of the curious attack of obfuscation Freud suffered on the Acropolis in 1904, one which, when he was eighty-one years old, he analyzed and traced to his having gratified the forbidden wish to excel his father.[66] In fact Freud himself mentioned the resemblance between that experience and the type of reaction we are considering.

Confirmatory of Freud's interpretation of his fainting attacks is the fact that on both the occasions there had just been an argumentative discussion on the topic of *death wishes,* and on both occasions Jung had reproached him for attaching too much importance to them. In Bremen Jung had been descanting at length on the significance of some prehistoric cemeteries that had been discovered in the neighborhood. Freud became restive and finally suggested that Jung's continuing with the theme must indicate the operation of some unconscious death wishes. Jung warmly repudiated this and asserted that Freud was too ready to make such interpretations. Then on the occasion in

[1] See Chapter 2, p. 55.

Munich in the discussion of Abraham's essay on Amenhotep, in which Abraham traced the Egyptian King's revolution to deep hostility against his father, Jung protested that too much was made of Amenhotep's erasing of his father's name and inscriptions wherever they occurred; any such death wishes were unimportant in comparison with the great deed of establishing monotheism.

Ferenczi optimistically hoped that now all would be well in the relations with Zurich,[67] but Freud had no such illusion. It is true that on parting Jung once more assured him of his loyalty and that on returning to Zurich he wrote a humble letter expressing again his great contrition and desire to reform. But in the next week something, at the nature of which one can only guess, happened in Zurich, since there came a letter to which the word "pert" would be a mild designation. After a further exchange on business matters another and final crisis occurred in the personal relationship. Freud had some time before pointed out to Jung that his conception of the incest complex as something artificial bore a certain resemblance to Adler's view that it was "arranged" internally to cover other impulses of a different nature. Others had commented also on the resemblance, and Jung resented the implication of having any connection with Adler, which indeed outwardly he had not; he found the comparison "a bitter pill." He now wrote angrily to Freud saying that "not even Adler's companions think that I belong to your group," this being a slip of the pen for "their group." [m] Since he had been insisting that his attitude to his new ideas was purely objective, Freud could not resist incautiously inquiring of him whether he was objective enough to pass an opinion on his slip of the pen. It was asking for trouble with a man in Jung's sensitive mood and by return of post there came an explosive and very insolent reply on the subject of Freud's "neurosis." [68] Freud told us he felt humiliated at being addressed in such a manner, and he could not make up his mind in what tone to reply. He wrote a mild letter but never sent it. A fortnight later, however, when writing on a business matter,[69] he proposed that they should discontinue their personal correspondence and Jung at once agreed. They continued to correspond on business matters and even a little on scientific ones for a few months longer, but that also ceased after the unpleasant experience at the 1913 Congress.

All this created a most awkward situation. Jung was still President of the International Psycho-Analytical Association and Editor of the

[m] This kind of slip is easy enough in German: one only has to write a capital letter instead of the small one with "*ihrer*."

Jahrbuch. He still had the function of holding the various societies together and constituting new ones. Cooperation in a necessarily emotional field of work is far from easy at the best of times, so it was gloomy to envisage it in the unpleasant atmosphere that now prevailed. Moreover, the increasing divergence of Jung's new outlook from Freud's proceeded to such an extent and was so fundamental that we began to ask what there was in common in the scientific work of the two groups, which may be called the Viennese and the Swiss for short, and how long there would be any point in any kind of collaboration.

Freud soon reconciled himself to the loss of Jung's personal friendship, much as he had enjoyed it for several years, and he turned to other friends, particularly Ferenczi. But he blamed himself for his misjudgment of Jung's personality and told us that after finding himself capable of making such a mistake he had better leave the choice of the next President to us, i.e. the "Committee." [70] But his future path seemed very obscure to him. There was no way of telling how long the tenuous official relationship with Jung would hold nor what was the best attitude to take about the whole problem. One thing, however, was clear to Freud. He would do anything he possibly could to avoid an open quarrel, still more any "scene" at which our opponents would rejoice. This was dictated not merely by political consideration, but especially by Freud's great dislike of personal quarrels.

Announcing to Ferenczi the breaking-off of personal relations with Jung Freud added: "I consider there is no hope of rectifying the errors of the Zurich people and believe that in two or three years we shall be moving in two entirely different directions with no mutual understanding. . . . The best way to guard against any bitterness is an attitude of expecting nothing at all, i.e. the worst. I recommend this to you. We shall fulfill our destiny by continuing our work as unperturbed by the noise as was the goldsmith of Ephesus." [71]

By the spring of 1913 there was uncertainty about what would happen at the coming Congress and whether the International Association would survive the split. In expressing his anxiety Freud wrote: "Naturally everything that tries to get away from our truths will find approbation among the general public. It is quite possible that this time we shall be really buried, after a burial hymn has so often been sung over us in vain. That will change a great deal in our personal fate, but nothing in that of Science. We possess the truth; I am as sure of it as fifteen years ago.* When Jones comes we shall consider

* The date of his writing *The Interpretation of Dreams.*

how to defend ourselves. You will all have more to do with it than I, since I have never taken part in polemics. My habit is to repudiate in silence and go my own way." [72]

Maeder wrote to Ferenczi that the scientific differences between the Viennese and the Swiss resulted from the former being Jews and the latter "Aryans." Freud advised Ferenczi to answer on the following lines. "Certainly there are great differences between the Jewish and the Aryan spirit.° We can observe that every day. Hence there would assuredly be here and there differences in outlook on life and art. But there should not be such a thing as Aryan or Jewish science. Results in science must be identical, though the presentation of them may vary. If these differences mirror themselves in the apprehension of objective relationships in science there must be something wrong." [73]

In our preliminary discussions about the approaching Congress we all agreed that our aim should be to maintain collaboration with the Swiss and do everything to avoid a break. We made a point of staying in the same hotel as the Swiss so as to avoid the appearance of strained relations.[74] In August Freud wrote to Ferenczi: "I am afraid that after all we shall get on [with the Swiss] worse than lies in our intention. But we will nevertheless keep to these intentions as long as possible." [75] I have described earlier the course of that disagreeable Congress at Munich in September 1913, when two-fifths of the audience abstained from voting in favor of Jung's re-election.ᵖ After it only formalities remained.

Jung wrote to Ferenczi reproaching him for not supporting his presidential candidature at the Congress, and Ferenczi replied in his characteristic downright fashion: "It is altogether untrue when you ascribe our attitude to Freud's reaction to your 'own scientific views.' So little is that the case that in spite of our deep differences we had decided, in accord with Freud's own suggestion, to vote again in favor of your being President. It was only the absolutely improper way in which you as Chairman of the Congress dealt with the suggestions we put forward, the quite one-sided and partial comments you made on all the papers read, and also the personal behavior on the part of your group, that caused us to protest by voting with blank cards." [76]

In October Freud happened to be describing in a lecture Breuer's separation from him because of his unwillingness to accept the sexual aetiology of the neuroses and for the first time the analogy with the present situation struck him.[77]

° *Geist.*
ᵖ Chapter 3, p. 102.

In October Jung wrote to Freud saying he had heard from Maeder that Freud doubted his *"bona fides."* He therefore resigned his editorship of the *Jahrbuch* and announced that no further cooperation with Freud was possible.[78] That was the last letter. Freud was anxious lest Jung secure control of the *Jahrbuch,* and he was so relieved when he came to a satisfactory arrangement with the publisher, Deuticke, that he sent me a triumphant telegram.[79] About the same time Jung wrote to me saying that the situation was "absolutely incurable," which was unfortunately only too true.

It was then merely a technical question of what form the separation should take officially. Ferenczi propounded a rather wild plan, to which he won Freud's assent. The Vienna, Berlin and Budapest groups were to petition Jung to dissolve the International Association, and I was to bring the British and American Societies the same action. I pointed out the drawbacks of such a plan. Jung had not yet recognized the British Society, so it could not act, and the Americans were extremely unlikely to do so. Brill was the only person in touch with the European situation and the rest would see no reason for such an extreme step. Then if Jung refused to dissolve we should have to resign and he would be left in possession. I could see no reason for hasty action without further consultation.[80] Abraham was similarly critical about the plan. Freud telegraphed to me at once: "Letter just received. Excellent. Will have moderating effect and will be sent to our friends at once. Abraham expresses himself similarly." In his next letter he wrote: "You see your advice and Abraham's have prevailed with us. I only called for a council feeling uncertain in these political matters. Ferenczi was the hotspur but he is giving in too. We do not want to lose any position by affective motives." [81]

We all met in Vienna that Christmas and agreed to await events.

In April 1914, Jung rather unexpectedly resigned his position as President, probably in response to what Ferenczi called the "salvo" of adverse reviews in the *Zeitschrift.* We unanimously decided that Abraham should act as interim President until the next Congress, which was to meet in Dresden in September.[82] I told Freud that "our Fabian policy had been justified." [83] Just before the outbreak of war Jung announced his withdrawal from the International Association, and we also heard that none of the Swiss proposed to attend the Congress.[84] This seems to have been a response to Freud's polemical essay[q] which had appeared in June, one which Ferenczi designated as the "bombshell." [85]

[q] See below.

Freud was under no illusion about the harm Jung's defection would do to psychoanalysis. In a letter to me he wrote: "It may be that we overrate Jung and his doings in the next time. He is not in a favour-able position before the public when he turns against me: i.e. his past. But my general judgment on the matter is very much like yours. I expect no immediate success but incessant struggling. Anyone who promises to mankind liberation from hardship of sex will be hailed as a hero, let him talk whatever nonsense he chooses." [86] Freud has been proved right in this forecast. As early as January 1914, Jung's conver-sion was hailed in the *British Medical Journal* as "a return to a saner view of life." To this day in certain quarters one hears of Jung as the man who purged Freud's doctrines of their obscene preoccupation with sexual topics. Then the general psychologists and others gladly seized on the opportunity to proclaim that since there were three "schools of psychoanalysis"—Freud, Adler and Jung—who could not agree among themselves over their own data there was no need for anyone else to take the subject seriously; it was compounded of un-certainties.

It was the last consideration, the claim that there were supposed to be many conflicting kinds of psychoanalysis, that impelled Freud to defend the title to his work by writing the polemical "History of the Psycho-Analytic Movement" [r] in January and February 1914. There he asserted that, better than anyone else, he had the right to know what psychoanalysis was, and what were its characteristic methods and theories that distinguished it from other branches of psychology. Of late years this claim has been more and more widely accorded to Freud.

[r] See p. 150.

6

CHAPTER

The Committee

I HAD BEEN DISTRESSED BY THE THREE DEFECTIONS NARRATED IN THE preceding chapter and foresaw the likelihood of further ones in the future.[a] The first two defections (Adler and Stekel) had been unpleasant enough and it was disturbing to hear from Freud, in July 1912, that now his relations with Jung were beginning to be strained. That month, while Freud was in Karlsbad, I was in Vienna and had a talk with Ferenczi about the situation. He remarked, truly enough, that the ideal plan would be for a number of men who had been thoroughly analyzed by Freud personally to be stationed in different centers or countries. There seemed to be no prospect of this, however, so I proposed that in the meantime we form a small group of trustworthy analysts as a sort of "Old Guard" around Freud. It would give him the assurance that only a stable body of firm friends could, it would be a comfort in the event of further dissensions, and it should be possible for us to be of practical assistance by replying to criticisms and providing him with necessary literature, illustrations for his work drawn from our own experience, and the like. There would be only one definite obligation undertaken among us: namely, that if anyone wished to depart from any of the fundamental tenets of psychoanalytical theory, e.g. the conception of repression, of the unconscious, of infantile sexuality, etc., he would promise not to do so publicly before first discussing his views with the rest. The whole idea of such a group had of course its prehistory in my mind: stories of Charlemagne's paladins from boyhood, and many secret societies from literature.

[a] A prediction which the subsequent forty years have on a number of occasions verified.

Ferenczi heartily concurred in my suggestion and we next put the matter before Otto Rank; I also wrote to Freud about it.[1] Rank of course agreed, but in the talk a curious episode occurred which stayed in my mind. Ferenczi, in his usual candid fashion, asked Rank if he thought he would remain loyal to psychoanalysis. I thought myself it was an offensive question to put to someone so devoted as Rank then was, and he was somewhat embarrassed to find a suitable reply. I mention it now because of the odd coincidence that those two were in years to come the only ones who did not stay faithful to our undertaking of mutual consultation. But Ferenczi must have been in a more apprehensive and suspicious mood than I perceived, since it turns out that only a few days later he was writing to Freud in this strain: "It has seldom been so clear to me as now what a psychological advantage it signifies to be born a Jew and to have been spared in one's childhood all the atavistic nonsense. Putnam also may easily desert us; you must keep Jones constantly under your eye and cut off his line of retreat." [2] Still, a couple of months later he felt he could assure Freud that "Jones and Abraham are unflinchingly steadfast." [3]

I then spoke to Sachs, my earliest and closest friend in Vienna, and soon after Ferenczi and Rank made contact with Abraham while on a visit to Berlin.[4] That Freud left us an entirely free hand and did not intrude into our arrangements may be seen from the following remark in a letter to me six months later: "Abraham has been here for three days. I am not informed how far Rank succeeded in gaining him to join our band." [5]

Freud himself was enthusiastic and answered my letter by return of post. "What took hold of my imagination immediately is your idea of a secret council composed of the best and most trustworthy among our men to take care of the further development of psycho-analysis and defend the cause against personalities and accidents when I am no more. . . . I know there is a boyish and perhaps romantic element too in this conception, but perhaps it could be adapted to meet the necessities of reality. I will give my fancy free play and leave to you the part of censor.

"I daresay it would make living and dying easier for me if I knew of such an association existing to watch over my creation.

"First of all: This committee would have to be *strictly secret* in its existence and in its actions. It could be composed of you, Ferenczi and *Rank* among whom the idea was generated. Sachs, in whom my confidence is unlimited in spite of the shortness of our acquaintance—and *Abraham* could be called next, but only under the condition of all of you consenting. I had better be left outside of your conditions and pledges: to be sure I will keep the utmost secrecy and be thankful for all you communicate to me. I will not drop any utterance about the matter before you have answered me, not even to Ferenczi. Whatever the next time may bring, the future foreman of the psycho-analytical movement might come out of this small but select circle of men, in whom I am still ready to confide in spite of my last disappointments with men. This plan would be another motive for my coming to London." [b] [6]

The ever-hopeful Freud greeted the formation of this group with joy. A year later he wrote to Abraham: "You cannot know what happiness[c] the cooperation of five such people in my work gives me." [7]

In October 1919, Freud proposed Max Eitingon as the sixth member of the Committee, which completed it. He replaced Anton von Freund, whose illness and subsequent death prevented him from becoming a member. The Committee began to function before the war, but it was after the war that it acquired its fullest significance for Freud, administratively, scientifically and, above all, personally. In the letter to Eitingon announcing his membership he wrote: "The secret of this Committee is that it has taken from me my most burdensome care for the future, so that I can calmly follow my path to the end." [8] Again, in a later letter to him, he wrote: "The care that weighs me down about the future I can best convey to you genetically. It comes from the time when psychoanalysis depended on me alone, and when I was so uneasy about what the human rabble would make out of it when I was no longer alive. In 1912, when we saw an example of these possibilities, the Committee was formed and took on the task of continuation along the right lines. Since then I have felt more light-hearted and carefree about how long my life will last." [9]

It was the following summer that the Committee first assembled as a whole. On May 25, 1913, Freud celebrated the event by presenting us each with an antique Greek intaglio from his collection which we then got mounted in a gold ring. Freud himself had long carried such a ring, a Greek-Roman intaglio with the head of Jupiter, and when some seven years later Eitingon was also given one there were the "Seven Rings" of the chapter heading in Sach's book.[10]

It was arranged that, as the founder, I was to act as Chairman of the Committee, and this I continued to do for most of its existence.

---

[b] At that time Freud was arranging to pay a visit to London, where I then was, together with Ferenczi and Rank.
[c] *welche Freude.*

Freud had all through his life many non-analytical friends, all of whom, so far as I know, remained faithful to him. He had three intimate friends who shared his scientific work, Breuer, Fliess and Jung, who had all parted from him. We were the last he was ever to make. Of the five pre-war members it was easy to say how Freud's affections were distributed. Ferenczi came easily first, then Abraham, myself, Rank and Sachs, in that order. I may also mention our ages. Ferenczi was the senior, being born in 1873; then Abraham, 1877; myself, 1879; Sachs, 1881; Rank, 1885. Rank had first met Freud in 1906, Abraham in 1907, Ferenczi and myself in 1908, and Sachs in 1910 (though he had attended his lectures for years before).

Freud conducted a regular and extensive correspondence for many years with those of us who were not in Vienna, and both sides of it have been preserved. On reading it all through (several times!) one is struck by several features. One is that Freud did not often mention the other friends in his letters; it is as if each relationship was distinct and personal. Nor would he repeat any news in the same terms; it would be described from different angles. Freud's letters, like his speech and his writing, were always distinctive; he would never use an obvious phrase. I will append a few of the more characteristic letters of Freud's from each set.

The contents of the letters also differ much more than one might have expected. Even the scientific points he would discuss read differently in the various sets. Let me give some account of the contents in each case.

The letters Freud wrote to his betrothed and to Fliess in earlier years expressed, among other things, the need to relieve inner tensions. None of his letters in later life have this character in any degree. The feelings displayed in them concerned essentially the recipients. Although he certainly enjoyed writing to them, and in this way maintained close contact, it was of their needs that he was primarily thinking and of how he could best help his friends.

Those to Ferenczi were by far the most personal. There would, it is true, be a certain amount of scientific discussion and from Freud's side some interesting pieces of technical advice. They sent patients to each other whose cases had, of course, to be discussed. Then there were plans for holidays together or for mutual visits. The scientific talks were often of a highly speculative character on many topics that never reached print and are therefore of special interest to a biographer. But there were two main themes that occupied a very great part of the whole correspondence, of more interest to a student of Ferenczi's personality than of Freud's. One was the constant discussion of Ferenczi's personal domestic problems, which were involved enough but which hardly concern us. It is enough to say that he took eighteen years to make up his mind to marry the lady of his choice, a step which Freud had throughout favored. Not that Freud was ever given to urging on anyone else any particular decision which should be his own. But Freud entered into his difficulties in the best fatherly fashion. He felt so fatherly towards Ferenczi that he not only wished he would marry his daughter, but at times would actually address him as "My dear Son." He worked hard to get Ferenczi over his neurotic difficulties and to train him to deal with life to an extent he never felt impelled to with his own sons. He encouraged Ferenczi to analyze his strong "brother complex," and would remonstrate with him over his antipathy to "outsiders." In this he had a great deal of success and during the many years Ferenczi was under his influence he proved a very good brother, and a friend with whom it was easy to get on. Then the second main theme of the correspondence was the monotonously tedious detail of an unusually severe hypochondria that always plagued Ferenczi. Freud showed the utmost patience in going over these details, in laughing at Ferenczi's fears of organic disease and in encouraging him in his efforts in self-analysis. Ferenczi was an excellent analyst and was also very good at analyzing himself. But he had the unfortunate peculiarity of not benefitting adequately from the self-analysis. It always remained too intellectual, often brilliantly so. Both he and Freud learned a good deal of general import from these efforts.

The correspondence with Abraham was totally different. The tone was throughout warm, but far less personal. The scientific content was objective and is the most valuable of the three sets. Abraham's attitude was that of a very senior pupil who could discuss matters seriously and unemotionally. He was learning, but he had no hesitation in saying when he had not yet been able to confirm this or that point from his own experience. Freud must have had a higher opinion of Abraham's intellectual powers than of any of the others, and in my opinion rightly so (I was merely intelligent!). He therefore welcomed confirmation from Abraham most of all. Not that this was always immediately forthcoming, as it would be with some of the others. Abraham once remarked to me that when Freud produced a new theory it took him some time to digest it and he was never satisfied until he could place it in relation to the central Oedipus complex. He was by no means a slow thinker, but he had not Ferenczi's lightning-like divination.

Freud's letters to me were again different. They were warm, even affectionate, and full of praise for my activity. Much of them was taken up with reports of a treatment he was conducting of a very difficult case, with a mixture of mental and organic symptoms, in a lady who stood in a personal relationship to myself. There would be many comments, often amusing ones, on the extensive reports I would send him of progress in America and England. He did not often volunteer accounts of any new theories, but would answer fully the numerous technical questions I kept putting to him. In the letters to all of us, however, there was always news of what he was writing at the moment, of publications, new editions, difficulties with publishers and the like.

Freud's personality cannot, any more than that of anyone else, be studied *in vacuo* but only in his relationships with other people, and for that purpose one needs to know something of the other people as well. Since the group under discussion meant so much to Freud, even at its inception, it is therefore desirable to say something about its members, not so much in respect of their scientific activities, the results of which are incorporated in the psychoanalytical literature, but more personally. It is always a delicate task to speak of one's friends, but I will try to perform it faithfully in accord with the ideals I have set before me in the whole biography.

Ferenczi—to use the name he and his family had adopted in place of their original surname, Fraenkel—was the senior member of the group, the most brilliant member and the one who stood closest to Freud. On all counts, therefore, we must consider him first. Of his past history and of how he came to Freud I have already said something.[d] Of the darker side of his life hinted at above, we knew little until many years later when it could no longer be concealed. It was reserved for communion with Freud. What we saw was the sunny, benevolent, inspiring leader and friend. He had a great charm for men, though less so for women. He had a warm and lovable personality and a generous nature. He had a spirit of enthusiasm and devotion which he also expected and aroused in others. He was a highly gifted analyst with a remarkable flair for divining the manifestations of the unconscious. He was above all an inspiring lecturer and teacher. Before an audience, even of one, his imagination worked at its best, and every theme flowered and developed in far-reaching directions. He had a bold imagination which readily carried him beyond the confines of the known. His honest and candid nature was such that he was extraordinarily prone to making slips of the tongue or other "symptomatic

[d] Chapter 2, p. 34.

actions" in a self-revealing fashion, which he would then gaily analyze in public. Among us he was called on this account the "King of Para-practics."

Ferenczi was for years the central figure in the International Psycho-Analytical Association. I may quote a passage from an address I gave to a later Congress, which will give some idea of what he meant. "My first thought on opening this Congress[e] is inevitably the painful one that for the first time in our history of twenty-six years we miss among us the founder of our Association. It costs an effort to picture a Psycho-Analytical Congress without Ferenczi. Until the last few years, when signs of his distressing malady were becoming unmistakable, he was the very life of every Congress. When it was his turn to deliver an address the hall was always thronged, and he never disappointed his audience. I do not need to recall to you the unforgettable vividness of his delivery, his inspired style, nor the characteristically frank and self-revealing quality of his speech. His personality radiated his interest in his work, and his enthusiasm for it. He was always at the free disposal of anyone whom he thought he could help."

Like all other human beings, however, he had his weaknesses. The only one apparent to us was his lack of critical judgment. He would propound airy, usually idealistic, schemes with little thought of their feasibility, but when his colleagues brought him down to earth he always took it very good-naturedly. Two other qualities, of which we then knew little, were probably interrelated. He had an insatiable need to be loved, and when years later this met with inevitable frustration he gave way under the strain. Then, perhaps as a screen for his over-great love of others and the wish to be loved by them, he had developed a somewhat hard exterior in certain situations, which tended to degenerate into a masterful or even domineering attitude. This became more manifest in later years.

Ferenczi, with his open childlike nature, his internal difficulties, and his soaring phantasies, made a great appeal to Freud. He was in many ways a man after his own heart. Daring and unrestrained imagination always stirred Freud. It had captured him with Fliess years before, and to some extent with Jung. It was an integral part of his own nature to which he rarely gave full rein, since there it had been tamed by a skeptical vein quite absent in Ferenczi and a much more balanced judgment than his friend possessed. Still the sight of this unchecked imagination in others was something Freud could seldom resist, and the two men must have had enjoyable times together when

[e] Lucerne, 1934.

there was no criticizing audience. When that happened there was always the risk of his native skeptical judgment yielding to the seduction of speculation, as certainly happened with Fliess and probably to some extent with Ferenczi. It was a side of his own nature which he displayed to me at times in the hours after midnight when we were relaxing after the time spent in more sedate discussions. It sometimes shocked me slightly, as it doubtless would have Abraham, since we were people always close to the realities.

Abraham was certainly the most normal member of the group. In the memoir I wrote after his death I have drawn a full-length sketch of both his character and his achievements, to which the reader may be referred.[11] In the present connection his distinguishing attributes were streadfastness, common sense, shrewdness and a perfect self-control. However stormy or difficult the situation he always retained his unshakable calm. Abraham would never undertake anything rash or uncertain; it was he and I, usually agreeing with each other, who supplied the element of judgment in our decisions. He was—I will not say exactly the most reserved—but the least expansive of us. He had none of Ferenczi's sparkle and engaging manner. One would scarcely use the word "charm" in describing him; in fact Freud used sometimes to tell me he found him "too Prussian." But Freud had the greatest respect for him. Intellectually independent, he was also emotionally self-contained, and appeared to have no need for any specially warm friendship. He was not closer to any one of us than to the others. Although there was nothing in the nature of a clique in the Committee one could remark that Freud and Ferenzci were close, Rank and Sachs similarly, while both Abraham and myself were rather more apart.

If Abraham had any failing it was his invariable optimism. This made him a little insensitive to the effect certain actions might have on the feelings of other people; he always hoped and expected they would respond as objectively as he did.

One always seemed to associate the names of Rank and Sachs together. That was not only because of the book they wrote in company[12] nor because they were the joint Editors of *Imago*. They were great friends and always worked harmoniously together. They were the only members of the Committee who, being lay, did not practice psychoanalysis (until after the war). Being the only Viennese in the Committee they were the ones I had come to know best on my numerous visits to Vienna. Yet, despite all this, they were very different personalities.

A difficulty in describing Otto Rank, whose original surname was Rosenfeld, is that he presented two quite different personalities before and after the Great War; I never knew anyone change so much. His personal experiences during the war brought out a vigor and other manifestations of his personality we had never suspected. I shall confine myself here to the pre-war Rank, leaving until the appropriate time an account of the subsequent changes.

Rank came from a distinctly lower social stratum than the others, and this perhaps accounted for a noticeably timid and even deferential air he had in those days. More likely it had to do with his unmistakable neurotic tendencies which in later life were to prove so disastrous. I always regretted that the war interfered with the arrangements he had made to come to me in London for analysis; afterwards he could not be spared from Vienna. He had been trained in a technical school and could handle any tool expertly. Freud induced him to take a University degree. I never knew how he lived, and suspect that Freud must have, partly at least, supported him; it was Freud's habit to do such things quietly without letting anyone else know. He would often say that if any of us became rich his first duty should be to provide for Rank. Once he said to me that in the Middle Ages a clever boy like Rank would have found a patron, adding, however, "It might not have been easy since he is so ugly." It so happened that none of the Committee was well-favored in looks. Rank would have made an ideal private secretary, and indeed he functioned in this way to Freud in many respects. He was always willing, never complained of any burden put upon him, was a man of all work for turning himself to any task, and he was extraordinarily resourceful. He was highly intelligent and quick-witted. He had a special analytic flair for interpreting dreams, myths and legends. His great work on incest myths,[13] which is not read enough nowadays, is a tribute to his truly vast erudition; it was quite mysterious how he found the time to read all that he did. One of the compliments I treasure in my life was when he asked me wherever I had found all that material in one of my non-medical essays; that the omniscient Rank should be impressed signified much. Rank had also a keen eye for practical affairs and would assuredly have been very successful had he entered the world of finance; there are rumors that he employed this capacity to good effect in his later years in Paris. For years Rank had a close almost day-to-day contact with Freud, and yet the two men never really came near to each other. Rank lacked the charm, among other things, which seemed to mean much to Freud.

Hanns Sachs was the least closely knit member of the Committee. As a colleague he was an amusing companion, the wittiest of the company, and he had an endless stock of the best Jewish jokes. His interests were primarily literary. When we had, as so often, to discuss the more political aspects of administration he was always bored and remained aloof, an attitude which stood him in good stead when he emigrated later to America where he wisely confined himself to his technical work. He was completely loyal to Freud, but his spells of apathy did not please Freud, so that he was the member in least personal contact with him.

Eitingon was marked out, among other respects, in being the only psychoanalyst in the world who possessed private means. He was thus in a position to be of great assistance in various analytical undertakings, and was always generous in doing so. He was entirely devoted to Freud, whose lightest wish or opinion was decisive for him. Otherwise he was rather easily influenced, so that one could not always be sure of what his own opinion was. He felt his Jewish origin more acutely than the others, except possibly Sachs, and was very sensitive to anti-Semitic prejudice. His visit to Palestine in 1910 foreshadowed his final withdrawal to that country at the first moment of Hitler's ascendancy more than twenty years later. Eitingon had three special claims to Freud's gratitude which Freud could never forget. He was the first person who, from interest in psychoanalysis, visited him from another country.[f] Secondly, he was of invaluable material assistance to Freud's undertakings, particularly the "*Verlag.*" Finally, Eitingon's personal devotion was such that Freud could be confident in retaining his friendship in any circumstances. On the other hand one cannot suppose that he thought specially highly of his intellectual abilities.

Of the five members of the Committee—six later with Eitingon— I should judge Abraham and Ferenczi to have been the best analysts Abraham had a very sure judgment even if he lacked some of Ferenczi's intuitive penetration. There was no idea of a training analysis in those days. I think I was the first psychoanalyst to decide on a personal analysis. Freud not being available for a reason I gave earlier, I went to Ferenczi in Budapest and had in 1913 a few months of intensive analysis, spending two or three hours a day at it. It helped me a great deal with my personal difficulties and gave me the irreplaceable experience of the "analytic situation"; it also gave me the opportunity of appreciating Ferenczi's valuable qualities at first hand. He himself had learned a great deal from Freud's comments on his own self-

---

[f] See Chapter 2, p. 31.

analysis, and both in 1914 and in 1916 he spent three weeks in Vienna being analyzed by Freud before being abruptly recalled to his military service each time. None of the other members ever had any regular personal analysis. It is remarkable how well Abraham got on without any help at all, which shows that one's original character and temperament are of the highest importance for success.

Apart from helping to damp down Abraham's optimism and Ferenczi's extravagances my own contribution to the Committee was essentially to give them a broader view of the outside world. The Viennese circle had a certain limited outlook, which was in some ways even rather provincial. In those days I was traveling widely in both America and Europe and had the habit of frequenting International Congresses of all sorts where one learns a great deal about personalities and prevailing opinions apart from the papers read. I had been made a member of the American Neurological Association, the *Gesellschaft der deutschen Nervenärzte* (Society of German Neurologists), the *Gesellschaft für experimentelle Psychologie* (Society for Experimental Psychology) and other bodies and was acquainted with the leading figures in various fields and countries. That gave me the opportunity of gauging the progress of psychoanalytical ideas in various places and the variety of resistances they were being met with. The response to the ideas was by no means identical in different countries, and the difficulties experienced by analysts similarly varied. So I was able at times to bring a breeze of fresh air into the somewhat hothouse atmosphere engendered by not straying from home. This position of being a mediator between East and West, being accused from each side of being an advocate for the other, brought me into great difficulties later on, but I look back with satisfaction on having in the long run prevented the split that several times appeared imminent.

We were all freethinkers, so there was no religious bar between us. Nor do I remember finding any difficulty from being the only Gentile in the circle. Coming myself of an oppressed race it was easy for me to identify myself with the Jewish outlook which years of intimacy enabled me to absorb in a high degree. My knowledge of Jewish anecdotes, wise sayings and jokes became under such tutelage so extensive as to create astonishment among other analysts outside this small circle. For my Jewish readers I will quote an amusing example, though it relates to a tragic situation. When the Nazis entered Vienna we tried to save whatever was possible and they decreed that only an "Aryan" should be allowed to conduct the Psychoanalytical Clinic. Unfortunately the only member of the Vienna Society answering to this description had just fled over the mountains to Italy. On hearing this I cried out *"O weh; unser einziger Sabbat-Goy ist fort,"* a remark that dispelled for a moment the gloom of the gathering.

I became, of course, aware, somewhat to my astonishment, of how extraordinarily suspicious Jews could be of the faintest sign of anti-Semitism and of how many remarks or actions could be interpreted in that sense. The members most sensitive were Ferenczi and Sachs; Abraham and Rank were less so. Freud himself was pretty sensitive in this respect. He must have wondered how the only foreigner—the only one, for instance, whose mother tongue was not German—would intermingle with a group otherwise so compact, but (referring to Rank) he reassured me: "You may guess what pleasure it gives me to see your friendly relationship to him, to Ferenczi and the other members of the Committee you yourself founded." [14]

My own failings are probably well enough known, so there is no need to expound them here. I think myself that the chief one in those days was an unduly critical attitude towards the shortcomings of others, and I learned a great deal from observing Freud's delightful tolerance.

We were all blessed with a good sense of humor, particularly Freud himself. I remember how he amused us by saying that the best sign of the acceptance of psychoanalysis would be when the Viennese shops advertised "gifts for all stages of the transference." That has not happened in Vienna, but I am told it has in New York.

Academic titles meant so much in Vienna that Freud was under the impression that the same was true elsewhere. When I was given the title of Professor he told me it gave him more pleasure than when that happened to him, and he cherished the hope that some day Abraham, Ferenczi and Rank would become Docents.[15]

The Committee undoubtedly fulfilled its primary function of fortifying Freud against the bitter attacks that were being made on him. It was easier to dissolve these into jokes when in a friendly company, and we could repel some of them in our writings in a way he did not care to undertake; he was therefore set free for his constructive work. As time went on other functions also became important. Frequent meetings, either all together or a few at a time, together with a regular correspondence among ourselves, enabled us to keep in touch with what was going on in the world of psychoanalysis. Moreover, a unitary policy formulated by those best informed and possessing considerable influence was invaluable in dealing with the innumerable problems that kept arising, disagreements within a society, the choice of suitable officials, the coping with local oppositions, and the like.

The Committee functioned perfectly for at least ten years, which was remarkable for such a heterogeneous body. After that internal difficulties arose which somewhat impaired it. The fate of the individual members, in death, exile or dissension, will emerge as the story unfolds; it reflects the unpredictability of life in general. But as the sole survivor I have the pleasant memory of the years when we were a happy band of brothers.

Some letters from Freud to myself have already been quoted. Here are three typical ones, one addressed to Abraham and two to Ferenczi.

"December 16, 1910

"Dear Friend:

"I am happy to hear from you again, and especially something good and very promising. By this I refer to your Segantini[g] which I am looking forward to reading in the holiday recess. But don't hurry in your work. I hardly have any holidays. Except for the two days at Christmas every day is the same, and only Sunday is a real holiday. I can't send your manuscript to press at once, since they have at present Jones's Hamlet study (translated into German) and for the next in the series I have accepted a juridical essay, his first one, by a talented young Swiss called Storfer. After that, however, your Segantini comes as soon as possible.

"I am to meet Bleuler in Munich. At least I have proposed that, though I have not yet got his answer. He is a curious fellow. I expect to read his Apologia in the *Jahrbuch* this week.

"Our *Zentralblatt* would like to have a good paper from you.

"My own work, just finished, is on Schreber's book and tries to solve the riddle of paranoia. As you can well imagine, I have followed in the direction indicated in your work on the psycho-sexual differences between hysteria and dementia praecox. When I was pursuing these thoughts in Palermo I was specially pleased with the formula that megalomania signifies a sexual over-estimation of the ego. On returning to Vienna I found that you had said the same in the clearest manner. Naturally I shall have to plagiarize you extensively in my work.

"I think I can also explain the difference between dementia praecox and true paranoia.

[g] Abraham's booklet on the Swiss painter Giovanni Segantini.

"I would gladly have another talk with you about all these matters, but the need to earn gives one no respite.

"Things are going well in America. Brill has now translated the *Three Essays on the Theory of Sexuality* and Putnam has written a splendid Preface for it. That old man is altogether a wonderful acquisition.

"I hope your wife and the children are all well.

"Cordial greetings
"your
"Freud"

"26.XI.1908

"*Lieber Herr Kollege,*

"I am very sorry indeed to have to put off your visit on Sunday, and do so very much against the wish of my family[h] so I must at least tell you the many reasons for it. First of all we have a patient in bed; in the second place we expect a lengthy visit from new relatives; and thirdly I feel so tired from missing my morning shower which has kept me fit and fresh for twenty-two years that I am obliged to rest for the whole of the Sabbath. But I should like to spend some hours with you chatting about our science. So I propose that you postpone your visit to one of the next Sundays, by which time everything should be better, or at latest Christmas time when we shall certainly expect you. I take it that your decision to postpone your Wednesday visit[i] is not final.

"You need not regret having been rude to Salgó; in my opinion it would not be easy to be unjust to him. The applause that greeted you in the *Gesellschaft der Aerzte* [Society of Physicians] was doubtless more for your personality than for the subject, but still it is all to the good. A dream book in a foreign language is much to be desired and would be highly interesting. I am constantly urging the English to produce one, but till now no one has taken the idea up. But sometime it must come about.[j]

"I am working at present—if one can call my pace working, since apart from Sunday I scarcely write a couple of lines—on a 'General Exposition of the Psychoanalytic Method,' of which there are at the moment 24 pages. I think it should be quite valuable for those who

[h] *Corona* (Viennese idiom).
[i] To the meeting of the Society.
[j] A prediction not yet fulfilled, at least in the form Freud intended.

are already carrying out analyses. Those who are not will not be able to understand a word of it.[k]

"Brill has published a fine analysis of a case of dementia praecox in Morton Prince's *Journal*; it dates from his Zurich days. He, Jones, Abraham and Jung are of course in regular correspondence with me. I hope to hear soon of the half-volume,[l] which should appear in January, but which will hardly be on time. Otherwise the stream of work flows on smoothly without my having time to notice the results.[m] What I have learned I usually appreciate in the autumn. An indifferent attitude towards my patients has certainly been for long one of the points. Jung very rightly remarked that one has to cure hysteria with a sort of dementia.

"Technique and mythology share in my few free hours the rudiment of interest I still have. The summer with its rich impressions lies years ago behind me and I find it quite incredible that after this working year there should be another summer.

"With cordial greetings
"Yours
"Freud"

"November 17, 1911

"Dear Son:[n]

"You ask for a quick response to your emotional letter, and today I should very much like to work, being cheerful on account of good news which I shall presently tell you of. I shall answer you briefly and not say much new. I am of course familiar with your 'complex troubles' and must admit I should prefer to have a self-confident friend, but when you make such difficulties then I have to treat you as a son. Your struggle for independence need not take the form of alternating between rebellion and submission. I think you are also suffering from the fear of complexes that has got associated with Jung's complex-mythology. A man should not strive to eliminate his complexes but to get into accord with them: they are legitimately what directs his conduct in the world.

"Besides you are scientifically on the best road to make yourself independent. A proof of it is in your occult studies, which perhaps

[k] See Chapter 9, p. 231.
[l] Of the *Jahrbuch*.
[m] *Niederschläge*.
[n] Freud twice addressed Ferenczi in this fashion, half jocularly, half analytically.

because of this striving contain an element of undue eagerness. Don't be ashamed of being for the most part of the same opinion as myself and don't demand of me personally more than I am willing to give. One must be glad when as a great exception someone manages to get on terms with himself without any help. You surely know the old saying: 'The untoward things that don't happen are to be counted on the credit side.' °

"Now for the news:

"Karger is calling for a fourth edition of *The Psychopathology of Everyday Life* in 1912.

"Our Frenchman in Poitiers who has been silent since January has sent me today a letter, a contribution for the *Zentralblatt* (on Homosexuality and Paranoia, with reference to two writers in the *Jahrbuch* you know of),ᵖ and a reprint of an admirable paper in the *Gazette des Hospitaux* (p. 1845, 84 Année; Nr. not evident). It is called '*Le Rapport affectiv dans la cure des Psycho-névroses.*' It is on a high level and it specially praises an essay by Ferenczi. Try and read it as soon as you can. I will write and ask him to send you a copy.

"Now farewell and calm yourself down. With fatherly greetings,

"your
"Freud"

* *Was einem nicht zukommt, ist Rebach.*
ᵖ Himself and Ferenczi.

7

The War Years

IN HIS JUDGMENT OF POLITICAL EVENTS FREUD WAS NEITHER MORE NOR less perspicacious than another man. He followed them, but had no special interest in them unless they impinged on the progress of his own work. 1914 was the first time they did so.

To understand Freud's attitude towards what older people still call the Great War it is necessary to recall the main circumstances of its outbreak, and for the sake of a younger generation I will do so, however briefly. The Croats had long been oppressed by their Hungarian masters, who were bent on Magyarizing them. Many of them looked yearningly towards their southern Slav brothers, or cousins, who lived in an independent state over the frontier. That state, then called Servia, was at the moment flushed with her successful victories in the two recent Balkan wars and her nationalist feeling, at a high pitch, strongly sympathized with her oppressed relatives. The Austrian Government had for some time been alarmed at this mutual attraction, fearing that if it went further it might portend the beginning of the dissolution of the ancient Austro-Hungarian Monarchy, to which indeed—in a way they could not foresee—it presently led. Freud himself seemed to share this opinion. As early as December 8, 1912, he wrote to me that the political situation in Austria was stormy and that they must be prepared for bad times ahead. I knew he was referring to the relations with Serbia, and perhaps also Russia—always the bugbear, then as now, of the Austrians. But he presumably took the conventional Viennese view of the difficulties, for I recollect his saying to me a little later, "The Serbians are so impudent." [a] Since I had just

frech.

been studying the history of Croatia I found the remark rather one-sided.

On June 28 the world was startled by the news that the heir to the throne, the Archduke Franz Ferdinand, had been assassinated by a Bosnian, an Austrian subject who had been inspired by conspirators in Serbia. This was the opportunity for which the Austrian Government had been waiting, urged on by their hot-headed military advisers, to settle scores once for all with the country they instinctively blamed for the deed. Franz Ferdinand himself had been planning to extinguish the Serbian hopes of union with the Croats by granting the latter autonomy, thus removing their grievances and resuscitating their old loyalty to the Hapsburg regime. In a letter to Ferenczi[1] on that day Freud wrote: "I am writing while still under the impact of the astonishing murder in Serajevo, the consequences of which cannot be foreseen." When the Archduke's body was conveyed through Vienna in the dead of night with little ceremony Freud sagely remarked: "There is something dirty going on behind this." [b] Less sage was the remark he made to a patient [c] the same day that, had Franz Ferdinand come to the throne, it would certainly have meant war with Russia, implying that the danger of that was now less.

There followed, however, for some weeks only an ominous silence. Freud seems to have been deceived by this, for otherwise he would hardly have allowed his youngest daughter to leave for Hamburg on July 7, and certainly not to continue her journey to England, where she proposed to spend a couple of months, on July 18. Then at last came the ultimatum to Serbia on July 23. The Foreign Minister, Count Berchtold, hoped this time to bluff his counterpart, Sazanov, in St. Petersburg, and thus repeat the discomfiture his predecessor, Aehrenthal, had administered to the Russian Isvolsky only six years before. It was an unforgivably reckless playing with fire.[d]

Serbia's acceptance of the ultimatum, which Sir Edward Grey described as the most formidable document he had ever known addressed by one sovereign state to another, was not quite complete, so Austria promptly declared war and bombarded Belgrade. Russia, the big brother, mobilized so as to induce Austria to retreat. Germany regarded this act as a *casus belli* and promptly declared war on Russia

[b] *Da ist was Faules dahinter.*
[c] The "Wolfman."
[d] When I talked with Count Berchtold some twenty years later in his castle in Moravia he did not evince any sign of his overwhelming responsibility for the ruinous blow dealt at European civilization.

and France. To crush the latter rapidly she hacked her way through Belgium, whose neutrality Prussia had sworn to respect, and this clinched the inevitability of Britain's entry.

In the first two or three years of the war, Freud certainly sympathized completely with the Central Powers, the countries with which he was so closely associated and for whom his sons were fighting; this was mingled, however, with increasing skepticism about their ultimate victory. He even turned against his beloved England, who now had become "hypocritical." He evidently accepted the German version that Germany was being "encircled" by envious neighbors who had been plotting to destroy her. It was only late in the war that the Allies' "propaganda" aroused his suspicions about the moral issues involved, so that he then became doubtful about both versions and could stay *au dessus de la mêlée.*

Throughout the war I was able to keep in contact with him by sending letters to friends in Holland, Sweden, Switzerland, and even Italy, which they then forwarded to Vienna. Putnam also used to send me regularly the letters Freud was able to write to him before the entry of America in 1917. Since then, of course, a mass of information has come to light on how he had spent the war years and what his various responses had been. We may consider this chronologically.

Like so many people at that time Freud and his circle, despite a warning letter I wrote him, were slow to apprehend the gravity of the international situation. Their thoughts were absorbed by the coming Congress in September and the question of whether the Swiss members would have resigned from the International Association before it took place. It was not until July 27 that Ferenczi found he had to give up his projected visit to England because, being on the active list, he was not allowed to leave Hungary. Only then did he begin to have doubts about the Congress, on the grounds that perhaps foreigners might not like to come! As for the ever optimistic Abraham, he still on July 29 counted on the Congress being held, and as late as July 31 was sure that no great power would declare war on another (the day that Germany did). As a result his family got badly stranded in a village on the Baltic coast, unable to get away. Ludwig and Boehm had come to Berlin from Munich in readiness to attend the Congress. Freud had begun to have doubts on July 26 about the feasibility of holding the Congress. On the 29th he wrote to Eitingon, "There are shadows falling on our Congress too, but one cannot predict what things will be like in another two months. Perhaps by then most of them will be in order again." On the same day, however, he wrote to Abraham that "in another fortnight we shall be either ashamed of our present excitement or else near to a decision of history that has been threatening for decades."

Freud's immediate response to the declaration of war was an un-expected one. One would have supposed that a pacific *savant* of fifty-eight would have greeted it with simple horror, as so many did. On the contrary, his first response was rather one of youthful enthusiasm, ap-parently a re-awakening of the military ardors of his boyhood.[2] He even referred to Berchtold's feckless action as "a release of tension through a boldspirited deed,"[e] and said that for the first time in thirty years he felt himself to be an Austrian.[3] After Germany had handed round her three declarations of war he wrote: "I should be with it with all my heart if only I could think England would not be on the wrong side."[4] He was quite carried away, could not think of any work, and spent his time discussing the events of the day with his brother Alexander.[5] As he put it: "All my libido is given to Austro-Hungary." He was excitable, irritable, and made slips of the tongue all day long. Oddly enough, Ferenczi displayed the last symptom also and "as a medically trained hypochondriac regarded it as the onset of a G.P.I. [general paralysis of the insane]."

Even at the outset, however, there was some doubt about the issue of the war. Freud wrote to Hitschmann: "We have won the campaign against the Swiss, but I wonder if the Germans will end the war vic-toriously and if we shall be able to hold out till then. We must strongly hope so. The rage[f] of the Germans seems to be a guarantee for it, and the Austrian re-birth[g] is promising."[6] He said he was too restless to do any writing and had no patients to occupy him. There were only certificates to write. But Freud did not readily help neu-rotics to avoid conscription. He was of the opinion that they should all try to help in the common interest and that it would do them good to do so. He contented himself with certifying a particular diagnosis.

This mood, however, lasted little more than a fortnight and then Freud came to himself. Very characteristically he described this by means of a Jewish anecdote in which a Jew who had resided in Ger-many for years and adopted German manners returns to his family where the old grandfather, by examining his underclothes, decides that the German part was only veneer. Curiously enough, what

[e] *Das Befreiende der mutigen Tat.*
[f] *Furor.*
[g] *Wiedergeburt.*

brought about the reversal of Freud's feelings was a loathing for the incompetence his newly adopted fatherland was displaying in its campaign against the Serbians. To be held up and even defeated by the very people Austria had contemptuously set out to annihilate showed again the hopelessness of such a fatherland, to whom it was not worth belonging. There remained only the hope that the big brother Germany would save them, and from then on that remained the only hope. After the crushing Austrian defeats in Galicia that same month Freud commented, "Germany has already saved us." [7] A week later, again, he was rejoicing in the German victories, but confessed he was "shaken to the core" [h] in his disappointment at the performance of the Austrian army.[8] He had already given up hope of a rapid end to the war, so that "endurance becomes the chief virtue." [9] Abraham in reply pointed out that France and Russia were already defeated, so there remained only England and "there we may rely on Krupp and Zeppelin." A little earlier Freud had made the mournful reflection that after the war it would be long before one could visit England and perhaps also Italy; it would even be unpleasant to visit Germany where it would be hard to put up with their haughtiness, "unfortunately a justified one." [10]

In the July of 1914 Freud was feeling worn out after a year of very hard work and of distressing complications. He felt specially in need of seclusion in which he could concentrate on the articles he had long promised for Krauss's *Handbuch*.[11] So he was relieved that Ferenczi, who for the past six years had spent his holidays with him, had this time formed the intention of passing them with me in London, coming in the first week of August. Freud's summer plans had been to go to Karlsbad for intestinal treatment on July 12, from there to Seis in the southern Dolomites for his holiday proper, then to the Psycho-Analytical Congress Abraham was arranging in Dresden on September 20, and after that to Holland to deliver a lecture at the University of Leyden on September 24. His daughter would join him there on her return from England and he would escort her home.

Naturally only the first item in this program could be carried out. Freud stayed at the Villa Fasolt on the Schlossberg near Karlsbad with his wife until August 5, when he returned to Vienna by a roundabout journey via Munich. It was the first time he had been there without van Emden's company, so he had an altogether peaceful time except for the doings in the outer world. Eitingon was to have

[h] *aufs heftigste erschüttert.*

paid him a visit at Karlsbad, but on July 29 Freud advised him not to risk the difficult journey from Berlin.

In the second week of the war his eldest son, Martin, volunteered for the Army and became a gunner. With his characteristic humor he gave as his motive the wish to visit Russia without changing his "Confession."[1] He was then in Salzburg and was sent to be trained in Innsbruck where his father paid him a visit in the first week of September.[12] Freud's daughter Anna, who it had seemed might be marooned in England, got home safely in the third week of August, having traveled via Gibraltar and Genoa in the care of the Austrian Ambassador. I see from one of my letters of that time that I had volunteered to escort her to the Austrian frontier "by one of the numerous routes available," such was one's innocence in those happy days of what governments could do in blocking the old freedom of travel. Federn, who had been lecturing in America, had a more adventurous time. As his ship on which he was returning, the *Kronprinzessin Caecilie*, neared France it was warned by radio to go back to New York. When he ultimately got to Trieste on a neutral ship he was so impressed by the business-like way in which the British Navy searched it at Gibraltar that he became the only one in the Viennese circle who from the beginning disbelieved in Germany's final victory.

This was the first August Freud had spent in Vienna for thirty years and he was naturally at a loose end. He nevertheless decided not to begin practice before his customary October 1. He wrote to Abraham[13] that he now had the full leisure in his study for which he had often longed, but added wryly: "That's what fulfilled wishes look like."[j] He spent the time in minutely examining and describing his collection of antiquities, while Otto Rank made a catalog of his library.

On September 16 he left Vienna for twelve days on a visit to his daughter Sophie in Hamburg. Announcing this approaching journey to Eitingon he expressed the hope of sharing the jubilation over the expected fall of Paris while in Germany.[14] And from Hamburg, a town with which he was very familiar, he wrote that for the first time he did not feel he was in a foreign city; he could talk of "our" battles, "our" victories, and so on.[15] On the return journey he spent five hours with Abraham in Berlin: they were not to meet again for exactly four years.

[1] In Czarist times everyone could visit Russia except Jews.
[j] *So sehen erfüllte Wünsche aus.*

On the last day of the month Ferenczi came to Vienna to be analyzed by Freud, but this was unfortunately interrupted after three weeks by his being called up. Ferenczi served as a doctor in the Hungarian Hussars, where he had to acquire the art of riding. For the first couple of years he was stationed in Pápa, with only very occasional visits to Budapest.

In October came the "splendid news" of the fall of Antwerp. By then Freud had resumed practice, but with only two patients, both Hungarian; in the next month the number dropped to one. This was when he wrote the long case history, since known as the "Case of the Wolfman." [k] It was, however, four years before it could be published.

In the first few months of the war several of the letters Freud and I wrote to each other did not arrive, and the first I got from him was dated October 3. Two days after the war was declared I had told him of the universal belief in England that Germany would lose in the long run, and even ventured to repeat this in a later letter. Reporting it to Ferenczi he said I talked about the war "with the narrow-minded outlook of the English." [16] A letter of October 22 he entrusted to a friend, a Professor of Archaeology in Rome, who could smuggle it through uncensored to a neutral country. In it he gave all his news, about Anna's safe arrival, his eldest and youngest sons being in the Artillery, that he was writing a case history, and that the loss of Eder (who had at that time gone over to Jung) was not at all a pity. He was astonished to hear that I had seven analyses daily and did not think there were so many on the whole Continent. Then there was the wise warning: "Don't forget that now there is much lying," [l] a maxim epitomized in the saying that in war truth is the first casualty, one now too familiar to the world.

On November 11 he wrote to Ferenczi that he had just heard of his beloved brother Emmanuel's death in a railway accident. This must have been a great grief to Freud, since his fondness for this half-brother had been quite unbroken from his earliest childhood. Some months later he made a characteristic comment on it to Abraham:[17] "Both my father and half-brother lived to be eighty-one, so my prospect is gloomy." [m] There was also the loss of the famous raider, the *Emden*, to be mourned; Freud said he had got quite attached to her. A fortnight later he sent Ferenczi a letter which contains several interesting statements, which one would give a deal to know more

[k] See Chapter 11, Case V.
[l] *jetzt viel gelogen wird.*
[m] Another twenty-three years of hard life to be borne!

about. One was that he had finally solved to his satisfaction the psychological problem of space and time! I think this refers to the notion that the former concept is related to the topographical nature of the mind, particularly of the unconscious, while the latter is absent in the unconscious and is confined to the more conscious layers. He had also solved that of the conditions under which the emotion of anxiety becomes manifest.[n] Then there is an allusion to his superstitious belief about the date of his death, about which more transpires later.

Freud told Eitingon at this time that he was writing hard, doubtless the papers published in 1915 which we shall note presently. But evidently he was also thinking hard as well; it was one of his very productive spells that recurred from time to time.

The polemical essay,[o] which led to Jung's resignation from the International Association, had appeared before war broke out. Freud had been concerned about the reception the essay would get in various quarters, and he was glad to get the following letter from Putnam, to whom he had sent a copy in advance.

"July 7, 1914

"Dear Dr. Freud:

"I think your historical sketch, with its characteristically honest statement of the present situation, is *very fine* and impressive. It is a model to all the rest of us in the way of clear thinking and intelligent expression.

"Sincerely Yours
"James J. Putnam"

The letter assuaged Freud's fears lest Putnam's puritanism might make him sympathize with Jung's rejection of sexuality.

The essay had one unfortunate reverberation in America. Jung had published in *The Journal of Nervous and Mental Disease* a translation of his long paper which displayed his divergence from Freud's teachings, so I wrote to Jelliffe, the Editor, suggesting that he ask Brill to publish Freud's essay in the same periodical to reach the same audience. I also made the same suggestion to Brill. Apparently he had thought of publishing it in *The Journal of Abnormal Psychology*, and when Jelliffe told him, mistakenly, that I had given him the rights of translation and that he was employing someone else, Dr. Payne of Rochester, he wrote a letter of complaint to Freud.[18] For some reason

[n] *Angstentbindung.*
[o] Chapter 14, No. 23.

Brill was not going through an easy time just then and he suffered a good deal from suspiciousness. He had conjured up the belief that Freud was displeased with him for not expressing his satisfaction with the "History"—the letter in which Brill had done so never reached Freud—and was punishing him by giving the translation to Payne; furthermore I was in some way at the bottom of it all. We both tried to calm him down by reassuring him that he had the sole rights and was also the best judge of where to publish, but it was the beginning of a sulky silence that for years grieved Freud.

On November 11 Ferenczi sent Freud the startling "news" that Garibaldi's son with a small army, had invaded the Tyrol, had been captured, and had been sent back to Italy so as not to disturb her neutrality. On his side Freud voiced the opinion that unless Germany won the war before Christmas the English would transfer a Japanese army to France and then they would certainly lose. Early the next month he was very satirical and even bitter about the Austrian efforts to capture Belgrade after three months. But Abraham tried to cheer him up by saying the Austrians would long ago have crushed the Serbians had not the latter received (imaginary) powerful help from outside: furthermore, he thought the war situation was much more favorable than they were allowed to know and that peace overtures from the Entente could be expected at any moment.

In December Freud's spirits were low, and he begged Abraham to come and cheer him up. They were not improved by an offer of asylum from Trigant Burrow in Baltimore, which, as he wrote to me, "shows what the Americans think of our chances." [19] To Abraham he wrote that helplessness and poverty were the two things he had always hated most, and that it looked as if they were not far off.[20] He was not yet alone; Hanns Sachs had been rejected by the military on account of his nearsightedness, while Otto Rank, his other literary assistant, was trying to avoid conscription, "fighting like a lion against his Fatherland." [21]

There was often some intellectual woman, usually a patient or student, in Freud's life whose company he specially enjoyed. At this time it was Lou Andreas-Salomé, who had studied with him before the war. She was a woman with a remarkable flair for great men, and she counted a large number among her friends, from Turgenieff, Tolstoy and Strindberg to Rodin, Rainer Maria Rilke and Arthur Schnitzler. It was said of her that she had attached herself to the greatest men of the nineteenth and twentieth century: Nietzsche and Freud respectively. Freud greatly admired her lofty and serene character as something far above his own, and she had a full appreciation of Freud's achievements. So in this depressing autumn he wrote her a postcard: "Do you still believe that all the big brothers[p] are so good? A word of cheer for me?" She did her best to rise to the occasion, and Freud spoke to Abraham of the "really moving optimism" in her letter.[22] He himself replied as follows: "What you write gives me the courage to come in on another note. I do not doubt that mankind will surmount even this war, but I know for certain that I and my contemporaries will never again see a joyous world. It is all too hideous. And the saddest thing about it is that it has come out just as from our psychoanalytical expectations we should have imagined man and his behavior. Because of this attitude I have never been able to agree with your blithe optimism. My secret conclusion was: since we can only regard the highest civilization of the present as disfigured by a gigantic hypocrisy it follows that we are organically unfitted for it We have to abdicate, and the Great Unknown, He or It, lurking behind Fate, will sometime repeat such an experiment with anothei race." [23]

Freud's productivity, however, was still at its height, as often happened when he felt in poor health or low spirits. He was not only writing hard, but thinking hard. Inner concentration was taking the place of interest in the dismal happenings in the outer world. After mentioning to Ferenczi some of his new ideas, he added: "Even without these I may say of myself that I have given the world more than it has given me. Now I am more isolated from the world than ever, and expect to be so later too as the result of the war. I know that I am writing for only five people in the present, you and the few others.[q] Germany has not earned my sympathy as an analyst, and as for our common Fatherland the less said the better." [24]

The ideas in question we shall give in Freud's own rather military language. "I live, as my brother says, in my primitive trench: I speculate and write and after severe battles have got through the first series of riddles and difficulties. Anxiety, Hysteria and Paranoia have capitulated. How far the successes can be followed up remains to be seen. But a great many beautiful ideas came up: the choice of neuroses, for example. The regressions are quite settled. Some progress in the phases of development of the ego. The importance of the whole matter depends on whether it will prove possible to master the really dy-

---

[p] An allusion to her six brothers who were all very good to her, and also to the Great Powers.

[q] Abraham, Ferenczi, Rank, Sachs and myself.

namic, i.e. the pleasure-pain problem, which my preliminary attempts make me rather doubt." [25] Ferenczi visited Freud for a day or so a week later and no doubt the two thrashed out some of these problems together.

The day after this talk Freud wrote to Abraham: "The only satisfactory thing going on is my work, which is in fact leading, despite recurrent pauses, to noteworthy new ideas and conclusions. Recently I succeeded in defining a characteristic of the two systems Bw (consciousness) and Ubw (the unconscious) which almost makes both of them comprehensible, and which yields what I think is a simple solution of the relation of dementia praecox to reality. All cathexes of objects make up the unconscious. The system Bw signifies the connecting of these unconscious ideas with the concepts of *words*: it is this that gives the possibility of something becoming conscious. The repression in the transference neuroses consists of withdrawing libido from the system Bw, i.e. in separating the ideas of objects and words. In the narcissistic neuroses[r] the repression withdraws libido from the unconscious ideas of objects, naturally a much more profound disturbance. Hence the changes in speech in dementia praecox, which in general treats the ideas of words as hysteria does that of objects, i.e. it subordinates them to the 'primary process' with its condensations, displacements and discharge. I could now write a complete treatise on the theory of neuroses with chapters on the fate of instincts, on repression and on the unconscious if only the pleasure in working were not disturbed by my bad mood." [26]

Freud had adumbrated this interesting theory before[s] and he always adhered to it. Ferenczi asked him how it could be applied to congenital deaf-mutes who have no conception of words. His reply was that we must widen the connotation of "words" in this context to include any gestures of communication.[27]

The following are extracts (in translation) from the last letter of the year.

"December 25, 1914

"Dear Jones,

"Your letter came just on Christmas Eve and, like your earlier efforts to keep in touch, has greatly moved me and given me great pleasure. I have repeatedly used Dr. van Emden's kindness to get answers through to you, but I do not know if you have received them.

---

[r] Psychoses.
[s] See Chapter 13, No. 6.

So when you do not get an answer I can't even let you know that it is not my fault. . . .

"I have no illusion about the fact that the flowering time[t] of our science has been violently disrupted, that there is a bad time ahead of us, and that the only thing we can do is to keep a glow of fire going on a few hearths until a more favorable wind will allow it to blaze up again. What Jung and Adler have left of the movement is being ruined by the strife of nations. Our Association can as little be kept together as anything else that calls itself International. Our periodicals appear to be coming to an end; perhaps we may manage to keep the *Jahrbuch* going. Everything that we tried to cultivate and care for we have now to let run wild. Naturally I am not anxious about the ultimate future of the cause to which you show such a touching devotion, but the near future, in which alone I can be interested, seems to me to be hopelessly clouded over, and I should not take it amiss of any rat whom I see leaving the sinking ship. I am now endeavoring to bring together in a sort of synthesis what I can still contribute to it, a work which has already brought out a good many new things. . . .

"Hold fast till we meet again.

"your loyal
"Freud"

1915

On the Continent it still looked as if the Central Powers would win the war. Germany repulsed all the offensives in the west and won great victories against the Russians. Freud's mood was fairly hopeful. At the beginning of the year he remarked that the war might be prolonged, even as late as October.[28] "Our mood is not so radiant here as in Germany, and the future seems unpredictable to us, but still the German strength and confidence exerts its influence." [29] Abraham, of course, had no doubts: "The tension is very high because of the blockade of England.[u] Our previous experience leads us to expect that one day something astonishing will be published." [30] About that time Freud for once expressed himself as being optimistic about victory in the coming battles and then peace,[31] and a month later he wrote, "My heart's in the Highlands; my heart is not here. That is to say, it is in the Dardanelles, where the fate of Europe is being decided. Greece will declare war on us in a few days, and then we shall not be able to visit the towns I have most loved of any I have seen." [32] He thought

[t] *Blütezeit.*

[u] By submarines.

that peace with Italy would be maintained on the condition of Austria relinquishing some territory. "We shall have to visit San Martino in a foreign country, but we keep Karersee, which personally I prefer of the two." [33]

But the Austrian cynical jokes were beginning, and Freud quoted the one about the retreats in Galicia being only designed to tire out the enemy.[34]

In the spring he reflected: "It is a consoling thought that perhaps the war cannot last so long again as it has already. . . . The tension about the expected events is great. Do you think that *everything* will be satisfactory?" [35] In the summer he thought the war might last another year,[36] but he was still hopeful of victory. "Like many other people I find the war more unbearable the better its prospects." [37] By the autumn the mood became darker. "I don't believe that peace is near. On the contrary there will be an increase in bitterness and ruthlessness in the coming year." [38] "The long duration of the war crushes one and the endless victories combined with the increasing hardships make one wonder if after all the perfidious English calculation[v] may be correct." [39] He had evidently not been confronted by Abraham's letter ten days before which announced that the war had already been won and that all that remained was to get the enemy to admit it; Abraham likened it to an analysis where the resistance to the truth was ultimately broken.

Naturally there was considerable anxiety about the two sons who were fighting: Martin, the eldest, in Galicia and Russia; Ernst, the youngest, against Italy after her entry into the war that April. Martin had already won a decoration for special gallantry. Oliver, the other son, was engaged on engineering work throughout the war, constructing tunnels, barracks, and so on; he had qualified as an engineer the same day as Anna qualified as a school teacher. Freud had several dreams about calamities to his sons, which he interpreted as envy of their youth. On one occasion there was a particularly vivid one about Martin which made Freud wonder if it were not an example of clairvoyance, so he wrote to make enquiries. It so happened that a few days later Martin remarked on bullets passing through his sleeve and his cap.[40] I asked him recently if he recollected the incident, and he tersely replied, "How could I? You got a bullet through your cap every time you showed your head above the trenches."

Freud made desperate efforts to save the psychoanalytical periodi-

[v] Lord Kitchener's prediction at the outset that the war would last three years.

cals, so as to preserve some measure of continuity in the work. He succeeded with the *Zeitschrift* and *Imago* at the cost of sacrificing a projected book by publishing its chapters in them, but the *Jahrbuch* never appeared again after 1914. He had to do most of the editing, Abraham and Ferenczi being so inaccessible. Then in June Rank was called up, as was Sachs in August; after twelve days training in Linz, however, Sachs was released. Freud wrote saying that he seemed to be repeating his early period of great productivity but of complete loneliness.[41] The Vienna Society ceased meeting when war broke out, but meetings were resumed in the winter and took place every three weeks.[42] Practice, of course was meagre. Early in the year there were still only two or three patients,[43] all Hungarian aristocrats. Freud commented on the remarkable fact of my having eleven, but by the end of the year he had himself as many as six.

Except for Ferenczi, who managed to dash to Vienna two or three times, Freud had hardly any visitors in this year, nor indeed in the ones following. A specially interesting one, however, was Rainer Maria Rilke, who was training for military service in Vienna. Freud enjoyed the evening Rilke spent with the family.[44]

On July 3 Freud reported to Abraham that he had been away for several days inspecting a house in Berchtesgaden. He had previously spent three summers there and now he liked the neighborhood more than ever, probably "through transferring to it the libido that used to belong to Italy, now lost." From there he went on July 17 to Ruofshof, Karlsbad, more enjoyable than ever for its quiet emptiness. Then on August 12 he returned to Berchtesgaden to be within reach of his mother at Ischl, where she was about to celebrate her eightieth birthday. He spent several weeks there, at the Pension Hofreit, Schönau. Leaving on September 13 he traveled via Munich and Berlin to Hamburg to stay with his daughter Sophie and enjoy the company of his first grandchild. After a fortnight there he went back to Vienna, paying a visit to Frau Abraham[w] in Berlin on the way, partly again to see the children there, of whom he was always fond.

Freud's correspondence in this year, although less in quantity than hitherto, contained many features of interest, and I will relate some extracts from it. There are two letters of special personal interest written to Putnam, which Putnam sent on to me. The following two paragraphs are from the first of the two, dated June 7, 1915. The second one will be quoted later.[x]

[w] Abraham was already on service.
[x] Chapter 16.

"My chief impression is that I am far more primitive, more humble and less sublimated than my dear friend in Boston. I perceive his noble ambition, his keen desire for knowledge, and I compare with that my way of restricting myself to what is nearest, most accessible and yet really small, and my inclination to content myself with what is within reach. I do not believe that I lack the appreciation for what you are striving towards, but what frightens me is the great uncertainty of it all; I have an anxious temperament rather than a bold one and willingly sacrifice a great deal to have the feeling of being on firm ground.

"The unworthiness of human beings, even of analysts, has always made a deep impression on me, but why should analyzed people be altogether better than others? Analysis makes for _unity_, but not necessarily for *goodness*. I do not agree with Socrates and Putnam that all our faults arise from confusion and ignorance. I think that too heavy a burden is laid on analysis when one asks of it that it should be able to realize every precious ideal."

It is interesting to think that Freud's prediction (in the second letter) that further knowledge might throw light on the genesis of nobler feelings was to a considerable extent borne out only a few years later in the investigation of the genesis of the conscience and super-ego. Putnam himself must have been very disappointed in Freud's reply, since in a letter to me not long after he wrote in a very sad strain about finding no one willing to accept the ideas he regarded as so precious.[45]

The next passages are from the correspondence with Ferenczi. He related to Freud the experience of conducting an analysis with his Commandant while riding together on horseback, which he termed the first "hippic psychoanalysis" on record.[46] Then he suddenly conceived the idea that Freud closely resembled Goethe and adduced a number of features in common, such as their love of Italy—one, you might suppose, common to most northerners. It is an opinion that has been expounded at length also by Wittels.[47] Freud's reply is of interest. "I really think you are doing me too much honor, so that I get no pleasure from your idea. I do not know of any resemblance between myself and the great gentleman you cite, and that not because of modesty. I am fond enough of the truth—or let us rather say of objectivity—to dispense with that virtue. A part of your idea I should explain from the similar impression that anyone gets when, for example, they see two painters using their brush and palette; but that doesn't tell you anything about the equal value of the pictures.

Another part comes from some similarity in your emotional attitude to both men. Let me admit that I have found in myself only one attribute of first quality: a kind of courage that is not affected by conventions. By the way, you also belong to the productive type and must have observed the mechanism of production in yourself: the succession of boldly roving phantasy and ruthlessly realistic criticism." [48]

Ferenczi, however, was not to be put off and produced more points of similarity. Whereupon Freud answered: "Since you persist in this comparison with Goethe I can myself make some contributions to it, both positive and negative. The former is that we both stayed in Karlsbad; and then there is our respect for Schiller, whom I regard as one of the noblest personalities of the German nation. Of the latter kind is my attitude towards tobacco which Goethe simply loathed, whereas for my part it is the only excuse I know for Columbus's misdeed. Altogether I am not oppressed by any sense of greatness." [49]

Then there is a personal note on the amount of writing Freud was doing at that time. "My productivity probably has to do with the enormous improvement in the activity of my bowels. I will leave it open whether I owe this to a mechanical factor, the hardness of the present-day bread, or to a psychical one, the changed relationship to money that is forced on us. At all events the war has already meant a loss to me of 40,000 Kronen [$8,104.00]. If I purchase health through it I can quote the beggar who told the Baron that for his health nothing was too dear." [50]

I will now select a few passages on scientific topics from this correspondence. An interesting discussion of the relation between human experiences in the glacial epoch and the variety of neuroses which may be historically connected with them I propose to incorporate in a later chapter dealing with the general theme of prehistory.

Some of us had criticized Freud's use of the term "paraphrenia" on the grounds that Kahlbaum had employed it in another sense, but Freud said he was resolved to keep his usage.[51]

He casually mentioned that an intuition had disclosed the censorship in the obsessional neurosis as functioning between the preconscious and consciousness rather than between the unconscious and the preconscious.[52]

In another letter he asked Ferenczi if he knew that there was such a thing as criminality due to the sense of guilt,[y] and that stammering could be caused by a displacement upwards of conflicts over excremental functions.[53]

[y] See Chapter 14, No. 27.

Communication with Abraham was less easy. It often took a fortnight for a letter to travel from Berlin to Vienna, and in April Abraham was transferred to Allenstein, in a distant part of East Prussia. He was to remain there for the rest of the war, and at the end of the year his family joined him there.

The most important matter Freud discussed with Abraham in 1915 was a theme of common interest to them, the psychology of melancholia. This will be considered in the appropriate section.[z] They had also an interesting exchange on Freud's essay on war.[aa]

Freud remarked to Abraham on the curious periodicity of his working moods: "At present I am as in a polar night and am waiting for the sun to rise." [54]

The most intriguing remark, however, was that he had at last obtained insight into the primal basis of infantile sexuality.[55] No more was said about this, but one may perhaps wonder whether he was already thinking of the change in his views about sadism and masochism which he announced nine years later and which went together with his theory of a death instinct.

In his essay on "Repression," that had just appeared, Freud spoke of a secondary repression being brought about both by the action of the ego and by the attraction of unconscious matter associated with the idea in question: thus a push and a pull. Finding this slightly ambiguous I put the following questions to him. "You describe the action of the unconscious in causing part of the repression in a different way from that in which I had conceived it, which was as follows: The attraction of previous, primitive unconscious material involves the newer associated material in the same orbit of feeling as itself, thus investing it with this feeling and causing it in consequence to be subjected to the same forces of repression as the older material. In other words, the latter involves the newer material in its own fate, i.e. repression, but in both cases the actual repressing force acts from above, from the 'higher' agencies (though, of course, not necessarily from conscious ones). Am I wrong in this, or can it be reconciled with your rather different phraseology?" [56] In his next letter he agreed that my formulation was more precise, and since there has at times been misunderstanding on the point I think it worth recording.

Freud was now in his sixtieth year, and the thought of approaching age always weighed on him. He superstitiously believed he had only another couple of years to live. He was therefore in a mood to attempt

[z] Chapter 13, No. 8.
[aa] Chapter 14, No. 26.

something like a synthesis of his most profound psychological conceptions and to add whatever he still felt he had to give to the world; the intention had been germinating in his mind for a few years. Four years before he had told Jung he was "pregnant with a great synthesis," and that he had the plan of beginning to write it that summer.[57] The present mood must have been accentuated by the experiences of an indefinitely long war, the hardships of which he might well not survive. To this I attribute his plan, which he announced to all of us, to write twelve essays and incorporate them in a book which presumably would be published after the war. The title of the book he gave variously as *Zur Vorbereitung der Metapsychologie* (Introduction to Metapsychology),[58] *Abhandlungen zur Vorbereitung der Metapsychologie* (Introductory Essays on Metapsychology)[59] and *Uebersicht der Uebertragungsneurosen* (A General Review of the Transference Neuroses).[60]

The conception "metapsychology" plays a central part in Freud's theory of the mind. By it he wished to designate a comprehensive description of any mental process which would include an account of (a) its dynamic attributes, (b) its topographical features, and (c) its economic significance. The term itself, which so far as I know Freud invented, occurs first in a letter to Fliess in 1896,[61] and in a letter two years later he wrote apologetically about using it.[62] Its first published appearance was in 1901,[63] but it does not occur again until 1915, in the great essay on "Repression."

Freud began writing this series on March 15, 1915, and wrote to Abraham on that day announcing the fact. In three weeks he had completed the first two, those on "Instincts and their Vicissitudes" and on "Repression." [64] The next one, on "The Unconscious," which he said was his favorite, took another fortnight.[65] The last two, on "The Metapsychological Supplement to the Theory of Dreams" and "Mourning and Melancholia' were finished in eleven days more.[66]

These five essays are among the most profound and important of all Freud's works. The originality of his penetration into the theory of the mind in them was so novel that they need very careful study. That they could all have been composed in the space of six weeks seems scarcely credible: yet it happened. Such a furor of activity would be hard to equal in the history of scientific production.

But Freud did not rest. In the next six weeks he had written five more essays, though two of them, on "Consciousness" and "Anxiety" respectively, still needed a little revision. He told Ferenczi he had just completed the essay on "Conversion Hysteria" and was about to write one on the "Obsessional Neurosis," to be followed by a "General Synthesis of the Transference Neuroses." [67] In another fortnight he told me that the whole twelve of the series were "almost finished," [68] and early in August they were completely so.[69]

When we consider this tremendous outburst of productivity and bear in mind the other contributions Freud wrote in this year it is plain that the war had greatly stimulated his working powers. As it went on, however, it necessarily had the opposite effect.

Now comes a sad story. None of the last seven essays were ever published, nor have their manuscripts survived. And the only single allusion to them in any correspondence is one some two years later when he mentioned his original intention of publishing them all in book form, "but now is not the time," [70] (evidently because of the war difficulties in publishing). I can't understand now why none of us asked him after the war what had become of them. And why did he destroy them? My own supposition is that they represented the end of an epoch, the final summing up of his life's work. They were written at a time when there was no sign of the third great period in his life that was to begin in 1919. He probably kept them until the end of the war, and then when further revolutionary ideas began to dawn which would have meant completely re-casting them he simply tore them up. We can only hope that the ideas in them have not been completely lost and that many of them have been silently incorporated in later writings.

Freud's attitude in this year of wishing to sum up his life's work is borne out by his behavior at the same time about his annual University lectures.[bb] He decided to give them for the last time. Everything seemed to be closing down.

In 1915 four other papers were published.[71] The first was a short account of a case that appeared to run counter to the explanation of paranoia Freud had previously put forward. The next, called "Observations on Transference Love," [72] was the third and last of the series of "Recommendation on Technique." [cc] A more original paper, though perhaps less useful to the therapeutist, was called "Some Character-Types Met with in Psycho-Analytic Work." [dd] [73] Last of them was a couple of essays "Thoughts for the Times on War and Death," [ee] [74] which have often been reprinted in various forms and

[bb] See Chapter 8, p. 218.
[cc] See Chapter 9.
[dd] See Chapter 14, No. 27.
[ee] See Chapter 14, No. 26.

have had a considerable vogue among the laity also. It was written, like the other papers just mentioned, early in the year.

Altogether 1915 had been a very eventful year, excitingly terrible, but withal stimulating. It was undoubtedly one of Freud's most productive years.

1916

This year proved to be a very dull one in contrast to the last. It began unauspiciously for Freud through Otto Rank being transferred in January to Cracow to edit the main newspaper there.[75] With the exception of a month's holiday in Constantinople in the coming August[76] Rank was marooned in Cracow for the rest of the war, and could only pay a couple of fleeting visits to Vienna. He told me afterwards that he had become recognized as a specialist in abuse of Lloyd George and was often consulted in this connection. Those years in Cracow were fateful for the rest of his life. He underwent remarkable character changes in them and also suffered two very severe attacks of depression that foreshadowed his later disorder.

Rank's absence was a serious blow to Freud, with Abraham and Ferenczi at a distance, since he depended on him for essential help in his editorial and publishing activities. Now there was no one left but Hanns Sachs, but Sachs rose to the occasion and Freud was full of his praise. Freud's chief preoccupation for the remaining years of the war was somehow or other to keep at least two of the three psychoanalytical periodicals going. They represented all that was left of the psychoanalytical movement. By dint of helping to fill the contents himself with papers written specially for that purpose, reducing the size of the periodicals, and then—when it came to the worst—letting them appear less frequently, Freud succeeded in his aim. Ferenczi urged that the word "International" be omitted from the title of the *Zeitschrift*, it being no longer applicable, but I begged that this should not happen and my own name remained as Co-editor throughout the war. At the end Freud was proud to think that this was the only scientific periodical that had kept the international flag flying[tt] despite the frightful bitterness between the nations in those days.

On New Year's Day Freud sent greetings to Eitingon and added: "It is hard to say anything about the war. There seems to be a calm before the storm. No one knows what is coming next, what it will lead to and how long it will last. It is not impossible that the English prediction will prove to be right, though it is to be hoped only as re-

[tt] I cannot vouch for this being entirely true.

gards the duration of the war and not its issue. The state of exhaustion here is already very great, and even in Germany they are no longer unhesitatingly optimistic." He mentioned that his eldest son had been made a Lieutenant and the youngest one a Cadet; both were now fighting on the Italian front. The other son, Oliver, was constructing a tunnel in the Carpathians and had taken a bride with him there. A month later Freud told Ferenczi he was reading four newspapers a day.[77] Now he was expecting war with America. That spring I mentioned that I had eleven patients, with three waiting for a vacancy, and that I had bought a car and a house in the country. Relating this news to Ferenczi Freud commented: "Happy England. That doesn't look like an early end to the war." [78] In a letter to Sachs that summer I quietly gave it as my opinion that we were nearly halfway through the war, a prediction that came almost exactly true. After it was over they told me this had caused a sensation, since they were at every moment expecting the end. The ever-hopeful Abraham tried to arrange a Congress in Munich that September. By then, however, the frontier between Austria and Germany was closed, and Freud disdained to use the pretext of a Congress to pass over.[79]

Abraham was now head of a hospital with seventy-five beds and at the end of the year his wish was granted to change from surgical work to psychopathology. Ferenczi also was transferred from Pápa to Budapest, where he had charge of a Neurological Clinic. Eitingon, fortunately for Freud as it turned out later, spent his time serving in Hungary. Freud's son-in-law, Max Halberstadt, had been wounded in France,[80] and was later on discharged from the army.

In February Freud had a bad attack of influenza[81] and about that time was suffering also from prostatic trouble.

That May Freud attained the age of sixty. He moaned to Eitingon[82] that he was on the threshold of old age,[gg] and wrote to Abraham, "As the result of the notices in the Berlin newspapers my birthday could after all not be kept so secret as I had wished. Particularly those at a distance, who did not know of my wishes, bestirred themselves and have given me plenty to do in thanking them. Even from Vienna I got so many flowers that I can no longer expect any funeral wreaths, and Hitschmann sent me on a "speech" which was so moving that I can request when the time comes to be buried without any funeral oration." [83] When it fell to my lot to deliver that oration, more than twenty years later, I knew nothing of Hitschmann's earlier discourse.

[gg] *Greisenalter,* a stronger expression.

The food shortage was already making it hard to arrange any holidays in Austria, and the closing of the frontier excluded both Freud's beloved Berchtesgaden and also any visit to his daughter in Hamburg. She came to Vienna in the middle of November, however, and spent six months with her parents. Freud himself left on July 16 for Bad Gastein,[84] a beautiful spot at the foot of the Tauren mountains. He had intended to pass all his summer holiday there, but the conditions were so unsatisfactory that after a week he went over to Salzburg and stayed five weeks there at the Hotel Bristol, the site of the first Congress. At the end of August, however, he returned to Gastein for a fortnight and got back to Vienna on September 15, earlier than had been his custom.[85] In the middle of the holiday he wrote, "One has to use every measure possible to withdraw from the frightful tension in the world outside; it is not to be borne." [86]

The correspondence with Ferenczi that year was mainly taken up with discussion of the latter's neurosis, which was narrated in great detail and which was interfering with some vital decisions in his life. Freud's own comments were brief and simply encouraging rather than analytic. In fact he gave the advice that one should make important decisions independently of any analysis, which should either precede or follow such decisions but not accompany them.[87] In the middle of June Ferenczi came to Vienna for three weeks and was analyzed for two hours a day; but this was again abruptly brought to an end through his military duties.

The only general remark of interest in their correspondence was that Freud told him that cocaine, "if taken to excess," could produce paranoid symptoms, and that cessation of the drug could have the same effect.[hh] Altogether, drug addicts were not very suitable for analytic treatment because every backsliding or difficulty in the analysis led to further recourse to the drug.[88] Another remark, which one may perhaps connect with that, was an admission that his passion for smoking hindered him in the working out of certain psychological problems.[89]

In 1915 Freud mentioned the matter of the Nobel Prize. "The granting of the Nobel Prize to Bárány, whom I refused to take as a pupil some years ago because he seemed to be too abnormal, has aroused sad thoughts about how helpless an individual is about gaining the respect of the crowd. You know it is only the money that would matter to me, and perhaps the spice of annoying some of my com-

[hh] To avoid any possible misapprehension I should add that this had no personal reference to Ferenczi.

patriots. But it would be ridiculous to expect a sign of recognition when one has seven-eighths of the world against one." [90] A year later Abraham informed Freud that Bárány had proposed Freud's name for the next Nobel Prize.[91] Freud admitted that the money would be very welcome since his last patient was just finishing.[92] When he heard that Bárány had been appointed to a chair in Sweden (at Upsala) he said that might raise his chances from 5 to 6 per cent, but would make no difference to the final result;[93] he unfortunately proved right in his prediction.

A few days later he told Ferenczi that he had no patients at all and saw no prospect of any others.[94] Nevertheless he was in a good mood which he attributed to President Wilson's *démarche* which he thought should be taken seriously.[ii]

The last three of the five essays which have been previously mentioned as being written in 1915[jj] were published in the present year. The only other publication was the first part of the *Introductory Lectures*. Freud's only scientific activity in this year was the preparation of the further lectures to be delivered in the winter session of 1916-1917. He finished writing them early in November.[95] The only hint of further ideas was his announcement at the end of the year that he had begun to study Lamarck's writings.[96] The outcome of this was to be seen in years to come. Compared with the previous one it was almost a fallow year.

1917

The year 1917 was to prove still more dismal and even less productive than the last one. Freud's earlier enthusiasm for a German victory had by now evaporated, and he became more and more pessimistic about the outcome of the war.

His comments on the accusations against Germany which the Entente made in their reply to President Wilson's note were as follows. "The first impression of the New Year was an extract from the Entente's reply. It is hard to know what to make of it. If they are able to maintain these lies for two and a half years things don't look so bad, for then their rejection of peace terms may also be deceitful. It is a different matter if they are in the right with their accusations, for that would mean that our Governments have lied to us so much that one can have no judgment in the matter." [97] Abraham, however,

[ii] An allusion to Wilson's suggestion that both sides should state their essential war aims.
[jj] See p. 185.

was still hopeful of the submarines defeating England and thus bringing peace.[98]

Then came the first Russian revolution. "How much one would have entered into this tremendous change if our first consideration were not the matter of peace." [99] In April he wrote to Ferenczi "I believe that if the submarines do not dominate the situation by September there will be in Germany an awakening from illusions that will lead to frightful consequences." [100] A couple of months later he felt sure that there was no hope of peace in 1917 and that the war would continue until the Americans arrived.[101] Later on he reported having a letter from me "in regular English style" saying that the German resistance was so strong that it might still take some time to overcome it.[102]

In the autumn he must have felt the war was lost.[103] "I judge the situation with extreme pessimism and believe that unless there is a parliamentary revolution in Germany we must expect the war to go on until a complete downfall. I think we should take seriously the assurances of the English about their intentions, and we also have to admit the failure of the submarine war. So the future is pretty dark for us." Abraham, on the contrary, thought that after the victory of Caporetto peace could be expected soon.[104]

By the end of the year there were plain signs that the truth was seeping through and that Freud had lost all sympathy for Germany— not that he had gained much for the other side. Writing to Abraham he said, "I feel bitterly hostile to the idea of writing as I feel toward many other things. To the latter belongs your dear German Fatherland. I can scarcely imagine traveling there even when it becomes physically possible. In the quarrel between the Entente and the Central Powers I have definitely got to the position of Heine's Donna Blanca in the *Disputation* in Toledo:

'Doch es will mich schier bedünken. . . .' [kk]

"The only cheerful news is the capture of Jerusalem by the English and the experiment they propose about a home for the Jews." [105]

Freud's favorite sister Rosa lost her only son, Hermann Graf, a youth of twenty, who was killed on the Italian front in the summer.[106] It was the only loss the family sustained in the war. Despite many hazardous adventures and hardships his two fighting sons came safely through the war.

But the population behind the front suffered severely too, especially

[kk] An allusion to the final passage of the long religious disputation where the Queen sums up: "All I can say about it is that both parties stink."

in Austria. In his letters Freud had to complain many times of the bitter cold and the difficulty of procuring enough food to keep in health; there was very definite undernourishment in those years. From time to time Ferenczi and von Freund managed to smuggle flour, bread and occasionally a few luxuries from Hungary by various complicated maneuvers, but such help was very precarious. Jacobus Kann, a brother of an ex-patient, also did much by supplying them with food from Holland. Freud's study could not be heated, so letters could only be written with freezing fingers, and all idea of scientific writing had to be given up in the winter months. All sorts of other difficulties, which need not be detailed here, made life in Vienna very hard. Yet, after mentioning some of them, Freud could add, "Curiouslv enough, with all that I am quite well and my spirits are unshaken. It is a proof of how little justification in reality one needs for inner well-being." [107] Rheumatism was now being added to his prostate trouble,[108] so he was lucky to have the inner resources he hinted at.

At the end of the year something happened which our later knowledge might be tempted to call sinister. He had gone very short of his beloved cigars, which naturally was distressing. "Yesterday I smoked my last cigar and since then have been bad-tempered and tired. Palpitation appeared and a worsening of a painful swelling in the palate which I have noticed since the straitened days [cancer?]. Then a patient brought me fifty cigars, I lit one, became cheerful, and the affection of the palate rapidly went down. I should not have believed it had it not been so striking. Quite à la Groddeck." [109] That was six years before the real cancer attacked him there, and one knows that surgeons speak of a "pre-cancerous stage." The connection with smoking is unmistakable.

The question of relief from the summer heat and dust of Vienna that year was extremely difficult. It was impossible to obtain accommodation in the country in Austria, either in Gastein or even in the near-by Semmering. After very complicated efforts Ferenczi solved the problem by finding a spot in the Tatra Mountains in what is now Slovakia. So the family set out on the evening of June 30, earlier than was Freud's custom, and spent two months there. The location was the Villa Maria Theresia, Csorbató, some 4,000 feet high. It was cold there, and they had a deal of stormy weather, but Freud enjoyed the neighborhood and was even able to indulge in his favorite holiday occupation of finding mushrooms. Ferenczi himself stayed there for a fortnight, and Sachs for three weeks. Eitingon and Rank also managed to pay a visit of a day or two. A sister of my wife's, Grete Ilm, a well-known actress, was also of the party and she cherishes many memories of the interesting time there. Freud returned to Vienna on the last day of August, stopping at Budapest on the way.

Freud's practice was naturally very variable during the year. It had started badly without a single patient.[110] It had improved by April, but in June there were only three.[111] After the holidays, however, there were nine for the rest of the year.[112] Still his earnings could not at all keep pace with the alarming increase in prices. They could only stave off "the inevitable bankruptcy." [113]

In May Freud had been grieved to hear of Johann Stärcke's death in Holland.[114] He was one of the most promising analysts and his death was accounted a specially great loss. Then Rank, who in the summer had rallied from his winter depression, was at the end of the year suffering from another severe attack.[115] Ferenczi also was a source of anxiety. In February he was discovered to be suffering from pulmonary tuberculosis as well as from Graves' disease (exophthalmic goitre), and he had to spend three months in a sanatorium on the Semmering.[116]

On the other hand news came of three valuable accessions. One was Anton von Freund, a wealthy brewer of Budapest, to whom both Freud and Ferenczi became very attached; we shall hear much of him later. Then Groddeck appeared on the scene and sent Freud his writings. He was favorably impressed by Groddeck; Ferenczi was less so at first, although he came to think highly of him later. A great surprise was an announcement that Otto Pötzl was to give a lecture at the University in which he would describe some experimental work on dreams that confirmed Freud's theories. Freud went to hear it and reported the strange feeling he had at being once more in Wagner-Jauregg's auditorium and this time listening to one of his assistants supporting psychoanalysis.[117] He invited Pötzl to attend the meetings of the Vienna Society. Later on Pötzl succeeded Professor Pick in Prague, and some ten years later succeeded Wagner-Jauregg as Professor of Psychiatry in Vienna.

It is not to be expected that in the depressing circumstances of this year Freud was in much mood for working. At times he would complain that the tension of the war situation was too great to let him think of writing. The increasingly dismal outlook at times even impaired his joy of living. In a letter to Ferenczi's betrothed he wrote, "I have occasionally spells of disliking life and relief at the thought of there being an end to this hard existence. At such moments the thought weighs on me of our friend being so much in need of care." [118] Naturally the approach of winter, with the forlornness of unheated rooms, was the worst time. When it looked as if the paper shortage was bringing his periodicals to an end he wrote to Abraham, "It would be good if your review of the *Introductory Lectures* could see the light of day before the world comes to an end. When the *Zeitschrift* ceases to appear our role is for the time being played out." [119] "I have been working very hard, feel worn out and am beginning to find the world repellently loathsome. The superstition that my life is due to finish in February 1918 often seems to me quite a friendly idea. Sometimes I have to fight hard to regain ascendancy over myself." [120] But when Ferenczi protested at such an idea Freud replied, "When I read your letter I looked down on your optimism with a smile. You seem to believe in an 'eternal recurrence of the same' [II] and to want to overlook the unmistakable direction of fate. There is really nothing strange in a man of my years noticing the unavoidable gradual decay of his person. I hope you will soon be able to convince yourself that it doesn't mean I am in a bad mood. I work splendidly the whole day with nine ninnys, and I can hardly control my appetite, but I no longer enjoy the good sleep I used to." [121]

Freud's literary output in 1917 was, as might be expected, not extensive. He had at the beginning of the year written a paper under the title of "A Difficulty in the Path of Psycho-Analysis." [122] It described the three great blows man's pride had suffered at the hands of science, his displacement from the center of the universe, then from a unique position in the animal world, and lastly the discovery that he was not master of his own mind.

The main publication of the year was the second half of the *Introductory Lectures*. These had been finished in the early spring, and the book appeared in June. Then on the train journey from Csorbató to Vienna[123] Freud wrote the little paper on Goethe: "A Childhood Recollection from *Dichtung und Wahrheit*." [124] In September he was writing[125] the anthropological essay on "The Taboo of Virginity," which he had started in the January before;[126] it was published in the following year.

But the actual publications are not a full index to Freud's productivity in this year. There was one important theme that occupied his thoughts at intervals throughout the year. It was a study that he and Ferenczi were jointly undertaking on the bearing of Lamarckism on psychoanalysis. Abraham knew nothing about it, so Freud sent him

[II] A quotation from Nietzsche.

the following summary. "Our intention is to place Lamarck entirely on our basis and to show that his 'need' which creates and transforms organs is nothing other than the power of unconscious ideas over the body, of which we see relics in Hysteria: in short, the 'omnipotence of thoughts.' Purpose and usefulness would then be explained psychoanalytically; it would be the completion of psychoanalysis. Two great principles of change or progress would emerge: one through (autoplastic) adaptation of one's own body, and a later (heteroplastic) one through transmuting the outer world." [127] This train of thought ran through much of Freud's more speculative period in the last part of his life.

1918

In the summer of this year two events greatly heartened Freud and redeemed the year from being an entirely sad and dreary one. Of these we shall speak presently. Before the last month of the war there is only one mention of it in any of the correspondence of this year. Freud had evidently resigned himself, like many Austrians, to being dragged along by Germany to the bitter end. The great offensive of March, which the British called the "Ludendorf push," aroused a momentary hope of another victory, but not of peace itself. "I suppose we have to wish for a German victory and that is (1) a displeasing idea, and (2) still improbable." [128] He apologized for not being more cheerful, saying he was tired of life.

The privations brought about by the war kept on increasing. Apart from the serious matters of food and heating there were endless smaller ones that constantly thwarted the activities of daily life. The Freud family were better off for food than most Viennese because of the constant efforts Ferenczi and von Freund made to get some through to them by hook or crook; they used, or misused, their military position for this end in various ingenious ways. Meat had always been Freud's main dish, and the great scarcity of it irked him; weeks or months could go by with very little appearing on the table. He repeatedly expressed his gratitude for the help he received and his pleasure at the thought of having such loyal friends. This help, however, came to an end in October when Hungary separated from Austria and all communication was cut.

In February a patient he had cured left Freud in his will ten thousand Kronen, a sum nominally equivalent to $2,026.000, but actually hardly worth the quarter of that. He "played the rich man," distributing it among his children and relatives.[129]

Freud's moods continued rather variable in the first half of the year. He evidently felt there was little to look forward to. "We have only grim resignation left." [130] The thought of Abraham's steadiness always cheered him up. "My alternation of courage and resignation takes shelter in your even temperament and your indestructible sense of vitality." [131] Three months later he wrote, "My Mother will be eighty-three this year and is no longer very strong. I sometimes think I shall feel a little freer when she dies, for the idea that she might have to be told that I have died is a terrifying thought." [mm] He had long cherished his belief that he would die in February 1918, and often referred to it in a resigned tone.

In May an artist, Schmutzer, a successfully treated patient, made an etching of Freud. He admired it, but, as is usual on such occasions, was not pleased with the likeness.[133]

After the cheering experiences of the summer, to which we shall next turn, Freud's mood became much happier and remained so. The story of the first of the two heartening events is as follows. The Hungarian, Dr. Phil. Anton von Freund, whose name was mentioned earlier, had recently had a sarcoma of the testicle removed and not unnaturally was apprehensive of recurrences. It precipitated a neurosis, for which Freud treated him with success. Being uncertain of life, however, he turned his thoughts to philanthropic plans for disposing of his vast fortune and decided to devote it to the furtherance of psychoanalysis. Freud referred him to Ferenczi and that summer plans began to take a concrete form. Freud had had endless trouble over his publications, both of books and periodicals. They arose not only from the extreme shortage of printing paper, type, labor and so on, but from his publisher, Heller, being a pretty difficult person. So he conceived the idea of founding an independent publishing firm of his own, to which I shall refer as the *Verlag*, which should give him independent control of such projects. This was what von Freund was now arranging, first in conjunction with Ferenczi, and then with Rank's more expert help. At first the idea was to establish it in Budapest where the money was, but after the war Freud insisted it should be in Vienna.[134] By then a quarter of a million Kronen had been transferred to Freud's account in Vienna, but it began to look very doubtful whether the Hungarian authorities would allow the main sum of the fortune to leave the country.

This gave Freud the feeling that after all there was something in

^{mm} etwas. wovor man zurückschreckt.[132]

the future to live for, and his mind began to busy itself with all sorts of plans concerning psychoanalytical literature.

Freud also made a less important plan, to be carried out from the interest of the money he had. It was to found a *prix d'honneur* to be given each year for the best essays, one medical and one non-medical. The first award was divided between Ernst Simmel and Abraham for the medical essay and given to Theodor Reik, a man whom Freud described as "one of our best hopes," for the non-medical one. In the following year the awards went to August Stärcke and Géza Róheim respectively, but the custom soon lapsed.

The other cheering event of this year was the decision to hold a Congress in the summer holidays. The holiday problem this year had been even more perplexing than in the previous one, but ultimately Ferenczi managed to procure accommodation in the same place, in the Tatra Mountains. Freud, with his daughter Anna, embarked on a ship on July 5 for Steinbruch in Hungary where they stayed for a couple of days with relatives of von Freund's. His wife in the meantime had undertaken an adventurous journey to Schwerin to visit her second daughter Sophie. The rooms in Csorbató were available only until the end of August, but others were then found at the Villa Vidor in Lomnicz not far away, and late in September a move was made to Budapest.

The moving spirit in arranging for such a Congress to be held in war time was of course the energetic Abraham, and in fact he started preparing his paper for it as early as March.[135] It was at first planned to hold it in Breslau, but at the beginning of September it was decided to change to Budapest, which Freud now declared to be the "center of the psychoanalytical movement." [136]

The Fifth International Psycho-Analytical Congress was held in the hall of the Hungarian Academy of Sciences on September 28 and 29, 1918. It had several peculiar features. Because of the war it could not be truly international, but we subsequently agreed to give it this official status and to accept its decisions. Freud's wife and his son Ernst participated as guests, the only occasion on which any of Freud's family (except of course the professional Anna Freud) attended any psychoanalytical Congress. It was the first Congress at which official representatives of any Government were present, in this case of the Austrian, German and Hungarian Governments. The reason for their attendance was the increasing appreciation of the part played by "war neuroses" in military calculations. A book by Simmel early that year,[137] together with the excellent practical work performed by Abraham, Eitingon and Ferenczi, had made an impression, if not on the general medical public, at least on the high-ranking army medical officers, and there was talk of erecting psycho-analytical clinics at various centers for the treatment of war neuroses. The first one was to be in Budapest.[138] As yet there was no realization of the imminent loss of the war, an event which naturally changed the whole situation.

The Mayor and Magistrates of Budapest outdid themselves in demonstrations of hospitality. The new Thermal Hotel, Gellért-fürdö, was reserved for the participants of the Congress, a special steamer on the Danube placed at their disposal, and various receptions and dinners given. Altogether, the atmosphere was most stimulating and encouraging. Ferenczi was chosen as the next President of the International Association. In the following month more than a thousand students petitioned the Rector of the University that Ferenczi be invited to give a course of lectures there on psychoanalysis.[139] Budapest was at its highest point.

Forty-two analysts and sympathizers took part in the Congress. The only two from neutral countries were Drs. van Emden and van Ophuijsen from Holland; there were no Swiss. Three came from Germany, and all the rest from Austro-Hungary. Freud read a paper on "Lines of Advance in Psycho-Analytic Therapy." [140] For some curious reason Freud did really read this paper, thus departing from his otherwise invariable rule of delivering a lecture or address without any notes. For this he incurred great disapproval from the members of his family who were present; they maintained he had disgraced them by breaking a family tradition.

Although he kept aloof as far as possible from the formal ceremonies he could not fail to be moved by the prevailing enthusiasm and the bright prospects unexpectedly opening for the extension of his work. A few days afterwards he wrote to Ferenczi "I am revelling in satisfaction and my heart is light, since I know that my 'Sorgenkind,' my life's work, is protected by your and the others' cooperation and its future taken care of. I shall watch the better times coming, even if I do so from afar." [141] Ferenczi replied that he had heard that story of watching from afar ten years ago when Freud withdrew to make room for Jung.

A disturbing incident just before the Congress was a serious illness that attacked Sachs. He was taken to a Budapest hospital and only managed to travel to Vienna on October 15. There Freud considered he was a doomed man,[142] but a prolonged cure at Davos saved his life and after it he settled for a while in Switzerland.

Freud had heard little from Pfister during the war, but in this October the correspondence was revived on the occasion of Pfister's publishing a new book.[143] After praising it, Freud said he disagreed with two points: the criticism of his views on infantile sexuality and that on ethics. "On the latter point I will give way to you; the topic lies far from my interests and you have the care of souls. I don't rack my brains much about the problem of good and evil, but on the whole I have not found much of the 'good' in people. Most of them are in my experience riffraff, whether they proclaim themselves adherents of this or of that ethical doctrine, or of none at all. You cannot say that, perhaps not even think it, although your experiences in life can hardly have been different from mine. If there is any question of ethics I avow I have high ideals, from which sad to say most people I have known diverge. . . . From a therapeutic point of view I can only envy you the possibility of sublimation that religion affords. But the beauty of religion certainly does not belong to the domain of psychoanalysis. Naturally our ways part at this point in therapy; and it may stay so. By the way, how comes it that none of all the pious people discovered psychoanalysis; why did they have to wait for a quite godless Jew?" [144] Pfister answered this letter at length, proclaiming a more favorable view of mankind, and then came to Freud's last question. "In the first place you are not a Jew, which my endless admiration for Amos, Isaiah, Jeremiah, with the men who composed Job and the Prophets, makes me greatly regret; and in the second place you are not so godless, since whoever lives for the truth lives in God and whoever strives for the freeing of love 'dwelleth in God.' If you would fuse your own contribution with the great world harmony, like the synthesis of notes in a Beethoven symphony into a musical whole, I could say of you 'There never was a better Christian.' " [145]

Freud's practice was very good in the first part of the year; indeed, at one time he was treating ten patients a day.[146] At the end of the war, with the uncertainties of the time, his practice virtually disappeared for a while. [147] The general privations also increased then, so much so that he found them "scarcely to be borne." [148]

In the last year or two Freud had had reason to fear, with the fall in the value of his earnings, that his financial circumstances would end in bankruptcy. His brother-in-law, Eli Bernays, suspecting that his financial situation could not be good, sent him a considerable sum of money from New York before America entered the war in 1917; it was a welcome recompense for the way Freud had helped him on his leaving for America more than a quarter of a century before. That, however, had long been exhausted.

Then came the downfall, with the break-up of the Austro-Hungarian Empire. Freud said he could not suppress his gratification at this outcome. A fortnight later he wrote: "The times are frightfully tense. It is a good thing that the old should die, but the new is not yet here. We are waiting for news from Berlin[nn] which should announce the beginning of the new. But I shall not weep a single tear for the fate of Austria or Germany." [149] Not that he expected anything good from Wilson,[150] and I know that afterwards he was very indignant with him for misleading Europe by making so many promises he was in no position to fulfill.

To Abraham he wrote: "Naturally we hope for some improvement in a few weeks or months. When one has no means of foretelling the future it would be wrong not to hope rather than fear. I doubt that we shall become compatriots.[oo] *Vederemo*." [151]

Freud had much to say to Ferenczi on the future of Hungary, a country with which he had had so many associations. "I know that you are a Hungarian patriot and in that connection have to expect some painful experiences. It would seem that the Hungarians are deceiving themselves into thinking that they alone will escape diminution of their country because the outside world has a special love or respect for them—in short, that they are 'exceptions.' Hence their rather undignified hurry to dissolve the bond with Austria and break with Germany although German troops twice saved Hungary in this war; hence also their haste to join the Entente. Disappointment will surely come and will bring bad times with it. All the defects Hungarians show as politicians threaten to avenge themselves. So withdraw your libido in good time from your Fatherland and put it at the disposal of psycho-analysis, else you are bound to feel miserable." [152] "That Hungary has decided not to regard the mystic glamour of St. Stephen's Crown as the highest thing in the life of a nation has specially pleased me. Once more a bit of romanticism less; mankind is much too full of such stuff." [153]

"I expect frightful things in Germany—far worse than with you or with us. Just think of the dreadful tension of these four and a half years and the awful disappointment now that this is suddenly re-

[nn] About the conclusion of peace.
[oo] Alluding to the attempted union of Austria and Germany.

leased. There will be resistance there, bloody resistance. That William is an incurably romantic fellow; he misjudges the revolution just as he did the war. He doesn't know that the age of chivalry came to an end with Don Quixote. Don't let yourself be too concerned about the fate of Hungary; perhaps it will lead to a recrudescence of such a gifted and virile nation. As for the downfall of old Austria I can only feel deep satisfaction. Unfortunately I don't consider myself as German-Austrian or Pan-German.[154]

"I should like to feel a great deal of sympathy for the Hungarians, but I can't bring myself to. I can't get over the ferocity and the lack of sense in that quite uncultivated people. I was assuredly not an adherent of the old regime, but I doubt if it is a sign of political wisdom to kill the cleverest of the many Counts and to make the stupidest of them a President.[pp] Our psychoanalysis has also had bad luck. No sooner had it begun to interest the world because of the war neuroses than the war comes to an end, and when for once we come across a source of wealth it immediately dries up. But bad luck is a regular accompaniment of life. Our Kingdom is evidently not of this world." [155]

Ferenczi made an effort to surmount his local patriotism and view things from a distance. "When seen *sub specie* psychoanalysis all these frightful happenings appear only as episodes in a still very primitive social organization. And even if our hopes deceive us and human beings stay the victims of their own unconscious to the bitter end we have been privileged to glance behind the curtain; knowledge of the truth can compensate us for much we have to do without and even for much suffering." [156]

The Austrian revolution was not a very stormy affair. Sachs parodied it to me by describing imaginary placards: "The Revolution will take place tomorrow at two-thirty; in the case of unfavorable weather it will be held indoors." But it provided the only occasion in his life when Freud was under fire. It happened in the Hörlgasse when he was strolling with his daughter Mathilde. They ran for it and were soon out of danger. It stays in my mind that the same thing happened to me in an attempted revolution in Zurich a few months later. I mention the incidents as a contrast with the present epoch, when few people in Europe have not been exposed to either cannon fire or bombs.

Freud wrote to me the day before the final armistice: "Everything

[pp] Karólyi.

has turned out just as you predicted at the beginning." [157] A few weeks later came another letter.

"December 22nd, 1918

"Dear Jones,*

"Extremely glad to have got your letter. I trust you have heard all that has happened in Budapest and at the Congress. I prefer writing English, however rusty it has become, remembering you could never read my German handwriting which has not improved since. You must not expect me or any of ours in England next spring. I am sure you cannot conceive what our condition really is. But you should come over as soon as you can, have a look at what was Austria, and bring my daughter's boxes with you. Needless to say we are all of us impatient to get your contributions to the *Zeitschrift* and see you taking an active part in the new career opening for 'her' (*Zeitschr.*). . . . Life is harsh you know already. Good-bye, dear Jones.

"yours affectionately

"Freud"

On the last day of the year it was my mournful duty to inform Freud of the death of a dear friend, J. J. Putnam, the month before. They had not been able to communicate with each other for a couple of years. Freud had the highest respect for Putnam's character and personality, and he felt his death as a great loss.

Things looked so bad in Austria, and indeed were so, that Freud was advised, not for the first time in his life, to emigrate to another country. Ferenczi was optimistic about the prospects of psychoanalysis in Hungary, where five analysts (!) had recently come together to re-start the Society, and he urged Freud to settle there.[158] Sachs advised him to come to Switzerland.[159] Pfister, while supporting this suggestion, passed on a letter from me in which I assured Freud I could guarantee an existence for him in England.[160] An ex-patient offered him a house in The Hague, vacated by her brother who was settling in Palestine. Freud, however, never even considered any of these proposals. His post was still in Vienna.

The war had left one personal anxiety, and that a considerable one. For many weeks there was no news whatever of Freud's eldest son, Martin, so all sorts of possibilities lay open. Ultimately the rumor came that his whole troop had been captured by the Italians, but it was not until December 3 that a postcard came to Vienna baldly announcing his presence in an Italian hospital. It was not until the end of the following August that he was released.

Since Freud's main anxiety during the war concerned the safety of his sons it would seem apposite to give a brief account of their doings in those years. Martin, who had enlisted in the first few days, served in the Horse Artillery. Most of the time he spent in Galicia where he underwent many dangerous and exhausting experiences, was engaged in a number of battles and distinguished himself for bravery. He was decorated several times and was soon made an officer. He was several times transferred to the Italian front and back again and was there in the last year of the war when he took part in the battles of Caporetto and the Piave. His whole troop was taken prisoner after the break-down of the Austrian army, when fighting had ceased.

Oliver, the second son, had not been accepted for the army at his physical examination, but instead of proceeding with his engineering studies thought he should try to supplement his father's greatly diminished income by obtaining a remunerative post. The first one had to do with building annexes to a hospital in the outskirts of Vienna, and during this time he lived at home. Then he got another job in March 1915, helping to construct a camp at Purgstall, about three hours from Vienna, but in May, when he was on leave, his father had a serious talk with him and advised him to return to his studies. He did so and successfully got through his examination in June. He was then employed in constructing a tunnel under the Jablonica Pass in the Carpathians in Eastern Silesia. It was a task of exceptional difficulty and of great military importance, and he worked very hard there for fifteen months. While he was there his father paid him a visit in the Easter of 1916. It was a twelve-hour journey, and he stayed two days and a night. He accompanied his son on an inspection of the unfinished tunnel, which was a gymnastic performance involving climbing over a number of ladders and so on. In December 1916, Oliver joined the army, entering a battalion of sappers. For three months he was stationed at Cracow, where Otto Rank was also, and after that at Krems on the Danube from where it was possible to pay visits to Vienna. He was made a Corporal in July and did some instructing, which came in useful in his later life. In November he was assigned to a field company in Galicia, but by then the war with Russia was over. There his work was the building of a bridge over a tributary of the Dniester. In June 1918, his company was transferred to the other end of the Austrian Empire, past Trieste to Conegliano on the Piave front, an enjoyable journey that occupied ten days. He saw some severe fighting there, after which his company was withdrawn. He had reached the rank of Cadet and was about to be made a full officer when the final break-up took place; later when living in France he was glad he had not got higher, since there were many restrictions in that country against former enemy officers. Late in October 1918, they were being shipped to Bulgaria where a last desperate stand was to be made, but Hungarian soldiers seized their train and redirected it to Austria.

Ernst, the youngest son, had the pleasantest experiences of all and thoroughly enjoyed the war. He enlisted in October 1914, and was received with the reproachful remark "You enlist now when the war is nearly over!" On hearing this Freud commented that the officer should be transferred to the Higher Command! Ernst spent the winter in Klagenfurt where friends of his father's introduced him to a rich social life. He was then moved to Neunkirchen, where his father and uncle paid him a visit. In the following autumn, 1915, he was transferred to the Bukowina and even spent a few hours on Russian soil. After a month, however, he was moved to the Karst (the Carso plateau in Istria) where he passed the rest of his active service. There he had a hairbreadth escape when all the rest of his platoon were killed. He was decorated for bravery and soon after was posted to Lavarone, in a country he knew well from holiday times. Following the Assiago battle he was made Adjutant and kept that post till the end of the war. After serving at the front for twenty-four months he was invalided with a duodenal ulcer and was also infected with tuberculosis. The rest of the time he spent in various hospitals, including a sanatorium in the Tatra at the time his parents were there on holiday. That is how he had the opportunity of attending the Budapest Congress of 1918. He was at home when the October revolution broke out. He met his brother Martin only once when on service and once again when on leave, the occasion when the accompanying photograph was taken.

All three sons set foot on Russian soil during the war.

Despite the extreme shortage of printing paper and type Freud succeeded in publishing in 1918 the fourth volume of his *Sammlung kleiner Schriften;* with its 717 pages it equalled all the three previous ones put together. It contained two long papers that had not appeared elsewhere. One was the extremely important "History of an Infantile Neurosis," one of his series of long case histories. The other, "The Taboo of Virginity," was a continuation of his anthropological studies initiated by *Totem and Taboo.* We shall come back to these later.

Like the previous two this was a fallow year for Freud so far as original ideas are concerned. There was no hint of the coming recrudescence that startled us all in the following year. Periodicity was of Freud's nature, as of that of most original thinkers.

1919

Peace was not made until the following summer, so in the meantime conditions kept worsening in Germany and especially in Austria, or what was now left of it. Freud sadly complained that "all the four years of war were a joke compared with the bitter grimness of these months and doubtless also of the ones to come." [161] To me he wrote a couple of days later as follows:

"January 15, 1919

"Dear Jones,*

"I concede that all your predictions about the war and its consequences have come true, but I should be sorry if we could not meet before June. . . .

"I have had no news from America these two years and I feel the loss of dear old Putnam grievously. He was a pillar of psychoanalysis in his country and behaved most truly and gallantly towards me in opposition to the whimsical, unreliable Stanley Hall. I had no notion what had become of the movement there beyond the pond, whether psychoanalysis had not been dethroned by Adlerism or some other invention, so I found some consolation in your favorable report.

"These last months are becoming the worst we have had to endure while this war lasted. My eldest son is still a prisoner in Italy. We are all of us slowly failing in health and bulk, not alone so in this town I assure you. Prospects are dark. I am ready to confess that fate has not shown injustice and that a German victory might have proved a harder blow to the interests of mankind in general. But it is no relief to have one's sympathy on the winning side when one's well-being is staked on the losing one.

"yours sincerely
"Freud"

I had only favorable reports to send of the progress of psychoanalysis in England, and mentioned that I was treating ten patients a day, with sixteen waiting for the next vacancy. Unfortunately I promised that before long food and money would be plentiful, to which Freud skeptically replied: "As regards your promise of plenty of food and money in a short time, I will try to believe you, as all your prophesies during this war have come true. But it strikes me that you did not add in clear language where that plentiness would be, with ourselves or in England." [162]

The only change in the situation as time went by was for the worse. In March came the story that meatless weeks were to be replaced by meatless months, which Freud stigmatized as a very poor joke.[163]

Freud's practice had by now revived and he was treating nine or ten patients a day.[164] But the thousand Kronen they brought in were worth only a tenth of their previous value. On the first day of the year he wrote to Ferenczi: "We have often talked about the alternative of self-adaptation versus altering the outside world. Now my capacity for adaptation is on strike and as to the world I am powerless. I remain ill-humored and must avoid infecting other people so long as they are young and strong."

At first he was destitute of new ideas, but soon some good ones came on the subject of masochism.[165] He was enthusiastic about a paper of Ferenczi's on technique,[166] which he described as "pure analytic gold."[167] He was happy to hear of Ferenczi's marriage at the beginning of March; now he would be relieved from the anxiety of looking after him.[168] On the other hand there was bad news about the other Hungarian friend, von Freund, who had at last developed a recurrence of his sarcoma and whose days must now be numbered.

In March Freud sent the news that he had suddenly become productive. Several years before he had told Ferenczi that his real periods of productivity came every seven years. The time was now ripe for a further re-emergence of his productive powers, one which was in some ways the most astonishing of all. This is a fitting place, therefore, to interrupt the chronological story.

In spite of the more than trying conditions in Vienna at that time Freud had quite rallied from the pessimism induced by the war. During the war, following the defections of Adler, Stekel and the Swiss group, he had felt that the psychoanalytical movement had shrunk to the dimensions of half a dozen serious supporters, and its future prospects seemed dark enough. But the possibilities opened up by the undertaking of the new *Verlag* and the enthusiastic atmosphere of the Budapest Congress were at the end of the war followed by stirring news of great progress being made in Berlin, New York and London. The letters he was receiving from Abraham and myself showed that the news was not illusory, and that the world at last was really opening its arms to receive Freud and his work. We shall see in the next volume how Freud responded to this widening prospect.

2

PART

WORKS

IN THE PERIOD HERE UNDER CONSIDERATION, WHICH WAS THAT OF
Freud's most voluminous production, he wrote some seventy-five
papers, essays, books and prefaces. On the whole they are characterized by detailed working out of the fundamental theories he had
already put forward rather than by the novel discoveries of the earlier
period and the philosophical vision of the final one. The libido theory
is amplified to its fullest extent and its applications explored in diverse fields. The clinical contributions are of outstanding importance.
But Freud was already reaching beyond the clinical sphere and making studies in the fields of religion, aesthetics, pre-history and pure
psychology. In a review of the total output perhaps the outstanding
contributions are the long case histories and the books on the theory
of sexuality and on totemism respectively.

It has seemed conducive to an easier appreciation of this vast production to group the items into seven chapters according to their
main theme, the contents being then considered chronologically. It
is of course inevitable that there is a little overlapping in such a classi-
fication, since a given paper may be concerned with more than one
theme.

8

CHAPTER

Expositions

All of Freud's writings contain some elements of exposition of his theories or methods, but in some of them this is more prominent than the new contribution to knowledge he is making. To mention an example at random: his little paper (1910) on psychogenic disturbances of vision[a] has in addition to the technical contribution an excellent exposition of his views about the dynamic nature of the unconscious and the significance of repression in general. There is, however, a small collection of essays or lectures that had no other aim than to expound to a wider public the general ideas of psychoanalysis. As a rule they were composed in response to a particular invitation, an example being his little book *On Dreams*[1] which Löwenfeld asked him to write for the purpose of conveying to the educated public in a simpler form the essence of his great work on the subject.

Freud readily responded to such invitations. He would have echoed sympathetically Servetus' statement uttered so long ago as 1531: "That I may not withhold from others that which I possess myself and gratefully acknowledge, which may be of use to my fellow-men, I throw aside fear and proclaim what I believe to be the truth." [2]

Freud had a very special gift for exposition. What wins one's admiration is not only his quite extraordinary power of marshalling in simple phrases the most complex material. Nor is it his beautiful command of language, with its feeling for the *mot juste*, though its Viennese grace and flexibility add greatly to its charm. It is above all the candor and simplicity of the writer. His expositions succeed in per-

[a] Chapter 10, No. 4.

suading largely because they do not set out deliberately to do so. He divines with an unfailing understanding the difficulties in the mind of the reader, the exact nature of their criticism or opposition, and he can put all this into words more clearly than the reader himself. This is done with such evident fairness, with such frank admission of the doubtful points in what he has to put forward, that his complete honesty carries one away and one feels inclined to give credence to whatever such a man may have to say. If William James wrote textbooks of psychology as if they were novels and his brother Henry wrote novels as if they were textbooks on psychology, Freud may be said to have combined the two aims in an enchanting degree.

(1) In the years here under consideration the first publication coming under the present heading is the little book already mentioned, *On Dreams*.[3] Published in 1901, it was reprinted in 1911 and 1921, the former being an enlarged version and containing especially new material on the topic of symbolism. The book still gives a fresh impression even to those familiar with the greater work on the subject.

(2) In 1905 Freud contributed to a collective work of two volumes edited by Kossmann and Weiss and entitled *Die Gesundheit* an essay some twenty-six pages long on "Mental Treatment." [4] Since it was addressed to a lay audience he had to begin at the beginning and explain how it is possible for mere words to exert an influence on a state of health. But words were originally connected with magic, and modern psychology salvages what truth there is in that ancient belief. They are after all the most powerful means through which one person can influence another. He then discussed at length the interrelationship between mental and physical processes. The common bodily expressions of emotion are familiar enough, but Freud maintained two further less well-known theses: first, that emotions can also involuntarily influence bodily processes, e.g. digestion, that are not under the control of the will; and secondly, that no mental process, even "pure" thought, is quite free from affect and therefore without some delicate influence on the body. When such influences are used therapeutically, i.e. in psychotherapy, the personality of the doctor is of undeniable significance. In this connection there is a sentence which Freud regarded as so important as to italicize it and which has a prophetic bearing on the modern administrative trends in medicine: *"If the patient's free choice of doctor were to be abrogated it would signify the removal of an important condition for mentally influencing the patient."*

Freud had some pages on cures brought about under the influence of religious belief and of mass emotion. It is quite wrong to deny their reality, but they are explicable by natural means. Then came a long account of hypnotism, its effects and its drawbacks. The latter had recently stimulated a search for more radical and trustworthy measures, but this is the only hint he gave of the existence of psychoanalysis.

The whole essay could still be read profitably today by the large majority of doctors, provided they pondered on the simple wisdom it so clearly expresses.

(3) Under this rubric may also be mentioned, although they are only in part expository, a series of volumes entitled *Sammlung kleiner Schriften zur Neurosenlehre*. There were five volumes in the series, which appeared respectively in 1906, 1909, 1913, 1918, and 1922. Most of them had several subsequent editions, but in unaltered form. Of the first of the series only 340 were sold in the first two years, but all the thousand copies of its second edition (1909) were sold in the same time, as were also those of the third edition (1920). Freud received 900 Kronen ($182.34) for the first of the series, 936 ($189.63) for the second and 1400 ($283.64) for the third respectively. They were for the most part collections of previously published papers, but the fourth volume contained two important ones that were published there for the first time.

(4) In September 1909 Freud gave five lectures at Clark University, Massachusetts, on the occasion of the twentieth anniversary of its foundation.[5] When published, under the title of *Five Lectures on Psycho-Analysis*, they proved to be very popular: eight editions of them were published in German, and they were translated into ten foreign languages. The German edition of 1500 copies was sold out in the first two years. Freud received 432 Kronen for it ($87.52). Altogether some 33,000 have been sold; 1900 were destroyed by the Nazis.

The lectures were delivered *extempore* without any notes and Freud had prepared them in his mind only a couple of hours before. Freud was loth to write them out afterwards—they seemed then *vieux jeu* and his mind had already moved on to preoccupation with the fascinating problem of Leonardo—but Deuticke, his publisher, had insisted on having them despite Freud's protest that there was nothing new in them.[6] By the end of October only half a page was written, and a month later only three pages.[7] They were finished in the second week of December.[8] His memory in such matters was so good, however, that they did not depart much from the original delivery.

The lectures were couched in the simplest possible terms and enlivened by some characteristic anecdotes and analogies. In one of the latter Freud likened an hysteric's out-of-date emotions concerning some traumatic episode in his childhood to the idea of a modern Londoner's gazing at the Charing Cross statue of Queen Eleanor and mourning the death it commemorates of the Queen who died over six hundred years before; the well-known phrase from his *Studies in Hysteria,* "hysterics suffer from reminiscences," is quoted here.

The first lecture was mainly historical, and in it Freud gave a somewhat exaggerated amount of recognition to the part Breuer had played. He gave a brief account of the Anna O. case, with its lessons of catharsis, the *conversion* of undischarged affect into somatic symptoms and its relation to consciousness. In the second lecture he came to the beginnings of psychoanalysis proper and its emergence from the period when hypnotism had been the chief device employed to recover lost memories. There followed an account of the phenomena of *resistance* and *repression.* He described the theory of symptoms as substitutive products replacing the repressed impulses, but at the same time being compromises between these and the repressing agencies. The third lecture was devoted to the technique of psychoanalysis. Freud here brought out the resemblance between neurotic symptoms and a patient's thoughts in free association, both of which contain elements from the repressed material as well as from the repressing agencies. The analyst has to detect the allusions to the former rather as crude ore has to be refined to obtain the precious metal. The two other technical devices are the interpretation of dreams, which Freud called "the most secure basis of psychoanalysis," and the observation of the many kinds of slips, of the tongue, etc., which he had described in his little book *The Psychopathology of Everyday Life*[b] and which nowadays go under the generic name of "parapraxes." He compared the value of psychoanalysis to the psychiatrist with that of histology to the anatomist, and criticized the opponents who passed judgment without troubling to learn his methods as resembling an anatomist who should repudiate our knowledge of finer structures by refusing to use a microscope.

In the fourth lecture Freud came to the delicate topic of sexuality. He gave a clear account of infantile sexuality, including the already famous Oedipus complex, and remarked that sexuality in childhood was plain enough to observe for anyone who would open his eyes, that in fact it needed a certain art to be able to overlook it. He admitted

See Chapter 14.

that he used the term "sexuality" with a wider connotation than was customary, but raised the question whether his use was too wide or the common one too narrow (for reasons of repression). In replying to the rhetorical question of why there should not be other essential causes of neurotic symptoms than sexual ones he said—more colloquially than in the subsequently printed version[9]—"I don't know either. I should have nothing against it. I didn't arrange the whole affair. But the fact remains. . . ."[c] He then went on to explain the occurrence of fixation at various points in development and compared the results found in psychopathology with the morbid consequences found in general pathology of inhibitions in the process of organic development, such as a cleft palate.

The last lecture was of a more general nature. He began by discussing the flight into phantasy that so commonly tries to compensate for the lack of satisfaction afforded by reality. He then took up the matter of the various outcomes of phantasies. This comprises the problem of better adaptation to reality or its alternative in the creation of neurotic symptoms, and he called attention to the exceptional case of the artist who retains the phantasies but uses his special talents to achieve an indirect relation to the outer world. Then came an account of *transference*, both in psychoanalytic treatment and outside it. He stated that in his opinion the study of transference phenomena provided the most convincing proofs of the theory of psychoanalysis. This led to the topic of *sublimation*, and Freud pointed out the limitations of this process. He illustrated the theme by the story of the peasants who tried to accustom a horse to doing with less and less food every day until at the end when they were on the point of success it unaccountably died. Similarly no machine can turn the *whole* of its energy into available heat or electricity; something is necessarily lost in internal friction. He also dealt with certain fears or criticisms concerning psychoanalysis: for instance, the fear that forbidden impulses if admitted to consciousness might run riot. He explained the reasons why such impulses necessarily lose strength in consciousness and why, through coming under better control, they have less power to create disturbances than when in their dissociated state inaccessible to any influence. Freud considered there were two principal intellectual difficulties in the way of accepting psychoanalytical findings. One was that we were not accustomed to apply the laws of strict determinism to

[c] *"Ich weiss es auch nicht. Ich hätte nichts dagegen. Ich habe die ganze Sache nicht gemacht. Aber Tatsache bleibt. . . ."*

mental processes in the way any scientific investigation of them must. The other was the fear, just alluded to, that the admission of unconscious processes might lower our cultural standards.

(5) In the Spring of 1911 Freud wrote a short paper for the Australasian Congress in Sydney[10] in circumstances that have been mentioned earlier.[d] At the Congress there were also papers by Jung, "On the Doctrine of Complexes," and Havelock Ellis, "The Doctrines of the Freud School."

Freud managed to compress an astonishing amount of information about psychoanalysis into a very few pages, but the content is so well known and is to be found in so many other publications that no summary of it is needed here. Freud took the opportunity of pointing out three respects in which his work came into sharp antagonism to Janet's: (a) It refused to trace hysteria directly to a congenital hereditary degeneration. (b) It offered in place of a mere description a dynamic explanation by a play of mental forces. (c) It referred psychical dissociation not to a congenital disability but to a special process called "repression."

(6) In 1912 Freud was invited by *Scientia*, an important international periodical published in Italy and devoted to the study of the relationships between the different branches of science, to expound the claims of psychoanalysis on the interest of the educated public, together with the bearing it might have on other branches of science. This essay, "The Claims of Psycho-Analysis to Scientific Interest," [11] thirty pages long, is much more comprehensive than the last one mentioned. It did not appear in a German publication until it was incorporated in 1924 in the *Gesammelte Schriften* (Collected Writings).[12] Oddly enough, it will appear in English for the first time in Strachey's *Standard Edition*.

In it Freud insisted that although psychoanalysis began as a method for investigating and treating neurotic affections it was equally applicable to so-called normal phenomena, where it could stand in its own right and should not be regarded as something simply transferred there from psychopathology. On the contrary, he asserted the value that the study of normal dreams had for psychopathology, where it had conquered for psychology a field that had previously been thought to belong to physiology. There was even a note of triumph over the way in which psychoanalysis had "restricted the physiological mode of thinking," a striking contrast from the days of twenty years before when physiology was to him Science *par excellence* and when he had

[d] Chapter 3, p. 77.

made desperate attempts to describe mental processes in physiological —more strictly, in physical—language. Commenting on the older medical view that dreams are of purely somatic origin without any meaning or significance, he remarked, "What speaks against the physiological conception is its unfruitfulness; for the psychoanalytical one it can be claimed that it has been able to make an intelligible interpretation of thousands of dreams and has used them to achieve a knowledge of intimate mental life." [13] He then made the somewhat surprising statement that it was with the interpretation of dreams that psychoanalysis entered on its "destiny of opposing official science," one which one would have expected him to make in connection with the subject of infantile sexuality and the sexual origin of the neuroses. But Freud never failed to give—and rightly so—dream analysis a preeminent position. "There is general agreement (among analysts) that the interpretation of dreams is the foundation stone of psycho-analytic work and that its results constitute the most important contribution psychoanalysis has made to psychology." [14] "One may well say that the psycho-analytic study of dreams has given us the first glimpse into the hitherto unsuspected realm of a depth psychology. Revolutionary changes in normal psychology will be needed in order to bring it into accord with these new discoveries." [15]

From the numerous conclusions of psychoanalysis that must prove important to general psychology Freud selected two points in particular: the primacy of affective processes in mental life, and the unsuspected extent to which they interfere with the intellect in both healthy and ill people.

In this section of the essay Freud had naturally given an account of the main tenets of psychoanalysis. He called special attention to the resemblances between dreams and psychopathological processes; to mental conflict; repression of certain impulses; reaction-formations on the part of the repressing agencies with substitutive formations on the part of the repressed; omnipresence of the processes of condensation and displacement.

The second section of the essay was devoted to the interest psychoanalysis has for certain non-psychological branches of knowledge, and Freud considered eight of these in order.

(a) *Interest for Philology:* Here Freud called attention to the astonishing resemblances between what may be called the language of the unconscious and the characteristics of ancient tongues. In both cases there is no means of expressing negation, ideas are ambivalent in that the same word may express either of two opposite meanings, symbolism plays a prominent part, and the mode of thought is curiously elliptical with the omission of connecting links. The word "archaic" applies equally to both. Then he called attention to the conclusions of the Swedish philologist, Sperber, concerning the remarkable importance of sexual expressions in the early development of language and the extraordinary ramifications emanating from them. Unconscious language is not only verbal, but can express itself in bodily form. As examples of its great variety he cited the example of the unconscious idea of pregnancy, which may express itself in hysteria through persistent vomiting, in the obsessional neurosis as a fear of infection, and in dementia praecox as a suspicion of being poisoned.

(b) *Interest for Philosophy:*   Philosophers have conceived of the unconscious either in mystical or transcendental terms or else as a matter of physiology that did not concern them. Now the study of its actual nature and contents must raise anew the old problem of the relation between body and mind in a different fashion from before. Then philosophies are much more individual and personal than other branches of knowledge, so that a deep knowledge of early individual development, with its influence on adult thinking, should throw a light on many presentations, if only by making them more easily comprehensible. But Freud was careful to refrain from asserting that in this way one could pass any judgment on any particular philosophical view; this could only be done on its own merits.

(c) *Interest for Biology:*   The important part accorded by psychoanalysis to the sexual instinct must concern biologists. Here Freud made two special points. One was the conception of this instinct transcending the simple aim of propagation in its search for gratification, and the wide extent of erotic activities beyond the genital organs themselves. In the other he compared the psychoanalytical concept of sexuality as something with an independent life of its own often opposed to the main personality with Weismann's conception of an immortal germ plasm to which animal bodies become temporarily attached. He mentioned how his favorite word *"Trieb"* (drive) was a transitional concept between psychological and biological modes of expression, and how the biological distinction between "male" and "female" becomes in psychology one between "active" and "passive," features that refer not to the instinct itself but only to its goals. The topic of bisexuality was naturally not omitted.

(d) *Genetic Interest:*   Psychoanalysis does not merely resolve complex products into their elements, as chemistry does, but traces them back to earlier activities from which they have been derived: it is not static, but dynamic and genetic. Freud pointed out how much more seriously psychoanalysis takes the old adage "the child is father of the man" than is usually done. The discovery of the vital importance the earliest impressions of life have for everything later gives the paradox, which Freud had long solved, of how it is that just these important memories are lost to consciousness. A still more astonishing discovery was that the early mental processes continue to exist side by side with the more complex products that are later developed from them, and that at any time there may be a "regression" back to them, giving them fresh life.

(e) *Interest for the History of Civilization:*   The first application of psychoanalytical knowledge here was to the elucidation of myths and fairy tales, the dreams of early mankind. But it could be used to throw light on the great institutions of civilization: religion, morality, law, and philosophy. There is an inner connection between the mental achievements of the individual and those of the community, since they both arise from the same dynamic sources. The main activity of the mind is to procure the release of tension. Some of this is obtained by direct gratification, but there remains a considerable proportion that has to search for any available indirect forms. According to Freud, it was this free amount of energy that created our various social institutions. The primitive belief in the "omnipotence of thoughts," of which there are still many relics, has to be modified by increasing contact with reality; we have there the passage from the animistic phase through the religious one to the scientific one. Myths, religion and morality may be regarded as attempts to procure compensation for the satisfactions lacking in reality.

(f) *Interest for the Theory and History of Art:*   Art is a special form of the attempt to gratify otherwise unsatisfied wishes, both for the artist and his audience. "Art constitutes an intermediate territory between the wish-denying reality and the wish-fulfilling world of phantasy." Psychoanalysis is able as a rule to trace the source of those wishes from the manifest content of the art form to their origins, but, according to Freud, it can throw no light on the nature of the artistic talent itself. "Whence the artist derives his creative capacities is not a question for psychology."

(g) *Interest for Sociology:*   A great deal of our social feeling is derived from the sublimation of particular unsatisfied erotic wishes. Undue repression leads to unsocial attitudes; this is the end state of every neurosis, and Freud likened it to the monastic life in earlier ages. On the other hand, social demands play an important part in the creation of neuroses by imposing ever greater restrictions on direct gratification. These restrictions then become internalized, inherited, and self-imposed—a view that became more prominent in Freud's later writings on sociology.

(h) *Interest for Pedagogy:* Only someone who has an understanding of a child's mind can become a good educator, but he has to overcome the difficulty interposed by the amnesia of the most important part of his own childhood life. Psychoanalysis affords access to this, and should thus prove of inestimable value to teachers. Freud laid stress on the tolerance needed in the upbringing of young children, and this can only be based on appreciation of the fact that manifestations repugnant to adult standards are often concerned with stages in development through which the child has inevitably to pass. Our finest virtues are often derivatives of such lowly origins.

(7) In 1917 appeared what proved to be, and deservedly so, Freud's most popular book, known in English as *Introductory Lectures on Psychoanalysis.*[16] There were five German editions, in addition to several pocket ones issued, and more than fifty thousand copies were sold. The book was first published in three separate parts, the first in July 1916, the other two in May 1917; Freud revised it twice, but without making any fundamental changes. It was translated into sixteen languages, including Serbian, Hungarian, Hebrew and Chinese; it was even printed in Braille. There have been five English editions and two American ones.

The story of its inception is as follows. On October 23 and 30, 1915, Freud began giving his accustomed lectures on "An Introduction to Psychoanalysis." He found, evidently to his surprise, an audience of seventy, a great contrast to the audience of three when he gave his first lecture on dreams only fifteen years before; in the following month it had mounted to over a hundred.[17] So he decided to prepare them more carefully than usual, and after a little reflection made up his mind to publish them in book form. The acute Rank at once interpreted this as a plan to make further lectures unnecessary, and he was right.[18] Freud had been lecturing for thirty years, and no doubt felt he had done his duty by the ungrateful University; these lectures were his last.

He wrote the first four lectures beforehand. The next eleven, those on dreams, he wrote immediately after delivering them.[19] When it came to the more difficult topic of the neuroses, however, he wrote them out fully some time beforehand and then committed them to memory; as early as September 1916, he had nine of the thirteen already written for the coming session.[20]

In these lectures Freud displayed at its height his gift for exposition, and the book would wring admiration for them alone. He led his audience on so gently and persuasively, with the fullest and fairest discussion of any possible objection, that they must have found it hard not to be won over. There is a quite charming passage where he suddenly warned them that by accepting some apparently impeccable proposition they were unwittingly committing themselves to more far-reaching conclusions than they could have realized, conclusions which then in their turn he gradually made more acceptable by further exposition.

The book is made up of three sections, but it really consists of two distinct halves. The first half, with two sections treating of the psychopathology of everyday life and of dreams respectively, was delivered in the winter of 1915-1916. The subject matter, taken from normal mental life, consisted of material of a kind available to the audience from their own experience. Assuming their disappointment at having to consider such trivialities as slips of the tongue Freud pointed out how many important matters in life have to be divined from faint indications. A glance of the eye or a faint involuntary pressure of the hand may speak volumes to a lover. Again, in the field of jurisprudence, circumstantial evidence from an accumulation of clues, each perhaps slight in itself, is often found to be more conclusive than the more doubtful direct evidence of eyewitnesses. And the supposed objector who suggested that such slips are meaningless accidents which might just as well have happened otherwise was reproved, since in that way he would be throwing overboard the whole scientific outlook based on strict determinism; even the religious outlook was more consistent when it taught that not a sparrow should fall to the ground without the express will of the Heavenly Father. So Freud led his audience on through the range of these various slips to recognizing the existence of mental dissociation. Finally he pointed out that the effect of such slips was by no means always trivial, such as with self-injuries, fatal "accidents" and even greater catastrophies.

The next section, on dreams, is also a masterpiece of exposition. Freud described his theory of dreams so many times that it was a constant source of wonder to us how he managed each time to infuse into it such freshness and novelty. Even psychoanalysts thoroughly familiar with the subject-matter could read each new presentation with absorbed interest as if they were reading of it for the first time. Freud devoted eleven lectures to this theme after the four on the everyday slips, but even so he felt he had given only an imperfect account of that extraordinarily rich topic. His little book *On Dreams*[*] is a simpler and more didactic introduction to it, but the present exposition is perhaps the more instructive. This is because it proceeds by discussions in which the various difficulties in apprehension are carefullly and patiently examined in detail. The first lecture was devoted to the preliminary difficulties, such as the vagueness and uncertainties of the material itself. Then the main themes follow: the technique of interpretation, the contrast beween manifest and latent content, the nature and function of the censorship, the simple features of dreams in childhood, the various mechanism of distortion employed in the "dream work," the sources of the stimuli and the unconscious wishes they set in action, and so on. There is also some account of the repressed wishes of the unconscious, of incestuous and death wishes from infancy, etc.

The last lecture was devoted to the difficulties that still remain, and Freud considered four of them in particular. The first of them concerns the uncertainties of interpretation, whether a given element is to be read literally or symbolically, whether a phrase has to be inverted or not, and the various possibilities of arbitrary and subjective interpretation. Freud conceded that such work does not attain the certainty to be found in mathematics, but he pointed out that all conclusions in scientific work are in the nature of varying degrees of probability rather than of absoluteness and that in most work the trustworthiness of the results depended largely on the skill and experience of the worker. With dream interpretation he maintained that a competent analyst reaches a very high level of probability in his interpretations. He drew the analogy of the original uncertainty in the deciphering of cuneiform hieroglyphics, and also remarked on how with certain languages, such as Chinese and ancient Egyptian, slight indications are necessary for understanding which of various possible meanings is intended. Another kind of hesitancy is induced through the impression that so many of the interpretations give of being farfetched and depending on a play on words of a kind foreign to our waking consciousness. All that, however, is of the nature of the unconscious system, which is alien in essence.

Then came the unhappy admission that certain people, hitherto regarded as psychoanalysts, had put forward different ideas about

[*] See p. 210.

the meaning of dreams. There was Maeder's suggestion that dream
life represents an attempt at adaptation to current and future tasks,
what he termed the "prospective tendency" of dreams; Silberer's belief that all dreams have two meanings, the psychoanalytical one and
the "anagogic" one in which higher aims of the mind are represented;
Adler's statement that all dreams have both a masculine and a feminine interpretation. In Freud's judgment the element of truth in all
these suggestions had been unjustifiably generalized, and the fallacy
in such cases lay in an imperfect realization of the profound difference
between the manifest and the latent content of a dream.

In conclusion he discussed the objection raised that the dreams of
a patient often depended on which analyst he attended, that there
was a similarity in the dreams of a given analyst's patients. This also
may happen, but the inference sometimes drawn from it was again
due to the same confusion between manifest and latent content. Remarks made by an analyst could often be the stimulus to a dream,
just as those made by anyone else or, for that matter, any bodily stimulus. But how the patient's dream-making activity worked up such
stimuli was a purely internal matter that was not susceptible to any
outside influence. "One may often influence a dreamer *about* what
he shall dream, but never *what* he actually dreams."

The third section, which is really the second half of the book, consisted of thirteen lectures delivered in the following winter. They differ from the first set in that they deal with material inaccessible to
the members of the audience and so had to assume a more didactic
form. They retained, however, the discussions of the supposed objections and difficulties on the part of the audience that made the
earlier lectures so attractive. The subject matter is not the theory
of psychoanalysis itself, still less a description of how to employ the
method, but an account of the psychoanalytical theory of the psychoneuroses. These lectures probably constitute the best introduction to
that subject.

In them Freud ranged widely, and at times deeply, over all aspects
of the psychoneuroses, and it is only possible here to comment on a
few of his characteristic statements. He began, for instance, by dis-
avowing his belief in the old proverb that strife is the father of things,
and by expressing his dislike for scientific polemics, which are usually
unfruitful and mostly personal. He pointed out that to discover the
meaning of neurotic symptoms through analysis involved the fateful
step of recognizing the existence of the unconscious. Then, speaking of
therapy, he showed that there is more than one kind of knowing; one

can know something with one part of the mind and yet not know it with another. He remarked on the tendency of neurotics to be willing in the long run to disclose everything except some special part of their mind that was to be held in reserve, and on the importance of ruthlessness in not sparing that reserved area, from which fresh symptoms might later once more develop. Nor could any particular field, such as perhaps state secrets, be exempted as an exception; if it were announced that criminals were to be exempt from arrest in any particular area it would be impossible to apprehend them.

Freud dealt at length with the problems of aetiology and repeatedly insisted on the need for several factors to converge before a neurotic symptom could be constituted. The elements of such a summation, however, are reciprocal; if one factor is specially strong the other ones need not be so, and vice versa. There was, to begin with, the hereditary predisposition, which in a few cases is all-important and in others hardly at all. It consists of the deposit of ancestral experiences. This was always Freud's view of heredity: "If nothing is acquired nothing can be inherited." [21] What are nowadays called "primal phantasies," e.g. pictures of parental coitus, fears of castration, etc., were once long ago realities. Then comes the factor of inhibited development at any given stage. This may be innate as often happens in organic development, leading there, for instance, to such incidents as an undescended testicle or a patent inguinal canal. Or it may be increased by actual experiences at those stages, leading to the very similar situation Freud called "fixation." These points of fixation remain throughout life as foci of special attraction, points to which libidinal energy can easily "regress" when difficulties or obstructions occur. This feature of regression was one to which Freud attached special importance, but he was careful to insist on a matter that is sometimes overlooked: that regression of energy cannot take place unless there is something to regress to, something that draws it back. The obstruction that dams up the libido and sets regression in train Freud termed sexual privation in the broad sense, but he included under this term not only external privations but above all internal ones due to previous repression.

While he maintained that every neurotic symptom is a disguised substitute for sexual gratification he made it clear that this was only half of the story. Strictly speaking, a symptom is, particularly in hysteria, a compromise formation between the libidinal wish and the repressing force exercised from the side of the ego. Moreover, the wish in question is typically not an adult desire for sexual intercourse, but one of the early partial components that go to make up the adult instinct. In other words, it is an impulse belonging to childhood—an additional reason for its meaning being easy to overlook. It was the existence of these numerous components in childhood that had led Freud to describe childhood sexuality as "polymorphous-perverse," an expression that gave rise to a great deal of indignation. In this connection he uttered his famous dictum that every neurotic symptom was the negative of a sexual perversion; which of the two comes about depends largely on the degree of repression present. Neuroses always signify a conflict between the sexual and the ego group of instincts. When they appear to be due to a conflict between two different sexual impulses, e.g. masculine and feminine, that is because the ego has accepted one of the two more than the other; in technical language, one impulse is more "ego-syntonic" than the other.

A still further factor enters into the formation, or more especially into the maintenance, of neurotic symptoms—the advantage the person gains from it. Freud made here a distinction between a "primary gain" (paranosic gain) and a "secondary gain" (epinosic gain). The former is the advantage the ego has from its flight into disease in place of enduring the painfulness of some situation. The secondary gain is the advantage the personality may subsequently obtain through exploiting the neurotic illness once it is established. This latter feature is sometimes so obvious, notably in domestic life, that at first sight it may be mistaken for the motor of the whole neurosis.

Freud drew an interesting contrast between dreams and neuroses, the inner mechanisms of which are so nearly identical: the distorting processes, presentation of a repressed infantile wish as fulfilled, etc. With a neurosis, however, the ego has to impose a far stronger negative to such wishes than it does in dream life. Here it can afford to be more tolerant because in sleep there is little or no access to motility and therefore no danger of the wishes being translated into action.

A special lecture was devoted to the fundamental problem of morbid anxiety (*Angst*). He endeavored to distinguish between "real" or objective anxiety, that related to an actual external danger, and "morbid" anxiety. The healthy state is one of readiness to perceive danger and a preparedness to deal with it. This normally should lead to decisions about the most expedient protection, whether flight, defense or attack. When, however, the process goes on to develop a full state of anxiety the biological advantages are diminished or lost, very evidently so in the case of panic. Freud was still puzzled about the source of the affect of morbid anxiety, a problem he solved years later. On the one hand he still insisted on his old opinion that anxiety was simply transformed libido, and he did not know how to combine this idea with the notion of its signifying a flight of the ego from its libido.[22] Furthermore, when he used the expression "transformation of libido into anxiety," in one place he slightly qualified it by adding, "or, better, discharge of libido in the form of anxiety." [23] But still there remained the fact that "real anxiety" is evidently an expression of the self-preservative instinct of the ego, and therefore had apparently a different source from that of "morbid anxiety." Freud confessed that here was a gap in his theory which up till then he was unable to fill.[24]

The last chapter was devoted to the subject of therapy, not to the technique of carrying it out, but to the problem of how psychoanalysis produced therapeutic results. It was mainly taken up with a discussion of transference and suggestion, with a long debate on the difference between the latter and psychoanalysis. It was commonly asserted at that time, and the objection is still occasionally raised by the uninformed, that analysis was merely a more subtle form of suggestion and produces its results in the same way. There exists no more complete answer to this criticism than that which Freud gave at length in his concluding lecture, the last he was ever to deliver, and it can be recommended to those who wish to examine the matter with an open mind.

Freud concluded with a very moving expression of his dissatisfaction at the way in which he had tried to perform his task. He candidly admitted and enumerated the various deficiencies in his presentation, his only excuse being the enormous complexity of the various topics with which he had dealt. It was a revealing measure of his true humility and also of the high standards he cherished in scientific work and teaching.

(8) The remaining one of Freud's writings to be considered in the present context is a little essay published in 1917 in *Imago*, the periodical concerned with the non-medical applications of psychoanalysis. It was written at the request of Ignotus, a Hungarian friend, for a paper he could publish in his Hungarian magazine *Nyugat*. Hanns Sachs persuaded Freud to publish it a couple of months later in German.[25] It bore the title of "A Difficulty in the Path of Psychoanalysis," meaning a difficulty in the way of apprehending and accepting its main tenets. The chief expository part was an apologia for his libido theory, more especially in connection with his recently postulated conception of narcissism. The reproach of one-sidedness in

studying sexual processes in such detail he countered with the assertion that it implied no denial or neglect of the manifold other interests with which mankind is concerned, although they did not lie in his own direct path. "Our one-sidedness is like that of the chemist who traces all compounds to the force of chemical affinity. In doing so he is not denying the force of gravity, a matter he leaves to the physicist." [26]

Freud then expounded the three heavy blows which the narcissism, or self-love, of mankind had suffered at the hand of science. It was a set of ideas he had already mentioned briefly in the course of his lectures: [27]

(a) *Cosmological:* The first serious blow to wound man's pride came from the astronomers, and is linked with the name of Copernicus. Hitherto, despite a few suggestions from the ancient Greeks, particularly Aristarchos, it had been taken for granted that our earthly home was the center of the universe around which the sun, moon and stars revolved—as it were, in recognition of our importance. When it had to be recognized in the sixteenth century that we dwelled on a minute fragment of matter, one of a countless number that revolved, man suffered the first blow to his pride.

(b) *Biological:* The aspect of man's pride to be wounded by biological discoveries, those associated with the name of Darwin, was his belief in his unique status in the animate realm. This was not a primordial belief like the former one. On the contrary, both savages and children readily take for granted a closeness to other animals which is shown in the ideas of descent from them, of sharing their language, and so on. With the development of civilization, however, man came not simply to assume a position of domination over other animals, but fundamentally to deny any innate community with them: the power of reason, the possession of an immortal soul, were his prerogatives alone. The demonstration of his essential affinity with other animals, and his descent from them, was the second great blow to man's pride. (Incidentally, this admission had been generally made only in respect of man's body, not his mind; it was Freud's work that is gradually extending it to the latter.)

(c) *Psychological:* The last stronghold of man's pride has also been assailed. It was the belief that at the center of his personality there resides something, whether called his ego or his soul, that is informed about all that goes on within him, and has a full knowledge of his motives and interests; and that furthermore he possesses an instrument, "will-power," which exercises command and control over the rest of his personality. Psychoanalysis has shown irrefragably that both these beliefs have only a very partial validity. Consciousness is far from knowing about everything that goes on in the mind, even about most important aspects of it, and man's power of controlling either his thoughts or his impulses is much less than he had deceived himself into believing.

This conclusion, it is true, had many times been enunciated by philosophers. Schopenhauer in particular had insisted on the importance of the "unconscious will" and also of the unsuspected significance of the sexual instincts. But it was only when psychoanalysis replaced abstract propositions by material demonstration that it began to dawn on man that he is not "master in his own house." The recognition of unconscious processes, hardly yet begun, would prove of momentous significance both for science and for life.

Abraham mildly remarked of this paper that it had the appearance of a personal document, whereupon Freud replied: "You are right in saying that the enumeration in my last paper may give the impression of claiming a place beside Copernicus and Darwin. But I didn't want to give up the interesting train of thought on that account, and so at least put Schopenhauer in the foreground." [28]

9

CHAPTER

Contributions to Technique

THE TECHNIQUE OF CARRYING OUT A PSYCHOANALYSIS IS LARGELY A matter of experience. The complexity of the human mind is such that it is impossible to enumerate all the particular situations and difficulties that may arise in the course of an analysis. A prerequisite, however, for the ability to make good use of such experience is a personal freedom and harmony, attainable only through personal experience of analysis, that enables one to detect at least an echo in oneself of any emotional reaction displayed by the patient and thus to comprehend its significance. Freud once remarked, as long ago as 1882, that it gave him an uncanny feeling whenever he was unable to gauge someone else's emotions through his own,[1] a remarkable premonition of his future analytic capacity.

With this freedom the analyst's mind should be flexible enough to apprehend all the infinite variety of emotional attitudes he may encounter. The analyst works, however, not only with his unconscious but also with his conscious mind, and it has proved possible to assist him in his work through more or less didactic instruction concerning general principles, just as a chemist can learn by supplementing, though not replacing, his necessary laboratory experience with lectures and reading. Freud naturally felt it incumbent on him to help those who were adopting his methods by imparting to them the knowledge he had painfully acquired through experience. His own technique had changed very greatly from its first tentative beginnings in the early nineties. Many refinements had been evolved, discrimination established between the more important data and the less, and unnecessary and even deleterious elements eliminated.[a]

Freud had of course already given many indications of the nature of his technique. Three valuable papers in the years 1904-5 had expounded enough of it to enable those of us at a distance to venture on applying it.

(1) The first of these, in 1904, was actually entitled "Freud's Psycho-Analytic Method"; it was written about the middle of 1903. It appeared anonymously as a chapter of Löwenfeld's book *Psychische Zwangserscheinungen* (Psychic Compulsion Phenomena), a notable book in its own right, but two years later Freud republished it, this time under his name, in the first series of his *Sammlungen*.[2] It was the only one he ever wrote with such a comprehensive title, since he never again felt like giving the impression that he was covering the whole ground. Indeed this paper itself consists of a very general description only and it contains a sentence on the most important part of the method which runs: "Freud has not yet published the details of his technique of interpretation."

Beginning with an account of the early cathartic method Freud indicated the fundamental changes he had instituted in it, principally the replacement of hypnosis by the investigation of "free associations." Stress was laid on the importance of repression and resistance, but not on the curious and important phenomenon of transference. He stated that: "The objection to hypnosis is that it conceals the resistance and for this reason obstructs the physician's insight into the play of the psychic forces. Hypnosis does not do away with the resistances: what it does is to avoid them, and thus yields only imperfect information and transitory therapeutic success." Now he no longer even asked his patients to close their eyes, as he had done only four years before.[3] He concluded with a number of contraindications which forbid the use of the method, some of which have since proved no longer refractory.

(2) On December 12, 1904, Freud delivered an address before the College of Physicians in Vienna on the subject of "Psychotherapy."[4] which he also included in the same volume. Freud remarked that it was eight years since he had addressed that College on the subject of hysteria. He was, however, confounding two occasions: one when he delivered three lectures on hysteria before that College *nine* years earlier, on October 14, 21 and 28, 1895 (never published by him, but

[a] An example of the latter is that in the nineties Freud had permitted himself unrestricted social intercourse with his patients.

reported at length in the Vienna medical press); the other a lecture on the "Aetiology of Hysteria" *eight* years earlier, on May 2, 1896, before the *Verein für Psychiatrie und Neurologie* (Society of Psychiatry and Neurology). The present occasion was the last time he ever addressed a medical audience in Vienna.

It was a most persuasive plea for studying the mode of action of psychotherapy, one which he expounded more fully in the paper he published shortly after on "Mental Treatment"; [b] but there is no reason to think that it met with any positive response from the side of the audience. He countered the belief that psychoanalysis is a form of suggestion by asserting that there is "the greatest possible antithesis" between the two. This he illustrated by citing Leonardo da Vinci's contrast between painting and sculpture. The former works *per via di porre* by adding something, paint, to the blank canvas, just as suggestion consists in adding something that it is hoped will counteract the morbid ideas. On the other hand, sculpture works *per via di levare*, by taking away from the rough stone all that hides the surface of the future statue contained in it, just as analysis reveals what was previously hidden. He explained the mode of action of psychoanalysis by contrasting the state of unconscious ideas with that of conscious ones which are subject to control. The various objections to psychoanalysis, the sexual aspects, the fear of harm, etc., were faithfully dealt with. The whole paper is enlightening and still full of interest.

Freud expressed in this lecture the opinion that further advances in technique should make it possible to influence certain psychoses therapeutically—a prediction now at last being fulfilled. He also remarked that as yet (end of 1904) no colleague had inquired of him how to carry out a psychoanalysis. By that time he had, it is true, a few pupils, but he was probably referring to colleagues of his own standing.

(3) By far the most valuable contribution to technique, however, that Freud made in those years was his account of the well-known Dora analysis. This is described at some length in another chapter,[c] but stress needs to be laid here on its purely technical aspects. For the first time one is allowed to see Freud at work, to observe how he deals with various situations in the analysis, how and when he interprets the material brought before him and, above all, the skillful and indispensable use he makes of dream interpretation.

[b] Chapter 8, No. 2.
[c] Chapter 11, No. I.

(4) "Notes on a Case of Obsessional Neurosis": This essay con stitutes one of the series of case histories that will presently be described.[d] It is mentioned here for the following reason. It was Freud's custom to destroy both his manuscript and the notes on which it was based, of any paper he published. By some odd chance, however, the day-to-day notes of this case, written every evening, were preserved, at least those for the best part of the first four months of the treatment, and James Strachey has edited and published a translation of them in conjunction with the case history itself.[5] This material is invaluable as affording a unique opportunity for watching Freud at his daily work so to speak: his timing of interpretations, his characteristic use of analogies to illustrate a point he was making, the preliminary guesses he would make privately which might subsequently be either confirmed or disproved, and altogether the tentative manner in which such piecemeal work proceeded. To a practicing analyst in particular such a glimpse behind the scenes is of absorbing interest.

Some features in Freud's technique at that time are of special interest. He gave his patients, for instance, fuller expositions of the theory of psychoanalysis than he did later on, or than is customary nowadays, but in his essay he made it clear that his object in doing so was not in the least to induce any conviction in the patient, but simply to provoke him to produce more relevant material. Then, from the unpublished notes, we learn that Freud permitted a more familiar attitude towards his patients than he did later, or has been the method since used by analysts. He no longer, it is true, invited them to meals with his family, as he had done in the eighteen-nineties, but he would still occasionally have refreshments brought in during the session for both himself and the patient.

(5) The widening of interest in his work that the Salzburg Congress in 1908 betokened evidently stimulated Freud's wish to give a further account of his method and thus help those who were beginning to use it. So some six months after the Congress he embarked on a systematic exposition of technique, which he proposed to publish under the title of *Allgemeine Technik der Psychoanalyse* (A General Account of the Psychoanalytic Technique). He wrote to Abraham that he had not yet decided where to publish it, perhaps in the second series of the *Sammlung* which were to appear in the following year.[6] By the next month he reported that he had already written 36 pages some weeks ago, but was so tired from the day's work that it was not making progress.[7] To Ferenczi he said it should run to fifty

[a] Chapter 11, No. III.

pages by Christmas when he would submit it for his approval. "It should be very valuable for those who are practicing analysis; those who are not will not understand a word of it." [8] A few days later he told Jung that it had been refused acceptance once and that if no one else would take it he would publish it in the first half-volume of the new *Jahrbuch*,[9] but by February he saw he could not get it ready in time and decided to postpone finishing it till August, when it would appear in the second half-volume.[10] This was still his intention in June, when he said that after writing up the case of the "Man with the Rats" [e] he would devote a couple of weeks of the holiday to finishing the work on technique.[11] When the time came, however, he was so tired and his thoughts so occupied with the coming visit to America that he made up his mind to do no more writing that year.[12] Another reason for postponing it till the following year was that he wished Ferenczi's paper on transference [13] to have priority.[14] In the following year, however, he announced there was no question of its appearing in the *Jahrbuch* and that it would be all the better for lying in a drawer.[15]

When I visited Freud in the summer of 1909 he told me he was proposing to write a little memorandum of maxims and rules of technique which he intended to distribute privately among only those analysts nearest to him. The news naturally aroused my expectations, but there again nothing came of the project. One suspects some unsureness or dissatisfaction in Freud's mind on the matter, the nature of which is hard to divine.

From that moment nothing more was heard of the project, nor have those precious pages been preserved. "Suddenly, as rare things will, it vanished." A year later, he announced his intention of digging up his "old work" on technique,[16] but by then he no longer felt like attempting to expound the whole subject, and formed a new plan of writing half a dozen essays on special aspects of it. This, as we shall see, he carried out.

(6) He first took up the subject again in the interesting address he gave before the Nuremberg Congress in April 1910, on "The Future Prospects of Psycho-Analytic Therapy." [17] He commented on how much more strenuous the treatment had been to both patient and analyst in its inception when it was confined to pressing the patient to give utterance to his thoughts. The arts of timely interpretation and of studying the transference manifestations had already made it easier. He further pointed out how the aim of the treatment had

* Chapter 11, No. III.

shifted from the mere elucidation of the symptoms to that of the complexes in general, and since then to the direct investigation of the resistances. The knowledge of typical symbols had been a recent addition. He now called attention to the occurrence of counter-transferences, and demanded a thorough and constant self-analysis of them. He expressed the hope that when psychoanalysis gained more recognition and respect the therapeutic task would be somewhat eased. He depicted ruefully his early days when he was regarded much as a gambler with a secret system. "It was really not agreeable to be operating on people's minds while colleagues, whose duty should have been to assist, took a pleasure in spitting into the field of opera-tion, and while at the first signs of blood or restlessness in him the patient's relatives threatened one." All that a gynecologist may do in certain eastern countries is to feel the pulse of an arm which is stretched out to him through a hole in the wall. "And his curative results are in proportion to the accessibility of their object; our op-ponents in the West wish to restrict our access to our patients' minds to something very similar."

He concluded with some important remarks on the attitude of society to neurotic troubles and the prophylaxis that could come about through a more honest knowledge of their meaning. But he warned against therapeutic fanaticism. There was also a place for neurosis in the world and some patients would be worse off if deprived of the secondary gain their illness brings them.

(7) A few months later, also in 1910, Freud published an article which unfortunately is still very much in place. It was on what he called "wild analysis." [18] He discussed, illustrating it by a well-chosen example, the muddle and harm that can be produced by doctors ap-plying his theories without taking the trouble to understand them, or by attempting to carry out a psychoanalysis without first learning how to. As he said, the technique of psychoanalysis cannot be learned from books, but only, like other medical interventions, from those who have mastered it. He would have been sad had he known that by now there are hundreds of "practitioners" in need of this obvious exhor-tation.

In the years 1911-1915 Freud published a series of six papers on technique which later he grouped together when re-issuing them as part of his fourth series of the *Sammlung Kleiner Schriften zur Neurosenlehre* (1918).

(8) The first one of the six, published in December 1911, was entitled "The Handling of Dream-Interpretation in Psycho-Anal-

ysis." [19] If a patient knows that dreams are very important his resistance may make use of the knowledge in two opposite ways. He may bring none at all, under the impression that then the analysis cannot proceed; he has to be shown that its progress can be independent of dream material, after which he will in due course produce some. Or he may overwhelm the analyst with a mass of dreams far beyond what is possible to analyze in the given time. The most important point was that the analyst should not put his scientific interest in interpreting any dream before the therapeutic rule of keeping touch with the current thoughts and emotions occupying the patient's mind. He may be confident that any dream material that would appear to be lost by not completely interpreting an interesting dream will surely recur in one form or another.

(9) A paper on "The Dynamics of Transference." [20] published a month later (January 1912), was one that helped analysts to get a clearer understanding of the obscure problems of this regular occurrence. After comparing the manifestations of transference in psychoanalysis with those in other medical situations Freud dealt with the enigma of their being both an indispensable help in the treatment and at the same time the greatest hindrance to its progress. He dissected the various elements of hostility, affection and unconscious sexuality, and explained how it is that the personal transference is always used as a resistance when a repressed complex is touched on.

In this paper Freud made two important statements. He expressed the opinion, which exposed him to much criticism, that all positive feelings, of sympathy, friendship, confidence, and so on, are derived from sexual sources, however completely the direct aim of the impulses has been concealed or altered. "Originally it was only sexual objects that we knew."

The other point was that when unconscious material emerges it often shows the typical features of the "Primary Process" he had discovered in connection with his investigation of dreams.[21] Instead of simply recalling the repressed memories, or rather impulses, the patient tries to repeat them in action: thought and behavior are one on that level. It was Ferenczi's inclination to encourage unduly this tendency of patients that many years later led to his divergence from Freud's teachings.

About that time, in 1912, Freud's wish to give fuller instruction to those employing his methods was strengthened by the unhappy dissensions that had recently taken place, which he felt sure were largely due to the correct technique not being adhered to. He still felt unable, however, to compose a complete exposition, and indeed that is inherently no more possible than describing on paper every detail of an engineer's or laboratory worker's skillful performances; the almost infinite variety of situations forbids it. Only general principles or guiding lines can be laid down, and the application of them left to practice and experience. This Freud now essayed in a special series of four papers, a part of the series of six mentioned above. He published them between 1912 and 1915, and gave them the general title of "Recommendations for Physicians Practising Psycho-Analysis." They are all of the utmost practical value.

(10) The first of these,[22] published in June 1912, dealt with the fundamental question of the mental state of the analyst during his work, a theme suggested to him by Ferenczi.[23] It is essential that his attention be what psychologists distinguish as passive or receptive; Freud used the apt expression "evenly-hovering attention." He should not pay more attention to one piece of the material than another, or regard one as more important than the other; mostly its significance appears only a good deal later, so that one should avoid pre-judgments. For the same reason he should not make notes during the analysis, either for the purposes of the treatment or for scientific purposes, nor should he encourage the patient to make notes or to think over any special matter beforehand. Unprejudiced spontaneity is the ideal for both parties, the analysts's attitude being the complement of the patient's attempts at free association.

Freud again laid stress on the importance of the analyst's own analysis, and very truly stated that if he neglects this "he will be penalized, not merely by an incapacity to learn more than a certain amount from his patient, but by risking a more serious danger, one which may become a danger for others. He will easily yield to the temptation of projecting as a scientific theory of general applicability some of the peculiarities of his own personality which he has dimly perceived; he will bring the psychoanalytic method into discredit, and lead the inexperienced astray." How many times has this prediction been fulfilled since those words were written!

Freud also warned against other mistakes that may easily be made. The analyst should not encourage the patient by narrating part of his own inner life; a mutual analysis of this sort would make the further investigation of the transference impossible. In other words, the analyst should act simply as a mirror to the patient. Furthermore, he should imitate the surgeon's attitude during an operation by keeping his personal feelings in the background and concentrating on performing his task to the best of his ability. Another danger is excessive ambition, whether of a therapeutic or a cultural nature. One should never demand of the patient more than lies in his native capacity.

(11) The next paper, "On Beginning the Treatment," [24] published in January and March of the following year (1913), dealt with the various problems that arise at the inception of the treatment. This paper is full of worldly wisdom garnered from his years of experience. What to say to the patient in the first interview, how much to explain, arrangements about time and money, the suitability of various cases, are among the matters he treated. Freud was always very apt at analogies, and here he remarked that those who are learning "the noble game" of chess soon find out that only the openings and the end game permit of systematic presentation; much the same applies to a psychoanalysis. He admitted, however, that even here the variations among patients are so great that none of the rules he proposes has any absolute validity; they all may have to be altered according to the case. One can only describe an average procedure.

It was Freud's custom to accept a strange patient at first only for a couple of weeks, during which the patient was to follow the analytic rules although the physician would refrain from interpretation. His reason for so doing was not only to decide on the suitability of the case but also to make sure, so far as possible, that the neurotic symptoms were not covering a more serious psychosis. He maintained that this gave one a far better chance of making a correct diagnosis than any number of ordinary interviews. For the psychiatrist a mistake in this connection has only academic interest, but for the psychoanalyst it might bring discredit on his work. Long talks before the treatment, or a previous acquaintanceship with the physician, are deleterious, because of the likelihood of a ready-made transference, so that the analyst has not the opportunity of studying its gradual development. One should be distrustful of patients who wish to postpone beginning treatment, however plausible their reason may seem. If the analyst, as his duty sometimes demands, decides to treat the wife or child of a friend he must reckon with losing that friendship, whatever the outcome of the analysis.[*]

There followed wise and characteristically honest remarks on the difficult matters of money and of length of treatment. Freud related that he had for ten years treated one or two patients daily without any fee, and he enumerated the difficulties it entailed in the analysis.

[*] From a somewhat similar personal experience of this kind with **Freud** himself I am glad to say that this statement does not invariably hold.

He gave an amusing example of the preposterous expectations on the part of patients, as well as of doctors, concerning the supposed length of the treatment, ascribing those expectations to the prevailing ignorance of the strength and depth of mental forces and the total obscurity surrounding a neurotic affection. It is regarded like the "maiden from afar," [g] no one knows where she came from and so is prepared for an equally mysterious departure. That a psychoanalysis is necessarily a long business is due, not only to its inherent difficulty, but also to the "timelessness" of the unconscious and the slowness with which deep changes can be brought about. Similarly it is unreasonable to demand that only certain symptoms should be analyzed and the rest left. As Freud put it, any man can beget a whole baby, but no one can create a head or arm alone.

He then explained why he adhered to the "ceremonial" of asking the patient to lie rather than to sit,[25] a matter that caused difficulties in the early days when American patients found it in some way humiliating. He mentioned the historical source of the custom as dating from the days of hypnotism and also the personal point that he did not like being stared at for many hours of the day at close quarters. These, however, are extrinsic factors. More important is the necessity for the analyst to be in a position to give free rein to his thoughts without the patient detecting them from the play on his features, which would impair the purity of the transference phenomena. He did not mention on that occasion the other advantage of the supine position assisting the state of relaxation which is so desirable. Incidentally, it is not true, as several critics have recently suggested, that it was Freud's embarrassment at approaching sexual topics that led him to insist on the supine position for his patients; his direct honesty gave him complete freedom here.

Stress was naturally laid on the fundamental rule of never withholding any thoughts under any pretext whatever. It is quite indifferent with what material one starts; this should be left entirely to the patient.

In conclusion he confessed his complete helplessness over one difficult matter, the treatment of patients' relatives. One has to reckon in any case with their invariable hostility and dissatisfaction.

(12) A more difficult paper was on the subjects of "Recollecting, Repeating, and Working Through," [26] published in December 1914. It concerned the constant struggle in every analysis between the analyst's endeavor on the one hand to get the patient to recollect the

[g] An allusion to Schiller's *Das Mädchen aus der Fremde.*

buried memories and impulses, and to assimilate them mentally, and the patient's tendency on the other hand to substitute for this a repetition in action, a tendency which when carried out in daily life may result in conduct detrimental to the patient's interests. The best way to deal with the problem is to concentrate the repetition in the transference situation where it is under control. Freud then drew the important distinction between on the one hand simply discovering the nature of a given resistance, with the conveying of it to the patient, and on the other hand the allowing him to "work through" the knowledge and thoroughly to assimilate it. This is one of the chief reasons for the length of the analytic work, but Freud said it cannot be obviated since it is connected with a curious feature of the unconscious mind, its "timelessness."

(13) The last paper of this extremely useful series, published in January 1915, the one which in Freud's opinion was the best of them,[27] was on the matter of "Transference Love," [28] a topic about which there are many popular misconceptions. Freud handled this delicate topic in a masterly fashion. Without falling back on any conventional morality he expounded with the utmost clarity the principles that should guide the analyst, and the precise reasons for them. The clearness of mind that integrity of character gives could nowhere be better illustrated than in this little paper. For instance, someone else might have denied to the patient that her love was real on the grounds of its blindness to reality, its compulsiveness and its demonstrable origin in prototypes of her childhood. But Freud honestly admitted that these are features applicable to all examples of falling in love, which is the reason why it verges on the abnormal, so that one cannot on such grounds deny the reality of the patient's feelings. The practical problem has to be tackled on quite another basis.

In a letter to Abraham, Freud mentioned that he had completed the two last papers we have been considering before being upset by the news of the outbreak of the war.[29]

(14) On September 28, 1918, Freud addressed another Psycho-Analytical Congress, at Budapest, on a similarly broad theme as that of the Nuremberg Congress. It was entitled "Lines of Advance in Psycho-Analytic Therapy." [30] He had written it at Steinbruch in Hungary while spending a few days there with the family of his friend, Anton von Freund, on his way to his summer holiday in the Tatra Mountains.[31]

Freud began by justifying his choice of the word analysis in the analogy with chemical analysis. Neurotic symptoms are highly complicated productions which it is necessary to resolve into their elements. Some writers—Bezzola was the chief among them—had drawn the conclusion that an analysis should logically be followed by a synthesis, a demand still occasionally made by the misinformed, but Freud animadverted strongly against this. He stigmatized it as an idea destitute of thought, an empty extension of an analogy and an unjustifiable exploiting of a name. The name was little more than a suitable label for purposes of distinction, not a definition or program. No simple analogy would be equal to describing the complex nature of mental processes, though, incidentally, it might be remarked that even chemical elements that have been artificially isolated mostly seek spontaneously for other affinities. Furthermore, psychoanalysis actually itself promoted synthesis by removing the repressions that have acted as blocks between different parts of the mind and thus prevented a harmonious unity; the dynamic element in them saw to it automatically that fresh means of expression are sought for and found, once they are set free to do so.

The main part of the address was devoted to discussing a recent paper by Ferenczi,[32] of which Freud thought very highly. Freud had long ago replaced the activity of hypnotic suggestion by the more passive technique of psychoanalysis, but Ferenczi had raised the question whether this technique could not be improved by introducing various very different forms of activity. Freud agreed that much could be done along these lines. Knowing the essential part played by privation in the genesis of neurotic symptoms, he suggested it was important to see to it that some element of privation or abstinence continue throughout the treatment as a constant stimulus to the motives for recovery, but he was very careful to explain what he meant by that. It was not at all a matter of general privation, and by no means necessarily one in the sphere of sexuality, but specific ones to be carefully chosen in reference to the individual's need and the particular features of the analysis at each stage. Great improvement was commonly followed by a search for gratification (by no means always the simple sexual ones) which when successful tends to neutralize the patient's spur to progress. When a certain quantity of libido had been freed by the analytic procedure it would automatically seek for some alternative mode of gratification in place of the neurotic symptoms and this has the effect of diminishing the patient's motives for further progress unless the analyst follows the new paths and obstructs them. Or the patient may discover some other form of suffering that would relieve his sense of guilt and also diminish his motives. Freud remarked that an unhappy marriage and physical disease were the commonest ways of keeping a neurosis at bay; they satisfy the need for suffering and self-punishment demanded by the repressions.

The other danger is that the patient seeks gratification in the transference situation of the analysis itself and Freud warned against indulging the patient in the many different ways possible. If life is made too comfortable, as often happens in sanatoria for nervous maladies, the patient is no better equipped to face life than before. Freud here criticized the tendency of certain Swiss analysts to guide their patients' lives in particular directions, to instruct them about what their aims in life ought to be, or get them to adopt the analyst's personality as a model. He also objected to Putnam's endeavor to foist a particular philosophy on his patients.

There are other forms of activity to which Freud made allusion. One was urging some phobic patients to endure the anxiety evoked by certain dreaded situations rather than to wait for the end of the analysis, which otherwise could be indefinitely postponed. Again, severe cases of obsessional neurosis call for certain changes in technique by allowing the analysis itself to become part of the obsessional tendency and then forcibly intervening.

Freud concluded by envisaging the future when the State would take serious cognizance of the cost and the vast amount of suffering and inefficiency resulting from neuroses, transcending that, for instance, caused by tuberculosis, and would take the same responsibility for the treatment of poor patients as is done with other disorders. Now, thirty-five years later, there are slight indications of moves in this direction in Britain, and it is very interesting to reflect on the particular suggestions Freud made at that time.

Freud made four contributions on the practical use of dreams in the course of treatment.

(15) The first one, published in 1911,[33] was entitled "Additional Remarks on the Interpretation of Dreams." It was never reprinted in either of the German collections of Freud's works, and in the *Standard Edition* in English it has been incorporated into the main text.[34] It was mainly concerned with the elucidation of various symbols.

The second, a much more important paper which was published in

December 1911,[35] initiated the series of six papers on technique mentioned earlier (No. 8).

(16) Then there is a slight, but interesting, paper[36] on a dream that bore testimony to an actual event which the dreamer had denied. It was a dream of someone else related to Freud by a patient, and it is instructive to compare the interpretations they both gave.

(17) A more serious contribution may be mentioned here, although it was not written until 1923. It was entitled "Remarks on the Theory and Practice of Dream Interpretation."[37] It consisted of ten sections dealing with separate themes. Freud first distinguished several methods of beginning the interpretation of a dream according to circumstances. He then described various ways in which different types of dreams make their appearance during a treatment, and discussed the important question of the clinical use to be made of a dream one has been able to interpret. He passed to the problem of the extent to which the suggestive influence of the analyst is able to influence dreams, and made here a sharp distinction between the effect of this on preconscious material and that on the unconscious proper; it is a theme he thrashed out very thoroughly. The paper also contained some important remarks on the "repetition-compulsion," a new conception that was greatly occupying his mind at the time.[h]

Two other short papers may be mentioned under the heading of technique.

(18) One is a set of little examples of incidents during analytic treatment.[38]

(19) The other contains some examples of what Freud termed *déjà raconté* on the analogy of the well-known phenomenon called *déjà vu*.[39] It happens at times that a patient is completely convinced he has already told the analyst something which he could not have done. The intention to do so had been so strong, and yet prevented by some resistance, that in his memory it is confounded with the act itself of narration. It is somewhat akin to the explanation Freud had proffered years before of the *déjà vu* phenomenon. He added the striking remark when a patient says about some unconscious material that he had known it all along the analysis is complete; some part of the patient's mind had truly known it all along.

We may conclude this chapter with a letter Freud wrote on January 4, 1928, congratulating Ferenczi on a paper he had just written on technique.[40]

[h] This will be discussed in Volume III.

"Dear Friend,

"Yesterday's post brought two rare things: a report from San Paulo in Brazil that a psychoanalytical group has been formed there which seeks acceptance in the International Association, and your letter with New Year's greetings which for twenty years I have cordially reciprocated. We are both of us aware of the powerlessness of our thoughts and of the influence of our attitude towards each other.

"Your accompanying production, which you will find enclosed, displays that judicious maturity you have acquired of late years, in respect of which no one approaches you. The title is excellent and deserves a wider provenance, since the 'Recommendations on Technique' I wrote long ago were essentially of a negative nature. I considered the most important thing was to emphasize what one should *not* do, and to point out the temptations in directions contrary to analysis. Almost everything positive that one *should* do I have left to 'tact,' the discussion of which you are introducing. The result was that the docile analysts did not perceive the elasticity of the rules I had laid down, and submitted to them as if they were taboos. Sometime all that must be revised, without, it is true, doing away with the obligations I had mentioned.

"The only criticism I have of your paper is that it is not three times larger and divided into three parts. There is no doubt that you have much more to say on similar lines, and it would be very beneficial to have it.

"All that you say about 'tact' is assuredly true enough, but I have some misgivings about the manner in which you make those concessions. All those who have no tact will see in what you write a justification for arbitrariness, i.e. subjectivity, i.e. the influence of their own unmastered complexes. What we encounter in reality is a delicate balancing—for the most part on the preconscious level—of the various reactions we expect from our interventions. The issue depends above all on a quantitative estimate of the dynamic factors in the situation. One naturally cannot give rules for measuring this; the experience and the normality of the analyst have to form a decision. But with beginners one therefore has to rob the idea of 'tact' of its mystical character.

"Yours sincerely,
"Freud"

10

CHAPTER

Clinical Contributions

IN THE COURSE OF YEARS FREUD MADE A NUMBER OF SHORT CONTRIBU-
tions, including descriptions of his cases, to the Vienna Society. Few
of these have been published, but it is intended to publish the whole
of the "Minutes" of that Society in Freud's time, and they will include also his contributions to various discussions.

The most important of Freud's clinical contributions in the present
period are the classical case histories which will be discussed in the
following chapter.

(1) Of the shorter ones the first was a paper, written in 1908 by
request for the first number of Hirschfeld's new *Zeitschrift für Sexualwissenschaft*, entitled "Hysterical Phantasies and their Relation to
Bisexuality." [1] In it Freud stressed the basic importance of phantasies
for the creation of hysterical symptoms. Such phantasies may be intimate daydreams that have undergone repression or they may never
have been conscious. Only unconscious phantasies can produce symptoms. Hysterical symptoms are nothing but unconscious phantasies
that have come to expression through "conversion." In long-standing
cases a symptom may come to represent several such phantasies, provided the latter are themselves interconnected.

Psychoanalytic investigation can regularly trace the source of these
phantasies to the sexual life. They originally accompanied masturbatory acts, but may persist when these are abandoned. They are closely
related, though in an inverse way, to sexual perversions because they
spring from the infantile, as yet dissociated, components of the sexual
instinct.

Freud summed up his experience on this subject in the following formulas:

(a) An hysterical symptom is the memory-symbol of certain active (traumatic) impressions and experiences.

(b) Hysterical symptoms are substitutes, produced through "conversion," for the revival of these traumatic experiences by association.

(c) Hysterical symptoms are, like other mental products, the expression of wish-fulfillments.

(d) An hysterical symptom is the realizing of an unconscious phantasy that gratifies the fulfillment of a wish.

(e) An hysterical symptom serves the purpose of sexual gratification and represents a part of the sexual life of the person (corresponding to one of the components of his sexual instinct).

(f) Hysterical symptoms are equivalent to the recurrence of a form of sexual gratification which had been really experienced in infantile life and has since been repressed.

(g) Hysterical symptoms arise as a compromise between two opposing affective or instinctual trends, of which one is striving to find expression for a partial impulse or component of the sexual constitution while the other is concerned to suppress it.

(h) An hysterical symptom may come to represent various unconscious non-sexual impulses, but it cannot dispense with some sexual significance.

"Among these various definitions the seventh [g] is the one that most exhaustively presents the essence of an hysterical symptom as the realizing of an unconscious phantasy and, together with the eighth [h], recognizes the proper significance of the sexual factor."

It is noteworthy that Freud had as long ago as 1896, in a letter to his friend Fliess, clearly indicated the structure of hysterical symptoms as a *compromise* between opposing forces, sexual and non-sexual,[2] and a year later had given a full account of the significant part played by phantasies in this connection.[3] In the manuscript in which he discussed them he concluded that phantasies have the function of either blocking the earliest memories by replacing them or of refining them into a more acceptable form. Incidentally, he had also pointed out the analogy between infantile amnesia and hysterical amnesia.[4]

(2) In 1909 Freud wrote a section for Otto Rank's *Myth of the Birth of the Hero*,[5] which was not reprinted separately until the *Gesammelte Schriften* were issued in 1924. It concerns a particular phantasy which, because of its sexual nature, will be considered in the

chapter on the Libido Theory. But it has also its clinical importance, since the phantasy in question is more pronounced in neurotics.

(3) In the same year Freud wrote by request a paper for the first number of the *Zeitschrift für Psychotherapie und medizinische Psychologie*, a new periodical that Moll was founding. Such requests were evidence of the growing recognition of Freud's work. Freud had previously given an account of the theme to the Vienna Society on April 8, 1908, where it was discussed. The paper was on "Hysterical Attacks." [6] It is one of his neatly polished papers where every sentence contains something of note. He began by comparing the phantasies, which such attacks always represent, with day and night dreams, and pointed out that the same repression makes use of similar mechanisms: condensation, multiple identification, reversal in the chronology, and here also the special one of the antagonistic reversal of the motor innervation. If such attacks are traced to their ultimate origin one can determine a regular order of development: (a) Auto-erotic activity with no ideational accompaniment; (b) The same, accompanied by a phantasy which expresses itself in the action; (c) Renunciation of the action while the phantasy is retained; (d) Repression of the phantasy, but its disguised recurrence in an hysterical attack; (e) Disguised repetition in motor form of the erotic act.

Contrary to the usual neurological teaching he maintained confidently that the passage of urine and biting of the tongue may occur in such attacks, which therefore cannot be distinguished from epilepsy by such manifestations.

(4) In the following year a short paper of a similar kind was also written for an occasion, as part of a special number which a medical periodical organized in honor of Prof. Königstein, an old friend of Freud's. Writing to Ferenczi, Freud remarked that it had no value [a] since it was only written for an occasion,[7] but we might well differ from his opinion here.

Since Königstein was a well-known ophthalmologist it was appropriate that Freud should contribute something in that field, and he chose the topic of the psychoanalytic conception of "Psychogenic Visual Disturbance." [8] Actually he confined himself to the one example of amaurosis, hysterical blindness. In such cases there is an unusual repression of the wish to see forbidden things. There is probably also an unusual degree of erotization of the eye itself, so that the other non-erotic functions of the eye get involved in the repression. Freud illustrated the theme from the legend of Lady Godiva and re-

[a] *Es taugt nichts.*

marked that this was not the first occasion when neurosis throws light on mythology. Most of the paper is an expository apologia for the general psychoanalytic point of view, a performance Freud always carried out with great skill.

(5) On April 20 and 27, 1910, there was a discussion in the Vienna Psycho-Analytical Society on "Suicide in Children." It was afterwards published as a brochure.[9] A paper was read by Professor Oppenheim, a teacher of Latin, and Freud opened the discussion. He remarked that schools, in fulfilling their function of weaning children from their early family life, often erred by exposing them too brusquely to the full severities of adult life, and were often not tolerant enough concerning the right of immature individuals to dally in certain stages of development—even if they are of an unpleasant kind. In closing the discussion he admitted that little light had been thrown on the fundamental causes of suicide: on whether disappointed libido alone was sufficient to account for it or whether there was some renunciation of life on the part of the ego (the last remark seems to foreshadow Freud's later idea of a death instinct). We could only progress further with the problem after a full study had been made of melancholia and prolonged grief. Seven years later Freud himself carried this out.[b]

(6) A little later three evenings of the Society were devoted to discussing the problems of masturbation. This sexual topic will be described in the appropriate chapter.[c]

(7) In 1911 Freud related in the recently founded *Zentralblatt für Psychoanalyse* two examples of patients unwittingly betraying repressed incest phantasies.[10] In both cases they did so by ascribing their idea to the physician.

(8) On October 30, 1912, Freud gave a short account of a case history to theVienna Society. It has not yet been published anywhere. It was a severe psychotic case in a young married woman and after four months' analysis a dream, unfortunately not recorded, revealed the main features of her infantile sexual activities. Freud took the data from the case to argue against Adler's "masculine protest" explanation of the neuroses and to expound its foundation in ideas of castration, as with the "inferiority complex." He made the significant remark: "In the male a castration complex almost regularly stirs the wish to be female."

(9) We now come to two papers of a more weighty nature. One of

* See Chapter 13, No. 8.
* See Chapter 12, No. 16.

them, published in 1912 and entitled "Types of Onset of Neurosis," [11] dealt with the various ways in which a person may become afflicted with a neurosis. To clarify the problem Freud classified the factors in four groups, although he admitted that pure examples of each are exceptional.

(a) The simplest type is where the neurosis comes about as the result of a more or less sudden libidinal privation.

(b) It may come about not through any such change in the outer world but because of the person's failure to meet certain demands of reality which would lead to satisfaction.

(c) The infantile fixation may be so strong that the person never really emerges from childhood and so can never be said to have enjoyed a period of mental health.

(d) In this type there has been no change in the outer world, no special new demands from it, no special infantile fixation, but a purely internal, probably organically determined, change in the libidinal economy, such as always happens at puberty or during the climacterium. What is common to all types is a damming up of the libido beyond the capacity of the ego to cope with it.

Freud remarked here that neuroses are not due to the appearance of any extraneous "cause of disease," and that there is no qualitative difference between healthy and neurotic people since they are both faced with the same task—the control of libido.

Freud animadverted against the prevailing habit of dividing the aetiological factors in the neuroses into endogenous and exogenous. The true state of affairs is more complex and is best described as a certain psychical situation which can be reached in a variety of ways with the different factors varying in their relative strength.

It is interesting to note that Freud had foreshadowed many of these points in another connection in an earlier paper.[d] [12] A simple way of stating the whole matter is that neurosis comes about whenever, for whatever reason, reality is felt to be unbearable.[13]

(10) The other paper was also on the subject of aetiology: "The Predisposition to Obsessional Neurosis." [14] It was read at the Munich Congress in September 1913. Freud related an interesting case where a phase of hysterical symptoms was followed by a quite distinct obsessional neurosis, and used it to illustrate the difference in the aetiology of the two affections. This was one of the several occasions where Freud admitted a previous error: in this case his former belief that hysteria was the result of passive experiences in infancy, obses-

---

[d] Chapter 13, No. 2.

sional neurosis of active ones.[15] He now correlated the latter condition with either a fixation at, or a regression to, a special stage in the development of the libido which he here described for the first time. This was the now well-recognized "anal-sadistic phase," a characteristic pregenital one. In his opinion, although an object-relation is present in this phase, there is as yet little differentiation between male and female.

The paper contains a number of stimulating thoughts which other workers have since extended. For instance, Freud suggested that among those who subsequently suffer from an obsessional neurosis, the development of the ego, including intellectual capacity, proceeds ahead of the libidinal development. He then wondered whether this is not an important characteristic of mankind in general, which might account for its moral nature. His reason for this idea was the evidence that in the infant's development hate comes before love, so that moral reactions against it are brought about to make friendly relations possible.

In the same year Freud published two short papers containing material from his clinical practice.

(11) One was entitled "Two Lies Told by Children," [16] He began with the rather cynical remark that it is understandable how children lie in imitation of adult lies, but he was concerned here with more complex and pathetic situations where a child is impelled by a deep inner conflict to lie and thus to impair its relationship with the persons he loves. He related in his unemotional manner two stories which were really tragedies. In each case the child had been compelled from internal difficulties to have recourse to lying in a fashion that proved fateful for all the later development. Freud pointed out how such suffering and subsequent mental injury could be spared children if only psychological understanding of their complex minds—such as he himself displayed here—were more widespread.

(12) The other paper was a small collection of scattered analytical examples from his daily work.[17] One was of a patient who was sensitive about anyone gazing at her feet. It was traced to an experience in childhood when she had tried to imitate her brother's way of urinating, wet her feet and got heartily laughed at by her brother. In another section Freud comments on unexpected self-criticisms on the part of a patient. This comes either from identification with someone else whom the patient dare not criticize or from covering a wish to boast about some other quality, such as when a woman, secretly proud of her charms, deplores a supposed lack of intelligence. Then

Freud makes the important statement that when symptoms are alluded to in a dream the rest of that dream will contain some explanation of the cause of the symptom.

In 1912 Professor Krauss of Berlin invited Freud to write the sections on "Hysteria" and the "Obsessional Neurosis" for a new comprehensive encyclopedia of medicine he and Professor Brugsch, also of Berlin, were planning.[18] Freud told us we were to keep this news a dead secret—I can't think why. But he said that it made psychoanalysis at last an official part of general medicine—"extremely official,"[e][19] and it evidently meant a great deal to him. Abraham reported that Krauss was friendlily disposed towards psychoanalysis.[20] There was apparently no urgency about writing the articles for such a huge encyclopedia which would take many years. In October, however, Freud was disturbed at finding, perhaps from some prospectus, that a Berlin neurologist, Kutzinski, had also been invited to write articles on the same two subjects.[21] It seemed a very odd and irregular arrangement, and Freud wrote to Professor Brugsch, who was concerned with the details of preparing the work, to ask what it meant and how he pictured the co-operation between the two writers on the same subjects. Getting no reply he wrote again twelve days later, this time in a registered letter. There was still no reply, so he wrote to Krauss. This brought a rather vague letter from Brugsch saying that various theories of hysteria had to be represented, hence the choice of two men.[22] Abraham surmised that Krauss had been influenced by Professor Bonhöffer, who was antagonistic to psychoanalysis and whose Assistant was Kutzinski.[23] Freud now made two proposals to Brugsch and asked him to choose between them. Either he would withdraw altogether or the two topics could be left to Kutzinski and Freud would write an extensive one entitled "A Psychoanalytical Presentation of the Psychoneuroses."[24] Brugsch accepted the latter proposal, and Freud wrote to announce the good news.[25] All now seemed in order and Freud set his mind to the task, which he had never before attempted, of giving a really comprehensive account of the whole subject, almost of his life's work. His mind was preoccupied about that time with the difficulties concerning Jung, and it was only in the summer of 1914 that he got down to the actual writing. Towards the end of July of that year he wrote saying he was glad he was going to be undisturbed in his holiday at Karlsbad, either by van Emden or Ferenczi who often spent that time with him, since he needed the isolation to concentrate on the difficult task in front of him.[26] In that week, however, the

[e] *höchst offiziell.*

Great War broke out and occupied all thoughts. Four months later he was informed that the manuscript, which was due to be delivered by April 1, 1915, would not be wanted, doubtless because of the war, before the end of that year or the beginning of 1916.[27]

Since the matter was no longer urgent Freud appears to have postponed it. The stimulus it had given to his thoughts, however, in the endeavor to think out all the fundamental problems involved must have been what brought about his great spurt of activity that lasted until the end of 1915 and led him to compose the twelve important essays on theory.[f] So Krauss' invitation had a valuable sequel.

What then happened about the promised article is a little obscure. We are not even sure whether it ever got written; it was certainly never published. The two articles in question were written by Kutzinski.[28] In the middle of 1915 Freud reported that he had just finished writing a "review of the transference neuroses," [29] but whether this refers to the article in question or to one of the essays on theory which he afterwards destroyed is not clear. Late in 1917 there are several somewhat sarcastic allusions to Krauss,[30] to whom he was then writing on behalf of Abraham's application for a docentship, and a remark about "the course taken by the negotiations for the Encyclopedia" which has a sinister ring. Then, soon after the war, Freud mentioned to Abraham that Krauss and Brugsch had reminded him of his promise to write the essay in question, but he was going to ask them to give him more space than the 48 pages they allotted; they wanted it by the spring (of 1920).[31] Six months later they asked him to sign a contract binding him to deliver the manuscript by the autumn. This compelled a decision and he told Abraham he was inclined to give up the whole plan; he could only summarize the *Introductory Lectures*, since to re-write the whole subject was a task that could no longer hold his interest.[32] As I have suggested, the publications of 1915-1917 represented the end of an epoch; he was now full of the new ideas he was developing. We may, therefore, feel pretty sure that the essay never got written, or at least never got further than a first draft.

Freud now proposed that Abraham undertake the task for him, to which with some misgiving he consented. I know no more about the story, but surmise that the Editors decided it must be Freud or no one. So the "highly official" incorporation of psychoanalysis in an authoritative medical encyclopedia did not come to pass. In 1920, however, this was a far smaller matter than it would have been in 1912.

[f] See Chapter 13, p. 316.

In the early part of the war Freud wrote three more important papers that may be called clinical.

(13) The first was a description of an interesting case of paranoia in a woman of thirty.[33] He had previously come to the conclusion that paranoia was dependent on repressed homosexuality, but had not enough experience to claim it as a general rule. He said in a letter that he had learned this from Fliess,[34] without mentioning whether directly or on reflection. Only two years before that letter he had presented a case of female paranoia before the Vienna Society and then did not mention the matter of homosexuality.[g]

The present case, indeed, appeared to contradict the conclusion, since the patient's complaint was that a man, her lover, was trying to harm her. The cautious Freud, however, was not satisfied with her first account and went deeper into the history. He then found that the real persecutor was after all a woman, an obvious mother substitute, and that the man, whom she suspected of being in love with the old woman, derived his pathological significance from that source. Freud took the opportunity of pointing out some delicate mechanisms of displacement which he had found characteristic of paranoia.

(14) In the same year, 1915, there was an original paper of general as well as clinical interest which bore the title of "Some Character-Types Met With in Psychoanalytic Work." [35] There are three of them, which he entitled respectively: "Exceptions"; "Those Wrecked by Success"; "Criminals from a Sense of Guilt." They will be described in a later chapter.[h]

(15) In 1916 there was one short paper, entitled "A Connection between a Symbol and a Symptom." [36] Analysts had been familiar with the symbolic meaning that a head—e.g. in dreams of beheading —or a hat may have in dreams, where they can represent the idea of the male genital. Freud here discussed some symptoms in which the same symbolism is used. One was the case of an obsessional patient whose head, laid in the groove of a small pillow artificially arranged to imitate the female genital organ, had this same meaning. Then there are the obsessional patients who weave the most complicated meanings into the simple act of greeting by taking off one's hat.

(16) We have now to mention two works that appeared in 1917, both of which are considered more fully in other chapters, but which have important bearings on clinical work. The first of them was the last section of the *Introductory Lectures*, that devoted to the study of

<hr>

[g] November 21, 1906.

[h] Chapter 14, No. 27.

the psychoneuroses.[1] It is the widest review Freud ever wrote of this huge subject, and, although cast in a didactic form, it probably followed on the lines he had intended to write for the Krauss encyclopedia. At the end of the course of lectures Freud expressed his great dissatisfaction with the way he had performed the task. This one would ascribe not so much to any personal inhibition as to his recognition of the number of problems in this field which were as yet imperfectly solved. He evidently felt that the attempt to present a really comprehensive review of the subject was still premature, and would doubtless have continued to feel so throughout the rest of his life. Increased knowledge only led to the discovery of still further problems whose existence had been previously unrecognized.

This work is none the less the best introduction we possess to the study of the psychoneuroses. More than that, it contains a number of considerations, for instance on the subject of anxiety, which were at the time fresh contributions.

(17) The other of the two works is that on "Mourning and Melancholia." [37] Freud himself regarded this essay as one in his series on metapsychology, so we shall consider it in the chapter on Theory. But it has obvious clinical bearings, and it is still the best account available of the psychology of manic-depressive insanity. It is the light Freud threw here on the inner nature of the various forms of pathological depression that has since opened the way to therapeutic successes with this painful malady.

In the great World War attention was widely drawn to the problem of "war neuroses," then more often called "shell shock" or "war shock," and the many thousands of cases came to have even purely military aspects. For the first couple of years the neurological view prevailed that the condition was simply due to minute disturbances in the cortex of the brain, but clinical investigations gradually revealed a more complex state of affairs. The occurrences of such neuroses among soldiers who had not been near the battle front made this conclusion certain. It was often possible to perceive a connection between the neurosis and mental conflicts involving unavowed motives. This was an essential part of psychoanalytical theory, and it might have been supposed that those who had been unfriendly to the subject would now admit that if one part of the theory was correct it was possible that the other also, namely the sexual aetiology, might be correct. Instead of which it became customary to announce that,

______

[1] See Chapter 8, No. 7.

since sexual factors were not obvious, whereas the aetiological factor of war strain mostly was, Freud's theory had been actually disproved.

Abraham, Ferenczi and myself, although out of contact with one another, came quite independently to very similar conclusions concerning the psychological nature of these war neuroses. They differed from the more familiar ones of peacetime, in which there are conflicts over libidinal attachments to other people ("object-libido"), in that the internal conflicts affected the narcissistic (self-love) aspects of the libido.

(18) Our contributions were published at the end of the war in a collective brochure,[38] for which Freud wrote a Preface.[39] He said he would not have written it but for Ferenczi and Jones.[40] The volume is easily available, but I will add here a passage from a letter to Ferenczi, and a letter of more general interest to myself, which expound his views more fully. It is very noteworthy that although Freud had no personal experience whatever of such cases (except for the traumatic neuroses of peacetime) he showed a deeper insight into the nature of these conditions than any of us.

"27.X.1918

"Dear Friend,

". . . I am generally at present without ideas, but a few occur to me in the morning on waking. I will put at your disposal the last of these, to do with the traumatic war neuroses. Probably it is only a dream.

"It is a question of a conflict between two ego ideals, the customary one and the one the war has compelled the person to build. The latter is concerned with relations to new objects (superior officers and comrades) and so is equivalent to the cathexis of an object; it might be called a choice of object not consonant with the ego.[j] Thus a conflict can come about just as in the ordinary psychoneuroses. The theory of it would be that a *new* ego has been developed on the basis of a libidinal cathexis of an object, and the former ego strives to displace it. There is thus a struggle within the ego instead of between ego and libido, but fundamentally that comes to the same thing.

"There is a certain parallelism with melancholia, where also a new ego has been instituted, but no ideal—merely a new ego on the basis of an object-cathexis that has been abandoned.

"Yours
"Freud"

[j] I.e. the previous ego.

"Feb. 18th, 1919

"Dear Jones,*

". . . I too enjoy our correspondence sincerely after so long a break of intercourse. Your last letter touched so many points of interest that I am at a loss which to begin with.

"As for good old Putnam I have acted exactly as your letter proposed. Nr 2 will contain a short notice of his decease, now rectified by your giving the date, and will promise a full article on his life and merits accompanied by his photo, already reproduced by our care. You are the fittest man to do the article. Don't forget to mention how he resisted Adler's temptings. . . .

"My health is all but perfect. I am growing an old man and am prepared to die a poor man. Martin's captivity is pressing hard on my spirits. Don't you know anyone who is traveling to Genoa where he is detained?

"I derived great pleasure from the perusal of your new Papers in that second edition. Sachs is busy with the "Symbolism," the "Anal Traits" (to appear in No. 2) have been revised in the proofs today, and the paper on war-shock is remitted to the translator as a highly valuable addition to the *"Discussion über Kriegsneurosen"* which will be given out as the first publication of the new *Internationale Psychoanalytische Verlag.* I took the responsibility to decide in this way as we have not time to wait for the return of letters. It is clear and clever and may well have merited its success in England. The first part, the theory of the *"Ichkonflikt"* is congruous with my utterances on this matter at the last meeting of the *Psa Vereinigung.* Later on it seems you are losing the contact with the item of the "traumatic neurosis." What you say on the relation to narcissistic anxiety is excellent, hits the point, but it is too short and may not sufficiently impress the reader. Let me propose to you the following formula: First consider the case of the traumatic neurosis of peace. It is a narcissistic affection like dementia praecox, etc. The mechanism may be guessed. Anxiety is a protection against shock (*Schreck*). Now the condition of the Tr. Neurosis seems to be that the soul had no time to recur to this protection and is taken by the trauma unprepared. Its *"Reizschutz"* [k] is overrun and the principal and primary function of keeping off excessive quantities of *"Reiz"* [l] frustrated. The narcissistic libido is given out in the shape of the signs of Anxiety. This is the mechanism of every case of primary repression; a traumatic neurosis

[k] Defense against stimuli.
[l] Stimulation.

is thus to be found at the bottom of every case of "Transference Neurosis."

"Now in the case of war there is the conflict between the habitual and the fresh warlike ideal. The first is subjugated, but when the "shell" arrives this older ego understands that it may be killed by the ways of the Alter Ego. Its opposition leaves this new master of the ego weak and powerless, and thus it, the Ego as a whole, comes under the aetiology of the traumatic neurosis. The difference between peace and war is that with the former the ego is strong but surprised, with the latter it is prepared but weakened. In this way the war neurosis is a case of internal narcissistic conflict within the ego, somewhat analogous to the mechanism of Melancholy, exposed in the 4th Volume of the *Schriften* I sent you by care of Emden. But I have made no analysis of a case of war shock.

"Your intention to purge the London Society of the Jungish members is excellent.

"Your plans about the English Journal seem reasonable enough. But the matter cannot be discussed by letters. Try by all means to meet Rank in Switzerland in the *first* half of March. He cannot postpone this journey any longer.

"To be sure it would be best, nay too good, if we could expect you here in Vienna in the course of April.

"Take my best love and let us look forward to a better future.

"Yours truly
"Freud"

. . .

11

CHAPTER

Case Histories

Freud published six lengthy case histories, all in the years at present under consideration. No complete account of an analyzed case can be published; it would occupy many volumes and would be quite unreadable. But these six essays of Freud's far excel, both in presentation and in original content, anything any other analyst has attempted. They are in the first rank of the classics of psychoanalytical literature.

I

Fragment of an Analysis of a Case of Hysteria[1]

The first of them has already been mentioned in another connection[2] and some account given of the circumstances under which it was completed. It was the well-known "Case of Dora," as it is generally called. The essay was rightly termed "A Fragment," since the imperfect analysis lasted only eleven weeks, at the end of 1900.[3] But there is no analyst who would not be proud to have unraveled so much of a difficult case in that short time.

To the unusual story of its publication I related earlier,[4] which has since been described in fuller detail by James Strachey,[5] I can now add a curious detail which has just come to light. In 1909 Freud told Ferenczi that Brodmann, the Editor of the *Journal für Psychologie und Neurologie*, had refused to publish the Dora case.[6] We know that when in January 1901, he offered the paper to Ziehen and Wernicke, the Editors of the *Monatsschrift für Psychiatrie und Neurologie* in which it was ultimately published, it was immediately accepted, and when Freud sent them the manuscript in the following

June it was with the expectation it would appear that autumn. He must then have asked for it back and kept it for another four years before he could bring himself to run the risk of being charged with professional indiscretion. It is entirely mysterious why he should have offered it to another periodical after it had been already accepted. The only suggestion that occurs to me is that he had doubts whether Ziehen and Wernicke, both severe critics of his work, would accept it after really reading the manuscript; he had indeed wondered how long they would go on allowing him to "lay cuckoo's eggs" in their nest.[7] And if it aroused their disapproval, it would jeopardize *The Psychopathology of Everyday Life* which he was about to send them. So one may perhaps surmise that he sent it to Brodmann as a second string between that January and June. Then after his refusal, and after the safety of the *Psychopathology* had been assured (he corrected the proofs of this in May), he could let Ziehen have the manuscript. It then may well have been Ziehen's expressing some doubts about the propriety of publishing such indiscretions, combined with Brodmann's outright refusal, that made him return the manuscript to its drawer for another four years.

The story itself of the case reads rather like a novel, though Freud remarked that were he making a novel out of it he would, for aesthetic reasons, omit various disturbing issues which show how much more complicated life is than art which necessarily abstracts. It concerned two unhappily married couples, one being Dora's parents. Her mother developed a *Hausfrau* neurosis as an indirect form both of gratification for herself and as revengeful discomfort for her husband. He solved his situation by a liaison with his friend's wife. The lady enriched her life by indulging in a warm, but platonic, homosexual relationship with Dora. Dora therefore had two reasons to be jealous of her father's connection, jealousy both of him and of the other lady. The latter's husband, here called Herr K., was enamored of Dora, paid her attention for a couple of years, and then when she was eighteen years old, began a speech intended to avow his love for her and the hope of marrying her after obtaining a divorce, which would not have been difficult. Dora, however, struck him in the face, fled, complained to her parents and clamored for the relationship with the other couple to be entirely broken off.

Dora was a disagreeable creature who consistently put revenge before love; it was the same motive that led her to break off the treatment prematurely, and to retain various hysterical symptoms, both bodily and mental.

Freud had, incidentally, previously treated the father for a luetic affection of the nervous system, and he very firmly gave it as his opinion that parental syphilis is an important predisposing factor to neurosis in the offspring. This is one of the respects in which further observations have not borne him out.

Besides the study of the particular case the essay contains a great number of interesting expositions of Freud's views on various psychopathological topics: a description of the various motives in hysteria,[8] its organic basis in the form of what he called "bodily compliance," [9] the negative relation of neurotic symptoms to repressed sexual perversions,[10] and so on.

Freud's main object, however, in publishing the case was to illustrate the value the interpretation of dreams has for analytic treatment. Indeed he asserted that unless one had learned this art one could not hope to penetrate into the structure of a neurosis. Here two dreams are related and analyzed as far as the resistance of the patient would allow. They afford brilliant illustrations of Freud's skill even at that relatively early stage of his work, of his delicate penetration and the bold, perhaps not invariably accurate, use he made of his unusual powers of intuition. The analysis of the dreams revealed in Dora sexual love for her father, for Herr K. and for his wife, all of which had been so repressed as to be totally unknown to her. They also disclosed the extraordinarily complicated interplay of various emotions besides those of love, especially hatred, disgust and jealousy.

This first case history of Freud's has for years served as a model for students of psychoanalysis, and although our knowledge has greatly progressed since then, it makes today as interesting reading as ever. It was the first of Freud's post-neurological writings I had come across, at the time of its publication, and I well remember the deep impression the intuition and the close attention to detail displayed in it made on me. Here was a man who not only listened closely to every word his patient spoke but regarded each such utterance as every whit as definite and as in need of correlation as the phenomena of the physical world. At the present day it is hard to convey what an amazing event it was for anyone to take the data of psychology so seriously. Yet that it should less than half a century after seem a commonplace is a measure of the revolution effected by one man.

Dora's neurosis was, of course, not dispelled by such a short treatment, but she never resumed it. She married, as Freud mentioned later,[11] and died a few years ago in New York.

In the second edition of *The Psychopathology of Everyday Life*

(1907) Freud related an incident which illustrated not only the point he was making there concerning strict determinism, but also how his dislike of compromise and concessions could conflict with his natural considerateness for others. He was lecturing on the Dora case and one of the two women in the audience (Dora Teleki) had that name. His sense of delicacy made him cast about for another name to apply to the patient whose very intimate sexual life he was about to describe. But without realizing it at the time he fell out of the frying pan into the fire by automatically using another name, this time taken from the surname of the second woman in the audience.[12]

II
Analysis of a Phobia in a Five-Year-Old Boy[13]

The second case history was very different and perhaps equally surprising, since it was the first published account of a child analysis. It is commonly referred to as the "Little Hans Case." The parents of the five-year-old boy had for some years been adherents of Freud—in fact among the first. Freud had treated the wife before she was married, and the husband had been an early attendant at Freud's lectures. It was the father, not Freud, who conducted the analysis. Freud himself had only one interview with the boy during it, but he had frequent consultations with the father, who consented to the case being published.[14] Freud had two years previously published a short account of two aspects of the case. In one, where the boy is called Herbert, it is concerned with the sexual curiosity of children;[15] in the other, written a year later, with a three-year-old boy's correctly divining the truth about childbirth from observing the pregnancy of his mother.[16] The present essay is a long one, extending to 134 pages, and there are some *longueurs* in the course of the father's stenographic protocol, but the running comment Freud made, and still more his concluding chapter, give it more than an historical interest.

The historical interest itself is certainly great, for it was not only the first therapeutic application of psychoanalysis to a young child, but also the first opportunity of checking by direct observation of a child the novel conclusions Freud had reached about infantile development from his analyses of adult patients. He had from these studies drawn inferences about the general occurrence of the Oedipus complex in infancy, of castration fears, and the significance of extra-genital erotogenic zones of the body. All these were clearly illustrated in the analysis of this five-year-old boy.

The case itself, which need not be detailed here, was one of a phobia that soon supervened on an anxiety state that developed at the age of four and three quarters, some nine months after the birth of a baby sister. The phobia was the impossibility of going out of doors lest a horse there should bite him. Incidentally Freud remarks on how difficult it often is to ascertain the precise content of a phobia. The repression in the neurosis may extend to the symptom itself, which becomes surrounded by an aura of vagueness. Before one can cure it one has to come to close quarters with it, to be clear about its precise nature. The result of this preliminary step is often to exacerbate the patient's distress in a way that to the uninformed brings discredit on the treatment. It was not, however, a difficulty that arose in this particular case.

The father used the unorthodox method of questioning in detail and often had to help the child by putting into words what he was finding hard to express. Freud, therefore, had to meet the obvious objection that the conclusions reached were simply due to the father's suggestions. Freud commented on the curious change that had taken place in respect to the importance of suggestion. In his early days, 1887 to 1889, he had, in insisting on the importance of suggestion, been opposed to prevailing medical opinion, and now this had gone to the opposite extreme when everything possible was attributed to it. Actually he had been conducting a little experiment on the matter. He had refrained from telling the father of important connections he had himself foreseen, so that the father had to flounder until the child himself made them clear. Then there was a phase when the child brought out important ideas which came as a surprise to both the father and Freud. Altogether Freud behaved with extreme caution, and repeatedly urged avoiding interpretations until further material be forthcoming. To one's surprise he even refrained from advising the father to enlighten the boy on the male role in procreation, although he said he would have done so himself.

In later years Freud was to postulate a phallic phase in development, one in which both boys and girls imagine the sex difference as one between presence or absence of penis rather than in terms of two sets of organs;[17] it is still a much disputed concept. He might have quoted in his support the present case. Little Hans was convinced that all living beings possessed a penis—it was his distinction between animate and inanimate matter—and on inspecting his baby sister could only hope that, although her "widdler" was very small, it would grow. Freud here could not resist a jibe at the philosophers of the Wundt school who insisted that consciousness was the one and only distinguishing criterion between mental and physical, and who, when faced with data from which one is bound to infer the activity of mental processes in spite of complete unawareness of them, fall back on the evasive description of them as "subconscious";[a] to which Freud dryly remarked: "The widdler will grow." The *total absence* of consciousness could not be admitted.

Freud classified the "Little Hans Case" as one of anxiety hysteria, a term he had recently recommended to Stekel when the latter was writing a book on anxiety states. The therapeutic result was excellent. It must have been greatly favored by the little patient's personality; he was an exceptionally attractive and intelligent child and fundamentally healthy-minded. He was genuinely fond of his father and had a strong positive transference to the Professor, who he was convinced could relieve him of his trouble if only his father wrote fully enough to him. Freud was not only satisfied with the immediate results of the analysis in dispelling the phobia, but expressed the hope that it would benefit the boy in his later life. This prediction was fully borne out. One of the pleasantest surprises in Freud's life was when fourteen years later a tall and sturdy young man called on him and presented himself with the words: *"Ich bin der kleine Hans"* (I am little Hans). What puzzled him, however, was that all memory of the analysis had completely vanished. All that remained was a faint memory of the holiday in Gmunden where an episode had occurred that was the starting-point of the neurosis.

In spite of the success of the experiment it is very remarkable that for once Freud refrained from making a generalization. Instead of perceiving that a new and most fruitful field for psychoanalytic therapy had been opened up, and that from its very prophylactic nature child analysis must hold out great possibilities, he evidently regarded the case as a lucky exception, one from which no general therapeutic conclusions could be drawn. In his opening paragraph he wrote: "No one else, in my opinion, could possibly have prevailed on the child to make such avowals. The special knowledge by means of which the father was able to interpret the remarks made by his five-year-old son was indispensable, and without it the technical difficulties in the way of conducting psychoanalysis with so young a child would have been insuperable. It was only because the authority of a father and of a physician were united in a single person, and because in him both affectionate care and scientific interest were combined, that it was

* *dunkelbewusst.*

possible *in this one instance*[b] to apply the method to a use to which it would not otherwise have lent itself." The brilliant successes of child analysis since then, and indeed inaugurated by the study of this very case, prove that here Freud's customary insight had deserted him. It seems a curious thing to say of the very man who explored the child's mind to an extent that had never before been possible that he should nevertheless have retained some inhibitions about coming to too close quarters with it. It is as if some inner voice had said "Thus far and no farther." We remarked earlier[18] on the slowness with which Freud was willing to admit the existence of infantile sexuality, particularly in its allo-erotic aspects, and to the end of his life he displayed certain reservations about the limits of what it was possible to accomplish in child analysis and the exploration of the more remote and hidden regions of the earliest mental processes.

There are many other noteworthy statements in connection with the "Little Hans Case." One concerns the frequency with which analysis of the boy's spontaneous play was used in interpreting and understanding what was going on in his mind. This feature was seized on later by Hermine von Hug-Hellmuth, and then far more profitably by Melanie Klein, as a cardinal device in the application of psycho-analysis with young children.

Freud made two important remarks about castration fears. One added in 1923 was that they could arise without there ever having been any direct threats of the sort.[19] The other was his opinion that they constituted the deepest source of anti-Semitism, because of the Jewish practice of circumcision.[20]

A sentence that has a bearing on Freud's various views concerning instincts is that "the thirst for knowledge seems to be inseparable from sexual curiosity." [21]

A few bisexual phantasies of the little patient gave occasion to a general excursus on the topic of homosexuality.[22] Freud expressed the opinion that there was no such thing as a homosexual instinct (*Trieb*) and that the essence of the condition lay simply in a displacement in the sex of the object. This he accounted for by a fixation on what he would later call the phallic phase, the belief that the existence of a penis was necessary to physical integrity.

The explanation that in this case the morbid anxiety had resulted from repression of the boy's aggressive tendencies, hostility towards his father and sadism towards his mother, accorded, Freud admitted,

[b] Here underlined.

with Adler's recent postulate of a special aggressive instinct, and yet he declined to follow Adler in this conclusion. He thought Adler had gone wrong in selecting a feature, aggressiveness, common to all instinctual life, and then regarding it as the one and only key to the understanding of all psychological problems. It was only many years later that Freud himself postulated an instinct of the kind, one, however, that differed in essential respects from Adler's, and which was inferred on quite different grounds.[c]

At the close Freud discussed whether the bringing of repressed complexes into consciousness (perhaps especially with children) can be harmful. He compared his opponents' warnings with the advice Dogberry in *Much Ado About Nothing* gives his constables to have nothing to do with such rabble as thieves and housebreakers who are not fit company for honest men. And in a footnote there is a further tilt at them: he wonders where they get the knowledge they are so confident about, that sexuality plays no part in the causation of the neuroses; if they consider it improper to allow patients to talk about such matters then their only source of information must be confined to Freud's own writings.

Soon after the case was published in the first number of the new *Jahrbuch*, Freud, in answering a letter of mine, wrote: "I am glad you see the importance of *Klein* Hans. I never got a finer insight into a child's soul." [23]

III

Notes on a Case of Obsessional Neurosis [24]

The third essay in this series is much more than a case history. Basing himself on a condensed and somewhat fragmentary account of a difficult case Freud discussed at length the peculiar features of the puzzling condition termed obsessional neurosis. Freud expressed the opinion that for the study of unconscious processes the investigation of this neurosis was more instructive than that of hysteria.

The patient was a lawyer nearly thirty years of age. He had suffered from obsessional impulses and fears since early childhood, but they had become more severe in the past four years. Naturally they had greatly impeded his progress in life, both professionally and personally. Some of the current symptoms related to episodes that had occurred during recent army maneuvers in which he had taken part as a reserve officer. Because of a peculiar symptom in the case we used to refer to the patient as "The Man with the Rats."

* This will be discussed in Volume III.

The analysis began on October 1, 1907, and it lasted only eleven months. The result was brilliant and the patient was afterwards very successful in his life and work. Unfortunately he was killed during the First World War.

Freud's analytic powers showed at their best in his unraveling of this case. His delicate and ingenious interpretation and elucidation of the most tortuous mental processes, with their subtle play on words and thoughts, must evoke admiration and were hardly surpassed in any other of his writings.

After a month's treatment Freud took up two evenings at the Vienna Society, October 30 and November 6, in describing the early picture of the case. Federn has since published the minutes of those meetings.[25] In the discussion Freud again spoke and said among other things: "In general a human being cannot bear opposed extremes in juxtaposition, be they in his personality or in his reactions. It is this endeavor for unification that we call character. In regard to persons near to us extremely opposed emotions may be so strong as to become completely unbearable."

From time to time Freud reported to the Vienna Society on the progress of the analysis, the case being by then familiar to the members. Thus on November 20, 1907, he gave the explanation of the patient's extraordinary method of praying; on January 22, 1908, he described the solution of the pince-nez symptom; and finally, on April 8, 1908, the most complicated symptom of all, the obsession about rats that gave the case its familiar title.

Some six months after the treatment began Freud gave a much fuller account of the case, this time at the Salzburg Congress on April 27, 1908. There he could talk more freely about personal details in the case than he could write for publication, but it was of course not feasible to record it at the time.[d]

In an earlier chapter I have mentioned how, as a remarkable exception to his general custom, Freud preserved the day-to-day notes he made on this case during the first few months, and have pointed out the value of these for the study of Freud's technique at that period.[e]

Freud was engaged on writing his work on technique[f] when he found he could not complete this in time for the next volume of the *Jahrbuch*, so he suddenly had the idea of writing up the present case history for it,[26] nearly a year after the treatment had come to an end.

[d] See Chapter 2, p. 42.
[e] Chapter 9, p. 230.
[f] Chapter 9, No. 5.

It was not easy to compose, both because of the inevitable compression and because of the need for greater discretion in print. He said it taxed his powers of presentation to the full. "How bungling are our attempts to reproduce an analysis; how pitifully we tear to pieces these great works of art Nature had created in the mental sphere." [27] Nevertheless he finished the writing within a month and sent it off on July 7, 1909. He was still thoroughly dissatisfied with his effort and was much relieved when Jung praised it.[28] It was published in the second number of the first volume of the *Jahrbuch für psychoanalytische und psychopathologische Forschungen*, edited by Jung, which it was decided to found at the time of the Salzburg Congress.

In his opening remarks Freud made some modest apologies about the necessarily incomplete account he could give of the case, not only because of its extraordinary complexity but also for motives of discretion, the patient being well known in Vienna. He explained how it is that intimate secrets could be more easily mentioned than the trivial details of personality by which a person could be readily identified, and yet it is just these details that play an essential part in tracing the individual steps in an analysis.

Freud interspersed the account of the analysis with general comments, some of which will be mentioned presently, and then added a general theoretical chapter which is a contribution of the utmost value to our understanding of this baffling neurosis. When one compares it with the previous knowledge of the subject, which had been cast in purely intellectual terms, it can fairly be called a revolutionary progress.

A contrast was established between the form of repression operative in the obsessional neurosis and in hysteria. In the latter case amnesia of the important complexes is the rule, whether the subsequent symptoms are bodily or mental. More characteristic of the obsessional neurosis is the retention of the complex in consciousness, but with a dissociation of its affect. The starting-points of the neurosis, and even its motive, are mentioned by the patient in a tone of complete indifference, he being quite unaware of their significance. Strictly speaking, such patients do not suffer from obsessive ideas so much as from an obsessional type of thinking. Another typical mechanism, similar to one often employed in wit, is that of ellipse, in which an important intermediate thought is omitted. This breaks the connection between two thoughts and makes them incomprehensible.

Freud made clear a very useful distinction between the primary and the secondary defenses built up in the course of development of the neurosis. The neurotic process does not cease with the original dissociation, but continues in confused trains of thought where purely rational ideas are throughout intermingled with illogical ones characteristic of the unconscious. These secondary products Freud proposed to term "deliria," using the word in its French rather than its English sense. He gave beautiful examples of them from the present case.

These defenses account not only for the element of confusion in the symptoms themselves, making it very difficult for either the patient or the analyst to define them clearly, but also for the general uncertainty that pervades the patients' mental life. They give the impression of being actively attracted towards uncertainty, which is one reason why their obsessional thinking is so prone to occupy itself with topics that inherently contain elements of uncertainty, such as death and immortality. Freud noted two useful devices for ascertaining the precise form of the obsessional thoughts when they are clouded with uncertainty. One is that the text of them often occurs in dreams in an unaltered form. The other is that when several obsessive thoughts follow each other in time they are essentially identical in meaning, however unrelated they may appear, and that the first of them to occur is apt to be the original form.

Correspondingly, opportunities for certainty are avoided, and Freud here quoted the cases where clocks are abolished lest they introduce that element into a part of the patient's life.

The tendency to *doubting* is one of the two cardinal symptoms of the obsessional neurosis, the recurrent sense of *compulsion* being the other. Freud explained in a convincing fashion how one is the counterpart of the other. The doubting is the result not only of the defensive measures alluded to above, but more fundamentally to the deep ambivalence between love and hate that dominates the patient's life. Indeed, Freud saw in the sharpness with which these two emotional attitudes are separated one of the main characteristics of this neurosis. The doubting is in the last resort the patient's doubt about his capacity to love, so constantly is this interfered with by its opposite. Freud commented on the sadistic component of the hate, but it was only four years later that this was localized to the "anal-sadistic" tendencies in particular. The sense of compulsion comes from an attempt to over-compensate for the doubt and uncertainty. When an impulse manages, in however disguised a form, to find expression, then all the pent-up energy behind the inhibiting uncertainties lends it force and it *has* to be carried out at all costs; the alternative would be a state of unbearable anxiety. The impulses, mental or physical, always represent either an erotic act or the direct prohibition of one, and this is another reason for its compelling force. Highly characteristic of this neurosis is a regression from action to thought, and the act of thinking itself becomes sexualized so that it represents a part of the patient's sexual activity.

As commonly happened in Freud's specialized studies, he was able to select a particular feature that lent itself there to intensive investigation and then on the basis of that knowledge to throw light on more general human characteristics. Two striking examples of this procedure are to be found in the present essay. He had observed that obsessional patients are terrified of their thoughts—more strictly, of their wishes—coming true in the outer world, and that an important part of their minds believes in their power to do so. Thus to "think" of someone's death put that person in dire danger. Freud gave this belief the name of "Omnipotence of Thoughts." [g] It was not long, however, before he was able to correlate it with various primitive beliefs in the efficacy of magic[h] and also with corresponding attitudes in the unconscious mind. Thus there is a layer in all minds where this curious belief holds, though the expressions of it vary endlessly.

The other example is akin to this, Freud observed, and the present patient illustrated it in lavish measure, that obsessional patients are very superstitious, though usually in individual ways. They believe, for instance, that if they think of someone and meet him soon after that there is an inherent connection between the two facts. Freud related this tendency to the characteristic dissociation mentioned above that breaks the connection between two thoughts so as to blot out their significance. The "endopsychic perception," as he termed it, of the repressed connection becomes projected into the outer world, where significant connections are believed to be perceived in purely accidental occurrences. This feature, so highly developed in this particular neurosis, throws light on the nature and genesis of *superstition* in general.

The fact that the sense of smell was unusually highly developed in this particular patient gave Freud occasion for some remarks on a

---

[g] Freud remarked some years later[29] that it was from the "Man with the Rats" he first learned the significance of this feature. Indeed he said then that the actual term came from this patient, but in the original record, to be published shortly, it reads "Omnipotence of Wishes," which actually is the more accurate of the two phrases.

[h] See Chapter 14, No. 19.

theme that several times recurred in his writings: the importance of man having assumed the upright posture. Basing himself on what we know of the very great importance of the sense of smell in the sexual life of animals, but perhaps also influenced by the stress his friend Fliess laid on the same connection,[30] Freud suggested that the extensive deterioration of this sense in man resulting from his adoption of the upright posture must play a great part in predisposing human beings to neurotic disorders and, put more generally, in explaining why civilization singles out the sexual instinct for repression. We have here an example of how much less timid Freud was in indulging in speculation going beyond the actual data than he had been in his earlier years. It was a propensity to which he gave increased rein as he grew older. The idea itself he put forward here may, of course, prove in the future to be of considerable significance, but he certainly went beyond what we actually know.

Another theme on which Freud had something noteworthy to say was that of auto-erotism. He remarked that most neurotics are inclined to ascribe their troubles to adolescent masturbation, whereas most doctors are skeptical on the point. In his opinion the patients are nearer the truth, but they overlook two essential considerations. One is that such practices reanimate the effect of infantile masturbation—typically at the age of three to five—in which Freud saw the source of neurotic disturbance. The other is that masturbation is not to be regarded as a simple entity but as the expression of most diverse sexual components, including the phantasies they give rise to, so that any harmful effect is not to be ascribed to the simple act itself.

A little later he laid great stress on the regressive distortion brought about by adolescent masturbation. It leads to a re-interpretation of childhood memories in terms of the present, so that misdemeanors of that period are now given a sexual meaning they did not then have and, further, that simple auto-erotic activities of that period are now invested with an allo-erotic significance (personal love) through identifying them with the adolescent's present emotions. One cannot help sensing here a certain shyness on Freud's part, which we have remarked more than once, in attaching the full weight it deserves to infantile sexuality. He summed up his views at that time as follows: "The content of the sexual life of infancy consists in auto-erotic activity on the part of the dominant sexual components, in traces of object-love, and in the formation of that complex that deserves to be called *the nuclear complex of the neuroses;* it is the complex that comprises the child's earliest impulses, alike tender and hostile, towards its parents and brothers and sisters after its curiosity has been awakened—most often by the arrival of a new baby." [31]

IV

Psycho-Analytic Notes on an Autobiographical Account of a Case of Paranoia [32]

The fourth lengthy study, published in 1911, is remarkable inasmuch as Freud had never seen the patient. It is based almost entirely on an autobiographical book written by a patient who had partially recovered from a severe attack of paranoia. He was an intelligent man of the highest character who had risen to the position of *Senatspräsident* in Saxony; this title, it may be remarked incidentally, had nothing to do with any political senate, but meant that he was the presiding judge in a division of an Appeal Court. The theory of the condition, however, was in no wise derived from this particular study, but had been previously formulated by Freud from his clinical experience. The secret of paranoia he said he had learned from his friend Fliess. [33]

After having made his very important contributions to our knowledge of hysteria and obsessional neurosis Freud now turned to the still more obscure problems of the psychoses. He had fifteen years before made a tentative approach to the study of paranoia, though his conclusions then could only be stated in general psychological terms. [34] The present incursion into the field of psychiatry, however, was, in Freud's own words, the boldest he had yet undertaken. [35] He expected from it "scornful laughter or immortality or both." [36]

Freud had come across Schreber's autobiography in the summer of 1910, seven years after it had been published, and he discussed it at some length with Ferenczi in September during the holiday they spent together in Sicily. As soon as he got home he asked Dr. Stegmann of Dresden to send him any further particulars he could ascertain about Schreber's life, [37] and he continued to study the book that autumn. The essay itself he composed in the first part of December. [38]

Apart from its content, a certain historical interest is attached to this essay. It was during the discussion of it with Ferenczi to which I have just referred that the first signs of mutual dissatisfaction were visible, though this only became manifest some twenty years later. And it also proved to be the starting point of the differences between Freud and Jung. There were some slightly ambiguous passages, a not infrequent occurrence in Freud's writings, German being a less precise language than English or French, and Jung understood one of them in a sense Freud had not intended. On the basis of it he started a train of ideas without at first realizing that he was deviating from Freud's. So this essay had its fateful associations.

The patient, Dr. Schreber, had an attack of nervous disorder in 1885, and was for fifteen months in a clinic under the care of the distinguished psychiatrist, Professor Flechsig of Leipzig. At the end of this time he was discharged, full of gratitude and affection, completely cured, and he remained so for the next ten years. His condition during this attack was labeled "hypochondria."

Then, only three weeks after assuming his responsible position as *Senatspräsident*, he fell ill with a far more serious affection. This time he was under care for six years, when he was discharged in a perfectly normal mental state except for certain fixed delusions. This serious illness had two distinct phases. In the first one, which lasted about a year, he suffered from extremely distressing delusions of persecution. He imagined he was being the victim of horrible homosexual assaults at the hand of his former physician, Flechsig, who before long was aided and abetted by God Himself. In the second phase he had voluptuously accepted this destiny, but at the hands of God. This was accompanied by various religious and megalomanic ideas according to which he would become a feminine savior of the world and breed a new and superior race of human beings.

Freud's detailed unraveling of the many aspects of these ideas is extremely fascinating, and he achieved as complete a picture of their significance and genesis as was possible from the imperfect data available. The really valuable part of the essay, however, lies in a concluding chapter he wrote on the "Mechanism of Paranoia." Apart from the general theory he propounded, which will presently be sketched, the chapter contains a number of pregnant remarks, each of which would serve, as some already have, as a starting point for extensive investigations. As an example of these we may quote a single sentence in which he said, "Paranoia resolves, while hysteria condenses." [39] By that he meant that in hysteria each symptom is derived from a condensed accumulation of impressions relating to many aspects of a number of people towards whom the patient had had some important affective attitude. In paranoia, on the other hand, every single one of them becomes once more disentangled and presented as a separate idea or hallucination. This latter procedure is identical with that which Rank has shown to be characteristic of myths and legends, as also of various religions such as the Greek one, where a set of different feelings about one significant person or God is presented in the guise of many, each of which representing one of the feelings in question.

Another example is to be found in a footnote where Freud gave it as his opinion that any complete theory of paranoia must include one of the hypochondria which regularly accompanies it. He suggested that hypochondria bears the same relation to paranoia as the anxiety neurosis does to hysteria[40]—a thought-provoking remark.

Freud had inferred in all his cases a distinct connection between repressed homosexuality and paranoia, but since his experience was not an extensive one he asked Ferenczi and Jung to examine their clinical material to see if they could confirm his conclusion. This they were both able to do in an unqualified manner, but evidently Freud had himself felt pretty sure on the point. He had in fact informed Ferenczi of his conclusion about this essential connection in one of the first letters in their correspondence.[41]

He then gave a brilliant analysis of the way in which the four typical paranoic delusions are related to that underlying complex. They represent, of course, denials of it or defenses against it. Starting with the simple formula (in the case of a man) "I love him," he pointed out that each of the three words could be denied separately, producing in consequence three of the most typical paranoic delusional ideas. If the verb of the sentence be denied, we have "I do not *love* him—I *hate* him." Even this attitude, however, is not admitted directly to consciousness. By the mechanism of projection so common in paranoia it is exteriorized in the form of "He hates (and persecutes) me," after which the patient feels justified in his own hatred. There we have the most frequent delusion of paranoia, that of persecution. If the object of the sentence is denied, we have "I do not love *him*—I love *her*." The projection turns this into "She loves me," where we get the well-known delusion of erotomania, the belief that every woman is in love with him. Freud acutely remarked that such patients may mislead one into inferring an exaggerated heterosexuality unless one notices how their loving is strictly dependent on *first* being loved. If now the subject of the sentence is denied, we get "It is not *I* who loves him—it is *she* who does"; in other words, the distressing delusions of jealousy. Here the projection does not need to come into play, because what two other people do is an external matter, whereas in the first two cases the patient is concerned with his own inner perception, an unbearable one, and so has to project it. There is still another possibility, that all three words are denied, which signifies "I don't love at all; I don't love anyone." Since, however, the erotic instinct must find some expression it falls back on the subject and invests it with libido. The result is the megalomania which in some degree or other is present in all cases of paranoia. Freud uses here the term "narcissism." [42] The term occurred for the first time in his writings in the book on Leonardo (1910),[43] but still earlier (November 10, 1909) he had told the Vienna Society that narcissism was a necessary intermediate stage in the passage from auto-erotism to allo-erotism. It was shortly before he introduced it as a regular stage in erotic development.[1]

Freud was of the opinion that the paranoic withdrawal of love from its former object was always accompanied by a regression, and he defined this as a regression from the previously sublimated homosexuality (social feeling) to narcissism. The half-way stage of manifest homosexuality, therefore, is omitted.

It was in this essay that Freud began to distinguish between different forms of repression or, as they were later called, defenses. He held that the kind of repression operative was more closely related to the phases of libidinal development than is the symptomatology of a neurosis, which depends on other factors as well. He stated that no repression could take place except in connection with a previous "fixation," [44] that is a failure on the part of the instinctual urge to pass a given stage in development. He divided the stages in repression into three: (a) the initial fixation, (b) the repression proper, and (c) the breaking down of this repression with the "return of the repressed." It is, of course, that last phase which is so important in psychopathology.

Although the mechanism of projection is so prominent in paranoia Freud hesitated to regard it as the most significant one, recalling its frequency in other conditions and indeed in normal mental activity. He promised to deal more fully with the problem on a future occasion, but, as with all workers in science, his hopes were only partially fulfilled. As to the nosological status of paranoia Freud agreed with Kraepelin that it should be grouped together with the various forms of dementia praecox rather than being considered a distinct entity. The likelihood of its purer forms deteriorating into "dementia" is, however, very variable. Freud expressed at this point his dislike of the nomenclature. He found the term "dementia praecox" particularly clumsy and Bleuler's substitution of "schizophrenia" only permissible so long as one forgets the meaning of the word, i.e. that it describes

---

[1] See Chapter 12, No. 19.

a normal state of affairs. He proposed instead the word "paraphrenia," and it is perhaps unfortunate that it has not been adopted.

Freud came to the conclusion that the prominent symptoms of paranoia, e.g. the various delusions, are not, strictly speaking, part of the disease proper, but represent more or less successful attempts at a healing process. This idea has, on the other hand, been generally accepted.

There is an interesting discussion of the frightful symptom in which the patient believes in the imminent, or even recently effected, destruction of the world.[45] Freud was uncertain whether this could be explained simply through the patient's total withdrawal of libidinal feeling from the outside world, i.e. from people, and suggested that a withdrawal of interest on the part of the ego might also be involved.

Freud wrote a short, but significant, addendum to the Schreber essay in which he linked Schreber's acquired power of staring at the sun without harm to the old belief that eagles can do this and will disown any offspring that cannot. Many similar folk beliefs show that the idea is based on the faith that one's ancestor (really one's father) will do one no harm if one treats him well; children of a cobra totem must not injure the animal and he will not bite them. This element in the case "shows how well-grounded is Jung's assertion that the power of creating myths is not extinct, but still produces in the neuroses the same psychical products as in the most ancient times. I should like here to mention a hint I gave some time ago, to the effect that the same holds good for the creative powers of religion. We shall soon have to extend a conclusion that we psychoanalysts have long since maintained and to add to its individual ontogenetic content an anthropological phylogenetic one. We have stated that in dreams and in neuroses we find once more the child with all the peculiar features of its mode of thought and feeling. Now we may add: also savage, primitive man as he is revealed in the light of archaeology and ethnology." [46]

Several interesting further studies of the Schreber case have been made subsequently by other writers. The most notable contributions are those by M. Katan,[47] two of which were read at International Psycho-Analytical Congresses. He explained very clearly the defensive function of the hallucinations as being in part a discharge phenomenon, and he was able to trace some of the sources of the psychosis to indications in the pre-psychotic period. Herman Nunberg discussed the problem of the different ways in which in neuroses and psychoses the ego deals with the earliest infantile material.[48] Melanie Klein has

Sigmund Freud, 1906, age 50.

Group, Worcester, Massachusetts, September 1909.
A. A. Brill, Ernest Jones, Sandor Ferenczi, Freud,
Stanley Hall, C. G. Jung.

Sigmund Freud, *1913, age 57. Sketch by John Philipp.*

WEIMAR CONGRESS, SEPTEMBER 1911

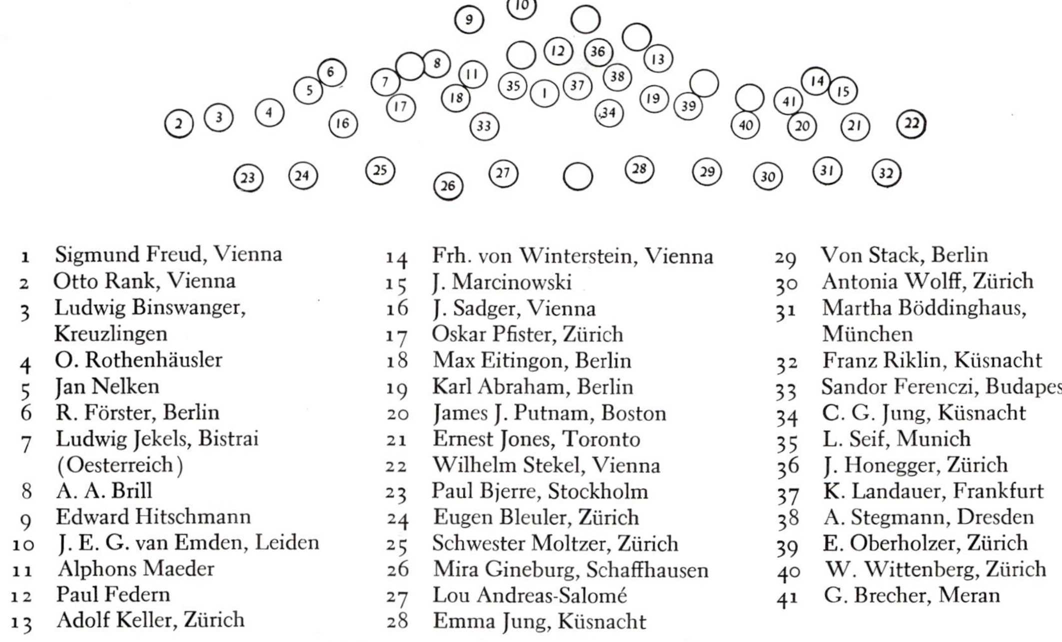

1 Sigmund Freud, Vienna
2 Otto Rank, Vienna
3 Ludwig Binswanger, Kreuzlingen
4 O. Rothenhäusler
5 Jan Nelken
6 R. Förster, Berlin
7 Ludwig Jekels, Bistrai (Oesterreich)
8 A. A. Brill
9 Edward Hitschmann
10 J. E. G. van Emden, Leiden
11 Alphons Maeder
12 Paul Federn
13 Adolf Keller, Zürich
14 Frh. von Winterstein, Vienna
15 J. Marcinowski
16 J. Sadger, Vienna
17 Oskar Pfister, Zürich
18 Max Eitingon, Berlin
19 Karl Abraham, Berlin
20 James J. Putnam, Boston
21 Ernest Jones, Toronto
22 Wilhelm Stekel, Vienna
23 Paul Bjerre, Stockholm
24 Eugen Bleuler, Zürich
25 Schwester Moltzer, Zürich
26 Mira Gineburg, Schaffhausen
27 Lou Andreas-Salomé
28 Emma Jung, Küsnacht
29 Von Stack, Berlin
30 Antonia Wolff, Zürich
31 Martha Böddinghaus, München
32 Franz Riklin, Küsnacht
33 Sandor Ferenczi, Budapest
34 C. G. Jung, Küsnacht
35 L. Seif, Munich
36 J. Honegger, Zürich
37 K. Landauer, Frankfurt
38 A. Stegmann, Dresden
39 E. Oberholzer, Zürich
40 W. Wittenberg, Zürich
41 G. Brecher, Meran

Sandor Ferenczi, 1913.

Ernest Jones, 1920.

Karl Abraham, 1912.

Otto Rank, 1924.

Hanns Sachs, 1914.

Max Eitingon, 1922.

Ernst Freud, Martin Freud and Sigmund Freud
Salzburg, August 1916.

Sophie and Martha Freud, circa 1912.

Minna Bernays, circa 1912.

inhibition and eccentricity, until an attack of gonorrhoea in his seventeenth year[1] when he collapsed with his present illness.

For more than four years Freud struggled without making any progress. The patient continued faithfully, but his inner resistance was so great that the work done made no impression on him. Choosing his moment, however, Freud announced that he intended to break off the treatment in whatever stage it was in at the time of his summer holiday in July (1914), and he resolved to keep to his word. It was a risky procedure, one that has often been abused since, but in this case its effect was to break the resistance, and the chief part of the analysis was completed within a few months, early in July. The patient went back to Russia in a state of mental health he had never before known and was able to cope with the various exigencies awaiting him.

The patient was the son of a Russian lawyer in Odessa who was also a very wealthy landowner; he had died in 1907. The Bolshevik revolution stripped him of all his possessions and left him quite penniless. In the spring of 1919 he escaped with his life and found his way again to Vienna. There Freud analyzed him for another four months (November 1919 to February 1920 inclusive) on account of an obstinate hysterical constipation which then yielded for good. On this occasion Freud not only treated him without a fee but regularly collected from his colleagues and pupils sums of money that sustained the patient and his invalid wife for the next six years, years when making a livelihood in stricken Vienna was a highly precarious undertaking.

The patient remained free of any serious neurosis for twelve years after Freud's first treatment and then developed one of an entirely different kind, in fact a paranoic psychosis. This time Ruth Brunswick treated him for four or five months (October 1926 to February 1927), and what she came across then formed a most instructive counterpart to Freud's earlier analysis.[54] The patient, however, came back to her two years later and she treated him at various times for several years. Her last report of him was in 1940 when he was in excellent health, and a similar one has recently been published by Muriel Gardiner.[55]

Freud remarked about the direct analysis of a child, such as in the "Little Hans case," that it was probably more convincing to those who had doubted the importance of infantile sexuality, but that it did not reach the deepest layers as one could with the fuller cooperation of an adult; the adult analysis of infancy was, therefore, far more instructive. Yet in the present case even he was astonished at some of

[1] Ruth Brunswick incorrectly gives the date as his nineteenth year.[53]

the conclusions he was compelled to accept. "On the whole the results of the analysis coincided quite satisfactorily with our previous knowledge, or could readily be embodied into it. Many details, however, seemed even to me so extraordinary and incredible that I have felt some hesitation in asking other people to believe in them. I got the patient to make the strictest criticism of his recollections, but he could find nothing improbable in them and adhered firmly to them. The reader may at all events rest assured that I am myself only reporting what I encountered as an independent experience, uninfluenced by any expectation of mine. So there was nothing left but to recall the wise saying that there are more things in heaven and earth than are dreamed of in our philosophy. And anyone who could manage to eliminate his preexisting convictions still more thoroughly could no doubt discover more such things." [56]

Although he came to a final decision, one which further experience of similar cases has amply confirmed, Freud was evidently in a state of considerable doubt over some essential points when writing this essay. It is interesting that he ascribed this state of mind partly to "a lurking doubt about whether we shall win the war." [57] That was, be it noted, as early as November 1914.

An important influence in the patient's early development was the witnessing of parental intercourse, with various peculiar details, at the age of eighteen months. The patient could not recollect the incident, which ever since has gone under the name of "primal scene," but the mass of converging evidence was so convincing that in Freud's judgment the reconstruction reached the same degree of certainty as an actual memory. It is interesting that in this he placed the greatest reliance on dream analysis, always his main stand-by when in any doubt. He discussed at length whether this primal scene was an unconscious memory of an actual event or a phantasy of the patient and concluded that the effect is identical in both cases. This is a conclusion of far-reaching importance.

Much of Freud's discussion of the case was concerned with the problem of whether the early traumas or phantasies dated from very early life or from later phantasies that had been projected backward into the past. This is a matter of fundamental importance to the whole of Freud's theory of development. It also has endless ramifications. If, for instance, these pathogenic agencies may date from later life, being then projected backwards, it opens the door to all the cultural variations and influences, stressed particularly of late by Karen Horney, which can for the most part be excluded if we are concerned only with the first couple of years of life. From a meticulous study of the data present in this case Freud showed irrefutably that the theories recently propounded by Adler and Jung were contradicted in the crucial test of factual experience.[58]

A cardinal feature of the case consisted in complicated defensive reactions against an unusually strong tendency to a homosexual solution of the Oedipus situation. Freud analyzed the various neurotic products of this conflict so thoroughly that they never recurred. But twelve years after the end of the treatment other symptoms, occasioned by the news of Freud's serious illness, began to appear, and they were the motive for Ruth Mack Brunswick's subsequent analysis. In essence they represented a quite different attempt at expressing the old homosexual trend, this time a paranoic manifestation. This also, however, yielded to treatment, and the analyst was able to make some interesting reflections on the relation between this phase and the complexes Freud had dealt with in his earlier analysis.

Like the others, this essay contains a number of statements and hints of a wider import than their immediate application to the case itself. For instance, Freud suggested that many patients whose case is diagnosed as manic-depressive insanity are really suffering from defects left over after a spontaneously cured obsessional neurosis. Again, in his opinion the emotion of shame is especially linked with the development of control over the urinary function. And in an unobtrusive footnote in the same connection he gave a hint of the view he developed many years later about primitive man's conquest of fire.[59]

Freud remarked on how difficult it was to speak accurately about the unconscious mind of a young child, since the distinction between the two mental systems only gradually develops.

In Freud's experience every adult neurosis is built on an infantile one, but he did not make the generalization, now widely accepted, that every child necessarily passes through a stage of neurosis.

Freud expressed his belief that instinctive knowledge of the fundamentals of life, including sexual knowledge, was not confined to the lower animals but must also be assumed for man. He even applied this idea clinically in the present case. Thus the inherited tendency to connect the fear of castration with the image of the father may compete with personal experience, as here, of castration threats emanating from a mother or her substitute. There is an interplay between the two, individual and inherited experience, and the result varies in different people according to the relative strength of the two factors.

Freud began to write his account of the case early in October, 1914, only three months after finishing the analysis.[60] By the end of the month he had written 54 pages[61] and early in November the whole 116 pages.[62] He had intended to publish it in the *Jahrbuch*, but the difficulties of the war brought that periodical to a premature end. The essay was too large for the *Zeitschrift*, so Freud put it in a drawer, hoping against hope that the *Jahrbuch* could re-appear. This hope had vanished by the end of the war, so Freud published the essay in the fourth series of his *Sammlung Kleiner Schriften* in 1918.

VI

The Psychogenesis of a Case of Female Homosexuality[63]

The last case resembled the first one in so far as the patient was a girl of eighteen and the analysis a short one. But this time it was Freud, more alive to the significance of resistance than twenty years earlier, who broke off the treatment. The history is remarkable in that the patient was so determined to retain the sole "symptom" for which she was being analyzed that she could afford to let the analysis of it proceed quite freely: her resistance was not against the analysis itself, only against its having any effect. Consequently Freud was able to obtain complete insight into the genesis of her case, and it is from that point of view that he recorded the history.

Freud remarked how much more conspicuous a part male homosexuality plays in the world, socially and legally, than female homosexuality, and, perhaps for that reason, how much more attention psychologists have paid to it. He therefore seized the opportunity he had of unraveling a case of the latter to make an important contribution to our knowledge of the condition.

The patient was desperately in love with a lady many years older than herself, and when a rebuff from her led to a serious attempt at suicide the alarmed parents persuaded her to consult Freud. She was not neurotic and did not regard her condition as pathological, but she consented for their sake. Freud commented on how unfavorable such a motive is for carrying through a psychoanalysis, and both for that reason and because of the nature of the condition he expressed himself very non-committally to the parents. He seemed to be skeptical in general about the prospects of bringing about changes in a homosexual case. He had succeeded only in specially favorable cases where heterosexual urges were also present or where the person had strong motives for desiring a change in his condition. Where the homosexual attitude is complete it is very difficult to persuade the patient that the pleasure he might obtain heterosexually could ever compare with that he had already experienced in the other direction. Much is gained if the path to heterosexual gratification is opened, even if the person remains bisexual; then he has at least the choice.

In some cases, such as in this one, a psychoanalysis passes through fairly distinct phases. In the first one the analyst is the more active person, interpreting the material and calling the patient's attention to the nature and meaning of his conflicts, whereas in the second phase it is the patient who takes charge of the progress in the work and plays the really active part. Writing in 1920 Freud was able to draw the analogy with the two phases in traveling, one even more valid nowadays. The first one is occupied with the complicated preparations, passports, visa, etc., but even when all that is accomplished and one takes one's seat in the train one is from a physical point of view not a step farther from one's starting-point. Nevertheless one has done much that is essential for the actual journey itself. In the present case the first phase was carried out successfully and both Freud and the patient obtained a clear insight into the essential nature and genesis of her condition. Only very slight progress, however, was made beyond this. Freud perceived that a powerful motive maintaining the homosexuality was the impulse to be avenged on her father, so he broke off the treatment and advised the patient, after thinking matters over, to be analyzed by a woman. Whether she ever followed this advice we do not know.

The causative agents in the case were familiar enough, to an analyst almost banal. What was peculiar was the patient's particular reaction to them. She had passed through a pronounced Oedipus phase in her childhood, but had not emerged from it by the familiar way of transferring her love to another male than her father and working through the rivalry with her mother or hostility toward her. Instead she responded, but in an exaggerated fashion, in the way many people do when disappointed in love: namely, by identification with the lost object. According to Freud, this is one way of regressing towards narcissism. It had the advantage of avoiding the conflict with the mother. Freud considered that not enough attention had been paid to this motive of *evasion*, one which plays an important part in the genesis of homosexuality. Incidentally he said he saw no necessity for introducing the term "Electra complex" to describe this particular reaction to the Oedipus situation.

In discussing this analysis Freud made some interesting reflections on the subject of determinism. As with many other cases, he felt satisfied that he could trace back the causal links quite comprehensively from the end product to the very beginning, but he was equally clear that were one to proceed in the reverse direction there would be no such certainty. Over and again one could see that such and such an aetiological agency might have led to several different effects, and one could only say in any particular case that it led to the one it actually did. Why it did so instead of leading to any of the other directions open to it no one could say. The explanation of the difficulty, however, is simple enough. It is that our knowledge of the causal agencies is purely qualitative, and that we have at present no prospect of making it quantitative. If a given conflict ends in a certain way one can say that one side of it was stronger than the other, but there is no means of predicting this beforehand since we have no method for measuring the strength of mental "forces."

Freud was able to unravel the various motives impelling this patient to her attempted suicide and he took the opportunity of making a general statement about suicide, one he had already adumbrated elsewhere in his writings.[m] "Perhaps no one can find the psychical energy to kill himself unless in the first place he is thereby killing at the same time someone with whom he has identified himself, and is directing against himself a death wish which had previously been directed against the other person." [64]

Until the patient had committed this desperate act neither she, nor of course her parents, had any idea of the strength of the passion moving her. Freud commented here on the frequency of such occurrences, on how often people are unaware of the strength of their love until some relatively slight incident reveals it by the intensity of their response.

In his concluding remarks on the theme of homosexuality in general Freud insisted on the necessity of distinguishing between inversion of a sexual attitude and inversion of the sex of the object, two different things which may or may not go together in a given case. Although he was impressed by the then recent experimental work of Steinach, which has since not been very well substantiated, Freud did not attach much importance to the presence of somatic changes in the direction of the opposite sex. He did not think there was any close correlation between them and homosexual tendencies, although it might be slightly closer with women than with men. He regarded the concept of an inborn "third sex" as unsupported by the evidence and having been put forward for tendentious reasons. The mistake made in most literature on the subject was the isolating of one factor at a

[m] See Chapter 10, No. 5.

time at the expense of the actual aetiological complexity. Any general conclusions must at least take into account the psychoanalytic discovery that homosexuals always have to begin with a pronounced fixation on the parent of the opposite sex. They must also be based on an axiom which Freud had acquired from his friend Fliess, and about which he could never be shaken: namely, the natural bisexuality **of** not only all human beings, but of all living creatures.

12

CHAPTER

The Libido Theory

IT IS WELL FIRST TO BE CLEAR HERE ABOUT WHAT PRECISELY FREUD meant by the word "libido" and what by the "libido theory." The sexual instinct he regarded, like everyone else, as a psycho-physical process, having both bodily and mental manifestations. By "libido" he essentially meant the latter, in whatever form they may be displayed.

Here are Freud's own words on the matter. "The popular view distinguishes between hunger and love, seeing them as representatives of the instincts that aim at self-preservation and reproduction of the species respectively. In associating ourselves with this very evident distinction we postulate in psychoanalysis a similar one between the self-preservative or ego instincts on the one hand and the sexual instincts on the other; that force by which the sexual instinct is represented in the mind we call 'libido'—sexual longing—and regard it as analogous to the force of hunger, or the will to power, and other such trends among the ego-tendencies." [1]

But Freud was seldom meticulous in adhering to precise definitions, and there are passages which give the impression that sometimes "libido" might be equivalent to "sexual instinct" in both its bodily and mental aspects. Thus in one place it is defined simply as "the force by which the sexual instinct expresses itself." [2] Again, in a passage written in 1915: "We have defined the concept of libido as a quantitatively variable force which could serve as a measure of processes and transformations occurring in the field of sexual excitation. We distinguish this libido in respect of its special origin from the energy which must be supposed to underlie mental processes in general, and we thus also attribute a qualitative character to it." [3] He could even speak of the organic basis of the libido. Thus, alluding to the "disturbances of the sexual processes, the processes which determine in the organism the formation and utilization of sexual libido," he adds: "It is scarcely possible to avoid picturing these processes as being in the last resort of a chemical nature." [4] This idea of Freud's can be traced as far back as 1894. [5]

As early as 1909 Jung was complaining to Freud about his difficulty in explaining to his pupils the concept of libido and begged him for a fuller definition. Freud tersely replied that he could give no clearer one than he had already. Only two years later Jung equated the concept with Bergson's *élan vital*, with life energy in general, and thus robbed it of its distinctive sexual connotation.

Then comes the vexed question of what Freud included under the term "sexuality." He has been bitterly criticized for using it in an unduly broad sense and applying it to processes which other people do not call sexual. Even writers sympathetic to his work, such as Sir Arthur Tansley, [6] have expressed regret at the trouble he might have spared himself had he only used phrases like "love" or "desire for union" in place of the starker word. Freud was wont to remark, however, that when one begins by agreeing to such compromises to veil one's real meaning from deference to outside opinion one is on a slippery path and may not know where to stop. By "sexual" Freud meant "sexual" in the ordinary sense, but he widened the popular conception of what things *are* sexual. The psychoanalytic study of early childhood and the knowledge of adult perversions compelled him to recognize that sexuality has many manifestations besides the simple genital union of coitus. The instinct does not begin in this finished form, the one where it obviously serves the end of reproduction. On the contrary, it has to pass through a rather complicated development before this stage of what Freud termed "genital primacy" is reached. It begins diffusely from the excitability of many "erotogenic zones" of the body. He maintained, for instance, just as a Hungarian pediatrician, Lindner, [7] had twenty years before him, that the infant is impelled to suck not only by hunger, the need for nourishment, but also by the desire for erotic gratification even when it is not hungry. This is continued later as thumb sucking, the sucking of other objects, such as pencils, and in adult life as amorous kissing or, in perverse cases, as fellatio. There is an unbroken line in this development, so Freud saw no reason for refusing it the same name "sexual" throughout. Just as he had widened the conception of "mental" from its popular connotation of "conscious," so he widened the range over which the term "sexual" could justifiably be applied. I once used the analogy of oxygen to illustrate this. When it was first discovered, oxygen was considered to be only a certain gas with particular properties. But further knowledge led it to be applied also to ozone, a gas with a different molecular weight. Indeed, it had to be admitted later that oxygen could exist in a non-gaseous form, even in solids such as saltpeter.

By the "libido theory" Freud meant the investigation of all these manifestations and the tracing out of the complicated paths they may follow in the course of development. He sometimes used it in a more restricted sense, especially in his early years, as referring only to examining the part played by the libido in the psychoneuroses.

The beginnings of the libido theory go back to the early nineties of the last century when Freud came across the importance of sexuality in connection with the "actual neuroses," neurasthenia and the anxiety neurosis. At that time the physiological basis of sexuality was prominently in Freud's mind, and indeed it never left it. But soon afterwards his discovery of the essential part played by sexual processes in the psychology of other neuroses, the psychoneuroses of hysteria, etc., turned his attention to the more mental aspects of the instinct. The theory was then extended step by step in accord with his increasing experience. There was the part played by auto-erotism in childhood with the conception of "erotogenic zones" in non-genital parts of the body, the significance of precocious stimulation by adults, and then—most important of all—the recognition of the rich sexual phantasy life of children which at first he thought began just after puberty and was projected backward into infancy, but which he later found originated in infancy itself.

The chronology of Freud's gradually deepening knowledge in this field has been fully described earlier in this biography,[8] when stress was laid on what seems to us now with our hindsight the slow tempo of Freud's progress and the almost timid reluctance, covering a revolutionary boldness, with which he accepted his gradually accumulating knowledge and insight. The conclusion was reached that Freud had before the turn of the century discovered all the essential phases in sexual development, although his expositions up to that time were still tentative and imperfect. He was certainly the first not only to assert that infants normally experience sexual sensations, but to give a complete description of their variety. But for some reason it was not until 1905 that he published to the world a full account of his startling discoveries and conclusions in this field. Even so signs remained of his earlier hesitations. In the *Three Essays on the Theory of Sexuality* (1905) there is a simple footnote saying that children between three and five are capable of choosing a love object; it is true, this is repeated in the text, but with little elaboration. In the first two editions of *The Interpretation of Dreams* (1900 and 1909) there is an odd passage in which it is assumed that children have no sexual desires; [9] it was Jung who called Freud's attention to it and got him to expunge it in the third edition (1911).

Logically one would have expected Freud to publish a book on this subject immediately after finishing *The Interpretation of Dreams*, since the two themes were intimately connected, had been worked out together, and constituted Freud's two most important discoveries. Indeed, this seems to have been his own intention at first. On October 11, 1899, just a month before the dream book was published, he wrote to his friend Fliess: "A theory of sexuality is likely to be the dream book's immediate successor," [10] and three months later he wrote: "I am putting together material for the theory of sexuality and waiting till some spark can set ablaze what I have collected." [11] Why the spark was so long in coming we do not know. Probably it simply had to wait for one of those outbursts of activity that seem to have been periodical with Freud: eight years later he did in fact refer to 1905 as one of his periodic years.[12] Or he might well have wished to accumulate more experience to confirm his novel conclusions. At all events he turned aside to work also at the material that was to produce his book on jokes, a theme which had been suggested by the curious play on words that so often occur in dreams. There was after all a continuity in his interests in those years. By 1905 both books were ready to be printed.

(1) In that year came two pronouncements by Freud on the subject of sexuality: the famous *Three Essays* and a short chapter in a book by his friend Löwenfeld. This book *Sexualleben und Nervenleiden* (Sexual Life and Neurotic Suffering), had already given some account of Freud's views in its earlier editions, but for the fourth edition the author persuaded Freud to describe them in a special chapter entitled "My Views on the Part Played by Sexuality in the Aetiology of the Neuroses." [13]

In it Freud gave an historical account of his views. The fact that they had changed considerably in accord with further experience distinguished them from mere speculation which needs no such

change. He began with an account of the "actual neuroses," neurasthenia and the anxiety neurosis, which had early called his attention
to the importance of the sexual factors in aetiology, and opened his
eyes to the possibility of their being operative in the psychoneuroses
also. Breuer and he had combined Charcot's views on traumatic
hysteria after physical accidents with their experience of psychical traumas in early life. At first Freud had thought that symptoms derived
directly from such traumas, but on discovering that often they had
not really happened he came to recognize the importance of phantasies for pathogenesis. It followed from this that the form of the supposed traumas, whether active or passive, could no longer be regarded
as determining the kind of psychoneurosis, as he had previously
thought, and that more importance had to be attached to the constitution itself. Instead, however, of employing the general concept
of "hereditary constitution," Freud replaced it by the more specific
one of "sexual constitution," one which evidently varies in different
individuals. At the same time he had recognized the significance of
repression, which may affect in different cases varying components
of the sexual instinct.

In all the changes in Freud's conceptions of aetiology the two factors of "sexual" and "infantile" remained constant. But he laid stress
on the complexity of pathogenesis in addition to these invariable
factors, so that a psychoneurosis may be brought about by a summation of various agencies reached in many different ways.

(2) In 1905 there appeared one of the most fundamental of Freud's
books, the *Three Essays on the Theory of Sexuality*.[14] It was this publication that brought the maximum of odium on his name; much of
it still remains, especially among the uneducated. The book was felt
to be a calumny on the innocence of the nursery. Yet, as James
Strachey well says,[15] "It stands, there can be no doubt, besides his
Interpretation of Dreams as his most momentous and original contribution to human knowledge."

A thousand copies of the first edition were printed, and it took
more than four years to sell them although they were only cheap
paper-covered booklets. Twice that number were printed of the next
two editions (in 1910 and 1915 respectively), and they were sold
in the same time. Freud was paid two hundred and sixty-two Kronen
($53.08) for his labors. The book has been translated into nine
languages, including Czech, Hungarian and Japanese; there have been
several English translations. There were six editions published in
Freud's lifetime, and Freud made more changes in this book than in

any other except, perhaps, *The Interpretation of Dreams* itself. James Strachey's remarkable editing has only now made it possible to distinguish and estimate these changes in the various editions. He calls attention to the startling fact, easily overlooked by the casual reader, that the entire sections on the sexual theories of children, on the pregenital organization of the libido, and on the libido theory itself, including especially the new idea of ego-libido (narcissism), made their first appearance in the third edition, ten years after the original publication.

In his Preface Freud insisted that the conclusions he put forward were all based on psychoanalytic investigations only and so are to be regarded as contributions to a subject that will need to be amplified by studies in other spheres: biological, physiological and sociological.

The book was divided into three parts. The first one dealt with the various deviations of the sexual instinct. These are often so dissociated from possibilities of reproduction or even of genital activity, that they alone would justify the extending of the concept "sexual" beyond the popular use of the word. Freud divided the apparently heterogeneous mass of these deviations into two broad groups, according to whether there is a deviation in the *object* of the instinct or in its *aims*. The former comprises changes in the sex, age, or even species of the object. With homosexuality, which he preferred to call "inversion," he discussed fully the problem of congenital or acquired factors, protesting against the tendency to one-sided emphasis in the matter. He fully accepted the conception of inborn bisexuality, which he had acquired from Fliess. What he had found in the case of inversion was that the subjects had passed through a very early stage of fixation on their mothers, and had then identified themselves with them. The objects from whom they later obtain gratification are narcissistic mirrors of themselves, loved as they had wished their mothers to love them.

The deviations in the *aims* of the instinct again fall into two subgroups: anatomical transgression, and fixations on preliminary stages. In connection with the former, where other parts of the body, mouth, anus, etc., or even articles of clothing (fetishism) take the place of the genital organs, Freud attached importance to the over-estimation of the object that so often accompanies sexual attraction. If this is excessive it is not easily compatible with genital activity, which therefore tends to be replaced by substitutes.

Here Freud, in a casual footnote, threw out the suggestion which Ferenczi and I developed later, that the peculiar relationship between a hypnotist and his subject depends on an unconscious sexual attitude, particularly a masochistic one, on the part of the latter. The suggestion had been rather more fully stated in the same year in a paper which remained unknown until after his death. This is, therefore, worth quoting here: "It may be remarked, by the way, that, outside hypnosis and in real life, credulity such as the subject has in relation to his hypnotist is shown only by a child towards his beloved parent, and that an attitude of similar subjection on the part of one person towards another has only one parallel, though a complete one —in certain love relationships where there is extreme devotion. A combination of exclusive attachment and credulous obedience is in general among the characteristics of love." [16]

In the second sub-group certain components of the sexual instinct which are normally only contributory agencies leading up to the final act are singled out to replace it. There is a dwelling on a preliminary stage of the whole process and such an accentuation of it that it may constitute the entire action. Here two paired components are the most prominent: the desire to look at or to be looked at, which when perversions are termed "scopophilia" and "exhibitionism" respectively; then the more familiar sado-masochism. It is noteworthy that when either one of such pairs is pronounced its opposite will always be so as well, with either conscious or unconscious manifestations.

Most of the "deviations" function in a mild form in normal life. The features that justify one in calling them pathological are *exclusiveness* and *fixation*. They then are perversions rather than mere perversities.

There follows a discussion of sexuality in the psychoneuroses, where Freud once more insisted that the part it plays is the only constant factor in those affections and their most important source of energy. The symptoms are disguised sexual functioning on the one hand and expressions of the ego's resistance on the other. An unexpected finding was that the sexual impulses creating and maintaining the symptoms are only in small part of a "normal" kind; more often they are "perverse" impulses, and most of the perversions mentioned above may be found behind neurotic symptoms. This led to his formulating the well-known sentence: "Neuroses are the negative of the perversions." It does not follow, however, as one might hastily suppose, that neurotics and perverts are closely related. A more probable explanation of the finding is that in the neuroses there is such an unusually strong repression that the libido is forced to seek collateral channels for expression. Nevertheless the two conditions, neurosis and perversion, may well co-exist.

In a short passage on instincts (*Triebe*) Freud suggested that what distinguishes one from another and gives them their specific quality is their *source* and their *aim*. The source is always a stimulation arising in some part of the body, and the aim is the allaying of this stimulus. At this point he introduced the concept of "erotogenic zones," [a] i.e. areas of the body that have the capacity to give rise to erotic sensations. Such zones may cover a wide area, but they are much more sensitive in some areas than in others: the genital organs and the alimentary orifices are prominent in this connection.

The second, and most original, section is devoted to the topic of "Infantile Sexuality." Freud found the reason why the very existence of this has been so largely overlooked, or denied, in the fact of infantile amnesia: few people can recollect much from the first three years of their life, so fateful for the formation of their personality, years in which the child can display the most complicated emotions. That is also why much more interest has been taken in the inheritance from distant ancestry, while the nearer prehistoric period, that of infancy, is ignored.

Freud expressed the view, then so startling but now widely accepted, that the infant is capable of erotic sensations from the beginning of life, that its sexual instincts undergo a progressive development until about the age of four, after which no further progress is made until puberty. The years of standstill, from about four to eleven, he termed a "latency period," an expression Fliess had suggested to him. He is here commonly misunderstood as implying that there are no sexual manifestations during these years, which may or may not be so according to the individual development. The earliest manifestations of sexuality are characterized by their arising in connection with important non-sexual bodily functions, such as feeding or defecating, by their activity being auto-erotic, and by their aim being the satisfaction of stimuli emanating from an erotogenic zone. Of these early or pre-genital activities Freud distinguished two phases: the oral, and the anal-sadistic; later Abraham divided each of them into two.[17]

According to Freud there are three phases of masturbatory activity: that of early infancy, that of the highest point of infantile sexual development (about the age of four), and that of puberty respectively.

The instinctive desire to acquire knowledge, which usually becomes active about the age of three or four, Freud considered took its origin in several sources, but one of the most important is the need to obtain

[a] A word doubtless coined on the model of the "hysterogenic zones" familiar in hysteria.

sexual information. Here he mentioned the conclusions children most often come to: the cloacal theory of birth and the sadistic conception of parental intercourse.

Childhood sexuality contains other elements besides autoerotic activity. Erotic attraction for a particular person is common between the ages of two and five, and may not happen again until the time of puberty.

The section ends with a very suggestive passage on the interaction of sexual and non-sexual processes. The zone of the lips and mouth subserve both. As a result, when there is excessive repression of the erotic component we may find an inability, or refusal, to eat—a frequent neurotic symptom. Again, the observation that intense concentration on intellectual work, especially in studying, is often accompanied by sexual excitation explains why the latter, when strong, is so distracting to such work. Incidentally, this is the kernel of truth in the popular belief that neuroses come from over-work. Most neurotic symptoms are not in the sexual sphere but in that of other functions; the explanation is the common interaction of the two, so that repression of the one may affect the functioning of the other. A striking example is that of hysterical blindness, where disturbance of the scopophilic element can inhibit the whole visual capacity.[b]

The third section is devoted to the changes that come about at the time of *puberty*. Here again Freud insisted on the complicated nature of sexual development, of how the final stage of genital primacy is reached only through many evolutionary changes in the elementary components which comprise the beginnings of the instinct. These changes are influenced both by the inborn sexual constitution and by the experiences of life, especially early life, and they are therefore subject to many inhibitions, fixations and deviations in the course of development. All this accounts for the extraordinary variation in the sexual nature and habits of human beings.

Many of the early components, then discrete, find a function in adult life in affording what Freud termed "preliminary pleasure," or "fore-pleasure," which he distinguished from the "end pleasure" that procures final and complete satisfaction. Obvious examples are the acts of looking, touching with hand or lips (kissing). These familiar facts set Freud a problem he was able only partially to solve at this period. Since such acts, for instance kissing, institute an urge towards further more intense excitation Freud concluded that they must imply a state of tension. Now tension, he always maintained, means "un-

[b] For an exposition of this see Chapter 10, No. 4.

pleasure," since it impels towards discharge and relief. On the other hand there is no doubt that the acts themselves are pleasurable, and no one wants to bring pleasure to an end. How resolve this antinomy? It was twenty years before Freud was able to find some solution.

At this point Freud cast back to the organic basis of excitation. The suggestion that physical pressure on the walls of the seminal vesicles is an explanation fails before its inapplicability to children, to women and to eunuchs, where it is absent. So Freud extended his notion of a chemical basis for the excitation to the whole body, including the internal organs. This was a speculation that took him beyond our actual knowledge at the time.

He then had a section on the differentiation between man and woman, one which is only completed at or after puberty. The accent falls, as throughout in his writings, on the importance of the male impulse. He maintained that the female child's libido is more male than female, because her autoerotic activity concerns predominantly the clitoris. He even made the obscure suggestion that perhaps all libido, being like all impulses in its nature active, is essentially male.[18] At puberty the fresh wave of repression affects in females particularly the clitoritic sexuality, and the modesty and reserve resulting from it exercise a special attraction for men, whose over-estimation of the preciousness of the loved object is proportionate to it. The fact that with males the principal sexual organ remains the same throughout, while with females a transition has to be effected from clitoris to vagina—one that often fails to take place—is the reason why women, having a more complicated development, are more prone to sexual troubles and to neurosis than are men.

Then comes an important section on the significance for later life of early sexual attitudes and experiences concerning the parents. Freud laid stress on the harm that can be done by spoiling and over-exciting a young child. This is described very much in physical terms, and it is noteworthy how little is said about the importance of infantile phantasy. Of the well-known Oedipus complex Freud remarked: "recognition of it has become the shibboleth that distinguishes supporters of psycho-analysis from their opponents."[19]

At the end of the book is a long summary of its main contents. In it Freud called attention to a theme that occupied him very much in later years: namely, the opposition between civilization and freedom of sexual development. He also commented on a factor in aetiology which subsequent investigation has not confirmed. He had observed that in more than half of the cases of psychoneurosis he treated the father had suffered from syphilis. This high proportion led him to the conclusion that syphilis in a parent, even if it did not produce symptoms in the children, deleteriously affected the "sexual constitution," thus rendering such children more liable to neuroses.[20]

In subsequent editions extensive passages were added, among which should be specially mentioned the insertion on "Ego-Libido" in the third edition, 1915.

After considering this weighty book we may now turn to a number of slighter papers several of which were *pièces d'occasion* written by request.

(3) On November 12, 1906, Freud gave an address on "Sexual Abstinence" before the *Sozialwissenschaftlicher Bildungsverein* (Society for Education in the Social Sciences),[c] Freud so seldom expressed himself on the interesting question of how he thought his new researches would bear on current social customs and institutions that one would greatly like to know the contents of this particular pronouncement. Unfortunately, however, all we know is the bare fact of the lecture.

(4) The first of the written papers to appear, on "The Sexual Enlightenment of Children," [21] was published in 1907 in the periodical *Soziale Medizin und Hygiene*, at the request of a Hamburg colleague.[22] In it Freud was very scathing on those who doubt the propriety of such enlightenment and he quoted some touching examples of distress where it had been withheld. His advice was that it should be continuous from the first, keeping pace with the child's curiosity and intelligence. It is in this paper that he first mentioned little Hans [d] (under the name of Herbert); it was before the boy had developed the neurosis that Freud studied.

(5) Two years later, on May 12, 1909, Freud had occasion to give a much fuller exposition of his views on this subject in the course of a discussion at the Vienna Society, the details of which will shortly be published. He laid stress on one particular harm that may ensue from ignoring a child's need for enlightenment: namely, that in this way the subject of sexuality in general can become inextricably associated with the idea of forbiddenness, with fateful consequences in married life.

(6) The next paper, entitled "Civilized Sexual Ethics and Modern Nervousness," was published in 1908 in *Sexualprobleme*, a continuation of the periodical *Mutterschutz*.[23] It was almost Freud's first

[c] Minutes of the Vienna Society, October 17, 1906.
[d] See Chapter 11. Case II.

excursus into the field of sociology, and it is inspired throughout by warm humanitarian feeling. It was in essence a protest against exorbitant demands of society, especially in the sexual sphere, on the life of the individual. The grounds of his protest are as valid now as then, but in some respects the paper has an interest as a period piece. It depicts a civilization in many ways different from our present one, and it can be said that some of the important changes in the past half century are the direct result of Freud's own work.

The starting point of the paper was a book of von Ehrenfels' called *Sexualethik* (Sexual Ethics). Two of his main points are quoted, apparently with approval: (a) The prevailing sexual morality of civilization is characterized by the transference of feminine demands on to the sexual life of the man, with deprecation of any sexual intercourse outside of marriage. This leads to a double moral life, with evil consequences for honesty and humanity. (b) The glorifying of monogamy paralyzes the process of selection, which is the only hope of improving the human constitution, a hope which humanitarianism and hygiene has already reduced to a minimum.

Freud then quoted several writers who were alarmed at the increase of neurotic affections. They drew a terrifying picture of the severe conditions of life at the beginning of the century which read strangely to those of us who look back on that epoch as a golden age. Apparently the world was full of uncertainty and restlessness, and anxiety stalked everywhere. The essential trouble was the incredible speed of communication in those days!

Freud at this point set himself the task of expounding an aspect of the harm done by civilization that was seldom mentioned: the effects of the restrictions on sexual activity. So far as neuroses were concerned this was the essential cause. Freud admitted that the achievements of civilization had been brought about by the suppression of instincts, but he raised the question whether the limit of this process had not been reached, and whether the gain to civilization was not being more than counterbalanced by the loss to it through the harm it does. He maintained that the capacity for sublimation differed considerably among different people, but that it was never unlimited; as in physics, the conversion of one type of energy could only produce a certain amount of the other into which it was transformed.

Freud spoke of three phases in sexual development: first the undifferentiated one unrelated to the reproductive process; then the restriction of it to such activity (genital) as may lead to reproduction; and thirdly, the restriction of even this to legitimate reproduction (in marriage). Many people are not able to endure even the first of these restrictions, perversions or neuroses being the result of their efforts. The second and third are endured without harm only by a minority.

Freud did not consider that total abstinence could be borne by most people without harm to their powers of initiative, their energy, their self-confidence or their mental health. Nor was he satisfied that marriage only provided a satisfactory solution. Diminished potency on the man's side and frigidity on the woman's are far commoner than is generally admitted, and the necessity for anti-conceptional measures lead to dissatisfaction or actual harm according to the method used. The existence of a double morality, even when not officially recognized, is an admission of this state of affairs. Women suffer more than men from the prevailing morality. Only a mentally healthy woman can successfully endure marriage. And any intellectual inferiority shown by women as a whole he would explain not, as Moebius did, by any biological difference, but by the stricter morality imposed on women which leads to general inhibition of the thinking powers as surely as religious beliefs do.

In short Freud was in favor of revolutionary changes in society, though he pointed out it was hard to effect radical reforms in any one sphere alone. He made no suggestions in detail of what reforms should be brought about, that not being the province of a physician, but he insisted that his experience of neuroses was a powerful supporting argument for the need of them.

(7) The next paper, on "Sexual Theories of Children," was published in the same periodical in the same year.[24] In it Freud described certain typical "theories" that children are apt to build to satisfy their sexual curiosity. In his opinion, the chief stimulus to such curiosity is the fear of being displaced by new rivals appearing and the wish to find out how it happens so as if possible to prevent it. Observation of animal life and of pregnant women teach children that the baby grows inside the body, leaving the two further questions of how it got in and how it gets out. The commonest answer to the latter is that it emerges from the rectum, one which is often replaced later by the more respectable idea of the navel. There is therefore no reason why men as well as women should not bear children. According to Freud, most boys believe to start with that women are built like themselves, and the discovery that that is not so commonly gets bound up with their fear of castration.

The pressing forward impulses in the penis are thwarted by ignorance of the vagina. Similarly ignorance concerning semen baffles the attempt to find out what is put into the women to start conception, and recourse is had either to the idea of urine or to something being swallowed. That conception may come about from a kiss alone seems to be a purely feminine idea.

Freud then dealt at some length with the child's "sadistic conception of coitus." This is often confirmed by resistances on the part of an unwilling mother, when parental intercourse is overlooked or heard, by quarrels during the daytime, and by the observation of menstrual blood on sheets or garments.

Some children think that childbirth follows almost immediately after intercourse and Freud quotes an amusing story of Marcel Prévost's illustrating this.[e]

In this paper Freud was chiefly concerned to show the effects in later life that result from these thwarted speculations of childhood, and he illustrated the theme from several clinical cases.

(8) The next paper, on "Hysterical Phantasies and their Relation to Bisexuality," appeared, also in 1908, in Hirschfeld's *Zeitschrift für Sexualwissenschaft*.[25] It was actually written for the *Jahrbuch für sexuelle Zwischenstufen*,[26] but just then the Editor, Hirschfeld, founded his new periodical. In it Freud briefly stressed the significance of phantasy life in the creation of psychoneurotic symptoms. He stated his conclusions in eight formulations, the content of which has been noted elsewhere in the present volume.[f] He added that very often such symptoms are fed by both masculine and feminine phantasies, although this happens only in long-standing cases. When that is so no therapeutic progress may be achieved until both components have been dealt with. Freud did not agree, however, with Sadger's dictum that this aetiology is invariable.

(9) In the same year Freud made his first excursus into characterology with a short article entitled "Character and Anal-Erotism," which was published in Bresler's *Psychiatrisch-Neurologische Wochenschrift*.[27] It certainly produced an effect, chiefly undesirable. The very idea of connecting the erotic excitability of one particular part of the body, and that such a lowly one as the anus, with spiritual qualities such as character traits seemed to be the most outrageous thing Freud had yet done. I was working at Kraepelin's Psychiatric

[e] Bernard Shaw indicates the same theme in his play, *Caesar and Cleopatra*.
[f] Chapter 10, No. 1.

Clinic in Munich at the time, and I well remember the jeers with which the psychiatric staff there greeted it, vying with each other in ribald remarks.

The literary form of the article was not particularly happy, nor did Freud exercise his persuasive powers in leading up to the theme. He bluntly stated that in his analytical experience persons whose pleasure in anal sensations had been unusually great in infancy were apt to develop in later life what he called a triad of character traits: orderliness, economy or even miserliness, and obstinacy. Since then the correlation Freud then established has become almost a commonplace of general knowledge, and the contributions such sources can make to the formation of character have been studied in considerable detail.[28] But at the time there is no doubt that the paper in question much increased the odium with which his name was becoming associated.

Freud had mentioned this triad of character traits in a letter two years previously,[29] and it is probable that his knowledge of it went back still earlier.

(10) 1909 was a still more prolific year in this field. First should be mentioned the "Little Hans Case," already described in the preceding chapter for its clinical interest.[g] But it is essentially a study of the conflicts arising in the course of the sexual development of a very young child, and thus afforded first-hand evidence of the existence and importance of childhood sexuality.

(11) On February 24, 1909, Freud read a paper before the Vienna Society on the "Genesis of Fetishism" (*Zur Genese des Fetischismus*). It has never been published.

(12) In the same year Freud wrote a fascinating section for a very original book by Otto Rank, *The Myth of the Birth of the Hero*. It was entitled "The Family Romance of Neurotics." [30] The particular phantasy with which it dealt is characteristic of those who have had difficulties as children in emancipating themselves from the authority of their parents. The usual overestimation of parents in early childhood is so pronounced with them as to be hard to renounce. The discovery later on that the parents are no more wonderful than other people, together with the feeling—so common in future neurotics—of not being loved enough, gives rise to the phantasy that perhaps they are adopted children and that the real parents are kinder and in every way superior to the apparent ones. The phantasy is commoner with boys and is often accompanied by ideas of the mother

[g] Chapter 11. Case II.

having been unfaithful; it is the father who is displaced more often than the mother, motives of hostility and rivalry also playing their part here.

There are endless varieties of this basic phantasy. Sometimes in a large family it may be reversed: the younger child believes he is the only legitimate one, the older ones having been adopted. Fundamentally it is the emotion of love rather than hate that gives rise to the phantasy. The substituted father, although of higher social status, bears many features taken from the actual one. The wish really is the longing that the early situation of childhood could be brought back, "when the father was the most distinguished and powerful man and the mother the dearest and loveliest woman."

Freud had first come across this phantasy in paranoia [31] and only later recognized its occurrence among neurotics and even normal people.

(13) In 1910 F. S. Krauss, the Editor of the periodical *Anthro-pophyteia*, published there a letter from Freud which he had asked him to write, giving his opinion of the value to psychologists of the collection of obscene jokes and anecdotes to which Krauss's periodical was devoted.[32] Freud made two points in this connection. The first concerned the correspondence between many of those jokes and the widened conception of sexuality which Freud was maintaining in the face of great indignation. He took the example of jokes having to do with the act and product of defecation, a topic which his researches had shown him to have a sexual connotation of varying intensity among normal people, especially children, as well as among neurotics. The extraordinary prevalence of such jokes, as shown by Krauss's collection, and the fact that, like all jokes, they were designed to provoke pleasurable amusement, could only be explained by Freud's conclusion on this matter. Otherwise one would have to assume that the whole population were sexual perverts in the full sense. And if such jokes had no underlying sexual connection they would evoke nothing at all but disgust, as indeed they do with people whose emotional life has undergone considerable repression.

The other point he made, concerning the technique of jokes, we shall consider in another connection.[h]

(14) In the same year Freud began writing a series of essays which he then collected under the title of "Contributions to the Psychology of Love," and we may consider them together. At a meeting of the Vienna Society four years before (November 28, 1906) he had an-

* See Chapter 14, No. 3.

nounced his intention of writing an essay or book on the "Love life of man," and probably then had a more extensive production in mind. It was a field hitherto reserved for creative writers, but, as Freud said, they have to mould the knowledge gained from intuition and experience into a form in accordance with their artistic needs, whereas the ruder hands of science are allowed no such "poetic license."

The first of them, on "A Special Type of Choice of Object made by Men," was published in the *Psychoanalytisches Jahrbuch*.[33] Freud gave an account of the theme to the Vienna Society on May 19, 1909, and there was a discussion of it at the next meeting (May 26). He actually wrote the essay itself in the summer of the following year, finishing it before leaving for his holiday.[34] At the end of May only one line had been written.[35]

For the type of man in question four conditions have to be fulfilled before he is moved to fall in love, and at first sight they appear very disparate.

(a) The woman has to belong to some other man. It may happen that no attraction is felt for her until she becomes engaged or married.

(b) Her reputation must be not entirely chaste. This varies from a tendency to flirtation to the extremes of promiscuity. Jealousy and mistrust always develop, although, curiously enough, not in respect of her legitimate partner.

(c) A sense of preciousness and uniqueness is attached to her in a much higher degree than is usual. And these attributes may become attached to one woman after another, to a whole series that fulfill the necessary conditions.

(d) The man has a constant phantasy of saving her from various imaginary dangers.

Freud, as the result of his analytical experiences with men of this type, was able to find a formula that covered all these various conditions. They represent one of the many outcomes of an early and pronounced fixation on the mother. With the type of men in question this fixation has lasted beyond the time of puberty. That explains the remarkable transference of exalted feelings from one woman to another, each in turn being the only woman in the world, all of them, however, being merely substitutes for the truly irreplaceable image in the unconscious. The disreputableness of the object surprisingly comes from the same source, dating from the discovery of parental intercourse when the mother is indulging in the forbidden acts and is untrue to her son. The first condition is easily understood as a rivalry with the father, the "owner" of the desired woman. The phantasy of saving, a theme which Otto Rank had extensively illustrated in his mythological studies, represents in the unconscious the desire to beget a child by the woman; Freud expounded in some detail the connections between these rather distant ideas.

As might be expected, there are numerous variations of the type here described. Freud's account was of the most typical and well-developed features.

(15) The second essay, published two years later in the same periodical, was "On the Universal Tendency to Debasement in the Sphere of Love." [36] Here Freud extended his vision beyond his professional sphere and raised questions of universal import to mankind.

He began with an exposition of the clinical findings on the subject of male impotence: the importance as aetiological factors of infantile fixations, the barrier of incest, and the later privations during adolescence. The essential point is the difficulty in fusing feelings of tenderness such as are appropriate toward a loved mother with sensual urges that seem incompatible with them.

Since everyone is subject to these influences one must ask why they do not always produce the same unfortunate result. One might, it is true, point to the varying strength of the factors in individual cases, but Freud did not burke the problem in that fashion. On the contrary, he boldly asserted that the unfortunate result is general, though of course of varying intensity. In other words, no civilized man is completely potent, can enjoy intense love together with the maximum of sensual pleasure. The respect for the partner that the former brings always inhibits to some extent the latter, and many men are only capable of intense physical pleasure with a woman socially, morally or aesthetically of a lower order.

With women a corresponding difficulty sometimes comes about from similar causes. The sense of forbiddenness in the years before marriage may become so closely associated with sensual longing that then they are anaesthetic when it is not present; they can enjoy intercourse with a lover but not with a husband.

Freud wisely remarked that psychoanalytic investigation can only be concerned with seeking explanations, not with giving advice. Reformers may avail themselves of the new knowledge, but psychoanalysis cannot predict the results of their efforts nor assure that they will not bring in their train new evils.

In a concluding section Freud opened a wide vista on the relation between the achievements of civilization and the privation on which they are necessarily built. No satisfactory compromise seems possible between them, so one has to be resigned to renunciation and suffering as the unavoidable lot of civilized man. It is even possible that further renunciations might lead to extinction of the human race.

He also raised the question whether there is not something inherent in the nature of the sexual instinct that prevents full gratification. Two factors, he suggested, are perhaps responsible for this: the two separate phases in human sexual development, in infancy and at puberty; and the anatomical proximity of the genital to the excremental organs.

(16) The third essay in the series did not appear until 1918. It was first published in the fourth series of Freud's *Sammlung kleiner Schriften zur Neurosenlehre*, under the title of "The Taboo of Virginity." [37] It concerns a problem in the fields of both sociology and anthropology, fields where Freud had already made important explorations. It was written in September 1917, but times were bad for publishing just then. Telling Ferenczi of it Freud jokingly added "You see, nothing is too small for me." [38]

Krafft-Ebing had described cases of extreme "thraldom" where a wife completely merges her personality in that of her husband; mild indications of this process are common enough in lasting marriages. Freud correlated its intensity with the amount of sexual resistance that the husband overcomes at the outset of marriage. A woman often feels a peculiar bond between her and the man with whom she first experiences intercourse; hence the significance of virginity in civilized life.

Freud then discussed the paradoxical custom of many primitive races where the opposite appears to hold, where every precaution is taken to ensure that some man *other* than the husband, preferably a senior or priest, performs the act of defloration. This, however, is not because such tribes regard the act with indifference; on the contrary, it has even more significance than with us. It comes under the heading of the taboo system, and care is taken that he who breaks the taboo, and suffers the consequence of doing so, is someone other than the man who has to spend his life with the woman concerned.[1] The problem is the nature of the danger against which the taboo has been instituted. Freud traced it to the transition the woman passes through in exchanging her original clitoritic (masculine) attitude for

---

[1] Many indications of this are to be found in customs of classical and even modern times. A faint trace of it is our custom of the best man having the privilege of claiming the first kiss after the wedding ceremony.

the vaginal (feminine) one of adult life. An ancient part of her mentality resents her being made into a woman and generates hostility towards the man who brings it about. It is from this hostility that the custom in question protects the future husband.

Freud supported this conclusion from his analytical experience. He explained the frequency of sexual anaesthesia among women in the same way, though here the woman's reaction is one of inhibition only rather than revengeful hostility. There are cases, however, where the latter appears in unexpected and inappropriate forms; for instance, when a loving wife may strike her husband even during a satisfying intercourse.

Freud concluded with a discussion of Hebbel's *Judith und Holofernes* and showed how the poet's intuition had discerned this theme behind the Biblical version of the story where it is suppressed.

(17) In 1910, not for the first time, the Vienna Psycho-Analytical Society held a discussion (May 25, June 1 and 8) on the topic of "onanism," masturbatory and other forms of auto-erotic activity. The main part of it was published two years later in book form to which Freud contributed introductory and closing remarks.[39] In the latter he listed the points on which there was general agreement, those where there were divergent opinions and those where there was still great uncertainty.

Freud defended against Stekel the conclusions he had reached years before on the aetiological importance of onanism in neurasthenia, but he admitted now that psychoanalysis of such patients could be therapeutically useful in enabling them to deal better with their sexual problems. There was general agreement that the significance of onanism, with the feelings of guilt attaching to the practice, lies in the phantasies, conscious or unconscious, that accompany or incite it. The harmful effects that it may give rise to Freud saw in three factors: (a) the organic consequences connected with excessive indulgence combined with inadequate satisfaction, (b) the habitual attitude of seeking gratification without making any efforts in the outer world (finding a partner, etc.) (c) through the favoring of infantile aims and the retention of psychical infantilism, which is the basis of the psychoneuroses.

(18) In 1913 Freud wrote a Preface to the German translation of J. G. Bourke's *Scatologic Rites of all Nations*.[40] This remarkable study of folklore and religion revealed how extraordinarily widespread in the most diverse cultures has been the interest attaching to the excremental functions. Freud commented on the confirmation the

book gave of his view that the infant derives great pleasure and interest from such functions, although that interest has to be largely diverted in the course of education. The book also confirmed Freud's other conclusion that there is an intimate association between excremental and sexual processes, notably in infancy, and even to some extent in later years. (A *roué*, for example, is said to have had "a dirty past.") The broad and tolerant attitude Freud here displayed contrasts with the violent emotions that such topics often evoke.

(19) In 1914 Freud made one of his radical revisions of his views on the structure of the mind in an important essay entitled "On Narcissism: An Introduction." [41] It caused some bewilderment among his adherents until we were able to assimilate its numerous implications. To convey the impression this essay made on psychoanalysts I may reproduce the comments I made on it some twenty years ago. [42]

"The second phase in the development of Freud's ideas on instinct dates from 1914, when he published a disturbing essay 'On Narcissism.' (I will explain in a moment why I use the word 'disturbing.') Self-love appears in its purest form in a sexual perversion Havelock Ellis was the first to describe by the name "narcissistic," referring to the well-known myth of the Greek youth who fell in love with himself. But it is easy to detect numerous other manifestations of the same tendency elsewhere. They are to be found in the megalomania of insanity, in the attention the hypochondriac devotes to his body, in various observations easily made on children, on the aged, on patients desperately ill, and even in the phenomena of normal love. Common to all these fields is a remarkable reciprocity between the love of self and the love of others, between what analysts term narcissism and object-libido respectively: when one increases the other diminishes, and vice versa. Freud supposed with good reason that the libido to begin with is all collected in the ego, that self-love is the beginning of all love. When it flows outwards we call it object-love, love for other objects than the self. That unfortunately it can flow back again, be once more withdrawn into the ego, is a familiar enough fact. In most marriages there are times later on when one partner reproaches the other that he (or she) does not love as much as formerly, that he (or she) has become "selfish." And, as hinted above, there are many typical situations in life, such as in disease, after an accident, in old age and so on, when the tendency to this withdrawal into self-preoccupation and self-love is apt to become pronounced.

"Now the reason why I called Freud's essay 'On Narcissism' a disturbing one was that it gave a disagreeable jolt to the theory of instincts on which psychoanalysis had hitherto worked. The observations on which the new conception of narcissism was founded were so unmistakable and easily confirmed that we had to accept it unreservedly, but it was at once plain that something would have to be done about the theory to which we were accustomed. For if the ego itself was libidinally invested, then it looked as if we should have to reckon its most prominent feature, the self-preservative instinct, as a narcissistic part of the sexual instinct. Adverse critics of psycho-analysis had always overlooked one half of the unconscious conflicts to which Freud had called so much attention and had charged him, *tout court*, with "reducing everything to sex," with "seeing nothing in the mind but sex." They were, it is true, supported by the fact that at that time most of Freud's discoveries had been in the field of repressed sexual impulses and very little in the other half of the mind. But he could easily rejoin that his main point was the fact of a conflict between sexual and non-sexual impulses, a "fifty-fifty" view of the mind. Now, however, that the ego itself was to be regarded as libidinal, were not the critics right from the start when they denounced Freud's tendency to "reduce everything to sex?" And what had become of his famous conflict? It is true that the psychoneuroses, his proper field of study, could still be described in terms of conflict: namely, that between narcissistic and object-libido. But did this mean that the only conflict was that between one form of sexual instinct and another form, that there was no other source of conflict in the mind? These and similar questions were thronging our minds just as the Great War broke out, and Freud was not able to give any answer to them until after its termination.

"Actually the case was not so serious as I have just portrayed, and the fallacy in my presentation of it is doubtless plain. To say there is reason to suppose that the ego is strongly invested with libido is clearly not the same thing as saying it is composed of nothing else.[1] Various other possibilities remained open. And the critics were quite wrong in asserting that Freud was aiming at a monistic libidinal conception of the mind. On the contrary, he was as obstinately dualistic as ever. But he was hard put to it to demonstrate one side of the conflict, to define any non-narcissistic components of the ego. His scientific career had received an apparent check, by no means for the first time."

[1] In a letter to me Freud neatly defined narcissism as "the libidinal complement to the egoism of the self-preservative instinct."

Freud twice in his life made fundamental changes in his theory of instincts. The present important essay represents the first of the two; the second time was eight years later. One is thus impelled to inquire into the circumstances of its composition, and if possible to relate it to Freud's mood and interests at the time. The first mention of it in his correspondence was in June 1913, when he said that the conception was to ripen during the summer vacation.[43] He added that it was intended to clear up his scientific difference with Adler, but one would think that at that time he had Jung more in his mind. A short description of narcissism also appears in the third section of the totem book, one which he wrote at the end of 1912.[44] He began writing the present essay in Rome in the third week of September 1913, and finished a rough draft before leaving there at the end of the month.[45] On February 21, 1914, he wrote to me that he intended beginning the final version "tomorrow." From the middle of February[46] he worked at it more systematically and completed it in a month.[47] He was very dissatisfied with the result. He wrote to Abraham: "The narcissism was a difficult labor [k] and bears all the marks of a corresponding deformation." [48] "That you accept what I wrote about narcissism touches me deeply and binds us even closer together. I have a very strong feeling of vexation at its inadequacy." [49]

Now in those two months, January and February 1914, Freud was also engaged in writing his "History of the Psycho-Analytic Movement," which he said he was doing "fuming with rage." [50] The one essay was the counterpart of the other. The one on narcissism dealt objectively with, among other things, the scientific differences between him and Adler and Jung; the other was of a more polemical nature. They were published in the same number of the *Jahrbuch der Psychoanalyse*, 1914. We are therefore justified in associating the two and in concluding that the stimulus to both came from the disagreements that had caused him so much distress in the previous couple of years.

Freud based his conception of narcissism on evidence drawn from many sources, but the main stimulus to forming it would seem to have come from his reflections on the nature of dementia praecox which Jung's writings had recently stirred. Jung had from his studies of dementia praecox come to the conclusion that libido, in the sexual sense in which Freud used the word, could not be distinguished from mental energy in general, so that for him it ceased to have any specific

---

[k] *schwere Geburt.*

meaning. He even maintained that Freud, in his Schreber analysis,[1] had been forced to come to a similar conclusion. In the present essay Freud contradicted him and gave his reasons for maintaining the distinction. He went on to add some valuable suggestions about the nature of this malady, making important further contributions to our knowledge of psychiatry in general. Thus he distinguished between the type of introversion that occurs in the psychoneuroses, where the withdrawn libido invests phantasies of other people, and that in dementia praecox where it is used to invest the ego itself.

Freud also dealt with some of Adler's conclusions. Accepting the descriptive aspects of the "masculine protest," which indeed contained nothing new to psychoanalysis, he gave his reasons for regarding Adler's explanation of it as quite inadequate and expounded the psychoanalytical one—its basis in the fear of castration.

The data on which Freud based the conception of narcissism were the manifestations of megalomania, i.e. the subjective over-estimation of self-importance, together with the magical belief in the "omnipotence of thoughts," to be found in dementia praecox, in the ideas of primitive races and in those of early childhood; in the last of these Ferenczi's contribution had been important. Furthermore, Freud instanced the self-absorption that takes place during sleep, during a painful illness when the patient withdraws both his love and his interest from the outside world, and in certain forms of passionate love, which, according to Freud, afforded the best evidence of all. Again there is the condition of hypochondria which Freud had had to study at close quarters during the last few years in his endeavor to help his friend Ferenczi, who was a severe victim of that affliction. He took the opportunity of making some important contributions to our knowledge of this distressing condition. In doing so he extended the libido theory by applying the idea of erotogenicity, formerly confined to certain areas of the surface of the body, to the internal organs as well.

The essay is particularly rich from many points of view. It contains, for instance, a study of the two (always two!) fundamental ways in which one chooses the object of one's love. They have been given the names of narcissistic choice and anaclitic choice respectively. In the former case the object corresponds with the picture of oneself (or a part of oneself), of what one used to be, or of what one would like to be. In the second case, where there is an association with non-sexual attributes of the parents, the choice falls, according to the

[1] See Chapter 11, Case IV.

sex, on a woman who tends, supports, helps or a man who protects. Freud expounded and illustrated these various types.

Again it was in this essay that Freud put forward his conception of an "ego ideal," one somewhat related to "conscience," though not identical with it. It is an agency in the mind that is invested with narcissistic libido, and Freud discussed at some length its ultimate origins. Coupled with this is a dissertation on the significance of the ego ideal for social life, the various identifications it may establish, and the impetus it may yield.

(20) Immediately after writing the two important essays just mentioned Freud read a paper before the Vienna Society, on March 11, 1914, on "A Case of Foot Fetishism"; it was never published. It concerned a man of forty-seven who had always been impotent. The case was under treatment for only a short while and without success. Freud assumed a primary excess of erotogenicity in the foot with such cases; in the present one there was premature excitation of it by a very abnormal mother who used to caress and kiss it to excess. The patient suffered serious intimidation in the sexual sphere at two periods of his life, once in childhood when his father threatened to castrate him, and again at puberty when he was surprised by the caretaker of his block of flats when attempting to have sexual relations with a girl. As a child he would lie with his head between his sister's thighs, and the sight of the female genital organ increased his fear of castration. When he was married he would dream that his wife was equipped with male organs. The sister in question had deformed legs from rickets, and it was her small foot that constituted his first ideal of a lovely and attractive organ—the foot. The perversion was evidently fixed by his seventh year, when he fell in love with his governess's foot. By then it had acquired the symbolic meaning of a male genital organ.

The interest in smell common in such cases was here replaced by pronounced visual curiosity. The patient as a child would creep on the floor like a dog in the hope of being able to see beyond the foot, but the excitement remained fixed at that point. The most important factor in the case Freud saw in the patient's masochistic attitude, which had been largely brought about as a reaction to the intimidation.

(21) In 1916 Freud interrupted his important series of theoretical papers to publish a more clinical one on "The Transformation of Instincts, with Special Reference to Anal Erotism." [51] Anal erotism seldom remains in its original form, and the indirect forms of expression it finds are very diverse. The present study, however, was not

really a comprehensive investigation of these various forms of expression, but was confined to consideration of the complicated relationships obtaining in the unconscious between three concrete and fundamental ideas: those of feces, child and penis respectively.

The first of these is in the nature of things the one that earliest arouses the infant's attention, and it soon becomes associated with the notion of giving or refusing to give; the latter, if pronounced, develops into the character trait of defiance. Feces are, therefore, the first gift, and all later gifts, whether bestowed or received, may reanimate this ancient association. As is well known, money often becomes a symbol for feces, as is illustrated by numerous expressions such as "filthy lucre," etc.

The association with the idea of a child probably dates back to the infantile view that it is born from the alimentary canal, the most obvious way in which things emerge from the body. It links also with the idea of a gift, and we still speak of a woman "presenting" her husband with a baby.

The associations of these two ideas with that of a penis naturally follow a different course in the two sexes. With both sexes a rod of feces may be regarded as a projecting organ, of course a part of oneself. With the male, however, its detachability and the subsequent loss of it assimilates the idea to that of castration, and anal-erotic derivatives, such as defiance, get fused with the castration fears that invariably develop; miserliness and fear of poverty are familiar manifestations. With the female much depends on how strong is her wish to possess a penis of her own. This very early becomes equated with the wish to bear a child, but the course of development is very far from simple. For instance, the later attraction towards a male is not always connected with the wish to bear a child by him. He may also be regarded as an appendage to a penis, and so constitute a way of obtaining that early desired object. Naturally the two wishes, for a penis and for a child, may combine, but often in very complicated ways.

Freud's analysis of this developmental theme is a very delicate one and reveals the unexpected complexities of it.

(22) Much of the libido theory was also expounded in Freud's *Introductory Lectures on Psycho-Analysis* (Chapters XX and XXI) published in 1917.[52] Since the exposition there takes a more conversational form it is easier reading than the *Three Essays* and constitutes an admirable introduction to them. It is indeed the path one would most recommend as the first approach to Freud's views on this subject.

(23) In 1919, at a time when he was still more engrossed with theory, Freud turned aside to publish a purely clinical study that reminds one of his earlier days. It was entitled "A Child Is Being Beaten," and was published in the *Zeitschrift für Psychoanalyse*.[53] It was a detailed study, some thirty pages long, of a particular erotic phantasy which is by no means uncommon. Freud had treated several cases in which it occurred and had been able to make a satisfactory analysis of it in six of them. He gave here a masterly analytic study of his experience.

The phantasy is of peculiar interest because of its offering great difficulties in the analysis. It is accompanied by very considerable shame and guilt, and it is hard to obtain any further details than the simple statement " a child is being beaten," an idea which in all cases is accompanied by pleasurable sensations relieved by masturbation. It is even hard to get clues to the identity of the victims, which are mostly "some boys," or of the person carrying out the beating. The genesis of the phantasy proved to be in important respects different in the two sexes.

With girls there are three phases in the genesis of the phantasy. The first of them, which had once been conscious, is of a non-sexual character. It expresses the wish that her father would beat, or otherwise show his displeasure to, another child of whom the subject was jealous. In the second phase, which is entirely unconscious, this wish has been changed into the phantasy of being beaten by the father, and this is accompanied by masochistic pleasure. In the third, conscious phase the father has been replaced by a teacher or person of similar standing, and the child being beaten is now a stranger. The latter is often a boy because the subject's repression of the incestuous wishes frequently sets up a regression to the earlier masculine wishes of the girl. The beating is therefore not only a punishment for the incestuous genital wishes, but a regressive (sexual) substitute for them.

Freud was not able to discover a primitive non-sexual phase of the phantasy with boys. It seems to begin with a masochistic wish to be beaten by the father, presumably a distortion of the simple wish to be loved by him. This becomes changed into the phantasy of "a boy" being beaten by a woman, evidently a substitute for the mother. With boys it is therefore throughout passive; with girls some sadistic gratification probably enters as well into the phantasy.

In this connection Freud added some important general remarks on the nature of sexual perversions. The chief one is that a perversion is the relic, or heir, of the Oedipus complex that usually finds its final thwarting about the age of four, and this explains the fact that manifest perversions hardly ever begin to show themselves before the age of five or six.

Freud then employed his analysis of the phantasy in question to test the validity of two suggestions that had been made to "sexualize" the process of repression. According to them, the conflict giving rise to psychoneuroses would be between two sexual impulses, a conclusion always alien to Freud's way of thinking. He does not mention the author of the first one, but it was certainly his former friend Fliess.[54] This was that the repressing agency corresponds with the dominant sex attitude of the subject, the repressed material emanating from the opposite one. In men the unconscious would consist of feminine impulses, in women of masculine ones. Freud had no difficulty in demonstrating the incompatibility of this view with the facts of analytic observation.

The second suggestion, this time a sociological rather than a biological one, had been put forward by Adler under the well-known caption of "masculine protest." Here the repressing force is supposed to proceed from masculine wishes in both sexes, the feminine one being repressed as unworthy and inferior. Freud subjected this suggestion to a very careful scrutiny in the light of his results in the analysis of the phantasy here under discussion, and again showed conclusively that it did not tally with the facts. He also agreed with other analysts that the feeling of inferiority on which Adler had laid such emphasis is simply an expression of the castration complex universally present in various degrees of strength.

13

Contributions to Theory

WE HAVE HERE TO CONSIDER EIGHT IMPORTANT PAPERS OF FREUD'S.
While some of them contain elements of a purely expository nature,
their main content consists of contributions to theoretical knowledge.

(1) The first one, entitled "The Antithetical Sense of Primal
Words," appeared in 1910 in the *Jahrbuch der Psychoanalyse*.[1] The
occasion for writing it was Freud's finding by chance a little brochure
that had been published by a German philologist, Abel, in 1884. This
afforded some explanation of an apparently incomprehensible observation Freud had made years before in his investigation of dream life,
and, incidentally, a confirmation of the trustworthiness of his technique.

Freud was enormously pleased at coming across this brochure. He
wrote at once to Ferenczi: "A little discovery I made a few days ago
has given me more pleasure than twelve articles of Aschaffenburg's
could.[a] A philologist called Abel had published in January 1884 a
brochure, *Der Gegensinn der Urworte* (The Antithetical Sense of
Primal Words), in which he maintained no more and no less than that
in many languages, old Egyptian, Sanskrit, Arabic and even in Latin,
opposites were designated by the same word. You will easily guess
what part of my discoveries about the unconscious is thereby confirmed. It is a long time since I have felt so victorious." [2]

Freud had observed that dream language was unable to express any
negative concept, that the words "no" and "not" were simply omitted
in it. Two results follow. Opposite ideas are often in dreams fused
into a single entity. Furthermore, a single image is capable of repre-

` An ironic allusion to one of his bitterest opponents.

senting both the plus and the minus aspects of itself, so that it is often hard to know at first sight which of the two opposite meanings is intended. This curious occurrence displays one more of the striking ways in which dream language differs from that of consciousness—to be more precise, of how the "primary process" differs from the "secondary process."

Now the interest of Abel's brochure was that in it he demonstrated just the same features in an old language, that of ancient Egypt. There it was common for a given word to be used for either of two opposite meanings. Thus, for example, a word could mean either "strong" or "weak." The two meanings were distinguished in writing by drawing a little figure after the word, in the one case an upright sturdy man, in the other a bent cripple. It is supposed that in speech the two meanings were distinguished by some appropriate gesture in place of these "determinatives." It would seem that early man could not apprehend such attributes unless there was a simultaneous allusion to its opposite, with which it was being contrasted. A "strong man" could not be understood unless one expressed it as "stronger than a weak man." As time went on man learned to apprehend concepts that stood alone without this simultaneous contrast. What happened then was that a gradual distinction was made between the opposite meanings by modifying the word for one of them. It would still happen even then that two such words would be fused into one, as Freud had observed in dream life.

Abel was able to find numerous traces of this curious primitive use in various other languages, even in Germanic ones. In Latin, for instance, *altus* meant "high" and "deep," *sacer* both "holy" and "accursed." The process of modification also can be traced. In Latin *siccus* means "dry," while *succus* means "juice." These modifications are naturally more visible where a language has changed considerably. Thus the old Saxon *bat* meaning "good" corresponds with the English word "bad"; the German *kleben* meaning "to adhere to" with the English "cleave" (to separate)[b] as well as "to cleave to" (to adhere). The English word "without" seems to be an example of two words of opposite meanings being fused, since "with" corresponds with the German *mit* (together with). It is, however, more complicated, since the word "with" originally had the meaning of "out," one still indicated in such words as "withdraw," "withhold," etc.

[b] These two meanings of "cleave" come from different roots which probably derived from a common one long ago and then came together again in the same word in modern times.

Freud remarked further on another resemblance between the Egyptian language and that of dreams: that one may find words, as well as situations, simply reversed. The same is often to be observed in the early play with words in which children indulge while learning to speak.

This whole train of thought is a brilliant confirmation of Freud's view, expressed in *The Interpretation of Dreams*, that dream language is typically archaic in nature and represents a regression to the most primitive mode of thought.

The empirical findings of Abel in philology and of Freud in dream interpretation, both pointing to a primitive form of language, had, interestingly enough, been anticipated as early as 1870 by the English philosopher Alexander Bain on purely theoretical grounds. "The essential relativity of knowledge cannot but show itself in language. If everything that we can know is viewed as a transition from something else, every experience must have two sides; and either every name must have a double meaning, or else for every meaning there must be two names." [3]

Still more remarkable is the fact, which Stekel pointed out,[4] that Schubert in his book *Die Symbolik des Traumes* (The Symbolism of Dreams) (first edition 1814) had commented on the ambivalence of words in dreams and also in various languages. It is a book that Freud often quoted, and he must have read that passage. So we have here yet another example of Freud noting a discovery, forgetting it, and then rediscovering it in another connection.

(2) A year later, in 1911, Freud published, also in the *Jahrbuch*,[5] what was to prove one of the classics of psychoanalytical literature. It was a short paper entitled "Formulations on the Two Principles of Mental Functioning."

Freud started composing this paper in June 1910, and evidently did not find it easy. He told Jung he was plagiarizing some of the ideas in Jung's libido essay, a year before the differences in their conceptions became manifest.[6] On October 26 he gave an account of the theme before the Vienna Society, but apparently the audience found it too difficult to assimilate at once. At all events Freud reported that their response was so unsatisfactory that at the end he was displeased himself with the ideas he had presented; it would have been better if he had told them something about the Schreber case.[7] He had as usual spoken without notes, and it was only in December that he committed the theme to paper;[8] it was finished at the end of January 1911.[9]

It was essentially a further exposition of ideas already hinted at in the seventh chapter of *The Interpretation of Dreams*. But the concluding remarks in it show that for Freud the ideas were now serving as a starting-point for further thoughts that were as yet unripe.

It begins with the observation that in every neurosis the patient turns away from reality, and, moreover, does so because he finds it, or some part of it, unbearable. This sentence alone, apart from very many other ones in Freud's writings, shows how unjustified is the reproach which has been levelled against him that he neglected the importance of the social environment in the genesis of the neuroses.

The two principles Freud here established, which he termed the "pleasure-principle" and the "reality-principle" respectively, are really extensions of the distinction he had pointed out fifteen years before between the "primary system" and the "secondary system" of mental functioning. It was this distinction on which rests Freud's chief claim to fame: even his discovery of the unconscious is subordinate to it.

In the primary system, such as operates in the young infant, in dreams and to a large extent in waking phantasies, the pleasure-principle dominates the scene. No mental process has any other purpose than to elicit pleasure and avoid unpleasure. It is its failure to procure adequate satisfaction that compels the further step of taking reality into account. Now it is no longer what is pleasurable that counts but also what is real. This is the transition from the earlier principle to the later one, a transition that is never fully completed.

Freud then makes eight comments on the consequences of this fateful change.

(a) A series of changes in the "psychical apparatus" becomes necessary. Both consciousness and the sense organs achieve a heightened significance and have to attend to various qualities beyond that of pleasure alone. The function of Attention is developed, so as to be prepared for the new impressions. They are noted and gradually a Memory is developed. Repression, or flight, is to some extent replaced by Judgment. Motor discharge, instead of being inchoate as earlier, is organized in the direction of Behavior. This is carried out through a process of Thought, which is in essence a probing action, a seeking in various directions with the least possible expenditure of energy.

All these features had been already adumbrated in the "Project" Freud had composed in 1895.[10] Even the phraseology is almost identical.

(b) The difficulty of passing from one principle to the other is shown by a special region being reserved where the earlier pleasure principle may still reign. This is the phantasy life, the continuation of the play of children.

(c) The transition in question takes place only gradually and does so earlier and more fully in connection with the "ego impulses" than with the sexual ones. Their responses to the necessities and privations of life are different. The latter impulses, which soon find gratification auto-erotically, remain much longer under the domination of the pleasure principle, often for the rest of life. This is the weak spot in our mental organization, and it also accounts for the important part played by the sexual impulses in the aetiology of the neuroses. Freud expounded this theme more fully later in his *Introductory Lectures*.[11]

(d) The transition betokens not an abrogating of the pleasure principle, but the providing of a more secure basis for it. A momentary pleasure with uncertain consequences is renounced in order to gain in a new way one that will come later but be more sure. The aim of both principles is in the last resort the same. Nevertheless the internal impression made by the change of method is so powerful that it is mirrored in a special religious myth—that of reward in the next world for the privations and renunciations in this one.

Freud quoted here a sentence from Bernard Shaw illustrating the superiority of the reality principle. "To be able to choose the line of greatest advantage instead of yielding in the direction of the least resistance." I had recently got him to read *Man and Superman*, and he told me he inserted this quotation to show he had profited by it. But he never came to like Shaw's writings, probably because of their widely differing conceptions of womanhood.

(e) Education is evidently based on the same process. Friendliness from the teacher is the bribe that hastens it. Freud remarked that with a spoiled child, who feels sure of being loved anyhow, the stimulus is less, but he did not mention the opposite case of the child who has received insufficient affection.

(f) Artistic creativeness achieves a novel combination of the two principles. The artist is a man who refuses to accept the necessary privations of life and turns from reality into the world of phantasy where his unsatisfied wishes receive imaginary gratification. He then, however, uses his special gifts to find a way back to reality, or a new form of it, by creating works that appeal to similar dissatisfactions in other people.

(g) While the ego is passing through its transitional phase the sexual instinct is moving from its original auto-erotism toward love of an object. Freud here throws out an idea that he developed a year later.[c] It was that the type of neurosis occurring depends on the relative stages in development the ego and sexual instincts have reached respectively when any block occurs in the evolution.

(h) The character of unconscious mental processes that we find most alien, and which is therefore very hard for us to assimilate, is the way in which they equate thoughts with real happenings. It is therefore often not easy to distinguish the fulfillment of a wish in phantasy from the memory of a happening, a difficulty which in his earlier days had led Freud seriously astray.[12]

This short paper represents one of the dividing lines in the development of Freud's thought. Although it would appear little more than a clearer and fuller presentation of what he had for some years promulgated, there are hints that he was then about to search for more profound conceptions of mental structure.

(3) The next paper on theory, "Some Remarks on the Concept of the Unconscious as Used in Psycho-Analysis," was in 1912 when the Society for Psychical Research in London asked Freud for a contribution to a Medical Supplement it was preparing of their *Proceedings*.[13] Freud wrote it in English, which was corrected in London;[14] it was Hanns Sachs who translated it into German for publication in the *Zeitschrift*.

Freud concentrated on defining the sense in which the word "unconscious" was used in psychoanalysis. Starting from the latent memories which are too weak to enter consciousness unless they are specially stimulated he proposed for them the name "preconscious." The experiments of post-hypnotic suggestion, however, prove that such memories can be active and produce effects without themselves entering consciousness. He described the cases of dual personality, the French *double conscience*, as cases where consciousness alternates from one area to another—and that in spite of the examples, such as Morton Prince's Sally Beauchamp, where the one personality claimed to be *aware* of what was going on even when the other personality was "on top." Freud's reason was that philosophers had misgivings enough in being asked to accept the idea of unconscious mental processes, and that they would surely boggle at the suggestion of an "unconscious consciousness."

He then established the cardinal distinction between this preconscious and what he called the unconscious proper, i.e. the processes that are not able to enter consciousness but which are nevertheless

[c] See Chapter 10, No. 9.

capable of producing indirect effects and so must be considered as active. With this distinction went his conception of a barrier maintained by an active force, repression. He supported it by reference to the group of slips in everyday life, so easily accessible to observation, and above all to the results of dream analysis. He did not miss the opportunity of emphasizing the importance of the latter. "Psychoanalysis is based on dream analysis; the interpretation of dreams is the most complete piece of work that the young science has so far accomplished." [15]

He then expressed the opinion that every mental process begins as an unconscious one; only subsequently is it decided whether it is to be allowed to pass the barrier into consciousness or remain unconscious. This pronouncement was a significant advance on his earlier opinion that the unconscious consists of ideas that have been expelled from consciousness, and it is one that has not even yet supplanted the latter with the general public.

Finally he laid stress on the third feature of the unconscious as the term is used in psychoanalysis; namely, that it constitutes a distinct system of mental processes with laws of its own that differ widely from those with which we are familiar in consciousness.

Two years later the profounder conceptions hinted at above began to appear. The other five papers we shall consider here are of a much more technical nature than any previous ones. They were all written in the spring of 1915 and were published in the *Internationale Zeitschrift für Psychoanalyse*, three of them in 1915, and two in 1917. They represent a summing up of Freud's ideas at that time, the nearest approach to a synthesis he ever wrote. But they are more than a simple summary, since they contain a number of important new conceptions. In Freud's judgment some of them, particularly the third and fourth essays, were comparable to the famous concluding section of *The Interpretation of Dreams*, 1900, the highest level of thought he had hitherto reached.[16]

These five papers are all that remain of the twelve essays Freud wrote in 1915 on metapsychology. The unhappy story of their fate was described in a previous chapter,[a] together with an account of the circumstances under which they were composed and the motives impelling Freud at that time.

(4) The first of the series was entitled *"Triebe und Triebschicksale,"* [17] which has usually been translated as "Instincts and Their

[a] Chapter 7, p. 186.

Vicissitudes." The German word *Trieb* is less committal than the English "Instinct," which definitely implies an inborn and inherited character. Other words such as "urge," "impulsion" or the more colloquial and expressive American "drive," have been suggested as translations, but none of them is entirely satisfactory. On the whole the word in Freud's writings more often means "instinct" in our sense. But he has an interesting preliminary passage deprecating in a young and growing branch of science a too eager proclivity to tie oneself at the beginning to strict definitions. Nevertheless, in an addition he had made to the third edition of the *Three Essays on the Theory of Sexuality* in the same year, he had made a very good approximation to a definition: "By an 'instinct' (*Trieb*) is provisionally to be understood the psychical representative of an endosomatic, continuously flowing source of stimulation, as contrasted with a 'stimulus' (*Reiz*), which is set up by *single* excitations coming from *without*. The concept of instinct is thus one of those lying on the frontier between the mental and the physical. The simplest and likeliest assumption concerning the nature of instincts would seem to be that in itself an instinct is without quality, and, so far as mental life is concerned, is only to be regarded as a measure of the demand made on the mind for work. What distinguishes the instincts from one another and endows them with specific qualities is their relation to their somatic sources and to their aims. The source of an instinct is a process of excitation occurring in an organ and the immediate aim of the instinct lies in the removal of this organic stimulus." [18]

Starting from a scheme of reflexes he stated that an instinct is a stimulus to the mind, but only one of such stimuli. Its characteristic is that it emanates from the interior of the body. The result is that the mind has to deal with it differently from the method (of simple withdrawal) that can be employed with external stimuli. Furthermore, it differs from the latter in being continuous until relief is obtained. A better name for an instinctual stimulus is "need."

It is the chief function of the nervous system (and mind) to master stimuli, to control them or abolish them in the aim of restoring the previous state of rest. With instincts this ideal aim is impossible because of their constant action, so the activity can hope only to *diminish* the amount of excitation. Freud then, in accord with the pleasure-unpleasure principle, equated this excitation with unpleasure and the relief from it as pleasure. He went on to discuss some conceptions used in connection with instincts: their impulsive force (*Drang*), aim, object and sources. Here he brought forward the concept of "aim-inhibited" instincts, those that proceed a certain distance in the direction of satisfaction and are then inhibited.

Coming to the nice question of how many, and which, instincts one should take into account, he remarked that, although there is no objection to enumerating a considerable number, play instinct, social instinct, etc., it is worth asking whether the ultimate sources of these are not more fundamental. If so, they would fall into a small number of groups. He himself proposed to use two such "primal instincts" (*Urtriebe*): namely, ego or self-preservative instincts and the sexual ones. He called this a purely temporary "auxiliary hypothesis," to be discarded whenever our further knowledge finds it desirable to do so, and he stated that his choice had been dictated by his early experience of finding that the psychoneuroses proceed from a conflict between the two groups in question. Ample support for it, moreover, is to be found in the field of biology, which has to contrast the activities of the individual with the permanent importance to the race of the germ plasma of which the individual is the temporary bearer.

Freud confined himself here to an analysis of the ways in which the sexual instinct seeks expression, and that for the obvious reason that it had been the one psychoanalysis had at that time most extensively investigated. His hope, however, that further studies would do the same for the ego-instincts was gratified in the following decade.

Freud listed under four headings the processes that may be followed by the sexual instinct: "Reversal into an opposite"; "Turning round upon the subject"; "Repression"; "Sublimation." In this essay he dealt with only the first two of these.

The first of them has two forms: a conversion from activity to passivity, such as from sadism to masochism, or pleasure in looking to pleasure at being looked at. This reversal affects only the aim of the instinct. The other change, one in content, is the turning of love into hate.

With the turning against the self, on the other hand, what is essential is the change of object.

In Freud's opinion both of these processes are initiated during the narcissistic phase of development and continue to carry traces of this.

The paper contains an important discussion of the status of sadism as seen from a purely clinical point of view. Freud was within a few years to change radically his views on this topic, but then on other grounds than clinical ones. He argued here that the infliction of physi-cal pain is not an original feature of sadism, but becomes associated with it only by the roundabout way of the pain experienced in masochism proving sexually exciting.

Freud did not find it easy to fit into his scheme the facts concerning love and hate, their interchangeability, co-existence, ambivalence, and so on. He approached the problem in this way. He first noted the three opposites: loving-hating; loving-being loved; loving or hating versus indifference. He then reflected that mental life altogether is dominated by three polarities: subject (ego)—object (outer world); pleasure—unpleasure; active—passive. The self is passive towards external stimuli, but active through its instincts. Later in development there seems to be a certain correlation between active and masculine on the one hand, passive and feminine on the other, but Freud said that this is by no means so regular and exclusive as is generally assumed.

The first of these he designated as the polarity of reality, the second as an economic polarity and the third as a biological polarity.

Since the infant's sexuality is at first gratified auto-erotically it must begin by being indifferent on this score to the outer world, but when it obtains gratification from the outside also, in connection with the bodily needs of the ego, the situation is changed. Freud considered that then the infant introjects these external sources of pleasantness into itself, and at the same time projects on to the outer world the unpleasant tension arising from its instincts.

It is noticeable here that Freud spoke only of the absorption of the good and the expulsion of the bad. Some years later Melanie Klein amplified the statement by laying stress on the two opposite processes.[19]

This results in what he called a "purified pleasure ego" in place of the earlier actual one, so that a contrast was established between pleasure in the subject and unpleasure in the object. This is the beginning of hate. But he would not regard hate as being specially bound up with sexuality. The ego hates all objects (in the outer world) that signify privation, whether of sexual or of ego satisfaction. So love and hate do not stand in a simple relation to each other; it is only through a rather complicated development that they come later to represent opposites. Hate emanates essentially from the ego group of instincts, but through the similarity in expression of hate and the sadistic component of the anal-sadistic phase of libidinal development hate may enter into a close association with love, leading to the familiar ambivalence in human relations.

This last theme of the genesis of love and hate, here presented in a condensed fashion, is perhaps the most valuable part of this essay, one which marks the beginning of a further development in Freud's thought.

A striking feature of the essay is the prominence in it of one set of contrasts, and one pair of opposites, after another. It vividly illustrates a peculiar feature of Freud's thinking throughout his life, his constant proclivity to dualistic ideas. Any kind of pluralism was quite alien to him. Someone once said facetiously that he had never learned to count beyond the number two. This tendency must have arisen in great part from the deep impression made on him by the phenomenon of conflict, which typically is between two opposing forces, but it must also have corresponded with something deep and characteristic in his nature about which it may be possible to say more later.

(5) The second paper in this series is simply entitled "Repression," [20] an ancient theme to which Freud had for years given much anxious thought. Since many of its problems are bound up with those of the unconscious, a subject Freud dealt with only later in this series, the paper represents a far from finished study and we are left with the impression that the problems it raises are much more complicated than one expected to find. A few outstanding points, however, may be selected for emphasis.

Seven years earlier (June 3, 1908) he had told the Vienna Society that in his opinion repression affected only sexual impulses. All other effects were secondary. He never retracted this.

An instinctual impulse may be repressed through a conscious condemnation. Repression is a half-way stage to this from the primitive flight by means of which the mind escapes from an unpleasant external stimulus. The condition for repression of an impulse is that, although gratification of it would be pleasurable, its incompatibility with other agencies of the mind would produce unpleasure, and—this is the important point—the latter would prove to be the stronger.

Repression is not a defensive mechanism that is present from the beginning. It can take place only after the distinction between the unconscious and consciousness has been effected. Before it the simpler defensive mechanisms of reversal into the opposite and turning against the self operate.

Freud then spoke of a "primal repression" where the mental representative of an instinct is not allowed to enter consciousness. This always goes with a "fixation" of the instinct on the idea concerned. Later repressions, where ideas are either kept from consciousness or expelled after having been present in it, can come about only when they are associated with one of the primal repressed ideas. The latter exercise an attraction on it, without which no effort on the part of consciousness would succeed in expelling it. The laity commonly apprehend only the latter, less important, feature of repression, overlooking Freud's fuller statement.

Repression does not prevent further activity on the part of the repressed ideas. They may organize themselves in groups, produce various derivatives, and above all pullulate in phantasy so that when the analyst first brings them to consciousness the patient is terrified at their imaginary strength and horrified at their outrageousness.

The indirect effect of repressed ideas is extraordinarily variable. The likelihood of one of their derivatives becoming also repressed depends on two factors: its nearness or remoteness in association with one of the primal ideas; and the state of activity in which the latter happens to be at the moment. There are, however, some techniques by which the conditions of pleasure-unpleasure production are altered so that a repressed idea may for a moment enter consciousness; the best known of these is wit, including jokes.

Repression does not signify a fixed state of affairs, something that happens once and for all. It is, on the contrary, highly mobile, varying in its intensity from time to time. A repressed idea may, therefore, be admissible to consciousness on one occasion and not on another, or in one context and not in another.

Freud discussed separately the fate of a repressed idea and that of the accompanying affect, which he equated with the psychical energy of the impulse in question. The fate of the two is by no means identical, and Freud laid stress on the frequency with which in these circumstances the affect is "transformed" into anxiety.

Freud ended the paper with some clinical comparisons of the different ways in which repression operates in three of the psychoneuroses. The only one of these in which repression achieves its aim of abolishing the accompanying affect is in some cases of conversion hysteria, where Charcot had already commented on what he called *"la belle indifférence des hystériques."*

(6) The next essay, entitled "The Unconscious," [21] is not only the most extensive one of the series—it is forty pages long—but also the most important. It was perhaps the most fundamental contribution to psychology Freud had made since *The Interpretation of Dreams* fifteen years before. Even Freud himself, who was so often dissatisfied with his productions, was of opinion that it was the best thing he had written for years.[22]

It began with the statement that the unconscious embraces more than what is repressed; the latter forms only a part of it. Freud had insisted on this years before;[23] indeed, there was a broad hint of it in a letter to Fliess as early as 1896.[24] The belief that Freud's unconscious contains only disreputable ideas that had to be repressed has not yet, however, been shaken in the popular mind.

The essay has seven sections. The first one is a brilliant exposition of the necessity and legitimacy of the conception that there is an unconscious mind. To condense the well-marshalled arguments here would impair their precision, but if any philosophers remain who still insist on equating "mental" entirely with "conscious" they may be recommended to study them.

Freud then pointed out that the word "unconscious" is used in more than one sense. At times it is purely descriptive, e.g. a part of the mind devoid of consciousness, and at other times it has a more systematic meaning, i.e. a part of the mind with peculiar characteristics. The two do not invariably go together. Mental processes originating in the unconscious may pass through a barrier, which he likened to a censorship, and thus reach another region of the mind. Even then, however, they are not necessarily conscious, although they possess the attribute of being "admissible to consciousness." They are then termed "preconscious," and have only a further slight barrier to pass before entering consciousness. This topographical conception of different mental systems raises the question of what happens in the passage from one to the other. Does a new imprint of the idea in question get made in the second locality, so that there would be two of them, or does some change take place in the original impression and in its original place? Freud seemed for the moment to favor the latter view. In this topographical discussion he was careful to avoid, indeed to deny, any connection with the anatomy of the brain, a former love he had long forsaken, and he was more than skeptical about any attempt to correlate consciousness with the cerebral cortex and the unconscious with lower centers of the brain. It may prove that he was over-skeptical in this.

The third section dealt with the matter of unconscious feelings. Freud admitted that it may not be strictly accurate to speak of unconscious affects or emotions, but in practice it was justifiable on the following grounds. Repression may entirely inhibit the development of any affect, such as usually accompanies an instinctual activity. When it fails to do so then the affect comes to consciousness by getting attached to some more or less distant derivative of the unconscious idea, or, thirdly, it is converted into anxiety and perhaps may be so converted within the unconscious system itself. When one speaks of unconscious affects one is using a shorthand expression for one of the two former cases; referring that is to say, to the affect that should belong to the impulse in action.

In Freud's opinion the real aim of repression, if such a teleological expression is permissible, is to inhibit all affects. This is of interest in connection with the Breuer-Freud principle of "abreaction" in therapy.

The fourth section has to do with the dynamic aspects of repression, and now Freud was able to get further with the problem than he could in the paper on repression itself. He operated with the word "cathexis" (*Besetzung*), which roughly means a "charge of energy." A repressed idea, being capable of activity, must retain its cathexis. But an idea that has once been in the preconscious and is repressed in the manner described above (attraction plus repulsion) has first to have its cathexis withdrawn before repression can occur. That, however, is not enough; otherwise the procedure would have to be endlessly repeated. So Freud postulated a "counter-cathexis," to which the cathexis withdrawn from the preconscious idea probably contributes, and it is this that maintains the repression.

He then remarked that these considerations are of an economic order, implying matters of quantity, an addition to his former dynamic conception. He proposed to use the word "metapsychology" to denote such a comprehensive study of any mental process as would include an account of its *dynamic, topographical* and *economic* aspects, i.e. as full an account as could possibly be given. In the present state of our knowledge this was evidently an ideal, one to be approached only after extensive further investigations. He nevertheless offered a tentative exposition of a metapsychological description of the process of repression in the three transference neuroses. It was a successful effort, the most interesting part being a detailed account of the different phases in the genesis of phobias. One notes that here for the first time Freud used the "signal" analogy which he was to develop extensively in his later writings on anxiety;[25] he had, it is true, used it in a somewhat different connection years before (in 1895 and 1899).[26]

The next section is concerned with the special characteristics of the unconscious "system." In this system there is no negation, no doubt, and no degree of certainty: everything is absolute. It is only the censorship emanating from the higher preconscious system that modifies this quality of absoluteness. The kernel of the unconscious consists of wishes proceeding from instinctual excitation, just as in the later conception of an Id.[e]

Freud then enumerated the main characteristics of the system as follows: (a) There is no sense of contradiction in the unconscious. Opposite or incompatible ideas exist happily side by side and exert no influence on each other. (b) Condensation of ideas and displacement of affect from one idea to another takes place freely without the least inhibition. These are features of what Freud had in *The Interpretation of Dreams* described as the "primary process" [27] and here he generously gave Breuer credit for his share in distinguishing between the primary and secondary processes. (c) The unconscious has no conception of time. Ideas and impulses from different ages are telescoped together, and only the present exists. (d) The unconscious has no relation to outer reality, which is replaced by a sense of psychical reality. When there is a wish for something to happen it simply happens.

Freud then contrasted these features with those of the preconscious system. He laid stress here on its inhibiting effect, partial or complete, on the free movement of displacement that occurs in the primary process, and said in this connection that in his opinion Breuer's conclusions about there being two states of cathectic energy in mental life, one a "tonic" bound state, the other a "freely mobile" one, represented the most penetrating insight we possess up to the present into the nature of nervous energy.

The sixth section, on the inter-communication between the two systems, is perhaps the most valuable part of this essay. Freud gave a much needed warning against over-simplifying the conclusions stated above. The unconscious is not a mere deposit, something done with. On the contrary, it is alive and has many kinds of relationship with the higher systems, even occasionally cooperation. The separation between it and the other systems is far from sharp: in pathological states, particularly in insanity, they may get mixed in a confused way and even interchange their characteristics.

There are some derivatives of the unconscious which seem to have opposite characteristics. On the one hand they are highly organized, free of any inner contradictions, and so are hardly to be distinguished from preconscious thoughts. Yet on the other hand they are not capable of entering consciousness, and so still belong to the primary system. They may even enter the preconscious, but the censorship be-

• See Volume III.

tween this and consciousness recognizes their origin and bars further progress. Freud was referring here to the unconscious phantasies of the normal as well as those of the neurotic.

This and other considerations show that the single feature of "being conscious" bears no simple relationship to the distinction between the systems nor to the conditions that determine repression. Much of what can be conscious is only occasionally so, being otherwise latent; much that shares the usual attributes of the conscious mind can nevertheless not be admitted to consciousness, and the function of attention itself also restricts the range of consciousness. It is not only what is repressed that does not enter consciousness, but a great part of the excitations that move the ego itself, i.e. processes of exactly the opposite nature to that of the repressed ideas. So Freud came to the conclusion that in the striving for a full metapsychological conception of mental processes one should learn to emancipate oneself from what he called the mere symptom of "being conscious." But he also noted that the function of consciousness is not restricted to its being simply a perceptual organ: it probably also implies a "super-cathexis," a higher step in mental organization.

It may happen that even an intensely repressed impulse fuses with a dominating one proceeding from the ego. Then the repression is temporarily abrogated, and the impulses combine in their action.

It is remarkable how the unconscious of one person may react to the unconscious of another, a fact worthy of special investigation.

How far the preconscious can influence and produce changes in the unconscious is very hard to estimate. But Freud asserted that any such changes must be very slow and hard to bring about.

The last section is an attempt to bring our knowledge about the unconscious, novel as it is, into some relation with any previous knowledge of the mind. Freud turned for this purpose to the study of schizophrenia. Here he commented on the various features, rejection of reality, restriction of transferences, tendency to apathy, etc., that made him call it a narcissistic affection. It would appear that the repressed impulses cease searching for objects, even in phantasy, and withdraw towards the self. This in itself, however, throws no light on the problem just mentioned, but he found in the study an unexpected clue. This was the peculiar part played by speech in this disorder. In the first place the patients' utterances, and their play with words, commonly center on some part of their body, so that Freud speaks of their "organ language." Then such patients treat words on the lines of the Primary Process, condensing words and displacing their cathexis with the greatest freedom. Their symptoms also are often built on resemblances between words instead of ideas as with the transference psychoneuroses. So it would seem that in renouncing the cathexis of objects such patients retain a cathexis of the designating words.

From this Freud concluded that the essential distinction between the unconscious system and the preconscious and conscious ones is neither the forging of new impressions of an idea in another locality nor any functional changes in their cathexis on the same spot, but the addition in the higher systems of a verbal concept to the more concrete one present in the unconscious. What repression really effects in the psychoneuroses is that the discarded idea is not to be expressed verbally. Patients often say that what they glimpse cannot be put into words.

Freud remarked that this was a piece of insight he had already expressed in *The Interpretation of Dreams*, 1900, but it was only now that he grasped its full significance and was able to make full use of it in constructing his theories. He had made the point not only in *The Interpretation of Dreams*,[28] but several times in his correspondence with Fliess in 1895 and 1896.[29] Indeed the idea was probably in his mind even earlier, since there are hints of it in his discussion of the meaning of words in his book *On Aphasia* in 1891.[30] This appears to be another one of Freud's ideas that he forgot and then recaptured more than once.[31]

(7) In the following year, 1916, Freud interrupted the series to publish a more clinical paper on the transformation of certain instinctual processes[f] and in the next year, another theoretical paper appeared, the "Metapsychological Supplement to the Theory of Dreams." [32] In a footnote to it he said he had originally intended to publish in book form a collection of essays, of which the present and the succeeding one would form chapters, under the title of "Preliminary Material for a Metapsychological Theory." It is a pity the plan never came to fruition. What seems to have happened was that Freud's interests, now deeply engaged in formulating a theoretical basis for psychoanalysis, were on the point of leading him to still more radical conceptions, which will be considered in the next volume of this biography. He was now in the sixties and about to enter on his final more philosophical phase, a reversion to early tendencies that had long been held in check.

The present essay adds little to the theory of dreams Freud had propounded seventeen years before, but it rounded it off in a more

[f] See Chapter 12, No. 21.

polished form by taking into account the metapsychological points of view he had recently been developing.

He began by remarking how advantageous it is for the pursuit of psychoanalysis to include comparisons with more normal states of mind, such as dreaming, grief and falling in love. Here he confined himself to the first of these. The withdrawal of interest in the outer world, which is an indispensable condition for sleep, means that one is thereby reverting to the womb-like state, with its accompaniments of rest and warmth; indeed many people adopt a foetal position when they sleep. In the psychoneuroses we are familiar with the two manifestations of *temporal* regression, that of the ego to the level of hallucinatory wish-fulfillment and that of the libido to the primitive state of narcissism: The same is to be observed in dreams, which are completely egoistic in nature. The narcissistic interest in the body, which Freud termed the libidinal complement to egoism, accounts for the interesting occurrence in which bodily disturbances are revealed during sleep long before they manifest themselves in waking life.

Dreaming implies a disturbance of this peaceful state of affairs. The wish to sleep is interfered with, not only by occasional external stimuli, but by certain unresolved thoughts of the previous day which have retained a certain amount of cathexis that resists the general withdrawal of interest from the outer world. They only have enough strength, however, to impair the wish to sleep when they are reinforced by unconscious instinctual excitations with which they have, either at the time or during sleep, entered into association. That can only mean that the unconscious has been able to retain some of its cathexis during sleep. This resistance of the unconscious to preconscious influences, e.g. the wish to sleep, is one of its most important characteristics.

The dream wish thus formed cannot find expression along motor paths during sleep, or only in the exceptional case of somnambulism, nor can it penetrate into consciousness where it would create a delusional belief, as happens in insanity. It follows a particular and quite unexpected path, regressing via the unconscious to the perceptual system itself—one with which consciousness has special links. The feeling of conviction that dreams give is thus akin not to delusions, but to hallucinations, i.e. to processes that operate through the sensorium; this brings the character of dreams very close to the hallucinatory psychoses. This regression may be termed a *topographical* one in distinction to the temporal ones mentioned above. In it presentation of words (*Wortvorstellungen*) are reduced to the primitive presentation of things (*Sachvorstellungen*), which then undergo the typical displacements and condensations of the Primary Process. Here there is a sharp difference between dreams and schizophrenic processes; in the latter it is the words themselves which are treated like things and subjected to the influence of the Primary Process. But, on the other hand, one may say that in dreams there is a topographical regression which does not take place in schizophrenia.

In this connection Freud discussed the nature of *hallucinations*. They cannot be explained by a simple regression of the kind that takes place in dreams. Something must also have happened to the "criteria of reality," which Freud regarded as an institution of the ego and placed in what he called the "perceptual consciousness." He inferred that hallucinations can never be an early symptom in any psychosis, but can come about only after some impairment of that institution of the ego.

He concluded by illustrating in a sentence the value topographical considerations of the process of repression have for our understanding of various conditions. Withdrawal of cathexis affects all systems in dream life (though the unconscious one less than the others): it affects the preconscious system in the psychoneuroses; the unconscious system in schizophrenia; and the conscious system in the hallucinatory psychoses (Meynert's amentia).

(8) The last essay in the series deals with both a normal condition and an abnormal one: "Mourning and Melancholia." [33] Apart from his few remarks on schizophrenia and "amentia" this is the only serious attempt Freud made to discuss the metapsychological implications of any psychosis. He admitted the special nosological difficulty about melancholia, that it does not appear to be a unity and that its status is still uncertain. Nevertheless he was sure that a considerable number of cases were purely psychogenic in their nature, even if other cases had an organic, e.g. a toxic, origin.

Freud had expounded the views expressed in this essay in a discussion at the Vienna Society on December 30, 1914, on the occasion of a paper Tausk read on melancholia.

Just as in the previous paper he had contrasted normal dreaming with narcissistic disorders such as schizophrenia, Freud here took as his basis the contrast between normal mourning and pathological depression. It was the same comparison and contrast that had inspired Abraham in one of his most original studies,[34] and Freud's paper constitutes an extension of Abraham's conclusions. Freud had written a draft of the essay in February 1915 and sent it to Ferenczi with the request to forward it then to Abraham.[35] Abraham made some lengthy comments on it, but the closing of the frontier between Germany and Austria at that time delayed his letter for several weeks. He was concerned to ascertain the psychological difference between the obsessional neurosis and melancholia, two conditions that have much in common, and he suggested that, although sadism was important in both, the oral factor played the part in melancholia that anal-erotism does in the obsessional neurosis. Here is Freud's reply: "Your comments on melancholia I found very valuable. I have unhesitatingly incorporated in my essay what I found useful. The most valuable point was your remark about the oral phase of the libido; the connection you had made between mourning and melancholia is also mentioned. Your request for criticism was easy to fulfill; I was very pleased with everything you wrote. I will only lay stress on two points: that you do not emphasize enough the essential part of my hypothesis, i.e. the topographical consideration in it, the regression of the libido and the abandoning of the unconscious cathexis, and that instead you put sadism and anal-erotism in the foreground as the final explanation. Although you are correct in that, you pass by the real explanation. Anal-erotism, castration complexes, etc., are ubiquitous sources of excitation which must have their share in *every* clinical picture. One time this is made from them, another time that. Naturally we have the task of ascertaining what is made from them, but the explanation of the disorder can only be found in the mechanism—considered dynamically, topographically and economically." [36] That was written on the day when Freud finished writing the essay, but because of the delay in publishing periodicals occasioned by the war it did not appear until two years later.

When I had the opportunity of reading the essay after the war finished I wrote to Freud reminding him how he had expounded the theme of it to me as long ago as January 1914.[37] I think we may take it, therefore, that the stimulus to investigating the subject had proceeded from Abraham's paper on it in 1911.

Mourning takes place after a severe loss of a loved person or of an abstraction such as fatherland, freedom or other ideal. We do not regard it as pathological because we are confident that it will pass, or greatly diminish, with time. We see no reason for interfering, and even think that to do so would be harmful. Some people, on the other hand, develop in similar circumstances a melancholic depression, which may be lasting. It resembles grief in the painfulness of the mood, in the withdrawal of interest from the outer world (except in so far as it may be connected with the lost person), in the inability to turn one's affection towards anyone else (who then would partly replace the lost one), and in an incapacity to undertake anything that has nothing to do with the loved person. As we say, the sufferer is so "absorbed" in the mourning that he has little left over for any other purpose in life. There is, however, one very striking difference between normal mourning and melancholia. With the former the pain and other manifestations are limited to the reaction to the loss of an external object, whereas melancholia gives the impression of there being an internal loss as well; there is a poverty of the ego, a sense of personal unworthiness.

Freud explained the economics of the "work of mourning" as follows, although he was puzzled at its extraordinary painfulness. Reality asserts that the loss is permanent and that continued preoccupation with it is not only futile, but would diminish the value of the rest of life. On the other hand, something struggles intensely against accepting this renunciation; as Freud puts it, human beings are always unwilling to abandon any "libido position." And, although normally reality is the victor in the end, its demands cannot be fulfilled forthwith. The withdrawal has to take place step by step, from every single memory of the lost one in detail—a task for which much time and energy is needed. If this is successfully carried through the person becomes once more free and uninhibited.

With melancholia one often cannot tell, nor does the sufferer know, what loss he has actually suffered. So one has to infer that, in contrast with the conscious loss in the case of grief, here there is a loss of some unconscious object. One is puzzled to know what really the melancholiac is absorbed in. Then there is the extraordinary sense of poverty in the ego. With grief the world has become poor and empty, with the melancholiac it is himself who has become so. He is worthless, useless and morally despicable; he vilifies and debases himself and commiserates with his relatives for being connected with such an unworthy person. Nor does he recognize that anything strange has come over him; he has always been worthless. Furthermore, there is a tendency, more dangerous than in any other psychosis, to destroy this worthless person through suicide.

Two things, however, are noticeable about these bitter complaints. First that the patient's behavior does not accord with them. So far from concealing his unworthiness in shame he is apt to insist on it or even to parade it. Nor does he behave like a person who gets only his deserts. He is ready to protest against the way he is treated, to complain he is unjustly treated, and so on. Then, secondly, if one listens carefully one observes that many of his complaints about himself would logically apply more accurately to another person, usually one the patient has been fond of.

The mechanism of melancholia now becomes clearer. The patient has suffered from some disappointment or loss in regard to a loved person, and, unlike what happens in normal mourning, rapidly withdraws the libidinal attachment. The libido thus released is, however, not free to seek fresh attachments, nor does it simply return to the self. There is effected an intimate identification of the self with the idea of the previously loved person, and a splitting of the ego is brought about. One part of the ego, the self-criticizing institution that we call the conscience, turns against the rest of the ego, now identified with the person to whom the reproaches apply.

This course of events comes about only under certain conditions. One is a strong fixation on a particular object, and nevertheless a weak and easily detachable libidinal cathexis of the object. Freud accepted Otto Rank's penetrating suggestion that this can happen only when the original choice of loved object had been effected on a narcissistic basis. Characteristic also is a regression to the anal-sadistic level, which accounts for many of the clinical features of melancholia, e.g. fear of poverty and tendency to self-destruction.

Freud called attention to the distinction between the process of identification in hysteria and other psychoneuroses when compared with that in psychoses. With the former condition cathexis of the actual object is preserved, or even intensified, whereas with the latter it is withdrawn. The ambivalence of love and hate in the latter is also connected with this particular regression. The same ambivalence occurs in the obsessional neurosis, but there it remains related to the outside object.

The problem of mania, which so often (although of course not always) alternates with melancholia, is a more difficult one and this was Freud's first attempt to cope with it; in later years he was able to pursue it further. Here he regarded it as representing a triumph of the patient's ego over the despised object with whom for a time there had been such a close identification. Put a little differently, it is the joy of the narcissistic ego at being freed from the hated and despised object that had in the melancholic phase overpowered it.

14

CHAPTER

Non-Medical Applications
of Psychoanalysis

ALTHOUGH THE PSYCHOANALYTIC INVESTIGATION OF THE PSYCHONEU-
roses was the basis of all Freud's work, affording as it did first-hand
access to the deeper layers of the mind, he was from the very beginning aware that the conclusions he had reached in this way had far
wider validity. Moreover it was in this wider bearing of his work that
he was primarily interested. He wanted to know how the mind works,
what makes it work, and the laws of its working. Then since his discoveries pertained to the more primitive and less rational areas of the
mind he was interested in any way in which they come to expression,
especially the products of phantasy—whether in neuroses, myths, legends, folklore, or custom. He was less concerned with the adaptations
to reality, the workings of the intellect in science and other realms.
Still the ways in which the deeper unconscious can influence or interfere with the smoother operations of the intellect did fall within his
sphere. It follows that the collection of writings we shall consider in
the present chapter is decidedly heterogeneous.

The proof that Freud's interest in the normal, non-medical, aspects
of psychology was an early one is given in the fact that the first two
books he wrote alone after his neurological period were devoted to
such topics: the psychology of dream life, and the "slips" that interfere
with normal mental functioning. His understanding of both these
topics came early, from 1895, the year from which psychoanalysis may
be dated.

(1) *The Interpretation of Dreams* was considered in the previous
volume, as was also a little book belonging to the present period
(1901), entitled *On Dreams*.[1]

Freud revised extensively the various editions of *The Interpretation of Dreams*. The new *Standard Edition*[2] makes it for the first time possible, thanks to James Strachey's careful editing, to ascertain precisely when each addition or omission was made. The most important additions were those made to the third and fourth editions, in 1911 and 1914 respectively; some of the former were published independently.[3] At the time of the third edition, in 1911, Freud formed the plan, which was never carried out, of writing an entirely new book on dreams, one based on more detailed analyses of patients' dreams than had been possible with his own personal ones.[4] This would have necessitated expounding the theory of the psychoneuroses, which he had avoided doing in his original book. Rank was to contribute the section on dreams in mythology and literature, which in fact he did in the fourth edition of *The Interpretation of Dreams* in 1914. But pressure of work and the need to express his ever-expanding ideas made it impossible to carry out the more ideal plan.

Freud, however, made in these years a number of separate contributions to the subject of dreams, the chief of which have been noted in previous chapters.[a] It was a theme so pre-eminently interesting to him that over and again in papers devoted to other topics we find allusions to some aspect of dream theory or interpretation.

(2) *The Psychopathology of Every Day Life*, 1904.[5] Its main theme —the influence of unconscious processes in interfering with conscious functioning—was sharply criticized at first by psychologists, but has been more widely accepted and generally known than any other of Freud's teachings. The phenomena in question have since been given the generic name of "parapraxes."

The first indication we have of Freud's interest in the subject is contained in a letter to Fliess, August 26, 1898,[6] in which he related how he had been unable to recall the name of Julius Mosen, the author of a well-known poem on Andreas Hofer, *Zu Mantua in Banden*. The analysis showed (a) that he had personal reasons for repressing the name Mosen, (b) that the repression was determined by infantile material, and (c) that the names occurring to him as substitutes in the effort to recollect were, just like neurotic symptoms, compromises between the repressing and the repressed factors. He added that he had "long" suspected the mechanism operative in the forgetting of names, but had not been able to confirm it so strikingly before. In the next letter but one, that of September 22,[7] he related the Signorelli example which plays a prominent part in the first chapter

* Chapter 9, Nos. 8, 15, 16, 17; Chapter 13, No. 7.

of the book. As I hope to expound in a revised edition of Volume I of this Biography, it was connected with a significant episode that must have played an important part in the inception of Freud's self-analysis.

The first chapter is called "The Forgetting of Proper Names." Freud had six years previously published the content of it in a simpler form in the *Monatsschrift für Psychiatrie und Neurologie*, where it had been entitled "The Psychical Mechanism of Forgetting." It had the function of popularizing in an easily recognizable form his theory of "repression." He had, indeed, written a more technical paper on the theoretical relationship between "forgetting" and "repression" in that same year (1898), but he never published it.[8]

In the following year, and in the same periodical, Freud published a highly interesting paper on "Screen Memories," i.e. the memories that come back to one as a cover for other associated, but repressed, memories. The interest of the paper, however, was not only scientific, since it was subsequently noticed that the story in it was a remarkable autobiographical fragment presented in an anonymous guise.[9] Evidently for personal reasons, Freud did not include it in the present book, where it would logically belong, nor was it reproduced until the *Gesammelte Schriften* were put together in 1925. An allusion in a letter to Fliess dated January 9, 1899, must refer to it.[10] He sent off the paper in May 1899.[11]

The rest of the book had also been published in the same *Monatsschrift* in 1901 [12] but it was revised before appearing in book form three years later.

The chapter on "The Forgetting of Proper Names" is followed by three others dealing with other instances of forgetting: of words, sentences, impressions and intentions. With all these Freud was able to demonstrate the same mechanism. Then there were chapters on slips of the tongue, and slips of the pen, where the slip is a compromise between the word intended and a repressed thought. Occasions where an "unintentional" slip carries an unmistakable meaning are common enough. No woman could fail to read one into it if after a quarrel her husband "forgot" their wedding anniversary, or if a lover "forgot" an appointment; still more blatant, if in a love embrace her husband uttered the words "darling Molly," in place of the wifely Jane. So to follow Freud further in his extension of such interpretations is not hard for the psychologically minded. But if they do so, as Freud pointed out, they are taking a more serious step than they may at once appreciate: nothing less than recognizing the existence of unconscious mental processes, which, moreover, are in conflict with the conscious ones.

In four other chapters Freud extended his interpretation to more complicated mental acts, in which strange and apparently meaningless things are done "accidentally." Some of them may be serious enough, leading to fatal results. Freud related a fascinating series of diverse examples of such performances.

The last chapter in the book has far-reaching conclusions. In it Freud solved the old dilemma between determinism and free will by showing how decisions which appear to be entirely spontaneous and uncaused are nevertheless determined by deeper motives of which the person may have no knowledge at all. He also in that connection threw an interesting light on the psychological significance of superstitions.

The book had more favorable reviews than most of Freud's, and even the *Neue Freie Presse* found the ideas interesting. It has probably been the most popular of Freud's writings.

The first edition of the book contained ten essays; two more were added in the second edition three years later. The book ran through ten editions in Freud's lifetime, and was translated into twelve languages (including Serbian and Japanese). Further illustrative examples were constantly added, to which we enjoyed contributing, so that the last edition is nearly four times the size of the original one.

(3) In 1905, one of Freud's periodic years of fruitful activity, he published, besides the Dora analysis and the important *Three Essays on Sexuality*, a book entitled *Jokes and their Relation to the Unconscious*.[13] It appeared just after the other book.[b] A thousand and fifty copies were printed, which took seven years to sell. Freud received 644 Kronen ($130.47) for it. It was reprinted three times, in 1912, 1921 and 1925 respectively, but without any alterations. Because of the play on words it is a specially difficult book to translate, and the attempt has been made only in English, French, Russian and Spanish.

Freud's stimulus to investigating the subject seems to have been Fliess's reproaching him for relating so many bad jokes, with often a play on words, from his analytical experiences, particularly of dreams, which Freud used to relate to him.[14] He naturally excused himself by saying it wasn't his doing—the things kept recurring in the course of analytic work. It made him wonder, however, why such phenomena were to be observed so often in unconscious material, and whether there was any special connection between the latter and the familiar

[b] Incidentally, the publisher, Deuticke, gives the wrong *Verlag* number for it.

conscious jokes. He unravelled the problem as early as 1897,[c] but after that was engaged in the great work on *The Interpretation of Dreams*. Then he was further stimulated by a book *Komik und Humor* (1898) by Theodor Lipps, a man of whom he thought highly; he read it in July 1898.[16] The complex topic, like that of sexuality, needed much research and pondering before it could be committed to paper, and it was in 1905, more than five years after the dream book, that these two appeared. It is nevertheless important to note that the three books just mentioned all belong together and were all derived from the same sources of investigation. All three really belong to the late nineties.

The book constitutes Freud's major contribution to the subject of aesthetics. It deals with the unconscious sources of pleasure in jokes, wit and humor. It contains some very fine and closely reasoned writing, and needs considerable concentration to appreciate fully. Perhaps for that reason it ranks as the least well known of Freud's writings, and the field covered is the one that has been least explored subsequently by other psychoanalysts. It is a pity, since it is a most rewarding work. An early effort, which Freud praised, was made by Ferenczi to extend the investigation to the theme of riddles.[17]

The pleasurable effect of jokes depends on two factors: a special *technique* and the *tendency* of the joke. In a joke with a play on words the commonest technique is that of condensation, a mechanism familiar from the analysis of dreams. In a joke with thought behind it several technical means may be employed: displacement of the thought from the essential to a trivial idea; the establishing of unexpected connections between disparate ideas; indirect presentation by means of allusion, analogy, etc.; the use of illogical trains of thought.

As to the *aim* of jokes Freud distinguished between the harmless ones, where only the technique is concerned, and the tendentious ones. If the latter are analyzed it will be found that their main sources are either aggressive or erotic. Similar techniques are employed in both cases, harmless and tendentious, and Freud described the pleasure obtained through them alone as "preliminary pleasure," which in the tendentious jokes leads to a deeper source of pleasure from themes which are in a state of repression. It is well known what things may be said "in joke" that could hardly be uttered in a serious vein. The essential psychological mechanism of jokes is the "saving in psychical expenditure" through the short cuts achieved in defying the laws of logic.

`He had some idea of it even four years before that.[15]

The psychogenesis of jokes goes back to the young child's fondness for playing with words as if they were objects. Three or four stages in development can be traced according to the increasing repression after the age of four and the gradual acceptance of logic and reality. Jokes take one back to the earlier periods where such pleasurable play was allowed.

Jokes have a social function. They need an audience, one that can be provoked to laughter. This distinguishes them from the similar mechanisms, displacement condensation, etc. at work in dreams. Their function is to gain pleasure, whereas in dreams it is to avoid unpleasure.

Freud then dealt with the nature of the *comic*, from its naïve forms to more complicated ones. Like other writers he laid stress here on the factor of contrast between the comic person and the audience. A plus in bodily activity or a minus in mental activity evokes this sense. It has, unlike a joke, no direct connection with the unconscious. Humor is a defense against unpleasure, and the energy set free from dealing directly with the latter becomes itself a source of pleasure.

To summarize: Wit spares an expenditure in inhibition, comic in thought, humor in feeling. "All three," in Freud's words, "take us back to the state of childhood in which we were not aware of the comic, were incapable of wit and did not need humor in order to feel happy in life."

The book had a long favorable review in the Vienna *Zeit* of June 4, 1905, but not much notice was taken of it by the academic periodicals.

(4) At the beginning of 1906 Freud wrote a short paper on the rather unexpected theme of "Psychopathic Characters on the Stage." It has never been published in German, but Max Graf, to whom Freud presented the manuscript, preserved it, and an English translation of it appeared in 1942.[18] A genius throws out and bestows precious productions lavishly, such as the present one, like spray from a fountain. Freud never mentioned it and perhaps forgot even its very existence. It is a thoughtful little essay, of only half a dozen pages, and it contains a considerable number of ideas which could well bear extensive development.

In a condensed fashion Freud expounded the conditions under which certain forms of art affect an audience and how they achieve their purpose. Lyric poetry and ritual dancing were mentioned in turn, but his main theme was the drama. The reasons why physical suffering is seldom permissible on the stage, while mental suffering plays a large part, were discussed. The importance of rebellion was emphasized, whether, as in the religious dramas of Greece, it is directed against the Divinity itself, or, as in social dramas, against social institutions, or, as in the dramas of character, against a powerful opponent. This leads to the more purely psychological drama where the struggle that causes the suffering is fought out in the hero's mind itself, a struggle between different impulses.

These familiar conflicts between "love" and "duty" may turn into psychopathological drama when the suffering in which the audience takes part is between a conscious impulse and an unconscious repressed one. Taking the example of *Hamlet* as a text Freud stated three conditions that have to be fulfilled before the theme is acceptable to the audience and will be enjoyed. He then commented on the failure of these conditions in a recent play by Hermann Bahr, which had evidently been the occasion for these reflections.

(5) In June 1906, Freud was invited by Löffler, the Professor of Jurisprudence, to address his seminar at the University. Löffler's students were studying recent work, initiated by Hans Gross's[d] pupils, Wertheimer and Klein, on the possibility of detecting criminals by the use of association experiments. Jung had himself published a little book on the subject earlier that year, and it was no doubt that which stimulated Freud's interest in the matter.[19] The title of his lecture was "Psycho-Analysis and the Ascertaining Truth in Legal Proceedings." [20] It was published the same year in Gross's *Archiv für Kriminalanthropologie und Kriminalistik*.[21]

Freud first recapitulated the main facts of Jung's association experiments with his discovery of objective signs indicating the activity of a hidden complex, and pointed out how he had previously expounded in his *Psychopathology of Everyday Life* the basic assumption of psychical determinism that underlay such experimental findings. He went on to compare the procedure with the technical devices used in the psychoanalysis of neurotics. The outstanding difference here between criminals and neurotics is that, although in both cases it is a matter of divining something hidden, what is hidden in the former case is something consciously known to the criminal which he is at pains to conceal, whereas the neurotic is concealing something from himself. Further, although there is opposition (resistance) to the discovery in both cases, it is wholehearted in the case of the criminal, while at least a part of the neurotic's mind is cooperating with the investigation. It would be a matter of further experience to ascertain whether

---

[d] The father of Otto Gross, mentioned earlier.

these distinctions make a difference, and if so what, in the response to the association experiment.

A further problem lay in the fact that a guilty conscience may so often be found that signs of a complex may be elicited which do not in fact relate to the particular crime under investigation. It was indeed this reflection of Freud's that as time went on was to prove a fatal stumbling block in what at first promised to become a useful aid to the legal profession.

(6) In 1907 Freud published in the first number of the new *Zeitschrift für Religionspsychologie* a paper entitled "Obsessive Acts and Religious Practices." [22] It was the first of three occasions in which he broached the important topic of religion, the others being in 1912 and 1927. He gave the paper before the Vienna Society on March 2, 1907, on which occasion Jung was present.

Freud began with a purely descriptive comparison and contrast between the ceremonies of the obsessional neurotic and of religious practices (praying, bowing, kneeling, etc.). In both cases there is a sense of inner compulsion and a more or less vague apprehension of misfortune (punishment) if the ceremonies are omitted. There are two striking differences. The obsessive acts are, especially at the onset of the disorder, performed in strict privacy, whereas the religious ones are shared with a community. Then the former concern trivial doings and appear quite senseless in contrast to the enormous importance of the ideas accompanying the religious ones.

Psychoanalysis has shown, however, that the obsessive acts also symbolize important attitudes and deal with weighty matters. They spring from a consciousness of guilt and fear and are designed to ward off certain temptations together with the punishments that yielding to them may bring. Conscience plays a similar part in connection with religion, and in neither case is the source of the bad conscience fully recognized. In the obsessional neurosis the repressed impulses that have to be kept at bay are typically sexual ones; in religion they may also be so, but more characteristically are selfish or aggressive (antisocial) ones. The shifting in the former case on to trivialities may to some extent be noticed also in religions where the practice of the ceremonial act becomes the main object and replaces the original lofty meaning of the attitude; hence the tendency in religions to recurrent reforms that strive at restoring the original significance of the ideas.

Freud summed up the contrast by saying that the obsessional neurosis may be regarded as a pathological counterpart of religion, an individual religiosity, while religion may be called a universal obsessional neurosis.

(7) On February 20, 1907, Freud gave before the Vienna Society a running commentary on a book recently published by Paul Moebius called *Die Hoffnungslosigkeit aller Psychologie* (The Hopelessness of all Psychology).

Freud attributed the pessimism in the title to the fact that the book was written just before the author died. The final conclusion of the book also, which asserted that the mental life of man was the only imperishable and essential part, pointed to the dying man's hope of an immortal life. Freud remarked that such personal considerations can never be completely excluded. It takes a very normal person to create a new picture; otherwise it is always distorted.

It turned out, however, that Moebius' pessimism applied only to academic or empirical psychology, the psychology which, as he put it, stopped short at the unconscious. He had reached this conclusion from the study of animal psychology, and, moreover, he distinguished between ("relative") unconscious processes that could at times become conscious and those that could not—what he called the "absolute unconscious"; they correspond closely with the psychoanalytical "preconscious" and "unconscious." Freud was puzzled that Moebius had never taken any notice of his work, since they reached very similar conclusions. Moebius also based himself on the same two fundamental instincts as Freud: that of self-preservation and that of reproduction. He considered dread (*Angst*) to be the most important manifestation of the life instinct, but Freud, while agreeing with this, would add to it his own conclusion that neurotic anxiety was an expression of a disturbance and threat to do with the sexual instinct.

Freud contradicted Moebius' opinion that the unconscious must always remain hidden and inaccessible, and mentioned the technical methods which, as he said, signified "a conquest of the unconscious." Various passages in the book aroused his suspicion that, in spite of statements to the contrary, Moebius had not really emancipated himself from the old idea that "mental" and "conscious" were identical concepts.

(8) Early in the same year Freud published, as the first volume in a series he had just established, *Schriften zur angewandten Seelenkunde*, a charming little book which was in effect a psychoanalysis of a novel. It was not the first one he had made, but the first he had published. As early as 1898 he had sent to his friend Fliess a very neat analysis of Conrad Ferdinand Meyer's *Die Richterin*, in which he traced the

source of the theme to a repressed memory on the author's part of an early sexual relationship with his sister.[23] The present analysis, entitled *Delusions and Dreams in Jensen's "Gradiva,"* [24] was a study of a story the well-known Danish writer Wilhelm Jensen, had published four years previously. It was Jung who had called his attention to the novel and he told me Freud had written his little book on it expressly to give him pleasure. If so, it must have been before they actually met each other. That accords with the high esteem in which Freud already held Jung at that time, the first year of their acquaintance. The book was twice reprinted and was translated into five languages, including Russian and Japanese.

Freud greatly enjoyed composing this little book. He had written it in the open air during his summer holiday (1906), in what he called "sunny days";[25] it appeared in May 1907.

The *Gradiva* book is one of the three of Freud's writings to which the word "charming" can most fittingly be applied, the other two being, in my opinion at least, the book on Leonardo and the essay on the "Three Caskets." It is written with such delicacy and beauty of language as to rank high and to compel admiration for its literary qualities alone. In fact some reviewers, such as Moritz Necker in the Munich *Allgemeine Zeitung,* praised above all his masterly prose, "which many professional writers must envy."

The story is of a young archaeologist who falls in love with a bas-relief of a Grecian girl who has a particularly striking gait. His phantasies about her assume a delusional form and he becomes convinced that she perished in the eruption that overwhelmed Pompeii in 79 A.D. He is drawn there and finds the girl, who may be a spirit or a living maiden. She recognizes his mental state and successfully undertakes to cure him, with the inevitable happy result. She then turns out to be a childhood playmate whom the youth had completely forgotten, but who still lived in the same town as himself.

Freud furnished a fine and detailed analysis which it is a joy to read. He was full of praise for the novelist who had correctly divined in every respect the psychological processes at work. The ancient time of two thousand years ago when the pair were supposed to have known and loved each other is equated with the forgotten period of their actual childhood. The repression that blotted this out corresponds with the interment of Pompeii under ashes, but in neither case is there destruction, only burial. Not only the various symptoms, but most of the turns of speech used by the couple in the story, are shown to be compromises formed with contributions from both the current archaeological material and the repressed erotic longings. Freud pointed out how exactly the story corresponded with his own experience with patients, and raised the question whether both he and the novelist were mistaken in recognizing such ideas as repression, the unconscious, and the formation of compromises, or whether they were both right in the face of prevailing medical opinion. Naturally he had no doubt about the answer.

The relief with which the hero of the story fell in love may be seen in the Vatican Museum, where Freud discovered it that September.[26] After Freud published his book it became fashionable among analysts to have a copy of the relief on their walls. Freud had one himself in his consulting room.

Jung praised the book highly, at which Freud was very gratified. He replied that Jung's acceptance of the ideas was more valuable to him than that of a whole medical congress, and he regarded it as a presage of future acceptance by such congresses. He admitted that the book contained nothing really new, but "it allows us to enjoy our wealth," [27] i.e. of insight.

About that time several analytic studies of great writers were being published, by Hitschmann, Sadger and Stekel, and Freud on several occasions discussed the proper method of dealing with such problems. He severely criticized Sadger's unimaginative attitude and praised Hitschmann's more tasteful approach. Max Graf read a paper on "The Methods used in the Study of the Psychology of Creative Writers" (December 11, 1907), and Freud confirmed his conclusions, adding some important ones of his own which will shortly be published. He considered that pathographies added very little to our knowledge, but psychoanalytic studies could throw light on the motivation of such writers and so become a useful contribution to biographical research.

Freud was naturally interested in the possibility of connecting the motives he had unravelled in the *Gradiva* with the personality of the writer and at once sent Jensen a copy of his book, doubtless with an accompanying letter. Jensen answered friendlily and agreed that the analysis coincided with his own aim and intention in describing the story. He ascribed this to his own intuition, perhaps aided by his own early medical studies! He had never heard of Freud's works. Encouraged by this Freud wrote asking him for any information about the source of the ideas. All he could get from Jensen on this matter, however, was that he had never seen the original relief, only a copy in the Munich Museum, and that the idea of the story occurred to to him while engaged on some other work which he had put aside to compose the *Gradiva*; it was written in an uninterrupted flow.[28] Freud read Jensen's letter to the Vienna Society on May 15, 1907.

Some six months later Jung called Freud's attention to three other stories by Jensen all of which had extremely similar themes: *Der rothe Schirm* (The Red Umbrella), *Im gothischen Hause* (In the Gothic House), and the autobiographical *Fremdlinge unter den Menschen* (Strangers Among People). In Jung's opinion they all pointed to an early emotional experience between brother and sister.[29] Freud promptly read these stories and on December 11, in the discussion on Graf's paper before the Vienna Society, put forward a hypothetical explanation of the source of Jensen's inspiration. In his childhood Jensen must have been very attached to a little girl, possibly a sister, and suffered a great disappointment, perhaps through her death. Presumably the other child had some physical disability such as a club-foot, which in the story Jensen converted into a beautiful gait; it was the sight of this on the relief that suggested the idea. So Freud wrote again to him. Jensen did not answer the question about the physical disability, said he had never had a sister or other young relative, but told Freud that his first love had been a little girl with whom he had grown up together and who died of consumption when she was eighteen. Many years later he had got fond of another girl who had reminded him of her, and this one died suddenly. So some at least of Freud's hypothesis was correct, and perhaps all of it.

Moritz Necker also published an enthusiastic review in the Vienna *Zeit* of May 19, 1907, saying that Jensen's intuition had provided a striking confirmation of Freud's theory of dream life.

(9) In 1908 there were four contributions the contents of which extended beyond the medical sphere. The first one, on "Civilized Sexual Ethics," was considered in a previous chapter[e] and is mentioned here because it was the first occasion on which Freud made any pronouncement on social problems.

(10) The second one, on "Character and Anal-Erotism," was also considered in the same chapter.[f] It was Freud's first contribution to the study of how various character traits come to be formed. In the next two or three years more were to follow.

(11) The Vienna Society held discussions on Nietzsche's writings on April 1 and October 28, 1908. On the first occasion Hitschmann read a section of Nietzsche's *Genealogie der Moral*, and raised several

[e] Chapter 12, No. 6.
[f] No. 9.

questions for discussion. Freud related, as he did on several other occasions, how he had found the abstractness of philosophy so unsympathetic that he gave up studying it. Nietzsche had in no way influenced his ideas. He had tried to read him, but found his thought so rich that he renounced the attempt.

In the second discussion Freud enlarged on Nietzsche's puzzling personality. Here he had a number of stimulating suggestions to make, the publication of which I may not forestall by repeating here. But he several times said of Nietzsche that he had a more penetrating knowledge of himself than any other man who ever lived or was ever likely to live. From the first explorer of the unconscious this is a handsome compliment.

(12) The other paper in 1908 was on a theme that had always fascinated Freud. It was entitled "The Creative Writer and Day Dreaming," [30] and it appeared in an early number of a new periodical called *Neue Revue*. One notices that Freud was already becoming well enough known for it to be customary to seek contributions from him. He lectured on the subject of his paper on December 6, 1907, before a private audience of ninety, admitted by ticket, at the art salon of the publisher, Hugo Heller. It was the nearest he ever got to a public lecture in his life.[31] Reporting it to Jung, Freud said that the writers and their ladies who were present must have found it hard to digest, but anyhow it was breaking into a new field where one could comfortably settle down. He had talked more about phantasy than about creative artists, but next time he would make that good.[32] This he did a couple of years later in his study of Leonardo. The lecture itself had been received with warm applause, a contrast to the stony silence of earlier lectures to medical audiences in Vienna, and it was fully reported in *Die Zeit* of December 7, 1907.

Freud always had an immense respect for artists, possibly tinged with some envy.[33] He seemed to take the romantic view of them as mysterious beings with a superhuman, almost divine, afflatus. That he could ascertain the nature of their genius was too much to expect, but he tried at least to comprehend the sources of their inspiration; that was the theme of the present paper.

Most of the paper is taken up with describing the characteristics of daydreaming, an activity Freud traced to the play of children though it differs from it in dispensing with actual objects which the child uses for its purpose. The similarity with night dreams was mentioned, and the nature of repressed wishes considered. Then there are the pathological phantasies of neurotics which lie behind their symptoms, and the phantasies of whole nations as interpreted in their myths, sagas and legends. The source of poetic creation lies also in phantasy and Freud supposed that such writers are stirred by some current experience that stimulates a forgotten memory in childhood, which in its turn is depicted in the form of a fulfilled wish and projected into the future.

If anyone related his most intimate phantasy it would probably repel his hearer or at least leave him cool. The creative writer must therefore possess some special talent that enables him to evoke quite different feelings in his audience. He does so by first supplying by various technical devices what Freud called a "preliminary" pleasure —a purely formal or aesthetic pleasure akin to that operative in jokes—and this enables the deeper repressed sources of pleasure to be accepted by the audience. Its final effect is brought about by a release of tension.

When Freud sent Abraham a reprint of this paper he had just received from him the manuscript of a book in which Abraham expounded at some length the parallels between dreams and myths which Freud had adumbrated in the present paper.[34]

(13) The "Three Contributions to the Psychology of Love" considered in Chapter 12 may also be regarded as studies in the formation of character. Moreover, some of the conclusions Freud expounded in them, e.g. of the effect on potency of the restrictions imposed by civilization, will have far-reaching sociological consequences when they are taken into account.

(14) In 1910 Freud published another book containing a study, not this time of a writer, but of a great artist. *Leonardo da Vinci and a Memory of his Childhood* appeared as Heft 7 of the series *Schriften zur angewandten Seelenkunde.*[35] It was the first real psychoanalytic biography. In it Freud took as a starting point the sole memory Leonardo ever recorded from his childhood, a unique occurrence which in itself gives it a special significance, and he submitted to a very detailed analysis both the meaning of the memory and its influence on Leonardo's later life and work. The memory was of a bird flying to the baby in his cradle and working its tail to and fro in his mouth, a recondite enough notion. Perceiving in the idea of the bird's tail the symbolism of both nipple and penis, Freud related the phantasy to the known facts of Leonardo's infancy. He was an illegitimate child and lived alone with his mother for the first few years until his father, who had married a wife who bore no children, took him away and adopted him. Freud then described Leonardo's

struggles between his artistic and his scientific interests, with the ultimate victory of the latter, and illuminated his curious difficulty in completing any task. In connection with Leonardo's known homosexual attitude and his abhorrence of heterosexuality Freud had a good deal to say of general interest on the origin and nature of this inversion. The book is a comprehensive study of Leonardo's life and personality, for whose greatness Freud had the utmost respect. Quoting the common saying that Leonardo could be regarded as an Italian Faust, he expressed the opinion that he resembled rather Spinoza. One has a strong impression that Freud's interest in him was partly personal, since he dwelt on many aspects, for instance the passion for natural knowledge, that were equally true for himself. His correspondence of the time shows how deeply engrossed he was in the subject.

One cannot help being struck throughout the book by Freud's vast literary knowledge, a burden he wore lightly and of which he never made any display. The book has many discursions apart from its main theme, on art, religion, etc., to which I hope to recur in other connections.

Freud's interest in Leonardo's psychology may be dated from October 1909, just after his return from America. It seems to have been aroused, not as one might have supposed, by reading of the childhood memory which gave him the text for his book, but by reflections on the stimulating effect of thwarted sexual curiosity in childhood. This is the account he gave of it in a letter to Jung in October,[36] when he said he had a patient with the same constitution as Leonardo though without any genius, and also mentioned that he was obtaining from Italy a book on Leonardo's youth.[37] It was there that he came across the childhood memory of the bird at the baby's mouth.

In the next month he mentioned his interest to Ferenczi[38] and described his conclusions to him while on a night journey between Budapest and Komorn. Later he borrowed from Eitingon two books he had been unable to obtain in Vienna.[39] As his own essay shows, he read very extensively in the Leonardo literature. On December 1 he related his discovery and interpretations before the Vienna Society. Before the end of the year he had written three of the five lectures he had delivered *ex tempore* in America that autumn, but he now put them aside for three months to work at his more absorbing theme. He found it hard going and in the first fortnight he had written only a few lines.[40] In another month he had written fifteen pages; he was hard at work all day, and wrote only a few lines each evening and a few pages on Sundays.[41] When one considers the concentration and research which the book evinces one must be astonished at Freud's working powers; anyone who has conducted psychoanalyses for eleven or twelve hours a day will know what that means. Nevertheless the book was finished and sent to the printers in the first days of April.[42]

When Freud told me he was writing the book I was naturally eager to hear about it and sent him Walter Pater's famous description of the Mona Lisa, but it turned out he already knew this. Here is his reply: "You must not expect too much of Leonardo who will come out in the next month, neither the secret of the Vierge aux Rochers nor the solution of the Mona Lisa puzzle; keep your hopes on a lower level, so it is likely to please you more. Many thanks for the page from Pater; I knew it and had quoted some lines out of the fine passage. I think L. was 'bimanual,' but that is about the same thing as left-handed. I have not inquired further into his handwriting,[g] because I avoided by purpose all biological views, restraining myself to the discussion of the psychological ones." [43]

Ferenczi had serious misgivings about the reception the book would have, for "nothing more shocking has been written since little Hans." He feared that because Freud interpreted visions he would be called a visionary; "that is the logic of the logicians." Freud replied: "Don't be concerned about the Leonardo. I have long written only for the small circle which every day widens, and if the other people didn't rail about the Leonardo I should have gone astray in my opinion of them. What those others say now is a matter of indifference. We shall all of us get more gratitude and posthumous fame from psychoanalysis than would be good for us now while we are in the midst of the work." [44]

Löwenfeld wrote to Freud describing at length the "horror" the book had evoked even among well-meaning people, but Freud said this left him unmoved because he was so pleased with it himself.[45] It was certainly one of his favorite works, and even ten years later he said that the Leonardo was "the only pretty thing" he had ever written.[46]

The book appeared at the end of May 1910, and Freud received 324 Kronen ($65.64) for it. Of the edition of 1500 copies 573 were sold in the first six months. The rest were sold by 1919, when a second edition was called for. The only mild concession Freud made then was to replace the word "homosexuality" in one passage by "in-

[g] An allusion to Leonardo's mirror writing.

version." He also added the footnote about the custom of circumcision among Jews being an important source of anti-Semitism, it being evidently connected with the theme of castration. The third edition of 1575 copies appeared in 1923, for which Freud received 1,765,800 worthless Kronen. Half of this edition remained for the Nazis to destroy in 1938. The changes made in the various editions were largely verbal.

Strange responses came from Switzerland. Jung discovered in the sacred picture which Freud reproduced in his book the outlines of a vulture.[47] Pfister promptly discovered a more convincing one, which he described at great length in a subsequent essay;[48] he found that the tail of the vulture pointed at the child's mouth, as in Leonardo's early memory. Now by this vulture hangs a tale. In the book Freud had made a good deal of the mythological associations of this bird, which in Egypt was regarded as a Mother-Goddess (*Mut*) though equipped with a male organ, and since it was often cited in Catholic theology he thought it likely that Leonardo was aware of the maternal symbolism.

Now comes Mr. Strachey with what he mildly calls "an awkward fact." [49] Freud had quoted Leonardo's original passage where the bird is called a *nibbio*.[h] But *nibbio* means kite, not vulture, which in Italian is *avoltoio*. In the German books on Leonardo it is correctly given as *Hühnergeier*, but in Herzfeld's translation of Leonardo on which Freud mainly relied it is given as simply *Geier* (vulture). It was a singular lapse in Freud's knowledge of natural history. Kites were as common in Italy as vultures in Egypt, but whether the similarity between the two is close enough to leave undisturbed the equations with the Goddess—and this unessential part of Freud's argument—must be left to the experts to decide. The same comment applies to the significance in this connection of the Egyptian legend of the child who permanently sucks at the breast of the Vulture-Goddess.[50] At all events the appearance of the two birds is unlike enough to diminish the significance of the Swiss observations.

(15) In the letter to F. S. Krauss mentioned earlier[i] Freud made two special points. The second one was this. In his book on jokes he had maintained the thesis that in the more complicated form he called "tendentious jokes" there are two sources of pleasure or amusement. One is the "preliminary pleasure" afforded by certain technical devices; the other is the release of pleasurable feeling derived from

[h] Leonardo spells the word with one "b."
[i] Chapter 12, No. 13.

deeper unconscious sources. Among the latter an important part is played by erotic motives. Now the collection of openly obscene jokes that Krauss was engaged in collecting contained material which Freud considered of great value for investigation of the unconscious. That was the second reason why he expressed his approval of the undertaking.

(16) In December 1911 Freud published a short note in the *Zentralblatt* on the "Significance of a Sequence of Vowels."[51] Stekel had made the acute observation that in dreams the correct name is often replaced by another one which has only the order of the vowels in common with it. Freud now quoted a striking example from the history of religions. The name of God was so taboo among the ancient Hebrews that only the four consonants of it are known, so that to this day it is impossible to say how it was pronounced. Vowels were therefore borrowed from another Hebrew word for Lord; *Adonai*, hence ultimately the modern Jehovah.

(17) "Great is Diana of the Ephesians":[52] Under this title Freud described (in February 1912) a remarkable instance of continuity in religious worship. This was the only original point in the short paper, which is essentially a summary of the account of a story which a French archaeologist, Sartiaux, had recently published. It evidently appealed to Freud's interest in religious mythology, as well as to his sense of the dramatic.

The Ionians had conquered Ephesus in the eighth century, B.C. and found there an ancient cult of a Mother Goddess. They merely rechristened her Artemis (Diana) after their own Goddess, and the cult continued. It became an ancient Lourdes, with pilgrims, temples, souvenirs and so on, one of the greatest in the world. When the Apostle Paul visited Ephesus and gathered a number of converts to his new Christian religion he tried to destroy the old cult. Whereupon the goldsmiths and other traders who saw both their Goddess and their livelihood threatened rioted with the famous slogan: "Great is Diana of the Ephesians." Paul had to leave hurriedly and was succeeded by the gentler John the Evangelist, who, following Jesus' request, had taken charge of the Virgin Mary and had brought her with him. In the course of the fourth century the first basilica to the Madonna was erected, so the city had its Mother Goddess again. Recently she appeared in a vision to a German girl, Katherina Emmerich, and told her where she had lived and slept when in Ephesus. Both the house and the bed have been found, and Ephesus is once more the goal of pious believers in a Mother-Goddess.

(18) On October 20, 1912, Freud read a short paper before the Vienna Society entitled "The Fate of Two Women." It has never been published. The one woman was Charlotte, the ex-Empress of Mexico, who became permanently insane after returning to Europe in the vain endeavor to save her husband from the execution awaiting him. The insanity first showed itself when pleading with Napoleon, and its chief symptom was the delusion of being poisoned. The only places where she felt safe were with the Pope and in an orphan home near Rome.

Freud maintained that the insanity could not be the inevitable result of her tragedy, and contrasted her fate with that of the ex-Empress Eugénie of France who retained the balance of her mind in spite of equally severe blows. Analytical experience has shown that the delusion in question arises as a defense against a forbidden wish to bear a child (from the father). Freud had authentic reasons for knowing that Charlotte's husband, Maxmilian, had been completely impotent and had never attempted coitus. So she, like Lady Macbeth, had turned all her energies into ambitious plans and could not endure reality when these foundered. That she should only feel safe with the Pope or in the nursery was understandable.

(19) *Totem and Taboo:*[53] This important work needs some introduction. It was composed in one of the septennial years with which Freud associated his highest periods of creative activity and he himself at one moment ranked the work as the best he had ever written.[54]

The theme of religion could never have been far from Freud's mind. There were occasional allusions to religion in earlier writings, and there was the paper mentioned above in which he compared its ceremonies to obsessive acts. The first indication of his interest having been aroused later is a letter to Ferenczi[55] in which he made, almost casually the announcement that on the previous night, the last day of the year (1909), when thoughts are apt to turn to serious matters, the idea had occurred to him about the meaning of religion: "Its ultimate basis is the infantile helplessness of mankind." But, he added, "I don't intend to elaborate it." [J]

Nothing more was heard of the subject until August of the following year (1911), when he informed me that he was engaged on something that was likely to occupy him for some years, i.e. "the psychology of religious faith and ties. I know I am following a crooked way in the order of my works (i.e. 'working'), but it is the order of unconscious connections." [56] A couple of days later he gave Ferenczi the same news

[J] *Ausführung schenke ich mir aber.*

and added: "I am entirely Totem and Taboo." [57] In the following month he described his new theory to Abraham at the Weimar Congress in 1911.[58] So the whole work must have been ripe in his mind that summer. What had stirred his mind to the work in that unexpected direction at just that time?

This question is not hard to answer. For the past couple of years Jung had been delving deeply into the literature of mythology and comparative religion, and the two men had had talks together about it. A year before the Weimar Congress Freud had read in manuscript the first part of Jung's great essay *"Wandlungen und Symbole der Libido,"* [59] and he was already beginning to be unhappy at the direction of Jung's researches. Jung was deriving rather uncertain conclusions from that far-off field and transferring them to the explanation of clinical data, while Freud's method was to see how far the assured conclusions derived from his direct analytical experience could throw light on the more distant problems of man's early history. It was doubtless these considerations that spurred him to see what contributions he could himself make.

There is, however, the further question why Freud did not follow Jung in investigating the realm of Greek mythology and comparative religion with which he was already so familiar, and chose instead to hark back to the quite unfamiliar field of Australian Aborigines and their curious customs. This also can be answered. As far back as the case of Little Hans with his phobia of horses, Freud had been aware of the unconscious significance of animals and the totemistic equation between them and the idea of a father. Abraham and Ferenczi had also been reporting similar cases, even where the neurotics' totem was an inanimate object such as a tree. Then in 1910 there appeared Frazer's massive four-volume work on *Totemism and Exogamy,* which gave Freud plenty of food for thought; Wundt's *Völkerpsychologie* he read only later.

After getting back to Vienna from the Weimar Congress in September, 1911, Freud at once plunged into the vast material he had to master before he could expound his ideas concerning the resemblances between primitive beliefs and customs and the unconscious phantasies of his neurotic patients. He was evidently starting on one of his great productive periods. He wrote to me: "There are a great many things boiling in my head, but they are very slow to come out, and I always find it hard to conform completely to another's thoughts. I cannot do everything myself, and the contributions of others, say Jung for example, are of the highest importance. . . . I am working hard on the psychogenesis of religion, finding myself on the same track with Jung's 'Wandlungen.' " [60] On the same day he wrote to Ferenczi: "I am not pleased with anything here, and am in that bodily and mental state to which I am accustomed during intensive inner work—or, rather, the preparation for such. It is a kind of misery; I am rarely productive when I feel well. I read and read and it ferments. Whether it will come to anything I don't know." [61]

A few weeks later he unburdened himself as follows: "The Totem work is a beastly business. I am reading thick books without being really interested in them since I already know the results; my instinct tells me that. But they have to slither their way through all the material on the subject. In that process one's insight gets clouded, there are many things that don't fit and yet mustn't be forced. I haven't time every evening, and so on. With all that I feel as if I had intended only to start a little liaison and then discovered that at my time of life I have to marry a new wife." [62]

By the middle of January 1912 Freud had finished the first of the four essays that were to make up the book, the one on the "Horror of Incest among Primitive Peoples." He was in a light-hearted mood: "not as if it were good, but because it is finished—that's the good thing about it." [63]

In the next month there was further news: "My contribution 'Inzestscheu,' is by no means famous, but the next two articles may prove much better. The second is entitled 'Tabu und Ambivalenz' and will I hope show up the essence of that marvellous 'taboo'; it is half written and all finished in thought. The third is not yet shaped in a definite form; it will bear the name: 'Die Magie und die Allmacht der Gedanken.' These three papers I conceive as forerunners of another more important one which intends to proclaim 'Die infantile Wiederkehr des Totemismus.' I have got all the books you indicated to me: Crawley; Bourke (*Scatalogical Rites*); Hartland (*Paternity*); Pearson (*Grammar of Science*), so I need not trouble you for sending me one of these from Toronto. I am now even in possession of the Encyclopedia Britannica, 11th Band, 1911." [64]

Alluding to the same (first) essay he told Ferenczi: "My essay in *Imago* has already been reprinted twice, in *Pan* and in the *Neues Wiener Journal*. It is the most lifeless thing I have ever written, and excusable only by my being a tyro and for the sake of the taboo essay that is to follow." [65]

Freud was now getting tired and also found it hard to steal an hour for the work, so to force himself on he announced a paper at the Society. This was the second essay, on "Taboo." He gave it on May 15, 1912, and it took him three hours: he humorously added in a letter: "it occasioned several fatalities." [66] Ferenczi wrote to him a couple of months later: "Your idea that the deferred obedience of the Brother Clan is the source of religiosity is excellent. I recollect your saying to me last year in Klobenstein that religion is something that the son has." [67]

In the next month Freud was enjoying himself reading Robertson Smith's *Religion of the Semites* and finding in it confirmation of the ideas he was inclined to think too daring. I remember talking with him about that time and his enthusiasm over the book. He had hardly ever been so pleased with any book. "To read it was like gliding in a gondola." There was, however, duller stuff to wade through. In October he was working on the third essay (on Magic). "Wundt makes me furious. To have to read such balderdash after eleven hours at analysis is a hard punishment." [68] Nevertheless he lectured on it to the Vienna Society on January 15, 1913, an occasion which is still well in my mind.

We then pass to April of the same year. "I am now slowly composing the fourth of the *Übereinstimmungen*, that on totemism, which is to close the series. It is the most daring enterprise I have ever ventured. On religion, ethics and *quibusdem aliis*. God help me!" [69] He told Ferenczi at the same time that it would take him two or three months,[70] but with a great spurt it was finished in a month.

The next couple of months yielded passages of exceptional interest to the historian of Freud's moods and personality. Everything went well during the writing itself. "I am writing Totem at present with the feeling that it is my greatest, best, perhaps my last good work. Inner confidence tells me that I am right. Unfortunately I have very little time for the work, so I have continually to force myself into the mood afresh and that injures the style." [71] A few days later: "I am working on the last section of the Totem which comes at the right moment to deepen the gap [k] by fathoms; reading and polishing will take me all my time before the 15th of June. I have not written anything with so much conviction since *The Interpretation of Dreams*, so I can predict the fate of the essay." [72] As it turned out, its reception was not unlike that of the other book. He told Abraham that the essay would appear before the (Munich) Congress and "would serve to make a sharp division between us and all Aryan religiosity. For that will be the result of it." [73] On the same day, after the book was

[k] Between him and Jung.

finished, he wrote also to Ferenczi: "Since *The Interpretation of Dreams* I have not worked at anything with such certainty and elation. The reception will be the same: a storm of indignation except among those near to me. In the dispute with Zurich it comes at the right time to divide us as an acid does a salt." (May 13, 1913.)

A fortnight later, however, there was quite another tone. As so often happens after a great achievement, elation was replaced by doubt and misgiving. With this change Freud's pugnacious attitude also softened. "Jung is crazy, but I don't really want a split; I should prefer him to leave on his own accord. Perhaps my *Totem* work will hasten the break against my will." On June 4, 1913, he lectured at the Society on the theme, an experience which usually depressed him. On June 11 he sent the early galley proofs of the book to the three of us. "There is nothing in these; they belong to the thicket behind which the Princess sleeps. Later on you will get the interesting part, which is also a disturbing one. I have reverted very much from my original high estimate of the work, and am on the whole critical of it. I should be very happy if you could lighten my task with any suggestions and will wait for your reply before correcting the last part." [74] "My high estimate of the Totem work has not quite returned. It is too uncertain; it would be too beautiful. I have inserted some softening passages, but will wait for your and Jones's comments." [75] He wrote to me at the same time asking for my opinion and comments, since he had lost his early confidence. He marked this passage "confidential." He told me in conversation shortly after that he was specially anxious about my opinion because I was the only analyst with some knowledge of the subject.[1] I was in fact very familiar with all the sources of his material.

Ferenczi and I read the proofs together in Budapest and wrote to Freud in a similar strain. We suggested he had in his imagination lived through the experiences he described in his book, that his elation represented the excitement of killing and eating the father, and that his doubts were only the reaction. When I saw him a few days later on a visit to Vienna and asked him why the man who wrote *The Interpretation of Dreams* could now have such doubts he wisely replied: "Then I described the wish to kill one's father, and now I have been describing the actual killing; after all it is a big step from a wish to a deed."

We seemed to have reassured Freud. "I thank you both sincerely and cordially for your explanations and contributions, all of which I

[1] Before the days of Róheim!

accept. The subjective explanation of my doubts must be well founded, for a great part of my confidence has come back since hearing from you. . . . After your reports I have decided not to weaken anything. . . . Jones's suggestions concern extensions which I should love to undertake, but one could hardly stop at the hints alone. I have broken off everywhere so as to make an essay and not a book. A great deal of what Jones brings forward is so very much his own that I should like to see him develop it himself in his own way.[76]

Naturally Abraham also sent a favorable report, which evoked this grateful answer. "Your judgment about the Totem work was specially important to me, since after finishing it I had a period of doubt about its value. Ferenczi, Jones, Sachs, Rank have expressed themselves as you have, so that I have gradually regained my confidence. The way in which you try to prove to me the value of the work, by making contributions, additions and drawing your own inferences, is wonderful; of course the best way. I am prepared for unfriendly attacks, which naturally will not disturb me." [77]

On June 30, 1913, we celebrated the occasion by giving Freud a dinner, which we called a totemic festival, on the Konstantinhügel in the Prater. Loe Kann presented him with an Egyptian figurine which he adopted as his totem.

After this introduction let us now consider the actual content of this important work. The first section, on the "Horror of Incest," is concerned with the extraordinarily ramified precautions primitive tribes take to avoid the remotest possibility of incest, or even a relationship that might distantly resemble it. It is evident they are far more sensitive on the matter than any civilized peoples, and infringement of the taboo is often punished with instant death. Freud inferred that the corresponding temptation must be greater with them, so that they cannot rely as we do on deeply organized repressions. In that respect they may be compared with the neurotics who often have to establish complicated phobias and other symptoms that serve the same purpose as the primitive taboos. Freud had some particularly interesting passages on family difficulties in our civilization, notably on the great problem of what to do about mothers-in-law.

The second section, four times as long as the first, is entitled "Taboo and the Ambivalence of Feelings." Freud ranged here over the vast field of taboos, with their almost infinite variety. To the believer a taboo has no reason or explanation beyond itself. It is autonomous, and the fatal consequences of outraging it are equally spontaneous. Its nearest parallel in modern times is the conscience, which Freud defined as that part of oneself which one knows with the most un-questioning certainty.[m] The passages on consciousness and the sense of guilt are especially noteworthy.

The tabooed person or object is charged with prodigious powers for both good and evil. Anyone touching it, even accidentally, becomes similarly charged: for instance, by eating a scrap of food the Ruler has thrown away, even if the consumer is innocent of its source. Months of complicated procedures, mostly consisting of various privations, may, however, purify him. The essential prohibition in a taboo is contact, and Freud likens this to the *délire de toucher* of obsessional neurotics, which is similarly feared to be followed by some terrible misfortune.

Freud drew a close parallel between what might be called the symptomatology of primitive taboos and that of obsessional neurotics. With both there is (1) a complete lack of conscious motivation, (2) imperiousness arising from an inner need, (3) the capacity of being displaced and of infecting other people, and (4) the leading to ceremonial performances designed to undo the harm feared. Since the latter consist of deprivations, Freud inferred that the taboos them-selves originally meant a renunciation of something towards which there was a temptation, but which has for some important reason become forbidden. When a person has transgressed a taboo he be-comes himself taboo lest he arouse the forbidden desires in his neighbors.

Freud then discussed in detail three particular taboos. (1) The curious treatment of slain *Enemies*. Their decapitated heads may be caressed, fed, and begged for forgiveness—a remarkable example of ambivalent feeling. (2) Those concerning *Rulers*, whether kings or priests. Here there is a most astonishing complexity of attitude. There is on the one hand awe for the Ruler and great precautions to ensure his safety, everything from tides and winds to fertile crops and success in war depending on his continued functioning. On the other hand he may be subjected to such severe restrictions as at times to make his life hardly worth living. Indeed there are countries where, since no one is willing to occupy that position, a successor has to be dragged by force into it, much as a new Speaker of the House of Commons is led to the Chair against a show of resistance. When things go wrong it is assumed that the Ruler has lost his powers, or is for bad motives failing to employ them; he at once becomes an object of contumely and is likely to be slain. Freud had no difficulty in showing that what

[m] Compare the German *Gewissen* and *gewiss*.

runs through the whole of this complexity is the unavowed attitude of ambivalence on the part of the subjects. (3) Those concerning the *Dead*. To touch a corpse is in many parts of the world taboo, and those who have to do so become themselves taboo. The departed spirits readily become evil demons, against whose power all sorts of precautions have to be taken. Psychoanalysis has revealed the frequency of unconscious hostility towards loved ones and the many results of this ambivalency, one which comes most to expression on the occasion of a death. It is only when deep changes take place in this attitude that it becomes possible, as in the East, to revere ancestral spirits as helpful beings.

What emerges is that primitive peoples have a more intense capacity for ambivalent feelings than civilized ones, or, put otherwise, that the latter have progressed further towards reconciling opposing feelings. Freud maintained that this comparative study illustrated the value investigations of the psychoneuroses, with their unconscious content, may have for the elucidation of problems in the field of anthropology and historical sociology. He pointed out, however, an important distinction between the unconscious impulses that are repressed in the two fields: with the neuroses these are typically sexual in nature, while with the primitive taboos they concern various anti-social impulses, predominantly aggression and murder.

"The neuroses on the one hand display striking and far-reaching resemblances with the great social production of art, religion and philosophy, but on the other hand they have the appearance of being caricatures of them. One might venture the statement that hysteria is a caricature of an artistic creation, the obsessional neurosis a caricature of religion, and paranoic delusions a caricature of a philosophical system."

The third essay was on "Animism, Magic and the Omnipotence of Thoughts." Accepting the usual division of the stages of human development into the animistic, the religious and the scientific, Freud expressed his agreement with Marett's conclusion that there must have been a still earlier, "pre-animistic" one, which Marett had termed "animatism." In it the outer world was believed to be animated in detail by various purposes, all of which bore on the well-being or misfortune of mankind. The development into animism, where it was peopled with souls or demons, betokened a progress, since man's wishes were through projection delegated in part to the spirits around him. Freud suggested that this progress signified a gain achieved through a partial renunciation. Hence pure magic, the technique whereby man influenced his neighbors, his enemies, and the world outside, must have preceded the use of sorcery, i.e. the various methods by which man hoped to control the spirits. Naturally both activities could co-exist.

Freud then quoted examples of the more typical magical procedures. There were the imitative types of magic, which operated by the principle of similarity: one might stick a pin into a wax image with the intention of wounding the person represented by the image, or one might stimulate the fruitfulness of crops by giving the fields the example of sexual intercourse. The other kind, operating by the principle of contiguity, is illustrated by the custom of burning something belonging to the hated person, his hair or nail parings, so that the same thing should happen to him as a whole. Frazer described the process of magic as "men mistaking the order of their ideas for the order of nature, and hence imagining that the control which they have, or seem to have, over their thoughts, permits them to exercise a corresponding control over things." Freud, however, wished to penetrate beyond this static description, one belonging to the association psychology of the nineteenth century, and to learn something of the dynamic factors at work. The basis of magic he saw in man's exaggerated belief in the power of his thoughts, or more exactly his wishes, and he correlated this primitive attitude with the "omnipotence of thoughts" that is to be found both in neurotic phantasies and in the mental life of young children. Marett had as early as 1900 described such attitudes in primitive tribes as a kind of solipsism, and Freud maintained that it was an index of pronounced narcissism.

It was above all the phenomenon of death, with its accompanying ambivalent conflicts, that, according to Freud, impelled man to change his outlook on life and invent evil demons, which were then to prove the precursors of mythological beings and the divinities of religion.

The fourth section, by far the most important of all, was called "The Infantile Return of Totemism." It was the one to which the rest of the book led up.

Totems were in all probability originally animals, though later on plants might also function as such. To the clan which traced its descent from a particular species (by maternal inheritance) it was strictly forbidden to kill that kind of animal. On the contrary, one had to care for it and it in its turn would protect its clan. McClellan, who first described this primitive religion in 1865, considered that it was linked with exogamy, the practice that forbade any sexual relations between members of the same clan, i.e. those sharing the same totem and totemic name. Later writers have doubted the essential connection between the two, but Freud accepted the more general belief in it.

He then discussed the numerous explanations of totemism that had been offered, most of which are obviously very sophisticated. He had the advantage of being familiar with the attitude of young children to animals, their capacity for close identification with them and the frequency with which they select one species to fear inordinately. Psychoanalysis had regularly found that the feared animal was an unconscious symbol of the father who was both loved and hated. The totemistic "ancestor" of the clans of primitive people must have the same significance, and from that point of view the various features of taboo, ambivalence of feeling, and so on, are easily comprehensible.

As for exogamy, which is nothing but a complicated insurance against the possibility of committing incest, Frazer had produced overwhelming reasons for supposing that primitive people had a peculiarly strong temptation towards incest, far stronger than civilized people. He knew nothing, of course, of its importance in young children. It was, therefore, easy for Freud to perceive the connection between totemism and exogamy. They simply represented the two halves of the familiar Oedipus complex, the attraction to the mother and the death wishes against the rival father. From this point of view everything falls readily into place.

Then comes the nice question of the historical origin of these great primordial institutions from which all later religions seem to have derived through elaboration and modification. Here Freud was supported by a suggestion of Darwin's, that early mankind must have resembled the higher apes in living in small hordes consisting of one powerful male and several females. Atkinson saw that this state of affairs would inevitably lead, as among so many of the larger animals, to the possessive male's prohibiting incest among his younger rivals. Freud's special contribution at this point was to assume that periodically the growing sons banded together, slew and devoured the father. That raises the question of the fate of the "brother clan" who would be left. Freud postulated ambivalent feelings towards the dead father, stimulated also by the difficulties arising from the quarrels and rivalries among the brothers. This would lead to remorse and a delayed obedience to his will in the matter of access to his women, i.e. a barrier against incest.

At this point Freud took into account Robertson Smith's important writings on the subject of sacrifice and sacrificial feasts. In these the totem is ceremonially slain and eaten, thus repeating the original deed. It is followed first by mourning and then by triumphant rejoicing and wild excesses. In this way the permanent community of the society, both among themselves, and also with their ancestor whose virtues they had just absorbed, is maintained.

After thousands of years the totem became a god, and the complicated story of the various religions set in. Freud did not pursue the theme further in this direction, but he proffered some interesting reflections on the earliest form of Greek tragedy where the Hero, in spite of warnings from the chorus, pursues a forbidden path and meets his merited doom. Freud suggested that this was an inversion—he called it a hypocritical one—of the original meaning where the brothers, here represented by the Chorus, were the transgressors, and the hero simply a victim.

There is a notable sentence at the end where Freud spoke of "the beginnings of religion, morality, social life and art meeting in the Oedipus complex." Then lastly he debated the question whether the social development he had postulated could not as well be accounted for by reactions of guilt against the sons' hostile *wishes* alone, which one knows commonly happens in individual development. This was a lesson he had learned through personal experience years before at a bitter cost.[78] On the other hand, there is also good reason to believe that with an infant, before the powers of self-restraint and a knowledge of reality have developed, a wish is the same as action; there is no intermediate pause for reflection. Freud thought it probable that the same must have been true of primitive man, who had as yet little to restrain him. So, he concluded, "In the beginning was the deed."

Freud was right in his prediction that the book would be badly received. Outside analytical circles it met with complete disbelief as one more personal phantasy of Freud's. Anthropologists united in discounting his conclusions and in maintaining that he had misunderstood the evidence. I have, however, not come across any of their criticisms that contained serious arguments; mere expressions of disbelief seemed as adequate to them as similar expressions seemed to psychologists when Freud published his *Interpretation of Dreams*.

(20) In 1913 Freud published a little paper on "The Occurrence in Dreams of Material from Fairy Tales." [79] He gave two illustrations of how the memory of fairy tales in childhood could be used in dreams to conceal current thoughts, and he pointed out that the

analysis of such dreams could be made to elucidate the latent meaning of the fairy tales themselves. The second of the two examples he
quoted was taken from the analysis of what we called the "Wolfman,"
previously described.[n]

(21) On March 19, 1913 Freud read a paper before the Vienna
Society on "Presentation in Dreams."

(22) In the same year Freud published a little essay entitled "The
Theme of the Three Caskets." [80] It is one of the two most charming
things he ever wrote, the other being the *Gradiva* book. Most students
of Freud's writings have, apart from an estimate of their scientific
value, a personal fondness for some favorite, and I may say that this
is mine. Its delicacy, combined with the gentle way in which Freud
leads the reader from one layer of the mind to a deeper one until
he reaches the deepest of all, gives it an attraction that always makes
the re-reading a pleasure.

It begins with a comparison between Bassanio's choice of the
leaden one in the scene of the three caskets in *The Merchant of
Venice* and Lear's demand for love from his three daughters, the
muteness of the lead being equated with Cordelia's silence. Various
mythological sources and parallels were drawn upon and a fine analysis made of the underlying themes. Ultimately he concluded that the
number three relates to the three chronological aspects of womanhood: the mother who gives one life; the loving mate who is chosen
by influences dating from the mother; and Mother-Earth (the Goddess of Death) to whom we return at the end.

It would be interesting to know what had stirred the theme in
Freud. He was occupied with the dull work of correcting proofs in
the spring of 1912 when the idea suddenly occurred to him that there
must be a connection between the two Shakespeare scenes just mentioned and the judgment of Paris. He also recalled how Paris in the
libretto of *Die schöne Helena*[o] was impelled to give the apple to the
third Goddess, Aphrodite, who had "stood aside mutely." He announced the connection to Abraham briefly and said he intended to
follow it up.[81] But only a few days later he sent a concise, but complete, account of his conclusions to Ferenczi,[82] and at the same time
described them to me during one of my visits to Vienna. Both Rank
and Sachs had helped him to trace the mythological material he
needed.

What of the themes of love and death which are the content of

* Chapter 11, Case V.
* *La Belle Hélène,* by Ludovic Halévy and Henri Meilhac.

the paper? There was the approaching engagement of his second daughter Sophie, which was formally announced in the following month. Then he had been much impressed by the new symbols of death (a topic never far from his mind), which Stekel had recently discovered and described in a book he had published the year before.[83] And a year later he mentioned to Ferenczi[84] that his interest in the theme must have been connected with thoughts of his three daughters, particularly of the youngest, Anna. And she it was who a quarter of a century later was by her loving care to reconcile him to the inevitable close of his life.

(23) "The History of the Psycho-Analytic Movement." [85] Whatever uncertainty may exist about the workings of Freud's unconscious mind about this time there can be no doubt about what most occupied it consciously. That was the approaching break with Jung. Personal relations had already disappeared and the only questions remaining were how far was Jung diverging from the fundamental principles of psychoanalysis and how long it would be profitable, or even possible, to continue any cooperative work with him. The Munich Congress in September 1913, had seemed to give a decisive answer in the negative to these questions, but Jung was still the President of the International Psycho-Analytical Association. Freud was always very averse to anything like a personal quarrel, and yet the cleft between the two men, and between their respective supporters, was rapidly widening. To Freud the most dignified procedure seemed to be for each to draw silently apart and leave the other to go his way in peace. The difficulty in the way of this solution, however, was that Jung was long in admitting his desertion of psychoanalysis and did not see why he should not hold radically different views from Freud. There was, of course, no reason at all, as Freud was the first to point out. But what troubled Freud was what he called sailing under false colors. He became more and more annoyed at Adler and Jung continuing to call their work psychoanalysis, thereby causing endless confusion in the minds of those outside the whole field. As he insisted, the founder of psychoanalysis must be the person best qualified to judge what was psychoanalysis and what was not. So, very reluctantly at first, he felt called upon to take some active step to defend his work.

What Freud decided on at that juncture, in the months following the Munich dissension, was to write two essays to clear up the confusion, and indeed he wrote them almost simultaneously in the first three months of 1914. One was the essay "On Narcissism," [p] in which

[p] Chapter 12, No. 19.

he took the opportunity of discussing on a purely objective level the differences between his views and those of Adler and Jung. This was the scientific contribution. The other was more avowedly polemical, one of the only two polemical essays Freud ever wrote; the other one had been his only direct answer to a critic.[86]

The essay, seventy pages long, is an historic document. Freud headed it with the quotation *"Fluctuat nec mergitur."* [q] It is divided into three parts. The first, necessarily autobiographical, section related the early beginnings of psychoanalysis when Freud was alone after the separation from Breuer. As always, Freud was generous about the part played by Breuer in its inception. This section contained several novel pieces of information, notably an account of the three hints Freud had received concerning the sexual aetiology of the neuroses and had then forgotten.

The second section related the history of the psychoanalytical movement after 1902, the support and international recognition it had gained since then.

The third section continued the narration up to the time of writing and ended with an account, twenty pages long, of the dissensions with Adler and Jung. Freud admitted the inner struggle it had cost him to bring such matters into public discussion, on which his opponents would gleefully seize, but he was above all concerned to make clear what in his opinion psychoanalysis was and what it was not. In Freud's opinion Adler's alternative theory was more important than Jung's; it was more consistent and had at least retained some connection with the theory of the instincts. (Subsequent history, however, has shown Jung's influence to have been the most lasting of the two.) This part of the essay contains a few personal expressions of a less objective nature which should be judged by the emotions that had been aroused by some painful experiences at the time. But Freud's main object was achieved of demonstrating the incompatibility of the diverging theories with the principles of psychoanalysis, and of enunciating the grounds on which he considered them to be retrogressive in character rather than, as had been claimed, an advance in the knowledge of psychoanalysis.

(24) "The Moses of Michelangelo." [88] As will be seen later, this essay is of special interest to students of Freud's personality. The fact alone that this statue moved him more deeply than any other of the

---

[q] The motto below the ship on the arms of Paris which he had once cited to Fliess as describing his indomitable mood.[87] It may be translated as "It tossed but does not sink."

many works of art with which he was familiar gives his essay on it a peculiar significance.[89]

What fascinated Freud about this statue was just that, the riddle of why it affected him so deeply. What did it mean, or rather what was the sculptor really portraying in it? Freud read widely on the subject and was still more intrigued when he found what a remarkable number of interpretations had been offered, and how greatly they differed from one another. In the essay he gave a rapid summary of the main ones, finding all but one of them unsatisfactory.

The statue portrays Moses in a particular posture and with a terrible expression of mingled anger, pain and scorn. It is evidently meant to represent a particular moment in his life, and most writers have connected this with the moment when on his descent from Mount Sinai bearing the Tables of the Law under his arm he catches sight of the backsliding Israelites dancing around their Golden Calf. But at that point interpretations diverge. Freud followed his usual method of delving deeper, not through the general impression of the whole, but through searching for minute and apparently casual clues. These he found by observing, which no one else had, that the Tables were held upside down, and that the right hand, clutching the majestic beard, had some puzzling features in its details.

The conclusion he came to was that the statue was not intended to represent Moses as about to start up and punish the disobedient people below, as so many commentators had assumed. On the contrary, Freud thought it could only be understood by postulating a *previous* movement, not a future one. Moses had been, it is true, on the point of starting up to denounce the rabble, and moreover had made certain movements in that direction. Then, however, observing that the precious Tables were about to slip from his grasp he contained himself with a mighty effort. The desire to preserve the Tables proved stronger than his anger (the contrary of the version in the Bible). "In this way he (Michelangelo) has added something new and more than human to the figure of Moses; so that the giant frame with its tremendous physical power becomes only a concrete expression of the highest mental achievement that is possible in a man—that of struggling successfully against an inward passion for the sake of a cause to which he has devoted himself." [90]

There is every reason to suppose that the grand figure of Moses himself, from Freud's early Biblical studies to the last book he ever wrote,[91] was one of tremendous significance to him. Did he represent the formidable Father-Image or did Freud identify himself with him? Apparently both, at different periods.

The history of Freud's interest in the statue itself is a long one. It is probable that he was familiar with reproductions of it, and of the plaster copy in the Vienna Academy of Art, long before he saw it in Rome, and it is perhaps noteworthy that he did not fail to visit S. Pietro in Vincoli, where it stands, on his very first visit to Rome in 1901. On a postcard to his wife from there he reported having seen it (on the fourth day after reaching Rome)[92] and then added four tantalizing words in brackets[r] which I will translate at greater length as "I have come to understand the meaning of the statue by contemplating Michelangelo's intention." It is certain, however, that this was not the interpretation he finally adopted, since he related that for long he felt on gazing at the statue that he expected Moses to start up at any moment.[93]

On these earlier visits—for he visited the church many times—he used to flinch at the angry gaze as if he were one of the disobedient mob. From that one must suppose that Moses stood for the angry father-image, with perhaps the glare of Brücke's formidable eyes.[94] One may recall also that 1901 was when his father-substitute, Fliess, had angrily discarded him in spite of Freud's attempts at reconciliation.

In the summer of 1912 he told me of his interest in the meaning of the statue, with his interpretation, and in September he reported from Rome to his wife that he was visiting Moses every day.[95] On returning to Vienna he plunged into the extensive literature on the subject, and in October had managed to get the English book he particularly wanted[96] whose interpretation had come nearest to his own.[97] At that time I sent him photographs from Florence of two statues in the Duomo there, one of which, by Donatello, was supposed to have provided Michelangelo with the stimulus for his great work.[98] This shook Freud badly, since it opened the possibility of the reason for the pose being a purely artistic one without any special ideational significance.[99] I then sent him two photographs from Rome,[100] and at his request had some also specially taken of the lower edge of the Tables.[101]

Nothing further happened for nearly a year, probably because of his doubts about the correctness of his interpretation. He was in Rome in the following September and of course that revived his interest. "I

[r] *"Plötzlich durch Mich. verstanden."*

have visited old Moses again and got confirmed in my application of his position, but something in the comparative material you collected for me did shake my confidence which is not yet restored." [102] Then at Christmas (1913) he decided to write the essay, and found while writing he felt surer of his ground.[103] It was finished on New Year's Day, 1914, but he still did not want to publish it. Finally he did so, but anonymously. The three of us protested at this, and pointed out that his style would at once identify the author. But he was adamant and even got cross with Ferenczi for persisting on the point.[104] The reasons he gave for his decision seem rather thin. "Why disgrace Moses by putting my name to it? It is a joke, but perhaps not a bad one." [105] To Abraham he gave three reasons: (1) "It is only a joke," (2) Shame at the evident amateurishness of the essay, (3) "Lastly because my doubt about my conclusion is stronger than usual; it is only because of editorial pressure (Rank and Sachs) that I have consented to publish it at all." [106] In the next month he consulted an artist on two occasions, but the evenings' talks resulting in nothing more than an exposition of general artistic principles with no opinion about the interpretation.[107] Only in 1924, when the *Gesammelte Schriften* were being issued, did Freud agree to withdraw his anonymity.

Thirteen years later Freud published a "Supplementary Note on the Subject of the Moses Statue." [108] It was based on a representation I had sent him of a statue of Moses which Nicholas of Verdun had made in the twelfth century. The interesting feature of this was that it represented Moses, down to the particular grasp of the beard, in just the pose Freud had postulated as preceding the one in which Michelangelo had depicted him in his famous work. Freud claimed this as confirming his interpretation of the latter as representing "the calm after the storm."

The winter of 1913-1914, following the unhappy Congress in Munich in the preceding September, was the worst time in the conflict with Jung. The *Moses* was written in the same month as the long essays in which Freud announced the seriousness of the divergences between his views and Jung's ("Narcissism" and "The History of the Psycho-Analytic Movement"), and there is no doubt that at the time he was feeling bitterly disappointed at Jung's defection. It cost him an inward struggle to control his emotions firmly enough to enable him to say calmly what he felt he had to say. One cannot avoid the pretty obvious conclusion that at this time, and probably before, Freud had identified himself with Moses and was striving to emulate the victory over passions that Michelangelo had depicted in his stupendous achievement. The backsliding mob were to him the many former supporters who had deserted him, and gone back on his work, in the last four years—Adler and his friends, Stekel, and now the Swiss. Indeed, he had expressed this very thought himself in a letter to Ferenczi written at the time of the separation from Stekel. "At the moment the situation in Vienna makes me feel more like the historical Moses[*] than the Michelangelo one." [109] But above all emotions was the overriding need to save something of his life's work, psychoanalysis, just as Moses had bent all his strength of will to preserve the precious Tables. Some of the doubt about his interpretation that kept disturbing Freud in what seems to us a really unnecessary degree may be attributed to his uncertainty about whether he would now succeed in self-mastery as Michelangelo's Moses did.

Twenty years later, on the occasion of an Italian translation of the essay, Freud wrote to the translator: "My feeling for this piece of work is rather like that towards a love-child. For three lonely September weeks in 1913 I stood every day in the church in front of the statue, studied it, measured it, sketched it, until I captured the understanding for it which I ventured to express in the essay only anonymously. Only much later did I legitimatize this non-analytical child." [110]

(25) Later in 1914 Freud was asked to contribute an article to a publication commemorating the fiftieth anniversary of the founding of his old school, which had in the meantime changed its name to that of the *K. K. Erzherzog Rainer Realgymnasium*; apparently Freud had joined the school in the second year of its existence. The article we may call "Some Reflections on Schoolboy Psychology." [111] It was written in the attractive light style of which Freud possessed the secret.

Freud discussed here the meaning of the extravagant ambivalence schoolboys often display toward their teachers, and the account of it is so vivid that one surmises Freud was drawing on his own memory. He then explained the manifestations as transferences from early childhood, when one's father is so much admired and loved, and yet envied and hated. The contribution was a gentle introduction to the theme of the Oedipus complex.

(26) "Thoughts for the Times on War and Death":[112] The external occasion for writing these two essays was pressure from the publisher, Heller, there being a dearth of material for the periodical *Imago*.[113] It is not unlikely that Heller suggested the theme itself. But there

[*] The Biblical one, who lost control of himself.

were of course more important inner motives as well. Freud, like all highly civilized people, was not only greatly distressed, but also bewildered, by the frightful happenings at the onset of the First World War, when so many things took place of which no living person had had any experience or any expectation. So these two essays may be regarded as an effort to clear his own mind about the most useful attitude to adopt to the current events. We may also think that they were designed to help others in a similar quandary to himself. The consolations he offered, however, were characteristically neither reassurances nor denial of any reality, but endeavors to clear one's mind by facing perhaps unpalatable truths. It is also typical of his generosity that he made no attempt to exploit the situation by pointing out that psychoanalytical conclusions about the nature of man had been right all along, although he could easily have done so.

But although he put forward no such claim in public he expressed it clearly enough in a letter he wrote a few months after the outbreak of the war to Dr. van Eeden, an acquaintance of his from the old hypnosis days.

Van Eeden, a Dutch psychopathologist, is now remembered more as a poet, essayist and social reformer; both Freud and I had been unsuccessful in getting him to accept psychoanalytical theories.

"Vienna, December 28, 1914

"*Verehrter Herr Kollege,*

"Under the influence of this war I venture to remind you of two assertions psychoanalysis has put forward which have assuredly contributed to its unpopularity.

"Psychoanalysis has concluded from a study of the dreams and mental slips of normal people, as well as from the symptoms of neurotics, that the primitive, savage and evil impulses of mankind have not vanished in any individual, but continue their existence, although in a repressed state—in the unconscious, as we call it in our language —and that they wait for opportunities to display their activity.

"It has furthermore taught us that our intellect is a feeble and dependent thing, a plaything and tool of our impulses and emotions; that all of us are forced to behave cleverly or stupidly according as our attitudes and inner resistances ordain.

"And now just look at what is happening in this wartime, at the cruelties and injustices for which the most civilized nations are responsible, at the different way in which they judge of their own lies, their own wrong-doings, and those of their enemies, at the general loss of clear insight; then you must confess that psychoanalysis has been right with both its assertions.

"Perhaps it was not entirely original in this. Many thinkers and students of mankind have said similar things, but our science has worked them out in detail and employed them to unravel many psychological riddles.

"I hope to see you again in better times.

"Ihr herzlich ergebener
"Sigmund Freud"

Van Eeden published this letter in a Dutch newspaper, *Uit De Groene*, January 17, 1915.

To Putnam Freud wrote that he was writing a paper on the disappointments brought about by the war, "which gives me no enjoyment to write, and will hardly please others." [114]

Only the year before another connoisseur of human nature, the Russian revolutionary Trotsky, had expressed similar sentiments: "The abstract, humanitarian, moralist view of history is barren—I know this very well. But this chaotic mass of material acquisitions, of habits, customs and prejudices, which we call civilization, has hypnotized us all, giving us the false impression that we have already achieved the main thing. Now comes the war and shows us that we have not even crawled out on our bellies from the barbarous period of our history." [115]

The first essay is entitled "The Disillusionment of the War." It is written in a philosophical frame of mind, the only emotion displayed being a tinge of sadness. The inevitable horrors of such a bloody war, with thousands of casualties a day, were bad enough, but what was specially depressing was the barbarous way in which it was being conducted. The ignoring of treaty and other international obligations, the ill-treatment of the wounded and prisoners, including the medical personnel, and the involvement of the civilian population: all such things signified a retrogression from the level of ethics and civilization which it had been hoped we had permanently reached. The reader must bear in mind that we had not yet been hardened by the forty years that were to follow.

Freud's main consolation was the reminder that the disillusionment was not altogether justified, since it was based on a great illusion that had been maintained up to the outbreak of that cruel and implacable war. "In reality our fellow-citizens have not sunk so low as we feared, because they had never risen so high as we believed. . . . The individual in any given nation has in this war a terrible opportunity to convince himself of what would occasionally strike him in peace time—that the State has forbidden to the individual the practice of wrongdoing, not because it desired to abolish it, but because it desires to have the monopoly of it, like salt and tobacco."

Freud pointed out that there were two kinds of moral behavior in peacetime, the outward manifestations of which were identical. One was displayed by those persons in whom the love instinct had mastered and controlled the underlying hostile ones that are always present. The other was the result of external control, a fear of punishment and disapproval from the community. The latter is therefore a more artificial, or, as Freud called it, "hypocritical" form of moral behavior, and it readily relapses when the external control is absent; according to Freud, this type is far commoner than the more genuine type of goodness. War, of course, not only abrogates such control but in many ways encourages the underlying cruel and dishonest tendencies. Despite the general theme of the essay Freud wrote in as cheerful a vein as could be expected, and was evidently trying to make the best, and not the worst, of things.

When Abraham read this essay in proof he called Freud's attention to the resemblance between the phenomenon of war and that of primitive totemistic festivals. In both cases the whole community combines to do things which were absolutely forbidden to the individual; common action was the necessary sanction for the murderous orgy.[116] Freud fully agreed with this comment,[t] and added: "It is interesting how any disturbance of mood in an author restricts his vision." He evidently thought that he should have perceived the analogy himself.

The second essay was on "Our Attitude to Death." He first delivered it at an address before his Jewish society, the B'nai B'rith.[117] He called it "an audacious lecture, containing much grim humor."[u][118]

Our attitude toward death includes a denial of its happening to ourselves or our loved ones; when it does so with the latter it is imputed to accident or disease, never to inevitability. There is a special attitude toward the dead; they must only be praised. "Consideration for the dead, who no longer need it, is dearer to us than the truth, and certainly, for most of us, is dearer also than consideration for the living." All this unreal attitude has a powerful effect on our lives. "Life

[t] *voll zutreffend.*
[u] *Galgenhumor.*

is impoverished when the highest stake in the game of living, life itself, may not be risked." We then have recourse to the world of fiction where heroes may die, and we with them in our imagination, a process that can be repeated indefinitely.

Freud then expounded his views on primitive man, with his pronounced ambivalence of emotions, and remarked on how much our own unconscious resembles the primitive attitude. "Our unconscious is just as inaccessible to the idea of our own death, as murderously minded toward the stranger, as divided or ambivalent toward our loved ones, as was man's in earliest antiquity. But how far have we moved from this primitive state in our conventionally civilized attitude toward death!" War strips us of the later accretions of civilization, and lays bare the primal man in each of us. We have thus to recognize that here, as in the illusions mentioned in the first essay, we are psychologically living beyond our means. If we took into account the true state of affairs we should make life again more endurable for ourselves. "To endure life remains, when all is said, the first duty of all living beings." So Freud concluded: "If you would endure life, be prepared for death." [119]

(27) "Some Character-Types met with in Psycho-Analytic Work": Later in 1915 Freud wrote for *Imago* one of his all too rare papers on character traits and their formation. It was characteristic of him that he should not attempt broad general estimates—he always felt the time was not ripe for great syntheses—but should focus his interest on some unusual feature the analysis of which might reveal something new. Here he chose three particular types of character traits that he had had to investigate in his work. The features he discussed are deeply ingrained, often hidden, and so become plain only during analysis.

The first of them he labeled the "Exceptions." After a disquisition of clinical value on the particular type of renunciations a patient has to make during a psychoanalysis Freud called attention to a class of persons who blankly refuse to do so since they regard themselves as exceptions to the iron laws of nature. With such people the explanation of much unreasonable, and also injurious, behavior turns on their secretly cherishing the belief that they are exceptions to the rule that society justly demands a certain standard of conduct; they are free of such rules. The analyses of such cases disclose that, usually in early life, the patient has in fact suffered unjustly from some ill-treatment or accident, so that he feels that society owes him some recompense, while he owes it nothing. Freud described as such a type King Richard

III, at least as delineated by Shakespeare, and he expressed his admiration for the skill with which the dramatist wins some degree of sympathy for the "hero" by adumbrating the meaning of his behavior rather than by bluntly insisting on it. In conclusion Freud suggested that women as a whole tend to regard themselves in the same light because of the part of the body they felt themselves in infancy to be deprived of.

The second type he called "Those Wrecked by Success." ▾ Being familiar with the rule that neurotic failure is the product of frustration it came as a surprise to meet with cases where the contrary appeared to hold: where people were well and happy until they had achieved some important goal, toward which they had perhaps striven all their life, and then fell ill and collapsed. The explanation is interesting. Here also the neurosis is the result of frustration, imposed by the conscience. Such a person is allowed to be well and efficient as long as he is pursuing the internally forbidden goal and it thus remains something in phantasy only, but when it is reached in reality his conscience steps in as if to say: "I let you play with that wish, but it must not be actually gratified."

Freud illustrated his theme by considering two examples from literature: Lady Macbeth and Rebecca West. He was of course very familiar with Shakespeare's *Macbeth,* but about this time he told Ferenczi he was making a special study of the play. "I have begun to study *Macbeth* which has long tormented me without my having been able to find a solution. How curious it is that I passed the theme over to Jones years ago, and now here I am so to speak taking it back. There are dark forces at work in the play." [120]

Freud felt that the theme of childlessness must be the key to the understanding of the tragedy. This suggestion had already been made by the Boston psychoanalyst, Isador Coriat, in his paper on the subject.[121] Freud could not, however, reconcile this idea with the time sequence presented by Shakespeare, and he made another suggestion which leads to still darker problems. It was that Lady Macbeth, the remorseless being who collapsed on attaining her ambitions, and her husband the faint-hearted person who became transformed into an implacable tyrant, were psychologically one and the same person; an example of what mythologists call "decomposition," a method adopted at times by Shakespeare. But the final solution of this obscure problem has not been reached, although Jekels, following Freud, carried it somewhat further a little time after.[122]

▾ *Die am Erfolge scheitern.*

Freud was more successful in the analysis of the other literary figure, Rebecca West in Ibsen's *Rosmersholm*. Here he followed closely the study Otto Rank had recently made of the same character,[123] but it is presented in his own inimitable style. Freud delicately dissected the three layers of Rebecca's sense of guilt and made clear the central theme of the whole tragedy.

The third type Freud called "Criminals from a Sense of Guilt." He quoted cases where some criminal act, such as theft, had been committed in order to provoke a punishment that would alleviate some unbearable sense of guilt arising from deeper unconscious sources, or at least to give the person a rationalized ground on to which they can displace some of the guilt and so make it bearable. These are people suffering from a deep, and usually unknown, sense of guilt, who seek relief in committing some forbidden deed on to the thought of which they can then displace the previously unbearable sense of guilt. Freud remarked that Nietzsche, in his *Also Sprach Zarathustra* had given broad hints of the same mechanism. Short as this section is, from it has come most of the modern work on the psychology of criminals and delinquents.

(28) "On Transience":[124] In November 1915, the Berlin Goethe Society invited Freud to contribute to a volume they were producing entitled *Das Land Goethes*, which was published in the following year. The main interest of the contribution is that it affords an irrefutable denial of the common belief in Freud's supposed pessimism.

He began by relating a discussion he had had with two friends in the summer of 1913. They maintained that the knowledge of how transient were all the beautiful things of the world, the products of both nature and man, took away the possibility of enjoying them. Freud asserted the contrary, but none of his arguments succeeded in convincing them. Thinking the matter over, he came to the conclusion that what was influencing them was the premonition of the grief they would suffer when the particular beautiful objects passed away, and that led him on to reflections about mourning. He admitted being baffled in the endeavor to ascertain the precise source of the pain this causes. Only two years later he was to embark on a thorough study of this problem.

He then commented on the enormous destruction the war had brought about, both materially and also in ideals, but he had made the observation that the sense of poverty resulting from the great reduction in the things left to admire had intensified the love for what was left, one's country, family and so on. But have the destroyed things lost their value through having been proved transitory? Freud denied this and opined that those who felt otherwise were still in a state of mourning. He then asserted that however painful this process may be it spontaneously comes to an end sooner or later, and then one's libido is free to seek fresh objects to admire or love. This would happen even after such a terrible and destructive war as they were then experiencing. "Once the mourning process is over it will be found that our high esteem for the productions of our culture has not suffered from discovering their frailty. We shall reconstruct all that the war has destroyed, perhaps on a better basis and more permanently than before."

This train of thought accords with a remark Freud once made to Marie Bonaparte: "It is the eternal changefulness of life that makes it so beautiful."

The paper also throws another light on Freud's personality. The terrible events of the war, and what he called the disillusionment it had induced, had evidently stirred Freud deeply. No doubt all sorts of old emotions were re-animated: horror, fear, and even his long forgotten military pugnacity. No wonder that for months he was in a state of great perturbation. But the present paper, even more than the essays on "Thoughts for the Times," shows how thoroughly he had mastered that perturbation and regained his calm through candidly facing his inner situation as well as the outside events.

(29) "A Mythological Parallel to a Visual Obsession": Freud read a short paper on March 15, 1916, before the Vienna Society; it was published in the *Zeitschrift* in the same year.[125]

It concerned an obsessional patient who was plagued by the curious hallucination of seeing his father's abdomen with the features of his face imprinted on it. Freud did not mention his interpretation of the symptom, but he was interested in various parallelisms that came to his mind from his vast reading. One was from Fuchs: *Das erotische Element in der Karikatur* (The Erotic Element in Caricature), 1901, (p. 248), where in an obscene caricature by Jean Veber, entitled "Indecent Albion," the Prince of Wales's face is painted on the buttocks of a female figure representing Britain. Then there came to his mind the Greek legend of Baubo's exposing her abdomen to bring a smile to the countenance of the mourning Demeter. A terracotta had been excavated at Priene in Anatolia depicting this scene, and with the woman's face on the abdomen. So the mythological imagination of the ancients persists in the psychoneuroses.

(30) "A Childhood Recollection from '*Dichtung und Wahr-*

heit.' " [126] This little essay in biography was written in September 1917,[127] in the first week after Freud's return from his holiday in the Tatra. Knowing Goethe's works so well from boyhood on, Freud must have long been familiar with the recollection Goethe mentioned, but he had paid no special attention to it until a patient related to him a similar experience. The memory was of indulging in an orgy of hurling crockery out of the window, which Freud now perceived from his patient's analysis to be an expression of jealousy of a younger brother with the wish to get rid of him. Even now he did not feel quite sure of his interpretation. Perhaps we may associate this remaining doubt, or inhibition, with a curious remark he made concerning the birth of Goethe's sister, Cornelia, when he was fifteen months old. "This slight difference in age practically excludes the possibility of her having been an object of jealousy." [128] He seems for the moment to have quite blotted out his own confession of years before about feeling guilty all his life because of his death wishes, based on jealousy, which he had cherished against his own little brother who was born when Freud was very little older than Goethe had been at the birth of his sister.[129] However, when a second patient narrated a similar experience, the analysis of which pointed to the same conclusion, he could no longer doubt the truth of his interpretation.

Freud related the story at a meeting of the Vienna Society on December 13, 1916, and asked if other members had any confirmatory material. At a later meeting, on April 18, 1917, Dr. Hug-Hellmuth produced reports of two similar cases, which Freud published as an appendage to his paper. Other confirmatory examples have since been recorded.[130]

3

PART

THE MAN

15

Mode of Life and Work

NO EXCITEMENTS CAN BE PROMISED IN THIS CHAPTER, SINCE THERE WERE none. Freud led a quiet and regular life, and in all these years the only thing that disturbed his equanimity was the recurrent dissension among his followers, an account of which has been given earlier.[a]

We may begin with a description of the physical environment of Freud's life. The Berggasse, so called because it slopes steeply down from a main street, consisted of massive eighteenth-century houses, typically Viennese, in which there were a few shops. The ground floor of No. 19 had a butcher's shop. The butcher's first name was Sigmund and his plate affixed on one side of the large entrance doors contrasted a little curiously with that of Prof. Dr. Sigm. Freud on the opposite side. The entrance to the main house was very wide, so that a horse and carriage could drive straight through it into the garden and stable behind. On the left as one entered were the concierge's quarters. I used to find it strange that, like other Viennese burghers, Freud had no latchkey to his house and had to awaken the concierge to let him in if he returned after ten o'clock. On the right there was a flight of half-a-dozen steps leading to the professional flat of three rooms which Freud occupied from 1892 to 1908. The windows of these rooms gave on to the garden behind. It was a separate flat which had previously been occupied by Viktor Adler, the founder of the Austrian Socialist party; Freud had once visited him there with a friend of Adler's. A noble flight of low stone steps then led to the next floor, called the mezzanine, and that is where Freud and his family dwelled.

[a] See Chapter 5.

On May 6, 1954, the World Federation for Mental Health, in virtue of a unanimous resolution passed a few months before, affixed on 19 Berggasse, Freud's old domicile, a tablet bearing this inscription (in German).

IN THIS HOUSE LIVED AND WORKED
PROFESSOR SIGMUND FREUD,
THE FOUNDER OF PSYCHO-ANALYSIS.
DEDICATED BY THE SIXTH ANNUAL
MEETING OF THE WORLD FEDERATION
FOR MENTAL HEALTH, VIENNA, AUGUST 1953.

In the nineteen-thirties the City Council proposed to re-name the Berggasse "Sigmund Freudgasse," thus following a graceful Viennese custom of commemorating famous physicians. Freud himself called the idea "nonsensical." Political conflicts intervened and the proposal was dropped. On February 15, 1949, however, the City Council decided to name a block of flats in the Ninth District of Vienna the "*Sigmund Freud-Hof.*" The tablet on it bears the inscription: "*Dr. Sigmund Freud, Professor der Neurologie an der Universität Wien. Begründer der Psychoanalyse. 1856-1939.*"

It was mentioned earlier how in the spring of 1908 Freud reorganized his domestic arrangements. Giving up his little flat of three rooms on the ground floor, which had constituted his own sanctum, he took over what had been his sister Rosa's flat on the first floor adjoining his own living one, so that he now occupied the whole of the floor. An opening was made so that he could pass from the new to the old flat without having to open the front door, and he regularly took advantage of this in the few minutes between patients. Another alteration was made to enable a patient to leave at the end of the hour without returning to the waiting room, so that two patients seldom encountered each other. The maid would at the appropriate moment retrieve the hat and coat and give them to the patient as he left.

Freud's own rooms were as follows. First there came a small waiting-room with a window giving on to the garden. It was commodious enough to hold in it the Wednesday meetings of the Vienna Society for several years until this grew too large. There was an oblong substantial table down the middle, and the room itself was decorated with various antiquities from Freud's collection. Between this and the adjoining consulting-room Freud had had double doors fitted, lined with baize and overhung on both sides with heavy curtains as well; this ensured complete privacy. With the analytical couch at his side Freud sat upright in a not too comfortable chair facing the window which similarly gave on to the little garden; in later years he used a high stool to support his feet. Chestnut trees there provided some protection from the evening sun. The garden was closed by a wall into which was set a pseudo-Renaissance recess or niche inside which was a cheap little statue of a young girl with a pitcher. Joel Shor, who visited Freud's old domicile recently, promoted the girl to an Aphrodite and suggested that it was Freud's constant staring at her that stirred him to discover his love for his mother! [1] I could think of many rebuttals of this extraordinary idea, but I will leave the choice to my readers.

The garden had originally been fairly extensive, but in the first years of the century stables with a coachman's flat above were built over part of it. This left untouched, however, that part of the garden on to which Freud's windows gave.

The consulting room itself contained also many antiquities, including a relief of the famous Gradiva, and they no doubt afforded useful stimuli to patients' phantasies. It led into an inner sanctum, Freud's study proper. This was lined with books, but there was room for cabinets of still more antiquities. The desk at which he wrote was not large, but was always neat. To dust it must have been a trial, since it was replete with little statues, mostly Egyptian, which Freud used from time to time to replace by others from his cabinets. The well-known etching of Freud by Max Pollak represents him seated at this desk with the little figures in front of him.

Freud's fondness for collecting Greek, Assyrian and Egyptian antiquities played an important part in his emotional life and afforded him great pleasure and interest. He seldom returned from his travels without some addition to his very considerable collection, and in later years friends and pupils who knew of his hobby made their own contributions. In 1910 a Hungarian farmer came across a Roman cemetery on his ground, and Ferenczi used from time to time to procure surreptitiously various objects from him which would be passed on to Freud.

Fortunately he was able to transfer the whole collection intact to his London home, where it is now displayed to great advantage. It was one of Freud's great pleasures to make presents from time to time of various objects from his collection, and several of us treasure such pieces. His son Ernst, who possesses several valuable selections, naturally chose them according to their artistic value, one which with

Freud was always secondary to their historical or mythological significance.

The living flat had three reception rooms and the bedrooms. Altogether no fewer than twelve of the old-fashioned Viennese porcelain stoves could be counted, and the children were proud to think that they were unique in their circle in possessing eleven desks in their home.

Naturally Freud's mode of life, and to some extent even his personality, was different in the working period in Vienna and the long summer holiday to which he always looked forward so much. In Vienna there was little besides work. It would begin with the first patient at eight in the morning, which meant rising soon after seven. It was never easy to get him up so early, since his hard work and late hours combined made him yearn for more rest than was allotted. However, a cold shower refreshed him. A barber appeared every morning to trim his beard and if necessary his hair. Impressed by the unusualness of his hirsute appearance in America Freud had his cheeks shaved on his return to Europe, but he decided to discontinue the practice after a few months; not long afterward he also sacrificed the fullness of his moustachios and beard which in later years were rather closely cropped. There was a hurried breakfast and a glance at the *Neue Freie Presse*. Each patient was given fifty-five minutes precisely, so that there was an interval of five minutes between each to clear his mind ready for fresh impression or to dash in and hear the latest news of the household. But he made a point of being punctual with his patients.

The family lunch was at one o'clock. This was the only time when the whole family would usually be together; the evening meal was often so late that the younger members had already retired to bed. It was the chief meal of the day, and was a substantial one of soup, meat, cheese, etc. and a sweet. Freud was specially fond of his meat dishes, and their disappearance in the war meant a considerable privation for him. He enjoyed his food and would concentrate on it. He was very taciturn during meals, which would sometimes be a source of embarrassment to strange visitors who had to carry on a conversation alone with the family. Freud, however, never missed a word of the family intercourse and daily news. Incidentally, I would contradict Helen Puner's innuendo when she writes: "Woe to the tardy child who showed such disrespect for the excellent food and Papa's schedule." [2] On the contrary, Freud on such occasions had a peculiar habit I have often witnessed and which the family themselves would comment on. He would point mutely at the vacant chair with his knife or fork and look inquiringly to his wife at the other end of the table. She would explain that the child was not coming in to dinner or that something or other had detained him, whereupon Freud, his curiosity satisfied, would nod and silently proceed with his meal. All he wanted was to be kept in touch with the family doings.

Unless he was exceptionally busy Freud was free from one to three, so after a few minutes rest he would proceed on his constitutional walk through the neighboring streets. It would be an opportunity for any minor shopping. Being a very swift walker Freud could cover a good distance in the time at his disposal. There would often be proofs to be delivered to his publishers, Deuticke and, later, Heller. And there was the important visit to the Tabak Trafik shop near the Michaeler Church to replenish his stock of cigars. Three o'clock was the hour for consultations, for which purpose Freud would don his frock coat. When Freud was forced to take an analytical patient at three it would necessitate holding any consultation at two. After that it was steady therapeutic work until nine in the evening, the hour for supper. When he was exceptionally busy Freud would even be at work with his patients until ten o'clock, which meant twelve or even thirteen analytic hours in the day.[3]

It seems a long run from one o'clock till nine without food, but it was only after he was sixty-five that Freud allowed himself the luxury of a cup of coffee at five o'clock.

Freud would relax with his family more readily at the evening meal than when he was in his preoccupied mood in the middle of the day. After it he would take another walk, this time with his wife, his sister-in-law or, later on, with a daughter. The length of these walks would vary. They usually began by proceeding to the Schottenthor and then along the Ringstrasse. The return might be via the Burghof or the Stubenring and back through the city (Innere Stadt) or the more enterprising way of continuing round the Ringstrasse and home along the Quai—two or three miles. Sometimes on these occasions they would drop into a café: in the summer the Café Landmann, in the winter the Café Central. When his daughters went to the theater, Freud would meet them at a particular lamp post near the theater and escort them home.

His eldest daughter tells a story of Freud's courtesy toward his family. When she was fourteen she was invited to walk on the right-hand side of her father during their strolls. A school friend who observed this told her it wasn't right; one's father should always be on the right-hand side. But the daughter proudly replied: "That is not so with *my* father. With him I am always the lady."

On returning home Freud would retire at once to his study to concentrate, first on his correspondence, which he invariably answered by hand, and then on whatever paper he was composing. Besides that there was the grind of preparing new editions and correcting proofs, not only of his own writings but also of the periodicals of which he was editor. He was never in bed before one in the morning and often much later.

There were a few interruptions in the routine just described. Every Wednesday there was the regular meeting of the Vienna Society, at which he always gave a paper or joined in the discussion. Every other Tuesday he would attend the meetings of his Jewish Lodge, the B'nai B'rith, where he occasionally also gave a paper. Saturday evening was a sacred one, since it was very rare for Freud to miss the enjoyable relaxation of his beloved card game of tarock. Usually he would drive to Königstein's house direct from the Hospital after he had delivered his weekly University lecture. Freud played a good deal of chess in coffee houses in the earlier years, but he came to find the concentration more of a strain than an enjoyment, and after 1901 he gave it up altogether. An evening spent at a theater was a rare event. It had to be something of special interest to him, such as a performance of a Shakespeare play or a Mozart opera before he could tear himself away from his work.

Sunday was of course a day apart, with no patients. In the morning Freud, accompanied by one or two members of his family, always paid a visit to his mother. There might be one or more sisters there too, and there would be much family gossip. Freud was always very much a family man, entered into any difficulties and no doubt proffered his sage advice. He did far more listening than talking on these visits, and when there was any serious problem, e.g. a financial one, he preferred to talk it over quietly with his brother Alexander at home. Occasionally he would call on a friend or there might be a visitor at home later in the morning, but this would happen only a few times in a year. Herzig, the Professor of Chemistry, might call or Professor Emanuel Loewy, the archaeologist, when he came back home from his work in Rome. In the afternoon Frau Professor would have her visitors, Anna Lichtheim, Bertha Hammerschlag, Frau Professor Königstein, the Rosanes couple, etc., and if it was anyone in whom Freud was interested he would drop into the drawing-room for a few minutes. In later years Sunday was Freud's favorite day for seeing psychoanalytical friends from abroad, when he could devote hours and hours to them. I have several times been with him till three in the morning, but in spite of my bad conscience at cutting his night's rest so short he found it hard to bring interesting conversations to an end. Ferenczi, although a member of the Vienna Society, would mostly choose a Sunday for visiting Vienna rather than the meeting day on Wednesday, since it meant a long private talk with Freud.

On Sunday evening his mother and all his sisters would come for a family meal, but Freud would get away to his own room as soon as it was over. If anyone wanted a private word with him, or some advice, she would have to pursue him there.

Sunday was also the day when Freud counted on doing most of his writing. We have seen how little time and energy were available for this on week days. To us nowadays it seems strange that he should be able to spend nine solid months of the year confined to the streets of a large city and not take a tram on a Sunday and refresh himself in the pretty country around that was so easily accessible, especially when we remember his passionate fondness for the country. But so it was. He and his friends had been brought up that way, so they continued their rather Ghetto-like existence. Moreover, he had a strong dislike of the famous Wienerwald, with the solitary exception of the Cobenzl. His children, who were all fond of it, could never drag him there. Whether this was because it grew no mushrooms, or whether it was too close to his hated Vienna, I cannot say, but he preferred to divide his life sharply between enforced work in the town and a complete change in the holidays to a distant and quite different country scene.

Sunday was the only chance to indulge in any aesthetic pleasures. Freud was fond of taking his children to visit the famous galleries of Vienna, both those of paintings and of the other art collections. The knowledge he had gained from his travels in Italy must have made his talks very enlightening. His own interests, however, lay rather in the great collections of Egyptian and other antiquities.

That Freud was a heavy smoker is generally known. His consumption averaged twenty cigars a day. That it might be called rather an addiction than a habit was shown by the extent to which he suffered when he was deprived of the opportunity to smoke. This happened in the last years of the war, and in still later years on grounds of health. When he had for the latter reasons to put up with denicotinized tobacco he pulled a very long face indeed. On the other hand he never had any inclination to drink to excess. There was a single exception in his life. The medical students were giving a dinner in honor of Professor Stricker, and everyone had to pay for what he drank. Being very poor Freud drank only beer, to which he was not accustomed. Suddenly everything went black and when he came to he found himself in bed, Gärtner and Wagner-Jauregg having carried him there.[4] As he wrote once to his betrothed, he had "no predisposition towards drinking." When a young man he had enjoyed wine, though never beer or spirits, and on his travels in Italy he would make a point of savoring the local wine. In Vienna, however, he never took any at all, and there could have been very little kept in the house. The three or four bottles of special wine which was Oscar Rie's regular Christmas present were reserved for particular social occasions, as was the Tokay which later on Ferenczi used to bring from the Royal cellars in Hungary. Nor were the family accustomed to partaking of wine; water was drunk at meals. This may well have been not because of any principle, but from a dislike of the faint mental obfuscation that even a slight drink induces; Freud wanted always to be clear-minded.

Freud's apparel was invariably neat and correct, though not smart or fashionable. Before the war he wore a dark lounge suit with a stiff white low collar and a ready-made black bow tie; his frock coat appeared only on special occasions. His headgear was the broad black hat then customarily worn in Vienna; silk hats were for the very rare ceremonial occasions which Freud was mostly successful in avoiding.

It is desirable to say something about Freud's married life, since various strange legends seem to be in vogue about it. In particular, Helen Puner's picture of it is very remote from that familiar to anyone with personal knowledge.[5] His wife was assuredly the only woman in Freud's love life, and she always came first before all other mortals. While it is likely that the more passionate side of married life subsided with him earlier than it does with many men—indeed we know this in so many words[6]—it was replaced by an unshakable devotion and a perfect harmony of understanding. In his letters to her when on holiday he constantly expressed his thoughts about her and showed her the most delicate consideration. Nor was it at all so that "Martha Freud epitomized the cleaning, brushing, tidying *Hausfrau* who neither rests nor wishes to while a cushion still remains to be plumped."[7] She was certainly a very competent housekeeper, with high standards, and ordering the duties of several servants and raising six children who were very often ill was a pretty full-time occupation. It would be far truer to say that with her the family came first than to suggest that housework came first. First of all of course was her husband, as she was first with him. And far from being a "governess type," she was a very cultivated lady to whom the graces of life meant a great deal. Her evening was given up to reading and thus keeping abreast with current literature, which she did to the end of her long life. It was a special pleasure to her when the great Thomas Mann, one of her favorite authors, was a guest, one of the many prominent literary figures of the day to be so. She was a perfect social hostess, which no real *Hausfrau* is ever able to be. She had little opportunity, or possibly desire, for pursuing purely intellectual studies, and she would hardly have been familiar with the details of her husband's professional work. But in his letters he makes casual allusions to his writings on *Gradiva*, Leonardo, Moses, etc. in a manner that implies knowledge on her part of them.

Then there was her sister, the well-known "Tante Minna," who lived with them for some forty-two years. One of the sons remarked to me that "Tante Minna" deserved a book to herself, so interesting and decided was her personality. She certainly knew more about Freud's work than did her sister, and he remarked once that in the lonely nineties Fliess and she were the only people in the world who sympathized with it.[8] She had more leisure for reading than her sister, and she also made the most exquisite embroideries. Her caustic tongue gave rise to many epigrams that were cherished in the family. Freud no doubt appreciated her conversation, but to say that she in any way replaced her sister in his affections is sheer nonsense.

His children were extremely astonished to read in a book by an American author about two supposed features of the relationship between them and their father. In the first place they learned there to their surprise that it was not in Freud's nature to give his children spontaneous simple affection and that he kept his natural feeling for them "walled in." There comes to my mind the memory of a daughter, then a big schoolgirl, cuddling on his lap in a manner that showed no doubt at all of his affection or his readiness to show it. To be with his children and to share their amusements was his greatest happiness, and he devoted his only spare time, when they were together on holiday, to them. Still stranger was it to learn what a stern father they were supposed to have had. Pictures have been drawn of a patriarchal severity in which awe of their father, and obedience to his lightest whim, constituted the basis of their upbringing. How very different was the truth, as they would all testify. On the contrary, it is perhaps possible to criticize Freud's education of his children on one point only—it was unusually lenient. To allow a child's personality to develop freely with the minimum of restraint or reprimand was in those days a very rare occurrence, and Freud may even have gone to the extreme in that direction—with, however, the happiest results in their later development. And this was as true of the sons as it was of the daughters. That they should have respected as well as loved him was an inevitable result of his personality, but it was entirely spontaneous, and any idea of compelling it by inculcating "awe" would have been quite alien to Freud's whole nature.

The children had of course their own friends, whom they used to bring to the house, but there were no formalities in their friendships. From time to time Frau Professor would say with a sigh, since she disliked formal occasions as much as her husband did, that she really ought to arrange a party for the children, which she described by the idiomatic phrase "biting into the sour apple," but somehow or other it never seemed to come off. On the other hand, they occasionally went to the parties of friends. In later years, for instance, Martin, Ernst and Sophie used to go to private dances every Saturday. But to give a dance of their own would have meant storing away the beds, bringing in a piano, and making various arrangements for which their crowded flat was not suited. In the early years the children paid a regular visit to Baronin Ferstl's to get their present from the Christmas tree. They were festively dressed for such occasions and had to be very well behaved. Incidentally, Freud had many years before remarked that it was important for children's self-respect that they should always be given good clothes.[9]

There was one very unusual feature of the family life in the Berggasse: the remarkable harmony in its atmosphere. Everything proceeded as on oiled wheels, in the most natural and inevitable fashion. The children had, like their parents, a highly developed sense of humor, so that life was full of jokes and there might also be a slight amount of mutual teasing. But there was never anything ill-natured or bad-tempered. None of them can remember anything like a quarrel among themselves, still less with either parent. There was never anything resembling a "scene." The whole atmosphere was free, friendly and well-balanced. Of few families can so much be said, and it is an eloquent witness to the love that pervaded their relationships. Freud himself was not a demonstrative man, not the sort of man who would think of kissing his wife in front of strangers, but the deep fount of affection that radiated from him inspired the whole family.

One thing Freud was determined on in the upbringing of his children, that so far as it lay in his power they should not experience any of the anxiety about money which had so marred his own early life. His plan was that they should have everything they wanted for both their pleasure and their education until they could earn their own living; after that they were not to expect anything. Any money he might leave was destined for his many dependents. In the end he gave money to his sisters before finally leaving Vienna and left what small fortune there was to a family trust from which his wife could draw at will. In the meantime the children were not only not to have any anxiety about money, but even to know as little as possible about it— nothing in fact beyond their own little allowances. In this he went rather to the opposite extreme, and it might have been easier for them had they been taught something of the part money necessarily plays in life. But again there were no bad consequences of this upbringing. His eldest daughter told me two stories illustrative of her early childhood in this connection. Once she saw her aunt paying money to a servant and asked her what it was for. On being told it was wages she vehemently asserted that her mother did nothing of the sort; their servants, and above all her Nannie, worked purely for love. When she was contradicted and told the truth she broke into tears and wept the whole night through. On another occasion she told a little boy friend that they were taking such and such a house for the summer holidays, and when he commented on the expense this would entail she was extremely astonished to hear that people had to consider such things; they never did at home.

Freud used to say that there were three things one should never economize on: health, education and travel.

Freud saw to it particularly that his children's holidays and travels should not be hampered by any lack of money. He would give them simply all that they wanted, and it speaks well for their characters that none of them ever abused this generosity. On the other hand his considerateness and sense of fairness would take into account the financial circumstances of any accompanying friend. This was most needed with his eldest son, whose chief friend happened to be a youth who was badly off. So when the two wanted to start off together on some mountain tour Freud would first make his son inquire how much money his friend was taking with him and then give him precisely the same, so that the friend should not be embarrassed.

Naturally Freud's main income came from his regular therapeutic work. Before the war his fees were 40 Kronen ($8.10), which was high for Vienna. Anything he earned from single consultations he regarded as a bonus and felt justified in reserving it for his favorite hobby—the collecting of antiquities. To Ferenczi Freud used to refer to such sums as proceeding from the *Nationalgeschenk* (Public Donation). Royalties, which for years were small sums, were divided among the children as presents. I related earlier the story about the horse ride that came from such a source.[b] Giving presents was one of Freud's great delights. So much so that he was too impatient to wait for the appropriate moment. Despite his wife's protests, a birthday present to a child always reached its destination on the evening before. Incidentally, this was not the only example of a vein of impatience in Freud's ardent nature. The daily arrival of the postman was an event he awaited with great eagerness. He not only greatly enjoyed getting letters but was apt to be impatient with his friends if they were not so swift in answering correspondence as he himself was. Waiting for a letter from his great friend Fliess in the eighteen-nineties was often a considerable torment. Of his later friends the one who chiefly perturbed him in this way was Jung, whose dilatoriness in correspondence was one of the first things that cooled Freud's affection for him; he said it reminded him of those Fliess days.[10]

It was unusual in those days in Austria for citizens to be meticulously exact in making their income tax returns, and Freud was probably no exception; it would not be surprising if he put the needs of his family before those of the Emperor's. On one occasion about 1913 the Department concerned wrote expressing their astonishment that his income was not larger "since everyone knows that his reputation extends far beyond the frontier of Austria." To which Freud tartly replied: "Prof. Freud is very honored at receiving a communication from the Government. It is the first time the Government has taken any notice of him and he acknowledges it. There is one point in which he cannot agree with the communication: that his reputation extends far beyond the frontier of Austria. It begins at the frontier." It was his ostracism in Vienna that hurt Freud far more than any criticisms of his work in other countries.

Freud was never interested in financial transactions. What money he was able to save he invested in insurance policies and in government bonds, never in stock exchange securities. All this was lost in the inflation following the war. When he could recover from this he again invested in government bonds, but sent the greater part abroad to be kept in a safer bank account. Toward the end of his life his son Martin, who had been a banker, took charge of his finances, and

[b] See Chapter 3, p. 79.

Freud left the matter entirely to him. His attitude to money was, when one thinks how greatly he suffered in youth from the lack of it, remarkably normal. It had its importance in the world of reality, but no emotional significance. He was generous much above the average, not only to numerous relatives, but to poor students with whose difficulties his own experience made it easy to sympathize.

Freud followed the local news and politics of his time, but did not feel much involved in them. He sympathized with the more progressive reforms proposed by the Socialist Party, but was not an adherent of socialism. His brother Alexander, who moved in government circles, was vehemently opposed to socialism, but Freud used merely to listen to his tirades with a quiet smile. He never voted for the Socialist Party in the elections, nor of course for their opponents, the violently anti-Semitic Christian-Social Party. There was also a small Liberal Party, which once or twice put up a candidate in Freud's district; when that happened Freud would vote for him.

Freud never had a serious illness before his late sixties. In the first forty years of his married life there are only two occasions recorded of his being confined to bed. The first was when he had the painful boil to which he refers in *The Interpretation of Dreams*.[11] The second was when he was suffering from a septic throat infection he had acquired on a visit to Prague. On the other hand there were constant minor disturbances of health. His letters to his friends were full of allusions to his intestinal disorders. At home only his wife knew of this. All his children knew about was an attack of indigestion every Sunday morning that he attributed to a rich dinner at Königstein's the evening before, one which always preceded the game of tarock. This, however, was not regarded seriously and became a family joke. The disorder in question, of which chronic constipation was the most prominent symptom, was very obscure. It was at different times diagnosed as colitis, inflammation of the gall bladder, simple indigestion or chronic appendicitis; he certainly had an attack of appendicitis when in Putnam's Adirondack camp in 1909.[c] All these conditions may well have been present in a man leading such a sedentary life, but the disorder was perhaps also in part a psychosomatic relic of the neurosis that had so troubled Freud in the days before and during his self-analysis. In his mid-fifties he several times underwent a regular "cure" at Karlsbad which would give him some temporary relief. His body, and particularly that area of it, he would refer to in his letters to Ferenczi, who had similar troubles, as his "poor Konrad," a phrase

[c] See Chapter 2, p. 50.

taken from Spitteler's *Imago*; it has a similar connotation to the phrase "Little Mary" which J. M. Barrie made popular in England thirty or forty years ago.

There were other troubles also, such as a good deal of "rheumatism." This was apt to attack his right hand and make writing difficult. It is also not surprising with someone so addicted to the use of the pen that there were occasional attacks of writer's cramp.[12] Then he was a life-long sufferer from severe migraine and recurrent sinus infections, in later years also from prostatic trouble.

Throughout his life Freud was much preoccupied with thoughts about death. There were reflections on its significance, fears of it and later on the wish for it. He often spoke and wrote about it to us, the burden of his remarks always being that he was growing old and had not long to live.[13] Fliess's "periodic" calculations had given Freud fifty-one years to live. As soon as this time had passed uneventfully Freud adopted another superstitious belief, which he told Ferenczi in 1910 he had held "for a long time":[14] that was that he had to die in February 1918. He kept looking forward to that date, usually with resignation and occasionally, in the dark days of 1917, with a sense of welcome. When that date in its turn passed quietly he made the characteristically dry comment: "That shows what little trust one can place in the supernatural." [15]

Holidays meant a very different life indeed for Freud. In the very train taking him out of his hated Vienna there must have been great sighs of contentment and relief. How he looked forward to getting away to the country. He said once to Pfister: "I long to see the land [d] as much as Columbus did." [16] For many months before, often as early as January, there had been discussions in the family and with friends about the most attractive spot to choose for the coming summer. Often he would make exploratory expeditions at Easter and send amusing reports back to his family. They were all connoisseurs in such matters, and the requirements were very specific: a comfortable house with a suitable room in which Freud could write if he felt so inclined, a certain altitude with sun and good air, pine forests near by for walks, a good supply of mushrooms, glorious scenery, and, above all, quietness and a remoteness from bandstands or other signs of crowding tourists.

Before the war Freud would sport on holiday a Tyrolese costume with visible braces, "shorts," and a green hat with a little *Gamsbart*

[d] In German "*Land*" means both "land" and "country."

(chamois brush) at its side. A stout walking-stick and in wet weather a shaggy Alpine cape completed the outfit. In later years this was replaced by "plus fours," and still later by a more sedate gray lounge suit. He had a special aversion to umbrellas. I remember his asking me in a slightly irritated tone, "Why ever do you carry an umbrella?" When I said I supposed it was a habit from having to wear a silk hat he replied: "Then try to give up the habit." He once told my wife that all an umbrella did was to keep its stick dry.

In early days Freud would divert himself with a game of bowls but for the most part exercise consisted of long walks. He was a remarkable walker, light, swift and tireless.

The most characteristic feature of Freud's holiday pursuits was his passion for mushrooms, especially for finding them. He had an uncanny flair for divining where they were likely to be, and would even point out such spots when riding along in a train. On an expedition for the purpose he would often leave the children and they would be sure to hear soon a cry of success from him. He would then creep silently up to it and suddenly pounce to capture the fungus with his hat as if it were a bird or butterfly. So Freud could be boyish enough on occasions. Another example of it was his habit of bringing his latest purchase of an antiquity, usually a small statuette, to the dinner table and placing it in front of him as a companion during the meal. Afterwards it would be returned to his desk and then brought back again for a day or two.

Then there was the endless detection of rare wild flowers, with a careful identifying at leisure. One of his daughters told me there were three things her father was specially desirous of teaching his children: a knowledge of wild flowers, the art of finding mushrooms, and the technique of the card game tarock. And he was completely successful in all of them.

Such expeditions were of course not confined to mushroom hunting. Any other delicacies, such as wild strawberries or blueberries, were also welcome additions to the dinner table. But the study of wild flowers, of which Freud had an extensive knowledge, was very important. To encourage his children in this he used to subscribe for years to *Cosmos*, a periodical devoted to natural history.

There were two manifestations during holiday times which are more usually associated with the feminine section of humanity. Freud had no sense of orientation and so could never find his way in the country. His sons tell me that on long walks they would be astonished when he started back for home in an absurdly wrong direction, but knowing this so well he would readily resign himself to their guidance. Again he was very unpractical about the details of traveling. Railway timetables were beyond his comprehension, and the more complicated tours were always arranged, first by his brother Alexander and later by his son Oliver, both of whom were experts in that field. Great precautions were taken to find the right train by arriving at the station an unconscionable time beforehand, and even then luggage might be misdirected or mislaid.

Freud would spend six weeks or so in this idyllic fashion and would then feel the need for more sophisticated pleasures. That nearly always meant a journey to Italy and very seldom quite alone. They have been fully recorded in earlier chapters.

That these foreign travels had to be undertaken without any member of the family came from the following circumstances. His wife was in any event a poor traveler and got ill or tired on the few times she tried to accompany him and to keep up with his pace. Mostly she would have found it hard to leave the children behind, since they were seldom free of one illness or another. The only alternative would have been to rent a house in the sunny south and travel there with the whole family, children, servants and all. That was beyond his means. Freud felt this conflict very much, and he often complained to his wife of how lonely he felt in her absence. In a letter from Palermo, where he was with Ferenczi, he wrote to her: "I am desperately sorry I can't manage to let all of you also see the beautiful things here. To be able to enjoy such things in a company of seven or nine, or even of three, I should have been, not a psychiatrist and allegedly the founder of a new direction in psychology, but a manufacturer of something generally useful like toilet paper, matches or boot-buttons. It is too late to learn that now, so I have to go on enjoying myself egoistically, but with a deep sense of regret." [17] On the same holiday he wrote from Syracuse to his youngest daughter: "I unthinkingly promised to bring you something nice from Sicily, but even you, with your multitude of wishes, would find it hard to discover something suitable, even in Palermo, the metropolis. There is nothing here except sulphur, papyrus and antiquities. I promise to make up for it in Vienna; I have been indulging myself so much that I should be only too happy to find something for you." [18]

He sent his wife a card or telegram every day, and a long letter every two or three days; constant contact was essential to him. And, even in an absence of a couple of weeks, there was often a yearning of homesickness for her.

There were some special features about Freud's Italian journeys, especially in the earlier ones, on which I have commented elsewhere.[19] One was the restless energy with which he would explore town after town, evidently eager to see in the time all there was. Another was the huge gusto and keen enjoyment of every minute. This contrasted with an initial anxiety before embarking on the expedition, one which at times reached an almost morbid intensity. Apart from the great intrinsic interest of the travels, one must therefore suppose that they represented something even deeper in his mind, something perhaps forbidden which was enjoyed all the more when a preliminary inhibition had been overcome.

I used the word "restless" because of the impression I got from the speed with which Freud covered the ground in his Italian journeys, gutting, as it were, town after town. But in fact it is not at all the right word. It is true that his tempo was fast and that he was extraordinarily untiring, but there was no haste, no hurrying away from one impression in search of others. On the contrary, he would spend hours and hours in one museum or other place of interest, very much concerned with the details of what he was examining. I may quote from a letter he sent to his daughter Anna when years later she was herself traveling in Italy.[e] "Very pleased at the way you are traveling. Evidently not the most obvious things that are supposed to be compulsory, but according to individual taste. No hurry, and dallying at what you enjoy." To which is added a characteristic postscript: "Always ready to telegraph money to you."

There is not much to be said about Freud's writing habits. To judge from their extent and from his correspondence he must have been fond of the physical act itself of writing, which he always did by hand. It was only in his late years, in his seventies, that his youngest daughter relieved him to some slight extent. Freud had not the Trollopian art of forcing himself to write so many hundred words a day. His composing had more the erratic quality of a poet's. He might go for weeks or even months without feeling that he had anything he wished to write. Then would come some urge of creation, a slow painful travail, the endeavor to write at least two or three lines a day, and finally a burst of expansion when an important essay would appear in a few weeks. By a few weeks one does not mean continuous writing: on the contrary, it meant snatching at high pressure the very few hours he could spare at the end of a day of toil.

[e] April 16, 1927.

I have described earlier in some detail the close association between this period of gestation and variations in Freud's bodily state.[20] He was a chronic sufferer from an obscure abdominal complaint. It was in this part of his person where production seemed to manifest itself to begin with. Increased discomfort, with various other symptoms of general malaise, always preceded Freud's best work. When, as happened sometimes, he was in a state of perfect health and in a euphoric mood there was no question of writing anything. "I have long known that I can't be industrious when I am in good health; on the contrary, I need a degree of discomfort which I want to get rid of." [21] There was also another personal motive that drove him on to write so much, apart of course from the scientific ones. He told Abraham that he simply had to write, otherwise he would not be able to endure doing so much analytic work.[22] He explained this to me by saying that listening and taking in so much all day long produced the need to give out something, to change from a passive recipient attitude to an active creating one.[23] There is no need, however, to descant here on the well-known unconscious symbolism of literary production.

The summer holidays were often a period when new ideas germinated, the after-result, no doubt, of the numerous impressions received from his patients in the preceding months of work. Then, on returning to Vienna in October, he would most often be in the mood to plunge into work. He had a belief, which he communicated to Ferenczi in 1913, that his best productions came about every seven years;[24] it was evidently a relic of his belief in Fliess' laws of periodicity. As a proof of it he cited the years of 1891, when he wrote his book *On Aphasia*, 1898 when he wrote *The Interpretation of Dreams*, 1905 the *Three Essays on the Theory of Sexuality*, and 1912 when he wrote *Totem and Taboo*. One should perhaps not spoil this pretty theory by pointing out that for its sake he seemed to confound the dates of "writing" with "publishing"; it would be more polite to add 1919, *Beyond the Pleasure Principle*; 1926, *Inhibitions, Symptoms and Anxiety*; and 1933, the *New Introductory Lectures on Psychoanalysis*.

When he wrote that, Freud seems to have forgotten the details of Fliess's calculation of fruitful activity every *seven and a half* years, since they fell in quite different years from those he now selected.[25]

Work of some sort or other was daily bread to Freud. He would have found a life of leisure unbearable. "I could not contemplate with any sort of comfort a life without work. Creative imagination and work go together with me; I take no delight in anything else. That would be a prescription for happiness were it not for the terrible thought that one's productivity depends entirely on sensitive moods. What is one to do on a day when thoughts cease to flow and the proper words won't come? One cannot help trembling at this possibility. That is why, despite the acquiescence in fate that becomes an upright man, I secretly pray: no infirmity, no paralysis of one's powers through bodily distress. We'll die with harness on, as King Macbeth said." [26]

It would have been affectation, of which Freud was never capable, to deny the evidence that, after many years of being notorious, he had at last, after the Great War, really become famous. He accepted it as a simple fact like any other and of course was glad of the increasing signs of recognition. But he did nothing in order to achieve fame; it was an incidental consequence of the work he was doing from other motives.

Freud once said, evidently speaking for himself but expressing it generally: "No one writes to achieve fame, which anyhow is a very transitory matter, or the illusion of immortality. Surely we write first of all to satisfy something within ourselves, not for other people. Of course when others recognize one's efforts it increases the inner gratification, but nevertheless we write in the first place for ourselves, following an inner impulse." [27] Freud had little need for such recognition, although he enjoyed it, and he always maintained that his years of loneliness, when the question didn't arise, had been the pleasantest. It is possible, however, that here he somewhat deceived himself.

He set little store by his writings, having once got out of his system what he wanted to express. When Rank, then in charge of the *Verlag*, insisted on publishing Freud's collected works in the *Gesammelte Schriften*, partly for pietistic and partly for commercial reasons, Freud had to acquiesce, but it is certain he would never have encouraged such a plan himself. This unconcerned attitude was most evident in the matter of his translations, where he was wont to grant rights somewhat heedlessly and indiscriminately. It cost his son Ernst a heavy labor years afterwards to disentangle the complicated and contradictory contracts that were discovered.

Freud had a modest enough estimate of himself. Here is a typical one. "I have very restricted capacities or talents. None at all for the natural sciences; nothing for mathematics; nothing for anything quantitative. But what I have, of a very restricted nature, was probably very intensive." [28]

I have several times been asked my opinion on how important was

Freud's Jewishness in the evolution of his ideas and work, particularly by correspondents who wish me to give an emphatically positive answer. There is one respect in which it unquestionably played an important part, one to which he often referred himself. The inherited capacity of Jews to stand their ground and maintain their position in life in the face of surrounding opposition or hostility was very evidently highly pronounced in Freud, and he was doubtless right in attributing to it the firmness with which he maintained his convictions undeterred by the prevailing opposition to them. That also holds good for his followers, who were for the most part Jews. When the storm of opposition broke over psychoanalysis in the years before the first World War the only Gentiles who survived it were Binswanger, Oberholzer, Pfister and myself.

Freud believed that the inevitable opposition to the startling new discoveries of psychoanalysis was considerably aggravated by anti-Semitic prejudice. Writing to Abraham on the early signs of anti-Semitism in Switzerland he said:[f] "In my opinion we have as Jews, if we want to cooperate with other people, to develop a little masochism and be prepared to endure a certain amount of injustice. There is no other way of working together. You may be sure that if I were called Oberhuber my new ideas would, despite all the other factors, have met with far less resistance." [29] It is hard to know how much truth there is in this judgment. It was not entirely borne out by my experience in England where we found quite enough "resistance" although in the first dozen years there were only two Jews in our Society.

The question of whether only a Jew could have contrived psychoanalysis is obviously much harder to answer. On the one hand it could be said that after all only a Jew actually did, but on the other hand it might equally be said there were countless millions of Jews who did not. So clearly there must have been more personal factors concerned, and some of these I shall try to elucidate in the following chapter. Some have suggested a connection between Freud's close attention to verbal detail, the striking patience with which he would unravel the meaning of phases and utterances, with the Talmudic gift of wrenching the uttermost meaning from single passages in Holy Script, one which, however, can be paralleled by many a mediaeval theologian or Scottish Presbyterian. This was Freud's own opinion, expressed perhaps half jocularly,[30] but I am myself not very impressed by the analogy, since it does not seem to me to accord very closely with Freud's type of mind. He was not at all given to arguing nor to

[f] Quoted earlier, p. 49.

wrestling over precise definitions or explications for their own sake. His type of mind was such as to penetrate through the material to something really essential beyond rather than to dally or play with it. He had, it is true, the quickness of thought and of observation, the acute intelligence, generally considered to be characteristic of Jews, but it would be presumptuous to claim that they possess a monopoly of these qualities. To sum up, what we can say with considerable assurance is that being Jewish accorded well with both Freud's personality and his work.[g]

The tenacity with which Freud maintained his hardly won convictions and his imperturbability in the face of outside "criticism," which was so often a mere expression of disbelief born of ignorance, have led many opponents into saying that he was dogmatic and cocksure, that he was never willing to admit any doubts. That such a conclusion is certainly untrue is demonstrable, not only from the numerous passages in his writings where he admitted the extreme tentativeness of various conclusions and above all their imperfection as final statements, but more especially from the many passages in his letters, some of which have been quoted in these two volumes, where he described how often he had been assailed by inner doubts and uncertainties. As he rightly claimed, he was a more severe critic of his work than any outsider could have been.

Freud never doubted that his work had a future, though he could form no opinion of how important it might prove to be. He was throughout encouraged by the thought that sooner or later the truth in his discoveries would tell. This was true even in the years before the Salzburg Congress, when he first learned of the wide support his ideas were already finding. Writing of his opponent Aschaffenburg he said: "What moves him is his tendency to repress everything sexual, that unwelcome factor so unpopular in good society. Two worlds fight with each other there, and whoever stands in the midst of life can have no doubt which will be the defeated and which the victorious one."[31] Some months before his first meeting with Jung he wrote to encourage him not to pay too much attention to the opposition they were both encountering: "After all, the great names in psychiatry mean very little; the future belongs to us and our ideas, and everywhere youth is actively siding with us. I notice it in Vienna where, as you know, I have systematically met with a deadly silence,[h] broken from time to time by some nonentity annihilating me; and

[g] See also Chapter II, Volume I, p. 22.
[h] *totgeschwiegen.*

where nevertheless I have in my lectures an audience of forty drawn from every faculty." [32] Shortly before the Congress he told Abraham: "I have no doubts about other workers following in my footsteps, whether that happens in my lifetime or not." [33]

A couple of years later he discussed the matter with his usual frankness in reply to New Year's wishes and compliments from Ferenczi: "It would be in vain for me to deny that the words with which your letter ushered in the New Year have given me great pleasure. I am not so insensitive to recognition as I am to blame. As to the question of the value of my work and its influence on the future development of science I myself find it very hard to form an opinion. Sometimes I believe in it; sometimes I doubt. I don't think there is any way of predicting it; perhaps God himself doesn't yet know. At all events the work should be of value to us at present, and I am heartily glad to be no longer alone in it. If I don't grow old I shan't get anything from it, but I certainly do not work because of the expectation of any reward or fame; in view of the inevitable ingratitude of humanity I do not expect anything either for my children later. All such considerations must play a very small role with us if we take seriously the global firm 'Fatum & Ananke.' " [i][34]

Two years later still, in the painful time he was going through with Jung, he wrote to Abraham: "I know what a hard time you are having in Berlin and I admire your imperturbable mood and steady confidence. The chronicle of our enterprise is perhaps not always cheerful but that may be true of most chronicles. Still it will make an interesting chapter[j] of history. For myself I do not expect much. We have a dark time in front of us; after that, recognition will shine only on the next generation. But we have the incomparable delight of the first insight into the new knowledge." [35] After the war was over he wrote: "I have finished sowing, though I shall not see the harvest." [36] And that was the year when Freud was on the point of sowing what were to prove some of his most fertile ideas. It will be long before their harvest is fully garnered.

Freud gave the final estimate of his work in his *Autobiography*:[37] "Looking back, then, over the patchwork of my life's labours, I can say that I have made many beginnings and thrown out many suggestions. Something will come of them in the future, though I cannot myself tell whether it will be much or little. I may, however,

[i] Destiny and Iron Necessity.
[j] *ein schönes Kapitel.*

express a hope that I have opened up a pathway for an important advance in our knowledge."

The three books Freud thought most highly of were *The Interpretation of Dreams*, the *Three Essays* and *Totem and Taboo*. But perhaps the one for which he had the greatest personal affection was his book on Leonardo.

It would hardly be becoming for a foreigner to dilate on the virtues of Freud's style in writing, but at least something should be said about this important feature of his personality. One has been told on very good authority that he was rated a master of German prose, and his receiving the high honor of the Goethe prize for Literature at Frankfurt in 1930 speaks for itself; it shows what connoisseurs of literature thought of his gifts. It would be truer to speak of his Austrian prose rather than German, since Freud showed a marked preference for what he called the *Geschmeidigkeit*[k] of the Austrian manner of writing, so different from the heavy German of more Northern writers.

It is rare for someone who is a real master of one language to be truly proficient in another one, and Freud was no exception to this rule. When he was asked once how many languages he knew his answer was "one, German." He found Italian more beautiful than Spanish, but considered German to be the most beautiful of all living languages; the only one that surpassed it was Ancient Greek.[38]

To judge from the voluminousness of his scientific writings and his correspondence Freud must have been a very ready writer. The fluency, however, never became ambagiosity; on the contrary, the ease and grace of his Viennese style are equalled only by the conciseness of expression. As every conscientious translator of his must admit, however, Freud was not an over-careful writer; at times, when questioned about an ambiguous phrase, he would reproach himself laughingly for *Schlamperei*,[l] a harsh term for even his ready self-criticism. There was lucidity, but also elision, in his swift pen.

His outstanding literary merit was the distinction of his style. This was noted as early as in his school years.[39] Even a foreigner like myself could recognize from a single paragraph whether it was written by Freud or by someone else. And I have noticed that when it was difficult—and it often was—to decipher some word in his handwriting it was useless to guess at various probable ones from the context; it

[k] Flexibility.
[l] Sloppiness.

would always turn out to be an unusual one I hadn't thought of. He had an enormously rich vocabulary, but he was the reverse of a pedant in words. When I asked him, for instance, why he spelled the word "*Narzissmus*" instead of the more correct "*Narzissismus*," his aesthetic sense was stronger than his philological conscience and he replied simply: "I don't like the sound of it."

It seemed impossible for him to write even simple sentences without infusing them with something of his originality, elegance and dignity. The same was true of his conversation: banality, even in the tritest matter, was alien to him and every remark would be trenchant, well-turned and distinctive. It was these qualities, with the extraordinary purity and felicity of his phrasing, that led many Germans to esteem him as a writer as others esteemed him as a man of science.

16

Character and Personality

I HAD HOPED THAT FROM THE INNUMERABLE DETAILS NARRATED IN Volume I of this Biography a definite figure would emerge. Not all the reviewers of the book, however, found this to be so, and I therefore feel it incumbent on me to attempt a full-length sketch of Freud as a man, his personality, character and mode of life; the last of these was described in the preceding chapter. In doing so one immediately encounters the biographer's characteristic dilemma in drawing a portrait of a great man. On the one hand he may put his greatness and the superbness of his virtues in the foreground, which has the effect of making him unrecognizable as a human being and risking the reader's turning away in boredom from such a just Aristides. On the other hand if the foreground is occupied by the features betraying an incomplete harmony of character, the foibles and weaknesses inseparable from humanity, the result may be simply a caricature of a personage, one possibly provoking among unsympathetic readers disdain or even in the worst case derision. Yet no one knew better than Freud that what makes one man distinguishable from his fellows is not a catalogue of his surpassing qualities, which can produce a quite colorless picture, but the peculiarities that go to make up a distinctive character, including even such eccentricities that border on the neurotic. Speaking of the way in which the tendency of many biographers to idealize their subject blurs the outlines of the personality and creates a cold effect he wrote: "This is regrettable, since in doing so they sacrifice the truth to an illusion and forego the opportunity of penetrating into the most fascinating secrets of human nature." [1] In other words, individuality resides in the combination of the harmoniously fused elements of a personality with those features that imply a less perfect fusion.

Freud's case well illustrates this thesis. He was the soul of honor and never deviated from the highest standards of ethical behavior in his personal life or from those of professional probity in his work. He was always kindly, considerate and generous, though most of his generous deeds were unknown to the outer world. He was a completely civilized being, to whom the idea of violence and cruelty was abhorrent; it would have taken a good deal even to drive him to fight and he would always go out of his way to avoid personal quarrels. He was one of the few people of whom it could genuinely be said that no common or mean thing was ever inputed to him, which is perhaps the essence of nobility. Throughout his life pettiness in any form was completely alien to him. He was one of those rare spirits that transcend the smallnesses of life and thus show us the picture of real greatness.

Having said these quite true things about Freud I may hope that the impression they make is not entirely colorless, yet it is plain that they do not really distinguish his personality from a number of other good people of whom similar things might be said. So it is necessary to search for more distinctive traits, which by their nature cannot produce the same perfectly rounded contours.

I have read a great many appreciations of Freud's personality, some written before his death and some after, and from them I propose to quote, a passage from Joan Riviere's descriptions which I find both just and illuminating.[a]

It is from an appreciation she wrote just after Freud's death.[2]

"I had met Professor Freud at The Hague in 1920, at the first International Congress of Psycho-Analysis held after the war. He impressed one as an exceptional personality. His appearance was not typically that of a medical man, nor was it particularly Jewish. The long pale face with grey beard and stooping shoulders were those of an intellectual and might have suggested a learned professor, but for two other essential characteristics. There was his lean but broad and sturdy figure, the rather stern expression and firm jaw, which bespoke a great reserve of dignity and hidden strength—an indomitable tenacity. He appeared somewhat aloof; in fact he could easily be bored by

[a] Quoted with Mrs. Riviere's and the editor's permission.

crowds and gatherings. His most striking feature, however, was the forward thrust of his head and critical exploring gaze of his keenly peering eyes. Finally, this rather awe-inspiring appearance was lightened by the glow of an enchanting humour, always latent and constantly irradiating his whole person as he spoke, which reassured one that the Olympian was indeed a mortal too. I knew already from his writings of his astonishing knowledge of literature; of his memory, especially for Shakespeare; and of his other tastes, his love of all antiquities, of Greece and Rome, and the art of earlier cultures. But on this occasion I first realised his amazing command of the English language. . . .

"These impressions were confirmed during 1922 when I studied with him and got to know him. Like his psychology, his personality was really one to concern itself with individuals. The aloofness, which was never indeed coldness or hauteur, but rather indifference to superficialities, vanished and one met a vivid, eager mind seizing on every detail with astonishing interest and attention. The vitality, the current of his great energy was felt. How he disliked preambles and polite nothings! My first analytic hour with him he opened—contrary to rule and inadvisably—saying: 'Well, I know something about you already; you had a father and a mother!' meaning, of course, 'Quick, I can't wait for you and your inhibitions, I want something to start with; give me an outline to get hold of!' He would allow himself liberties with his medium, like any master, until he recognised a new problem and bent himself as a student to that.

"But whether in analysis or not, his interest, with all its intolerance of preliminaries and its imperativeness, was curiously impersonal. One had always the impression of a certain reserve behind the eagerness, as though it were not for himself that he so peremptorily demanded to understand things, but for some purpose outside himself. There was a simplicity in this impersonal eagerness that was perhaps the most significant thing about him. He was so concentrated on the inquiry he was pursuing that his self functioned only as an instrument. His penetrating, attentive eyes had not only the simplicity and innocent clear-sightedness of a child—one for whom nothing is too small, and nothing either common or unclean—there was also in them a mature patience and caution, and a detached inquiry. The half-peering and half-piercing gaze beneath the heavy brows showed a power to see beneath the surface and beyond the boundaries of ordinary perceptions. But it also expressed a capacity for patient, careful scrutiny and for suspended judgment so rare as to be unrecognisable by many; his cool scepticism has even been misread as cynicism or pessimism. There was in him a conjunction of the hunter on an endless trail and the persistent immovable watcher who checks and revises; it was from this conjunction that his power of discovering and understanding the sources of the feelings and behaviour of men and women sprang. Indomitable courage and tenacity, coupled with an unswerving honesty, were the characteristics supporting his gifts of observation, his 'intrepid imagination' and insight, which led to his great achievements.

"Along with these qualities, to which essentially we owe his great work, his personality had many very human features which endeared him to his friends. The inimitable dry humour of his writings became in ordinary intercourse a charming gaiety and capacity for finding amusement in most situations and, though he could be tolerant and philosophical, he was apt to be both impatient and intolerant. His humour was often witty and barbed, and he could be choleric, resentful and unforgiving. Nor would I claim that he suffered fools gladly. He was compelled by destiny to be a great man in his work; but he lived his private life as an ordinary man, and he believed in that kind of life. He disliked pathological types and extremes of any kind. From this attitude of mind his intolerance of religion in my view largely derived; for religion tends to see life in black or white and cannot accept the compromises and complexities in it which are the subject matter of scientific psychology. Once when a heated discussion on political topics arose he was accused of being neither black nor red, Fascist nor Socialist; his amused reply was: 'No, one should be flesh color'—the colour of ordinary men. And again, apropos of a young scientist interested in psycho-analysis who might have proved of service to the new science, Freud said to me mournfully: 'But I can't regard it as normal, you know, that he has married a woman old enough to be his mother!' I could but laugh at the discoverer of the Oedipus complex; he met the laugh with a twinkle, but he was seriously disappointed.

"In later life a certain reserve, dislike of publicity and a concentration of interest on his work was characteristic of him; one surmises that this trait had developed as a result of the hostile reception for so long accorded to his discoveries. But he was no captious hermit; numerous eminent contemporaries, especially in the literary world, sought his acquaintance and met or corresponded with him; among these were notably Romain Rolland, Thomas Mann, Arnold and

Stefan Zweig. But any genuinely inquiring visitor, too, could always see him, and met with a frank and friendly reception. Whatever the outcome of the interview, those who preferred fair dealing to favours found nothing in him to alienate them. Above all, Freud was entirely without pose. He could be mistaken: but deception or disingenuousness were not to be found in his nature, and essential honesty was the hall-mark of his mind. He wrote: 'I can say I have made many beginnings and thrown out many suggestions. Something will come of them in the future, though I myself cannot tell whether it will be much or little.' These words sum up and express the fearlessness, the acceptance of truth and love of it which characterised him and inspired his work."

When a relative or friend composes a biography he sometimes tries to protect himself against unduly obtruding his personal view of the subject by adhering to an arid objectivity. I do not think any reader of Volume I would charge me with painting too dull a picture. Such a one would assuredly give a false impression of Freud, who was preeminently a man of strong feelings. I have, however, taken the precaution of consulting various friends who knew him well, asking them particularly what they considered to be Freud's most distinctive characteristics, and I shall take due account of their comments. As is natural, such answers differed. The characteristic chosen by one friend may be taken for granted by another and the stress laid elsewhere. Furthermore, it does not necessarily follow that what one remembers in a personality as an outstanding feature is of any fundamental importance; Mr. Gladstone's collars, so beloved of cartoonists, were not even the most prominent feature of his appearance. In attempting a total assessment of a personality, as I am here doing, I am aware of pitfalls on every side.

I once put that question to Anna Freud, the person who knew him most intimately in the last twenty or thirty years of his life. She unhesitatingly answered: "his simplicity." This was the feature that Mrs. Riviere also found "the most significant thing about him." We must give this answer all the value it assuredly deserves. Freud undoubtedly disliked anything that complicated life, both his own and that of others. It was a feature that extended to the smallest details of every day, the most personal matters. Thus he would own no more than three suits of clothes, three pairs of shoes, and three sets of underclothing. Packing, even for a long holiday, was a very simple matter. That the characteristic his daughter intuitively selected was not only a striking one, but one of fundamental significance, is shown by the ease with which the theme could be developed and the many other attributes which it illuminates. It was manifest, to begin with, in his very demeanor. Freud had a quiet manner and a simple dignity far removed from any pose, airs or pretentiousness. He had a pronounced aversion to such attitudinizing, or to anything smacking of humbug, hypocrisy or complicated intrigue. The epithets "vain" and "pompous" which I have seen applied to him are singularly unhappy inventions. His speech was direct and to the point; there were no phrases or circumlocutions. He could hardly be called subtle, nor did he set a high store on tactfulness except where it implied real considerateness for the feelings of others. Even my mild reputation for tactfulness in settling disputes was sufficiently alien to Freud's directness to evoke comment. On one occasion he said laughingly: "If Jones behaves in this diplomatic manner much longer we shall lose him to the League of Nations." It would not surprise me to hear that a stranger might even at times find his manner a little brusque. Yet he was a very accessible person, and would seldom refuse to see anyone wishing to call on him even if the caller's motive was one of idle curiosity.

With his intimates Freud would naturally relax into a very easygoing manner. In my memory of such times I think predominantly of his constant cheerfulness, his tolerant attitude and the general ease of intercourse, nor do I forget his very characteristic humor. Freud was not a really witty person, but he had a keen sense of the humorous aspects of life, and his comments on any piece of news would be very apt to take the form of quoting some amusing wise saying, proverb or, most often, a Jewish anecdote. But one always felt that the relationship was under his control. His affability and accessibility were there because he willed it so. One sensed an invisible reserve behind which it would be impertinent to intrude, and no one ever did.

We touch here on an arguable point. Freud always held very strongly that only he had the right to decide how much of his personality he would reveal to others and how much not: in a general way a quite understandable position. But there were features about his attitude that would seem to pass beyond that and to justify the word privacy being replaced by secrecy. For it would hold good when there were no particular reasons for the privacy or concealment; and then, again, its strength was really remarkable. Freud was far from being a reserved man in general; he expressed himself very freely on all manner of subjects and never withheld his opinions. But somehow he managed to convey the impression that only what he vouchsafed about his personality was a permissible topic and that he would resent any intimate questioning. He never spoke to his children about his youth and early years; most of the knowledge they have of it has come from the present work. The topic, though not expressly proscribed, seemed to be taboo, and they never raised it. In his middle years he would always tell us what he was engaged in writing, but in the last twenty years of his life he became secretive about it, even to his intimates; he would only say they should know in good time. Above all, as we have noticed earlier, there was a striking contrast between the rather unflattering picture he revealed to the world concerning his inner life, notably in the analysis of his dreams, and the quite complete reticence on the matter of his love life. The sacredness undoubtedly centered there, and we have remarked on the quite extraordinary precautions he took to conceal a most innocent and momentary emotion of love in his adolescence.[3] His wife was the only person on earth to know anything of that side of his life, and she was the only person to whom he related the Gisela incident in question.

Here is an almost amusing example of this sense of "privacy." In 1911 Jung suggested holding the Congress in Weimar in the middle of September. In letters to Abraham and Ferenczi Freud told them that he had "highly private reasons" for wanting the date postponed for a week.[4] Then a few days later, in a burst of expansiveness, he disclosed to Ferenczi the terrible secret that the anniversary of his wedding-day was on September 14, but he begged him to keep this information absolutely confidential.[5] It was too near to the forbidden topic.

One must suppose that in Freud's earliest years there had been extremely strong motives for concealing some important phase of his development—perhaps even from himself. I would venture to surmise it was his deep love for his mother.

On the other hand, oddly enough, Freud was not a man who found it easy to keep someone else's secrets. He had indeed the reputation of being distinctly indiscreet. It may be remembered that the final break with his friend Fliess came about over a matter of this sort. I had many personal examples of this rather unexpected trait of Freud's. He several times told me things about the private lives of colleagues which he should not have. At the time I excused him by reflecting that perhaps he was finding it hard to carry about painful information of the sort and that it was a relief to unburden himself to a foreigner whose discretion he could, truly enough, trust. Perhaps my guess here was not far out. It may well be that preserving his own secrets also was accompanied with a certain tension which he relieved in this indirect fashion.

When James Strachey went to study with Freud I wrote a letter of introduction, not entirely complimentary, telling Freud what little I knew of him at that time. In an early session Freud went into the next room, fetched the letter, and read it aloud to him. On another occasion I sent Freud some private information I thought he should have about a patient of mine he was treating—it was a question of surreptitious use of morphia—and told him it was important that the patient should not know of my communication. He wrote back assuring me he would keep the knowledge to himself, but it was not long before I received a furious letter from the patient complaining of my action.

Freud's preference for simplicity over complexity was closely connected with two other traits in his personality: his dislike of formality and his impatience of restriction. A little of the former attitude may be attributed to his having been brought up in a penurious environment with small opportunity for social intercourse and experience. In his early letters to his future wife he several times confessed to a sense of inferiority at not having acquired social graces and at not feeling at home in the arts of gallantry. In later years, however, he had evidently overcome such difficulties and, though one would hardly think of him as a man of the world, he could perform graceful deeds in a graceful fashion, such as making a present from his precious collection, and his social manners were beyond reproach.[b]

No, the matter goes deeper than that, and two sources of his dislike may readily be detected. One was his passion for simple and direct truthfulness with no sort of compromise. After all there is a certain air of falsity or even hypocrisy seldom absent from formal occasions, such as weddings where only the brightest hopes may be expressed or banquets in honor of esteemed colleagues where only lavish praise is the order of the day. Perhaps even stronger was Freud's aversion to doing things that are expected of one, where the spontaneity of the act is necessarily somewhat impaired. He liked to do agreeable things

---

[b] Perhaps an exception should be made here for his habit of hawking and spitting induced by his chronic catarrh and over-smoking. Western patients unaccustomed to such behavior could be disturbed by it, whereupon Freud would chide them for their squeamishness.

quite of his own accord, and, if possible, as a surprise. Then, with his entirely spontaneous and courteous manner, he was at his best, and the warmth of friendliness he conveyed was unforgettable. It is an attitude that accorded with his deep love of independence, with his dislike of being ordered or even "expected" to do something, of having his freedom of action interfered with in any way.

This dislike of complexity and of artificial restrictions had ramifying effects in Freud's character. He had little patience with the complex safeguards, especially legal ones, with which people often invest their relationships. If they trusted one another such safeguards were superfluous; if not, no safeguards would avert trouble: he was really scandalized when he heard that American psychoanalytical societies were in the habit of employing lawyers to formulate the rules that were to regulate the relationships between their members. This attitude was so fundamental that it created rather difficult problems when more elaborate matters of administration arose. Freud could see little reason for rules in a society, although we got him to tolerate a short list of statutes for the International Psycho-Analytical Association. It would happen at times that he would suggest some action which—it would be pointed out—contravened a particular rule or statute. "Then let us alter it; you can easily put it back again if you want to." He would often prefer to cut a Gordian Knot rather than to untie it. And yet there comes to my mind an incident which shows that the description I have just given is only a half-truth. Late in 1910 Jung made the very sensible suggestion that the *Correspondenz-Blatt* be merged in the new *Zentralblatt* and that this should also relieve the *Jahrbuch* of the task of reviewing the literature, a suggestion that was soon afterwards carried out. Freud, however, raised the objection that such action would be contrary to the statutes of the International Association and that they must wait till the next Congress to obtain warrant for the change.

More law-abiding people might have interpreted this attitude of Freud's as sheer arbitrariness, which would not have been a just epithet. It sprang from a more laudable source. What he was concerned about was that we should retain the freedom to make whatever at any juncture we felt to be the best decision without its being thwarted by a fixed rule. Still there were other occasions, such as in the matter of references to other analysts in his writings, where this could not be the explanation. Whereas in his neurological work Freud's bibliographical references had been scrupulously exact and comprehensive, when it came to his analytical writings this was no longer so. Rank once jokingly remarked that Freud distributed references to other analysts' writings on the same principle as the Emperor distributed decorations, according to the mood and fancy of the moment. More than that, he would re-distribute them. I remember his attributing an important conclusion of mine in a book he had read to the reviewer of the book; but then at the moment I was out of favor and he was in.

A part of this apparent arbitrariness came from a very unexpected element in Freud's personality, his black and white judgment of people. It is unexpected, because no one knew better than Freud what a composite mixture of good and bad qualities goes to make up a human being. Yet in his conscious life, and doubtless still more in his unconscious, they were for him mostly divided into good and bad—or, perhaps more accurately, into liked and disliked—with very little in between. And the same person could move from one category into the other from time to time. Still stranger with such a supreme psychologist was the fact, on which we were all agreed, that he was also a poor *Menschenkenner*[c]—a poor judge of men. Perhaps one should not call it strange, since the two characteristics go together. It was a respect, and a not unimportant one, in which Freud's emotions could bias his intellect. It is a theme to which we shall recur later.

I should now like to consider what element of truth there may be in some of the adverse comments that have been made on Freud's personality. I have several times read that he was a pessimist, arrogant and so disagreeable that he always had to quarrel with his friends. There is much to say on these charges, and I will take them in order. The question that I have been most often asked about Freud is what sort of man was he to work with. This is one that it is very simple to answer. I always found him easy and pleasant to work with, and I am sure anyone else in a similar position to myself would have said the same. He was a most cheerful, agreeable and amusing companion, and he seldom had much criticism to make about whatever plans we laid before him. One would now and then, it is true, run into one of his prejudices and they could be so adamant that there was nothing to be done but steer another course. And he was certainly given to entertaining prejudices. In an early letter to

---

[c] We have no English word for this. It means "One who has the intuitive capacity of correctly appraising the character and personality of other human beings."

Abraham he confessed: "You must know that I have a tendency to invent prejudices and to adhere to them." [6] But that had no bearing on our personal relations.

Now as to his supposed pessimism. He was certainly a cheerful person, so the worst that might be supposed was that perhaps he was one of those "cheerful pessimists" with whom we are familiar in life; it was indeed a phrase he more than once used to describe himself.[7] But it would not really be true. The proper word is certainly "realist," someone free of illusions. One can have a pessimistic attitude about life itself or about people. The former means that since one does not enjoy living it has little value for one. This was assuredly not true of Freud, since he had a huge capacity for enjoyment. It is true that he considered life to be inherently hard rather than easy, as his own experience had taught him. It was something primarily to be endured. If one was successful in doing so there was plenty in it to enjoy, and life was very well worth living. One need only refer to his little essay on "Transience," where he described as sheer nonsense the idea that the good things of life lose their value through their impermanence; if they lasted but a minute they could be good.[a]

When it comes to human beings the question is not so simply answered. People are apt to label as a pessimist anyone who has no illusions. Freud would perhaps have qualified for the epithet under that definition, since few men have been so bereft of illusions as he was. In his opinion there were some really noble beings in the world, beings of pure gold, but they were in a minority. The others were not so good as they appeared to be, although the pressure of the environment might compel them to behave reasonably well: let circumstances change and so would their behavior. Freud could be tolerant of this majority, with their weaknesses, but could not admire them. What about the future of mankind? There we touch on a characteristic attitude of Freud's toward time. He lived in the present. In spite of his fascination for the past, both of individuals and of the human race, and his belief that only through the study of it could one learn anything valuable and helpful, he seemed no longer to have any interest in his own past and never spoke of it. For him personally it was the present that mattered, including of course any plans for the quite immediate future. As for the future in general I do not think he spared it much thought. He was so aware of the enormous complexity of both material circumstances and of psychological motives that it was a waste of time to speculate on such an

[a] Chapter 14, No. 28.

unpredictable thing as the future. He had, however, no reason to be pessimistic about it. In a letter to Reik he wrote: "Although I agree with your judgement about the world and the present race of human beings I cannot, as you know, regard your pessimistic rejection of a better future as justifiable." [8]

Freud would have been in favor of any obvious social reforms, but on a longer view he was not sure that they would produce a really satisfactory civilization. Something more radical was needed, and he was a revolutionary rather than a reformer. At times he wondered if another species of creatures would replace mankind and create a better form of social life. At other times he thought that selective breeding was the best hope. But the fact remains that he hoped rather than despaired. For that was his nature.

Arrogant is really an absurd word to apply to Freud. If one wished one might use the word opinionated to describe the tenacity with which he held to his hard-won convictions, but it would be untrue if one meant that they were immovable and not open to revision. The gradual fashion in which Freud felt his way into the unknown, and the changes increasing experience brought about in his conclusions, are facts of history. Nor would it be easy for any great man of science to be otherwise than humble at heart. Freud wrote once: "He who begins to divine the magnificent concatenation of the Universe and its unalterable laws soon forgets his own self." [9] In the face of the vast unknown Freud's attitude could not be other than Newton's, with his pebbles on the beach of knowledge. He knew he had made "a few beginnings" and opened out a few paths, but where they could lead to he could not judge and did not try to. That again would be essaying the useless task of prophesying the future. He was not philosopher enough to imagine he had the capacity for constructing any finished system of thought; beginnings are far removed from anything of the kind. That naturally did not prevent him from having a personal fondness for what he had produced, much as if it were his offspring. His belief in the omnipotence of truth in the long run made him feel sure of the viability of his conclusions. Ignorant criticisms from without did not therefore disturb him; he recognized their transience. It was only when he felt that there was some danger from within of his creation being ruined that for once in his life he sprang to its defense. At the end of the first war, however, when he learned of the progress his ideas had made in distant countries, he felt reassured of their future. He wrote then to Ferenczi: "Psychoanalysis is now equal to all dangers." [10]

I doubt very much if Freud ever thought of himself as a great man, or that it ever occurred to him to measure himself with the men he considered great: Goethe, Kant, Voltaire, Darwin, Schopenhauer, Nietzsche. Marie Bonaparte once told him she thought he was a mixture of Pasteur and Kant. He replied: "That is very complimentary, but I can't share your opinion. Not because I am modest, not at all. I have a high opinion of what I have discovered, but not of myself. Great discoverers are not necessarily great men.[e] Who changed the world more than Columbus? What was he? An adventurer. He had character, it is true, but he was not a great man. So you see that one may find great things without its meaning that one is really great." On another occasion she referred to him as a genius. Freud retorted: "Geniuses are unbearable people. You have only to ask my family to learn how easy I am to live with, so I certainly cannot be a genius." Of one thing about himself he was always sure: that he had a poor intellectual capacity. There were so many things, e.g. in mathematics or physics, he knew he should never be able to understand where so many others easily could.

Was Freud an ambitious man? In the ordinary sense not. Social prestige and titles were intrinsically valueless things, though academic ones might help in his profession and the spread of his ideas. Fame itself meant very little personally, only in so far as it signified a more widespread knowledge of the important ideas. His ambition, such as it was, concentrated on the wish to see those ideas, by which he set great store, accepted.

He wished he could have been wealthy enough to indulge his delight in travel and in the study of antiquity, but it being evidently out of the question it could not be called an ambition. He knew he had to work hard to the end simply to earn a living. So he never strove for money as such. The thought of a Nobel Prize became a wish, though never a hope, only for the material reason that it would save him from the specter of bankruptcy he saw looming ahead during the war and which toward its end came very close.

The term "disagreeable" could not for a moment have been used to describe Freud by anyone who knew him or even had had the experience of his courteous reception. The use of it must proceed from various subjective sources, since the only slight objective one I can think of is that few of his photographs show him smiling. For some reason he very much disliked being photographed—perhaps it was too "formal" an action—and always scowled when he saw a

[e] *grosse Geister.*

camera pointed at him; another reason was his dislike of his aging appearance, a motive that operated even when he was only fifty-two. The best photographs of him are therefore snapshots taken when he was unaware; his son Oliver was expert at this game.

A man's relationship to his friends is a sphere where important aspects of his personality are necessarily revealed. Freud had a rich and complex personality, which, incidentally, may have been one reason for his liking for simplicity. His relationship to friends was certainly not always simple. If they could be covered by the word "quarrelsome," which his opponents have sometimes applied to him, the biographer's task would be much easier. And that he could not keep friends is negatived by the simple fact of there being a number of people besides myself still alive to tell the tale.

Freud had all his life several close personal friends from his social circle, Oskar Rie and Königstein being good examples. They were quite unconnected with his own work, and—perhaps for that reason— the friendships seem always to have pursued a smooth course. I do not know of any disturbance in them nor of any breaks in such friendships. Freud found it easy to maintain them, since he was never tempted to do anything that excited animosity. Something may well be said at this point about his moral nature.

Whatever the source of it—and Freud himself was constantly puzzled by this very problem—a moral attitude was so deeply implanted as to seem a part of his original nature. He never had any doubt about what was the right course of conduct. It was all so obvious that a favorite quotation of his was F. T. Vischer's saying: "Morality is self-evident." [f] It was only in late life that Freud was able to throw light on the origin of the moral sentiment.

His correspondence with Putnam was very revealing about his attitude to morality. In 1915 Freud read Putnam's recently published book entitled *Human Motives*. He wrote at once to Ferenczi about it, "It is a good and loyal book, but filled with the sense of religion which I am irresistibly impelled to reject. From the psychical reality of our ideas he directly infers their material reality,[g] and therefore God." [11] This was his letter to Putnam on the book.

"July 8, 1915

"Dear Dr. Putnam,

"Your book has arrived at last, long after it was announced. I

____

[f] *Das Moralische versteht sich von selbst.*
[g] *I.e. external, objective.*

have not yet finished reading it, but I have read what were for me the most important sections on religion and on psychoanalysis and yield to the impulse to write to you about it.

"You will assuredly not ask for praise and recognition from me. It is pleasant to think that it will make an impression on your fellow-countrymen and with many of them break down their deeply rooted resistance. On p. 20 I found the passage which I must regard as most applicable to myself: 'To accustom ourselves to the study of immaturity and childhood before proceeding to the study of maturity and manhood is often to habituate ourselves to an undesirable limitation of our vision with reference to the scope of the enterprise on which we enter.'

"I recognize that is my case. I am certainly incompetent to judge the other side of the matter. I must have used this one-sidedness to be able to see what is hidden, from which other people knew how to keep away. That is the justification of my defensive reaction. The one-sidedness had after all its own usefulness.

"On the other hand, that the arguments for the reality of our ideals do not make any deep impression on me does not prove very much. I cannot find any transition from the fact that our ideas of perfection have psychical reality to a belief in their objective existence. You know, of course, how little is to be expected from arguments. I will add that I have no dread at all of the Almighty.[h] If we ever were to meet I should have more reproaches to make to Him than He could to me. I should ask Him why He had not given me a better intellectual equipment, and He could not complain that I had not made the best use of my supposed freedom. (By the way, I know that everyone of us represents a fragment of life energy, but I don't see what energy has to do with freedom, i.e. absence of conditioning factors.)

"For I have to tell you that I have always been dissatisfied with my gifts and know precisely in what respects they are lacking, but that I consider myself to be a very moral person who can subscribe to the excellent maxim of Th. Vischer: 'What is moral is self-evident.' I believe that in a sense of justice and consideration for others, in disliking making others suffer or taking advantage of them, I can measure myself with the best people I have known. I have never done anything mean or malicious and cannot trace any temptation to do so, so I am not in the least proud of it. I am taking the idea of morality we are speaking of in its social meaning, not in its

[h] *der liebe Gott.*

sexual. Sexual morality as society, in its most extreme form the American one, defines it, seems to be very contemptible. I stand for an incomparably freer sexual life, although I myself have made very little use of such freedom: only in so far as I myself judged it to be allowable.

"The publicity with which moral demands are made often makes an unpleasant impression on me. What I have seen of religious-ethical conversions has not been very inviting. [Here comes an outspoken reference to Jung.]

"I see one point, however, in which I can agree with you. When I ask myself why I have always behaved honorably, ready to spare others and to be kind wherever possible, and why I did not give up doing so when I observed that in that way one harms oneself and becomes an anvil because other people are brutal and untrustworthy, then, it is true, I have no answer. Sensible it certainly was not. In my youth I never felt any special ethical aspirations, nor have I any recognizable satisfaction in concluding that I am better than most other people. You are probably the first person to whom I have admitted it. So one could cite just my case for your view that an impulsion toward the ideal forms an essential part of our constitution. If only more of this valuable constitution were to be observed in the others! I have the secret belief that if one possessed the means of studying the sublimations of instincts as thoroughly as the repressions of them one might come across quite natural psychological explanations which would make your philanthropic supposition unnecessary. But, as I said, I know nothing about it all. Why I—and incidentally my six adult children also—have to be thoroughly decent human beings is quite incomprehensible to me. There is another reflection: when the knowledge of the human soul is so imperfect that even my poor abilities have managed to make such rich discoveries it is evidently premature to decide for or against such assumptions such as yours.

". . . For the time being psychoanalysis is compatible with various *Weltanschaungen*. But has it yet spoken its last word? For my part I have never been concerned with any comprehensive synthesis, but always with certainty alone. This deserves that everything else be sacrificed to it.

. . .

"Yours very sincerely,
"Freud"

But Freud knew well that the *certainty* science offers is far removed from the Absolute, and he distinguished it sharply from the *certitude* for which so many people yearn. Marie Bonaparte once gave him Poincaré's *La Valeur de la Science* to read, and made the comment: "Those who thirst before everything for certitude do not really love truth." To which Freud replied: "That is so true. I have said that too somewhere, in another way. Mediocre spirits demand of science a kind of certainty which it cannot give, a sort of religious satisfaction. Only the real, rare, true scientific minds, can endure doubt, which is attached to all our knowledge. I always envy the physicists and mathematicians who can stand on firm ground. I hover, so to speak, in the air. Mental events seem to be immeasurable and probably always will be so."

As for morality, Freud would have found a deontological department of a university, such as exists nowadays, quite superfluous.

It was only when friends were at the same time cooperators in his work that difficulties could arise. The work itself was concerned with such deep emotions that difficulties might arise on both sides. Another analyst could run into emotional difficulties of his own which would distort his apprehension of the problems inherent in the subject. Then on Freud's side his discoveries meant to him something so ineffably precious that he was inevitably sensitive about any distortion by manhandling. This he could probably have dealt with objectively were it not that further complications arose from his emotional attitude toward helpers in general. On the one hand he welcomed them warmly and they had for him a profound significance beyond their practical value, but on the other hand that brought with it a sensitiveness about the risk of losing them. Not long after such friends began to gather round him he wrote to Eitington: "The affection of a group of courageous and understanding young men is the most precious gift that psychoanalysis has brought me." [12] And to Abraham he wrote: "I have always sought for friends who would not first exploit and then betray me." [13]

Freud's letters are full of such remarks. After the Committee was instituted it became evident that to the natural pleasure of friendship there was added an element of reassurance. Any doubts Freud had about his work or fears about the future fate of it could now be stilled. He had had a similar attitude to Jung previously, but with unfortunate results.

This need for reassurance, although it was not at all pronounced in Freud at that time of his life, must have stirred older and much more serious emotions of a similar kind. In those days, with Breuer and notably with Fliess, the need had been accompanied by two more disturbing attitudes: dependence and a corresponding over-estimation of the other person. As he himself remarked several times, they proceeded from the feminine side of his nature. The tendency to over-estimation persisted to some extent, however, and partly accounted for his deficiencies as a *Menschenkenner*. It was manifest with Adler and Jung, and to some extent with Ferenczi, Silberer and Tausk. The risk of subsequent disappointment was inevitable. Presumably these attitudes came from some impairment of self-confidence; certainly the two things went hand in hand. He remarked once to Ferenczi that the overcoming of his "homosexuality" had brought him a greater self-dependence.[14] The attitudes also represented an oscillation between over-trustfulness and distrust of others.

Freud's dislike of dependence and of having his freedom of action restricted, even by rules he might have made himself, was nevertheless much stronger than the opposite tendency that has just been mentioned. Freedom and independence were life-blood to him. In his earlier life he had loathed being dependent for his livelihood in practice on the good will of other physicians for whom more often than not he had little respect. The wish to be economically independent was always very strong with him. He did not want to owe anything to anyone. It is possible that his inability for years to repay Breuer what he had borrowed from him in his twenties was as important as any other factor for the break between them. When I asked him once why he minded old age so much he said it was because it made him dependent on others; he instanced as an example that he could no longer raise or lower the window of a railway carriage alone and had to ask someone else to do it for him. One must suppose that this trait of insisting on doing everything for himself, and managing his own affairs without any help or interference, had been developed very early in life, probably in the earliest infancy. There was perhaps a certain distrust in his attitude toward help. He would often express the opinion that life was essentially hard, that one had to earn for oneself every enjoyment one got, with the implication that, if one accepted anything good as a favor at the hands of another, one would probably rue it later or at least pay substantially for it; so it was better not to be beholden. We know that his early life was an exceptionally hard one; he was certainly not a spoiled darling of fate.

Freud used to say that an alternation of love and hate was apt to affect his relationships with men, and there is no doubt that it occasionally did. No such disturbing ambivalence, however, ever troubled those with women, where his attitude was much more consistent. To pass any judgment on it is not easy. The varying status of women in society has experienced such extraordinary changes in the history of humanity that the position prevailing in the last fifty years may perhaps not be so permanent as is now assumed. If judged by it alone Freud's attitude to women would probably be called rather old-fashioned, and it would be easy to ascribe this to his social environment and the period in which he grew up rather than to any personal factors. Whatever his intellectual opinions may have been in the matter there are many indications in his writings and correspondence of his emotional attitude. It would certainly be going too far to say that he regarded the male sex as the Lords of Creation, for there was no tinge of arrogance or superiority in his nature, but it might perhaps be fair to describe his view of the female sex as having as their main function to be ministering angels to the needs and comforts of men. His letters and his love choice make it plain that he had only one type of sexual object in his mind, a gentle feminine one. While women might belong to the weaker sex, however, he regarded them as finer and ethically nobler than men; there are indications that he wished to absorb some of these qualities from them.

There is little doubt that Freud found the psychology of women more enigmatic than that of men. He said once to Marie Bonaparte: "The great question that has never been answered and which I have not yet been able to answer, despite my thirty years of research into the feminine soul, is 'What does a woman want?' "[1]

Freud was also interested in another type of woman, of a more intellectual and perhaps masculine cast. Such women several times played a part in his life, accessory to his men friends though of a finer caliber, but they had no erotic attraction for him. The most important of them were first of all his sister-in-law, Minna Bernays, then in chronological order: Emma Eckstein, Loe Kann, Lou Andreas-Salomé, Joan Riviere, Marie Bonaparte. Freud had a special admiration for Lou Andreas-Salomé's distinguished personality and ethical ideals, which he felt far transcended his own.

Freud was quite peculiarly monogamous. Of few men can it be said that they go through the whole of life without being erotically moved in any serious fashion by any woman beyond the one and only one. Yet this really seems to have been true of Freud, since we must

[1] *Was will das Weib?*

consider the momentary excitement over Gisela Fluss at the age of sixteen to have been an intense phantasy rather than a personal attraction. Such men are fortunate indeed if all goes well with the great choice, as happened to Freud, but whether they are to be regarded as representing the true normality of males is a question that only social or psychological anthropology can answer. Freud's deviation from the average in this respect, as well as his pronounced mental bisexuality, may well have influenced his theoretical views to some extent, a possibility to be borne in mind when assessing them.

Freud undoubtedly exercised a remarkable attraction on members of both sexes, and this assuredly cannot be attributed to charm of manner or gallantry only. Women, even those who knew him only slightly or even not at all personally, often found irresistible his peculiar combination of confident strength with unfailing considerateness and tenderness; here was a man that could be trusted. They were also impressed by his evident interest in their own personality. Men also were as a rule struck by the air he gave of authoritative finality, a true father-image, by his transcendent knowledge and by his kindly tolerance; he was plainly a person they could look up to and perhaps take as a model.

Most students of Freud have been struck by what has been called his obstinate dualism; had he been a philosopher he certainly would not have been a monist nor would he have felt at home in William James's pluralistic universe. Running all through his work there is what Heinz Hartmann has called "a very characteristic kind of dialectical thinking that tends to base theories on the interaction of two opposite powers." This was of course most pronounced in his basic classifications: love-hunger; ego-sexuality; auto-erotism—hetero-erotism; Eros-Thanatos; life-death, and so on. I remember how alien this seemed to me, having been brought up in a biological school that thought of instincts in the plural. But the same fondness for pairs is to be found again and again: love-hate, exhibitionism-scopophilism, etc. It is as if Freud had a difficulty in contemplating any topic unless he could divide it into two opposites, and never more than two. That there was a fundamental conflict between two opposing forces in the mind was for him a basic fact.

One is naturally tempted to correlate this tendency with its manifestations in Freud's own personality. There was the fight between scientific discipline and philosophical speculation; his passionate love urge and his unusually great sexual repression; his vigorous masculinity, which shines through all his writings, and his feminine needs; his desire to create everything himself and his longing to receive stimulation from another; his love of independence and his needs of dependence. But such thoughts assuredly bring the risk of falsification from the lure of simplistic solutions.

Nevertheless I cannot but recall in this connection that Freud once told Jung that were he ever to suffer from a neurosis it would be of the obsessional type. That signifies, as Freud himself taught us, a deep ambivalence between the emotions of love and hate, and much in his own self-descriptions undoubtedly accords with this.

I will take the liberty here of reproducing some passages from an estimate of his personality which I wrote soon after Freud's death. They contain points of view it is necessary to put forward, and I feel that simply to paraphrase them now could only impair them.

"Future generations of psychologists will assuredly wish to know what manner of man it was who, after two thousand years of vain endeavour had gone by, succeeded in fulfilling the Delphic injunction: Know thyself. Their wish will not be one of simple curiosity; they will understand that to know Freud's personality will bring them closer to the inspiration of his achievement. They will, furthermore, have a legitimate scientific interest in trying to comprehend the precise balance of mental energies that made it possible for him to accomplish his Herculean feats. For Herculean they truly were. Few, if any, have been able to go as far as he did on the path of self-knowledge and self-mastery—even with the aid of the pioneer torch he provided with his methods and previous exploration, and even with the invaluable assistance of years of daily personal work with expert mentors. How one man alone could have broken all this new ground, and overcome all difficulties unaided, must ever remain a cause for wonder. It was the nearest to a miracle that human means can compass, one that surely surpasses even the loftiest intellectual achievements in mathematics and pure science. Copernicus and Darwin dared much in facing the unwelcome truths of outer reality, but to face those of inner reality costs something that only the rarest of mortals would unaided be able to give.

"Doubtless many qualities went to make up such an original mind as Freud's was, but he possessed certain notable ones in such a high degree that they must surely have played an important part in making possible his creative work. They thus deserve to be specially signalized, though it would be inappropriate here to offer conjectures about their source or inner significance. We know that purely intellectual gifts alone are inadequate for the purpose of endopsychic exploration. Freud possessed these, it is plain, in rich measure, though he himself did not esteem them highly. We look rather for what may be called traits of character, and here also Freud's endowment was outstanding.

"If one had to place one of these traits above all others it would probably be that of the amazing intellectual courage—the rarest and most transcendent form of courage—Freud displayed. When faced over and again with the dark unknown, and apparently unknowable, his impulse was always to press forward, undaunted by the possibilities of what he might encounter, and alone in an uncharted territory with no precursor or companion with whom to share his doubts. He possessed the quality of intellectual daring in the highest degree. Horror, fear, disgust at the revelations made within the depths of his own mind or in those of his patients: nothing restrained him—least of all the knowledge of what his colleagues would probably think of his findings. Perhaps the hardest obstacle of all to overcome was not the content alone of the unconscious material, but the extraordinary form it took. Never before had anyone dared to read sense and meaning into mental processes that so flagrantly ignored all the mental laws of logical exposition. Imagine meeting a race of beings whose minds were timeless, had no conception of a negative, were quite insensitive to contradictory juxtapositions and who expressed themselves by the curious devices of displacement, condensation, primitive symbolism and all the other mechanisms with which Freud has made us familiar. How many investigators in that situation would have ventured to think it possible to read sense into such a meaningless farrago? More over, with the material in question, that of dreams, neurotic and psy chotic phantasies, etc., he had been assured beforehand by all authori ties that it was by definition devoid of meaning, being the jumbled product of disorder in the organ itself of meaning—the brain; after all, Freud had been educated, not as a psychologist or mythologist, but in the tenets of orthodox neurology. Undeterred by this bias, however, Freud determined to examine the facts themselves and let nothing but their evidence influence his conclusions.

"What little we know of intellectual courage, that quality so seldom found even among men of distinction, indicates that it is closely akin to scepticism. Those possessing it do not take things for granted, nor are they affected by the opinions of others. They prefer to suspend their judgement until they can examine the matter personally and form their own opinion. Freud's indifference to the views of other people was one of his most highly developed characteristics, one so striking as to be observed in ordinary life by those who met him even casually. Certain aspects of it—in the way he insisted on coming to an independent decision even in small matters—were so pronounced as to evoke the epithets 'opinionated,' 'suspicious,' or even 'obstinate' on the part of the unsympathetic, where his friends would rather speak of his resolution, determination or independence of spirit. Be that as it may, it is of interest that on rare occasions faint hints would transpire of just the opposite qualities, namely of credulity or suggestibility, so that one might wonder if his pronounced independence had not in part been developed as a reaction to some early propensities of that sort. There can, however, be no doubt about the great value this quality of independence had both in the scepticism indispensable to his scientific inquiries and to the life of a pioneer these brought in their train.

"A mere tendency to doubt and to ignore conventional opinions cannot in itself lead to originality in any significant sense; it may end only in social eccentricity. It relates to true originality only when it is informed, i.e. only when the scepticism is founded on some objective reason and not on any personal foible. The elusive qualities of judgement, of critical power and especially of self-criticism are necessary to this end, and these qualities also Freud possessed in a high degree. He had a judicial mind, one which would unprejudicedly balance differing considerations and could with an intuitive sense of perspective distinguish the important from the unimportant, the essential from the irrelevant. By significant originality one must mean something more than flashes of insight, however brilliant and accurate these may be. With most of Freud's discoveries it is possible to point to precursors—indeed he himself called attention to them—who had made what may be called lucky guesses. Freud's merit lay in taking his new ideas seriously, in following them up in detail with unsparing labour, and in not resting until he had established them on a wide basis of correlation with other, known ideas. He once compared the difference in these two attitudes to that between a casual flirtation and a responsible marriage.

"For courageous scepticism to result in valuable originality it needs another quality besides judgement, namely, honesty of mind. With Freud this virtue was so immediate and innate that it infused his whole personality. And he was as honest with himself as with others. He was always the first to point out the imperfections and misapprehensions in his work, and in correcting them in the interest of greater accuracy he was indifferent to the charges brought against him of self-contradiction or fickle changeability. His sensitiveness to the inner voice of criticism, however, was accompanied by a remarkable resistance to any outside influence or pressure; here he displayed a moral courage in the face of bitter opposition, and a tenacity in his adherence to his hard-won convictions, that in themselves raise him far above most of his contemporaries. Honesty with Freud was more than a simple natural habit. It became an active love of truth and justice—the Goddess Maat of whom he wrote so warmly in his last book—and brought with it an equally strong dislike of any deception, ambiguousness or prevarication. Even the simplest form of compromise, a quality that would certainly have made his life easier, was anathema to him. He went so far here as to develop a dislike of the usual formalities of social relationships, conventional or otherwise, and laid little store by the common graces of life.

"Though not by nature devoid of the capacity for truculence and pugnacity Freud must early in life have decided that it was a quality not to be cultivated. He undoubtedly attached far more value to peaceful than to militant pursuits. Once only, at the outset of his career, did he enter into controversy with an opponent. All other attacks on his work—and no man could have had more—he answered in the same fashion as our great Darwin, whom he resembled in many other respects: namely, by simply producing a further piece of research. This attitude he adopted both from conviction and by temperament. He had little belief in the value of controversy in scientific matters. He observed how many other factors played a part in it besides the ostensible search for truth, factors such as the desire to prove oneself personally in the right, to score off an opponent, and so on; so he refrained from polemics as being something that wasted time and emotional energy and brought one no nearer to the goal. The greatness of his character thus showed itself both in his scientific work itself and in his attitude towards it.

"About one thing Freud was serious above all else and it became the driving force of his life. That was the search for knowledge. His mind was not of the philosophic or contemplative kind; it was a restlessly inquiring mind. He believed that knowledge was a real thing, not a mere point of view, and that within our limited powers much of it could be attained. But he also knew that in order to do so the strictest honesty was essential and that for this supreme goal one must be ready to sacrifice much else—not only time and endless labour, but *amour propre*, any reputation for consistency in the sense of fixity, and whatever personal feeling might threaten to interfere with the single aim of truth.

"In any discussion of psychical integrity one must always think of Freud as a supreme example of it. There is general agreement over the importance a 'strong ego' plays in bringing about psychical integrity and without doubt Freud possessed an immensely strong ego. We know that this is a concept not very easy to define, but it connotes two things which we find exemplified in a high degree with Freud: tolerance of anxiety, i.e. such mastery of it that it affects one but little, and a firm apprehension of reality. Above all else Freud was a realist.

"Side by side with the capacity to admit and face the evil of life, a capacity essential to the realist, went equally pronounced abilities to enjoy its good. Freud was a man keenly alive to the sublimities of human existence and also aware of how much the appreciation of little everyday things goes to make the good life. He was a man schooled to restraint in emotion, but his fundamental benevolence was unmistakable and constantly transpired in unostentatious fashion. He had great personal charm, though without any trace of that facile charmingness that so often passes for the real thing. A smile, the more attractive for its sincerity, was never far from his lips and his fondness for humour and wit (particularly with an ironical tinge) was proverbial among his friends. Though not demonstrative by nature he had, it was not hard to perceive, a deep fund of tenderness as well as kindliness. It is not surprising that he inspired devotion.

"One cannot describe the man Freud without laying stress on the fact that he was a Jew. Though never orthodox or in any way religious he held together with his people, was a Governor of the Hebrew University in Jerusalem, and took an interest in all that concerned the fate of Jewry. The Nazi intolerance of this spared him no more than it had Einstein. The fact itself is of more than personal interest, since it is doubtful if without certain traits inherited from his Jewish ancestry Freud would have been able to accomplish the work he did. I think here of a peculiar native shrewdness, a sceptical attitude towards illusion and deception, and a determined courage that made him impervious to hostile public opinion and the contumely of his professional colleagues."

After this long descriptive prelude I now propose to make the daring attempt of approaching as near as I can to the secret of Freud's genius. A bold endeavor; one can but fail.

Recurring to our original question about Freud's most prominent characteristics I propose to offer my own answer to it. When I first got to know Freud I could not fail to observe such manifest qualities as his directness, absolute honesty, tolerance, ease of approach and his essential kindliness. But I also soon noticed another feature which was more peculiar to him. It was his attitude about being influenced by other people's opinions. He would listen politely to them, would show interest in them and often make penetrating comments on them, but somehow one felt that they would make no difference to his own. It was like taking interest in something gazed at which did not really concern oneself personally. A superficial critic might call this attitude opinionated, or even obstinate, but we shall see that it signified something much more interesting.

This imperviousness in matters of opinion applied far less to questions of conduct. Although Freud had a strong will and always knew what he wanted, he was quite amenable here to suggestions from outside. He might not wish to read a paper at a Congress, but he could be persuaded to do so. In such ways he would always subordinate his own wishes. The giving way in deference to someone else's wishes was, however, not always wholehearted; at times he remained "of his own opinion still." James Strachey has told me of a rather amusing example of this. He was translating a passage about a writer with the unfortunate name of Looney who, Freud said, had converted him to the view that Shakespeare's plays had been written by the Earl of Oxford. Strachey knew that scholars regarded this supposition as hare-brained, and he patiently explained to Freud the connotation of the author's name in English which could only have the effect of adding risibility to derision. He therefore begged Freud to omit it. After a while Freud consented, but evidently only to mollify what he seemed to think was an absurd prejudice on Strachey's part, for in the American edition he re-inserted the compromising name.

Nor is the word "self-willed" really in place, since that refers typically to active wishes, an insistence on doing or getting something. This was hardly true of Freud. It was characteristically in negative resistance that his will displayed unusual strength. Once his will was really set he would not be driven or even guided in any particular direction.[1] "No" could be a powerful word to him. In his old age he would repeat the words *"nein, nein, nein,"* to the accompaniment of a vigorous shaking of the head that made me think how strenuously he must have resisted ministrations as an infant.

[1] A striking example of this was quoted in Chapter 2, p. 60.

Now Freud had inherently a plastic and mobile mind, one given to the freest speculations and open to new and even highly improbable ideas. But it worked this way only on condition that the ideas came from himself; to those from outside he could be very resistant, and they had little power in getting him to change his mind. I may cite an illustration from personal experience. Soon after the war I was in constant correspondence with Rank and his assistant over matters concerning publications. Freud wrote a letter reproaching me for my alleged dilatoriness and neglect in answering their letters and questions. I told him the truth was quite otherwise. It was I who had been troubled in this respect by the Viennese, so much so that I had been compelled to institute a system of not merely dating and numbering my letters, but of numbering each paragraph in the hope of getting it answered, and I appealed to his own experience over many years of my punctiliousness in swiftly attending to correspondence. All in vain. He continued from time to time to express the hope that I was improving.

I was at first puzzled by this resistiveness to outside opinion until I hit on what I consider to be the explanation of it, one which indeed the foregoing example illustrates. An intuition, soon confirmed by evidence, told me that side by side with Freud's great independence of mind and skeptical criticism of ideas there was also a concealed vein of the very opposite, and that his resistiveness was a defense against the danger of being too readily influenced by others. With a patient he was treating before the war, whose life history I knew intimately, I would come across instance after instance where he was believing statements which I knew to be certainly untrue and also, incidentally, refusing to believe things that were as certainly true. Joan Riviere has related an extraordinary example of this combination of credulity and persistence. During her analysis Freud spoke very angrily one morning of an English patient he had just seen who complained bitterly of monstrous, and indeed fantastic, ill-treatment she had suffered at the hands of an English analyst in Ipswich—of all places. Mrs. Riviere's cool mind at once perceived that this was a cock-and-bull story, but she contented herself with remarking that there was no English analyst of the name mentioned, that there never had been an analyst in Ipswich nor indeed anywhere in England outside London. That made no impression, and Freud continued his tirade against such scandalous behavior. Shortly afterwards, however, he received a letter from Abraham saying he had recommended an English lady to consult him and that she was a wild paranoiac with a fondness for inventing incredible stories about doctors. So poor Abraham had been the wicked analyst in Ipswich!

But there is on record unquestionable proofs of this credulousness against which Freud must have had to fight so hard. It is astonishing to read how in the nineties he had for years absorbed his friend Fliess's amazing numerological phantasies, and I am not even sure that he ever entirely freed himself from a lingering belief in them. So he knew from bitter experience the extraordinary extent to which his thinking could be influenced by someone who aroused his emotions.

Less astonishing, perhaps, and certainly more fateful for good, was the credulous acceptance of his patients' stories of paternal seduction which he narrated in his earlier publications on psychopathology.[15] When I commented to my friend James Strachey on Freud's strain of credulity he very sagely remarked: "It was lucky for us that he had it." Most investigators would have simply disbelieved the patients' stories on the ground of their inherent improbability—at least on such a large scale—and have dismissed the matter as one more example of the untrustworthiness of hysterics. Freud took them seriously, believed at first in their literal truth, and only after a few years of reflection made the discovery that they represented highly significant phantasies. It was the beginning of his appreciating the importance of the life of phantasy in the unconscious and of discovering the existence of repressed infantile erotism.

We must come to the conclusion, therefore, that this curious strain in Freud's nature, far from being an unfortunate weakness or deficiency, constituted an essential part of his genius. He was willing to believe in the improbable and the unexpected—the only way, as Heraclitus pointed out centuries ago, to discover new truths. It is doubtless a two-edged weapon. It led Freud at times into making serious misjudgments, possibly even ridiculous ones, but it also enabled him dauntlessly to face the unknown and thus to open up fields of knowledge that had remained closed to more judicial but pedestrian explorers.

It is an interesting thought that very possibly this trait may be a regular accompaniment to scientific genius. One can think of many great men of science whose simple-minded credulity in other fields than their own makes one sometimes blush to read about, as if one had inadvertently come across an unfortunate weakness in a hero. The great Newton's preoccupation with extraordinary theological speculations, and his search for the mythical Philosopher's Stone, may serve as an example. Yet I am suggesting that we are here concerned with not a weakness but an indispensable tool of genius.

The picture of Freud as a tediously patient and rationally factual investigator is, as we have seen, a very imperfect one. Patient and rational he undoubtedly was, but he was far more. The daemon of creative speculation,[k] which he had so ruthlessly checked in the early years of scientific work when he tied himself all day to the microscope, never really rested for long. His scientific rationalism of those days was broken into by the tumultuous urge of his love experience. Later on the emotional episode which Fliess helped to release his imagination, even if it also guided it for a time into fruitless directions. After his self-analysis he attained a balance that enabled him to tread surely through the mazes of his new province and for forty years to bring back invaluable reports of what he had found. Then, as we shall learn later, in the last twenty years of his life, he gave his speculative daemon a freer rein than ever before, with bewildering results that are as yet far from adequately appraised.

Beyond the self-discipline Freud had acquired in his early work he also possessed an innate power of self-criticism. This was infinitely more valuable and far more penetrating than the ignorant outpourings of what passed as "criticisms" of his work in the outer world. He himself was well aware of both its strictness and its value. It made him very independent of either praise or blame from others, which could never proceed from the insight his own conscience had. He wrote once to Ferenczi: "You were always ready to admire me.[l] Since I am very jealous of my powers of self-criticism in scientific matters in particular, I could naturally not have given any occasion for admiration. Self-criticism is not a pleasant gift, but next to my courage it is the best thing I have, and it has exercised a strict selection in what I have published. Without it I could have given three times as much to the world. I treasure it all the more since hardly anyone credits me with it."[17]

Valuable as it is in its place, self-criticism is a rather negative quality. It can decide what is wrong, but not necessarily what is right. For that some more positive quality is needed, but one that is hard to define and still harder to explain. It is a flair for choosing the essential in a collection of material, for divining correctly and confidently even in a limited number of observations certain connections which further research will confirm. One might even call it the capacity to know

---

[k] What he called "my phantastic self."[16]
[l] Referring to a recent holiday together in Sicily.

instinctively what is true. Freud possessed this in the highest degree, so close was he to psychical reality and so easily did he thread his way through a maze of psychological data. He was a born psychologist, and by that one means that he had a high and serious respect for the reality of psychological facts. They were as real and concrete to him as metals are to a metallurgist.

This power of divining truth postulates an unusually intense desire to do so. Freud not only had this, and evidently so, but I venture to surmise that it was the deepest and strongest driving force in his life. I am led to this conclusion by the feeling that much of what Freud said when he penetrated into Leonardo's personality was at the same time a self-description; there was surely an extensive identification between Leonardo and himself. There we learned that Leonardo was torn by two impulses: the passion for scientific knowledge and the passion for creating works of art. According to Freud, the scientific striving in the end proved stronger than the artistic one, and Leonardo's artistic output necessarily suffered thereby. Freud could never have become a painter, it is true, but I find it not unprofitable to ask what else he might well have become besides a great psychologist; in other words, what undeveloped talents had he as well. I can think of two. He might have become a creative writer, perhaps not a poet but a novelist—in fact he said so himself more than once. It was perhaps not chance that, before he ever met him, he once wrote to Arthur Schnitzler, the famous Austrian novelist and dramatist, that he felt his mind to be more akin to his own than anyone else's he had ever come across. For creative writing he had the technical literary qualities in a high degree, he had the necessary imagination, and he surely would have penetrated into the very heart of his characters. Or, on the other hand, he might have evolved a philosophy, one in which man's relation to nature and to the universe would be expounded. The ultimate questions of philosophy were very near to him in spite of his endeavor to keep them at a distance and of distrusting his capacity to solve them.

It is not hard to see what prevented Freud from following in either of these directions, and the answer takes us far into understanding Freud's inmost being. However beautiful a picture of human truths it might display, creative writing would after all have remained only a picture of the truth, not the literal truth itself. And the naked truth, stark if need be, was Freud's goal. Philosophy might or might not yield the ultimate truth—no one could say—but it evidently lacked certainty. And certainty, again, was Freud's goal. The final sentence in the letter to Putnam quoted above proves how central was this goal.

Freud's passion to get at the truth with the maximum of certainty was, I again suggest, the deepest and strongest motive in his nature and the one that impelled him toward his pioneering achievements. What truth? And why was the desire so overwhelming? In his study of Leonardo Freud maintained that the child's desire to know is fed by powerful motives arising in his infantile curiosity about the primary facts of life, the meaning of birth and what has brought it about.[m] It is commonly animated by the appearance of a rival child who displaces him in his mother's attention and to some extent in her love. We know that little Julius played this part in Freud's infantile life, and that he never ceased to reproach himself for being, through his hostile wishes, responsible for the intruder's early death.[19] We also know of the immense capacity for jealousy he manifested during his engagement to Martha Bernays and his inordinate demand for exclusive possession of the loved one. He had had, therefore, very good reasons for wanting to know how such things happened, how it was that intruders could appear and who was responsible for their doing so. It cannot after all be chance that after many years of distraction in other fields the one in which the chaste and puritanical Freud ultimately made his discoveries was in that of the sexual life.

Only in knowing the truth could there be found security, the security that possession of his mother would give. But to conquer the forbidding barriers between him and his goal needed not merely determination, but also superb courage to face the phantoms of the unknown. This undaunted courage was Freud's highest quality and his most precious gift. Whence could he have derived it other than from a supreme confidence in his mother's love?

Can we now from this point of view come to a nearer understanding of the other prominent features of Freud's character. If success was to be attained in the great search for truth, absolute honesty and complete integrity were essential; so much is evident. But why had he to be wholly independent in the search? He had not only to carry it out alone, but he fended off any influences from without, however apparently helpful, as if they were interfering distractions or even designed to lead him astray. That accords with the vein of distrust in his nature; in the last resort he could only trust himself in his vital

[m] As early as 1909 Freud had written, when discussing the child's mind, "The thirst for knowledge seems to be inseparable from sexual curiosity."[18]

quest. That being so, however, how are we to account for the opposite attitude he also exhibited at times? There was the tendency to believe stories told him by someone else, someone who seemed to have more power of revealing secrets than he had. There was Fliess, for instance, with his conclusion about the bisexual nature of all living things and his periodic law of the universe. What had become of Freud's distrust at such junctures? There must have been the belief that someone else really did know the answer to the riddles that unconsciously perplexed him. But would they tell him the truth? How often in later years did Freud complain of the times he had been "betrayed," to use his expression, by his friends; in turn Breuer, Fliess, Adler, Jung, had promised to aid or even inspire him in his great search and then deserted him. I think we are justified in the present context of replacing the word "betrayed" by "deceived." So after all he would have to find out for himself.

Our thoughts go back here to what we know of Freud's early childhood. There was, it is true, the old Nannie who had told him stories of heaven and hell which he had soon come to doubt; perhaps he had never taken them really seriously in view of his family's evident disbelief in her Catholic theology. We note, moreover, that never in his life did Freud accuse any woman of betraying or deceiving him. So it must have been a man who knew the secrets and only pretended to impart them to him. Well, there was his half-brother Philipp, so given to joking as Freud himself remarked, whom he suspected of being his mother's mate and whom he tearfully begged not to make his mother again pregnant.[20] Could one trust such a man, who evidently knew all the secrets, to tell the truth about them? It would be a curious trick of fate if this insignificant little man—he is said to have ended up as a peddler—had through his mere existence proved to have fortuitously struck the spark that lit the future Freud's determination to trust himself alone, to resist the impulse to believe in others more than in himself, and in that way to make imperishable the name of Freud.

Appendix

To C. G. JUNG, December 6, 1906
(In answer to the reasons Jung gave for not putting the topic of ther-
apy in the foreground of an exposition of psychoanalysis: the number
of unsuitable cases, the mistakes in diagnosis, and the fear lest inex-
perienced doctors think that psychoanalysis in therapy is easy and
thereby discredit it in their efforts to apply it.)

"I can unreservedly subscribe to your remarks about therapy. I have
had the same experiences, and for the same reasons have taken care
not to maintain in my writings more than that 'the method effects
more than any other.' I will not even maintain that every case of
hysteria is curable, let alone everything that goes under that name.
Since I am not concerned with the percentage of cures I have often
treated cases bordering on the psychotic, or delusional (delusions of
reference, blushing phobia, etc.), and in that way at least learned that
the same mechanisms apply extensively beyond the limits of hysteria
and obsessional neuroses. One cannot explain things to unfriendly
people. I have therefore kept to myself a good deal that I could have
said about the limitations of therapy and its mechanism, or mentioned
it in such a way as to be intelligible only to the expert. It would not
have escaped you that our cures come about through attaching the
libido reigning in the subconscious [a] (transference) which comes
about with more certainty in hysteria than elsewhere. Where this fails
the patient will not make the effort or else does not listen when we
translate his material to him. It is in essence a cure through love.

[a] *Unterbewusstsein.*

Moreover it is transference that provides the strongest proof, the only unassailable one, for the relationship of neuroses to love.

"I warmly welcome your promise to accord me provisional belief where your experience does not yet allow you to come to a decision—of course only until it does allow you to do so. I think I deserve that credit in view of my severe self-criticism, but I ask for such credit only of very few people."

Minutes of the Vienna Psycho-Analytical Society,
January 30, 1907

(*In reply to Eitingon's question whether there was such a thing as a special psychology of neuroses.*)

"This question has to be answered in a double way: yes and no. If the generally recognized psychology were correct one would need no special 'neurosis psychology.' As things are, however, one does."

To C. G. Jung, April 7, 1907

(*In answer to Jung's plea for using another word than sexual.*)

"I appreciate your motives in endeavoring to spare people 'the bite into the sour apple,' but I do not believe that you will have any success. Even were we to call the unconscious 'psychoid' it would still remain the unconscious; even if we were not to call the driving force in our broadened conception of sexuality 'libido' it would still remain the libido and every time we follow it up we should get back to the very thing from which the new nomenclature was supposed to divert us. We cannot avoid the resistances, so why not rather challenge them at once? In my opinion attack is the best defense. Perhaps you underestimate the intensity of these resistances when you hope to counter them with small concessions. What is demanded of us is after all that we deny the sexual instinct. So let us proclaim it."

To Karl Abraham, October 11, 1908

(*In the following year Bleuler and his wife, when visiting Freud in Vienna, repeated the same plea but more passionately. Freud called it a nostrum,*"[b] *and he added that neither of them was able to think of another word to replace "sexual".*)

To Karl Abraham, July 5, 1907

(*A comment on Abraham's paper contrasting hysteria with dementia praecox.*)

"(1) I have noticed that those patients who take a turn towards

* *Hausmittel.*

dementia and lose their similarity with hysterics yield their infantile sexual phantasies without any resistance, as if these have now lost their value—rather in the way a man who has decided not to marry throws away the souvenirs, ribbons and locks of hair that have now lost their value. I would furthermore connect this behavior with our conclusion that this turn essentially consists in a withdrawal of libido from sexual objects.

"(2) I have always thought that people whom we commonly call 'originals' and who later become unmistakably paranoic are those with whom the necessary development from auto-erotism to love of an object has been imperfect. With a certain number of dements this factor would therefore be the *predisposition* to later illness we have sought for. That agrees excellently with the outlook of general pathology where falling ill always signifies a regression in development (the evolution and involution of English authors)."[c]

To KARL ABRAHAM, October 21, 1907

"I am in full accord with your remarks on dementia, i.e. I have come myself to the same conclusions without being in a position to confirm them in actual material. I seldom see dements and hardly ever other severe types of psychosis. I can only repeat your words: the dementia of dementia praecox must have a different mechanism from that of senility, epilepsy, etc. What a muddle psychiatrists make out of the word is a matter of indifference. So the dementia of de mentia praecox must be capable of being resolved (*virtute*), a so called functional one. Its prototype would be the incredible momen tary stupidity we have to observe in our analyses when the piece of knowledge we are seeking has to work against great resistances. The intelligence simply won't go in the direction we want it to. With the disinclination to cathecticize objects which we assume to be operative in dementia praecox the phenomenon must naturally be on a grander scale. Another model—one which can't be used for scientific pur poses—would be the very remarkable imbecility we are accustomed to find in the arguments of our opponents, even of those who are otherwise highly intelligent. That is also only resistance.

"Now you want to examine the concept itself of "dementia" and to replace it in dementia praecox by another concept "inhibition of personality." Although such questions of definition are of little importance I cannot agree with you here. What for? No one regards "dementia" as anything but a symptom which can appear in the most

[c] Evidently referring to Hughlings Jackson.

diverse conditions. It only means that the intellect is not at the disposal of its necessary tasks. Whether that is because it isn't there, or because it is being used for some other purpose, or because this activity is forbidden, the name "dementia" tells us nothing. If anyone finds any pleasure in doing so he can so far as I am concerned say that dreams are demented; this abuse doesn't affect the mechanism that makes them demented. It is just like the case of a son who is hard up calling on his father to support him. If the father doesn't give him anything, that may be because he has nothing himself or because he doesn't like the son and won't give him anything. Up to a point that comes to the same for the son; he can starve in the one case as well as in the other.

" 'Personality,' like your Chief's[d] concept of the "ego," is a rather indefinite expression taken from surface psychology, and it doesn't contribute much to our understanding of the real processes, i.e. meta-psychologically. Only one can easily believe that by using it one has said something substantial."

To SANDOR FERENCZI, February 11, 1908

"From a theoretical point of view the case confirmed what I already knew, that in these varieties of paranoia it is a matter of the libido being detached from the homosexual component. All the women with whom she suspects her husband are really attractive to her as the result of a juvenile homosexual fixation. She struggles against this attraction and projects it on to her husband; her love for him has been strengthened by the detachment from women. Through the jealousy she then realizes in her husband her youthful ideal of incredible potency, etc."

To C. G. JUNG, February 17, 1908

"I think if some of my pupils were analyzed it would turn out that they are still waiting for the bacillus or protozoon of hysteria as confidently as the faithful do for the Messiah. It is to be hoped that then the differential diagnosis from dementia praecox will be very easy, since the parasite of hysteria should have only one rigid appendage, while dementia praecox would regularly have two and also take a different stain. Then we could leave psychology to the writers."

To C. G. JUNG, February 25, 1908

"I know that you are right when you say that I work really honestly. That is the reason why my knowledge is so piecemeal and why I am

[d] Bleuler.

mostly unable to offer any long connected presentation. I have excluded speculation as thoroughly as possible, and quite rejected any endeavor to "stop up the gaps in the universe." [e]

To C. G. JUNG, April 19, 1908
(In criticism of Jung's suggestion that the sexual aetiology of the neuroses was valid only for some cases.)
"I feel a fundamental aversion towards your suggestion that my conclusions are correct, but only for certain cases (points of view instead of conclusions). That is not very well possible. Entirely or not at all. They are concerned with such fundamental matters that they could not be valid for one set of cases only. Or rather: with such vital characteristics that one would have the right to designate those cases otherwise in which they are absent. As you know, so far no one knows anything about the supposed other kind of hysteria, dementia praecox, etc. There is only our kind or else nothing at all is known. *Au fond* you must be of the same opinion. So now I have confessed all my fanaticism!"

To KARL ABRAHAM, November 12, 1908
"The opposition against infantile sexuality confirms my opinion that the "Three Essays" represent an achievement of similar value to *The Interpretation of Dreams*."

To C. G. JUNG, November 29, 1908
"I can see that those who proclaim errors deserve well of humanity. They spur others on to find the truth, whereas those who proclaim the truth turn out to do harm inasmuch as they drive others into opposition against truth. Being original is also an aim in life."

To OSKAR PFISTER, February 9, 1909
"Lasting success in psychoanalysis certainly depends on the conjunction of two issues: the obtaining of gratification, and the mastery and sublimation of the obdurate instinct. If we generally succeed in the first respect it is for the most part because of the nature of our material: people who over a long period have been severe sufferers who do not come to a physician expecting moral elevation—often very inferior material. You on the other hand have young people with recent conflicts who are attached to you personally, and who are in a suitable state for sublimation and indeed for its most convenient form—re-

[*] An allusion to a passage in Heine's *Heimkehr*.

ligious sublimation. You do not of course doubt that in the first place your success comes about in the same way as ours, through the erotic transference to your person. But you are in the fortunate position of leading them on to God and reconstructing the conditions of earlier times, fortunate at least in the one respect that religious piety stifles neuroses. We no longer have this opportunity of settling the matter. People in general, whatever their racial origin, are irreligious—we also are mostly thoroughly irreligious—and since the other forms of sublimation through which *we* replace religion are commonly too difficult for most patients our cure generally issues in the search for gratification. Moreover, we do not see in sexual gratification anything forbidden or sinful in itself but recognize it as a valuable part of our vital activity. You know that our word 'erotic' includes what in your profession is called 'love' and is not at all restricted to gross sensual pleasure. Thus our patients have to seek in people what we are not able to promise them from the Land Above and what we have to refuse them personally. Naturally, therefore, it is much harder for us, and dissolving the transference impairs many good results.

"In itself psychoanalysis is neither religious nor the opposite, but an impartial instrument which can serve the clergy as well as the laity when it is used only to free suffering people. I have been very struck at realizing how I had never thought of the extraordinary help the psychoanalytic method can be in pastoral work, probably because wicked heretics like us are so far away from that circle.

"I hardly use the Association technique[f] at all nor do I see any advantage in it over the usual technique of 'free associations,' although this has not yet been fully described. I knew, and learn it again from your reports, that it is very valuable in refractory cases and indispensable for psychotic conditions like dementia praecox. That is because our neurotics suffer greatly and are very willing to cooperate."

To Oskar Pfister, March 18, 1909
(*A comment on a dream of one of Pfister's patients called Dietrich.*)
"The first dream runs: The girl jumped into the lake. I wanted to plunge in after her, but she held herself upright above the water and emerged quite dry.

"Dreams with this content are, as doubtless you have long known, *birth dreams*. The stork fetches children out of water. The piece of biological reality behind this is familiar to us all, hence the motive for giving this 'explanation.' To come out of water, therefore, is the same

[f] Jung's association experiments.

as being born, with the corresponding obverse: to enter water—to give birth. (Here we see a result of the insoluble connection between death and sexuality. When a poor woman wishes to escape from life she does so only by way of symbolically carrying out a sexual phantasy. She throws herself into water, i.e. she gives birth; or she leaps from a height, i.e. she drops;[g] or she poisons herself, i.e. she becomes pregnant.)

"Because of the ease of 'representation by its opposite' the symbolisms of giving birth and being born are often exchanged. In the well-known exposure myths of Sargon, Moses, Romulus, etc., the exposure in a basket or in water signifies the same as the subsequent rescuing out of the water. Both refer to birth. (Basket is box, casket, genitals, womb—from there we get to the Flood sagas.)

"In Dietrich's dream it runs that he wants to spring after the maiden who had thrown herself into the water, but she holds herself up alone and comes out of the water alone. Since this maiden is the Madonna, this trait means that he wants to help her to bear a child, but the Madonna bears the child as a virgin without any contribution from a man. Hence the allusion that follows: she is quite dry, the Immaculate Conception. The hesitation at the end of the dream, the doubt whether it is she, can only correspond to the dreamer's doubt about the Catholic doctrine, which he would like to accept, about the possibility of such an Immaculate Conception and Virgin Birth.

"Dietrich's statement that the dream was nothing new, that he had dreamed things of that kind before, agrees well with our interpretations. For it often happens that one sees a landscape in a dream and has the feeling: I have been here before. This landscape is then always the mother's genital organ, of which one can maintain more assuredly than of anywhere else that one has once been there; otherwise one would not be in the world. 'I have dreamed this dream before' has the same significance."

To Oskar Pfister, March 30, 1909
"The value of what we write must lie in the fact that it contains nothing that is accepted on the basis of authority, only what was to be offered as the result of one's own laborious work."

To Oskar Pfister, May 10, 1909
(*With regard to a silver paper weight Pfister had sent him.*)
"The Matterhorn now covers the unanswered letters on my writing

[g] *kommt nieder.*

desk. I am glad to accept the little fragment of Switzerland in the symbolic sense you intended, as a homage of the only country where I feel I possess something and know of strong and good men on my side. I am not thinking of defending myself. I have purposely allowed my personality to appear only as an example, never as a model, let alone as someone to be venerated.

"It is easy to give the Matterhorn another and less exalted meaning. The scale of 1:50,000 is about the same as the proportion in which our wishes get fulfilled or our resolutions carried out. By the way, it has struck me how little numbers mean to us. I find it extremely hard to believe that one only has to pile up 50,000 of such little blocks to reach the height of a giant mountain; I should have guessed it would take more than a million. I will mention yet a third signification of the Matterhorn. It reminds me of a remarkable man who visited me one day, a true servant of God, the very idea of whose existence seemed to me highly unlikely: that is of a man who has to bestow spiritual gifts on everyone he meets. So you did me good as well. After our talk I asked myself why ever I was not *really* happy, and I soon found the answer. I renounced the infeasible plan of becoming rich by honest means and decided not to replace a patient who had left; since then I have been well and cheerful and see how right your advice was. I have kept to this decision three times since then. Without your visit and your influence I should never have been able to do so; my own father complex, as Jung would call it, i.e. the impulse to correct my father, would never have allowed it."

To Karl Abraham, May 23, 1909

"I was familiar with your conclusion about agoraphobia being traceable to the spatial impressions of infancy; it is certainly important. The specific feature of claustrophobia seems to be ambitious phantasies that have vanished."

To C. G. Jung, June 18, 1909
(Commenting on difficulties that occur in analytic work.)

"I beg you not to react too strongly with contrition. Think of Lassalle's excellent analogy of the test-tube that breaks in the chemist's hand. 'With a slight frown at the obduracy of matter the research worker goes on with his work.' Small laboratory explosions cannot be avoided from the very nature of the material with which we work. Perhaps one has really not held the test-tube at the right angle or has heated it too quickly. One learns in this way which is at fault, the danger in the material or the handling of it."

To Oskar Pfister, July 12, 1909
(*In reply to some information about earlier writers.*)

"I am really very ignorant about my predecessors. If we ever meet up above they will certainly greet me ill as a plagiarist. But it is such a pleasure to investigate the thing itself [h] instead of reading the literature about it."

To Oskar Pfister, August 16, 1909

"Do you really want me to intrude on your plans of work with some advice? You needn't follow it, if other motives gain the upper hand. I regard the connection with the Prize as something quite irrelevant. If it doesn't hold you up, take the chance; if it disturbs you drop it. But complete the work itself straight away and not after years. Like the saying: *Jung gefreit hat nie gereut.*[1] Only the first impulse will give you the ardor and freshness of conception. If you continue to work you will in a few years think differently and more correctly about many things, will put individual problems in the foreground and divine deeper connections, but then you will speak a language intelligible only to our little group and therefore will make no impression on the large majority, whereas now in your transition from the common to the psychoanalytical mode of thought you will have the subjective power of carrying with you the uninitiated. I think that is what you want to do, and to stimulate is also something that matters."

Minutes of the Vienna Psycho-Analytical Society, November 10, 1909

"Dream symbols that do not find any support in myths, fairy tales, popular usages, etc., should be regarded as doubtful."

Minutes of the Vienna Psycho-Analytical Society, November 17, 1909
(*Discussion on the value of pediatric work for the verification of psychoanalytical theories.*)

"We expect it would turn out that the severe neuroses all have their prototypes in childhood life, so that we should find the kernels of the later neuroses in the disturbances of development in childhood. That is quite evident with, for example, the obsessional neurotics. This neu-

[h] *das Ding selbst zu befragen.*
[1] Happy is the wooing that's not long in the doing.

rosis is almost mono-symptomatically concentrated on one point at the age of six to eight, and is already completely formed. It is a question whether everybody has not passed through a kind of elementary neurosis in childhood years, and whether the inter-relationship be not still closer than we imagine, so that not only the elements but the very prototype itself originates in childhood. The later neurosis may well be only a magnification of a product, which one can only call a neurosis, of the later or middle years of childhood. In that event we should have a clear view of the source of neuroses and should have to interpolate the 'elementary neurosis' as an intermediate stage between the nuclear complex [j] and the subsequent severe neurosis. The pediatrist should be able to distinguish the layers of a neurosis that are psychically determined from the nucleus dating from the earliest years of life; furthermore, how much of this nucleus is to be attributed to development and how much to heredity. It may perhaps turn out that something else lies behind everything that is psychically determined.

"The objection that the hysteria of childhood appears to have no 'reminiscences' [k] behind it was brought forward also by Jung. Two points, however, are neglected here:

"(1) In a childhood hysteria occurring between six and eight we have no right at all to underestimate the previous history, since the decisive impressions occur in the years between two and four. The shortness of the period elapsing since these reminiscences is compensated by the magnitude of the changes that occur rapidly at this time of life.

"(2) If we assume that there is no repression without an organic kernel, then this organic repression must reside in the replacement of pleasurable sensations by unpleasurable ones. It is likely that man's assumption of an upright posture was one of the fundamental conditions of neurosis; the sense of smell was drawn towards repression because of being valueless. That is also the way in which the repression of coprophilic tendencies begins; the bigger the child gets the farther away is it from the ground. In this organic repression the psychical plays no part as yet; the replacement of pleasurable sensations by unpleasurable through repression may be regarded as a step in cultural advance. This repression makes possible an hysteria in earliest infancy, indeed even in an animal. . . . The whole theory of neurosis is in-

[j] I.e. the Oedipus complex.
[k] As in Freud's well-known dictum "hysteria consists of reminiscences."

complete so long as we have no more light on the organic kernel of repression.

"In the matter of anxiety one has to remember that children begin their experience of it in the act of birth itself. It is also noteworthy that every affect manifests itself originally as an hysterical attack. It is only a reminiscence of an event. Thus the pediatrist should be able to enlighten us about the origin of affects. Most children have a trauma. After it they behave like hysterics. I refer to the weaning from the breast, and this has to be taken into account as a significant psychical trauma to the pleasure of the nutritional impulse. . . . Such children can, for instance, come to dislike milk.

"The technique of this child study has not such poor prospects as it might seem. One will have to make use of an intelligent nurse (in specially favorable cases, of the mother herself) who will observe the child continuously and report anything of note—rather like the indirect observation of psychotic patients.

"The investigation of childhood life will for some time yet be dominated by the knowledge we gain from adults. But that is not the ideal state of affairs.

"The treatment of nervous disorders in children will always encounter one great difficulty: the parents' neuroses which will build a wall around the child's neurosis."

To C. G. Jung, November 21, 1909
(*With regard to "chimney sweeping," Anna O's term for the cathartic procedure.*)
"The reason why a chimney sweep is supposed to bring good luck is that sweeping a chimney is an unconscious symbol of coitus, which is something of which Breuer certainly never dreamed."

To C. G. Jung, December 2, 1909
"It will interest you to hear that we have become acceptable to the *Dürerbund*.[1] In this year's Christmas catalogue they have reviewed my publications at length and warmly recommended them: in such a turgid and unintelligible style, it is true, that my young daughter Sophie could say: 'It is good that you know what you are after, for you would never guess it from that.' Anyhow, according to Heller,

[1] *Dürerbund fähig.* The *Dürerbund* was a highly reputable book society which also published a review periodical.

such appreciation from the *Dürerbund* signifies great progress in the good opinion of the German nation.

"So now Germany is coming along! Aren't we (justifiably) childish to be so pleased with every little bit of recognition, when after all it doesn't in the least matter and moreover it is so certain that the final acceptance of our ideas by the world still lies in an indefinite future?"

To C. G. Jung, December 19, 1909
(*In reply to an objection of Jung's to Freud's clinical terminology—in this case, "omnipotence of thoughts"—which he feared would become permanently embedded in the nomenclature because of Freud'ʀ writings attaining the status of a gospel.*)

"Your surmise that after my departure my errors might be adored as holy relics amused me enormously, but I don't believe it. On the contrary, I think my followers will hasten to demolish as swiftly aʀ possible everything that is not safe and sound in what I leave behind, In psychoanalysis things often happen in an opposite fashion to the way they do elsewhere. Since presumably you will have the lion's share in this liquidation I will try to rescue some of the tenets that your doubts call in question."

To Sandor Ferenczi, January 10, 1910
(*In answer to a question of whether a man should relate his previous sexual experiences to his wife.*)

"That the sexual life of a man can be different from that of a woman surely belongs to the A B C of our conception of life, and it is only a mark of respect when one does not conceal this from her. Whether the demand of absolute truthfulness may not sin against practical considerations and against the aims of love itself I should not like to answer with an absolute negative. Truth is only the absolute goal of science, but love is a goal of life quite independent of it and conflicts between the two great powers are very well conceivable. I do not see any necessity for regularly subordinating one to the other as a matter of principle.

"I was for personal reasons very interested in the explanation of your medical tendencies in your dream analysis. I lack that passion for helping and I see now why; it is because I never lost any loved person in my early youth. The same personal motivation as with you I found with Fliess. The strong features of his personality, as well as the pathological, came from it. The conviction that his father, who died of erysipelas after suffering for many years from nasal suppuration, could have been saved was what made him into a doctor, and indeed into a rhinologist. The sudden death of his only sister two years later, on the second day of a pneumonia for which he could not make the doctor responsible, led—as a consolation—to the fatalistic theory of predestined lethal dates. This piece of analysis, very unwelcome to him, was the real reason for the break between us which he engineered in such a pathological (paranoic) fashion. . . .

"I will present you with some theory that has occurred to me while reading your analysis. It seems to me that in our influencing of the sexual impulses we cannot achieve anything other than exchanges and displacements, never renunciation, relinquishment or the resolution of a complex (Strictly secret!). When someone brings out his infantile complexes he has saved a part of them (the affect) in a current form (transference). He has shed a skin and leaves it for the analyst. God forbid that he should now be naked, without a skin! [m] Our therapeutic gain is a barter, as in the *Hans im Glück*[n] story. The last piece falls into the well only with death itself. The theoretical value of this conception lies in its approach to the processes of dementia praecox. Fortunately it has little practical value.

To Oskar Pfister, January 10, 1910

"All repressions operate on *memories*, not on experiences; the latter are at most repressed only in consequence. With the use of the word 'complex' one needs to be very cautious. However indispensable the concept may be for various manipulations and demonstrations, when it is a matter of theory one should be constantly concerned about what is concealed behind it and not be content with the word. It is surely too vague and inadequate."

To Ernest Jones, January 11, 1910 *

"In the matter of left-handedness I should be rather inclined to regard the organic factor as the primary one, not the psychical, but I have no proper judgement about it all."

To Sandor Ferenczi, February 13, 1910

"I have suddenly found in a case of erythrophobia ° an unsuspected old coprophilic instinct and think that is just as significant for this symptom as the pleasure in smell is for fetishism."

[m] The skin is evidently the transference.
* The Hans in Luck in Grimm's *Household Tales.*
° Nowadays called ereutophobia.

To Sandor Ferenczi, February 25, 1910

"I don't know why Putnam makes such high demands on psychoanalytic therapy, even after only three months of treatment. Surely he cannot have been spoiled by the success of earlier methods."

To Oskar Pfister, March 17, 1910

"I have, as you agree, done much to show the importance of love. My experience, however, does not confirm your view that it is at the basis of everything unless you add hate to it; which is psychologically correct. But then that at once gives a gloomy look to the world."

To Oskar Pfister, May 2, 1910

"What you term 'Compensation' I include under the concept of 'Sublimation' or the similar but clearer one of 'Reaction-formation.' "

To Oskar Pfister, June 5, 1910

"As for the transference it is altogether a curse. The intractable and fierce impulses in the illness, on account of which I renounced both indirect and hypnotic suggestion, cannot be altogether abolished even through psychoanalysis; they can only be restrained, and what remains expresses itself in the transference. That is often a considerable amount. The analytic rules fail us; one has to adapt oneself to the individuality of the patient and keep some personal note of one's own. In general I agree with Stekel that the patient should be kept in a state of abstinence, of unrequited love, and that is not always entirely possible. The more affection you allow him the more readily you reach his complexes, but the less the definite result since he disposes of the previous gratification in his complexes by exchanging them for what he experiences in the transference. The therapeutic result is very good, but it is quite dependent on the transference. One perhaps achieves a cure, but not the necessary degree of independence or a guarantee against relapse. It is easier for you in this respect than for us physicians, because you sublimate the transference on to religion and ethics, and that is not easy with seriously ill people."

To C. G. Jung, July 5, 1910

"I am more and more persuaded of the cultural value of psychoanalysis, and I could wish for someone bright enough to draw from it the legitimate inferences for philosophy and for social life. My impression is—but perhaps it is only the projection of my own jaded mood at present—that we are for the time being held up and are awaiting a fresh impetus. But I am not impatient."

To Oskar Pfister, July 19, 1910

"In the earlier catharsis the transference was a matter of course. It is like the omnipresence of the Divine Being. Present Herr P. and Frau A. Besides them the Almighty is also looking on, but that is obvious, so He is not mentioned. Difficulties arise only when the transference is hostile. . . .

"Your idea of polarization is excellent. I call it a defusion of opposites, in which several impulses are usually represented. It is as if the cook had put all the sugar in one corner of the dough and all the salt in another. Naturally it is all up with the taste."

To C. G. Jung, October 1, 1910

"I notice that you have the same way of working as I have: to be on the look out in whatever direction you feel drawn and not take the obvious straightforward path. I think that is the best way too, since one is astonished later to find how directly those circuitous routes led to the right goal."

To Oskar Pfister, November 6, 1910

"I am entirely in accord with your treating with suspicion every new symbol you hear of until your experience forces it on you. I do the same in regard to Stekel. But the best tool of psychoanalysis is still a knowledge of the peculiar idioticon [1] of the unconscious."

To Ernest Jones, November 20, 1910

(In reply to a suggestion that scopophilia (visual curiosity) is only a part of a wider group in which other sense organs should be included.)

"As for the sexual components, the *Schaulust* and *Exhibitionismus* are only given as samples and you are free to add the other sexual interests to the list, subsuming the whole of these tendencies in an *Erkenntnistrieb* [p] when you remember that *Erkennen* means *Coitiren* in the Bible ('and Adam knew his wife')."

To Sandor Ferenczi, December 6, 1910

"Imagine that we were back again in Palermo and that I was giving you one morning in the Hotel de France the following contribution

[p] Search for Knowledge.

to the notes on paranoia. For I have now overcome a mistake which
at that time held me up and can announce the following simple formulation:

"Let us divide up *Repression* into

(a) *Fixation*; (b) *The repression proper*; (c) *Return (Break-through)*.
(You are familiar with the meaning of these terms.) Then we get the
main statement:

I. *The Break-through occurs at the point of fixation.*

   That you know already. (But it was not clear.) The obscurity
   lay in the relation between the repression and the break-through.
   I had assumed the same mechanism and that was misleading.

II. *The Mechanism of the Break-through is independent of that of
    the Repression.* And now the third.

III. *The Mechanism of the Break-through depends on the Develop-
     ment of the Ego, that of the Repression on the Phase of the
     Libido.*

   "If that proves to be true let us slaughter a hundred oxen in
   spite of the meat shortage. It would work out so well. Hoche,
   Friedländer, Oppenheim, etc. on the Ara of the Hieron which we
   have seen.[q]

To ERNEST JONES, January 22, 1911

(*Anent my work* On the Nightmare.)

"I only want to remark to you as I did to Jung at Christmas-time
that we are to withstand the big temptation to settle down in our
colonies, where we cannot be but strangers, distinguished visitors, and
have to revert every time to our native country in medicine, where we
find the root of our powers."

To C. G. JUNG, April 4, 1911

"I have just read Silberer's paper. . . . I have to admit that only
now does the idea of the 'functional phenomenon' seem to be
proven, and I shall in future take it into account in interpreting
dreams. After all it is in essence nothing other than my 'endopsychic
perception.' "

To OSKAR PFISTER, May 28, 1911

"I quite understand why we all attach so little value to appearing
at Congresses. It is scarcely possible to have a public debate on psycho-

[q] An allusion to the Greek sacrificial altars they had recently seen together
in Sicily.

analysis; one has no common ground and there is nothing to be done against the lurking emotions. The movement is concerned with the depths, and debates about it must remain as unsuccessful as the theological disputations at the time of the Reformation."

To Ernest Jones, June 25, 1911

(In reply to a suggestion that the feeling of conviction of free will being stronger with unimportant acts could be correlated with the peculiar use the unconscious makes of unimportant mental material, e.g. in the formation of dreams.)

"Your remark on the feeling of conviction in small things and the relation of the unconscious to these trifles is quite just and very clever."

To C. G. Jung, October 13, 1911

"I do not doubt your interpretation of G.[r] and Gabani as a human being and gross sensuality respectively. It is striking that the conception of such pairs consisting of one noble and one common partner (mostly brothers) is a recurring motif in legends and literature. The last great descendant of the type is Don Quixote with his Sancho Panza (i.e. Paunch). Of mythological figures there occur to me the Dioscuri (one mortal, the other immortal) and any number of pairs of brothers and twins of which Romulus and Remus will serve as an example. Always one of them is the weaker and dies before the other. This ancient motif of an unequal pair of brothers serves in the Gilgamesch saga to represent a man's relationship to his libido.

"These old motifs were constantly re-interpreted (at last also in an astronomical sense), but where do they originally come from? It is not hard to see that the weaker twin who dies first is the after-birth, simply for the reason that it is regularly born with the child by the same mother. This interpretation we heard months ago from a modern mythologist quite ignorant of psychoanalysis, who for once forgot his science and therefore had a good idea. But you can read in Frazer's *Golden Bough*, Vol. I, in how many primitive peoples the placenta is still today called the *brother* or the *twin* and correspondingly treated, fed and cared for—which naturally does not last long. If there is a phylogenetic memory, which unfortunately will soon prove to be so, then the uncanniness of 'doubles'[s] has also this source.

"I only wanted to surprise you by saying that fundamentally Gabani

---

[r] Gilgamesh.

[s] *Doppelgänger.*

is the after-birth of Gilgamesh. There are all sorts of other surmises and connections here. What a pity that we can work together only in this fashion."

To SANDOR FERENCZI, November 17, 1911

"I believe you are suffering a little from the fear of complexes, which has got connected with Jung's complex-mythology. One should not try to eradicate one's complexes, but come to terms with them; they are the legitimate guiding forces of one's behavior in the world."

To C. G. JUNG, November 30, 1911

"I have misgivings about the way in which Frl. Spielrein tries to subordinate the psychological material to biological criteria; this dependence is just as objectionable as that on philosophy, physiology or cerebral anatomy. Psychoanalysis *fara da sè*[t] will make out on its own."

To C. G. JUNG, December 7, 1911

"I will meet your wish that I should explain my objection to exploiting mythological material at its surface value by quoting the example I had used in the discussion in our Society. Frl. Spielrein had made use of the story that in Genesis the woman appears as the seductress of the man by giving him the apple to eat. Now the myth in Genesis is probably a miserable, tendentious distortion by a priest's apprentice[u] who, as we know now, condensed in a quite witless fashion (as in a dream) two independent sources into one account. It is not impossible that the two sacred trees are there because he found *one* tree in each of his sources. The creation of Eve has something about it that is quite peculiar and singular. Rank recently suggested to me that a reversal could easily have been brought about in the myth. That would make the matter clear: Eve would be the mother from whom Adam was born, and we should then encounter the mother-incest so familiar to us, the punishment of which, and so on. Equally strange is the feature of the woman giving the man something to eat of a fertilizing nature (pomegranate). On the contrary, in its reversed form it is again something well-known: that the man gives a woman fruit to eat is an old marriage ceremony (i.e. the way in which Proserpine has to stay in Hades as Pluto's wife).

"In the light of these considerations I should maintain that the

[t] Will make good by itself.
[u] *Priesterlehrbub.*

manifest forms of mythological themes cannot without further investigation be used for purposes of comparison with our psychoanalytical conclusions. One has first to ascertain their latent original forms by tracing them back through historical comparative work so as to eliminate the distortions that have come about in the course of the development of the myth."

To ERNEST JONES, January 14, 1912*
(*In reply to a question whether he regarded the pleasure principle and the reality principle as distinct in nature, or, as I supposed, the latter only an extension of the former.*)
"Your question about the relation of the pleasure principle to the reality principle is answered in the paper itself in agreement to what you yourself suppose. The reality principle is only continuing the work of the pleasure principle in a more effectual way, gratification being the aim of both and their opposition only a secondary fact. Yet I am sure this paper of mine will produce much hesitation and wants a better thorough-going exposition. I was very much amused at your finding out my quotation from Shaw, as it was pointed directly to you as an indirect means of expressing my thanks to the giver."

To SANDOR FERENCZI, February 1, 1912
"As for your Chanticleer[2] it is simply delightful and will have a great future. You surely do not believe that I would confiscate it for myself; that would be too low of me. Only don't publish it until 'The Infantile Return of Totemism' is ready and I will quote it there. I hope you will still be able to fill the gap of whether the threat of castration happened *before* or *after* the adventure. That is very important. I have been thinking on the same lines as you about the theme of castration. We should greatly like to know whether the jealous Old Man of the Horde in Darwin's primordial family really used to castrate the young males before the time when he was content with simply chasing them away."

To SANDOR FERENCZI, March 18, 1912
"We must talk over at Easter your very interesting news of hypochondria. What I am sending you today is only a statement of the point of view I have held up to now: I have always felt the obscurity in the question of hypochondria to be a disgraceful gap in our work. The problem has seemed to me to be: characterization through a special organic source or in a special process. Influenced by my knowledge

of the obsessional neurosis I have opted for the latter, while you pre-fer the former. I thought of the process constituting hypochondria as the third 'actual neurosis,' so that it would be the somatic basis of paraphrenia just as the anxiety neurosis is that of hysteria. I thus take into account the erotogenic contributions from bodily organs which have got attached to the ego instead of to the general libido, but with a negative prefix.[v] Nothing consistent, however, has come of these thoughts, and I am not going to force things that won't fit together of themselves."

To SANDOR FERENCZI, April 21, 1912
(*In response to the request for advice.*)

"I am writing not to answer your question, since the dilemma you report does not allow any intrusion other than giving urgent advice, and I can't bring myself to do that. That is assuredly not because of any lack of sympathy, but from respect for another person's rights and from my concern lest our friendship get coupled with something else, undefinable."

To KARL ABRAHAM, June 3, 1912
"I have read your Egyptian study[3] with the pleasure I always derive from your way of writing and thinking, and I should like only to make two suggestions. I see you maintain that when a mother is specially prominent the conflict with the father assumes milder forms; I myself have no evidence for this and must assume you have had special ex-perience. Since I do not find the statement convincing I will ask you to revise it. In the second place, I have misgivings about presenting the King so definitely as a neurotic. It stands in sharp contrast with his extraordinary energy and achievement, and we associate the con-cept, which has become vague as a scientific term, rather with the idea of someone inhibited. We all have these complexes and must be careful not to call everybody neurotic. When we have fought against our complexes we ought to be spared the name. Perhaps your work would not lose anything if you designated it as a character study and keep neurotics in the background for the purpose of comparison. My knowledge of the literature does not enable me to judge the evidence for really neurotic symptoms in Amenhotep IV. If you have any you should quote it fully."

[v] I.e. unpleasurable instead of pleasurable.

To Ernest Jones, August 1, 1912

"The true historical source of repression I hope to touch on in the last of the four papers, but I may as well give you the answer now. Any internal—(damn my English)—*Jede innere Verdrängungsschranke ist der historische Erfolg eines äusseren Hindernisses. Also. Verinnerlichung der Widerstände, die Geschichte der Menschheit niedergelegt in ihren heute angeborenen Verdrängungsneigungen.*" [*]

To Sandor Ferenczi, October 20, 1912

"I have answered Maeder's letter as sharply and honestly as possible, and am curious to see what effect it will have. I don't think anything good comes of concessions and compromises. None of that matters; completing our work is the important thing. These fights, however, are good for that purpose; they keep one tense. Success always has a somewhat numbing effect; commotion on all sides provides as favourable conditions as did my earlier isolation."

To Sandor Ferenczi, February 10, 1913

"I have always thought that sexual physiology lies behind the 'actual neuroses' just as ego-psychology lies behind paraphrenia."

To Sandor Ferenczi, February 14, 1913

"I should like to criticize one point in your essay,[4] which seems to me the best and most important contribution you have made to psychoanalysis. In your discussion of the delicate question of the specific factors determining the choice of neurosis you associate the *content* of a neurosis with the stage in the development of the libido. Can one say that? Is it really the content? Surely what you mean is the *kind* of erotic impulse."

Minutes of the Vienna Psycho-Analytical Society, December 10, 1913 (A *discussion of Schizophrenia.*)

"The complex found behind the symptoms should not be mistaken for the cause of the disease. What is evident in dementia praecox is the withdrawal of the libido from external objects, hence the impossibility of a transference therapy. But this withdrawal is only partial

---

[*] Every *internal* barrier of repression is the historical result of an *external* obstruction. Thus: the opposition is incorporated within; the history of mankind is deposited in the present-day inborn tendencies to repression.

One can divine the mechanism of dementia praecox from the study of paranoia, from which the following statements appear probable:

"(1) The aetiology is the same as that of the other neuroses.

"(2) The apparent resemblance to other neuroses is far-reaching. The patients first react by the slighter methods of repression; then individual traits of dementia or paranoia get added to the neurotic ones.

"(3) Characteristic is the withdrawal of the libido on to the ego.

"(4) The division of the symptoms into three groups: the manifestations of regression; those of restitution; and those that remain at the end."

To Ernest Jones, March 25, 1914*

(This relates to Freud's writing "Jones's gospel" for Jung's gospel," a mistake he corrected in the letter.)

"Now my interesting 'Verschreiben' may have aroused your suspicion. But you remember I did not try to conceal it but even called your attention to it. . . . It is a common trick of my unconscious to supplant a person disliked by a better one (see the first dream on 'Irma's Injection'). It is equivalent to the thought: Why can he not be like you. It is veiled tenderness. You remember perhaps after the Munich Congress I could never utter the name 'Jung' but had to replace it by 'Jones.' "

To Karl Abraham, June 5, 1914

"I read your paper for the *Jahrbuch*[5] yesterday and will allow myself to congratulate you. In my opinion it is the best clinical contribution that has appeared in the whole five volumes: unrivalled in sureness, accuracy, wide range and interest. *Vivant sequentes.*"

To Karl Abraham, December 21, 1914

"The only thing that is progressing satisfactorily is my work, which in fact is, in spite of pauses, leading to worth-while new ideas and explanations. Recently I succeeded in defining the characteristics of the systems of Cs and Ucs[x] which makes them almost tangible, and with the help of which I think one can discern a simple solution of the relation of dementia praecox to reality. The system Ucs is composed of the cathexes of material objects: the system Cs corresponds to the association of these unconscious ideas with *verbal* ideas, and this makes them able to become conscious. Repression in the trans-

* Consciousness and unconscious.

ference neuroses consists in the withdrawal of libido from the system Cs, i.e. in detachment of the concepts of objects from those of words; repression in the narcissistic neuroses[y] signifies the withdrawal of libido from the unconscious ideas of objects—naturally a far more profound disturbance. So dementia praecox produces changes in language and in general treats the concepts of words just as hysteria treats those of objects; i.e. they subordinate them to the 'primary process' with condensation, displacement, discharge, etc."

To Oskar Pfister, October 9, 1918

"I have just read your little book[6] and quite believe you when you say that you wrote it gladly. I rejoice in its warmth. It displays all the fine attributes we value in you: your enthusiasm, your love for truth and for humanity, the courageous way in which you profess your opinions, your understanding and also—your optimism. It will without doubt render our cause good service. I mention this practical point, although, as you know, I don't attach much value to it.

"Now, praise is always short; strictures have to take longer. I am dissatisfied with one point: your contradicting my sexual theory and my ethics. I grant you the latter; ethics is far from my interest and you are a pastor. I don't cudgel my brains much about good and evil, but I have not found much 'good' in the average human being. Most of them are in my experience riff-raff, whether they loudly proclaim this or that ethical doctrine or none at all. That you cannot say out loud, perhaps not even think it, although your experience of life could hardly have been different from mine. If we must speak of ethics I admit to having a high ideal, from which most people I know sadly deviate.

"But when it comes to the sexual theory whatever makes you dispute the resolving of the sexual instinct into partial instincts to which our analysis compels us every day? Your contrary arguments are really not strong. Don't you see that the multiplicity of instincts goes back to the multiplicity of erotogenic organs? Fundamentally they all strive to find some expression in the future organism. And has the fact that all organs have combined into a living unity and that they influence, sustain and inhibit one another—even being dependent on one another in their development—prevented anatomy from studying and describing them separately; or prevented therapy from attacking an individual organ which has become the main seat of a pathological process? It is possible that internal therapy often forgets all this cor-

[y] I.e. psychoses.

relation of the organs; psychoanalysis is concerned with keeping in mind the inter-relation of instinctual life beyond the distinction between the partial instincts. In science one has first to take things apart and then put them together. It seems to me that you want to make a synthesis without a previous analysis (in psycho-analytic technique there is no need for any special synthetic work; the individual himself sees to that better than we could).

"That holds good for all instincts in so far as we can separate them. In your book you have not done full justice to the sexual instincts. You have nowhere said that these really differ from others in having a more intimate connection with, and a greater significance for—*not mental life in general, and this is what matters, the pathogenesis of neuroses.* This comes from their conservative nature, their intimate connection with the unconscious and with the pleasure-principle, and further the peculiarities of their development into a cultural norm.

"From a therapeutic point of view I can only envy your opportunity of bringing about sublimation into religion. But the beauty of religion assuredly has no place in psycho-analysis. Naturally our paths in therapy diverge here, and it can stay at that. Quite by the way, how comes it that none of the godly ever devised psychoanalysis and that one had to wait for a godless Jew?"

FROM OSKAR PFISTER, October 29, 1918 [z]

"As to your question why none of the godly discovered psychoanalysis, but only a godless Jew. Well, because piety is not the same as the genius for discovering, and because the godly were for a great part not worthy to bring such an achievement to fruition. Moreover, in the first place you are not a Jew, which my boundless admiration for Amos, Isaiah, the author of Job and the Prophets makes me greatly regret, and in the second place you are not so godless, since he who lives for truth lives in God and he who fights for the freeing of love 'dwelleth in God' (First Epistle of John, IV, 16). If you were to become aware of and experience your interpolation in the great universals which for me are as inevitable as the synthesis of the notes of a Beethoven symphony are to a musician I should say of you 'There never was a better Christian.' "

[z] Also quoted on p. 199.

Chronology

September 1901—Freud visits Rome for first time, accompanied by Alexander Freud.

September 1902—Freud visits Naples, Sorrento, Capri, with Alexander Freud.

October 1902—Initiation of "Psychological Wednesday Society." (Name changed to Vienna Psycho-Analytical Society in April 1908.)

1903—Paul Federn and Wilhelm Stekel commence practice of psychoanalysis.

1904—Publication of *The Psychopathology of Everyday Life.*

First application of psychoanalytic method by a foreigner: A. Stegmann, of Dresden.

September 1904—Freud visits Athens, with Alexander Freud.

Eugen Bleuler begins correspondence with Freud.

1904-1906—Swoboda-Fliess priority dispute.

1905—Publication of *Three Essays on the Theory of Sexuality,* Dora Analysis, *Jokes and Their Relation to the Unconscious.*

Edward Hitschmann, Ernest Jones and August Stärcke commence practice of psychoanalysis.

September 1905—Freud visits Italian lakes, with Minna Bernays.

April 1906—C. G. Jung begins correspondence with Freud.

January 1907—Max Eitingon visits Freud, first foreigner to do so.

March 1907—Jung visits Freud, accompanied by Binswanger.

May 1907—Publication of *Delusion and Dreams in Jensen's "Gradiva."*

September 1907—Jung founds Freud Society in Zurich.

Freud visits Florence and Rome, with Minna Bernays.

December 1907—Karl Abraham visits Freud.

February 1908—Sandor Ferenczi visits Freud.

March 1908—Freud acquires citizenship of Vienna.

April 1908—First International Psycho-Analytical Congress, Salzburg.

A. A. Brill and Ernest Jones visit Freud.

Freud expands living accommodations; destroys correspondence.

August 1908—Karl Abraham founds Berlin Society.

September 1908—Freud visits half-brothers in England.

Spends four days with Jung in Burghölzi.

1909—Freud founds *Jahrbuch der Psychoanalyse.*

February 1909—Marriage of Freud's eldest daughter, Mathilde.

April 1909—*Pfarrer* Pfister visits Freud.

September 1909—Lectures at Clark University, Worcester. Freud meets Stanley Hall, William James and J. J. Putnam.

April 1910—Nuremberg Congress. Founding of International Psycho-Analytical Association.

May 1910—Freud is made Honorary Member of American Psychopathological Association.

June 1910—Publication of *Leonardo da Vinci and a Memory of his Childhood.*

August 1910—Holiday at Noordwijk.

September 1910—Freud visits Paris, Florence, Rome, Naples and Sicily, with Ferenczi.

October 1910—Freud founds *Zentral-blatt für Psychoanalyse.*

1910-1912—*Three Contributions to the Psychology of Love.*

January 1911—Freud is made Honorary Member of Society for Psychical Research.

February 1911—A. A. Brill founds New York Society.

May 1911—Ernest Jones founds American Psychoanalytic Association.

June 1911—Alfred Adler resigns from Vienna Society.

September 1911—Freud spends four days with Jung at Küsnacht.
Weimar Congress takes place.

January 1912—Freud founds *Imago.*

April 1912—Freud visits Arbe, with Ferenczi.

May 1912—Freud stays with Binswanger at Kreuzlingen.

June 1912—Ernest Jones founds "Committee."

September 1912—Freud visits Rome, with Ferenczi.

October 1912—Wilhelm Stekel resigns from Vienna Society.

November 1912—Meeting with Jung and others in Munich.

December 1912—First book on psychoanalysis published in English.

1912-1915—Essay on *Technique.*

1913—Publication of *Totem and Taboo.*

January 1913—Freud founds *Zeitschrift für Psychoanalyse.*
Marriage of Freud's second daughter, Sophie.

March 1913—Freud visits Venice, with Anna Freud.

May 1913—Sandor Ferenczi founds Budapest Society.

September 1913—Munich Congress.
Freud visits Rome, with Minna Bernays.

October 1913—Jung breaks off relations with Freud.
Ernest Jones founds London Society.

December 1913—Freud visits daughter Sophie in Hamburg (also in September 1914 and 1915).

March 1914—*History of the Psycho-Analytical Movement.*

April 1914—Freud visits Brioni, with Ferenczi and Rank.
Jung resigns presidency of International Association.

August 1914—Jung resigns as member of International Association.

September 1914—Dresden Congress postponed.

November 1914—Death of Emmanuel Freud.

March-June 1915—Twelve essays on *Metapsychology.*

July-August 1916—Holiday in Gastein and Salzburg.

1916-1917—Freud gives University lectures for last time.

July-August 1917—Holiday in Tatra, Slovakia.

July-September 1918—Holiday in Tatra, Slovakia.

Summer, 1918—Von Freund founds *Verlag* publishing firm.

September 1918—Budapest Congress.

December 1918—Death of J. J. Putnam.

Short Title Index

Anf.   Marie Bonaparte, Anna Freud, Ernst Kris (eds.), *Aus den An-fängen der Psychoanalyse*. London: Imago, 1950.

Auto.   Freud, *An Autobiographical Study*. Translated by James Strachey. London: Hogarth, 1935.

C.   *Zentralblatt für Pychoanalyse*. Wiesbaden: J. F. Bergmann.

C.P.   Freud, *Collected Papers*. 5 vols. London: Hogarth, 1924-1950.

G.S.   Freud, *Gesammelte Schriften*. 12 vols. Vienna: Internationaler Psychoanalytischer Verlag, 1925-1934.

G.W.   Freud, *Gesammelte Werke*. 18 vols. London: Imago, 1940-1952.

I.   *Imago*. Vienna: Internationaler Psychoanalytischer Verlag.

I.J.   *International Journal of Psycho-Analysis*. London: Baillière, Tindall and Cox.

I.Z.   *Internationale Zeitschrift für Psychoanalyse*. Vienna: Internationaler Psychoanalytischer Verlag.

J.   *Jahrbuch für psychoanalytische und psychopathologische Forschungen*. Leipzig and Vienna: Franz Deuticke.

Minutes   Minutes of the Vienna Psycho-Analytical Society, 1906-1915.

Origins   Marie Bonaparte, Anna Freud, Ernst Kris (eds.), *The Origins of Psycho-Analysis*. Translated by Eric Mosbacher and James Strachey. New York: Basic Books, 1954.

S.E.   James Strachey (ed.), *The Standard Edition of the Complete Psychological Works of Sigmund Freud*. 24 vols. London: Hogarth and The Institute of Psycho-Analysis, 1953—.

Vol. I   Ernest Jones, *The Life and Work of Sigmund Freud*, Vol. I. New York: Basic Books, 1953.

Ab.   Letter from Freud to Karl Abraham.

Eit.   Letter from Freud to Max Eitingon.

E.J.   Letter from Freud to Ernest Jones.

Fer.   Letter from Freud to Sandor Ferenczi.

Jg.   Letter from Freud to C. G. Jung.

M.   Letter from Freud to Martha Freud.

Pf.   Letter from Freud to Oskar Pfister.

References to letters which Freud wrote in English are marked with an asterisk.

Reference Notes

CHAPTER 1

EMERGENCE FROM ISOLATION

[1] *On Aphasia,* E. Stengel, Trans. (New York: International Universities Press, 1953).

[2] *Anf.,* p. 340; *Origins,* p. 318.

[3] *G.W.,* X, 60; *S.E.,* XIV.

[4] *Auto.,* p. 87.

[5] W. Stekel, "Coitus im Kindesalter," *Wiener Medizinische Blätter,* April 18, 1895, pp. 242–44.

[6] *G.W.,* I, 444; *S.E.,* I.

[7] *The Autobiography of Wilhelm Stekel* (New York: Liveright, 1950), p. 107.

[8] Jan. 6 and 13, 1900.

[9] Jan. 29 and 30, 1902.

[10] *Jg.,* Jan. 3, 1913.

[11] Stekel, *Autobiography,* p. 113.

[12] Phyllis Bottome, *Alfred Adler* (New York: Putnam, 1939), p. 83.

[13] Stekel, *Autobiography,* p. 115.

[14] *G.W.,* X, 63; *S.E.,* XIV.

[15] Bottome, *op. cit.,* p. 90.

[16] Max Eitingon, "Aus der Fruhzeit der Psychoanalyse." Delivered in honor of Freud's eighty-first birthday. *Max Eitingon: In Memoriam* (Jerusalem: Israel Psycho-Analytic Society, 1950).

[17] Alfred Adler, "Drei Psycho-Analysen von Zahleneinfällen und obsedierenden Zahlen," *Psychiatrisch-Neurologische Wochenschrift,* VII (1905), 263.

[18] *Ibid.,* "Das sexuelle Problem in der Erziehung," *Die Neue Gesellschaft,* 1905, Heft 34.

[19] *Ibid., Studie über Minderwertigkeit der Organe* (Berlin, Vienna: Urban und Schwarzenberg, 1907).

[20] A. Meisl, "Das psychische Trauma," *Wiener klinische Rundschau,* XX (1906), Nos. 12 and 13.

[21] *Ibid.,* "Der Traum," *Wiener klinische Rundschau,* XXI (1907), Nos. 3, 4, 5, 6.

[22] I. Sadger, "Die Bedeutung der psychoanalytischen Methode nach Freud," *Centralblatt für Nervenheilkunde und Psychiatrie,* XXX (1907), 41.

[23] W. Stekel, *Die Ursachen der Nervosität* (Vienna: Hygienische Zeitfragen, 1907).

[24] *Ibid.*, "Nervöse Angstzustände und ihre Behandlung," *Medizinische Klinik*, III (1907), Nos. 35 and 36.

[25] I.Z., p. 545.

[26] *Vol. I*, 362.

[27] *Vol. I*, 362.

[28] *Vol. I*, 313–14.

[29] M., Sept. 4, 1902.

[30] *Anf.*, p. 359; *Origins*, p. 335.[a]

[31] *Anf.*, pp. 287, 295, 299, 314, 331, 340, 351; *Origins*, pp. 269, 276, 280, 294, 310, 317, 327.

[32] G.W., II/III, 199–202, 328–29, 403n, 443–44, 446n; S.E., IV, 193–97, 323–24; V, 398n, 441–442, 444n.

[33] G.W., II/III, 202; S.E., IV, 197.

[34] *Anf.*, p. 287; *Origins*, p. 269.

[35] *Anf.*, p. 299; *Origins*, p. 280.

[36] M., Sept. 24, 1907.

[37] I. Velikovsky, "The Dreams Freud Dreamed," *The Psychoanalytic Review*, XXVIII (Oct. 1941), 487.

[38] *Anf.*, p. 340; *Origins*, p. 317.

[39] Velikovsky, *op. cit.*, p. 490.

[40] L. Oehlschlegel, "Regarding Freud's Book on Moses," *The Psychoanalytic Review*, XXX (Jan. 1943), 67.

[41] Helen Walker Puner, *Freud: His Life and His Mind* (New York: Crown, 1949), p. 241–44.

[42] *Vol. I*, 167.

[43] *Anf.*, p. 359; *Origins*, p. 336.

[44] G.W., II/III, 446n; S.E., V, 444n.

[45] G.W., II/III, 403n; S.E., V, 398.

[46] Otto Rank, "Ein Traum der sich selbst deutet," *J.*, II (1910), 465.

[47] *Vol. I*, 23.

[48] G.W., II/III, 199n; S.E., IV, 194n.

[49] *Anf.*, p. 369; *Origins*, p. 344.

[50] Puner, *op. cit.*, p. 245.

[51] J. W. Goethe, *Wilhelm Meister's Apprenticeship and Travels*, Thomas Carlyle, Trans., Vol. I (London: Chapman and Hall, Ltd., 1824), p. 176.

[52] G.W., XVI, 250–51; S.E., XX.

[53] Personal communication from Freud to Marie Bonaparte.

[54] G.W., XVI; S.E., XX.

[55] G.W., X, 370; S.E., XIV.

[56] Personal communication from Freud to Marie Bonaparte, 1925.

[57] *Vol. I*, 336.

CHAPTER 2

THE BEGINNING OF
INTERNATIONAL RECOGNITION

[1] G.W., I, 81; S.E., II.

[2] XIX (1896), 401-14.

[3] *Vol. I*, 203.

[4] Havelock Ellis, "Hysteria in Relation to the Sexual Emotions," *The Alienist and Neurologist*, XIX (1898), 599-615.

[5] *Ibid.*, *Studies in the Psychology of Sex* (New York: Random House, 1906).

[a] My translation of portions of *Aus den Anfängen der Psychoanalyse* (*Anf.*) was prepared for this volume before publication of the English translation, *The Origins of Psycho-Analysis* (*Origins*) and will, therefore, differ slightly in some cases. However, the reader is referred to definite passages in *Origins* for the entire context.

[6] Scott Stevenson, *In a Harley Street Mirror* (London: Christopher Johnson, Ltd., 1951), p. 180.

[7] W. Warda, "Ein Fall von Hysterie; dargestellt nach der kathartischen Methode von Breuer und Freud," *Monatsschrift für Psychiatrie und Neurologie*, VII (1900), 301-18, 471–89.

[8] W. Strohmayer, "Zur Charakteristik der Zwangsvorstellungen als 'Abwehrneurose'," *Centralblatt für Nervenheilkunde und Psychiatrie*, XXVI (May 1903), 317–25.

[9] *Ibid.*, "Über die ursächlichen Beziehungen der Sexualitat zu Angst- und Zwangszuständen," *Journal für Psychologie und Neurologie*, XII (1908), 69–95.

[10] O. Juliusburger, "Beitrag zu der Lehre von der Psychoanalyse," Sitzungsbericht des Psychiatrischen Vereins (Berlin), Dec. 14, 1907, *Allgemeine Zeitschrift für Psychiatrie*, LXIV (1907), 1002-10; "Zur Psychotherapie und Psychoanalyse," *Berliner klinische Wochenschrift*, Feb. 8, 1909, pp. 248–50.

[11] A. Muthmann, *Zur Psychologie und Therapie neurotischer Symptome, eine Studie auf grund der Neurosenlehre Freuds* (Halle: Carl Marhold, 1907).

[12] Otto Gross, "Zur Differentialdiagnostik negativistischer Phänomene," *Psychiatrisch-Neurologische Wochenschrift*, VI (1904), 345–53, 357–63.

[13] *Ibid.*, *Das Freud'sche Ideogenitätsmoment und seine Bedeutung im manisch-depressiven Irresein Kraepelins* (Leipzig: F.C.W. Vogel, 1907).

[14] A. Stegmann, "Kasuistischer Beitrag zur Behandlung von Neurosen mittels der kathartischen Methode (nach Freud)," Zehnte Versammlung mitteldeutscher Psychiater und Neurologen (Halle), Oct. 22, 1904. Abstract in *Centralblatt für Nervenheilkunde und Psychiatrie*, XXVII (1904), 770.

[15] *Ibid.*, "Zur Aetiologie des Asthmas bei kindern," *Medizinische Klinik*, July 19, 1908, pp. 1113–16.

[16] C. G. Jung, *Zur Psychologie und Pathologie sogennannter okkulter Phänomene* (Leipzig: Oswald Mutze, 1902).

[17] *Ibid.*, "Experimentelle Beobachtungen über das Erinnerungsvermögen," *Centralblatt für Nervenheilkunde und Psychiatrie*, XXVIII (1905), 653.

[18] "Zwangshandlungen und Religionsübungen," *G.W.*, VII, 129; "Obsessive Acts and Religious Practices," *S.E.*, IX.

[19] L. Binswanger, "Freud'sche Mechanismen in der Symptomatologie von Psychosen," *Psychiatrisch-Neurologische Wochenschrift*.

[20] *Jg.*, Feb. 28, 1908.

[21] *Jg.*, Jan. 17, 1909.

[22] Abraham, "Über die Bedeutung sexueller Jugendtraumen für die Symptomatologie der Dementia Praecox," *Centralblatt für Nervenheilkunde und Psychiatrie*, XXX (1907), 409–15.

[23] Hanns Sachs, *Freud, Master and Friend* (Cambridge, Mass.: Harvard University, 1944), p. 35.

[24] Letter to Freud from *Ab.*, May 3, 1908.

[25] *Schiller's Briefwechsel mit Korner*, Vol. I (1847), pp. 381–85.

[26] *Ab.*, March 13, 1908.
[27] *G.W.*, VII, 381–463; *S.E.*, X.
[28] *G.W.*, II, 524; *S.E.*, V, 519.
[29] *M.*, April 29, 1908.
[30] *Jg.*, June 12, 1907.
[31] *Jg.*, Nov. 12, 1908.
[32] Letter to Freud from *Pf.*, Oct. 29, 1918.
[33] *Pf.*, Feb. 20, 1909.
[34] *E.J.*, June 27, 1908.
[35] *Fer.*, Feb. 12, 1909.
[36] *Fer.*, April 27, 1909.
[37] *Anf.*, p. 325; *Origins*, p. 304.
[38] *Ab.*, July 20, 1908.
[39] *Ab.*, July 23, 1908.
[40] *Ab.*, July 31, 1908.
[41] *Fer.*, March 23, 1909.
[42] *G.W.*, IV, 253.
[43] *Vol. I*, 24.
[44] *Fer.*, Jan. 10, 1909.
[45] *Ab.*, March 9, 1909.
[46] *Fer.*, Aug. 8, 1909.
[47] *Fer.*, July 25, 1909.
[48] *Fer.*, June 16, 1909; *Pf.*, June 13, 1909.

[49] *Fer.*, Oct. 27, 1908.
[50] *Fer.*, Feb. 7, 1909.
[51] *Vol. I*, 317.
[52] *Jg.*, June 4, 1909.
[53] Letter to Freud from *E.J.*, April 20, 1910.
[54] *Auto*, p. 94.
[55] *Pf.*, Oct. 4, 1909.
[56] *E.J.*, July 17, 1914.
[57] Letter from Freud to Hitschmann, Nov. 6, 1935.
[58] *G.W.*, IV, 38; *S.E.*, VI.
[59] *Fer.*, Jan. 2, 1910.
[60] *E.J.*, Jan. 27, 1910.
[61] Communication from Marie Bonaparte.
[62] *Vol. I*, 184.
[63] G. Modena, "Psicopatologie ed etiologia dei fenomeni psiconeurotici. Contributo alla dottrina di S. Freud," *Rivista sperimentale di Freniatria e Medicina Legale delle Alienazione Mental*, XXXIV (1908), 657–70; XXXV (1909), 204–18.

CHAPTER 3

THE INTERNATIONAL
PSYCHO-ANALYTICAL ASSOCIATION

[1] *Jg.*, Jan. 13, 1910.
[2] *Jg.*, Feb. 13, 1910.
[3] *Ab.*, March 21, 1910.
[4] *E.J.*, March 10, 1910.
[5] *Fer.*, Jan. 1, 1910.
[6] Letter to Freud from *Fer.*, Feb. 5, 1910.
[7] *Fer.*, Feb. 8, 1910.
[8] *Ab.*, Feb. 24, 1910.
[9] *Jg.*, Aug. 10, 1910.
[10] *Fer.*, April 24, 1910.
[11] *Pf.*, Nov. 6, 1910.
[12] *Jg.*, Nov. 25, 1910.
[13] *Fer.*, Dec. 29, 1910.
[14] *Pf.*, Jan. 2, 1912.

[15] *Fer.*, April 12, 1910.
[16] Letter to Freud from *Ab.*, Feb. 25, 1912.
[17] Letter to Freud from *Ab.*, Oct. 29, 1911.
[18] Letter to Freud from *Ab.*, Dec. 25, 1911.
[19] Letter to Freud from *Ab.*, April 19, 1908; *Fer.*, Feb. 1, 1914.
[20] *Jg.*, Sept. 25, 1907.
[21] J. J. Putnam, "Personal Impressions of Sigmund Freud and his Work, with Special Reference to his Recent Lectures at Clark University," *Journal of Ab-*

normal Psychology, IV (Dec. 1909 and Feb. 1910), 293, 372.

22 *E.J.*, Jan. 11, 1910.

23 *C.*, I, 137.

24 *G.W.*, IV, 38; *S.E.*, VI.

25 E. A. Acher, "Spontaneous Constructions and Primitive Activities of Children Analogous to Those of Primitive Man," *American Journal of Psychology*, XXI (1910), 114–50.

26 *Ibid.*, "Recent Freudian Literature," *American Journal of Psychology*, XXII (1911), 408–43.

27 B. Hart, "The Conception of the Subconscious," *Journal of Abnormal Psychology*, IV (Feb.–March 1910), 339.

28 *Fer.*, May 17, 1910.

29 *Eit.*, Dec. 30, 1909; *Fer.*, Jan. 1, 1910.

30 *Fer.*, June 5, 1910.

31 Letter to Freud from *Ab.*, Nov. 10, 1909.

32 *Fer.*, Dec. 12, 1909.

33 Letter to Freud from *Fer.*, Dec. 7, 1909.

34 *Jg.*, Dec. 3, 1910.

35 *Ab.*, Oct. 4, 1908.

36 G. Modena, "Psicopatologie ed etiologia dei fenomeni psiconeurotici; Contributo alla dottrina di S. Freud," *Rivista sperimentale di Freniatria e Medicina Legale delle Alienazioni Mentali*, XXXIV (1908), 657–70; XXXV (1909), 204–18.

37 *E.J.*, Oct. 31, 1909.

38 *Fer.*, April 10, 1910.

39 *Jg.*, March 25, 1911.

40 *Jg.*, May 2, 1910.

41 *Jg.*, May 26, 1910.

42 *Ab.*, Feb. 24, 1910.

43 *Pf.*, Jan. 10, 1910.

44 *Pf.*, April 26, 1910.

45 *Fer.*, May 17, 1910.

46 Personal communication from Freud to Marie Bonaparte, 1925.

47 Letter to Freud from M., Sept. 1, 1910.

48 Letter to Freud from *Fer.*, Sept. 27, 1926.

49 *Pf.*, Sept. 27, 1910.

50 *G.W.*, IV, 38; *S.E.*, VI.

51 *Fer.*, Oct. 3, 1910.

52 *Fer.*, Oct. 29, 1910.

53 *Fer.*, Jan. 10, 1911.

54 *E.J.*, Jan. 22, 1911.

55 *Jg.*, Feb. 17, 1911.

56 *Ab.*, Jan. 20, 1911.

57 *Fer.*, Aug. 11, 1911.

58 *E.J.*, Feb. 26, 1911.

59 Letter to Freud from *Ab.*, April 9, 1911.

60 *G.W.*, VIII, 317; *S.E.*, XII.

61 E. Hitschmann, *Freud's Neurosenlehre* (Leipzig: Deuticke, 1911).

62 *Fer.*, March 12, 1911; *Ab.*, March 14, 1911.

63 *Fer.*, May 2, 1911.

64 R. Morichau-Beauchint, "Le 'Rapport Affectif' dans la cure des psychoneuroses," *Gazette des Hospitaux*, LXXXIV (Nov. 14, 1911), 1845–49.

65 *E.J.*, Feb. 24, 1912.

66 *Fer.*, May 28, 1911.

67 *Fer.*, May 28, 1911.

68 Putnam to *E.J.*, Sept. 14, 1910.

69 *Jg.*, May 27, 1911.

70 Putnam to *E.J.*, June 15, 1911.

71 *Jg.*, Feb. 17, 1911.

72 *G.W.*, VIII, 429; *S.E.*, XII.

73 *E.J.*, Aug. 9, 1911.

74 M. D. Eder, "A Case of Obsession and Hysteria Treated by the Freud Psycho-Analytic Method," *British Medical Journal*, II (1911), 750.

75 R. A. Hunter and Ida MacAlpine, "Follow-up Study of a Case Treated in 1910 by 'the

Freud psycho-analytic method',"
British Journal of Medical Psychology, XXVI (1953), 64.

[76] *Fer.*, March 12, 1911.
[77] *Fer.*, May 28, 1911.
[78] *E.J.*, Aug. 9, 1911.
[79] *Fer.*, Oct. 5 and 21, 1911; Nov. 5, 1911.
[80] *G.W.*, VIII, 229; *S.E.*, XII.
[81] *Fer.*, April 10, 1911.
[82] *E.J.*, June 25, 1911.
[83] *M.*, July 10 and 12, 1911.
[84] *Fer.*, June 23, 1912.
[85] *Ab.*, Jan. 2, 1912.
[86] *Fer.*, May 30, 1912.
[87] *Fer.*, March 24, 1912.
[88] *Vol. I*, 202.
[89] *Fer.*, May 30, 1912.
[90] *Ab.*, June 3, 1912.
[91] *Fer.*, May 30, 1912.
[92] *Fer.*, July 20, 1912.
[93] **E.J.*, Aug. 11, 1912.
[94] Letter to Hitschmann, July 1912.
[95] *E.J.*, Sept. 3, 1912.
[96] **E.J.*, Sept. 7, 1912.
[97] *M.*, Sept. 16, 1912.
[98] *M.*, Sept. 20, 1912.
[99] *M.*, Sept. 25, 1912.
[100] **E.J.*, Dec. 8, 1912.
[101] *Fer.*, Oct. 27, 1912.
[102] **E.J.*, Oct. 28, 1912.
[103] **E.J.*, Nov. 8, 1912.
[104] *Fer.*, Dec. 2, 1912.
[105] *Ab.*, Dec. 16, 1912; *E.J.*, Dec. 26, 1912.
[106] *Fer.*, Oct. 28, 1912.
[107] **E.J.*, Oct. 30, 1913.
[108] *Pf.*, Oct. 9, 1913.
[109] *E.J.*, Jan. 1, 1913.
[110] Letter to Freud from *E.J.*, Jan. 18, 1913.
[111] *Fer.*, Feb. 10, 1913.
[112] *Ab.*, May 13, 1913.
[113] **E.J.*, July 23, 1913.
[114] *G.W.*, VIII, 441; *S.E.*, XII.
[115] **E.J.*, Sept. 21, 1913.
[116] *Fer.*, Sept. 11, 1913.
[117] **E.J.*, Oct. 1, 1913.
[118] *Ab.*, Oct. 12, 1913.
[119] *Ab.*, April 6, 1914.
[120] *Ab.*, June 6, 1914.
[121] *E.J.*, March 19, 1914.
[122] *Fer.*, Feb. 18, 1914.
[123] **E.J.*, Feb. 21, 1914.
[124] *Fer.*, Feb. 15, 1914; *Ab.*, Feb. 5, 1914.
[125] *Ab.*, May 13, 1914.
[126] **E.J.*, May 17, 1914.
[127] Stanley Hall, Preface to Freud, A *General Introduction to Psychoanalysis* (New York: Liveright, 1920).
[128] Régis et Hesnard, *La Psychoanalyse des Nervoses et des Psychoses* (Paris: 1922).
[129] *Ab.*, Jan. 2, 1912.
[130] *Fer.*, May 24, 1914.

CHAPTER 4

OPPOSITION

[1] *Fer.*, Feb. 16, 1911.
[2] *Ab.*, Oct. 18, 1910.
[3] *Fer.*, Feb. 14, 1916.
[4] *Ibid.*
[5] Spielmeyer, Review of Freud's "Bruchstück einer Hysterie-Analyse," *Centralblatt für Nervenheilkunde und Psychiatrie*, XXIX (April 15, 1906), 322–324.
[6] E. Bleuler, Letter to the Editor, *Centralblatt für Nervenheil-*

kunde und Psychiatrie, June 1, 1906, pp. 460–61.

7 Spielmeyer, Reply to Bleuler's letter, *Centralblatt für Nervenheilkunde und Psychiatrie*.

8 Gustav Aschaffenburg, "Die Beziehungen des sexuellen Lebens zur Entstehung von Nerven- und Geisteskrankheiten," 31. Versammlung der Süd-Westdeutschen Neurologen und Irrenärzte, May 27, 1906, *Münchener Medizinische Wochenschrift*, Sept. 11, 1906, pp. 1793–98.

9 Jung, "Die Hysterielehre Freud's. Eine Erwiderung auf die Aschaffenburg'sche Kritik," *Münchener Medizinische Wochenschrift*, LIII (Nov. 1906), 2301.

10 Ostwald Bumke, Review of Freud's "Bruckstück einer Hysterie-Analyse," *Schmidt's Jahrbücher der in- und ausländischen gesamten Medizin*, CCLXXXIX (1906), 168–69.

11 *G.W.*, I, 392; *S.E.*, III.

12 B. Rieger, "Über die Behandlung Nervenkranker," *Schmidt's Jahrbücher der in- und ausländischen gesamten Medizin*, CLI (1896), 193–198, 273–76.

13 O. Bumke, *Die Psychoanalyse: Eine Kritik* (Berlin· Springer, 1931).

14 *Jg.*, April 14, 1907.

15 Aschaffenburg, "Autorreferat," *Monatsschrift für Psychiatrie und Neurologie*, XXII (1907), 565–67; C. G. Jung, "Die Freud'sche Hysterielehre," *Monatsschrift für Psychiatrie und Neurologie*, XXIII (1908), 310–22.

16 *Comptes Rendus* of the International Congress of Psychiatry and Neurology, Amsterdam, 1908, p. 293.

17 T. Ziehen, Review of Jung's *Über die Psychologie der Dementia Praecox, Monatsschrift für Psychiatrie und Neurologie*, XXIII (1908), 565–66.

18 M. Isserlin, "Moderne Analyse psychischer Erscheinungen," 79. Versammlung deutscher Naturforscher und Aerzte, Dresden; "Über Jung's Psychologie der Dementia Praecox und die Freud'sche Forschungsweise in der Psychopathologie," *Centralblatt für Nervenheilkunde und Psychiatrie*, XXX (1907), 329–343.

19 Abraham, "Die Stellung der Verwandtenehe in der Psychologie der Neurosen," *Neurologisches Centralblatt*, XXVII (1908), 1150.

20 H. Oppenheim, "Zur Psychopathologie der Angstzustände," *Berliner klinische Wochenschrift*, XLVI (July 12, 1909), 1293–95.

21 *Ibid.*, "Pathologie und Therapie der nervösen Angstzustände," *Deutsche Zeitschrift für Nervenheilkunde*, XLI (1911), 173–94.

22 Letter to Freud from *Ab.*, April 7, 1909.

23 *Ab.*, Feb. 18, 1909.

24 Letter to Freud from *Ab.*, Feb. 11 and 17, 1911.

25 Letter to Freud from *E.J.*, May 4, 1910.

26 *Hamburger Aerzte-Correspondenzblatt*, April 4, 1910.

27 *Fer.*, April 24, 1910.

28 Hoche, "Eine psychische Epidemie unter Ärzten," Versammlung Süd-West Deutscher Ir-

renärzte (Baden-Baden), May 28, 1910, *Medizinische Klinik,* VI (1910), 1007–10.

29 *Fer.,* July 3, 1910.

30 **E.J.,* July 3, 1910.

31 *Jg.,* May 26, 1910.

32 *Jg.,* July 5, 1910.

33 A. Friedländer, "Über Hysterie und die Freudsche psycho-analytische Behandlung derselben," *Monatsschrift für Psychiatrie und Neurologie,* XXII (1907), 45–54; "Kurze Bemerkungen zu der Freud'schen Lehre über die sexuelle Aetiologie der Neurosen," *Neurologisches Centralblatt,* XXVI (Oct. 1907), 953; "Hysteria and Modern Psychoanalysis," *Journal of Abnormal Psychology,* V (Feb.–March 1911), 297–319.

34 *Ibid.,* "Hysterie und moderne Psychoanalyse," XVI, International Congress of Medicine, Budapest, 1909; "Autorreferat," *Monatsschrift für Psychiatrie und Neurologie,* XXVII (1910), 81–82.

35 *Ab.,* June 5, 1910; *Fer.,* June 5, 1910.

36 *Fer.,* Aug. 8, 1913.

37 Robert Sommer, *Klinik für psychische und nervöse Krankheiten,* V (1910).

38 O. Vogt, "Zur Kritik der psychogenetischen Forschung der Hysterie," *Zeitschrift für Hypnotismus,* VIII, 342; "Zur Methodik der aetiologischen Erforschung der Hysterie," *Zeitschrift für Hypnotismus,* VIII (1899), 65–83.

39 Letter to Freud from *E.J.,* Nov. 17, 1911.

40 *Fer.,* April 12 and 17, 1910.

41 *Fer.,* Dec. 3, 1910.

42 *Fer.,* Dec. 23, 1912.

43 Von Luschan, "Altweiber Psychiatrie," *Deutsche medizinische Wochenschrift,* XLII (Jan. 6, 1916), 20.

44 *Fer.,* Feb. 4, 1916.

45 *Journal für Psychologie und Neurologie,* X (1907), 201–13.

46 J. H. Schultz, "Psychoanalyse, die Breuer-Freud'sche Lehre, ihre Enstehung und Aufnahme," *Zeitschrift für angewandte Psychologie,* II (1909), 440–97.

47 C. Adam, *Die Psychologie und ihre Bedeutung für die ärztliche Praxis* (1921).

48 M. Isserlin, "Die psychoanalytische Methode Freuds," *Zeitschrift für die gesamte Neurologie und Psychiatrie,* I (1910), 52–80.

49 A. Kronfeld, "Über die psychologischen Theorien Freuds und verwandte Anschaungen," *Archiv für die gesamte Psychologie,* XII (1911), 130–248.

50 *Ab.,* Jan. 14, 1912.

51 Letter to August Stärcke, Aug. 25, 1912.

52 Kuno Mittenzwey, "Versuch zu einer Darstellung und Kritik der Freud'schen Neurosenlehre," *Zeitschrift für Pathopsychologie,* I (1912), 164–86, 369–421, 640–700; II, 79–119, 181–259, 445–80, 611–98; III, 128–52.

53 *Auto.,* pp. 89, 90; *G.W.,* XIV, 75; *S.E.,* XX.

54 *Pf.,* Feb. 20, 1909.

55 *Fer.,* Jan. 10, 1910.

56 *Fer.,* June 26, 1910.

57 *Fer.,* May 25, 1911.

58 Personal communication from C.P. Oberndorf.

59 *Vol. I,* 202.

60 *Vol. I,* 257.

61 *Pf.,* July 12, 1909.

62 **E.J.,* Dec. 18, 1910.

63 *Pf.,* Jan. 1, 1910.

64 Letter to August Stärcke, Feb. 25, 1912.

CHAPTER 5

DISSENSIONS

1 *G.W.*, X, 54; *S.E.*, XIV.

2 Jan. 11, 1929.

3 *Jg.*, April 9, 1908.

4 *Fer.*, Nov. 8, 1910.

5 *Fer.*, Nov. 23, 1910.

6 *Fer.*, April 6, 1911.

7 Phyllis Bottome, *Alfred Adler* (New York: Putnam, 1939), p. 91.

8 *Vol. I*, 402.

9 *G.W.*, XII, 222–25; *S.E.*, XVII.

10 K.M. Colby, "On the Disagreement Between Freud and Adler," *The American Imago*, VIII (Sept. 1951), 229–38.

11 *E.J.*, June 25, 1911.

12 *The Autobiography of Wilhelm Stekel* (New York: Liveright, 1950), p. 143.

13 *Fer.*, May 28, 1911.

14 *Fer.*, June 20, 1911.

15 *C.*, I, (June 1911), 433.

16 *Fer.*, July 5, 1911.

17 Bottome, *op. cit.*, p. 93.

18 Personal communication from Ludwig Jekels.

19 Personal communication from Paul Klemperer, Secretary of Adler's society.

20 *Fer.*, May 10, 1914.

21 *Jg.*, Nov. 11, 1909.

22 Stekel, *Die Sprache des Traumes* (Wiesbaden: Bergmann, 1911).

23 *Ab.*, April 11, 1911.

24 *Fer.*, April 2, 1911.

25 Putnam to *E.J.*, July 15, 1911.

26 *G.W.*, X, 90; *S.E.*, XIV.

27 F. Wittels, *Sigmund Freud: His Personality, His Teaching and His School* (New York: Dodd, Mead, 1924), p. 216.

28 *Fer.*, May 2, 1911.

29 Quotation from Scheftel's *Trompeter von Säkkingen* in personal communication.

30 Stekel, *Autobiography*, p. 131.

31 Stekel, "Die Verpflichtung des Namens," *Zeitschrift für Psychotherapie und medizinische Psychologie*, III (1911), 110–14.

32 *Fer.*, May 30, 1912.

33 *C.,I* (1911), 49–50.

34 *C.,I* (1911), 594.

35 *Fer.*, Oct. 27, 1912.

36 *Ab.*, Dec. 3, 1912.

37 *Ab.*, Nov. 3, 1912.

38 *Fer.*, Sept. 13, 1924.

39 Letter from *Jg.* to *E.J.*, Jan. 21, 1908.

40 *Ab.*, July 23, 1908.

41 Letter from *Jg.* to *E.J.*, Dec. 7, 1907.

42 *Fer.*, July 28, 1912.

43 *Pf.*, June 6, 1910.

44 Letter from *Jg.* to *E.J.*, May 15, 1909.

45 Letter from *Jg.* to *E.J.*, Feb. 25, 1909.

46 *Fer.*, Aug. 14, 1910.

47 *Fer.*, Dec. 29, 1910.

48 *E.J.*, Jan. 22, 1911.

49 *Fer.*, Feb. 8, 1911.

50 Letter from *Jg.* to *E.J.*, July 12, 1911.

51 *Fer.*, Oct. 21 and Nov. 9, 1911.

52 *Fer.*, Feb. 1, 1912.

53 *Fer.*, Dec. 29, 1910.

54 C.G. Jung, "*Wandlungen und Symbole der Libido*," Erster Teil, *J.*, III (1911), 120–227; Zweiter Teil, IV (1912), 162–464.

55 *E.J.*, Sept. 7 and 22, 1912.

56 *I.Z.*, I (1913), 391–403; II (1914), 72–82, 83–87.

[57] Edward Glover, *Freud or Jung* (New York: Norton, 1950).
[58] *Fer.*, July 20, 1912.
[59] *Ab.*, July 29, 1912.
[60] *Jg.*, Nov. 11, 1912.
[61] *Jg.*, June 13, 1912.
[62] *E.J.*, Sept. 21, 1912.
[63] *Vol. I*, 317.
[64] *Fer.*, Nov. 28, 1912.
[65] *Vol. I*, 7.
[66] *G.W.*, XVI, 250–57; *S.E.*, XX.
[67] *Loc. cit.*
[68] Letter to Freud from *Jg.*, Dec. 18, 1912.
[69] *Jg.*, Jan. 3, 1913.
[70] *E.J.*, Sept. 22, 1912; *Ab.*, Nov. 9, 1913.
[71] *Fer.*, Jan. 5, 1913.
[72] *Fer.*, May 8, 1913.
[73] *Fer.*, June 8, 1913.
[74] Letter to Freud from *Ab.*, July 6, 1913.
[75] *Fer.*, Aug. 3, 1913.
[76] *Fer.* to *Jg.*, Nov. 3, 1913.
[77] *Ab.*, Oct. 26, 1913.
[78] Letter to Freud from *Jg.*, Oct. 17, 1913.
[79] *E.J.* Nov. 8, 1913.
[80] Letter to Freud from *E.J.*, Nov. 4, 1913.
[81] **E.J.*, Nov. 13, 1913.
[82] *E.J.*, April 27, 1914.
[83] Letter to Freud from *E.J.*, April 22, 1914.
[84] *Ab.*, July 27, 1914.
[85] *Ab.*, June 25, 1914.
[86] **E.J.*, May 17, 1914.

CHAPTER 6

THE COMMITTEE

[1] Letter to Freud from *E.J.*, July 30, 1912.
[2] Letter to Freud from *Fer.*, Aug. 6, 1912.
[3] Letter to Freud from *Fer.*, Nov. 28, 1912.
[4] Letter to Freud from *Ab.*, July 24, 1912.
[5] **E.J.*, Dec. 26, 1912.
[6] **E.J.*, Aug. 1, 1912.
[7] *Ab.*, Dec. 10, 1913.
[8] *Eit.*, Oct. 22, 1919.
[9] *Eit.*, Nov. 23, 1919.
[10] Hanns Sachs, *Freud, Master and Friend* (Cambridge, Mass.: Harvard University, 1944).
[11] Karl Abraham, *Selected Papers on Psycho-Analysis* (New York: Basic Books, 1953).
[12] O. Rank and H. Sachs, *Die Bedeutung der Psychoanalyse für die Geisteswissenschaften* (Wiesbaden: Bergmann, 1913).
[13] O. Rank, *Das Inzest-Motive in Dichtung und Sage* (Leipzig: Deuticke, 1912).
[14] **E.J.*, July 10, 1913.
[15] *Ab.*, Dec. 21, 1914.

CHAPTER 7

THE WAR YEARS

[1] *Fer.*, June 28, 1914.
[2] *Vol. I*, 23.
[3] *Ab.*, July 26, 1914.
[4] *Ab.*, Aug. 2, 1914.
[5] *Fer.*, Aug. 23, 1914.
[6] Letter to Hitschmann, Aug. 1914.
[7] *Ab.*, Aug. 25, 1914.

8 *Ab.*, Sept. 3, 1914.

9 *Ibid.*

10 *Fer.*, Aug. 23, 1914.

11 *E.J.*, July 22, 1914.

12 *Fer.*, Sept. 6, 1914.

13 *Ab.*, Aug. 25, 1914.

14 *Eit.*, Sept. 15, 1914.

15 *Ab.*, Sept. 15, 1914.

16 *Fer.*, Nov. 25, 1914.

17 *Ab.*, July 3, 1915.

18 Letter from Brill to Freud, Oct. 27, 1914.

19 **E.J.*, Dec. 25, 1914.

20 *Ab.*, Dec. 30, 1914.

21 *Fer.*, Dec. 2, 1914.

22 *Ab.*, Dec. 11, 1914.

23 Lou Andreas-Salomé, *Lebensrückblick* (Zurich: Niehans, 1951), p. 368. Quoted by permission of her executor, Dr. Pfeiffer.

24 *Fer.*, Dec. 15, 1914.

25 *Fer.*, Dec. 15, 1914.

26 *Ab.*, Dec. 21, 1914.

27 *Fer.*, Jan. 18, 1916.

28 *Fer.*, Jan. 9, 1915.

29 *Eit.*, Jan. 17, 1915.

30 Letter to Freud from *Ab.*, Feb. 28, 1915.

31 *Ab.*, Feb. 18, 1915.

32 *Ab.*, March 4, 1915.

33 *Ab.*, March 15, 1915.

34 *Fer.*, April 4, 1915.

35 *Eit.*, May 9, 1915.

36 *Fer.*, July 10, 1915.

37 *Fer.*, Oct. 17, 1915.

38 *Fer.*, Nov. 15, 1915.

39 *Fer.*, Nov. 23, 1915.

40 *Fer.*, July 21, 1915.

41 *Ab.*, July 3, 1915.

42 *Eit.*, Jan. 17, 1915.

43 *Eit.*, *ibid.*; *Fer.*, April 8, 1915.

44 *Fer.*, Dec. 24, 1915.

45 Putnam to *E.J.*, Oct. 2, 1915.

46 Letter to Freud from *Fer.*, Feb. 22, 1915.

47 Fritz Wittels, *Freud and His Time* (New York: Liveright, 1931), Chap. I, "Goethe and Freud."

48 *Fer.*, April 4, 1915.

49 *Fer.*, April 23, 1915.

50 *Fer.*, April 23, 1915.

51 *Fer.*, July 31, 1915.

52 *Fer.*, Oct. 17, 1915.

53 *Fer.*, Nov. 26, 1915.

54 *Ab.*, Jan. 25, 1915.

55 *G.W.*, XIII, 369; *S.E.*, XIX.

56 Letter to Freud from *E.J.*, Dec 8, 1915.

57 *Jg.*, Feb. 12, 1911.

58 *E.J.*, June 30, 1915.

59 *Ab.*, May 4, 1915.

60 *Fer.*, July 12, 1915.

61 *Anf.*, p. 168; *Origins*, p. 157.

62 *Anf.*, p. 262; *Origins*, p. 246.

63 *G.W.*, IV, 288; *S.E.*, VI.

64 *Fer.*, April 4, 1915.

65 *Fer.*, April 23, 1915.

66 *Ab.*, May 4, 1915.

67 *Fer.*, June 21, 1915.

68 **E.J.*, June 30, 1915.

69 *Fer.*, Aug. 9, 1915.

70 *Ab.*, Nov. 11, 1917.

71 *G.W.*, X, 234–46; *S.E.*, XIV.

72 *G.W.*, X, 306–21; *S.E.*, XII.

73 *G.W.*, X, 364–91; *S.E.*, XIV.

74 *G.W.*, X, 324–55; *S.E.*, XIV.

75 *E.J.*, April 16, 1916.

76 *Eit.*, Aug. 26, 1916.

77 *Fer.*, Feb. 4, 1916.

78 *Fer.*, July 22, 1916.

79 *Ab.*, Aug. 27, 1916.

80 *Eit.*, March 26, 1916.

81 *Ab.*, Feb. 13, 1916.

82 *Eit.*, May 8, 1916.

83 *Ab.*, May 8, 1916.

84 *E.J.*, July 14, 1916.

85 *Eit.*, Sept. 7, 1916.

86 *Fer.*, Aug. 2, 1916.

87 *Fer.*, Jan. 18, 1916.

88 *Fer.*, June 1, 1916.

89 *Ab.*, Feb. 13, 1916.

90 *Fer.*, Oct. 31, 1915.

91 Letter to Freud from *Ab.*, Dec 10, 1916.

474   Reference Notes

92 *Ab.*, Dec. 18, 1916.
93 *Fer.*, Jan. 22, 1917.
94 *Fer.*, Dec. 22, 1916.
95 *Fer.*, Nov. 16, 1916.
96 *Fer.*, Dec. 22, 1916.
97 *Fer.*, Jan. 1, 1917.
98 Letter to Freud from *Ab.*, Feb. 11, 1917.
99 *Fer.*, March 25, 1917.
100 *Fer.*, April 30, 1917.
101 *Fer.*, June 15, 1917.
102 *Ab.*, Oct. 5, 1917.
103 *Fer.*, Oct. 9, 1917.
104 Letter to Freud from *Ab.*, Nov. 11, 1917.
105 *Ab.*, Dec. 10, 1917.
106 *Ab.*, July 13, 1917.
107 *Fer.*, Feb. 16, 1917.
108 *Fer.*, May 18, 1917.
109 *Fer.*, Nov. 6, 1917.
110 *Fer.*, Jan. 1, 1917.
111 *Fer.*, June 15, 1917.
112 *Ab.*, Nov. 11, Dec. 10, 1917.
113 *Ab.*, Oct. 5, 1917.
114 *Fer.*, May 27, 1917.
115 *Ab.*, Dec. 26, 1917.
116 *Fer.*, Feb. 21, 1917.
117 *Fer.*, June 8, 1917.
118 To Gisela Pálos, April 30, 1917.
119 *Ab.*, Nov. 11, 1917.
120 *Fer.*, Nov. 20, 1917.
121 *Fer.*, Dec. 16, 1917.
122 *G.W.*, XII, 3; *S.E.*, XVII.
123 *Fer.*, Sept. 24, 1917.
124 *G.W.*, XII, 15; *S.E.*, XVII.
125 *Fer.*, Sept. 24, 1917.
126 *Fer.*, Jan. 1, 1917.
127 *Ab.*, Nov. 11, 1917.
128 *Ab.*, March 22, 1918.
129 *Fer.*, Feb. 27, 1918.
130 *Eit.*, Jan. 1, 1918.
131 *Ab.*, Jan. 18, 1918.
132 *Ab.*, May 29, 1918.
133 *Ab.*, May 29, 1918; *Fer.*, June 2, 1918.
134 *Fer.*, Dec. 3, 1918.
135 *Ab.*, March 1918.
136 *Ab.*, Aug. 27, 1918.
137 Ernst Simmel, *Kriegs-Neurosen und psychisches Trauma: Ihre gegenseitigen Beziehungen dargestellt auf Grund psychoanalytischer, hypnotischer Studien* (1918).
138 Letter to Freud from *Fer.*, Oct. 8, 1918.
139 Letter to Freud from *Fer.*, Oct. 25, 1918.
140 *G.W.*, XII, 183-94; *S.E.*, XVII.
141 *Fer.*, Sept. 30, 1918.
142 *Fer.*, Oct. 20, 1918.
143 *Was bietet die Psychoanalyse dem Erzieher*, (Leipzig: 1917).
144 *Pf.*, Oct. 9, 1918.
145 Letter to Freud from *Pf.*, Oct. 29, 1918.
146 *Fer.*, March 3, 1918.
147 *Fer.*, Nov. 3, 1918.
148 *Fer.*, Nov. 27, 1918.
149 *Fer.*, Oct. 25, 1918.
150 *Fer.*, Oct. 16, 1918.
151 *Ab.*, Nov. 29, 1918.
152 *Fer.*, Oct. 27, 1918.
153 *Fer.*, Nov. 3, 1918.
154 *Fer.*, Nov. 9, 1918.
155 *Fer.*, Nov. 17, 1918.
156 Letter to Freud from *Fer.*, Dec. 26, 1918.
157 *E.J.*, Nov. 10, 1918.
158 Letter to Freud from *Fer.*, Nov. 11, 1918.
159 *Ab.*, Dec. 2, 1918.
160 Letter to Freud from *Pf.*, Dec. 30, 1918.
161 *Fer.*, Jan. 24, 1919.
162 *E.J.*, Feb. 18, 1919.
163 *Fer.*, March 17, 1919.
164 *Fer.*, Jan. 6, 1919.
165 *Fer.*, Jan. 24, 1919.
166 Ferenczi, "Zur psychoanalytischen Technik," *I.Z.*, V (1919), 181–92.
167 *Fer.*, Feb. 13, 1919.
168 *Fer.*, March 4, 1919.

CHAPTER 8

EXPOSITIONS

1 *Vol. I*, 362.
2 Michael Servetus, *De Trinitatis Erroribus*, Librum Septem.
3 *On Dreams* (New York: Norton, 1952); *S.E.*, V.
4 *G.W.*, V, 289–315; *S.E.*, VII.
5 *G.W.*, VIII, 1–60; *S.E.*, XI.
6 *Fer.*, Nov. 21, 1909.
7 *Fer., loc. cit.*
8 *Jg.*, Dec. 12, 1909.
9 *G.W.*, VIII, 41; *S.E.*, XI.
10 "On Psycho-Analysis," *Transactions of the Australasian Medical Congress*, Ninth Session, September 1911, VIII (1913), 839–42.
11 *G.W.*, VIII, 389–420; *S.E.*, XIII.
12 *G.S.*, IV, 310–43.
13 *G.W.*, VIII, 395; *S.E.*, XIII.
14 *G.W.*, VIII, 396; *S.E.*, XIII.
15 *G.W.*, VIII, 398; *S.E.*, XIII.
16 *G.W.*, XI; *S.E.*, XV, XVI.
17 *Fer.*, Nov. 23, 1915.
18 *Fer.*, Oct. 31, 1915.
19 *Fer.*, Nov. 15, 1915.
20 *Fer.*, Sept. 20, 1916.
21 *G.W.*, XI, 375–76; *S.E.*, XVI.
22 *G.W.*, XI, 420; *S.E.*, XVI.
23 *G.W.*, XI, 425; *S.E.*, XVI.
24 *G.W.*, XI, 426; *S.E.*, XVI.
25 *G.W.*, XII, 1; *S.E.*, XVII.
26 *G.W.*, XII, 5; *S.E.*, XVII.
27 *G.W.*, XI, 294; *S.E.*, XVII.
28 *Ab.*, March 25, 1917.

CHAPTER 9

CONTRIBUTIONS TO TECHNIQUE

1 *M.*, July 13, 1882.
2 *G.W.*, V, 1–10; *S.E.*, VII, 247.
3 *G.W.*, II/III, 105; *S.E.*, IV, 101.
4 *G.W.*, V, 13–26; *S.E.*, VII, 256.
5 *S.E.*, X.
6 *Ab.*, Nov. 12, 1908.
7 *Ab.*, Dec. 26, 1908.
8 *Fer.*, Nov. 26 and Dec. 26, 1908.
9 *Jg.*, Dec. 30, 1908.
10 *Fer.*, Feb. 2, 1909.
11 *Fer.*, June 13, 1909.
12 *Fer.*, July 4, 1909.
13 Ferenczi, "Introjektion und Übertragung," *J.*, I (1909), 422–57.
14 *Jg.*, June 3, 1909.
15 *Jg.*, Feb. 2, 1910.
16 *Fer.*, April 3, 1910.
17 *G.W.*, VIII, 104–15; *S.E.*, XI.
18 *G.W.*, VIII, 118–25; *S.E.*, XI.
19 *G.W.*, VIII, 350–57; *S.E.*, XII.
20 *G.W.*, VIII, 364–74; *S.E.*, XII.
21 *Vol. I*, 389 *ff*.
22 *G.W.*, VIII, 376–87; *S.E.*, XII.
23 *Fer.*, June 6, 1912.
24 *G.W.*, VIII, 454–78; *S.E.*, XII.
25 *G.W.*, VIII, 467; *S.E.*, XII.
26 *G.W.*, X, 126–36; *S.E.*, XII.
27 *Ab.*, March 4, 1915.
28 *G.W.*, X, 306–21; *S.E.*, XII.
29 *Ab.*, July 29, 1914.
30 *G.W.*, XII, 183–94; *S.E.*, XVII.
31 *Fer.*, June 18, 1918.

32 Ferenczi, "Technische Schwierigkeiten einer Hysterieanalyse," I.Z., V (1919), 34–40.
33 C., I (Feb. 1911), 187–92.
34 S.E., V, 360–66, 408.
35 C., II, 109–13.
36 G.W., X, 12–22; S.E., XII.
37 G.W., XIII, 301–24; S.E., XIX.
38 "Erfahrungen und Beispiele aus der analytischen Praxis," G.W., 40; "Observations and Examples from Analytic Practice," S.E., XII.
39 "Ueber fausse reconnaissance ('déjà raconté') während der psychoanalytischen Arbeit," G.W., X, 116–23; "Fausse Reconnaissance ('déjà raconté') in Psycho-Analytic Treatment," S.E., XIII.
40 Ferenczi, "Die Elastizität der psychoanalytischen Technik," I.Z., XIV, 197

CHAPTER 10

CLINICAL CONTRIBUTIONS

1 G.W., VII, 191–99; S.E., IX.
2 Anf., p. 177; Origins, p. 166.
3 Anf., p. 210; Origins, p. 197.
4 Anf., p. 262; Origins, p. 246.
5 Otto Rank, Der Mythus von der Geburt des Helden (Leipzig: Deuticke, 1909), p. 64–68.
6 G.W., VII, 235–40; S.E., IX.
7 Fer., April 12, 1910.
8 G.W., VIII, 94; S.E., XI.
9 Über den Selbstmord, insbesondere den Schulerselbstmord (Wiesbaden: Bergmann, 1910).
10 G.W., VIII, 227; S.E., XI.
11 G.W., VIII, 322–30; S.E., XII.
12 G.W., VIII, 234–35; S.E., XII.
13 G.W., VIII, 230.
14 G.W., VIII, 442–62; S.E., XII.
15 Vol. I, 262, 278.
16 G.W., VIII, 422–27; S.E., XII.
17 G.W., X, 40; S.E., XII.
18 Krauss und Brugsch, Specielle Pathologie und Therapie der inneren Krankheiten.
19 Fer., Oct. 2, 1912.
20 Letter to Freud from Ab., Feb. 14, 1913.
21 Ab., Oct. 12, 1913.
22 Ab., Oct. 29, 1913.
23 Letter to Freud from Ab., Oct. 14, 1913.
24 Ab., Nov. 11, 1913.
25 Fer. and Ab., Nov. 9, 1913.
26 E.J., July 22, 1914.
27 Fer., Nov. 9, 1914.
28 A. Kutzinski in Krauss und Brugsch, op. cit., X, 924; "Hysterie," 183–259, "Zwangs-zustände," 409–41.
29 Fer., July 12, 1915.
30 Fer., Aug. 20, 1917 and Ab., Dec. 21, 1917.
31 Ab., Jan. 6, 1920.
32 Ab., June 4, 1920.
33 G.W., X, 234–36; S.E., XIV.
34 Jg., Jan. 27, 1908.
35 G.W., X, 364–91; S.E., XIV.
36 G.W., X, 394–95; S.E., XIV.
37 G.W., X, 428–46; S.E., XIV.
38 Zur Psychoanalyse der Kriegsneurosen (Leipzig: Internationaler Psychoanalytischer Verlag, 1919).
39 G.W., XII, 321–24; S.E., XVII.
40 Fer., March 17, 1918.

CHAPTER 11

CASE HISTORIES

1 *G.W.*, V, 163–286; *S.E.*, VII, 7.

2 *Vol. I*, 362.

3 Freud gave an erroneous date later. See *Vol. I*, 362.

4 *Ibid.*

5 *S.E.*, VII, 3,4.

6 *Fer.*, Jan. 20, 1909.

7 *Anf.*, p. 349; *Origins*, p. 326.

8 *G.W.*, V, 202; *S.E.*, VII, 42.

9 *G.W.*, V, 201; *S.E.*, VII, 41.

10 *G.W.*, V, 210; *S.E.*, VII, 50.

11 *G.W.*, V, 286; *S.E.*, VII, 122.

12 *G.W.*, IV, 270; *S.E.*, VI.

13 *G.W.*, VII, 243; *S.E.*, X.

14 *G.W.*, V, 171; *S.E.*, X.

15 *Sammlung*, II (1909), 154; *G.S.*, V (1924), 137; *G.W.*, VII, 23.

16 *G.W.*, VII, 176; *S.E.*, IX.

17 *G.W.*, XIII (1924), 293; *S.E.*, XIX.

18 *Vol. I*, 321.

19 *G.W.*, VII, 246; *S.E.*, X.

20 *G.W.*, VII, 271; *S.E.*, X.

21 *G.W.*, VII, 247; *S.E.*, X.

22 *G.W.*, VII, 343; *S.E.*, X.

23 **E.J.*, June 1, 1909.

24 *G.W.*, VII, 381; *S.E.*, X.

25 Paul Federn, "Professor Freud; The Beginning of a Case History," *Samiksa*, I (1947), 305–311. Reprinted in *The Yearbook of Psychoanalysis*, IV (New York: International Universities Press, 1948), 14–20. Federn gave the second date incorrectly as November 16.

26 *Jg.*, June 3, 1909.

27 *Jg.*, June 30, 1909.

28 *Jg.*, Oct. 17, 1909.

29 *G.W.*, IX, 106; *S.E.*, X.

30 *Vol. I*, Chap. XIII.

31 *G.W.*, VII, 428; *S.E.*, X.

32 *G.W.*, VIII, 240–320; *S.E.*, XII.

33 *Ab.*, March 3, 1911.

34 *G.W.*, I, 392; *S.E.*, III.

35 *Fer.*, Dec. 16, 1910.

36 *Ibid.*

37 *Fer.*, Oct. 6, 1910.

38 *Fer.*, Dec. 16, 1910.

39 *G.W.*, VIII, 285.

40 *G.W.*, VIII, 292.

41 *Fer.*, Feb. 11, 1908.

42 *G.W.*, VIII, 297.

43 *G.W.*, VIII, 170; *S.E.*, XI.

44 *G.W.*, VIII, 303.

45 *G.W.*, VIII, 305–307.

46 *G.W.*, VIII, 319–20.

47 M. Katan, "Schreber's Delusion of the End of the World," *The Psychoanalytic Quarterly*, XVIII (1949), 60; "Schreber's Hallucinations about the 'Little Men'," *I.J.*, XXXI (1950), 32; "Further Remarks about Schreber's Hallucinations," *I.J.*, XXXIII (1952), 429; "Schreber's Pre-Psychotic Phase," *I.J.*, XXXI (1953), 43.

48 H. Nunberg, "Discussion of M. Katan's Paper on Schreber's Hallucinations," *I.J.*, XXXIII (1952), 454.

49 Melanie Klein, "Notes on Some Schizoid Mechanisms," *I.J.*, XXVII (1946), 108–110.

50 Ida Macalpine and R. A. Hunter, "The Schreber Case," *The Psychoanalytic Quarterly*, XXII (1953), 328–71.

51 *G.W.*, XII, 29–157; *S.E.*, XVII.

52 *Fer.*, Feb. 13, 1910.

53 *I.J.*, IX (1928).

54 Ruth Mack Brunswick, "A Sup-

plement to Freud's 'History of an Infantile Neurosis'," *I.J.*, IX (1928), 439.

[55] Muriel M. Gardiner, "Meetings with the Wolfman," *Bulletin of the Philadelphia Association for Psychoanalysis*, II (July 1952), 32. See also some interesting comments by Kurt Eissler, "The Effect of the Structure of the Ego on Psychoanalytic Technique," *Journal of the American Psychoanalytic Association*, I (Jan. 1953), 111–13; and Max Stern, "Trauma and Symptom Formation," *I.J.*, XXXIV (1953), 211–12.

[56] *G.W.*, XII, 34, 35.

[57] *Fer.*, Nov. 9, 1914; *Eit.*, Nov. 9, 1914.

[58] See particularly *G.W.*, XII, 137.

[59] *G.W.*, XII, 126.

[60] *Ab.*, Oct. 18, 1914.

[61] *Fer.*, Oct. 30, 1914.

[62] *Fer.*, Nov. 9, 1914.

[63] *G.W.*, XII, 271–302; *S.E.*, XVIII.

[64] *G.W.*, XII, 290.

CHAPTER 12

THE LIBIDO THEORY

[1] *G.W.*, XII, 4; *S.E.*, XVII.

[2] *G.W.*, XI, 323; *S.E.*, XVI.

[3] *G.W.*, V, 118; *S.E.*, VII, 217.

[4] *G.W.*, V, 158; *S.E.*, VII, 278. See also *G.W.*, V, 277; *S.E.*, VII, 113.

[5] *S.E.*, VII, 127.

[6] A. G. Tansley, *Mind and Life* (New York: John deGraff, 1952), p. 104.

[7] S. Lindner, "Das Saugen an den Fingern, Lippen, etc. bei den Kindern (Ludeln)," *Jahrbuch für Kinderheilkunde*, XIV (1879), 68.

[8] *Vol. I*, 321–23.

[9] *G.W.*, II/III, 136; *S.E.*, IV, 130.

[10] *Anf.*, p. 321; *Origins*, p. 300.

[11] *Anf.*, p. 330; *Origins*, p. 309.

[12] *Fer.*, July 9, 1913.

[13] *G.W.*, V, 149–59; *S.E.*, VII, 270.

[14] *G.W.*, V, 27–145; *S.E.*, VII, 123–245.

[15] *S.E.*, VII, 126.

[16] *G.W.*, V, 307; *S.E.*, VII, 296.

[17] Abraham, "Versuch einer Entwicklungegeschichte der Libido auf Grund der Psychoanalyse seelischer Störungen," *Neue Arbeiten zur ärztlichen Psychoanalyse*, Heft 11, (1924).

[18] See also *G.W.*, VII, 240; *S.E.*, IX.

[19] *G.W.*, V, 128; *S.E.*, VII, 226.

[20] *G.W.*, V, 138, 178n; *S.E.*, VII, 20, 21, 236.

[21] *G.W.*, VII, 19–27; *S.E.*, IX.

[22] *Jg.*, July 1, 1907.

[23] *G.W.*, VII, 143–67; *S.E.*, IX.

[24] *G.W.*, VII, 171–88; *S.E.*, IX.

[25] *G.W.*, VII, 191–99; *S.E.*, IX.

[26] *Jg.*, Feb. 25, 1908.

[27] *G.W.*, VII, 203; *S.E.*, IX.

[28] Ernest Jones, *Papers on Psycho-Analysis* (London: Baillière, Tindall and Cox, 5th ed., 1948), Chap. XXIV.

[29] *Jg.*, Oct. 27, 1906.

[30] *G.W.*, VII, 227–31; *S.E.*, IX.

[31] *Anf.*, p. 219; *Origins*, p. 205.

[32] *G.W.*, VIII, 223; *S.E.*, XI.

[33] *G.W.*, VIII, 66–77; *S.E.*, XI.

34 *Fer.*, April 24, 1910.
35 *Jg.*, May 26, 1910.
36 *G.W.*, VIII, 78–91; *S.E.*, XI.
37 *G.W.*, XII, 161–80; *S.E.*, XI.
38 *Fer.*, Sept. 24, 1917.
39 *Die Onanie: 14 Beitrage zu einer Diskussion der Wiener Psychoanalytischen Vereinigung* (Wiesbaden: Bergmann, 1912); *G.W.*, VIII, 332–45; *S.E.*, XII.
40 *G.W.*, X, 453–55; *S.E.*, XII.
41 *G.W.*, X, 138–70; *S.E.*, XIV.
42 Ernest Jones, *op. cit.*, pp. 158–160.
43 *Fer.*, June 17, 1913.
44 *G.W.*, IX, 109; *S.E.*, XIII.
45 *Ab.*, Sept. 21; *E.J.*, Oct. 1; *Fer.*, Sept. 22 and Oct. 1, 1913.
46 *Fer.*, Feb. 23, 1914.
47 *E.J.*, March 19, 1914.
48 *Ab.*, March 18, 1914.
49 *Ab.*, April 6, 1914.
50 *Fer.*, Jan. 12, 1914.
51 *G.W.*, X, 402–10; *S.E.*, XVII.
52 *G.W.*, XI, 313, 331; *S.E.*, XVI.
53 *G.W.*, XII, 197–226; *S.E.*, XVII.
54 See *Vol. I*, 402.

CHAPTER 13

CONTRIBUTIONS TO THEORY

1 *G.W.*, VIII, 213–21; *S.E.*, XI.
2 *Fer.*, Oct. 22, 1909.
3 Alexander Bain, *Logic*, Vol. I (1870), 54.
4 *C.*, I (Oct. 1911), 63.
5 *G.W.*, VIII, 230–38; *S.E.*, XII.
6 *Jg.*, June 19, 1910.
7 *Fer.*, Oct. 27, 1910.
8 *Fer.*, Dec. 16, 1910.
9 *Jg.*, Jan. 22, 1911.
10 See *Vol. I*, 379 *ff.*
11 *G.W.*, XI, 368; *S.E.*, XVI.
12 See *Vol. I*, 266.
13 XXVI, Part LXVI; *G.W.*, VIII, 430–39; *S.E.*, XII.
14 *E.J.*, Feb. 12, 1912.
15 *G.W.*, VIII, 437; *S.E.*, XII.
16 *Ab.*, May 4, 1915.
17 *G.W.*, X, 210–32; *S.E.*, XIV.
18 *G.W.*, V, 67; *S.E.*, VII, 168.
19 Melanie Klein, *The Psycho-Analysis of Children* (New York: Norton, 1932).
20 *G.W.*, X, 248–61; *S.E.*, XIV.
21 *G.W.*, X, 264–303; *S.E.*, XIV.
22 *Ab.*, April 1, 1916.
23 *Minutes*, Dec. 11, 1907.
24 *Anf.*, p. 177; *Origins*, p. 166.
25 *Hemmung, Symptom und Angst*, *G.W.*, XIV, 111; *Inhibitions, Symptoms and Anxiety*, *S.E.*, XX.
26 *Anf.*, p. 451; *Origins*, p. 429; *G.W.*, II/III, 608; *S.E.*, V, 602.
27 *Vol. I*, 389 *ff.*
28 *G.W.*, II/III, 580, 622; *S.E.*, V, 574, 617.
29 *Anf.*, pp. 177, 186, 453; *Origins*, pp. 164, 174–75, 431.
30 *Zur Auffassung der Aphasien* (Vienna: Deuticke, 1891), p. 75; *On Aphasia* (New York: International Universities Press, 1953), p. 77.
31 See *S.E.*, V, 611n.
32 *G.W.*, X, 412–26; *S.E.*, XIV.
33 *G.W.*, X, 428–46; *S.E.*, XIV.
34 Abraham, "Ansätze zur psychoanalytischen Erforschung und Behandlung des manisch-depressiven Irreseins und verwandter Zustände," *C.*, II (1912), 302–315.
35 *Ab.*, Feb. 18, 1915.
36 *Ab.*, May 4, 1915.
37 Letter to Freud from *E.J.*, Dec 7, 1918.

CHAPTER 14

NON-MEDICAL APPLICATIONS
OF PSYCHOANALYSIS

[1] *G.W.*, II/III; *S.E.*, V.

[2] Vols. IV and V.

[3] *E.g.*, Freud, "Nachtrage zur Traumdeutung," *C.* I (1911), 187.

[4] *Jg.*, Feb. 17, 1911.

[5] *G.W.*, IV; *S.E.*, VI.

[6] *Anf.*, p. 279; *Origins*, p. 261.

[7] *Anf.*, p. 282; *Origins*, p. 264.

[8] *Anf.*, p. 361; *Origins*, p. 337.

[9] See *Vol. I*, 24–25, 32–33.

[10] *Anf.*, p. 289; *Origins*, p. 270–71.

[11] *Anf.*, p. 299; *Origins*, p. 281.

[12] *Monatsschrift*, X, Heft 1, 1–32 and Heft 2, 95–143.

[13] *G.W.*, VI; *S.E.*, VIII.

[14] *Anf.*, p. 317; *Origins*, p. 297.

[15] *G.W.*, I, 251; *S.E.*, II.

[16] *Anf.*, p. 278; *Origins*, p. 260.

[17] *Fer.*, Feb. 11, 1908.

[18] *The Psychoanalytic Quarterly*, XI, 459; *S.E.*, VII, 305.

[19] C. G. Jung, *Die psychologische Diagnose des Tatbestandes* (Halle: 1906).

[20] *G.W.*, VII, 3–15; *S.E.*, IX.

[21] XXXVI (Dec. 21, 1906), Heft 1, 1–10.

[22] *G.W.*, VII, 129–39; *S.E.*, IX.

[23] *Anf.*, p. 273; *Origins*, p. 256.

[24] *G.W.*, VII, 31–125; *S.E.*, IX, 1.

[25] *Jg.*, May 26, 1907.

[26] *M.*, Sept. 24, 1907.

[27] *Jg.*, May 26, 1907.

[28] *Jg.*, May 26, 1907.

[29] *Jg.*, Nov. 2, 1907.

[30] *G.W.*, VII, 213; *S.E.*, IX.

[31] Communications from Oliver Freud and E. Hitschmann.

[32] *Jg.*, Sept. 8, 1907.

[33] See *Vol. I*, 111.

[34] *Ab.*, April 19, 1908.

[35] *G.W.*, VIII, 128–21 ; *S.E.*, XI.

[36] *Jg.*, Oct. 17, 1909.

[37] Scognamiglio, *Ricerche e Documenti sulla Giovinezza di Leonardo da Vinci* (1900).

[38] *Fer.*, Nov. 10, 1909.

[39] *Eit.*, Dec. 30, 1909.

[40] *Fer.*, Jan. 10, 1910.

[41] *Eit.*, Feb. 17, 1910.

[42] *Fer.*, April 3, 1910.

[43] **E.J.*, April 15, 1910.

[44] *Fer.*, June 6, 1910.

[45] *Jg.*, Aug. 8, 1910.

[46] *Fer.*, Feb. 13, 1919.

[47] *Pf.*, June 17, 1910.

[48] O. Pfister, "Kryptolalie, Kryptographie und unbewusstes Vexierbild bei Normalen," *J.*, V (1913), 146–51.

[49] Personal communication.

[50] J. Harnik, "Ägyptologisches zu Leonardo's Geierphantasie," *I.Z.*, VI (1920), 362.

[51] *G.W.*, VIII, 348; *S.E.*, XII.

[52] *G.W.*, VIII, 360; *S.E.*, XII.

[53] *G.W.*, IX; *S.E.*, XIII.

[54] *Fer.*, May 4, 1912.

[55] *Fer.*, Jan. 1, 1910.

[56] *E.J.*, Aug. 9, 1911.

[57] *Fer.*, Aug. 11, 1911.

[58] Letter to Freud from *Ab.*, May 25, 1913.

[59] *J.*, III (1911), 120–227.

[60] **E.J.*, Nov. 5, 1911.

[61] *Fer.*, Nov. 5, 1911.

[62] *Fer.*, Nov. 30, 1911.

[63] *Ab.*, Jan. 12, 1912.

[64] **E.J.*, Feb. 24, 1912.

[65] *Fer.*, April 21, 1912.

[66] *Fer.*, April 28 and May 16, 1912.

[67] Letter to Freud from *Fer.*, July 20, 1912.

[68] *Fer.*, Oct. 17, 1912.

[69] **E.J.*, April 9, 1913.

[70] *Fer.*, April 10, 1913.

[71] *Fer.*, May 1, 1913.

[72] *Fer.*, May 8, 1913.

[73] *Ab.*, May 13, 1913.

[74] *Fer.*, June 12, 1913.

[75] *Fer.*, June 17, 1913.

[76] *Fer.*, June 26, 1913.

[77] *Ab.*, July 1, 1913.

[78] See *Vol. I*, 300–304.

[79] *G.W.*, X, 2–9; *S.E.*, XII.

[80] *G.W.*, X, 24–37; *S.E.*, XII.

[81] *Ab.*, June 14, 1912.

[82] *Fer.*, June 23, 1912.

[83] W. Stekel, *Die Sprache des Traumes* (Wiesbaden: Bergmann, 1911).

[84] *Fer.*, July 9, 1913.

[85] *G.W.*, X, 44–113; *S.E.*, XIV.

[86] See *Vol. I*, 257.

[87] *Anf.*, p. 318; *Origins*, p. 298.

[88] *G.W.*, X, 172–201; *S.E.*, XIII.

[89] *G.W.*, X, 174; *S.E.*, XIII.

[90] *C.P.*, IV, 283.

[91] *Moses and Monotheism* (New York: Alfred A. Knopf, 1939).

[92] *M.*, Sept. 6, 1901.

[93] *Moses and Monotheism*, p. 269.

[94] See *Vol. I*, 39.

[95] *M.*, Sept. 25, 1912.

[96] *Fer.*, Oct. 20, 1912.

[97] W. Watkiss Lloyd, *The Moses of Michelangelo. A Study of Art, History and Legend* (1863).

[98] *E.J.*, Oct. 30, 1912.

[99] *E.J.*, Nov. 8, 1912.

[100] Letter to Freud from *E.J.*, Dec. 23, 1912.

[101] *E.J.*, Dec. 26, 1912.

[102] *E.J.*, Sept. 21, 1913.

[103] *E.J.*, Jan. 3, 1914.

[104] *Fer.*, Jan. 3, 1914.

[105] *E.J.*, Jan. 16, 1914.

[106] *Ab.*, Jan. 6, 1914.

[107] *E.J.*, Feb. 8; *Fer.*, Feb. 23, 1914.

[108] *G.W.*, XIV, 321; *S.E.*, XIII.

[109] *Fer.*, Oct. 17, 1912.

[110] Letter to Edoardo Weiss, April 12, 1933.

[111] *G.W.*, X, 204–207; *S.E.*, XIII.

[112] *G.W.*, X, 324–55; *S.E.*, XIV.

[113] *Ab.*, March 4, 1915.

[114] Putnam, March 9, 1915.

[115] Quoted from I. Deutscher, *The Prophet Armed* (New York: Oxford, 1954), p. 202.

[116] Letter to Freud from *Ab.*, April 26, 1915.

[117] See *Vol. I*, 330.

[118] *Fer.*, April 8, 1915.

[119] *G.W.*, X, 355; *S.E.*, XIV.

[120] *Fer.*, July 17, 1914.

[121] Isador Coriat, "Psychoanalyse der Lady Macbeth," *C.*, IV (1914), 384.

[122] L. Jekels, "Shakespeare's Macbeth," *I.*, V (1917), 170.

[123] Otto Rank, *Das Inzest-Motiv in Dichtung und Sage* (Leipzig: Deuticke, 1912), pp. 404–405.

[124] *G.W.*, X, 358–61; *S.E.*, XIV.

[125] *G.W.*, X, 398–400; *S.E.*, XIV.

[126] *G.W.*, XII, 15–16; *S.E.*, XVII.

[127] *Fer.*, Sept. 10, 1917.

[128] *G.W.*, XII, 20; *S.E.*, XVII.

[129] See *Vol. I*, 7.

[130] For instance J. Harnik, "Zum Hinauswerfen von Gegenständen aus dem Fenster durch kleine Kinder," *I.Z.*, VI (1920), 160–163.

CHAPTER 15

MODE OF LIFE AND WORK

[1] Joel Shor, "A Well-Spring of Psychoanalysis," *Psychoanalysis: Journal of Psychoanalytic Psychology*, II (1953), 27.

[2] Helen Walker Puner, *Freud: His Life and His Mind* (New York: Crown, 1949), p. 83.

[3] *Ab.*, July 4, 1914.

[4] Communication to Marie Bonaparte, 1928.

[5] Puner, *op. cit.*

[6] Letter from Emma Jung to Freud, Nov. 6, 1911.

[7] Puner, *op. cit.*, p. 83.

[8] Personal communication from Lucie Freud.

[9] *M.*, Sept. 5, 1883.

[10] *Jg.*, March 9, 1909.

[11] *G.W.*, II/III, 235–38; *S.E.*, IV, 229–32.

[12] *E.J.*, May 14, 1911.

[13] E.g. *Eit.*, May 7, 1914.

[14] *Fer.*, Jan. 10, 1910.

[15] *Fer.*, May 9, 1918.

[16] *Pf.*, June 13, 1909.

[17] *M.*, Sept. 15, 1910.

[18] Letter to Anna Freud, Sept. 18, 1910.

[19] Ernest Jones, "Freud's Early Travels," *I.J.*, XXXV (1954), 81–84.

[20] *Vol. I*, 343–46.

[21] *Fer.*, April 2, 1911.

[22] *Ab.*, July 3, 1912.

[23] *E.J.*, April 15, 1910.

[24] *Fer.*, July 9, 1913.

[25] *Anf.*, p. 321; *Origins*, p. 301.

[26] *Pf.*, March 6, 1910.

[27] Communication to Marie Bonaparte, 1925.

[28] Freud to Marie Bonaparte, 1926.

[29] *Ab.*, July 23, 1908.

[30] Communication from Marie Bonaparte.

[31] *Jg.*, Oct. 7, 1906.

[32] *Jg.*, Jan. 1, 1907.

[33] *Ab.*, March 1, 1908.

[34] *Fer.*, Jan. 10, 1910.

[35] *Ab.*, Jan. 2, 1912.

[36] *Ab.*, Dec. 15, 1919.

[37] *G.W.*, XIV, 96; *S.E.*, XX.

[38] Communication to Marie Bonaparte, 1926.

[39] *Vol. I*, 20.

CHAPTER 16

CHARACTER AND PERSONALITY

[1] *G.W.*, VIII, 203; *S.E.*, XI.

[2] Joan Riviere, "An Intimate Impression," *The Lancet*, Sept. 20, 1939, p. 765.

[3] *Vol. I*, 32.

[4] *Ab.*, May 18, 1911; *Fer.*, May 16, 1911.

[5] *Fer.*, May 21, 1911.

[6] *Ab.*, Jan. 17, 1909.

[7] *Pf.*, Oct. 9, 1913.

[8] Theodore Reik, *Freud als Kulturkritiker* (Vienna and Leipzig: Max Praeger, 1930) p. 64.

[9] *G.W.*, VIII, 142; *S.E.*, XI.

[10] *Fer.*, Sept. 5, 1919.

[11] *Fer.*, July 10, 1915.

[12] *Eit.*, May 10, 1912.

[13] *Ab.*, July 26, 1914.

[14] *Fer.*, Oct. 17, 1910.
[15] *Vol. I*, Chap. XII.
[16] *E.J.*, Aug. 9, 1912.
[17] *Fer.*, Oct. 17, 1910.

[18] *G.W.*, VII, 247; *S.E.*, X.
[19] *Vol. I*, 7.
[20] *Vol. I*, 10.

APPENDIX

[1] See *Vol. I*, 20*n*.
[2] "Ein kleiner Hahnemann," *I.Z.*, I (1913), 240–46.
[3] Abraham, "Amenhotep IV (Echnaton)," *I.*, I, 334–60.
[4] Ferenczi, "Entwicklungsstufen des Wirklichkeitssinnes," *I.Z.*, I, 124–238.
[5] Abraham, "Über Einschränkungen und Umwandlungen der Schaulust bei den Psychoneurotikern," *J.*, VI (1914), 25–88.
[6] Pfister, *Was bietet die Psychoanalyse dem Erzieher?* (Leipzig: 1917).

Index